Law and Public Policy

Laws exist to incentivize citizens to act in a certain manner, in accordance with the policies that a community has deemed correct. When those laws no longer serve the population for whom they were designed, policies, beliefs, and ideas must be re-examined to decide whether the community has changed. In this ground breaking new textbook, author Kevin J. Fandl examines the ideas and the rules we build to implement those ideas. While similar books have looked at public policy and public administration in an effort to explain how the government works, and others have considered the foundations of the legal system to understand the rulemaking institutions, this book develops a complete picture of society from idea to action—by examining laws through the lens of policy and vice versa. This holistic approach gives readers a chance to see not only why certain rules exist, but to understand the events that inspired them and how those rules have evolved over time. It offers students an opportunity not only to comprehend but to see themselves in the process of forming the structures that shape our society.

This textbook is divided into two sections. The first section provides readers with the tools that they will need to digest the policies and laws that surround them. These tools include a historical deep dive into the foundations of the governance structure in the United States and beyond, an important examination of civics and a reminder of the importance of engaging in the policymaking process, a careful breakdown of the institutions that form the backbone of the law and policymaking institutions in the United States, and finally critical thinking including practical tools to find reliable sources for news, research, and other types of information. The second section of the text comprises subject-matter analyses written by experts, beginning with a historical perspective followed by a careful examination of the key policies and laws that inform that field. Each chapter highlights key vocabulary, provides practical vignettes to add context to the writing, explores a unique global component to compare perspectives from communities worldwide, and includes a number of discussion questions and recommended readings for further examination. This textbook is tailored specifically for undergraduate and graduate students of public policy, to introduce them to the role of law and legal institutions as facilitators and constraints on public policy, exploring those laws in a range of relevant policy contexts with the help of short case studies.

Kevin J. Fandl is Assistant Professor and Director of Immersion Programs in the Fox School of Business at Temple University, USA.

Law and Public Policy

Kevin J. Fandl

NEW YORK AND LONDON

First published 2019
by Routledge
711 Third Avenue, New York, NY 10017

and by Routledge
2 Park Square, Milton Park, Abingdon, Oxon, OX14 4RN

Routledge is an imprint of the Taylor & Francis Group, an informa business

© 2019 Taylor & Francis

The right of Kevin J. Fandl to be identified as author of this work has been asserted by him in accordance with sections 77 and 78 of the Copyright, Designs and Patents Act 1988.

All rights reserved. No part of this book may be reprinted or reproduced or utilised in any form or by any electronic, mechanical, or other means, now known or hereafter invented, including photocopying and recording, or in any information storage or retrieval system, without permission in writing from the publishers.

Trademark notice: Product or corporate names may be trademarks or registered trademarks, and are used only for identification and explanation without intent to infringe.

Library of Congress Cataloging-in-Publication Data
Names: Fandl, Kevin J., editor.
Title: Law and public policy / [edited by] Kevin J. Fandl.
Description: New York, NY : Routledge is an imprint of the Taylor & Francis Group, an Informa Business, 2018. | Includes bibliographical references and index.
Identifiers: LCCN 2018011349 | ISBN 9780815373742 (hbk : alk. paper) | ISBN 9780815373919 (pbk : alk. paper) | ISBN 9781351243094 (ebk)
Subjects: LCSH: Public policy (Law)—United States. | Public policy (Law)
Classification: LCC KF450.P8 L39 2018 | DDC 342.73/041—dc23
LC record available at https://lccn.loc.gov/2018011349

ISBN: 978-0-815-37374-2 (hbk)
ISBN: 978-0-815-37391-9 (pbk)
ISBN: 978-1-351-24309-4 (ebk)

Typeset in Sabon
by Apex CoVantage, LLC

Contents

About the Author	vi
Contributing Authors	vii
Preface by Kevin J. Fandl	xi

1. A Historic Introduction to Law and Public Policy — 1
2. How the Government Works: A Foundation in Civics — 35
3. Institutions and Power—Congress, the Courts, and the President — 62
4. Separating Facts and Fiction—How to Become a More Effective Researcher and a More Critical Reader — 105
5. Economic Law and Policy — 124
6. Foreign Law and Policy — 157
   ASTRID SCHMIDT-KING
7. Security Law and Policy — 209
   COL. MICHAEL W. TAYLOR
8. Food and Agriculture Law and Policy — 243
   ANN C. BLISS AND AUTUMN T. JOHNSON
9. Environmental Law and Policy — 293
   INARA SCOTT
10. Employment Law and Policy — 323
    ELIZABETH BROWN, KEITH DIENER, LUCIEN DHOOGE, LEORA EISENSTADT, AND NATALIE PEDERSEN
11. Civil Rights Law and Policy — 352
    EHSAN ZAFFAR

Index — 378

About the Author

Kevin J. Fandl, J.D., Ph.D.

Kevin Fandl is an Assistant Professor of Legal Studies and Strategic Global Management at the Fox School of Business at Temple University, where he serves as the Academic Director of Global Immersion Programs and also the Executive Director of Temple's Center for International Business Education and Research. Kevin began his legal career as a Presidential Management Fellow working as an international trade specialist with U.S. Customs and Border Protection. He transitioned through many roles within the federal government, including Chief of Staff for the International Intellectual Property Rights Center and Senior Counsel to the Assistant Secretary of U.S. Immigration and Customs Enforcement.

Playing an important role in shaping immigration and trade policy for the federal government inspired Kevin to pursue a doctorate in Public Policy focused on international trade law. During that process, he received a Fulbright fellowship to teach trade law in Bogotá, Colombia for one year. His doctoral dissertation addressed the informal business sector within Colombia, a topic that he has written about extensively since. He continues to address law and policy issues related to Colombia and Latin America more broadly and advises on those issues for firms and international organizations around the world.

After a decade of federal government service and many years of international consulting on issues from immigration to foreign trade, Dr. Fandl transitioned to academia to pursue his passion for teaching and research. He continues to lecture frequently in Latin America, Europe and Asia on comparative law and policy matters. As an active researcher, he has published extensively in the field of international business law and policy and serves as an expert for international organizations and law firms on issues related to business law and policy. He has published 5 books and more than 30 journal articles in journals such as the American Business Law Journal, the Berkeley International Law Journal, and the Yale Law & Policy Review *Inter Alia*.

Kevin earned his B.A. in Philosophy at Lock Haven University, his M.A. in International Peace and Conflict Resolution at American University, his J.D. in law from American University, and his Ph.D. in Public Policy from George Mason University. He also holds a Certificate in International Human Rights Law from Oxford University. He has won many accolades for his leadership, his research and his teaching. He lives just outside Washington, D.C.

Contributing Authors

Ann C. Bliss received her J.D. from the University of San Diego. She practiced law in rural Wisconsin before taking office to serve the people of Columbia County by presiding over 10 years of family court calendars. She became a board member of her local food co-op in North Carolina in 2005. With a dedicated group of members, the TBC Food Co-op proudly launched Cobblestone Farmer's Market in Winston-Salem, North Carolina in 2010. Ann is a contributing author to *The Food Activist Handbook* by Ali Berlow (Storey Publishing, 2015). As a Visiting Professor of Practice at the Wake Forest University School of Business, Ann asks her students to introduce themselves with the same question every semester: Describe your favorite sandwich and how it reveals your philosophy of life.

Elizabeth Brown is an Assistant Professor of Business Law at Bentley University. She graduated with honors from Harvard College and Harvard Law School. Before joining Bentley, she practiced law in San Francisco, London, and Boston, advising senior executives at Fortune 500 companies on legal strategies and managing multimillion-dollar cases from inception to successful resolution. In addition to being a former law partner, she is also the former Executive Director in Boston of Golden Seeds, the largest source of angel funding for women entrepreneurs. She wrote the best-selling *Life After Law: Finding Work You Love with the JD You Have* and is a frequent speaker and writer on alternative law careers. Her wisdom on career change has appeared in *The Atlantic*, *Wall Street Journal*, and *ABA Journal*, among other publications. Liz also wrote the foreword to the American Bar Association's own career change guide, *Lawyer Interrupted*.

Lucien J. Dhooge After completing an undergraduate degree in history at the University of Colorado in 1980, Prof. Dhooge attended the University of Denver College of Law, where he received his J.D. in 1983. He received his LL.M. in 1995 from the Georgetown University Law Center, where he specialized in international and comparative law. Prior to coming to the Scheller College of Business at the Georgia Institute of Technology, Prof. Dhooge spent 11 years in private law practice and 12 years serving on the faculty of the University of the Pacific in California. Prof. Dhooge teaches international business law and ethics at the Scheller College of Business.

Prof. Dhooge has authored more than 55 scholarly articles, co-authored 14 books, and has presented research papers and courses throughout the world. Prof. Dhooge is the recipient of numerous research awards given by the Academy of Legal Studies in Business, including seven Ralph C. Hoeber Awards for excellence in research. He was designated the outstanding junior business law faculty member in the United States by the Academy in 2002 and received the Kay Duffy

Award for outstanding service in 2005. Prof. Dhooge was the program chair for the Academy's 2009 international conference in Denver, Colorado and served as Academy President in 2009–10. Prof. Dhooge is a past editor-in-chief of the *American Business Law Journal* and the *Journal of Legal Studies Education*.

Keith Diener is an Assistant Professor of Business Law and Ethics at Stockton University. Dr. Diener holds two doctoral degrees, in law and business ethics, and two masters' degrees, in international law and philosophy, from Georgetown University, Georgia State University, and George Washington University. He has published more than 20 articles and chapters. His work and research has received numerous awards from national and international law and ethics organizations. Keith has taught to undergraduate and graduate students for over a decade at many universities, including George Washington University, the University of Maryland—University College, and Stockton University. Prior to joining academia full-time, Dr. Diener maintained a successful business and employment law legal practice.

Leora Eisenstadt is an Assistant Professor in the Department of Legal Studies at the Fox School of Business at Temple University. Prof. Eisenstadt's areas of scholarship and interest include employment law, business law, race and the law, law and linguistics, work-family conflict, and sex discrimination. Her recent publications include *Suppressed Anger, Retaliation Doctrine, and Workplace Culture*; *Enemy and Ally: Religion in* Loving v. Virginia *and Beyond*; *Intent and Liability in Employment Discrimination* (American Business Law Journal); *Fluid Identity Discrimination* (American Business Law Journal); *Causation in Context* (Berkeley Journal of Employment & Labor Law); and *The N-Word at Work: Contextualizing Language in the Workplace* (Berkeley Journal of Employment & Labor Law).

Prof. Eisenstadt received her J.D., *cum laude* from New York University School of Law and her B.A. in History, *cum laude* from Yale University. From 2003 to 2004, she was a Fulbright Fellow in Israel studying equal employment opportunity law. She served as a law clerk to the Hon. R. Barclay Surrick in the Eastern District of Pennsylvania and spent several years in the Labor and Employment Group at Dechert LLP, litigating cases and counseling clients in employment discrimination issues, general employment matters, and Title IX–related litigation. Prior to joining the faculty at the Fox School, Prof. Eisenstadt spent two years as a Fellow and Lecturer in Law at Temple University's Beasley School of Law. Prof. Eisenstadt teaches courses on general business law, workplace law, and experiential learning in the legal profession.

Autumn T. Johnson started her career as a social worker in Arizona, an experience that compelled her to attend law school, where she focused on environmental law. After a clerkship and several years practicing in the private sector (where she simultaneously completed her MBA), she fell into teaching at Seattle University. A passion for teaching and an interest in policy took her to Boise State University, where she is the assistant director of the Energy Policy Institute, an adjunct professor in the College of Business and Economics, and a PhD student in Public Policy and Administration. Her research interests rest in environmental law and policy, including energy, food/agriculture, and water. She plans to write her dissertation on agriculture law and policy, specifically related to agricultural exceptionalism, the industrialization of agriculture, and policy change (or lack thereof).

Natalie Pedersen is an Assistant Professor of Legal Studies at Drexel University's LeBow College of Business. She graduated with honors from the Wharton School of the University of Pennsylvania and Harvard Law School. Before going to Drexel, she worked as an associate at Ballard Spahr Andrews & Ingersoll and as a clerk for the Hon. Marjorie Rendell of the U.S. Court of Appeals for the Third Circuit.

Astrid Schmidt-King is currently a Visiting Affiliate Assistant Professor of Law and Social Responsibility for the Sellinger School of Business and Management at Loyola University Maryland and serves as the Special Assistant for the presidentially appointed university task force focused on global engagement and the Chair of the Building a Better World Through Business initiative. Prior to pursuing a field in higher education, Astrid practiced law in the fields of immigration law and compliance in Washington, D.C. and New York. Astrid earned her B.A. in International Relations from New York University, J.D. from the University of Baltimore School of Law, LL.M. in Law and Government from the American University Washington College of Law, and M.A. in International Relations and Global Politics from Freie University in Berlin, Germany. Her thesis, *Reacting to Globalization's Socioeconomic Impact? The Recent Rise of Right-Wing Populist Movements in Developed Democracies*, examined why some developed democratic countries are experiencing a rise in right-wing populist movements while others are not, and it analyzed whether such movements act as vehicles for the (re)construction and/or (re)assertion of national and self-identity. Through a comparative case analysis (Canada, France, U.K., and U.S.), the research examined variables closely related to key measures of the socioeconomic impacts of globalization—migration, labor composition, employment and unemployment, trade, and inequality. Astrid was a Fulbright International Education Administrators (IEA) Seminar (Germany) recipient in 2010, a participant in the American Council on Germany's immigration delegation in Berlin in 2012, and was named a Presidential Fellow by the Association of International Education Administrators in 2013. She currently serves on the peer-review panel for the Fulbright IEA program in Germany.

Inara Scott is an Associate Professor in the College of Business at Oregon State University (OSU). Prior to arriving at OSU, she practiced environmental and energy law for almost a decade, both in private practice and as legal counsel and senior manager for two of Oregon's largest public utilities. She received her J.D. *summa cum laude* from Lewis and Clark Law School and her A.B. *summa cum laude* from Duke University. Her primary research areas include sustainable business and environmental law and regulation, with a particular focus on clean energy. Her research has appeared in the *American Business Law Journal, Harvard Environmental Law Review*, the *University of Pennsylvania Business Law Journal*, and the *Michigan Journal of Environmental and Administrative Law*.

Col. Michael W. Taylor, USAF (Ret.), received a B.A. from Berry College in 1993, a J.D. from the University of Georgia in 1996, and an LL.M. (Air and Space Law) from McGill University in 2006. Col. Taylor served on active duty in the U.S. Air Force for 21 years as a judge advocate before retiring in 2017. During his military service, he spent eight years as a legal advisor at the strategic and operational levels on matters involving outer space, airspace, cyberspace, nuclear weapons, international agreements, rules of engagement, and law-of-war detainees. He deployed to Qatar and Afghanistan and was selected to be a command staff judge advocate (senior legal counsel) three times. Since retiring, Col. Taylor has been teaching a variety of law-related subjects, including constitutional law, business law, and air and space law, to undergraduate students.

Ehsan Zaffar serves as Senior Advisor on Civil Rights and Civil Liberties at the Department of Homeland Security in Washington, D.C., where he advises the Secretary of Homeland Security and Department of Homeland Security components on the civil rights and civil liberties implications of existing and proposed national security policies, programs, and procedures. Mr. Zaffar leads the Department's efforts to implement UNHRC Resolution 16/118 to combat intolerance and violence against persons on the basis of religion or belief. He represents the Department on issues related to the Violence Against Women Act (VAWA) and issues concerning the LGBTQ community.

In addition to his policy work, Mr. Zaffar works to build resilience and diminish retaliation against diverse communities in the wake of domestic national security and natural disaster incidents. He has worked with victims on the ground after the tragic events at the 2013 Boston Marathon, the PULSE Nightclub in Florida, and at the AME Church in Charleston, South Carolina. He is the recipient of the Benjamin Franklin Award for Public Diplomacy from Secretary of State John Kerry and the Secretary's Award for Excellence from Secretary Jeh Johnson at the Department of Homeland Security.

Mr. Zaffar is a member of the adjunct faculties of the Washington College of Law at American University, Temple University's Fox School of Business, George Mason University, and George Washington University. He teaches courses on homeland security policy and civil rights, as well as privacy and surveillance law. He has been invited to testify as an expert by the United States Congress and has led workshops and trainings on his areas of expertise around the world, most recently in Spain, Indonesia, Saudi Arabia, and Macedonia.

Mr. Zaffar is a columnist at *U.S. News & World Report,* and his writing has appeared on CNN.com, *Slate,* and *The Huffington Post.* His books, *Understanding Homeland Security: Foundations of Security Policy* and *Legal, Ethical & Moral Dilemmas in First Amendment Jurisprudence,* will be published in fall 2018 by Routledge Press.

Preface

We live in a world of rules. With every step that we take, we interact with those rules, whether we are crossing the street, buying a car, or forming a multinational enterprise. Rules exist to protect us from ourselves, but they also exist to give us a sense of order and direction, putting our beliefs into practice. And over time, those rules change, molding to the changing dynamics of a society and the evolving demands of its citizens. These rules create opportunity and take it away, open doors and close them, and everything in between.

Public policy is about the development of this system of rules. Rules cannot exist in a vacuum—they need people to create them. These people form communities that share common beliefs and values, and they turn those beliefs and values into rules that they largely agree upon. Yet within those communities, there will always be dissent—the minority that disagrees with the rules advocated by the majority. Effective rules, thus, call for compromise. Public policy is the process of filtering those ideas—distilling them into workable compromises that give structure to the ideas and beliefs of the community.

Law is the transformation of policies into rules. In order for policies to function, they must have boundaries that create space by limiting action. Laws restrict the actions of the few in order to create opportunities for the many. Laws give contours to the policies advocated by the community, turning idea statements into action statements. Ultimately, our decisions to act are our own, so laws exist to incentivize us to act in a certain manner, in accordance with the policies that our community has deemed right for us. And when we disagree with those laws, we must re-examine our policies, and thus our beliefs and ideas, to decide whether our community has changed.

Of course, the *community* that I am referring to here could be easily substituted with the term *county*, *city*, *state*, or even *country*. And while compromise over policies within a smaller community may be relatively seamless, the larger the community becomes, the more diverse interests play a part in the development of those policies, and the more opportunity for conflict appears. Yet at all levels, the fundamentals are the same. We define our individual ideas and beliefs, share those within our local community to find points of agreement, craft policies that everyone can live with, and then build the rules necessary to implement those policies. As a member of that community, it is your responsibility to participate in that policy- and rulemaking process.

This is a book about law and public policy—about the ideas and the rules we build to implement those rules. Similar books have looked at public policy and public administration in an effort to explain how the government works. Still others have considered the foundations of the legal system to understand the rulemaking institutions. This book takes a different approach. By examining laws through the lens of policy, and vice versa, we develop a complete picture of society, from idea to action. This holistic approach gives readers a chance to see not only why certain rules exist but also how those rules evolved over time and the events that inspired them. It is an attempt to give readers an opportunity not only to see but also to participate in the process of forming the structures that shape our society.

This textbook is divided into two sections. The first section is meant to give readers the tools that they will need to digest the policies and laws that surround them. These tools include a historical deep dive into the foundations of the governance structure in the United States, and to a lesser extent, the entire world; an important examination of civics and a reminder of the importance of engaging in the policymaking process; a careful breakdown of the institutions that form the backbone of the law- and policymaking institutions in the United States; and finally, perhaps the most important tool of all, critical thinking and analysis and, as part of that chapter, practical tools to find reliable sources for news, research, and other types of information.

The second section of the text comprises subject-matter analyses. I have selected a number of key subject areas and asked experts in those areas to contribute their fundamental understanding of the laws and policies that inform each of those subjects. Those subject-based chapters begin with a historical perspective on the topic, followed by a careful examination of the key policies and laws that inform that field. Each chapter highlights key vocabulary, provides practical vignettes to add context to the writing, provides a unique global component to compare perspectives from communities worldwide, and includes a number of discussion questions and recommended readings for further examination. Though in no way a complete examination of law and policy subjects, the selected chapters serve as a lens through which any subject can be evaluated, critiqued, and improved.

My hope is that this text gives you the resources that you need to lead a better life—a life that allows you to see through the noise, understand the history, and construct critical ideas and insights that help to shape the communities that all of us would like to live in. Let's get started.

Kevin J. Fandl
Washington, D.C.

1 A Historic Introduction to Law and Public Policy

Introduction

Welcome to the study of law and public policy. You are about to embark on an exciting and highly practical learning experience that includes historical precedents, controversial cases, and current events that touch on this field. The field itself is a relatively new addition to many academic programs, though the ideas behind it have been around since ancient Rome. In this text, while we will certainly pay homage to those important roots, our focus will be on understanding the real-life implications of policies, laws, and cases that impact our lives.

The book is laid out in two substantive parts. The first part (Chapters 1–4) provides you with many of the tools that you will need to properly analyze laws and policies and apply a critical eye to that analysis. In this first part, we will discuss the theories of public policy, the relevant actors in the law and policy environment, the practice of governance, and tools to effectively analyze the actions of policymakers. In the second part (Chapters 5–11), we will focus on specific subject areas, such as economic policy and foreign policy, in order to better understand how the law and policy environments work together to create the rules and norms that guide individuals and businesses both domestically and abroad. Each of these chapters includes a number of case excerpts, real-world examples provided by expert practitioners, and enough background to give you a comprehensive understanding of why today's policies and laws are what they are. The purpose of part two of the book is to show you how laws and policies interact with our lives directly.

The goal of this book, the first of its kind, is to tie together concepts that are directly related but often overlooked, and to expose readers to the foundations that form the modern policy environment so that they can make better decisions about those policies for the future. The lessons in the following pages can be applied easily in a number of disciplines, from business to law to social science, as law and policy guide nearly every aspect of our lives and work. Failing to see and understand the interconnections between law and policy will undoubtedly lead to short-sighted and uninformed decision-making, which creates a harmful policy environment for all of us.

The Historical Antecedents to Public Policy

The Gilded Age

> *To the Victor belong the Spoils.*[1]

The United States federal government that we know today is far different from how it was originally operated—and perhaps from how it was originally intended. Today's professional cadre of government officials working alongside a limited number of political appointees gives our government a steady balance of historic expertise and routine adjustments of focus. Yet many of us take for granted the distinction between the career civil service and the political appointments process. The former consists of the thousands of government workers that applied for positions with particular government agencies, competed against others for those positions, and expect to hold those positions for an extended period of time. These career civil servants acquire expertise and know-how about their agency and its mission, and they usually have an interest in seeing that agency do good work.

A political appointee, on the other hand, is not usually someone who applied to work in a particular government agency, not usually someone with extensive experience in that sector, and not someone who intends to remain in the position they receive beyond the term of their appointment. These workers are donors to or friends of the incoming President or are otherwise recommended to the President as individuals who will carry forth the policy beliefs of that President. There are roughly 4,000 political appointees at any given time, about 1,400 of them serving as low-level Schedule-C appointees who work as policy advisors to the agency, guiding agency decisions to align with the beliefs of the administration.

This is not always how government has worked. In the beginning of the United States' democracy, elected officials were able to effectively replace the entire cadre of government workers with their own appointees. An incoming administration could effectively start over with his own staff across the entire federal government, which was small at the outset but quickly expanding in number. This turnover could have the effect of destroying the knowledge and experience that the existing employees had developed and would require agencies to start from scratch in putting together new policies. This was known as the spoils system.

Early administrations did not take advantage of this spoils system to an unethical degree. It was not until the administration of President Andrew Jackson in 1829 that we see the fundamental flaw in allowing a president to upset the system of governance. Jackson rotated approximately 20% of the existing government workforce out and replaced them with his own appointees. Most of those appointments went to those who helped Jackson accede to the presidency. As he himself said, "to the victor belong the spoils." Public outcry over these appointments and the resulting failures of government led to a push for reform.

The spoils system applied by President Jackson was no longer popular policy. However, the ability of an incoming President to place his or her supporters in key positions allowed that executive to more effectively carry out their policies through executive agencies that they relied upon. Completely eliminating such a system would have created conflict between the executive and his or her agencies, which would have placed a wedge between the President and civil servants who may have had competing interests. Allowing the President to appoint the heads of these agencies ensured that his or her priority policies were conveyed, even if ultimately they were not implemented completely by career civil servants.

The Civil Service Act of 1883, commonly known as the Pendleton Act, was an attempt by Congress to achieve a balanced policy that recognized the need for a president to appoint individuals that he or she trusted to carry out their policy ideas with the need to maintain a robust civil service sector that would maintain a consistent approach to governance.[2] Similar reforms had been happening already at the city level, but civil service reform became a federal matter following the assassination of President James Garfield in 1881 by a supporter who believed that he was owed a position in government in exchange for the help he had provided during the campaign. The Pendleton Act was passed by Congress in 1883.

The Pendleton Civil Service Reform Act was the beginning of the administrative state as we understand it today. Among other things, the Act established a commission responsible for developing merit-based rules for incoming government employees. They were empowered to develop a testing system that would rank candidates based upon their knowledge and skills, rather than their connections or political donations. Following the ranking of candidates under this new "competitive service" examination, conditional job offers would be made whereby the employee had to perform well in order to be converted to a permanent civil servant.

The creation of the civil service system kicked off an era of more effective governance and less politicized administration. Long-term strategies for growth could be put in place as policies outlasted administrations. This paved the way for what has been dubbed the **progressive era** in U.S. history, which fueled a new perception of public policy.

> **Progressive era**—period of social activism and political reform from the 1890s through the late 1920s.

The Progressive Era

The U.S. federal government of the 19th century was small and relatively weak. Those who were elected often became corrupted by a system that encouraged longevity at the expense of policy. Organizations of elected officials, known as **political machines**, saw their role as giving favors to connected businesses and individuals in exchange for ongoing patronage, which allowed them to keep their political positions. Elected office became a matter of power rather than policy, leading to a mob-like environment in many major cities.

> **Political machines**—small group of political supporters and businesses led by a single boss or small autocratic group.

This situation changed with civil service reforms of the late 19th century and the election of progressive politicians who were determined to stamp out political machines and the policies they purveyed. A new era had begun with the turn of the 20th century, one in which public demands for government reform grew louder and a shared goal of modernization of civil society came into focus.

Much like social media has dramatically influenced the elections of Presidents Obama and Trump, and will likely affect most future administrations, the rise of mass media—namely, magazines—and the use of investigative journalism known as **muckraking**, helped to bring concerns about corruption, anti-competition, and ineffective governance to the forefront of the voters' agenda. One of the prime examples of this effort involves the meatpacking industry and appeared in a series of articles by Upton Sinclair in 1906:

> **Muckraking**—searching for and publishing scandalous information about people.

> **[Excerpts From Upton Sinclair's "The Jungle"]**
>
> Promptly at seven the next morning Jurgis reported for work. He came to the door that had been pointed out to him, and there he waited for nearly two hours. The boss had meant for him to enter, but had not said this, and so it was only when on his way out to hire another man that he came upon Jurgis. He gave him a good cursing, but as Jurgis did not understand a word of it he did not object. He followed the boss, who showed him where to put his street clothes, and waited while he donned the working clothes he had bought in a secondhand shop and brought with him in a bundle; then he led him to the

"killing beds." The work which Jurgis was to do here was very simple, and it took him but a few minutes to learn it. He was provided with a stiff besom, such as is used by street sweepers, and it was his place to follow down the line the man who drew out the smoking entrails from the carcass of the steer; this mass was to be swept into a trap, which was then closed, so that no one might slip into it. As Jurgis came in, the first cattle of the morning were just making their appearance; and so, with scarcely time to look about him, and none to speak to any one, he fell to work. It was a sweltering day in July, and the place ran with steaming hot blood—one waded in it on the floor. The stench was almost overpowering, but to Jurgis it was nothing. His whole soul was dancing with joy—he was at work at last! He was at work and earning money! All day long he was figuring to himself. He was paid the fabulous sum of seventeen and a half cents an hour; and as it proved a rush day and he worked until nearly seven o'clock in the evening, he went home to the family with the tidings that he had earned more than a dollar and a half in a single day!

(Excerpt from Chapter 4)

The new hands were here by the thousands. All day long the gates of the packing houses were besieged by starving and penniless men; they came, literally, by the thousands every single morning, fighting with each other for a chance for life. Blizzards and cold made no difference to them, they were always on hand; they were on hand two hours before the sun rose, an hour before the work began. Sometimes their faces froze, sometimes their feet and their hands; sometimes they froze all together—but still they came, for they had no other place to go. One day Durham advertised in the paper for two hundred men to cut ice; and all that day the homeless and starving of the city came trudging through the snow from all over its two hundred square miles. That night forty score of them crowded into the station house of the stockyards district—they filled the rooms, sleeping in each other's laps, toboggan fashion, and they piled on top of each other in the corridors, till the police shut the doors and left some to freeze outside. On the morrow, before daybreak, there were three thousand at Durham's, and the police reserves had to be sent for to quell the riot. Then Durham's bosses picked out twenty of the biggest; the "two hundred" proved to have been a printer's error.

(Excerpt from Chapter 7)

And now in the union Jurgis met men who explained all this mystery to him; and he learned that America differed from Russia in that its government existed under the form of a democracy. The officials who ruled it, and got all the graft, had to be elected first; and so there were two rival sets of grafters, known as political parties, and the one got the office which bought the most votes. Now and then, the election was very close, and that was the time the poor man came in. In the stockyards this was only in national and state elections, for in local elections the Democratic Party always carried everything. The ruler of the district was therefore the Democratic boss, a little Irishman named Mike Scully. Scully held an important party office in the state, and bossed even the mayor of the city, it was said; it was his boast that he carried the stockyards in his pocket. He was an enormously rich man—he had a hand in all the big graft in the neighborhood. It was Scully, for instance, who owned that dump which Jurgis and Ona had seen the first day of their arrival. Not only did he own the dump, but he owned the brick factory as well, and first he took out the clay and made it into bricks, and then he had the city bring garbage to fill up the hole, so that he could build houses to sell to the people. Then, too, he sold the bricks to the city, at his own price, and the city came and got them in its own wagons. And also he owned the other hole near by, where the stagnant water was; and it was he who cut the ice and sold it; and what was more, if the men told truth, he had not had to pay any taxes for the water, and he had built the ice-house out of city lumber, and had not had to pay anything for that. The newspapers had got hold of that story, and there had been a scandal; but Scully had hired somebody to confess and take all the blame, and then skip the country.

(Excerpt from Chapter 9)

There were the men in the pickle rooms, for instance, where old Antanas had gotten his death; scarce a one of these that had not some spot of horror on his person. Let a man so much as scrape his finger pushing a truck in the pickle rooms, and he might have a sore that would put him out of the world; all the joints in his fingers might be eaten by the acid, one by one. Of the butchers and floorsmen, the beef-boners and trimmers, and all those who used knives, you could scarcely find a person who had the use of his thumb; time and time again the base of it had been slashed, till it was a mere lump of flesh against which the man pressed the knife to hold it. The hands of these men would be criss-crossed with cuts, until you could no longer pretend to count them or to trace them. They would have no nails,—they had worn them off pulling hides; their knuckles were swollen so that their fingers spread out like a fan. There were men who worked in the cooking rooms, in the midst of steam and sickening odors, by artificial light; in these rooms the germs of tuberculosis might live for two years, but the supply was renewed every hour. There were the beef-luggers, who carried two-hundred-pound quarters into the refrigerator-cars; a fearful kind of work, that began at four o'clock in the morning, and that wore out the most powerful men in a few years. There were those who worked in the chilling rooms, and whose special disease was rheumatism; the time limit that a man could work in the chilling rooms was said to be five years. There were the wool-pluckers, whose hands went to pieces even sooner than the hands of the pickle men; for the pelts of the sheep had to be painted with acid to loosen the wool, and then the pluckers had to pull out this wool with their bare hands, till the acid had eaten their fingers off. There were those who made the tins for the canned meat; and their hands, too, were a maze of cuts, and each cut represented a chance for blood poisoning. Some worked at the stamping machines, and it was very seldom that one could work long there at the pace that was set, and not give out and forget himself and have a part of his hand chopped off. There were the "hoisters," as they were called, whose task it was to press the lever which lifted the dead cattle off the floor. They ran along upon a rafter, peering down through the damp and the steam; and as old Durham's architects had not built the killing room for the convenience of the hoisters, at every few feet they would have to stoop under a beam, say four feet above the one they ran on; which got them into the habit of stooping, so that in a few years they would be walking like chimpanzees. Worst of any,

> however, were the fertilizer men, and those who served in the cooking rooms. These people could not be shown to the visitor,—for the odor of a fertilizer man would scare any ordinary visitor at a hundred yards, and as for the other men, who worked in tank rooms full of steam, and in some of which there were open vats near the level of the floor, their peculiar trouble was that they fell into the vats; and when they were fished out, there was never enough of them left to be worth exhibiting,—sometimes they would be overlooked for days, till all but the bones of them had gone out to the world as Durham's Pure Leaf Lard!
>
> (Excerpt from Chapter 9)

The conditions described in Sinclair's publication *The Jungle* and the corruption and ineptitude of government exposed in the mass media drove the progressives to develop an aggressive reform agenda. Their top priorities at the turn of the 20th century were:

- Eliminating corruption and graft in politics
- Improving education and investing in science and technology
- Empowering women with the right to vote
- Breaking apart corporations that became too large and powerful

The first progressive elected to the presidency was Theodore Roosevelt in 1901.

Progressives were able to achieve many of their goals, some through Constitutional Amendments. In order to reduce the power of political machines and political bosses, which largely controlled state legislatures, which elected Senators at the time, Congress enacted the 17th Amendment. The 17th Amendment required the direct election of Senators, bypassing state legislatures and allowing more independence in the voting process.

Improvements in education and science were happening largely at the state and local levels. Mass media was being used to help farmers learn new agricultural techniques that would help them with their crops—modernizing farming. Rural schools, which had been run as one-room operations led by local and often untrained women, were replaced with larger operations led by trained professionals. In cities, efficiency reforms were being implemented to help spread science and technology among the rapidly growing population.

The safety of food and medicines became a significant issue following a number of illnesses and deaths from the use of unregulated products and following the outcry over investigative journalist reports about safety in the food and drug industries. The **Pure Food and Drug Act** of 1906 was enacted as a first step in crafting federal regulations about the quality of food and drugs that will be sold to consumers (see Chapter 8 on Food Policy).

> Pure Food and Drug Act—first legislative attempt to regulate the food and cosmetic industry.

A less popular progressive policy at the time was prohibition—a ban on the manufacture, sale, and transport of alcoholic beverages. Some progressives saw this as a way to break apart the powerful liquor lobby, which held significant influence over the government. However, the push was largely driven by evangelicals, who believed that alcohol was to blame for a number of societal ills, from child abuse to poverty. Ultimately, Congress enacted the 18th Amendment, establishing the prohibition era.

Following passage of the 18th Amendment, federal prohibition officers began shutting down distilleries, vineyards, saloons, and any related business engaged in the sale or manufacture of alcohol. A **black market** quickly arose to satisfy the unmet demand for alcohol. That black market became violent at times, feeding the rise of mafia organizations in major cities that controlled illegal sales of alcohol. Al Capone made a name for himself during this era. He told one reporter, "All I do is to supply a public demand . . . somebody had to throw some liquor on that thirst. Why not me?" (Sullivan, 111).³ Prohibition was ultimately repealed in 1933 by the 21st Amendment, a policy change pushed by Catholics, among others.

> Black market—economic channel to sell goods not authorized for sale, such as liquor during Prohibition.

The economic policies of the progressive era departed significantly from those of the Gilded Age before it. During the prior era (see Chapter 5 on Economic Policy), government took a *laissez-faire* approach to the economy, allowing business to operate largely without government intervention or regulation. However, as corporations began to grow larger, small businesses and farmers began asking for government intervention. By the late 19th century, Congress had enacted two statutes (the Interstate Commerce Act and the Sherman Antitrust Act) to offer some relief to these groups through regulation of railroads and corporations. But an economic crisis between 1893 and 1897, followed by rising inequality in the very early 20th century, led progressives to take a different approach to economic policy.

Initial steps of the progressive era included the creation of the Federal Reserve in 1913 in order to stabilize and regulate the U.S. monetary system, and the Clayton Antitrust Act of 1914, which went further than the Sherman Act by providing details about the formation of large corporations through mergers and acquisitions, among other things. Key among the reforms of this time was passage of the 16th Amendment, which enabled the levy and collection by the federal government of the first personal income tax.

Progressives had become increasingly concerned about the growing gap between the rich and the poor. They had also become concerned about the need for government revenue, which, prior to 1913, had largely come from the imposition of import tariffs on foreign goods. Democrat Woodrow Wilson, along with his democratic Congress, secured passage of this Amendment, which initially focused only on taxes on the rich in an effort at redistribution. Following U.S. entry into World War I in 1917, the income tax became quite a useful tool in funding the costly war efforts (see Figure 1.1).

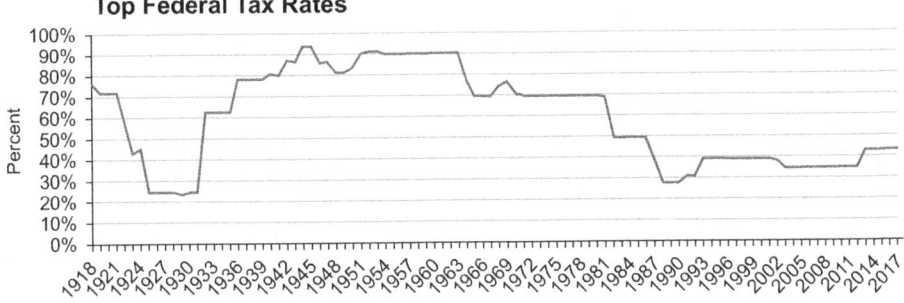

Figure 1.1 Top Federal Income Tax Rates (1913–2017).

Source: Bradford Tax Institute, https://bradfordtaxinstitute.com/Free_Resources/Federal-Income-Tax-Rates.aspx

The Public Policy Era Begins

The early 20th century was not simply a time of increasing federal tax rates and engagement in global warfare. It was also a time of reinvention in the U.S. government. There was a growing progressive movement against corruption and favoritism in the public sector and a new interest in using the government as an advocate for the citizenry, defending citizens against encroaching business interests and social injustice.

In his 1887 article, "The Study of Administration," Woodrow Wilson acknowledged the evolving need for a government that was capable of responding to the increasingly complex needs of society. Population growth, rising economic inequality resulting from growing business interests, and new social concerns led him to this conclusion. Wilson saw lawmaking and policymaking as two sides of the same coin. Legislators would enact laws that civil servants in the myriad federal and state agencies (as well as within some elements of the private sector) would apply on a practical level. He said, "[e]very particular application of general law is an act of administration."[4]

Wilson believed that the administration of government, what later became known as public policy, was a field of business. Organizational theory, administration, efficiency, and innovation were all areas that clearly intersected with the organization of the public sector. He argued that civil servants should be experts in their fields and should carry knowledge across administrations without the influence of politics on their decision-making. This would ensure that a more neutral, capable core of civil servants could carry on the business of governance.

Frederick Taylor, a mechanical engineer who wrote about efficiency during the Wilson Administration, published essays focused on the need to develop efficiency in government, as it had been developing in business:

> We can see our forests vanishing, our water-powers going to waste, our soil being carried by floods into the sea; and the end of our coal and our iron is in sight. But our larger wastes of human effort, which go on every day through such of our acts as are blundering, ill-directed, or inefficient, and which Mr. Roosevelt refers to as a lack of "national efficiency," are less visible less tangible, and are but vaguely appreciated.
>
> The search for better, for more competent men, from the presidents of our great companies down to our household servants, was never more vigorous than it is now. And more than ever before is the demand for competent men in excess of the supply.[5]

Taylor's approach, which became known as the Scientific Management Theory, drove a desire to utilize scientific methods to create efficiencies in government. He sought to reduce the amount of labor necessary to create significant economic output through the application of scientific methods. This approach influenced government as well through at least the Roosevelt Administration.

This theme of public policy as part of the field of business was picked up in the first text on public policy, Leonard White's 1926 *Introduction to the Study of Public Administration*. Much like Wilson had argued in his article decades before, White, who had worked in the Theodore Roosevelt Administration, felt that government needed to reflect the efficiencies and management techniques that were helping business of the day to become successful. Good management and good government went hand in hand, according to Leonard, and the study of management should be part of the study of government.

Wilson had made it apparent that public administration and public law are interconnected fields and that both required a clear understanding of management in order to function properly. White agreed on their relationship, noting that, "Public administration is embedded in law, and the student of the subject will often be with the statutes."[6] However, White emphasized that this connection can be "exaggerated," and the role of the lawyer in public administration should be deemphasized.[7] White preferred studying policy from the perspective of the government manager rather than the Supreme Court Justice, as Wilson might have preferred.

These early developments in the understanding of the field of public policy and administration drove a rethinking of how government should evolve to address the changing needs of society. Following on Taylor's observation that the demand for qualified civil servants outweighed the supply, new civil service position descriptions were developed to solicit individuals with appropriate training and skills to drive a competent administration. To fill those positions, new educational programs arose in the burgeoning field of public administration. The first graduate program in this field was the Maxwell School of Citizenship and Public Affairs established at the University of Syracuse in 1924 with the mission "to cull from every source those principles, facts, and elements which, combined, make up our rights and duties and our value and distinctiveness as United States citizens."[8]

At the same time that these new training programs and job opportunities were opening, philosopher Max Weber published his seminal 1922 text, *Economy and Society*.[9] That text was a sociology treatise that addressed a range of social and political topics; however, it also traced the rise of capitalism in the West and tried to explain what made Europe and the United States, in particular, so successful in establishing thriving economic environments. Weber argued that those countries had put in place bureaucracies and institutions that provided the tools necessary to protect nascent businesses and to facilitate their growth and opportunity. He concluded that this very bureaucracy formed the essential and necessary character of the West.

As these changes were taking place in administration, Congress was also taking a more aggressive role toward the regulation of business. They increasingly saw their role as a safety valve for consumers and workers against the rapidly expanding big-business sector. A number of statutes were passed in the late 18th and early 19th century that might be classified as assertions of the federal government's growing interest in playing a more prominent role in society and protecting citizens from the threat of business. Among others, these acts included:

- The Interstate Commerce Commission (1887) to regulate railroads
- The Sherman Act (1890) to prevent monopolies
    - Augmented by the Clayton and Federal Trade Commission Acts (1914)
- The Pure Food and Drug Act (1906) to regulate germs in food
- The Meat Inspection Act (1907) to regulate the quality of meat products
- The Federal Employers' Liability Act (1908) to incentivize private employers to reduce industrial accidents
- The Federal Reserve Act (1913) to protect currency and the U.S. economy

Along Came a Baker

The newfound power in the federal government may have produced a more stable economy and safer consumers, but at the same time, increasing government intervention met resistance from businesses large and small that felt constrained in their ability to grow. Some businesses believed that the government was encroaching on their freedoms and preventing them from the pursuit of the American dream. Economic powerhouses of the time, such as oil baron J.D. Rockefeller, railroad industrialist Andrew Carnegie, or banker J.P. Morgan, had all pursued their riches largely absent government oversight. New regulations, such as those mentioned previously, were seen by some businesses as prohibitive in their own economic pursuits. Joseph Lochner, a baker, was one of those people. His case follows.

Lochner v. New York, *198 U.S. 45 (1905)*

[Background] In the 1890s, conditions in bakeshops in New York were known to be unsanitary. An exposé published in a New York newspaper in 1894 highlighted many of these conditions,[10] including vermin and dirt as well as excessive working hours for employees. Protests and strikes ensued, led largely by bakers' unions in New York. In response, the New York state legislature unanimously passed the Bakeshop Act of 1895, and the Republican governor signed the bill into law.

Joseph Lochner, who owned Lochner's Home Bakery in Utica, New York, had been fined twice for violating the Bakeshop Act. After the second fine, Lochner sued the state, challenging their authority to regulate his business. He lost his case in the New York Appellate Term and the Court of Appeals. He appealed to the U.S. Supreme Court.

> The statute necessarily interferes with the right of contract between the employer and employees concerning the number of hours in which the latter may labor in the bakery of the employer. The general right to make a contract in relation to his business is part of the liberty of the individual protected by the Fourteenth Amendment of the Federal Constitution. Under that provision, no State can deprive any person of life, liberty or property without due process of law. The right to purchase or to sell labor is part of the liberty protected by this amendment unless there are circumstances which exclude the right. There are, however, certain powers, existing in the sovereignty of each State in the Union, somewhat vaguely termed police powers, the exact description and limitation of which have not been attempted by the courts. Those powers, broadly stated and without, at present, any attempt at a more specific limitation, relate to the safety, health, morals and general welfare of the public. Both property and liberty are held on such reasonable conditions as may be imposed by the governing power of the State in the exercise of those powers, and with such conditions the Fourteenth Amendment was not designed to interfere.
>
> The State therefore has power to prevent the individual from making certain kinds of contracts, and, in regard to them, the Federal Constitution offers no protection. If the contract be one which the State, in the legitimate exercise of its police power, has the right to prohibit, it is not prevented from prohibiting it by the Fourteenth Amendment. Contracts in violation of a statute, either of the Federal or state government, or

a contract to let one's property for immoral purposes, or to do any other unlawful act, could obtain no protection from the Federal Constitution as coming under the liberty of person or of free contract. Therefore, when the State, by its legislature, in the assumed exercise of its police powers, has passed an act which seriously limits the right to labor or the right of contract in regard to their means of livelihood between persons who are *sui juris* (both employer and employee), it becomes of great importance to determine which shall prevail—the right of the individual to labor for such time as he may choose or the right of the State to prevent the individual from laboring or from entering into any contract to labor beyond a certain time prescribed by the State.

***

It must, of course, be conceded that there is a limit to the valid exercise of the police power by the State. There is no dispute concerning this general proposition. Otherwise the Fourteenth Amendment would have no efficacy, and the legislatures of the States would have unbounded power, and it would be enough to say that any piece of legislation was enacted to conserve the morals, the health or the safety of the people; such legislation would be valid no matter how absolutely without foundation the claim might be. The claim of the police power would be a mere pretext—become another and delusive name for the supreme sovereignty of the State to be exercised free from constitutional restraint. This is not contended for. In every case that comes before this court, therefore, where legislation of this character is concerned and where the protection of the Federal Constitution is sought, the question necessarily arises: is this a fair, reasonable and appropriate exercise of the police power of the State, or is it an unreasonable, unnecessary and arbitrary interference with the right of the individual to his personal liberty or to enter into those contracts in relation to labor which may seem to him appropriate or necessary for the support of himself and his family? Of course, the liberty of contract relating to labor includes both parties to it. The one has as much right to purchase as the other to sell labor.

This is not a question of substituting the judgment of the court for that of the legislature. If the act be within the power of the State, it is valid although the judgment of the court might be totally opposed to the enactment of such a law. But the question would still remain: is it within the police power of the State?, and that question must be answered by the court.

The question whether this act is valid as a labor law, pure and simple, may be dismissed in a few words. There is no reasonable ground for interfering with the liberty of person or the right of free contract by determining the hours of labor in the occupation of a baker. There is no contention that bakers as a class are not equal in intelligence and capacity to men in other trades or manual occupations, or that they are able to assert their rights and care for themselves without the protecting arm of the State, interfering with their independence of judgment and of action. They are in no sense wards of the State. Viewed in the light of a purely labor law, with no reference whatever to the question of health, we think that a law like the one before us involves neither the safety, the morals, nor the welfare of the public, and that the interest of the public is not in the slightest degree affected by such an act. The law must be upheld, if at all, as a law pertaining to the health of the individual engaged in the occupation of a baker. It does not affect any other portion of the public than those who are engaged in that occupation. Clean and wholesome bread does not depend upon whether the baker works but ten hours per day or only sixty hours a week. The limitation of the hours of labor does not come within the police power on that ground.

It is a question of which of two powers or rights shall prevail—the power of the State to legislate or the right of the individual to liberty of person and freedom of contract. The mere assertion that the subject relates though but in a remote degree to the public health does not necessarily render the enactment valid. The act must have a more direct relation, as a means to an end, and the end itself must be appropriate and legitimate, before an act can be held to be valid which interferes with the general right of an individual to be free in his person and in his power to contract in relation to his own labor.

This case has caused much diversity of opinion in the state courts. In the Supreme Court, two of the five judges composing the Appellate Division dissented from the judgment affirming the validity of the act. In the Court of Appeals, three of the seven judges also dissented from the judgment upholding the statute. Although found in what is called a labor law of the State, the Court of Appeals has upheld the act as one relating to the public health—in other words, as a health law. One of the judges of the Court of Appeals, in upholding the law, stated that, in his opinion, the regulation in question could not be sustained unless they were able to say, from common knowledge, that working in a bakery and candy factory was an unhealthy employment. The judge held that, while the evidence was not uniform, it still led him to the conclusion that the occupation of a baker or confectioner was unhealthy, and tended to result in diseases of the respiratory organs. Three of the judges dissented from that view, and they thought the occupation of a baker was not to such an extent unhealthy as to warrant the interference of the legislature with the liberty of the individual.

We think the limit of the police power has been reached and passed in this case. There is, in our judgment, no reasonable foundation for holding this to be necessary or appropriate as a health law to safeguard the public health or the health of the individuals who are following the trade of a baker. If this statute be valid, and if, therefore, a proper case is made out in which to deny the right of an individual, *sui juris*, as employer or employee, to make contracts for the labor of the latter under the protection of the provisions of the Federal Constitution, there would seem to be no length to which legislation of this nature might not go. The case differs widely, as we have already stated, from the expressions of this court in regard to laws of this nature, as stated in *Holden v. Hardy* and *Jacobson v. Massachusetts, supra*. We think that there can be no fair doubt that the trade of a baker, in and of itself, is not an unhealthy one to that degree which would authorize the legislature to interfere with the right to labor, and with the right of free contract on the part of the individual, either as employer or employee. In looking through statistics regarding all trades and occupations, it may be true that the trade of a baker does not appear to be as healthy as some other trades, and is also vastly more healthy than still others. To the common understanding, the trade of a baker has never been regarded as an unhealthy one. Very likely, physicians would not recommend the exercise of that or of any other trade as a remedy for ill health. Some occupations are more healthy than others, but we think there are none which might not come under the power of the legislature to supervise and control the hours of working therein if the mere fact that the occupation is not absolutely and perfectly healthy is to confer that right upon the legislative department of the Government. It might be safely affirmed that almost all occupations more or less affect the health. There must be more than the mere fact of the possible existence of some small amount of unhealthiness to warrant legislative interference with liberty. It is unfortunately true that labor, even in any department, may possibly carry with it the seeds of unhealthiness. But are we all, on that account, at the mercy of legislative majorities? A printer, a tinsmith, a locksmith, a carpenter, a cabinetmaker, a dry goods clerk, a bank's, a lawyer's or a physician's clerk, or a clerk in almost any kind of business, would all come under the power of the legislature on this assumption. No trade, no occupation, no mode of earning one's living could escape this all-pervading power, and the acts of the legislature in limiting the hours of labor in all employments would be valid although such limitation might seriously cripple the ability of the laborer to support himself and his family. In our large cities there are many buildings into which the sun penetrates for but a short time in each day, and these buildings are occupied by people carrying on the business of bankers, brokers, lawyers, real estate, and many other kinds of business, aided by many clerks, messengers, and other employs. Upon the assumption of the validity of this act under review, it is not possible to say that an act prohibiting lawyers' or bank clerks, or others from contracting to labor for their employers more than eight hours a day would be invalid. It might be said that it is unhealthy to work more than that number of hours in an apartment lighted by artificial light during the working hours of the day; that the occupation of the bank clerk, the lawyer's clerk, the real estate clerk, or the broker's clerk in such offices is therefore unhealthy, and the legislature, in its paternal wisdom, must therefore have the right to legislate on the subject of, and to limit the hours for, such labor, and, if it exercises that power and its validity be questioned, it is sufficient to say it has reference to the public health; it has reference to the health of the employees condemned to labor day after day in buildings where the sun never shines; it is a health law, and therefore it is valid, and cannot be questioned by the courts.

The Court ultimately sided with Lochner and against the state's effort to regulate business. They found that the 14th Amendment to the U.S. Constitution contains an implicit freedom of contract principle that the state cannot easily infringe upon with regulations such as this. The result of the ruling was the start of what became known as the *Lochner Era*, which defined a period of judicial pushback against legislative and executive efforts to regulate business. No fewer than 159 statutes during this era were struck down by the Supreme Court as being overly restrictive on business, thwarting the efforts of the progressives to expand and enhance the role of government in society.

During the *Lochner Era*, the unrestricted growth of business led to strong economic growth alongside growing economic inequality and consumer safety issues. Figure 1.2 exemplifies the strong economic growth leading up to the 1929 stock market crash.

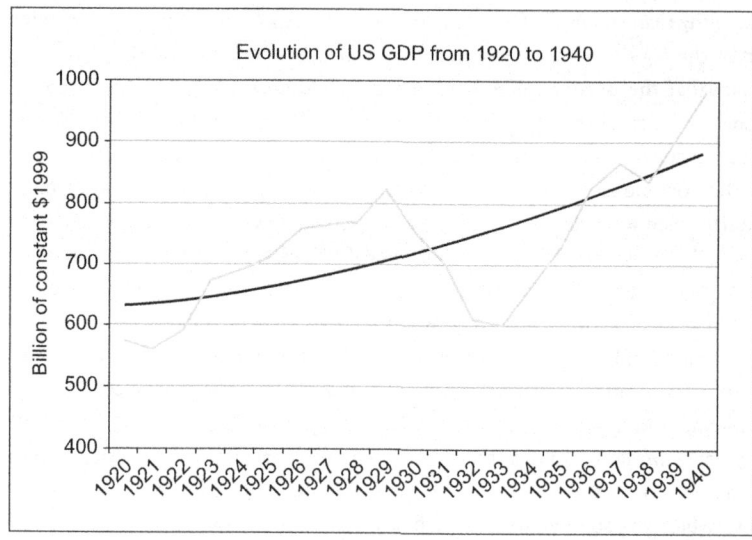

Figure 1.2 Economic Growth in the United States during the Lochner Era.
Source: Susan Carter, ed. *Historical Statistics of the US: Millennial Edition* (2006), series Ca9.

The Laissez-Faire Approach to Regulation of Business

The Roaring Twenties and the swift economic growth of that decade, which brought mass production of the automobile, movies, and radio, as well as jazz, also brought rising inequality and an increasing level of executive compensation that was out of line with previous decades during the Gilded Age. Reflecting the general sentiment at the time, President Calvin Coolidge said in 1927 that "the business of America is business."[11]

As reflected in the classic novel by F. Scott Fitzgerald, *The Great Gatsby*, the 1920s was a time of previously unheard-of wealth, vast inequality, and rapid economic development in the United States. As a number of new enterprises formed as corporations, including automobile and communications companies, a broader swath of investors began putting their earnings into companies, hoping to reap profits from the seemingly unstoppable American economic engine. Stock prices continued to rise throughout the decade with no apparent end in sight—that is, until 1929. The 1929 stock market crash and **bank run** quickly stopped the joyous consumerism and modernization period of the early 20th century.

Investors often act based upon expectations and perceptions of what the market will do. That was certainly the case in September of 1929, when British investor Clarence Hatry and his associate were jailed for fraud and forgery, causing the London stock exchange to crash. This set off a series of unfortunate events in the United States and elsewhere around the world. U.S. investors slowly began selling off stocks, lowering their value and generating a perception that the market had peaked and was now about to tumble. On October 24, 1929, known as *Black Thursday*, U.S. investors sold off roughly 11% of shares held on the market. Wealthy investor and stock exchange vice president Richard Whitney, at the behest of other wealthy investors, purchased significant shares in U.S. steel and other *blue chip* stocks above market price in order to give confidence to investors. This stabilized the market until the following week when, on *Black Tuesday*, 16 million shares were sold off and the market lost 12% of its value.

> **Bank run**—a large number of bank customers seeking to withdraw their funds at the same time, usually leading the bank to fail or close.

Following the crash, many banks that had used their clients' funds to invest in the now significantly devalued stock market went out of business. In addition, thousands of businesses closed and unemployment skyrocketed to 25%. As discussed in more detail in Chapter 5 on Economic Policy, this was the end of the Roaring Twenties and the start of the Great Depression.

As discussed later in this text, the Great Depression was likely made worse by other factors, including the increasing isolationism that led to laws such as the Smoot-Hawley Tariff Act of 1930 (see Chapter 5 on Economic Policy). For our purposes in this opening chapter, it is important to note that this was also a period in which the laissez-faire approach to governance was being challenged by progressives once again. It would be the pivotal moment in the development of the modern federal regulatory state that we know today, but it would take a number of social crises to generate the support for policies that would turn the government from a facilitator of business to an advocate for consumers.

Breaking Bad and the New Deal

President Franklin Delano Roosevelt was elected in 1932 in the midst of the Great Depression and a declining American economy. He ran on a platform that emphasized a radical departure from the past. His New Deal policies would place government at the center of the economy rather than business, giving far more centralized control to regulatory agencies (many of which his administration would ultimately create). And given the economic climate at the time, he had a great deal of support for his policies in Congress.

The first New Deal package that Roosevelt sent to Congress focused directly on the financial crisis. It included the Emergency Banking Act of 1933, the Federal Emergency Relief Administration, and the Securities Act of 1933, among others. All of these initiatives focused on shoring up the banking system and trying to prevent a crash like that of 1929 from happening again. The reforms easily passed the democratically controlled Congress with support by liberal Republicans.

The second New Deal package included more controversial reforms focused on the establishment of social protection schemes for workers. These included the Wagner Act, which protected labor union organizing; the Social Security Act, which provided financial support for the elderly; the Fair Labor Standards Act, which set rules for maximum hours and minimum wages for all workers; and the Works Progress Administration, making the U.S. government the largest employer in the country.

The first set of reforms achieved its intended effect of stabilizing the banking industry and building trust in the banking system once again. And the Works Progress Administration, among other reforms from the second package, brought unemployment down quickly. Similarly, Roosevelt used tax policy to both reduce economic inequality and to generate the revenue that the government would need to pay for the new social programs that it was rapidly implementing. This included a tax as high as 79% on incomes over $5 million.

By the time of the 1936 reelection, Roosevelt had garnered not only a more stable and prosperous economy but also widespread support for his policies and the Democratic party. Following his landslide victory in 1936, in which he won over 500 electoral votes, one *New York Times* reporter noted that his re-election was "the most overwhelming testimonial of approval ever received by a national candidate in the history of the nation."[12]

However rosy the state of affairs appeared on the outside, Roosevelt was well aware that he faced a significant legal hurdle for his New Deal policies at the U.S.

Supreme Court. The Court took a conservative turn during the previous Hoover Administration and included four justices—Pierce Butler, James McReynolds, George Sutherland, and Willis Van Devanter—who consistently voted conservative (known as the "Four Horsemen") and a fifth, Own Roberts, who swung in their favor on economic matters. The Court struck down many of Roosevelt's new policies, including the Agricultural Adjustment Act,[13] the Coal Conservation Act,[14] and the National Industrial Recovery Act,[15] among many others. Their decisions were based upon a very narrow interpretation of the Commerce Clause of the U.S. Constitution, which Roosevelt had contended gave the federal government wide discretion to regulate matters of the U.S. economy.

The Supreme Court's opposition to Roosevelt's attempt to insert the government—both state and local—into matters that affect business came to a head in the 1936 case of *Morehead v. New York ex rel. Tipaldo*.[16] The case involved a New York state law that declared it against the public policy of the state for a business to employ a female employee at an oppressive or unreasonable wage, which the Act defined as "both less than the fair and reasonable value of the services rendered and less than sufficient to meet the minimum cost of living necessary for health."[17] The complainant in the case, the owner of a laundromat that violated this Act, contended that the New York law should be deemed against public policy just as the federal minimum wage law (enacted under Roosevelt) had been.[18]

The Court, in a 5–4 decision, struck down the New York law on the same principles of the *Lochner* decision, stating that government was not empowered to limit the freedom of business to contract with society as they saw fit. Roosevelt saw this as the last straw and put in place a plan to change the Court's "horse-and-buggy definition of interstate commerce."[19]

In February 1937, Roosevelt stunned Congress with his request to appoint an additional Justice to the U.S. Supreme Court for every member over the age of 70 (the average age at the time was 71). If approved, this would have allowed him to appoint as many as six additional Justices to the Court. Whether Roosevelt intended for this proposal to actually be approved or to simply alert Congress and the Court to the fact that the Justices were aged and perhaps a barrier to his progressive policies is unclear. He noted in a speech that, "[t]his brings forward the question of aged or infirm judges—a subject of delicacy and yet one which requires frank discussion."

Roosevelt's Democrats held a significant majority in the Congress; accordingly, it was reported at the time that his proposal was likely to pass without much controversy. Whether it was this pressure or the growing public sentiment against the Court's defense of business over individuals, the Court took a swift turn in 1937 away from its laissez-faire past and opened the door to allowing progressives some room to regulate.

Parrish v. West Coast Hotel, 300 U.S. 379 (1937)

The appellant conducts a hotel. The appellee, Elsie Parrish, was employed as a chambermaid and (with her husband) brought this suit to recover the difference between the wages paid her and the minimum wage fixed pursuant to the state law. The minimum wage was $14.50 per week of 48 hours. The appellant challenged the act as repugnant to the due process clause of the Fourteenth Amendment of the Constitution of the United States. The Supreme Court of the State, reversing the trial court, sustained the statute and directed judgment for the plaintiffs. The case is here on appeal.

The appellant relies upon the decision of this Court in *Adkins v. Children's Hospital*, 261 U. S. 525, which held invalid the District of Columbia Minimum Wage Act, which was attacked under the due process clause of the Fifth Amendment. On the argument at bar, counsel for the appellees attempted to distinguish the *Adkins* case upon the ground that the appellee was employed in a hotel, and that the business of an innkeeper was affected with a public interest. That effort at distinction is obviously futile, as it appears that, in one of the cases ruled by the *Adkins* opinion, the employee was a woman employed as an elevator operator in a hotel.

The recent case of *Morehead v. New York ex rel. Tipaldo*, 298 U. S. 587, came here on certiorari to the New York court, which had held the New York minimum wage act for women to be invalid. A minority of this Court thought that the New York statute was distinguishable in a material feature from that involved in the *Adkins* case, and, that for that and other reasons, the New

York statute should be sustained. But the Court of Appeals of New York had said that it found no material difference between the two statutes, and this Court held that the "meaning of the statute" as fixed by the decision of the state court "must be accepted here as if the meaning had been specifically expressed in the enactment." That view led the affirmance by this Court of the judgment in the *Morehead* case, as the Court considered that the only question before it was whether the *Adkins* case was distinguishable, and that reconsideration of that decision had not been sought. Upon that point, the Court said:

> The petition for the writ sought review upon the ground that this case [*Morehead*] is distinguishable from that one [*Adkins*]. No application has been made for reconsideration of the constitutional question there decided. The validity of the principles upon which that decision rests is not challenged. This court confines itself to the ground upon which the writ was asked or granted.... Here, the review granted was no broader than that sought by the petitioner.... He is not entitled, and does not ask, to be heard upon the question whether the *Adkins* case should be overruled. He maintains that it may be distinguished on the ground that the statutes are vitally dissimilar.

We think that the question which was not deemed to be open in the *Morehead* case is open and is necessarily presented here. The Supreme Court of Washington has upheld the minimum wage statute of that State. It has decided that the statute is a reasonable exercise of the police power of the State. In reaching that conclusion, the state court has invoked principles long established by this Court in the application of the Fourteenth Amendment. The state court has refused to regard the decision in the *Adkins* case as determinative, and has pointed to our decisions both before and since that case as justifying its position. We are of the opinion that this ruling of the state court demands on our part a reexamination of the *Adkins* case. The importance of the question, in which many States having similar laws are concerned, the close division by which the decision in the *Adkins* case was reached, and the economic conditions which have supervened, and in the light of which the reasonableness of the exercise of the protective power of the State must be considered, make it not only appropriate, but we think imperative, that, in deciding the present case, the subject should receive fresh consideration.

***

The principle which must control our decision is not in doubt. The constitutional provision invoked is the due process clause of the Fourteenth Amendment, governing the States, as the due process clause invoked in the *Adkins* case governed Congress. In each case, the violation alleged by those attacking minimum wage regulation for women is deprivation of freedom of contract. What is this freedom? The Constitution does not speak of freedom of contract. It speaks of liberty and prohibits the deprivation of liberty without due process of law. In prohibiting that deprivation, the Constitution does not recognize an absolute and uncontrollable liberty. Liberty in each of its phases has its history and connotation. But the liberty safeguarded is liberty in a social organization which requires the protection of law against the evils which menace the health, safety, morals and welfare of the people. Liberty under the Constitution is thus necessarily subject to the restraints of due process, and regulation which is reasonable in relation to its subject and is adopted in the interests of the community is due process.

This essential limitation of liberty in general governs freedom of contract in particular. More than twenty-five years ago, we set forth the applicable principle in these words, after referring to the cases where the liberty guaranteed by the Fourteenth Amendment had been broadly described:

> But it was recognized in the cases cited, as in many others, that freedom of contract is a qualified, and not an absolute, right. There is no absolute freedom to do as one wills or to contract as one chooses. The guaranty of liberty does not withdraw from legislative supervision that wide department of activity which consists of the making of contracts, or deny to government the power to provide restrictive safeguards. Liberty implies the absence of arbitrary restraint, not immunity from reasonable regulations and prohibitions imposed in the interests of the community.

This power under the Constitution to restrict freedom of contract has had many illustrations. That it may be exercised in the public interest with respect to contracts between employer and employee is undeniable. Thus, statutes have been sustained limiting employment in underground mines and smelters to eight hours a day (*Holden v. Hardy*, 169 U. S. 366); in requiring redemption in cash of store orders or other evidences of indebtedness issued in the payment of wages (*Knoxville Iron Co. v. Harbison*, 183 U. S. 13); in forbidding the payment of seamen's wages in advance (*Patterson v. Bark Eudora*, 190 U. S. 169); in making it unlawful to contract to pay miners employed at quantity rates upon the basis of screened coal instead of the weight of the coal as originally produced in the mine (*McLean v. Arkansas*, 211 U. S. 539); in prohibiting contracts limiting liability for injuries to employees (*Chicago, B. & Q. R. Co. v. McGuire, supra*); in limiting hours of work of employees in manufacturing establishments (*Bunting v. Oregon*, 243 U. S. 426); and in maintaining workmen's compensation laws (*New York Central R. Co. v. White*, 243 U. S. 188; *Mountain Timber Co. v. Washington*, 243 U. S. 219). In dealing with the relation of employer and employed, the legislature has necessarily a wide field of discretion in order that there may be suitable protection of health and safety, and that peace and good order may be promoted through regulations designed to insure wholesome conditions of work and freedom from oppression.

The point that has been strongly stressed that adult employees should be deemed competent to make their own contracts was decisively met nearly forty years ago in *Holden v. Hardy, supra*, where we pointed out the inequality in the footing of the parties. We said:

> The legislature has also recognized the fact, which the experience of legislators in many States has corroborated, that the proprietors of these establishments and their operatives do not stand upon an equality, and that their interests are, to a certain extent, conflicting. The former naturally desire to obtain as much labor as possible from their employees, while the latter are often induced by the fear of discharge to conform to regulations which their judgment, fairly exercised, would pronounce to be detrimental to their health or strength. In other words, the proprietors lay down the rules and the laborers are practically constrained to obey them. In such cases, self-interest is often an unsafe guide, and the legislature may properly interpose its authority.

And we added that the fact

> that both parties are of full age and competent to contract does not necessarily deprive the State of the power to interfere where the parties do not stand upon an equality, or where the public health demands that one party to the contract shall be protected against himself.
>
> The State still retains an interest in his welfare, however reckless he may be. The whole is no greater than the sum of all the parts, and when the individual health, safety and welfare are sacrificed or neglected, the State must suffer.

It is manifest that this established principle is peculiarly applicable in relation to the employment of women, in whose protection the State has a special interest. That phase of the subject received elaborate consideration in *Muller v. Oregon* (1908), 208 U. S. 412, where the constitutional authority of the State to limit the working hours of women was sustained. We emphasized the consideration that "woman's physical structure and the performance of maternal functions place her at a disadvantage in the struggle for subsistence," and that her physical wellbeing "becomes an object of public interest and care in order to preserve the strength and vigor of the race." We emphasized the need of protecting women against oppression despite her possession of contractual rights. We said that,

> though limitations upon personal and contractual rights may be removed by legislation, there is that in her disposition and habits of life which will operate against a

full assertion of those rights. She will still be where some legislation to protect her seems necessary to secure a real equality of right.

***

With full recognition of the earnestness and vigor which characterize the prevailing opinion in the *Adkins* case, we find it impossible to reconcile that ruling with these well considered declarations. What can be closer to the public interest than the health of women and their protection from unscrupulous and overreaching employers? And if the protection of women is a legitimate end of the exercise of state power, how can it be said that the requirement of the payment of a minimum wage fairly fixed in order to meet the very necessities of existence is not an admissible means to that end? The legislature of the State was clearly entitled to consider the situation of women in employment, the fact that they are in the class receiving the least pay, that their bargaining power is relatively weak, and that they are the ready victims of those who would take advantage of their necessitous circumstances. The legislature was entitled to adopt measures to reduce the evils of the "sweating system," the exploiting of workers at wages so low as to be insufficient to meet the bare cost of living, thus making their very helplessness the occasion of a most injurious competition. The legislature had the right to consider that its minimum wage requirements would be an important aid in carrying out its policy of protection. The adoption of similar requirements by many States evidences a deep-seated conviction both as to the presence of the evil and as to the means adapted to check it. Legislative response to that conviction cannot be regarded as arbitrary or capricious, and that is all we have to decide. Even if the wisdom of the policy be regarded as debatable and its effects uncertain, still the legislature is entitled to its judgment.

There is an additional and compelling consideration which recent economic experience has brought into a strong light. The exploitation of a class of workers who are in an unequal position with respect to bargaining power, and are thus relatively defenceless against the denial of a living wage, is not only detrimental to their health and wellbeing, but casts a direct burden for their support upon the community. What these workers lose in wages, the taxpayers are called upon to pay. The bare cost of living must be met. We may take judicial notice of the unparalleled demands for relief which arose during the recent period of depression and still continue to an alarming extent despite the degree of economic recovery which has been achieved. It is unnecessary to cite official statistics to establish what is of common knowledge through the length and breadth of the land. While, in the instant case, no factual brief has been presented, there is no reason to doubt that the State of Washington has encountered the same social problem that is present elsewhere. The community is not bound to provide what is, in effect, a subsidy for unconscionable employers. The community may direct its lawmaking power to correct the abuse which springs from their selfish disregard of the public interest. The argument that the legislation in question constitutes an arbitrary discrimination, because it does not extend to men, is unavailing. This Court has frequently held that the legislative authority, acting within its proper field, is not bound to extend its regulation to all cases which it might possibly reach. The legislature "is free to recognize degrees

> of harm and it may confine its restrictions to those classes of cases where the need is deemed to be clearest." If
>
>> the law presumably hits the evil where it is most felt, it is not to be overthrown because there are other instances to which it might have been applied.
>
> There is no "doctrinaire requirement" that the legislation should be couched in all embracing terms. This familiar principle has repeatedly been applied to legislation which singles out women, and particular classes of women, in the exercise of the State's protective power. Their relative need in the presence of the evil, no less than the existence of the evil itself, is a matter for the legislative judgment.
> Our conclusion is that the case of *Adkins v. Children's Hospital, supra*, should be, and it is, overruled. The judgment of the Supreme Court of the State of Washington is *Affirmed*.

It might be said that *Parrish* signaled the end of the *Lochner Era*. The Court gave Roosevelt the first major win under his New Deal policies, even though the law in question was a state law that was relatively narrow in scope. Justice Owen Roberts, who had served as the conservative-leaning swing vote during much of the *Lochner Era*, became the liberal-leaning swing vote in *Parrish* and a number of subsequent cases upholding New Deal legislation. This switch, along with an announcement that Justice Van Devanter, one of the "Four Horsemen," would retire, led to the demise of the court-packing plan. Now that the Court appeared to be supporting a highly popular President's policies, Congress no longer saw a need to change the makeup of the judiciary.

The demise of the court-packing plan was seen as a victory for the sanctity of U.S. legal institutions. Whether Roosevelt's threat caused the Court to change its approach toward governmental power is uncertain, but this served as the beginning of a new era for government regulation—one that would be supported for decades to come by a deferential judiciary.

During this period of regulatory expansion, a number of cases of unregulated businesses causing societal harms inspired the creation of new rules and regulatory authorities. This began a new era of government regulation of business. A prominent example can be found as follows.

Massengill and Elixir Sulfanilamide

In 1937, no laws existed that would require a pharmaceutical company to test their products prior to marketing them to consumers. S.E. Massengill, a pharmaceutical manufacturer, created an elixir that combined sulfanilamide and diethylene glycol, a mixture that is poisonous to humans, with raspberry flavoring, and marketed the product to assist with a variety of ills. The company was unaware at the time of the poisonous nature of the mixture. At least 100 children and adults died as a result of taking the concoction. However, because no regulations were in place to prevent such an outcome, Massengill faced no liability. The company owner famously quipped, "We have been supplying a legitimate professional demand and not once could have foreseen the unlooked-for results. I do not feel that there was any responsibility on our part."[20] The Food, Drug, and Cosmetic Act was enacted the following year.

The progressive reforms that began in 1937 were largely interrupted by the onset of World War II. Once the United States reluctantly entered the war in 1941, the country shifted to a wartime economy and saw many of its working men depart for the war. Women entered the workforce in droves and began to change the nature of the economy and society. When men returned after the war, policies enacted in the Roosevelt administration provided opportunities for veterans to secure an advanced education, purchase homes in new suburban developments, and find work in an expanding government. This dramatically changed the structure of American society and the government's role in that society.

Much of the Roosevelt administration concentrated its efforts on domestic economic reforms. And while some major foreign policy achievements can be highlighted, such as the enactment of the Reciprocal Trade Agreements Act of 1934 and the delegation of congressional trade authority to the President (discussed in more detail in Chapter 6 on Foreign Policy), it was not until the rise of the Soviet Union and the more belligerent Eisenhower administration that foreign affairs became the focal point of public policy.

The laissez-faire capitalist state that had functioned during the *Lochner Era* was replaced with the centralized regulatory state model during the Roosevelt administration. Economists at the time had debated the merits of both approaches to stimulating economic growth, and it became clear in the post–*Lochner Era* that government stimulus and social security had positive economic effects. Yet this centralized control also gave rise to fears of oppression and anti-democratic elements. The rise of communism in the Soviet Union and the consolidation of economic and political power that began following World War II fueled this debate between capitalism and communism.

When Roosevelt died rather suddenly on April 12, 1945, his vice president, Harry Truman, took the helm. Unlike his predecessor, Truman took a more aggressive approach to maintaining democracy around the world. While Roosevelt had helped to dismantle the threat from Nazi Germany, Truman authorized the use of a nuclear bomb to stop the threat from imperial Japan. Truman also repelled North Korea when it tried to invade South Korea. And he implemented the Marshall Plan to rebuild Europe and helped to establish the North American Treaty Alliance (NATO) to defend democracy against the rising Soviet threat. Truman's public policy approach exemplified the growing complexity of the new world order and the need to respond simultaneously to multiple threats.

Truman's foreign policy approach focused largely on containing the Soviet threat. The "Truman Doctrine" emphasized a push for democratic principles worldwide. In explaining his policy, Truman told Congress: "it must be the policy of the United States to support free people who are resisting attempted subjugation by armed minorities or by outside pressures."[21] This became known as an internationalist foreign policy approach and led to such successes as the founding of the United Nations in 1945. However, toward the end of Truman's second term of office, his administration became mired in a corruption scandal, and he was criticized for allowing the rise of Chinese communism as well as Chinese intervention on behalf of North Korea, prolonging the Korean War.

The expansionist regulatory approach of the Roosevelt and Truman Administrations drew strong liberal support; however, it was also met with severe criticism about government overreach and a weakening of the democratic process. During their administrations, more executive agencies had been created to carry out their policies, and those agencies had been endowed with significant interpretive power to decide how legislation should be enforced in society. To some, this reflected executive overreach and a diminished sense of democracy at home.

The Administrative Procedure Act of 1946[22] (APA) was the response of Congress to the threat of executive overreach through regulatory agencies. Those agencies, which existed since the Interstate Commerce Act of 1887, took on a greater role in governance beginning in the early 20th century. Through their **rulemaking** powers, regulatory agencies were entitled to interpret statutory legislation and craft mechanisms to implement those statutes. Their interpretations often collided with the intent of the legislative drafters, creating conflicts in how laws would be enforced.

> Rulemaking—the agency-led process of making rules that give practical effect to legislation.

In the following case, the Court is being asked to decide whether agencies should be permitted to rely on their own interpretations of statutory language or whether they should be required to refer to "common law standards" for making their determinations. The case involved a union representing "newsboys," who argued that they should be considered employees within the meaning of that term in the National Labor Relations Act, which would allow them to organize as a union.

Nat'l Labor Relations Board v. Hearst, 322 U.S. 111 (1944)

The principal question is whether the newsboys are "employees." Because Congress did not explicitly define the term, respondents say its meaning must be determined by reference to common law standards. In their view, "common law standards" are those the courts have applied in distinguishing between "employees" and "independent contractors" when working out various problems unrelated to the Wagner Act's purposes and provisions.

The argument assumes that there is some simple, uniform and easily applicable test which the courts have used, in dealing with such problems, to determine whether persons doing work for others fall in one class or the other. Unfortunately this is not true. Only by a long and tortuous history was the simple formulation worked out which has been stated most frequently as "the test" for deciding whether one who hires another is responsible in tort for his wrongdoing. But this formula has been by no means exclusively controlling in the solution of other problems. And its simplicity has been illusory because it is more largely simplicity of formulation than of application. Few problems in the law have given greater variety of application and conflict in results than the cases arising in the borderland between what is clearly an employer-employee relationship and what is clearly one of independent entrepreneurial dealing. This is true within the limited field of determining vicarious liability in tort. It becomes more so when the field is expanded to include all of the possible applications of the distinction.

It is hardly necessary to stress particular instances of these variations or to emphasize that they have arisen principally, first, in the struggle of the courts to work out common law liabilities where the legislature has given no guides for judgment, more recently also under statutes which have posed the same problem for solution in the light of the enactment's particular terms and purposes. It is enough to point out that, with reference to an identical problem, results may be contrary over a very considerable region of doubt in applying the distinction, depending upon the state or jurisdiction where the determination is made; and that, within a single jurisdiction, a person who, for instance, is held to be an "independent contractor" for the purpose of imposing vicarious liability in tort may be an "employee" for the purposes of particular legislation, such as unemployment compensation. In short, the assumed simplicity and uniformity, resulting from application of "common law standards," does not exist.

***

It is not necessary in this case to make a completely definitive limitation around the term "employee." That task has been assigned primarily to the agency created by Congress to administer the Act. Determination of "where all the conditions of the relation require protection" involves inquiries for the Board charged with this duty. Everyday experience in the administration of the statute gives it familiarity with the circumstances and backgrounds of employment relationships in various industries, with the abilities and needs of the workers for self-organization and collective action, and with the adaptability of collective bargaining for the peaceful settlement of their disputes with their employers. The experience thus acquired must be brought frequently to bear on the question who is an employee under the Act. Resolving that question, like determining whether unfair labor practices have been committed, "belongs to the usual administrative routine" of the Board.

In making that body's determinations as to the facts in these matters conclusive, if supported by evidence, Congress entrusted to it primarily the decision whether the evidence establishes the material facts. Hence, in reviewing the Board's ultimate conclusions, it is not the court's function to substitute its own inferences of fact for the Board's when the latter have support in the record. Undoubtedly questions of statutory interpretation, especially when arising in the first instance in judicial proceedings, are for the courts to resolve, giving appropriate weight to the judgment of those whose special duty is to administer the questioned statute. But where the question is one of specific application of a broad statutory term in a proceeding in which the agency administering the statute must determine it initially, the reviewing court's function is limited. Like the commissioner's determination under the Longshoremen's & Harbor Workers' Act, that a man is not a "member of a crew" (*South Chicago Coal & Dock Co. v. Bassett*, 309 U. S. 251) or that he was injured "in the course of his employment" (*Parker v. Motor Boat Sales, Inc.*, 314 U. S. 244) and the Federal Communications Commission's determination [Footnote 36] that one company is under the "control" of another (*Rochester Telephone Corp. v. United States*, 307 U. S. 125), the Board's determination that specified persons are "employees" under this Act is to be accepted if it has "warrant in the record" and a reasonable basis in law.

Box 1.1: Executive vs. Independent Agencies

In discussing the role of regulatory agencies, it is crucial to distinguish between executive and independent agencies. Both agencies are created by an act of Congress and both types (in most cases) are subject to some congressional control and oversight, especially since Congress controls their budgets. However, an independent agency is specifically designed by Congress to be independent of executive control and oversight, whereas a regulatory agency is usually aligned with the policy priorities of the president.

An independent agency is most often operated by a set of commissioners appointed for staggered terms and usually with political party restrictions. The President is usually permitted to designate the chairperson of those commissions, but the President should not influence the actions of that commission. The first regulatory body in the United States was the Interstate Commerce Commission in 1887, which was established as an independent agency. Since that time, numerous other agencies have been established in this way, though the number is dwindling today. Some major examples include:

- The Central Intelligence Agency
- The Consumer Financial Protection Bureau
- The Federal Communications Commission
- The Federal Reserve Board of Governors
- The Federal Trade Commission
- The International Trade Commission
- The Nuclear Regulatory Commission
- The Securities and Exchange Commission
- The Social Security Administration

An executive agency, on the other hand, operates under much more executive oversight than an independent federal agency. These agencies are headed by a single administrator (often called a "Secretary"), appointed by the President as well as other senior appointments to the agency made by the President, such as Assistant Secretaries, Chiefs of Staff, General Counsels, and so forth. The President requires Senate approval of these appointments but retains broad discretion to remove appointees as he wishes. His power to control these agencies comes from the Appointments Clause of the U.S. Constitution.[23] Among others, these executive agencies include:

- All Cabinet Departments (i.e., State, Defense, Commerce)
- International Trade Administration (distinct from the ITC)
- Federal Bureau of Investigation
- Internal Revenue Service
- Food and Drug Administration
- Centers for Medicare and Medicaid Services
- National Institutes of Health
- U.S. Immigration and Customs Enforcement
- Customs and Border Protection

The APA was "the nation's decision to permit extensive government, but to avoid dictatorship and central planning."[24] At a time when the debate between capitalism and socialism was still strong in the United States, Roosevelt's broad expansion of federal government powers was seen as a definitive move toward socialism, which capitalists strongly rebuffed. The APA might be seen as an olive branch to those with concerns over Roosevelt's consolidation of regulatory power within the executive branch.

The statute has four basic principles:

1. Agencies will keep the public informed about their rulemaking activities;
2. Agencies will allow the public to participate in the rulemaking process;
3. Agencies will establish and follow uniform rules in rulemaking and adjudicating those administrative cases; and,
4. The courts will have the power to review agency rules.

Regulatory agencies were thus allowed to function as powerful rulemaking authorities subject to the demands of congressional oversight committees, led in policy-making directives by executive appointees, driven by bipartisan civil servants, and responsive to the public at large. As you might imagine, the potential for conflict both within the agency and between the agency and the three branches of government was significant. Nevertheless, these agencies serve a critical function in governance by ensuring that the laws enacted by Congress, and the policies developed by the executive, are reflected in the functional application and enforcement of rules and regulations upon our lives.

The End of the "New Deal" (for Now)

Dwight ("Ike") Eisenhower, who led American and allied forces through much of World War II, came to power with great popularity and fanfare. He was a moderate Republican who supported many of the New Deal policies put in place during the Roosevelt Administration, as well as the internationalist approach of the Truman Administration. His public policy approach focused on using deterrence and the threat of nuclear strikes to slow the rise of communism, especially in the Middle East. He was also responsible for significant changes to the U.S. Supreme Court, on which he replaced five justices during his two terms in office, including the new Chief Justice, Earl Warren. Eisenhower was also the first President subjected to the new Constitutional Amendment limiting presidents to two terms.

Eisenhower's vice president, Richard Nixon, who Eisenhower did not offer much support for, ran to succeed Eisenhower but lost to the young democrat from Massachusetts, John F. Kennedy. JFK presided over a number of important domestic policy issues, including the first lunar landing, the appointment of the first African American Supreme Court Justice, Thurgood Marshall, and a commitment to a balanced federal budget. His foreign policy concerns included the continuing threat of communism, the Cuban revolution and Soviet influence on the island, and the establishment of the Peace Corps to facilitate a better understanding by American young people of their world. Kennedy was unable to complete his signature piece of legislation, the Civil Rights Act, which was enacted shortly after his 1963 assassination.

Kennedy's vice president, Lyndon Johnson, continued and expanded upon Kennedy's civil rights policies. In addition to the signing of the Civil Rights Act of 1964, Johnson also advocated his Great Society public policy, which emphasized improved race relations, reduced desperation through the War on Poverty, and expanded access to healthcare for the sick and elderly through the Medicaid and Medicare programs. His liberal approach to governance returned American public policy in many ways to the New Deal period. A growing economy helped Johnson to achieve many of his goals with these policy approaches. Johnson also shepherded the Voting Rights Act of 1965 through Congress, which protected disenfranchised, mainly African American voters. He was also the last President to successfully enact comprehensive immigration reform. And finally, he was able to enact comprehensive reforms to immigration policy with the 1965 Immigration and Nationality Act, opening the door to larger numbers of immigrants from a greater number of countries.

Administrative Expansion: Social Protections and the Environment

Despite these successes, Johnson's Administration was overshadowed by the Vietnam War. Though Kennedy had already sent 16,000 American advisors to help South Vietnam fight back the communist North, Johnson felt it politically necessary to increase U.S. involvement through air assaults and ultimately ground troops. Beginning with the Gulf of Tonkin Resolution in August 1964,[25] which authorized the President to use the armed forces in South Asia without a congressional declaration of war, through the end of his term, the quagmire in Vietnam scarred his image as a liberal icon and successful domestic policymaker.

Johnson was entitled to run for a third term since his first term was the conclusion of President Kennedy's term and thus did not count toward the two-term limit. However, his popularity had dropped among both Republicans and Democrats, and Johnson decided not to run in the 1968 election. His replacement on the Democratic ticket was to be the popular Robert Kennedy; however, Kennedy, like his brother before him, was assassinated before he had the chance. Richard Nixon, who advocated an end to the Vietnam War, won that election against Johnson's former vice president, Hubert Humphrey.

Richard Nixon's legacy is obviously clouded by the Watergate Scandal and his resignation from office. However, he enacted certain policies that did a great deal to advance peace and prosperity in the world. On the advice of his Secretary of State, Henry Kissinger, Nixon organized the first meeting of a U.S. President and Chairman Mao of China. Fearing the influence of the Soviets on China, Nixon felt it important to create a positive bond with China with the hope that better economic and political relations would curb the rise of communism in South Asia. However, he was less successful politically in Vietnam, where Nixon authorized expansive "carpet bombing" and an expanded ground war in Cambodia. The Paris Peace Accords in 1973 ultimately led to a ceasefire and the withdrawal of American troops. North Vietnam attacked and took control over the South in 1975.

Nixon's principal policy focus was in the foreign arena. However, with rising inflation and a weakening economy at home, he found some limited success in his support for environmental issues. During his administration, numerous laws related to the environment and regulatory agencies to enforce them were established. Among these, the Environmental Protection Act, the Clean Water Act, the National Environmental Policy Act, and the Occupational Safety and Health Act.

Despite these added regulatory agencies and laws, the Nixon Administration also saw the expansive regulatory state as a threat to political power. If regulators were able to issue sweeping interpretations of statutes, policymakers' power would be diluted (see discussion of *Chevron* in Chapter 3). Accordingly, both the Executive and the Legislature began enacting rules to govern the actions of administrative agencies. This began with a 1971 White House rule requiring agencies to submit one-page summaries of proposed regulations before formally issuing them. This reining in of administrative agencies reached its pinnacle during the Reagan Administration.

Following Nixon's resignation, his vice president, Gerald Ford, took over. This was the worst economic period in the United States since the Great Depression. Ford already had tepid Republican support, and when Democrats made substantial midterm election gains in 1974, Ford all but lost the ability to enact his policies. He did support the Republican approach to administration, however: "A government big enough to give you everything you want is a government big enough to take from you everything you have."[26] Ford officially ran for office in 1976 but lost to Democratic challenger Jimmy Carter.

The Deregulatory Era Begins

Jimmy Carter was seen as an outsider in Washington, which was one of the reasons he was so popular on the heels of the Nixon crisis and interim Ford presidency. He did not play politics by catering to special interests or cajoling the support of Congress through favors, which ultimately created a rift between the Executive and his own Democratic Party, making the enactment of his legislative agenda particularly troublesome. His policy approach focused on responding to major societal issues at the time—the energy crisis and a deteriorating educational system. To remedy this, he spearheaded the creation of two new cabinet-level departments, one for Energy and one for Education.

Carter can also be said to have begun the process of deregulation that picked up substantial steam under the subsequent Reagan Administration. Carter facilitated the Airline Deregulation Act,[27] which was the first major deregulatory legislation enacted. On the advice of economists, he felt that airlines should be free to set their own fares and routes and that the market would do a better job in promoting competition and innovation in air travel. He also deregulated the beer industry, leading to the start of the micro-brewing industry that remains popular today.

However, a severe recession, as well as a deteriorating relationship with the Soviet Union and their invasion of Afghanistan in 1978, alongside the 1979 Iranian hostage crisis that led to the deaths of eight American servicemen, crippled his administration toward the end of his term. He left behind the impression that the government was unable to resolve many of the ills of society, including a tax increase that failed to stimulate growth, failed healthcare reform, and a worsening Cold War that could not eliminate communism. The path was paved for an outside Republican candidate.

In his inaugural speech, former actor and sports commentator Ronald Reagan stated, "In this present crisis, government is not the solution to our problems; government is the problem."[28] His platform was one of tax reduction and deregulation that emphasized economic recovery through business opportunity. Reagan's policy approach during his first term strongly emphasized economic recovery, and he began with a significant tax cut in 1981, followed by tax increases over the next seven years that undid a significant portion of that cut. He applied the supply-side economics approach of "trickle-down" economics, which, along with one of its most ardent supporters, Arthur Laffer, was modeled on the belief that wealthy business owners that receive tax breaks would share that wealth with their workers through investment and wage increases. He successfully cut inflation and enjoyed high economic growth rates throughout his two terms in office.

Unlike his predecessor, Reagan substantially increased the defense budget, using the threat of military strikes to curtail the expansionary efforts of the Soviet Union. He covertly supported a number of anti-communist movements around the world, including the mujahedeen in Afghanistan, led by Osama bin Laden, to rid that country of Soviets. He also continued with the process of economic deregulation by reducing the funding for the EPA, food stamps, and Medicaid, and signing into law the Garn-St. Germain Depository Institutions Act,[29] which authorized savings and loan banks to invest with money from savings accounts and to provide consumers with adjustable-rate mortgages. There is debate about whether this legislation caused or mitigated the effects of the 1986 savings and loan crisis.

Reagan's 1984 reelection was a landslide, sweeping him to victory with 525 electoral votes (the most ever by one candidate) and winning 49 out of 50 states. During his second term, Reagan launched the war on drugs to combat the growing crack epidemic with $1.7 billion in funding and new laws requiring stiff penalties and mandatory minimum sentences for low-level drug offenders. He also facilitated the enactment of the 1986 Immigration Reform and Control Act, which tightened restrictions on unlawful immigration while also providing amnesty to immigrants already unlawfully present in the United States. And perhaps most momentous, he helped to bring closure to the Cold War, which had been waning in the face of a rapidly deteriorating Soviet economy.

What we began seeing in these administrations was a growing role for government in economic stimulation, social program funding, and defense. Prior to the New Deal period, government had far fewer programs to fund and, consequently, far less need for revenue to pay for them. But with wars in Korea, Vietnam, and with ideologies such as communism, along with major regulatory programs such as the EPA, Social Security, and Medicaid, the government had become responsible for a broad array of what citizens considered to be essential programs.

Reagan left office with one of the highest approval ratings of any President, equivalent to Roosevelt before him and Clinton after. Reagan also left office with a significant deficit, nearly triple what it was when he took office. George H.W. Bush, who handily defeated Michael Dukakis in 1988, focused his public policy on economic recovery. However, he made the political mistake of promising something during the campaign that he would have to renege on shortly after winning the election: "Read my lips, no new taxes."[30] Facing a democratic Congress and a growing recession, Bush signed into law a tax increase that cost him party support.

Bush turned his attention to foreign policy, and the formal end of the Cold War through the 1991 announcement of a U.S.–Russia strategic partnership following the collapse of the Soviet Union. He continued to make headlines by spearheading an allied attack on Iraqi forces that had invaded neighboring Kuwait. The first Gulf War, which lasted only six weeks, was viewed as a major success in foreign policy and strategic planning. However, this success was not enough to overcome the growing domestic concern with the weak U.S. economy. Toward the end of his term, Bush negotiated the North American Free Trade Agreement (NAFTA), which had strong Republican support, but he was unable to see it through to enactment.

Democrat Bill Clinton came into office in 1992 and quickly began implementing a new social agenda. He signed the Family Medical Leave Act into law, raised taxes, and made a significant push for comprehensive healthcare reform through a nationalized healthcare system. The latter policy was strongly opposed by conservatives and ultimately failed as an initiative. He also signed into law, over some Democratic objection, the NAFTA agreement that his predecessor had negotiated.

Clinton won a second term (the first Democrat to do so since Roosevelt), but it was tainted since the beginning when an investigation into his conduct while in office, specifically an allegation of sexual harassment by Paula Jones and an affair with Monica Lewinsky, resulted in a grand jury investigation wherein Clinton lied under oath. He was impeached by the House of Representatives in 1998 and acquitted on all charges by the Senate in 1999. This scandal overshadowed the significant economic growth that occurred during his second term, including three years of significant surpluses. Despite the scandal, Clinton left office with very high approval ratings.

Clinton left office with substantial economic growth but increasing concerns over speculation from the rise of Internet companies. George W. Bush, the Republican President to succeed Clinton, oversaw the bursting of that bubble, kicking off his first term with a recession. Bush increased government spending by 60% in order to counteract the recession while pushing for a significant tax cut. Accordingly, national debt rose from around $5 trillion at the start of his term to over $11 trillion at the end of his term.

The "Bush Doctrine," coined by journalist Charles Krauthammer, initially referred to the Bush Administration's pullback from environmental accords, such as the Kyoto Protocol on Climate Change, and withdrawal from the anti-ballistic missile treaty between the United States and the former Soviet Union. However, following the terrorist attacks on the United States in September 2001, this doctrine largely shifted Bush's policy focus to what he called the "War on Terror." Beginning in early 2002, Bush engaged in a largely unilateral and preemptive approach to foreign military actions, starting with the invasion of Afghanistan to remove the Taliban from power and followed by the invasion of Iraq in search of weapons of mass destruction.

Like Clinton before him, Bush faced a significant image problem domestically (and in Bush's case, internationally as well). Rather than sex scandals, Bush was criticized for the failed search for weapons of mass destruction in Iraq in 2003 as well as for his response to Hurricane Katrina in 2005, one of the most destructive hurricanes on record. His treatment of terrorism suspects and unique interpretation of executive powers were challenged in court numerous times, and his failed push for comprehensive immigration reform due partly to dissension within his own party cost him political capital. Bush left office with low approval ratings and the albatross of starting a war on terror that would drag on for years to come.

Though Bush did not continue the deregulation of his predecessors, he did change significantly the domestic policy environment with two significant statutes: the USA Patriot Act of 2001 and the Homeland Security Act of 2002. The Patriot Act brought substantial changes to civil liberties in the United States by expanding the power of the government to conduct surveillance and searches of parties within the country under the guise of terrorism investigations. Though controversial in many respects, most of these permissions were supported by subsequent Democratic and Republican legislatures. The Homeland Security Act substantially restructured seemingly disparate government agencies engaged in foreign affairs and emergency management matters, such as international trade, disaster prevention, and immigration, into a single overarching department. Today, the Department of Homeland Security is the third-largest cabinet agency after Defense and Veterans Affairs. More detail on these changes can be found in Chapter 7 on National Security.

Public Policy in 140 Characters

Barack Obama made history in the 2008 presidential election by becoming the first African American to be elected to that office. He also made history with the appointment of two female Supreme Court Justices during his term, bringing the number of female Justices on the Court to three—the highest number ever. Obama came into office in the midst of the Great Recession, the most destructive global economic crisis since the Great Depression. The recession was caused largely by the housing boom and subsequent crash known as the subprime mortgage crisis (see Chapter 5 on Economic Policy) in 2007, at the end of the Bush Administration. Accordingly, Obama's policy at the outset of his first term focused on economic recovery.

With a Democratic Congress behind him, Obama enacted two major bills that would have lasting economic effects on the domestic economy. First, he signed the American Recovery and Reinvestment Act of 2009, which was a $787 billion economic stimulus package aimed at providing homeowners with relief from rising housing debts and to provide money for education, health, and infrastructure programs. The following year, in an effort to stem rising healthcare and insurance costs, Obama proposed and ultimately signed into law the Patient Protection and Affordable Care Act (ACA).

Obama took a significant policy turn from previous administrations with respect to foreign affairs. He condemned Israeli actions toward Palestine, he drew down combat operations in Iraq, he declared an end to the war on terror, and he began rapprochement with Cuba (see Chapter 6 on Foreign Policy). And though he had some successes, such as the killing of Osama bin Laden and a deal to stop Iranian nuclear proliferation, he also faced criticism for major downfalls, such as the attack on the American Embassy in Libya and the failed intervention to stop the Syrian civil war.

The Obama Administration was the first to truly capitalize on social media and popular broadcasts as a means of developing support for public policy positions. Obama regularly engaged with voters on apps such as Twitter and political satire shows such as *Real Time With Bill Maher*. This drew broad appeal among young voters and generated more robust discussions about political issues in classrooms and cafés. It can be seen as a new era in public policy communications.

This social media trend continued with the election of Donald Trump, a real estate mogul and political outsider, in 2016. Running on a platform of voter frustration with the perceived government overreach of the Obama Administration, including the requirement that individuals purchase health insurance under the ACA and use of executive authority to protect young immigrants who were brought to the United States as children unlawfully (through the Deferred Action for Childhood Arrivals [DACA]), Trump used his media prowess to zone in on the failures of the previous administration rather than the policy possibilities of his own administration.

Since taking office, Trump has taken steps to roll back many of the policy initiatives of the Obama Administration, including DACA, transgender individuals serving in the military (overturned by the judiciary), and the individual mandate of the ACA (through a legislative tax plan). However, his administration was tarnished at the outset by allegations of collusion or influence by Russia on the Trump campaign, leading to the appointment of a special prosecutor, as well as numerous sexual assault allegations against the President directly. His support in Congress has been tepid at best, weakening his ability to complete his policy agenda.

The policy environment of 2018, when this book was completed, can be summed up as follows: growing partisanship exacerbated by the broad use of social media channels to disseminate political viewpoints, many of which are unsubstantiated. The regulatory expansion that took place under the Obama Administration in areas such as energy, immigration, and healthcare is largely being rolled back in the current administration alongside a push for more states' rights.

Conclusion

This chapter was meant to provide an introductory overview of the evolution of the public policy environment in the United States in order to lay the groundwork for the more-detailed analyses in the following chapters. As the adage goes, those who do not learn their history are doomed to repeat it. This is no doubt the case in public policy—as you have seen in the discussion in this chapter, many of the issues that we face today, such as healthcare and economic stability, are the same issues that we have been attempting to deal with for decades, often with the same approaches. A better understanding of what the country looked like socially, politically, and economically over time can be dramatically helpful in designing appropriate public policies to address the issues of the day.

As a young country, the United States has found itself trying hard to define what it wants to be—a government with strong centralized control to guide with a firm hand the development of its society and economy, or a deferential body of last resort to provide only the most fundamental governmental necessities, such as national security, while leaving decision-making power to the states and the citizens. As the country came into its own and began developing a strong economy in the 19th century, government was seen as a mechanism to facilitate growth with standard setting, military operations, and later, intervention to protect free trade. This laissez-faire approach was sharply curtailed after the stock market crash of 1929 and the many reports of capitalist abuse of citizens. The New Deal period and the subsequent Great Society period reshaped American governance to emphasize a stronger and broader approach for government in the lives of citizens. Backlash against that expansion has recently appeared to be growing and likely led to the election of a wealthy capitalist that has appointed other wealthy capitalists in an attempt to sharply reduce government intervention in the private sector.

Thus, we may characterize the public policy process over time in the United States as a pendulum approach to policymaking, moving from left to right every so often and, seemingly, with more frequency in recent years. These dramatic shifts may be caused by a number of factors, but one that will be emphasized in this text is a diverse environment of awareness of the political and public policy process. Citizens today appear less interested and less aware of how the government works and how policy and laws are developed, which is one of the reasons I wrote this book. I believe strongly that by educating everyone about the relationship between the government and the governed, all of us will become more agile policy advocates of our own right, regardless of the positions that we take.

Notes

1. Senator William Learned Marcy (1832).
2. Ari Hoogenboom, *Outlawing the Spoils: A History of the Civil Service Reform Movement, 1865–1883* (1961).

A Historic Introduction to Law and Public Policy   33

3. Edward D. Sullivan, *Rattling the Cup on Chicago Crime* (1929).
4. Woodrow Wilson, *The Study of Administration* (1887).
5. Frederick W. Taylor, *Collection of Essays* 48 (1911).
6. Leonard White, *Introduction to the Study of Public Administration* 11 (1926).
7. *Id.* at 32.
8. Syracuse University home page, www.syracuse.edu
9. However, the German text was not translated completely into English until 1968, so its influence may have been less dramatic than that of others of the era.
10. *The Press* (New York), Sept. 30, 1894.
11. Calvin Coolidge, *Address to the American Society of Newspaper Editors*, Jan. 17, 1925, www.presidency.ucsb.edu/ws/?pid=24180
12. Arthur Krock, *Roosevelt Sweeps the Nation: His Electoral Vote Exceeds 500*, N.Y. Times, 1936.
13. *United States v. Butler*, 297 U.S. 1 (1936).
14. *Carter v. Carter Coal Co.*, 298 U.S. 238 (1936).
15. *Schecter Poultry Co. v. United States*, 295 U.S. 495 (1936).
16. 298 U.S. 587 (1936).
17. New York Act, Laws of 1933, c. 584.
18. *Adkins v. Children's Hospital*, 261 U.S. 525.
19. See Robert Dallek, *Franklin D. Roosevelt: A Political Life* 219 (2017).
20. Stephen Mihm, *A Tragic Lesson*, The Boston Globe, 2007.
21. Michael Beschloss, *Our Documents: 100 Milestone Documents from the National Archives* (2006).
22. Pub. L. No. 79–404, 60 Stat. 237 (1946).
23. Art. II, Sec. 2, Cl. 2.
24. George Shepard, *Fierce Compromise: The Administrative Procedure Act Emerges from New Deal Politics*, 90 Nw. U. L. Rev. (1996).
25. Pub. L. No. 88–408, 78 Stat. 384 (1964).
26. Gerald Ford, *Address to a Joint Session of the Congress*, Aug. 12, 1974, www.presidency.ucsb.edu/ws/?pid=4694
27. Pub. L. No. 95–504 (1978).
28. Robert K. Murray & Tim H. Blessing, *Greatness in the White House* 80 (1993).
29. Pub. L. No. 97–320 (1982).
30. BBC News, *Bush Wins with 'No New Taxes' Promise*, BBC News, Nov. 9, 1988.

Additional Learning Resources

Annotated Case Bibliography

The Growth of the Administrative State and Regulations

- *FTC v. Ruberoid*, 343 U.S. 570 (1952), discussing the rise of administrative agencies in the United States.
- *Buckley v. Valeo*, 424 U.S. 1 (1976), confirming the ability of Congress to place limits on campaign contributions, among other things.
- *Kolender v. Lawson*, 461 U.S. 352 (1983), striking down a California law that gave broad discretion to police to stop suspicious individuals.
- *Shelton v. Tucker*, 364 U.S. 479 (1960), upholding the right of association by striking down an Arkansas law requiring teachers to disclose group affiliations.
- *Church of Lukumi v. City of Hialeah*, 508 U.S. 520 (1993), striking down a law about animal slaughter that interfered with a group's freedom of religion.

The Relationship Between Reinvention and Constitutional Rights of Individuals

- *Adarand Constructors, Inc. v. Pena*, 515 U.S. 200 (1995), challenging a law that uses race and national origin to determine minority status.
- *Grutter v. Bollinger*, 539 U.S. 306 (2003), upholding the use of race in admissions at the University of Michigan law school.

- *Gratz v. Bollinger*, 539 U.S. 244 (2003), striking down the University of Michigan's use of race in undergraduate admissions for being too broad.
- *Cleveland Board of Education v. Loudermill*, 470 U.S. 532 (1985), providing for an administrative hearing when a civil servant is fired from his or her job.

Additional Readings

Robert V. Percival, *Who's in Charge? Does the President Have Directive Authority over Agency Regulatory Decisions?*, 79 Fordham L. Rev. 2487 (2011).

Leonard Dupee White, *Introduction to the Study of Public Administration* (1926).

Woodrow Wilson, *The Study of Administration*, 2 Pol. Sci. Quart. 197 (1887).

2 How the Government Works
A Foundation in Civics

> *A popular Government without popular information, or the means of acquiring it, is but a Prologue to a Farce or a Tragedy, or perhaps both. Knowledge will forever govern ignorance: And a people who mean to be their own Governors, must arm themselves with the power which knowledge gives.*
> —James Madison (1822)

Introduction

Declining civic engagement is a bit of a paradox. The average citizen was more engaged in U.S. politics 100 years ago than they are today, yet the role of government in our lives today is substantially more evident than it was 100 years ago. Over the last few decades, a precipitous decline in civic engagement and understanding of the political process has become evident. Today, most political or civic engagement by adults takes place among more educated, wealthier individuals. Yet even among those groups, a small minority of adults engage regularly in the discussion about politics and governance.

Just as civic engagement is diminishing, public trust in government has dropped precipitously. According to the Pew Research Center (2016), public trust began its steady decline in the midst of the Vietnam War, picking up speed during the Watergate Scandal, and ending up at an average of 20% of Americans who trust the federal government to do what is right most of the time across Democrats and Republicans (see Figure 2.1).

Compared to other developed countries, the United States falls far behind its peers in terms of voter turnout. With only about 55% of voting-eligible citizens participating in elections, despite over 86% of citizens being registered to vote, as compared to 87% voter turnout in Belgium, for instance, it becomes apparent that Americans are less engaged with politics than are citizens in similarly situated countries. Voter turnout seems to have been largely unaffected by declining trust in government in the 20th century, but lack of engagement in both voting and political dialogue suggests that Americans are unplugging from the government to a frightening degree.

One reason for the growing disinterest in politics and governance may be the limited exposure to civics education that our students receive in school. The number of civics classes being offered in American high schools just as teenagers come of age to vote has declined. A national examination conducted by the National Assessment of Educational Progress found that only 25% of American eighth graders were considered proficient on a national civics exam.[1] White and wealthier students did almost six times better than minority students on that exam.

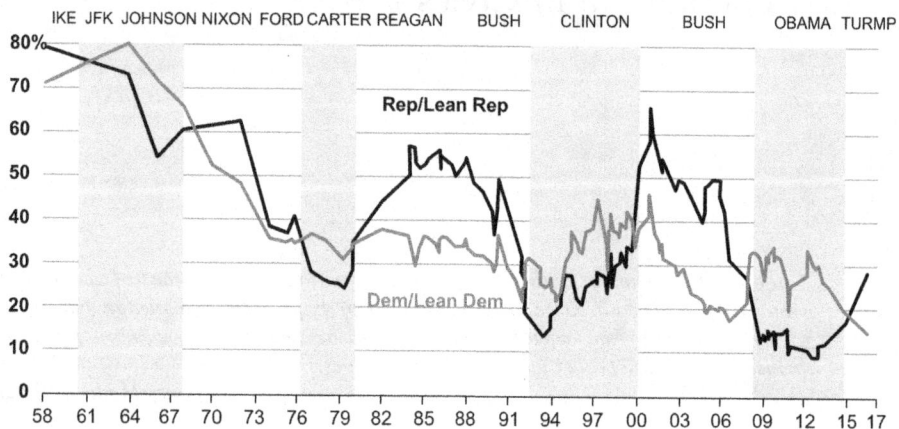

Figure 2.1 Public Trust in Federal Government.
Source: Pew Research Center (2016).

While all states require some form of civics education in secondary school curriculum, only ten states require teachers to be certified as proficient in civics or government. Additionally, the quality of content in those classes differs dramatically. A study by the Fordham Institute gave 28 states grades of D or F for the quality of their civics education programs. Former Supreme Court Justice Sandra Day O'Connor noted, "When I went to school, we had all kinds of courses on civics and government. . . . Today, at least half of the states don't even require high school students to take civics; only three states require it in middle school."[2] If schools fail to adequately train their pupils on the basics of civics and public policy, we will have an increasingly large cadre of uninformed voters who may not vote at all and, if they do, may be ill-equipped to understand the issues that they are voting on.

Some interesting statistics emphasize this point:

- Roughly 50% of Americans cannot correctly identify the three branches of government.

    (ABA, 2005)

- 35% of Americans cannot name even one branch of the federal government.
    (Annenberg Public Policy Center)

- After the 2016 election, 47% of millennials could identify the party that won the Senate.

    (Pew Research Center)

- 35% of Americans thought that Obamacare and the Affordable Care Act were different things.

    (Morning Consult poll)

Combine this with the increasingly complex system of political engagement, from shifting rules on monetary contributions by individuals, organizations, and businesses, to diverse voter identification and registration laws across states, and we are left with a system of weak political engagement and limited political knowledge. Regardless of your political persuasions, lack of awareness of how your political system functions and how to participate in it leaves you in the hands of elected officials that you did not necessarily choose. As the opening quote suggests, a country of ignorant voters is susceptible to being ruled by an intellectual elite that care little about the needs of the citizenry.

In Chapter 3 (Institutions and Power), we will focus on the three branches of government that create the rules for our society. You will learn that each of those branches has a unique role according to the U.S. Constitution, but that nevertheless, those roles often overlap with powers adopted by other branches. And you will also learn about the relationship between the federal and state institutions of governance in our federal system.

In this chapter, we take a political look at those institutions. How does the Constitution affix the role of the citizen in selecting those who will make the laws and regulations that affect their daily lives? How are elections structured and coordinated? And what role do political parties and other influencing organizations play in the political apparatus? This, then, is a chapter about civics. It is important to point out, however, that this is not a chapter about political debate or what we typically call *politics*. Rather, it is a chapter about political dialogue and engagement in the political process, a process that affects members of every political persuasion.

This chapter is structured as follows. We begin with some basic insights into the foundations of our electoral system by looking at how and why it was established as it was. We move on to an important discussion of the political party establishment. The two-party system, and in fact, parties in general, were not part of the Constitution, so where did they come from and why? We turn next to the role of voting and lobbying in the political process. And we round out the chapter with a look at the voting process, voter rights, and disenfranchisement.

Who Elects Whom? A Look at the Mysterious Electoral College

Donald Trump was elected President of the United States in November 2016, despite receiving approximately 2.9 million fewer popular votes than his opponent, Hillary Clinton. In other words, the majority of the U.S. population voted for Clinton, but Trump was elected regardless. This was not the first time in history that this occurred. In fact, it was the fifth. Al Gore won 540,000 more votes than his opponent, George W. Bush, in the 2000 election, but Bush was elected regardless. The same thing happened in the 1888 election of Benjamin Harris (90,000 vote difference), the 1876 election of Rutherford B. Hayes (250,000 vote difference), and the 1824 election of John Quincy Adams (38,000 vote difference). All of these unusual results are due to the American use of an electoral college.

The **electoral college** was the result of a compromise between the 13 original states over how to establish fair representation in the new federal government. In 1787, at the Constitutional Convention in Philadelphia, the delegates from the states debated between the establishment of a system similar to that of England, which popularly elects a Parliament that subsequently appoints a Prime Minister, or something different altogether.

> Electoral college—process established for the indirect election of the President and the Vice President in the United States.

38 How the Government Works

Virginia Plan—proposal by James Madison to create a two-house legislature, both elected proportionally by the states (giving more populous states more power).

James Madison from Virginia was the first to put forth a proposal. Known as the **Virginia Plan,** his proposal would create a bicameral (two-chamber) legislative body consisting of representatives elected directly by the people that serve three years in office and a second chamber consisting of older statesmen elected by state legislatures to serve seven-year terms. The number of representatives from each state would be based upon their state's population, giving large states an advantage over smaller states. The executive (later termed the "President") and also the judiciary under this plan would be selected by the legislature. Less populous states, especially Southern states with large slave populations, opposed this plan.

New Jersey Plan—proposal by William Patterson to create a single-house legislature with one vote per state representative (giving equal power to all states).

An alternative known as the **New Jersey Plan** was offered to counter the power that large states would have under the Virginia Plan. This plan would have created a unicameral system (one chamber) whereby the people elected their representatives directly and equally—one representative from each state, regardless of population. This was the approach that had been previously followed under the Articles of Confederation (the precursor to the U.S. Constitution). Under this plan, the legislature would still select the executive, but the executive would then select the members of the judiciary. This plan was also rejected.

Connecticut Compromise—final agreement on the design of the legislature that included two houses, the lower house elected proportionally and the upper house elected evenly by the states.

The final plan was known as the **Connecticut Compromise**, which created the electoral college. This compromise created a bicameral system with population-based representation in one chamber (the U.S. House of Representatives) and equal power in another chamber (the U.S. Senate). This allayed some of the concerns from the less populous states without significantly diluting the power of more populous states. And rather than allowing the legislature to appoint the Executive, the Connecticut Compromise established the electoral college to cast votes for the President and Vice President of the United States. This plan became part of the Constitution in Article I, as discussed later.

The Electoral College: The Unique American Way

Perhaps the most confusing aspect of the American voting process is the electoral college. In this section, we will try to lift the veil of uncertainty around this process so that we can fully understand how our votes work.

Elector—designated person who casts their ballot for the President and Vice President.

Simply put, the United States is a representative (rather than a direct) democracy. While we vote directly for our representatives in Congress, our choice for President and Vice President is made by someone else, called an **elector**. When you cast your ballot on election day, though the ballot identifies the candidates for President and Vice President, you are actually voting for a group of electors that have committed to cast your state's electoral votes for those candidates (see Figure 2.2).

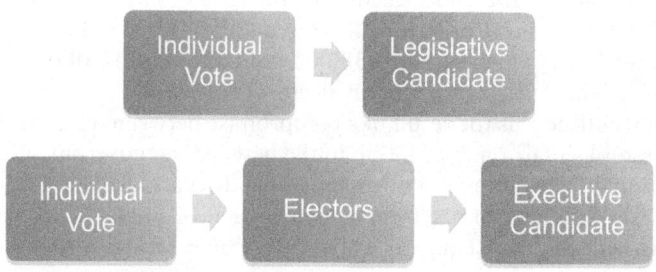

Figure 2.2a and 2.2b Direct and Indirect Voting in the United States.

Because of the Connecticut Compromise, discussed in the previous section, we have a system that uses middlemen and middlewomen to decide who the President and Vice President should be. In its original form, the electors were supposed to be selected by popular vote in each state and were then supposed to decide who *they* thought would be the best choice for President and Vice President. This changed in the early 1800s, when political parties began to form and realized that their party candidates would be more likely to win if electors were pledged to a single candidate. This new statewide system is now the most common mechanism for casting electoral votes.

How Does the Electoral College Work?

Each state is allotted a number of electors based upon their number of congressional representatives (House and Senate) at the time of the election. Washington, D.C., which is not a state and has no congressional representatives, is allotted a number of electors equal to the smallest state (three in 2018), thanks to the 23rd Amendment to the U.S. Constitution. In total, this means that (in 2018) there are 435 House delegates, 100 Senators, and 3 Washington, D.C. electors, for a grand total of 538 electors. A majority (270) is required to win an election.

An elector may be nominated by a state chapter of a national political party (e.g., the Republican or Democratic party), at a party convention, or by popular vote during the **primary**. Electors are most often affiliated with a particular party and, ultimately, a candidate, though some, known as *faithless electors*, refuse to align with a candidate prior to the election. An elector may not hold a position in the federal government as an elected or appointed official while serving as an elector.

Electors are chosen in the months leading up to the election. Election day is always on the Tuesday following the first Monday in November. This is the day that voters cast their ballots for congressional representatives as well as for the electors who will select the President and Vice President (most states do not name the electors on the ballot anymore). The electors will cast their ballots for the President and Vice President on the first Monday after the second Wednesday in December. Their ballots are certified by Congress in early January. The new President starts his or her term on January 20th at noon.

Today, all but two states (Maine and Nebraska) follow a *winner-take-all* approach to electing the President and Vice President. This means that a simple majority of the popular vote in each state will lead to the casting of all of that state's electoral votes to the popular candidate. Maine and Nebraska use the congressional district method, which allows each congressional district to vote independently. The two additional electoral ballots (from the two Senators) are cast via statewide popular vote.

The winner-take-all approach in most states leads to the interesting possibility that a presidential candidate may receive enough electoral votes to win but may lose the popular vote. The way that would happen is as follows: The number of ballots cast for a single presidential candidate in any state is only capped at the population of that state, but the number of electoral ballots cast is capped at the number of electors (see Figure 2.3). So even if a candidate won 100% of the popular vote in a given state, they would still only win the allotted number of electoral ballots for that state. Thus, other than in Nebraska and Maine, a candidate needs only half of any state's popular vote to propel them toward victory. The other half is just a popularity contest.

Frustration about the power of electors over direct citizens has been voiced by many politicians, especially Democrats, given the two recent losses of the presidency despite

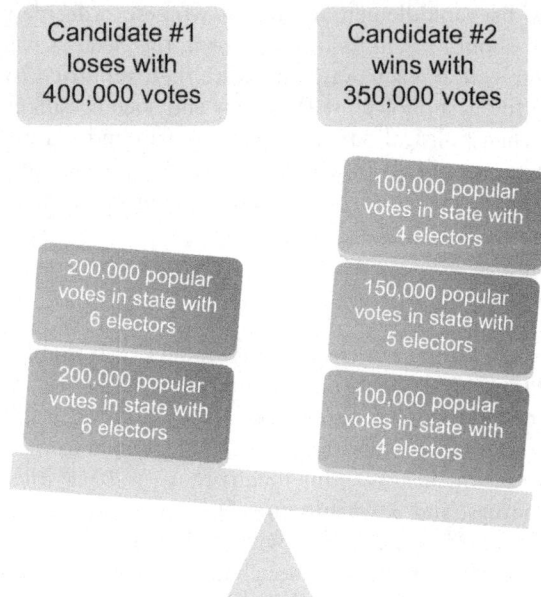

Figure 2.3 Hypothetical Five-state Contest Using an Electoral College.

popular vote victories. Democratic Senator Barbara Boxer tweeted on November 15, 2016, "[t]he presidency is the only office where you can get more votes & still lose. It's time to end the Electoral College." But these concerns have been around for some time. In 1934, Democratic Senator Alben Barkley said, "The American people are qualified to elect their president by a direct vote, and I hope to see the day when they will." Democratic Senator Birch Bayh was able to get a majority (51–48) vote to switch from an electoral college to a direct election system in 1979; however, he needed two-thirds of the Senate to support the bill, so the bill failed.

It is worth mentioning that a recent effort, begun in 2006, has proposed maintaining the electoral college in name alone, thus avoiding the need for a Constitutional Amendment. The National Popular Vote Interstate Compact asks states to commit to pledging their electoral votes to whoever wins the national popular vote. The pledge would only take effect if enough states sign on to commit 270 electoral votes or more. As of 2018, 10 states with 165 electoral votes have joined the compact. There is no guarantee that this process would avoid legal challenge, but given that states are ultimately able to put in place their own system for choosing electors, a solution like this may be viable.

The creation of the electoral college system is outlined in Article II of the Constitution:

U.S. Constitution Article II, Section 1, Clause 3

The Electors shall meet in their respective States, and vote by Ballot for two Persons, of whom one at least shall not be an Inhabitant of the same State with themselves. And they shall make a List of all the Persons voted for, and of the Number of Votes for each; which List they shall sign and certify, and transmit sealed to the Seat of the Government of the United States, directed to the President of the Senate. The President of the Senate shall, in the Presence of the Senate and House of Representatives, open all the Certificates, and the Votes shall then be counted. The Person having the greatest Number of Votes shall be the President, if such Number be a Majority of the whole Number of Electors appointed; and if there be more than one who have such Majority, and have an equal Number of Votes, then the House of Representatives shall immediately chuse [sic] by Ballot one of them for President; and if no Person have a Majority, then from the five highest on the List the said House shall in like Manner chuse [sic] the President. But in chusing [sic] the President, the Votes shall be taken by States, the Representation from each State having one Vote; A quorum for this Purpose shall consist of a Member or Members from two thirds of the States, and a Majority of all the States shall be necessary to a Choice. In every Case, after the Choice of the President, the Person having the greatest Number of Votes of the Electors shall be the Vice President. But if there should remain two or more who have equal Votes, the Senate shall chuse [sic] from them by Ballot the Vice President.

The original Article created confusion, largely because of the election of a president from one party and a vice president from another. This led the legislature to propose and enact the 12th Amendment in 1804:

U.S. Constitution Amendment XII (1804)

The Electors shall meet in their respective states, and vote by ballot for President and Vice-President, one of whom, at least, shall not be an inhabitant of the same state with themselves; they shall name in their ballots the person voted for as President, and in distinct ballots the person voted for as Vice-President, and they shall make distinct lists of all persons voted for as President, and all persons voted for as Vice-President and of the number of votes for each, which lists they shall sign and certify, and transmit sealed to the seat of the government of the United States, directed to the President of the Senate.

The President of the Senate shall, in the presence of the Senate and House of Representatives, open all the certificates and the votes shall then be counted.

The person having the greatest number of votes for President, shall be the President, if such number be a majority of the whole number of Electors appointed; and if no person have such majority, then from the persons having the highest numbers not exceeding three on the list of those voted for as President, the House of Representatives shall choose immediately, by ballot, the President. But in choosing the President, the votes shall be taken by states, the representation from each state having one vote; a quorum for this purpose shall consist of a member or members from two-thirds of the states, and a majority of all the states shall be necessary to a choice. *And if the House of Representatives shall not choose a President whenever the right of choice shall devolve upon them, before the fourth day of March next following, then the Vice-President shall act as President, as in the case of the death or other constitutional disability of the President.*

The person having the greatest number of votes as Vice-President, shall be the Vice-President, if such number be a majority of the whole number of Electors appointed, and if no person have a majority, then from the two highest numbers on the list, the Senate shall choose the Vice-President; a quorum for the purpose shall consist of two-thirds of the whole number of Senators, and a majority of the whole number shall be necessary to a choice. But no person constitutionally ineligible to the office of President shall be eligible to that of Vice-President of the United States.

The electoral college was established to ensure that less populous states had equal representation in the legislature to more populous states. Urbanization shifted the American landscape dramatically to concentrate large segments of the population in major cities within individual states, giving certain states, such as California and New York, substantially more popular votes than rural states. However, the electoral college system dilutes that power to some degree, ensuring that states like Iowa and Idaho remain important to political candidates.

An unfortunate perception of the electoral college is that it disempowers voters in more populous states. A Republican vote in a mostly Republican state may have less impact on a national election than a Republican vote with a simple majority of Republican voters, for instance. Thus, states that are more equally split in political positions tend to be the *competitive* races for national candidates, as they try to swing just enough voters to get the simple majority that they need to win the state. Consistently Republican or Democratic states thus get less attention by candidates.

Congressional Districts and Apportionment

By now, hopefully, you see the importance of the electoral college in determining the outcome of an election. And the electoral college depends directly upon two things: the number and the location of the state's representatives. The number of representatives depends on the state's population, which is recalculated every ten years by the U.S. Census Bureau. The census is conducted every decennial (e.g., 2010, 2020, 2030), and the results affect the following election cycle by either increasing or decreasing (or maintaining) the number of representatives and thus electors.

Every state is divided into congressional districts represented by a single congressperson. Those districts are required by the U.S. Constitution to be equally *apportioned* across the state:

> Representatives shall be apportioned among the several States according to their respective numbers, counting the whole number of persons in each State, excluding Indians not taxed. But when the right to vote at any election for the choice of electors for President and Vice-President of the United States, Representatives in Congress, the Executive and Judicial officers of a State, or the members of the Legislature thereof, is denied to any of the male inhabitants of such State, being twenty-one years of age, and citizens of the United States, or in any way abridged, except for participation in rebellion, or other crime, the basis of representation therein shall be reduced in the proportion which the number of such male citizens shall bear to the whole number of male citizens twenty-one years of age in such State.
> —14th Amendment, section 2, amending Article I, section 2, clause 3

In 1789, each representative had approximately 33,000 citizens in his district. Today, that number is about 720,000. Likewise, the number of representatives overall has increased due to increases in population and, historically, to the admission of new states. This means less attention for each voter as well as a much more diverse set of interests within each district. However, by drawing political district lines carefully, voters with similar interests can be grouped together. We turn now to how those lines are drawn.

United We Stand, Divided We Fall

The Constitution requires that each state draw their districts to equally apportion their population within those districts. This means that each district must be within 1% of the average population of all the districts. The courts take apportionment very seriously, and states must be very careful not to violate the intent of the apportionment clause. However, challenging apportionment at first may appear to be a **political question**, which the courts generally treat as non-justiciable (i.e., not able to be heard by the Court). However, in a landmark decision in 1962 known as *Baker v. Carr*, the Court decided that apportionment cases are not political questions but rather are questions of equal protection that merit judicial review.

> Political question—an issue that a court will not address because the political branches (executive and legislative) are the more appropriate forum for resolution.

To get a sense of the importance of equal apportionment, we review a case from 1964 in which a Georgia representative had 823,680 residents in his district while the average district in his state had 394,312 residents. Note that this case was dismissed by the lower courts as a non-justiciable political question, but based upon the precedent established in *Baker v. Carr*, the U.S. Supreme Court saw a need to address the important issue of apportionment.

Wesberry v. Sanders, 376 U.S. 1 (1964)

Appellants are citizens and qualified voters of Fulton County, Georgia, and as such are entitled to vote in congressional elections in Georgia's Fifth Congressional District. That district, one of ten created by a 1931 Georgia statute, includes Fulton, DeKalb, and Rockdale Counties, and has a population, according to the 1960 census, of 823,680. The average population of the ten districts is 394,312, less than half that of the Fifth. One district, the Ninth, has only 272,154 people, less than one-third as many as the Fifth. Since there is only one Congressman for each district, this inequality of population means that the Fifth District's Congressman has to represent from two to three times as many people as do Congressmen from some of the other Georgia districts.

Did Georgia's congressional districts violate the Fourteenth Amendment or deprive citizens of the full benefit of their right to vote?

***

This brings us to the merits. We agree with the District Court that the 1931 Georgia apportionment grossly discriminates against voters in the Fifth Congressional District. A single Congressman represents from two to three times as many Fifth District voters as are represented by each of the Congressmen from the other Georgia congressional districts. The apportionment statute thus contracts the value of some votes and expands

> that of others. If the Federal Constitution intends that, when qualified voters elect members of Congress, each vote be given as much weight as any other vote, then this statute cannot stand.
>
> We hold that, construed in its historical context, the command of Art. I, § 2 that Representatives be chosen "by the People of the several States" means that, as nearly as is practicable, one man's vote in a congressional election is to be worth as much as another's. This rule is followed automatically, of course, when Representatives are chosen as a group on a statewide basis, as was a widespread practice in the first 50 years of our Nation's history. It would be extraordinary to suggest that, in such statewide elections, the votes of inhabitants of some parts of a State, for example, Georgia's thinly populated Ninth District, could be weighted at two or three times the value of the votes of people living in more populous parts of the State, for example, the Fifth District around Atlanta. We do not believe that the Framers of the Constitution intended to permit the same vote-diluting discrimination to be accomplished through the device of districts containing widely varied numbers of inhabitants. To say that a vote is worth more in one district than in another would not only run counter to our fundamental ideas of democratic government, it would cast aside the principle of a House of Representatives elected "by the People," a principle tenaciously fought for and established at the Constitutional Convention. The history of the Constitution, particularly that part of it relating to the adoption of Art. I, § 2, reveals that those who framed the Constitution meant that, no matter what the mechanics of an election, whether statewide or by districts, it was population which was to be the basis of the House of Representatives.
>
> ***
>
> Who are to be the electors of the Federal Representatives? Not the rich more than the poor; not the learned more than the ignorant; not the haughty heirs of distinguished names more than the humble sons of obscure and unpropitious fortune. The electors are to be the great body of the people of the United States. (internal quotation and citation omitted).
>
> Readers surely could have fairly taken this to mean, "one person, one vote."
>
> While it may not be possible to draw congressional districts with mathematical precision, that is no excuse for ignoring our Constitution's plain objective of making equal representation for equal numbers of people the fundamental goal for the House of Representatives. That is the high standard of justice and common sense which the Founders set for us.

The same year that the Court strictly interpreted the apportionment clause for state representatives in the U.S. congress, they made a similar decision for state legislatures. In *Reynolds v. Simms*, the U.S. Supreme Court addressed the question of whether a state is obligated to re-apportion its state (or federal) congressional districts to maintain equality among those districts. In an 8–1 decision, the Court concluded that the 14th Amendment Equal Protection clause required re-apportionment to account for variances in population and to ensure equal representation.

> We hold that, as a basic constitutional standard, the Equal Protection Clause requires that the seats in both houses of a bicameral state legislature must be apportioned on a population basis. Simply stated, an individual's right to vote for state legislators is unconstitutionally impaired when its weight is in a substantial fashion diluted when compared with votes of citizens living in other parts of the State. Since under neither the existing apportionment provisions nor either of the proposed plans was either of the houses of the Alabama Legislature apportioned on a population basis, the District Court correctly held that all three of these schemes were constitutionally invalid. Furthermore, the existing apportionment, and also, to a lesser extent, the apportionment under the Crawford-Webb Act, presented little more than crazy quilts, completely lacking in rationality, and could be found invalid on that basis alone.

How to Draw a Vote: Redistricting and Gerrymandering

We learned in the previous section that states are required to reapportion their congressional districts following the decennial census if their populations have shifted. This is a process known as **redistricting**. States have the ultimate responsibility for deciding where they will draw the lines on the state map to establish congressional districts. Each state follows one of the following approaches to redistricting:

> Redistricting—adjusting the boundaries of a congressional district within a state.

- State legislative control (28 states)
- Independent or bipartisan redistricting commission (12 states)
- State legislative decision based upon independent commission recommendations (5 states)
- Political commission control (Arkansas)
- Single representative control (7 states)

Most states have rules for redistricting that are meant to promote fairness in the drawing of district lines as well as to comply with federal apportionment requirements. However, partisan politics play an increasingly significant role in this process.

Gerrymandering

Gerrymandering is the process of drawing congressional districts in a way that gives the party in power an advantage over the minority party, even if that minority party would have a majority of the popular vote in the district. Given that in the majority of states, redistricting is left to the state legislative bodies, the majority party at the time of redistricting may be motivated to redraw district lines in such a way that they can strengthen their representative power. How is this possible within the framework of the apportionment and equal protection clauses? It is easier than many people realize (see Figure 2.4).

> Gerrymandering—drawing congressional district boundaries in a manner that gives preference to voters of the party in power.

As Figure 2.4 demonstrates, creative line-drawing can take a state that has a majority of districts from one party and turn it into a state with a majority of districts from the other party, without changing any votes. The first iteration of the district map shows perfect representation, with all of the red districts together and all of the blue districts together. The second iteration is unfair because it leaves a blue majority in every district despite two-fifths of the population living in red districts. And the

46 How the Government Works

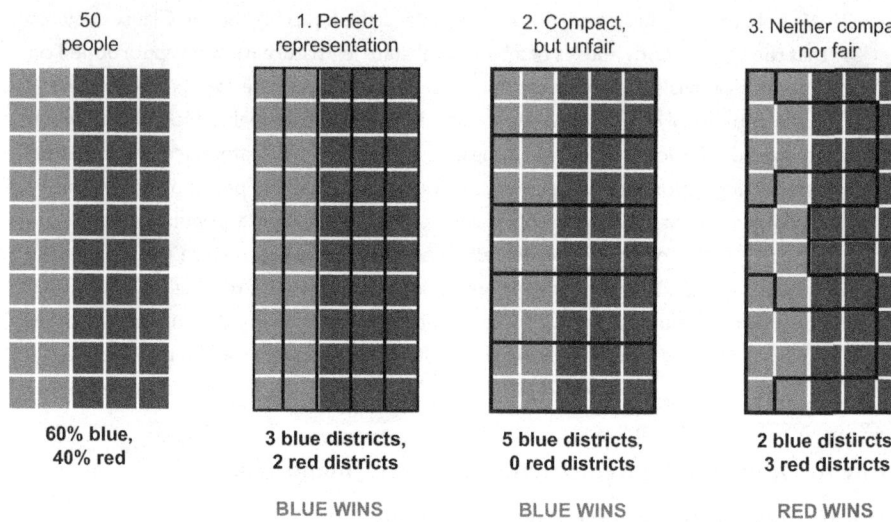

Figure 2.4 Distinct Ways of Dividing 50 Districts.
Source: Christopher Ingraham, *Washington Post* (March 1, 2015).

third iteration, also seemingly unfair, is the best representation of gerrymandering. Lines were drawn to minimize the power of blue districts in every instance through *cracking* and *packing*.

Cracking refers to the dispersion of voters from a particular political party among many districts to ensure that they are unable to join together to form a powerful voting block. This might involve splitting an urban district with a majority of Democratic voters, for instance, into multiple districts where those Democrats are mixed with Republican voters, thus diluting the power of the Democrats' vote. **Packing**, on the other hand, refers to the consolidation of voters of a single political persuasion into compact districts to minimize their overall effect on an election. By giving up some districts, the party drawing the lines can maximize the overall number of districts in which they will have a majority share.

Gerrymandering has been a political tactic for many election cycles. However, technology has enabled parties to become extraordinarily precise in drawing district lines to ensure proportionality of their population while maximizing political control. A number of lawsuits have challenged this process, though the Supreme Court has yet to provide clear guidance on what constitutes proper redistricting.

In Arizona, the state adopted an independent redistricting commission in 2000 via state constitutional amendment. In 2015, the state legislature challenged that amendment, arguing that only the state legislature should be permitted to apportion congressional districts. The U.S. Supreme Court disagreed and found that while redistricting is a legislative function, it can be carried out by other entities. *Arizona State Legislature v. Arizona Independent Redistricting Commission* (2015). That same commission was challenged the following year on the basis of the new district map that it drew, which was alleged to have favored Democrats by separating minority voters from white voters in accordance with the terms of the Voting Rights Act (see later section). The Court again upheld the commission's actions, finding that they had

> Cracking—a form of gerrymandering that breaks apart majorities of a single party in order to dilute their voting power.
>
> Packing—a form of gerrymandering that consolidates voters of one political party within a single district in order to dilute their voting power.

acted in good faith and in accordance with the Act. *Harris v. Arizona Independent Redistricting Commission* (2016).

In another recent decision, the Court upheld a Texas decision to count all residents, voting and non-voting, in determining proper population distributions. *Evenwel v. Abbott* (2016). This unanimous decision meant that all residents, including citizens, residents, and undocumented immigrants, could be counted as part of the state's population for purposes of redistricting, even though only a portion of those residents were eligible to vote.

Finally, in 2017, the U.S. Supreme Court struck down a North Carolina effort to redistrict in a partisan manner. In *Cooper v. Harris*, the Court examined racial bias in redistricting efforts. North Carolina had redrawn its congressional districts in a way that would create a majority black voter district by reallocating some black voters from other districts. The state claimed that it was trying to comply with the Voting Rights Act. The Court found the redistricting unlawful since it was based largely upon the race of the voters and because the state had no compelling interest in reallocating black voters other than a loose effort to comply with the Act.

As you may have noticed so far, while votes can determine the outcome of an election, the process is more complicated than pulling a lever or filling in a ballot. The power of a vote depends upon two things—the makeup of your district and the electoral college. Both of those elements are affected significantly by political parties, which work to consolidate votes for a single candidate by carefully organizing districts to favor their voters and by tying electors to single candidates rather than allowing them to independently choose how to cast their vote. In the next section, we consider the power of political parties and their unique origin.

Political Parties

> *[Political parties] gradually incline the minds of men to seek security . . . in the absolute power of an individual.*
> —President George Washington, Farewell Address, September 17, 1796

The U.S. Constitution is silent on the topic of political parties. Some of the founding fathers believed that political parties would undermine the country by creating factions and dividing people into general groups of belief. The first President was not a member of any political party and used his farewell address to express his concern over the risk of such parties leading to affiliation with individuals who become too powerful and despotic. His administration was the last (and only) to escape the grip of these parties.

The first political parties arose over the issue of federalism. One party—the Federalists—believed that there should be a strong central government to protect the rights of citizens. The competing party—the Democrat-Republicans—believed in states' rights and a weak central government. The Federalists were led by Alexander Hamilton while the Democrat-Republicans were led by Thomas Jefferson and James Madison.

The Democrat-Republican Party split in the early 1800s to become the Whig Party and the Democratic Party. The Whigs supported a federal government where Congress maintained most of the power and where the economy would be modernized and protected against foreign competition (see Chapter 5 on Economic Policy). The Democrats supported stronger executive power and fought against modernizing industry for fear that it would hurt individual taxpayers. The Whigs became largely defunct in 1850 following an intra-party split over the issue of slavery.

The Republican Party, which was established on the ashes of the Whig Party in 1854, became the leading party starting with the 1860 election of Abraham Lincoln, a Republican. Republicans supported business modernization, fought against slavery, and favored protecting American industry over foreign imports. Republicans maintained a majority in Congress until 1932, when the stock market crash and subsequent depression led voters to seek more controls over free markets.

The rise of the Republican Party and the ongoing support for the Democrat Party crowded out the political landscape and largely prevented the rise of competing parties. Arguably, when President Millard Fillmore, a Whig, left office in 1853 and was replaced by Democrat Franklin Pierce, a two-party system had been entrenched in the United States (with the small exception of President Andrew Johnson from the National Union party who served out the remainder of Abraham Lincoln's term after Lincoln's assassination). No candidate from outside these two parties has been elected to the presidency since.

Does this mean that third parties ceased to exist? Not at all. Today, although the national political landscape is composed of mostly Democrats and Republicans, there are also Independents (two Independent Senators as of 2018) and a variety of party members at the state and local level. Elected officials in statehouses include members of the Vermont Progressive Party, the Libertarian Party, the Green Party, the Working Families Party, the Independence Party of New York, and simply Independents. All total, as of 2018, 38 legislative and executive positions at the state level are occupied by affiliates of third parties.

Individuals are free to join any political party that they wish or none at all, and they can change their affiliation at will. Affiliating with a political party as a voter can help to generate support for particular candidates who align with the policies of that party and can likewise help that candidate fundraise on a recognized platform. Parties are eligible under federal election law to receive political contributions from voters that do not count toward that voter's campaign contribution limits for individual candidates. This means that a political party can develop a "war chest" that can be used to purchase advertising, host events, and take other steps to generate awareness of a candidate and his or her campaign. The downside of affiliating with a small party is the limited financial support it can offer a candidate.

Voting

Voter turnout is a key driver of election success. A politician may be very popular and well-funded, but if he or she cannot turn out enough supporters on election day, none of that matters. Today, only about half of the eligible population votes in presidential elections (every four years), and less than 36% participate in midterm elections (every two years). Compare this to last century when presidential elections enjoyed a voter turnout rate of 82% (1860 election) and a midterm turnout rate of 66% (1860 election). With the federal government engaged in more areas of life today, from business regulation to social protections, it is more important than ever before to ensure that all eligible voters participate in the election process.

There are over 500,000 elected officials in the United States, from local magistrates to the President of the United States. These officials have the power to make decisions that affect their constituents, and their positions depend on support from those constituents. If you are interested in running for office, there are many resources available to help you get started (see Box 2.1). In this section, we will focus on your critical role as a voter.

> **Box 2.1: Want to Become a Congressperson?**
>
> One of the best ways to influence public policy is to place yourself at the center of it by becoming a policymaker. And while there are many ways to make an impact, serving as a member of the U.S. Congress gives you access to the levers of power like nowhere else.
>
> If you want to run for Congress, you must meet the Constitutional requirements for holding office, which are as follows:
>
> - Be a U.S. Citizen (naturalized is acceptable) for at least seven years
> - Be at least 25 years old
> - Live in the state that you plan to represent
>
> If you meet those requirements and you are interested in exploring this possibility, consider talking with friends who have run campaigns or reading a book on running for office. Some recommendations can be found in the Additional Learning Resources section of this chapter.

Who Is Eligible to Vote?

States set their own rules for determining who is eligible to vote in an election. However, there are some constitutional guidelines ensuring that certain groups of individuals are not denied the right to vote. Grounds upon which voting rights cannot be denied include the following:

- National origin (citizens of any country can vote)

    (Naturalization Act of 1790)

- Race or color

    (15th Amendment, 1870)

- Gender

    (19th Amendment, 1920)

- Failure to pay a poll tax for federal elections

    (24th Amendment, 1964)

- Age (must be 18 or over)

    (26th Amendment, 1971)

Aside from these restrictions, states have some flexibility in setting down the rules for determining voter eligibility. For instance, some states restrict the voting rights of convicted felons. The breakdown of state laws with respect to criminal convictions is as follows:

- No loss of voter rights: Maine, Vermont
- Loss of right to vote while incarcerated only: Washington, D.C., Hawaii, Illinois, Indiana, Maryland, Massachusetts, Michigan, Montana, New Hampshire, North Dakota, Ohio, Oregon, Pennsylvania, Rhode Island and Utah

- Loss of right to vote until completion of sentence, probation or parole: Alaska, Arkansas, California, Colorado, Connecticut, Georgia, Idaho, Kansas, Louisiana, Minnesota, Missouri, New Jersey, New Mexico, New York, North Carolina, Oklahoma, South Carolina, South Dakota, Texas, Washington, West Virginia and Wisconsin
- Loss until completion of sentence and permission required for restoration: Alabama, Arizona, Delaware, Florida, Iowa, Kentucky, Mississippi, Nevada, Nebraska, Tennessee, Virginia and Wyoming

The estimated number of potentially eligible voters who cannot vote due to a felony conviction is over 5 million. Other laws restricting voter eligibility, such as laws prohibiting those with mental incompetence from voting, are generally not enforced.

Voter Registration

Before anyone can cast a ballot, they must register to vote in their district. This is a mechanism to ensure that the voter is eligible to vote based upon where they live, their age (over 18), and their citizenship status (only citizens can vote). Once registered, the voter is ready to vote in the primary and general elections.

Registration rules vary among states and have at times been controversial. Some states require voters to register in advance of an election, whereas others allow voters to register and vote on the same day. According to the Pew Charitable Trusts organization, 24% of eligible voters are not registered to vote. Some states, such as Oregon, California, West Virginia, Vermont, and Connecticut, automatically register individuals to vote when they apply for a driver's license. Other states provide mail-in registration options, same-day registration, or something similar.

On election day, a registered voter prior to 2006 needed only to appear at their local polling station and check their name off the registered voter roll before casting their ballot (though some states requested some identity document, none required it). However, beginning in 2006, states began implementing voter identification laws that required voters to produce some form of ID that proved their identity (see Figure 2.5). Indiana and Georgia were the first such states to do so, but 34 states have followed suit as of 2018. Most of these states contend that voter ID requirements reduce the possibility of voter fraud. However, evidence of voter fraud (e.g., convicted felons casting ballots) appears to be miniscule according to reports by the Brennan Center for Justice as well as the Commission on Federal Election Reform.

Some organizations, such as the American Civil Liberties Union (ACLU), have vociferously argued against voter ID laws, alleging that they unfairly discriminate against minority voters. Though the evidence on this assertion is also uncertain, courts have found that some strict voter ID laws, such as those enacted twice in Texas, appeared to disenfranchise minority voters and thus violated the Constitution. Ultimately, the question is whether the risk of voter fraud outweighs the risk of taking a vote away from an otherwise eligible American citizen.

It is worth noting that in most developed countries, voter registration is automatic (e.g., Finland, Italy, Iceland, Denmark, the Czech Republic, Chile) or required (e.g., Germany, Australia, Switzerland), ensuring that everyone who wants to vote is able to do so on election day. Most of the countries that do not automatically register their voters also offer same-day registration. Election day in most of the developed world is on a Sunday or over a weekend. In the European Union, election day runs from a Thursday through a Sunday. This allows for those who work to find ample time to cast their ballot.

How the Government Works 51

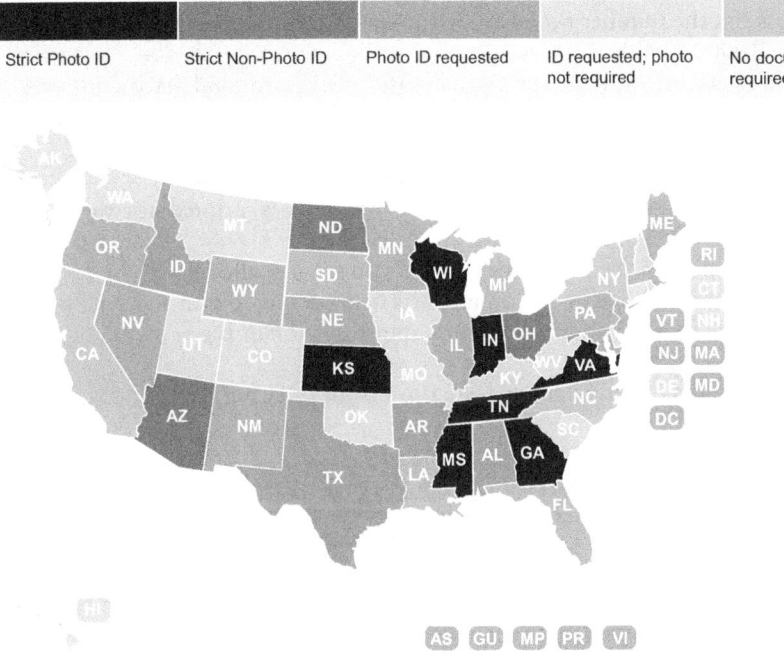

Figure 2.5 Voter ID Laws across the States (2018).
Source: National Conference of State Legislatures.

Disenfranchisement and the Voting Rights Act

Despite passage of the 15th Amendment in 1870, which guaranteed the right of African Americans to vote, discriminatory practices continued to disenfranchise many of those voters. One of the most common means to restrict the power of this group of voters was through the use of literacy tests (see Box 2.2). These tests, often unrelated to civics or governance in any way, proved difficult for voters with limited access to education (recall that public schools only began to be integrated in the South in the late 1950s).

Box 2.2: Literacy Tests

Many states employed tests to assess the cognitive abilities of voters as a means of eligibility. Since states have the ability to set their own rules for establishing voter eligibility, these tests might be permissible. However, some states used the tests to discriminate against African Americans and others with limited access to education.

In 1964 Louisiana, a test was given to all eligible voters. They had 10 minutes to complete the test, and a single wrong answer would result in failure and thus an inability to vote. Here are some of the questions asked on that test:

1. Draw a line around the number or letter of this sentence.
2. Circle the first, first letter of the alphabet in this line.

3. Above the letter X make a small cross.
4. Cross out the number necessary when making the number below one million: 10000000000
5. In the space below, write the word "noise" backwards and place a dot over what would be its second letter should it have been written forward.
6. Spell backwards, forwards.
7. Print the word vote upside down, but in the correct order.
8. Print a word that looks the same whether it is printed forwards or backwards.
9. Write right from the left to the right as you see it spelled here.
10. Divide a vertical line in two equal parts by bisecting it with a curved horizontal line that is only straight at its spot bisection of the vertical.

Source: Louisiana Voter Literacy Test, 1964 from the Civil Rights Movement Veterans web site.

The Voting Rights Act of 1965 was passed during the Civil Rights movement. Signed into law by President Lyndon B. Johnson, the Act sought to rectify recurring discrimination against racial and language minorities in their efforts to vote. The two major provisions of the Act focus on the prevention of state laws that restrict access to voting on the basis of minority status, and enhanced monitoring of states with a history of egregious discrimination. We examine these two provisions as follows.

Section 2 of the Act prohibits any state or local jurisdiction from establishing a "voting qualification or prerequisite to voting, or standard, practice, or procedure . . . in a manner which results in a denial or abridgement of the right . . . to vote on account of race . . . color, or language minority status." The law allows private individuals to sue a jurisdiction on the basis of their alleged denial of voting rights on the basis of discrimination. The law was originally interpreted by the Supreme Court to require proof that a voter eligibility rule intentionally discriminated (*Mobile v. Bolden*, 1980); however, subsequent amendments to the Act in 1982 applied a *results test* that examined the impact of the law rather than the intent.

To be successful on a claim under the Act, a voter must prove that they were either denied the right to vote or that their vote was *diluted* by the restriction. Most cases are brought under the vote dilution charge, which means that the effect of racial and language minority group votes is weakened due to a state law or policy, such as gerrymandering, to pack those minority groups into a limited number of districts to weaken their overall influence on an election.

Section 4 of the Act creates the *coverage formula*. This highly controversial section singled out states and localities as historically disenfranchising minority voters. Jurisdictions that employed literacy tests, moral character requirements, and similar measures targeting minority populations (all of which were no longer permitted) were placed on a list that made them subject to special provisions under the Act. The original list included the following states: Alabama, Alaska, Georgia, Louisiana, Mississippi, South Carolina, and Virginia, as well as an array of local jurisdictions in other states.

Jurisdictions that were subjected to the coverage formula had to comply with section 5 of the Act, which required those jurisdictions to acquire *preclearance* from the Attorney General before making any change to voting rules, no matter how minor. If the Attorney General objected to the change during the preclearance process on the basis of perceived discrimination, the jurisdiction would have the option to request judicial preclearance, which could overturn the decision of the Attorney General. If the objection withstood challenge, the jurisdiction would be prohibited from implementing their change.

The Supreme Court largely upheld the coverage formula initially, which was modified numerous times to include additional jurisdictions since 1965. However, a challenge to the Act arose in 2012 on the grounds of federalism that asked the Court to consider whether Congress had the Constitutional authority to re-authorize the Act in 2006 (in effect, whether Congress had the power to enact the law in the first place). In *Shelby County v. Holder*, the Court held that Congress did not have the authority to designate certain jurisdictions as subject to additional scrutiny as this violated state sovereignty and the principle of federalism. Thus, the Court struck down section 4 of the Act, which effectively terminated the applicability of section 5 since there would be no more covered jurisdictions.

How Do You Vote?

Given that this is a civics chapter intended to enhance each reader's participation in the public policy process, it is essential that we describe the process for casting your ballot in an election.

The first step in voting, as discussed earlier, is to register to vote. Since the 1993 passage of the National Voter Registration Act (the "motor voter" law), states are required to make voter registration easy and consistent. Today, potential voters can usually register to vote when they renew their driver's license, at schools, libraries, or by mail. Some states allow you to register to vote on election day (though most ask you to register in advance).

The second step is to cast your ballot. Yes, it is that easy. Register and vote. However, remember that there are two "elections" you will be able to vote in each two-year cycle. The first is the **primary** (sometime between January and June) and the second is the **general election** (in November).

The primary, which is not really an election, is where you are asked to select the candidates you prefer from within your political party (e.g., the Democratic candidate for Senator). These are elections from within your political party—they are not elections for national office. The primary is held early in the year when there will likely be multiple candidates running for a single position on behalf of a particular political party. Since only one candidate can run for a single position under that party's banner, voters choose those finalists during the primary. Note that most countries allow their political parties, rather than individual voters, to select the final candidates to stand for election, a process that the United States had followed in the past as well.

Your state may have an **open primary**, in which any registered voter can participate; a **closed primary**, in which only voters registered with that political party can participate; or a **caucus**, in which there is no vote but rather a meeting of party members to select final candidates. Eleven states (Iowa, New Mexico, North Dakota, Maine, Nevada, Hawaii, Minnesota, Kansas, Alaska, Wyoming, Colorado) and the District of Columbia use the caucus method. You do not need to participate in a primary or caucus to be eligible to vote in the general election in November.

The general election takes place on the first Tuesday after November 1 (the first Tuesday after the first Monday in November). This is where you will vote for your preferred candidate between (rather than within) political parties. Assuming you are

---

Primary—election held within a single party to determine which person will represent a particular political party in a general election.

General election—election held across political parties to determine which person will fill particular political positions.

Open primary—primary election in which any registered voter may participate.

Closed primary—primary election in which only voters registered for that political party may participate.

Caucus—type of primary election in which a meeting is held to determine political party candidates.

a registered voter in the jurisdiction in which you are voting, you will visit your local polling station (often a school or public building) and cast your secret ballot. You can use Google, Facebook, and many other electronic tools to identify your local polling station, determine the hours of operation, and confirm that you are registered to vote there.

Election day is not a national holiday and falls on a weekday, making it hard for some people to find the time to get out and vote. So to make it even easier, 33 states and the District of Columbia allow early voting, which means that you can cast your ballot prior to election day so that you can avoid any conflicts and crowds on that busy day. If you don't vote early and you won't be in town on election day, you can also cast an absentee ballot, usually by mail, from anywhere in the world.

Remember that each election cycle includes different offices being filled. The President and Vice President are elected every four years (i.e., 2016, 2020, 2024), whereas congressional representatives are elected every two years to serve six-year terms (i.e., 2016, 2018, 2020). Some elections are even held during *off years*, such as elections of some local officials (i.e., 2017, 2019, 2021). On election day, you will vote for local, state, and federal officials, as well as in some cases for local voter initiatives, which are utilized in 24 states and the District of Columbia as well as in several local elections.

Voting is easy and is still the best way to express your views on public policy in your community. The right to select the composition of your government was a hard-fought right and should not be ignored. Participate early and often in elections, as either a voter or a candidate, and spread the word to get the vote out far and wide.

Conclusion

The American identity is unique in many ways from other cultures. A diverse population with myriad ethnicities, races, religions, and languages unites around shared political values. Who we are as a nation is not easily defined, but it is something that politicians from all political parties try to determine in order to establish issue platforms and win elections. However, our affiliation with ideas depends to a significant extent upon our understanding of those ideas and the governing structures that will implement them.

As this chapter has hopefully made apparent, we (collectively) are becoming more ignorant of politics, more hesitant to engage in political dialogue, and more averse to participating in government as voters. Social media is allowing the rapid spread of false ideas that many voters are unable to distinguish from facts (see Chapter 4 on Critical Thinking), further skewing voter awareness and engagement in governance. We are perpetuating a cycle of political ignorance that injects an unhealthy distance between the government and the governed and that risks silencing the voice of the people in place of the voice of the elite. Only through the spread of facts and active dialogue around those facts can we create a healthy political environment in which most people participate, believe that their voice is being heard, and trust their government to act in their best interests.

Learning Activities

The Civics Game

Visit the following website to try your hand at a civics game that will test your knowledge of American government:
www.icivics.org

The Redistricting Game

Play the Redistricting Game from the Annenberg Center at the University of Southern California:

http://redistrictinggame.org

Test Your Civics Knowledge

The following questions are on the citizenship examination and are given to intending citizens as part of their requirements to receive U.S. citizenship. The answers can be found in Appendix A. Note that only 50 of the 100 questions are listed here. To view the complete test, visit www.USCIS.gov.

Principles of American Democracy

1. What is the supreme law of the land?
2. What does the Constitution do?
3. The idea of self-government is in the first three words of the Constitution. What are these words?
4. What is an amendment?
5. What do we call the first ten amendments to the Constitution?
6. What is one right or freedom from the First Amendment?
7. How many amendments does the Constitution have?
8. What did the Declaration of Independence do?
9. What are two rights in the Declaration of Independence?
10. What is freedom of religion?
11. What is the economic system in the United States?
12. What is the "rule of law"?

System of Government

13. Name one branch or part of the government.
14. What stops one branch of government from becoming too powerful?
15. Who is in charge of the executive branch?
16. Who makes federal laws?
17. What are the two parts of the U.S. Congress?
18. How many U.S. Senators are there?
19. We elect a U.S. Senator for how many years?
20. Who is one of your state's U.S. Senators now?
21. The House of Representatives has how many voting members?
22. We elect a U.S. Representative for how many years?
23. Name your U.S. Representative.
24. Who does a U.S. Senator represent?
25. Why do some states have more Representatives than other states?
26. We elect a President for how many years?
27. In what month do we vote for President?
28. What is the name of the President of the United States now (2018)?
29. What is the name of the Vice President of the United States now (2018)?
30. If the President can no longer serve, who becomes President?
31. If both the President and the Vice President can no longer serve, who becomes President?

32. Who is the Commander-in-Chief of the military?
33. Who signs bills to become laws?
34. Who vetoes bills?
35. What does the President's Cabinet do?
36. What are two Cabinet-level positions?
37. What does the judicial branch do?
38. What is the highest court in the United States?
39. How many justices are on the Supreme Court?
40. Who is the Chief Justice of the United States now (2018)?
41. Under our Constitution, some powers belong to the federal government. What is one power of the federal government?
42. Under our Constitution, some powers belong to the states. What is one power of the states?
43. Who is the Governor of your state now?
44. What is the capital of your state?
45. What are the two major political parties in the United States?
46. What is the political party of the President now?
47. What is the name of the Speaker of the House of Representatives now (2018)?

Rights and Responsibilities

48. There are four amendments to the Constitution about who can vote. Describe one of them.
49. What is one responsibility that is only for United States citizens?
50. Name one right only for United States citizens.

Notes

1. National Assessment of Educational Progress, Civics Assessment, https://nces.ed.gov/nationsreportcard/civics/
2. Mark Hansen, *Flunking Civics: Why America's Kids Know So Little*, ABA Journal (2011), www.abajournal.com/magazine/article/civics/#quiz

Additional Learning Resources

Civics Renewal Network, www.civicsrenewalnetwork.org/resources
iCivics Teaching Resources, www.icivics.org/teachers
Victor S. DeSantis & Tari Renner, *The Impact of Political Structures on Public Policies in American Counties*, 54 Public Administration Review 291 (1994).
Ronald Faucheux, *Running for Office: The Strategies, Techniques and Messages Modern Political Candidates Need to Win Elections* (2002).
Amanda Litman & Hillary Rodham Clinton, *Run for Something: A Real-Talk Guide to Fixing the System Yourself* (2017).
Richard M. Merelman, *Symbols as Substance in National Civics Standards*, 29.1 PS: Political Science & Politics 53 (1996).
Earnest A. Young, *The Constitution Outside the Constitution*, 117.3 Yale Law Journal 408 (2007).

Appendix A
Answers to Citizenship Test

Principles of American Democracy

1. What is the supreme law of the land?
   a. The Constitution

2. What does the Constitution do?
   a. sets up the government
   b. defines the government
   c. protects basic rights of Americans

3. The idea of self-government is in the first three words of the Constitution. What are these words?
   a. We the People

4. What is an amendment?
   a. a change (to the Constitution)
   b. an addition (to the Constitution)

5. What do we call the first ten amendments to the Constitution?
   a. the Bill of Rights

6. What is one right or freedom from the First Amendment?
   a. speech
   b. religion
   c. assembly
   d. press
   e. petition the government

7. How many amendments does the Constitution have?
   a. twenty-seven (27)

8. What did the Declaration of Independence do?
   a. announced our independence (from Great Britain)
   b. declared our independence (from Great Britain)
   c. said that the United States is free (from Great Britain)

9. What are two rights in the Declaration of Independence?
   a. life
   b. liberty
   c. pursuit of happiness

10. What is freedom of religion?
    a. You can practice any religion, or not practice a religion.

11. What is the economic system in the United States?
    a. capitalist economy
    b. market economy

12. What is the "rule of law"?
    a. Everyone must follow the law.
    b. Leaders must obey the law.
    c. Government must obey the law.
    d. No one is above the law.

System of Government

13. Name one branch or part of the government.
    a. Congress
    b. legislative
    c. President
    d. executive
    e. the courts
    f. judicial

14. What stops one branch of government from becoming too powerful?
    a. checks and balances
    b. separation of powers

15. Who is in charge of the executive branch?
    a. the President

16. Who makes federal laws?
    a. Congress
    b. Senate and House (of Representatives)
    c. (U.S. or national) legislature

17. What are the two parts of the U.S. Congress?
    a. the Senate and House (of Representatives)

18. How many U.S. Senators are there?
    a. one hundred (100)

19. We elect a U.S. Senator for how many years?
    a. six (6)

20. Who is one of your state's U.S. Senators now?
    a. Answers will vary. [District of Columbia residents and residents of U.S. territories should answer that D.C. (or the territory where the applicant lives) has no U.S. Senators.]

21. The House of Representatives has how many voting members?
    a. four hundred thirty-five (435)

22. We elect a U.S. Representative for how many years?
    a. two (2)

23. Name your U.S. Representative.
    a. Answers will vary. [Residents of territories with nonvoting Delegates or Resident Commissioners may provide the name of that Delegate or Commissioner. Also acceptable is any statement that the territory has no (voting) Representatives in Congress.]

24. Who does a U.S. Senator represent?
    a. all people of the state

25. Why do some states have more Representatives than other states?
    a. (because of) the state's population
    b. (because) they have more people
    c. (because) some states have more people

26. We elect a President for how many years?
    a. four (4)

27. In what month do we vote for President?
    a. November

28. What is the name of the President of the United States now (2018)?
    a. Donald J. Trump
    b. Donald Trump
    c. Trump

29. What is the name of the Vice President of the United States now (2018)?
    a. Michael R. Pence
    b. Mike Pence
    c. Pence

30. If the President can no longer serve, who becomes President?
    a. the Vice President

31. If both the President and the Vice President can no longer serve, who becomes President?
    a. the Speaker of the House

32. Who is the Commander in Chief of the military?
    a. the President

33. Who signs bills to become laws?
    a. the President

34. Who vetoes bills?
    a. the President

35. What does the President's Cabinet do?
    a. advises the President

36. What are two Cabinet-level positions?
    a. Secretary of Agriculture
    b. Secretary of Commerce
    c. Secretary of Defense
    d. Secretary of Education
    e. Secretary of Energy

f. Secretary of Health and Human Services
g. Secretary of Homeland Security
h. Secretary of Housing and Urban Development
i. Secretary of the Interior
j. Secretary of Labor
k. Secretary of State
l. Secretary of Transportation
m. Secretary of the Treasury
n. Secretary of Veterans Affairs
o. Attorney General
p. Vice President

37. What does the judicial branch do?
    a. reviews laws
    b. explains laws
    c. resolves disputes (disagreements)
    d. decides if a law goes against the Constitution

38. What is the highest court in the United States?
    a. the Supreme Court

39. How many justices are on the Supreme Court?
    a. nine (9)

40. Who is the Chief Justice of the United States now (2018)?
    a. John Roberts (John G. Roberts, Jr.)

41. Under our Constitution, some powers belong to the federal government. What is one power of the federal government?
    a. to print money
    b. to declare war
    c. to create an army
    d. to make treaties

42. Under our Constitution, some powers belong to the states. What is one power of the states?
    a. provide schooling and education
    b. provide protection (police)
    c. provide safety (fire departments)
    d. give a driver's license
    e. approve zoning and land use

43. Who is the Governor of your state now?
    a. Answers will vary. [District of Columbia residents should answer that D.C. does not have a Governor.]

44. What is the capital of your state?
    a. Answers will vary. [District of Columbia residents should answer that D.C. is not a state and does not have a capital. Residents of U.S. territories should name the capital of the territory.]

45. What are the two major political parties in the United States?
    a. Democratic and Republican

How the Government Works 61

46. What is the political party of the President now?
    a. Republican (Party)
47. What is the name of the Speaker of the House of Representatives now (2018)?
    a. Paul D. Ryan
    b. (Paul) Ryan

Rights and Responsibilities

48. There are four amendments to the Constitution about who can vote. Describe one of them.
    a. Citizens eighteen (18) and older (can vote)
    b. You don't have to pay (a poll tax) to vote
    c. Any citizen can vote (Women and men can vote.)
    d. A male citizen of any race (can vote)
49. What is one responsibility that is only for United States citizens?
    a. serve on a jury
    b. vote in a federal election
50. Name one right only for United States citizens.
    a. vote in a federal election
    b. run for federal office

3 Institutions and Power—Congress, the Courts, and the President

Introduction

We have already defined public policy to be the relationship between the government and the governed. How that relationship operates depends in large part on the nature of the institutions and the rules that define those structures. Weak institutions are associated with poor governance and poor relations between the government and governed. On the contrary, strong institutions are a hallmark of an effective government, regardless of the principles of its policies toward the governed. In other words, effective institutions are a necessary but not sufficient precondition to effective governance.

In this chapter, we will examine the key institutions in the United States that enact and interact with public policy. We will start with the three Constitutionally established branches, the legislative, executive, and judicial branches of government. We will then proceed to consider the relationship between those federal branches and the state governance structures that mirror them. Finally, we will take a comparative look at governance structures around the world.

A Trade Embargo Leads to a New Country

Our previous chapter on civics provided a more thorough background on the creation of the U.S. electoral process, but it would do a great disservice to our readers to offer an explanation of governmental institutions without paying heed to their formation. This requires us to step back in time to 1773.

The East India Company (discussed in Chapter 5 on Economic Policy) imported goods from South Asia into England, including tea. Prior to the Tea Act of 1773, tea from the East India Company had to be sold at auction in England, where it was taxed, and then exported to the colonies, where it would be sold at an inflated price.

Because of the British Navigation Acts, only tea sold by authorized British merchants was permitted to be sold in the colonies. That tea was taxed under the Townshend Acts of 1767, which raised revenue to fund the British occupying army and governors. Seeing an economic opportunity, some American merchants coordinated the import of tea from The Netherlands, which, though illegal, entered without tax and was thus in high demand. These tea smugglers imported twice as much tea from the Dutch as they did from the British.

As a means of both rescuing the struggling East India Company and of asserting control over the rebelling Americans, on May 10, 1773, the British Parliament enacted the Tea Act. This Act was in some sense a historic bailout of a failing company, one that had a long and important relationship with the British government.

The Act allowed the East India Company to sell its tea directly to the colonies without having to first enter into London and pay tax on it. This would allow the company to acquire a competitive advantage over the illegal exporters, who were selling untaxed tea that was considered of inferior quality. The Parliament hoped that this Act would reign in the smuggling and empower colonial rulers. The plan failed spectacularly.

As with any trade regulation, those who stand to lose economically tend to be the most vocal in response. In this case, the Sons of Liberty represented the interests of the American merchants that had been smuggling in the cheaper tea from The Netherlands. Even though economically the Act should have been well-received by Americans hoping for affordable English tea, the principle of the British asserting control over the tea trade and pushing colonists out was enough to garner support for a protest.

Protests began in September 1773, with calls for the arriving ships from England to return to England or face consequences. The protests were successful in Philadelphia, New York, and Charleston, and the ships left. In Boston, the British governor refused to let the protests stop the ships from entering the port. So, the Sons of Liberty boarded the ships and dumped the 342 chests of tea into the sea.

In response to the "Boston Tea Party," the British Parliament began enacting retaliatory legislation in a desperate effort to reacquire control over the colonies. The Prime Minister said,

> [t]he Americans have tarred and feathered your subjects, plundered your merchants, burnt your ships, denied all obedience to your laws and authority; yet so clement and so long forbearing has our conduct been that it is incumbent on us now to take a different course. Whatever may be the consequences, we must risk something; if we do not, all is over.[1]

Parliament enacted the "intolerable acts" (called the "coercive acts" in England) to punish those who interrupted the tea trade, authorizing the trial of British royal officials in England rather than the colonies, and so forth.

This string of events led to the Revolutionary War and the formation of the United States as we know it today. In order to respond to the intolerable acts, American colonists organized, at the behest of Benjamin Franklin, the first Continental Congress. That was a body of representatives from the 12 colonies that wished to participate (Georgia abstained). This 1774 body was divided in its desire to remain part of the United Kingdom or to declare independence. At the end of their first meeting, they decided to send a list of grievances to the British Parliament and to meet again if the crown failed to address them.

The British Parliament did not concede to the demands of the colonists and, accordingly, the Congress met again in May 1775. Within a year of that Second Continental Congress meeting, the Declaration of Independence had been drafted and was delivered to the King of England on July 4, 1776. The British responded with what became known as the American Revolutionary War. The war lasted until the Treaty of Paris, which was signed in September 1783.

At the start of the war, it became apparent that the colonies would not be able to function under former British laws as they were throwing off the chains of British rule. The second Continental Congress drafted the **Articles of Confederation**, which was a precursor to the U.S. Constitution. In 1781, toward the end of the war, those articles were ratified by the states. Interestingly, those articles in effect transferred only the powers that had formerly belonged to the King to the new federal government, retaining all of the existing colonial powers within the newly formed states.

> Articles of Confederation—the first Constitution of the United States, adopted in 1777 (ratified in 1781).

The Articles of Confederation proved to be very weak, along with the Continental Congress, which was tasked with enforcing this weak central government. Accordingly, in May 1787, a Constitutional Convention was organized to modify the articles in order to grant more power to the federal government. By 1789, it became clear that the original Articles of Confederation were unable to be sufficiently modified, so the U.S. Constitution was drafted instead. The Constitution established the federal government on March 4, 1789.

The United States Begins Operating

> *I agree to this Constitution, with all its Faults, if they are such; because I think a General Government necessary for us, and there is no Form of Government but what may be a Blessing to the People if well administered; and I believe farther that this is likely to be well administered for a Course of Years, and can only end in Despotism as other Forms have done before it, when the People shall become so corrupted as to need Despotic Government, being incapable of any other.*[2]
>
> —Benjamin Franklin (1789)

The Constitution of the United States in 1789 was, as Benjamin Franklin observed, a compromise. States were unwilling to accede a great deal of power to the federal government for fear that a strong central government would simply replace the tyranny that Britain had employed for decades hence. And each representative had his own idea as to what the role of a central government would be. In the end, the federal government that was created resembled a version of the Articles of Confederation before it but with language that would allow it to grow in the future.

The Lawmakers: Article I and the Legislative Branch

> *All legislative powers herein granted shall be vested in a Congress of the United States, which shall consist of a Senate and House of Representatives.*
>
> —U.S. Constitution Art. I, Sec. 1

The founding fathers met at the 1787 Constitutional Convention to form a government that would function effectively without overpowering the voice of the people that it represented. They did not want to replicate the governing structure of England, with a powerful King and weaker protections for the people. So the new government would give the stronger voice to the people and that would be done through the legislative body, which was created by the first article of the Constitution.

The legislative body consists of two branches: the House of Representatives and the Senate. The House is considered to be the chamber that is closest to the people considering their smaller districts and popular representation. This is similar to the House of Commons in the British Parliament. The Senate represents larger districts and thus is not as closely connected to their **constituents** as members of the House (note that the Senate is distinct from the British House of Lords in that the latter are not elected).

> Constituents—individuals within a certain voting district.

House of Representatives

The U.S. House of Representatives (as of 2018) has 435 voting members. The number of voting members from each state depends on the population of that state. Thus, the larger the population size, the more representatives that state has in the House.

The population size is recalculated every ten years during the decennial census (see Chapter 2 on Civics).

The House of Representatives is a powerful body. The leader of the House, who is nominated and selected by the party that holds the majority of seats (usually Republican or Democrat), is called the **Speaker of the House**. The Speaker holds that post until they retire from office, lose to a challenger from within their party, or fail to be reelected to office. The Speaker is the third-in-line to the presidency after the President and Vice President. The first woman to hold that post was Nancy Pelosi (Democrat from California) in 2007.

> Speaker of the House—the congressperson from the party in power chosen to speak on behalf of that chamber of congress.

Elections for the House of Representatives (discussed in more detail in Chapter 2 on Civics) are held every two years, and all seats are elected at the same time (in other words, they are not staggered). This means that a member of the House only holds office for two years before having to be reelected. If they are popular, however, they may serve as many terms as their constituents will allow.

U.S. Senate

The Senate was designed by the framers to be less directly accountable to the people and more focused on larger policy issues. Senators are expected to have more expertise in a broad array of important policy and legal issues, and to have a greater impact on public policy given their broader base of constituents.

The Senate is composed of 100 senators—two from each state, regardless of the population. This gives equal power to all of the states, allowing Iowa, with four House members, to be as influential in the Senate as California, with 53 House members.

Elections for Senators are held every two years; however, unlike in the House, Senators are elected to office for six-year terms. This was an effort by the founding fathers to provide more time for the Senate to focus on larger, longer-term issues facing the United States. The founders also wanted to ensure that the legislative and policymaking efforts of those senators were not tossed aside every six years with an election. So, they added section 3 to Article I of the Constitution, which states:

> Immediately after they shall be assembled in Consequence of the first Election, they shall be divided as equally as may be into three Classes. The Seats of the Senators of the first Class shall be vacated at the Expiration of the second Year, of the second Class at the Expiration of the fourth Year, and of the third Class at the Expiration of the sixth Year, so that one third may be chosen every second Year.
> —U.S. Constitution, Art. 1, Sec. 3

This effectively created staggered elections, allowing one-third of the Senate to be elected every two years. To determine which Senators would be elected in which election cycle, the Constitution created three classes of Senators, each with terms expiring in one of the three six-year election cycles. Each state has two senators and each of those senators is part of a different class:

Class 1 senators (up for election in 2018): Arizona, California, Connecticut, Delaware, Florida, Hawaii, Indiana, Maine, Maryland, Massachusetts, Michigan, Minnesota, Mississippi, Missouri, Montana, Nebraska, Nevada, New Jersey, New Mexico, New York, North Dakota, Ohio, Pennsylvania, Rhode Island, Tennessee, Texas, Utah, Vermont, Virginia, Washington, West Virginia, Wisconsin, and Wyoming

Class 2 senators (up for election in 2020): Alabama, Alaska, Arkansas, Colorado, Delaware, Georgia, Idaho, Illinois, Iowa, Kansas, Kentucky, Louisiana, Maine, Massachusetts, Michigan, Minnesota, Mississippi, Montana, Nebraska, New Hampshire, New Jersey, New Mexico, North Carolina, Oklahoma, Oregon, Rhode Island, South Carolina, South Dakota, Tennessee, Texas, Virginia, West Virginia, and Wyoming

Class 3 senators (up for election in 2022): Alabama, Alaska, Arizona, Arkansas, California, Colorado, Connecticut, Florida, Georgia, Hawaii, Idaho, Illinois, Indiana, Iowa, Kansas, Kentucky, Louisiana, Maryland, Missouri, Nevada, New Hampshire, New York, North Carolina, North Dakota, Ohio, Oklahoma, Oregon, Pennsylvania, South Carolina, South Dakota, Utah, Vermont, Washington, and Wisconsin

> **Senate Majority Leader**—the senator from the party in power chosen to speak on behalf of that chamber of congress.

The Senate spokesperson is the **Majority Leader**, and is selected at the start of each legislative session by the party with control over the Senate (usually Republican or Democrat). To become a Senator, a prospective senator must be a U.S. citizen, at least 30 years old, and must reside in the state they hope to represent. Finally, when voting on legislation, if there is a tie in the Senate, the Vice President presides as *president pro tempore* of the Senate and casts the deciding vote.

Congressional Policymaking and Law

It is important to bear in mind that the House and Senate often disagree over policy prescriptions to address important issues. Sometimes these differences are small, but often they are significant and can prevent the passage of legislation. Neither chamber is able to operate on its own—both must agree on all of the details of a piece of legislation before it can be presented to the President for signature, and thus enactment into law.

Some of our readers may have enjoyed the 1970s Schoolhouse Rock cartoon, *How a Bill Becomes a Law*. That was a public service–style attempt at informing voters about the legislative process. For our purposes, we can take this process through a bit more detail to understand what it takes for Congress to turn a policy idea into a piece of legislation that the President will be able to sign.

How a Policy Becomes a Law

Step 1. An idea is formulated. We often skip this step when studying legislation, but it is especially important today given the power of certain voting blocs and influential donors. A policy is a response to a demand for action from someone with enough power to influence their representative to craft legislation on their behalf. That demand for action could be based upon personal interests (e.g., protecting the rainforest) or systemic values (e.g., tax relief).

Step 2. A sponsor is found. Legislation can only be introduced by members of Congress, so the policy initiator must have at least one (preferably multiple bipartisan) sponsor(s) to support the bill. The draft bill is often written by the initiator, lobbyists, or aides, not the congressional sponsor.

Step 3. The bill is referred to specialized committees (e.g., the House Finance Committee) for focused review and analysis. In some cases, it is sent to multiple committees or split into parts that are sent to different committees. This decision is made by the Speaker of the House, the presiding officer in the Senate, or the parliamentarian in either chamber. A time limit is usually established to complete the review, and if it is not met, the bill dies. It is important to note that during this process, committees usually request comments from government agencies that would have to enforce the law, if enacted.

Step 4. *If the bill "makes it out of committee," it is brought to the floor of both the House and Senate.* However, there are important differences between the two. In the House, the bill will be debated following strict procedural rules that limit the amount of time for debate and that divide that time equally between those who support and those who oppose the bill. In the House, members can amend the bill only with changes that are associated with the underlying bill. In other words, they cannot add **riders** to the bill. In the Senate, on the contrary, debate on the bill is unlimited unless **cloture** is invoked. This means that any Senator could use a **filibuster** to talk a bill to death. In addition, unlimited amendments and riders can be added to the bill, meaning that an entirely unrelated bill could be added as an amendment to a proposed bill.

Step 5. *Once debate is closed, the members vote separately in their chambers.* If the very same bill passes both the House and Senate, it is sent to the President for signature. If different versions pass the two chambers, a Conference Committee is formed to resolve the differences. That committee prepares a report that is sent to both chambers for an additional vote. If it passes, the bill is sent to the President for signature.

Step 6. *Presentment.* All bills must be presented to the President for signature before becoming law, though that signature is not necessarily required in order to enact a law. Once presented, the President has three options:

- Sign the bill within ten days, in which case it becomes law.
- **Veto** the bill by sending an explanation for the veto to Congress. This veto can be overridden by Congress if both chambers pass the legislation with two-thirds of those members present in each chamber supporting the override.
- If Congress adjourns prior to ten days passing after presentment and the President does not sign, the bill is effectively vetoed (known as a "pocket veto").

> Rider—additional provision included in a bill, often with no relation to the subject of the bill itself.
>
> Cloture—a procedure used by Congress to end discussion and bring a bill to a vote.
>
> Filibuster—a procedure used to delay the calling of a vote on a bill.

> Veto—the executive action used to reject a bill that passed both houses of congress.

The Powers of Congress

In creating a limited government with **enumerated powers**, the founders intended for most of the authorities of the Congress to be clearly spelled out in the Constitution. However, they had the foresight to realize that times would change and that those powers would need to be expanded upon or reinterpreted as time went on. This evolutionary approach to legislative powers is evident in the constitutional amendment process (Article 5) and through the establishment of the judiciary (Article 3), both of which provide room for an expansion of federal powers.

The powers of the legislative branch are laid out in Article I, Section 8 of the Constitution:

> Enumerated powers—specific powers identified by the U.S. Constitution.

- The Congress shall have power to lay and collect taxes, duties, imposts and excises, to pay the debts and provide for the common defense and general welfare of the United States; but all duties, imposts and excises shall be uniform throughout the United States;

- To borrow money on the credit of the United States;
- To regulate commerce with foreign nations, and among the several states, and with the Indian tribes;
- To establish a uniform rule of naturalization, and uniform laws on the subject of bankruptcies throughout the United States;
- To coin money, regulate the value thereof, and of foreign coin, and fix the standard of weights and measures;
- To provide for the punishment of counterfeiting the securities and current coin of the United States;
- To establish post offices and post roads;
- To promote the progress of science and useful arts, by securing for limited times to authors and inventors the exclusive right to their respective writings and discoveries;
- To constitute tribunals inferior to the Supreme Court;
- To define and punish piracies and felonies committed on the high seas, and offenses against the law of nations;
- To declare war, grant letters of marque and reprisal, and make rules concerning captures on land and water;
- To raise and support armies, but no appropriation of money to that use shall be for a longer term than two years;
- To provide and maintain a navy;
- To make rules for the government and regulation of the land and naval forces;
- To provide for calling forth the militia to execute the laws of the union, suppress insurrections and repel invasions;
- To provide for organizing, arming, and disciplining the militia, and for governing such part of them as may be employed in the service of the United States, reserving to the states respectively, the appointment of the officers, and the authority of training the militia according to the discipline prescribed by Congress;
- To exercise exclusive legislation in all cases whatsoever, over such District (not exceeding ten miles square) as may, by cession of particular states, and the acceptance of Congress, become the seat of the government of the United States, and to exercise like authority over all places purchased by the consent of the legislature of the state in which the same shall be, for the erection of forts, magazines, arsenals, dockyards, and other needful buildings; and
- To make all laws which shall be necessary and proper for carrying into execution the foregoing powers, and all other powers vested by this Constitution in the government of the United States, or in any department or officer thereof.

The powers identified in Section 8 are the enumerated powers of Congress, but they are not they only powers Congress has. The very last clause of that section refers to the power to "make all laws which shall be necessary and proper for carrying into execution the foregoing powers." This language created a significant opportunity for Congress to develop what were known as **implied powers,** which were the powers to enact legislation that helps to achieve one of the purposes outlined in the enumerated powers.

One of the earliest examples of Congress capitalizing on this necessary and proper power was in the case of *McCulloch v. Maryland*. This case dealt with the decision by Congress to establish a national bank that would be exempt from state tax laws, despite the absence of that clear authority in Section 8.

> Implied powers—powers not clearly identified within the text of the Constitution but sufficiently related to be recognized by the judiciary.

McCulloch v. Maryland, 17 U.S. (4 Wheat) 316 (1819)

Congress has power to incorporate a bank

The Act of the 10th of April, 1816, ch. 44, to "incorporate the subscribers to the Bank of the United States" is a law made in pursuance of the Constitution.

The Government of the Union, though limited in its powers, is supreme within its sphere of action, and its laws, when made in pursuance of the Constitution, form the supreme law of the land.

There is nothing in the Constitution of the United States similar to the Articles of Confederation, which exclude incidental or implied powers.

If the end be legitimate, and within the scope of the Constitution, all the means which are appropriate, which are plainly adapted to that end, and which are not prohibited, may constitutionally be employed to carry it into effect.

The power of establishing a corporation is not a distinct sovereign power or end of Government, but only the means of carrying into effect other powers which are sovereign. Whenever it becomes an appropriate means of exercising any of the powers given by the Constitution to the Government of the Union, it may be exercised by that Government.

If a certain means to carry into effect of any of the powers expressly given by the Constitution to the Government of the Union be an appropriate measure, not prohibited by the Constitution, the degree of its necessity is a question of legislative discretion, not of judicial cognizance.

The Bank of the United States has, constitutionally, a right to establish its branches or offices of discount and deposit within any state.

The State within which such branch may be established cannot, without violating the Constitution, tax that branch.

The State governments have no right to tax any of the constitutional means employed by the Government of the Union to execute its constitutional powers.

The States have no power, by taxation or otherwise, to retard, impede, burthen, or in any manner control the operations of the constitutional laws enacted by Congress to carry into effect the powers vested in the national Government.

This principle does not extend to a tax paid by the real property of the Bank of the United States in common with the other real property in a particular state, nor to a tax imposed on the proprietary interest which the citizens of that State may hold in this institution, in common with other property of the same description throughout the State.

This was an action of debt, brought by the defendant in error, John James, who sued as well for himself as for the State of Maryland, in the County Court of Baltimore County, in the said State, against the plaintiff in error, McCulloch, to recover certain penalties, under the act of the Legislature of Maryland hereafter mentioned. Judgment being rendered against the plaintiff in error, upon the following statement of facts agreed and submitted to the court by the parties, was affirmed by the Court of Appeals of the State of Maryland, the highest court of law of said State, and the cause was brought by writ of error to this Court.

It is admitted by the parties in this cause, by their counsel, that there was passed, on the 10th day of April, 1816, by the Congress of the United States, an act entitled, "an act to incorporate the subscribers to the Bank of the United States;" and that there was passed on the 11th day of February, 1818, by the General Assembly of Maryland, an act, entitled, "an act to impose a tax on all banks, or branches thereof, in the State of Maryland, *not chartered by the legislature*," which said acts are made part of this Statement, and it is agreed, may be read from the statute books in which they are respectively printed. It is further admitted that the President, directors and company of the Bank of the United States, incorporated by the act of Congress aforesaid, did organize themselves, and go into full operation, in the City of Philadelphia, in the State of Pennsylvania, in pursuance of the said act, and that they did on the ___ day of _____ 1817, establish a branch of the said bank, or an office of discount and deposit, in the City of Baltimore, in the State of Maryland, which has, from that time until the first day of May 1818, ever since transacted and carried on business as a bank, or office of discount and deposit, and as a branch of the said Bank of the United States, by issuing bank notes and discounting promissory notes, and performing other operations usual and customary for banks to do and perform, under the authority and by the direction of the said President, directors and company of the Bank of the United States, established at Philadelphia as aforesaid. It is further admitted that the said President, directors and company of the said bank had no authority to establish the said branch, or office of discount and deposit, at the City of Baltimore, from the State of Maryland, otherwise than the said State having adopted the Constitution of the United States and composing one of the States of the Union. It is further admitted that James William McCulloch, the defendant below, being the cashier of the said branch, or office of discount and deposit did, on the several days set forth in the declaration in this cause, issue the said respective bank notes therein described, from the said branch or office, to a certain George Williams, in the City of Baltimore, in part payment of a promissory note of the said Williams, discounted by the said branch or office, which said respective bank notes were not, nor was either of them, so issued on stamped paper in the manner prescribed by the act of assembly aforesaid. It is further admitted that the said President, directors and company of the Bank of the United States, and the said branch, or office of discount and deposit have not, nor has either of them, paid in advance, or otherwise, the sum of $15,000, to the Treasurer of the Western Shore, for the use of the State of Maryland, before the issuing of the said notes, or any of them, nor since those periods. And it is further admitted that the Treasurer of the Western Shore of Maryland, under the direction of the Governor and Council of the said State, was ready, and offered to deliver to the said President, directors and company of the said bank, and to the said branch, or office of discount and deposit, stamped paper of the kind and denomination required and described in the said act of assembly.

The question submitted to the Court for their decision in this case is as to the validity of the said act of the General Assembly of Maryland on the ground of its being repugnant to the Constitution of the United States and the act of Congress aforesaid, or to one of them. Upon the foregoing statement of facts and the pleadings in this cause (all errors in which are hereby agreed to be mutually released), if the Court should be of opinion that the plaintiffs are entitled to recover, then judgment, it is agreed, shall be entered for the plaintiffs for $2,500 and costs of suit. But if the Court should be of opinion that the plaintiffs are not entitled to recover upon the statement and pleadings aforesaid, then judgment of *non pros* shall be entered, with costs to the defendant.

> It is agreed that either party may appeal from the decision of the County Court to the Court of Appeals, and from the decision of the Court of Appeals to the Supreme Court of the United States, according to the modes and usages of law, and have the same benefit of this statement of facts in the same manner as could be had if a jury had been sworn and impanneled [sic] in this cause and a special verdict had been found, or these facts had appeared and been stated in an exception taken to the opinion of the Court, and the Court's direction to the jury thereon.

The Court in *McCulloch* sided with the federal government on two important points. First, they agreed that the Congress has the power to read into the language of Section 8 in its efforts to pass legislation that would give effect to those enumerated powers (thus creating "implied powers"). And second, they confirmed that states may not impede the actions of the federal government, which reaffirms the **supremacy clause** found in Article 6 (discussed in further detail later).

Several other enumerated powers appear to give Congress, and not the states or other branches of government, substantial power over major policy concerns. And just as Congress has legislated in all of these areas, legal challenges over their power to do so have been brought and, in the majority of cases, the courts have sided with Congress. Some examples are as follows.

> Supremacy clause—a clause of the U.S. Constitution that expresses the authority of federal law over state law.

Immigration

Congress was given the power to set the rules for naturalizing new citizens. However, this power does not clearly say that Congress has the power to regulate immigration law. Thus, in the early years of the United States, some states took it upon themselves to set rules for admission by foreigners to the United States. A veritable hodgepodge of immigration laws was established, creating inconsistency and unpredictability for would-be immigrants. Eventually, state politics drove immigration policies, and as those policies offended foreign nations, immigration policy became a matter of federal concern.

> **Chy Lung v. Freeman, 92 U.S. 275 (1875)**
>
> ... the plaintiff in error was a passenger on a vessel from China, being a subject of the Emperor of China, and is held a prisoner because the owner or master of the vessel who brought her over refused to give a bond in the sum of $500 in gold, conditioned to indemnify all the counties, towns, and cities of California against liability for her support or maintenance for two years.
>
> *Secondly*, the statute of California, unlike those of New York and Louisiana, does not require a bond for all passengers landing from a foreign country, but only for classes of passengers specifically described, among which are "lewd and debauched women," to which class it is alleged plaintiff belongs.
>
> The plaintiff, with some twenty other women, on the arrival of the steamer *Japan* from China, was singled out by the Commissioner of Immigration, an officer of the State

of California, as belonging to that class, and the master of the vessel required to give the bond prescribed by law before he permitted them to land. This he refused to do, and detained them on board. They sued out a writ of habeas corpus, which by regular proceedings resulted in their committal, by order of the supreme court of the state, to the custody of the Sheriff of the County and City of San Francisco, to await the return of the *Japan*, which had left the port pending the progress of the case, the order being to remand them to that vessel on her return, to be removed from the state.

All of plaintiff's companions were released from the custody of the sheriff on a writ of habeas corpus issued by MR. JUSTICE FIELD of this Court. But plaintiff by a writ of error brings the judgment of the Supreme Court of California to this Court for the purpose, as we suppose, of testing the constitutionality of the act under which she is held a prisoner. We regret very much that while the Attorney General of the United States has deemed the matter of such importance as to argue it in person, there has been no argument in behalf of the State of California, the Commissioner of Immigration, or the Sheriff of San Francisco, in support of the authority by which plaintiff is held a prisoner; nor have we been furnished even with a brief in support of the statute of that state.

It is a most extraordinary statute. It provides that the Commissioner of Immigration is

> to satisfy himself whether or not any passenger who shall arrive in the state by vessels from any foreign port or place (who is not a citizen of the United States) is lunatic, idiotic, deaf, dumb, blind, crippled, or infirm, and is not accompanied by relatives who are able and willing to support him, or is likely to become a public charge, or has been a pauper in any other country, or is from sickness or disease (existing either at the time of sailing from the port of departure or at the time of his arrival in the state) a public charge, or likely soon to become so, or is a convicted criminal, or a lewd or debauched woman,

and no such person shall be permitted to land from the vessel, unless the master or owner or consignee shall give a separate bond in each case, conditioned to save harmless every county, city, and town of the state against any expense incurred for the relief, support, or care of such person for two years thereafter.

The commissioner is authorized to charge the sum of seventy-five cents for every examination of a passenger made by him; which sum he may collect of the master, owner, or consignee, or of the vessel by attachment. The bonds are to be prepared by the commissioner, and two sureties are required to each bond, and, for preparing the bond, the commissioner is allowed to charge and collect a fee of three dollars, and for each oath administered to a surety, concerning his sufficiency as such, he may charge one dollar. It is expressly provided that there shall be a separate bond for each passenger; that there shall be two sureties on each bond, and that the same sureties must not be on more than one bond; and they must in all cases be residents of the state.

***

It is hardly possible to conceive a statute more skillfully framed, to place in the hands of a single man the power to prevent entirely vessels engaged in a foreign trade, say with

China, from carrying passengers, or to compel them to submit to systematic extortion of the grossest kind.

The commissioner has but to go aboard a vessel filled with passengers ignorant of our language and our laws, and without trial or hearing or evidence, but from the external appearances of persons with whose former habits he is unfamiliar, to point with his finger to twenty, as in this case, or a hundred if he chooses, and say to the master,

> These are idiots, these are paupers, these are convicted criminals, these are lewd women, and these others are debauched women. I have here a hundred blank forms of bonds, printed. I require you to fill me up and sign each of these for $500 in gold, and that you furnish me two hundred different men, residents of this state, and of sufficient means, as sureties on these bonds. I charge you five dollars in each case for preparing the bond and swearing your sureties, and I charge you seventy-five cents each for examining these passengers, and all others you have on board. If you don't do this, you are forbidden to land your passengers under a heavy penalty. But I have the power to commute with you for all this for any sum I may choose to take in cash. I am open to an offer, for you must remember that twenty percent of all I can get out of you goes into my own pocket, and the remainder into the Treasury of California.

If, as we have endeavored to show in the opinion in the preceding cases, we are at liberty to look to the effect of a statute for the test of its constitutionality, the argument need go no further.

But we have thus far only considered the effect of the statute on the owner of the vessel. As regards the passengers, sec. 2963 declares that consuls, ministers, agents, or other public functionaries, of any foreign government, arriving in this state in their official capacity, are exempt from the provisions of this chapter.

All other passengers are subject to the order of the Commissioner of Immigration.

Individual foreigners, however distinguished at home for their social, their literary, or their political character, are helpless in the presence of this potent commissioner. Such a person may offer to furnish any amount of surety on his own bond, or deposit any sum of money; but the law of California takes no note of him. If is the master, owner, or consignee of the vessel alone whose bond can be accepted; and so a silly, an obstinate, or a wicked commissioner may bring disgrace upon the whole country, the enmity of a powerful nation, or the loss of an equally powerful friend.

While the occurrence of the hypothetical case just stated may be highly improbable, we venture the assertion, that, if citizens of our own government were treated by any foreign nation as subjects of the Emperor of China have been actually treated under this law, no administration could withstand the call for a demand on such government for redress.

Or if this plaintiff and her twenty companions had been subjects of the Queen of Great Britain, can anyone doubt that this matter would have been the subject of international inquiry, if not of a direct claim for redress? Upon whom would such a claim be made? Not upon the State of California, for, by our Constitution, she can hold no exterior relations with other nations. It would be made upon the government of the United States. If that government should get into a difficulty which would lead to war or to suspension of intercourse, would California alone suffer, or all the Union? If we should conclude that a pecuniary indemnity was proper as a satisfaction for the injury, would California pay it, or the federal government? If that government has forbidden the states to hold negotiations with any foreign nations or to declare war and has taken the whole subject of these relations upon herself, has the Constitution, which provides for this, done so foolish a thing as to leave it in the power of the states to pass laws whose enforcement renders the general government liable to just reclamations which it must answer, while it does not prohibit to the states the acts for which it is held responsible?

The Constitution of the United States is no such instrument. The passage of laws which concern the admission of citizens and subjects of foreign nations to our shores belongs to Congress, and not to the states. It has the power to regulate commerce with foreign nations; the responsibility for the character of those regulations and for the manner of their execution belongs solely to the national government. If it be otherwise, a single state can at her pleasure embroil us in disastrous quarrels with other nations.

We are not called upon by this statute to decide for or against the right of a state, in the absence of legislation by Congress, to protect herself by necessary and proper laws against paupers and convicted criminals from abroad, nor to lay down the definite limit of such right, if it exist. Such a right can only arise from a vital necessity for its exercise, and cannot be carried beyond the scope of that necessity. When a state statute, limited to provisions necessary and appropriate to that object alone, shall, in a proper controversy, come before us, it will be time enough to decide that question. The statute of California goes so far beyond what is necessary, or even appropriate, for this purpose, as to be wholly without any sound definition of the right under which it is supposed to be justified. Its manifest purpose, as we have already said, is, not to obtain indemnity, but money.

The amount to be taken is left in every case to the discretion of an officer, whose cupidity is stimulated by a reward of one-fifth of all he can obtain.

The money, when paid, does not go to any fund for the benefit of immigrants, but is paid into the general treasury of the state, and devoted to the use of all her indigent citizens. The blind, or the deaf, or the dumb passenger is subject to contribution, whether he be a rich man or a pauper. The patriot, seeking out shores after an unsuccessful struggle against despotism in Europe or Asia, may be kept out because there his resistance has been adjudged a crime. The woman whose error has been repaired by a happy marriage and numerous children, and whose loving husband brings her with his wealth to a new home, may be told she must pay a round sum before she can land, because it is alleged that she was debauched by her husband before marriage. Whether a young woman's manners are such as to justify the commissioner in calling her lewd may be made to depend on the sum she will pay for the privilege of landing in San Francisco.

It is idle to pursue the criticism. In any view which we can take of this statute, it is in conflict with the Constitution of the United States, and therefore void.

> *Judgment reversed, and the case remanded, with directions to make an order discharging the prisoner from custody.*

Following the *Chy Lung* case and others like it, immigration law and policy authority was largely consolidated within the federal government. State power to regulate immigration dissipated quickly and today is only permitted with respect to certain limited matters, such as licensing. The Court thus enabled the legislature to interpret the citizenship and naturalization clause in such as way that pushed out state policymaking power.

Commerce

The **commerce clause** is unique in two ways. First, as written, it seems to empower Congress only with the ability to regulate certain types of commerce—that which moves across state or international borders. And second, it is the clause that has been relied upon most by Congress when enacting a variety of "necessary and proper" laws, from agricultural quotas to civil rights laws. Much of this expansive interpretation of the commerce clause results from the language of a Supreme Court case in 1824. That case involved a dispute over monopoly licensing for control of trade routes along waterways in New York. The first key question in the case was, what regulatory power does the commerce clause give to congress, which the Court answered as follows:

> Commerce clause—a clause of the U.S. Constitution that provides the federal government with authority to regulate interstate and international commerce.

> the power to regulate; that is, to prescribe the rule by which commerce is to be governed. This power, like all others vested in Congress, is complete in itself, may be exercised to its utmost extent, and acknowledges no limitations, other than are prescribed in the Constitution.
>
> *(Gibbons v. Ogden, 22 U.S. 1 (1824))*

The second, and perhaps more important question, was how "interstate commerce" should be interpreted—narrowly or broadly, which the Court addressed as follows:

> The enumeration presupposes something not enumerated, and that something, if we regard the language or the subject of the sentence, must be the exclusively internal commerce of a State. The genius and character of the whole government seem to be that its action is to be applied to all the external concerns of the nation, and to those internal concerns which affect the States generally, but not to those which are completely within a particular State, which do not affect other States, and with which it is not necessary to interfere for the purpose of executing some of the general powers of the government. The completely internal commerce of a State, then, may be considered as reserved for the State itself.
>
> *(Gibbons v. Ogden, 22 U.S. 1 (1824))*

Justice Marshall, who authored the *Gibbons* opinion, chose a broad interpretation of commerce to include all matters not "completely internal" to the state. Again,

Congress capitalized on that interpretation in enacting legislation that took a broad view of the commerce clause. We consider one of these cases as follows.

Katzenbach v. McClung, 379 U.S. 294 (1964)

***

Ollie's Barbecue is a family owned restaurant in Birmingham, Alabama, specializing in barbecued meats and homemade pies, with a seating capacity of 220 customers. It is located on a state highway 11 blocks from an interstate one and a somewhat greater distance from railroad and bus stations. The restaurant caters to a family and white-collar trade with a take-out service for Negroes. It employs 36 persons, two-thirds of whom are Negroes.

In the 12 months preceding the passage of the Act, the restaurant purchased locally approximately $150,000 worth of food, $69,683 or 46% of which was meat that it bought from a local supplier who had procured it from outside the State. The District Court expressly found that a substantial portion of the food served in the restaurant had moved in interstate commerce. The restaurant has refused to serve Negroes in its dining accommodations since its original opening in 1927, and, since July 2, 1964, it has been operating in violation of the Act. The court below concluded that, if it were required to serve Negroes, it would lose a substantial amount of business.

On the merits, the District Court held that the Act could not be applied under the Fourteenth Amendment because it was conceded that the State of Alabama was not involved in the refusal of the restaurant to serve Negroes. It was also admitted that the Thirteenth Amendment was authority neither for validating nor for invalidating the Act. As to the Commerce Clause, the court found that it was

> an express grant of power to Congress to regulate interstate commerce, which consists of the movement of persons, goods or information from one state to another,

and it found that the clause was also a grant of power

> to regulate intrastate activities, but only to the extent that action on its part is necessary or appropriate to the effective execution of its expressly granted power to regulate interstate commerce.

There must be, it said, a close and substantial relation between local activities and interstate commerce which requires control of the former in the protection of the latter. The court concluded, however, that the Congress, rather than finding facts sufficient to meet this rule, had legislated a conclusive presumption that a restaurant affects interstate commerce if it serves or offers to serve interstate travelers or if a substantial portion of the food which it serves has moved in commerce. This, the court held, it could not do, because there was no demonstrable connection between food purchased in interstate commerce and sold in a restaurant and the conclusion of Congress that discrimination in the restaurant would affect that commerce.

***

Section 201(a) of Title II commands that all persons shall be entitled to the full and equal enjoyment of the goods and services of any place of public accommodation without discrimination or segregation on the ground of race, color, religion, or national origin, and § 201(b) defines establishments as places of public accommodation if their operations affect commerce or segregation by them is supported by state action. Sections 201(b)(2) and (c) place any "restaurant ... principally engaged in selling food for consumption on the premises" under the Act "if ... it serves or offers to serve interstate travelers or a substantial portion of the food which it serves ... has moved in commerce."

Ollie's Barbecue admits that it is covered by these provisions of the Act. The Government makes no contention that the discrimination at the restaurant was supported by the State of Alabama. There is no claim that interstate travelers frequented the restaurant. The sole question, therefore, narrows down to whether Title II, as applied to a restaurant annually receiving about $70,000 worth of food which has moved in commerce, is a valid exercise of the power of Congress. The Government has contended that Congress had ample basis upon which to find that racial discrimination at restaurants which receive from out of state a substantial portion of the food served does, in fact, impose commercial burdens of national magnitude upon interstate commerce. The appellees' major argument is directed to this premise. They urge that no such basis existed. It is to that question that we now turn.

***

As we noted in *Heart of Atlanta Motel*, both Houses of Congress conducted prolonged hearings on the Act. And, as we said there, while no formal findings were made, which, of course, are not necessary, it is well that we make mention of the testimony at these hearings the better to understand the problem before Congress and determine whether the Act is a reasonable and appropriate means toward its solution. The record is replete with testimony of the burdens placed on interstate commerce by racial discrimination in restaurants. A comparison of per capita spending by Negroes in restaurants, theaters, and like establishments indicated less spending, after discounting income differences, in areas where discrimination is widely practiced. This condition, which was especially aggravated in the South, was attributed in the testimony of the Under Secretary of Commerce to racial segregation. This diminutive spending springing from a refusal to serve Negroes and their total loss as customers has, regardless of the absence of direct evidence, a close connection to interstate commerce. The fewer customers a restaurant enjoys, the less food it sells, and consequently the less it buys In addition, the Attorney General testified that this type of discrimination imposed "an artificial restriction on the market," and interfered with the flow of merchandise. In addition, there were many references to discriminatory situations causing wide unrest and having a depressant effect on general business conditions in the respective communities.

Moreover, there was an impressive array of testimony that discrimination in restaurants had a direct and highly restrictive effect upon interstate travel by Negroes. This resulted, it was said, because discriminatory practices prevent Negroes from buying prepared food served on the premises while on a trip, except in isolated and unkempt restaurants and under most unsatisfactory and often unpleasant conditions. This obviously discourages travel and obstructs interstate commerce, for one can hardly travel without eating. Likewise, it was said that discrimination deterred professional as well as skilled people from moving into areas where such practices occurred, and thereby caused industry to be reluctant to establish there.

We believe that this testimony afforded ample basis for the conclusion that established restaurants in such areas sold less interstate goods because of the discrimination, that interstate travel was obstructed directly by it, that business in general suffered, and that many new businesses refrained from establishing there as a result of it. Hence, the District Court was in error in concluding that there was no connection between discrimination and the movement of interstate commerce. The court's conclusion that such a connection is outside "common experience" flies in the face of stubborn fact.

It goes without saying that, viewed in isolation, the volume of food purchased by Ollie's Barbecue from sources supplied from out of state was insignificant when compared with the total foodstuffs moving in commerce. But, as our late Brother Jackson said for the Court in *Wickard v. Filburn*, 317 U.S. 111 (1942):

> That appellee's own contribution to the demand for wheat may be trivial by itself is not enough to remove him from the scope of federal regulation where, as here, his contribution, taken together with that of many others similarly situated, is far from trivial.

We noted in *Heart of Atlanta Motel* that a number of witnesses attested to the fact that racial discrimination was not merely a state or regional problem, but was one of nationwide scope. Against this background, we must conclude that, while the focus of the legislation was on the individual restaurant's relation to interstate commerce, Congress appropriately considered the importance of that connection with the knowledge that the discrimination was but

> representative of many others throughout the country, the total incidence of which, if left unchecked, may well become far-reaching in its harm to commerce.

With this situation spreading as the record shows, Congress was not required to await the total dislocation of commerce. As was said in *Consolidated Edison Co. v. Labor Board*, 305 U.S. 197 (1938):

> But it cannot be maintained that the exertion of federal power must await the disruption of that commerce. Congress was entitled to provide reasonable preventive measures and that was the object of the National Labor Relations Act.

The Power of Congress to Regulate Local Activities

Article I, § 8, cl. 3, confers upon Congress the power "[t]o regulate Commerce ... among the several States" and Clause 18 of the same Article grants it the power

> [t]o make all Laws which shall be necessary and proper for carrying into Execution the foregoing Powers.

This grant, as we have pointed out in *Heart of Atlanta Motel*,

> extends to those activities intrastate which so affect interstate commerce, or the exertion of the power of Congress over it, as to make regulation of them appropriate means to the attainment of a legitimate end, the effective execution of the granted power to regulate interstate commerce.

Much is said about a restaurant business being local, but, "even if appellee's activity be local, and though it may not be regarded as commerce, it may still, whatever its nature, be reached by Congress if it exerts a substantial economic effect on interstate commerce."

The activities that are beyond the reach of Congress are "those which are completely within a particular State, which do not affect other States, and with which it is not necessary to interfere, for the purpose of executing some of the general powers of the government."

This rule is as good today as it was when Chief Justice Marshall laid it down almost a century and a half ago.

This Court has held time and again that this power extends to activities of retail establishments, including restaurants, which directly or indirectly burden or obstruct interstate commerce. We have detailed the cases in *Heart of Atlanta Motel*, and will not repeat them here.

Nor are the cases holding that interstate commerce ends when goods come to rest in the State of destination apposite here. That line of cases has been applied with reference to state taxation or regulation, but not in the field of federal regulation.

The appellees contend that Congress has arbitrarily created a conclusive presumption that all restaurants meeting the criteria set out in the Act "affect commerce." Stated another way, they object to the omission of a provision for a case-by-case determination—judicial or administrative—that racial discrimination in a particular restaurant affects commerce.

But Congress' action in framing this Act was not unprecedented. In *United States v. Darby*, 312 U.S. 100 (1941), this Court held constitutional the Fair Labor Standards Act of 1938. There, Congress determined that the payment of substandard wages to employees engaged in the production of goods for commerce, while not itself commerce, so inhibited it as to be subject to federal regulation. The appellees in that case argued, as do the appellees here, that the Act was invalid because it included no provision for an independent inquiry regarding the effect on commerce of substandard wages in a particular business. But the Court rejected the argument, observing that:

> [S]ometimes Congress itself has said that a particular activity affects the commerce, as it did in the present Act, the Safety Appliance Act, and the Railway Labor Act. In passing on the validity of legislation of the class last mentioned the only function of courts is to determine whether the particular activity regulated or prohibited is within the reach of the federal power.

Here, as there, Congress has determined for itself that refusals of service to Negroes have imposed burdens both upon the interstate flow of food and upon the movement of products generally. Of course, the mere fact that Congress has said when particular activity shall be deemed to affect commerce does not preclude further examination by this Court. But where we find that the legislators, in light of the facts and testimony before them, have a rational basis for finding a chosen regulatory scheme necessary to the protection of commerce, oar investigation is at an end. The only remaining question—one answered in the affirmative by the court below—is whether the particular restaurant either serves or offers to serve interstate travelers or serves food a substantial portion of which has moved in interstate commerce.

The appellees urge that Congress, in passing the Fair Labor Standards Act and the National Labor Relations Act, made specific findings which were embodied in those statutes. Here, of course, Congress has included no formal findings. But their absence is not fatal to the validity of the statute…for the evidence presented at the hearings fully indicated the nature and effect of the burdens on commerce which Congress meant to alleviate.

Confronted as we are with the facts laid before Congress, we must conclude that it had a rational basis for finding that racial discrimination in restaurants had a direct and adverse effect on the free flow of interstate commerce. Insofar as the sections of the Act here relevant are concerned, §§ 201(b)(2) and (c), Congress prohibited discrimination only in those establishments having a close tie to interstate commerce, *i.e.*, those, like the McClungs', serving food that has come from out of the State. We think, in so doing, that Congress acted well within its power to protect and foster commerce in extending the coverage of Title II only to those restaurants offering to serve interstate travelers or serving food, a substantial portion of which has moved in interstate commerce.

The absence of direct evidence connecting discriminatory restaurant service with the flow of interstate food, a factor on which the appellees place much reliance, is not, given the evidence as to the effect of such practices on other aspects of commerce, a crucial matter.

The power of Congress in this field is broad and sweeping; where it keeps within its sphere and violates no express constitutional limitation it has been the rule of this Court, going back almost to the founding days of the Republic, not to interfere. The Civil Rights Act of 1964, as here applied, we find to be plainly appropriate in the resolution of what the Congress found to be a national commercial problem of the first magnitude. We find it in no violation of any express limitations of the Constitution and we therefore declare it valid.

The judgment is therefore *Reversed*.

Legislative power can be found in several Section 8 clauses, from tax authority, to war power, to appropriations, but the commerce clause provides it with the foundation to enact laws that substantially affect the policy environment of the United States by regulating commercial activities and those affected by such activities.

We turn next to the executive branch, which in some sense is kept in check by the legislature's power of the purse. Since Congress maintains both tax and appropriation authorities, any action that the executive takes requiring government funding likely has to receive the support of the legislature first. But, as we will see, the executive has some independent powers of its own.

The Executive

The executive Power shall be vested in a President of the United States of America.
—U.S. Constitution Article II, Sec. 1

When we think about public policy on a grand scale, we tend to envision the President of the United States. We see that position as the focal point for developing and implementing the policies that drive social and economic development both domestically and abroad. And when we vote, we do so based upon our own principles, and we tend to select a President who mirrors those principles as much as possible. This powerful description of the President as policymaker-in-chief was not the historical vision of that post and, even today, it is not entirely accurate.

As we discussed in more detail in Chapter 2 on Civics, the founding fathers were uncertain as to how to establish the executive branch of government. One thought, supported by Thomas Jefferson, James Madison, and others, was to create a system similar to the British Parliament, which appoints the Prime Minister responsible for carrying out the day-to-day operations of the country. This would mean that the President is not directly elected by the people but rather that he or she would serve at the pleasure of the Parliament, and be able to be removed if Parliament lost confidence in his or her ability to govern. This approach would have left most of the power of governance with the legislative branch.

The Federalists, led by Alexander Hamilton, favored a strong executive branch that was led by someone who would be directly elected by the people. This person would serve as head of state, commander-in-chief of the armed forces, and indeed, the principal policymaker for the country. Though the founding fathers included checks and balances to prevent consolidation of power in any single branch, the Federalist approach gave much more power and independence to the President than the Jeffersonian approach. Ultimately, the Federalist vision prevailed.

What Is the Executive Branch?

When you think of the executive branch, you may picture the President, or perhaps the White House, but in reality, it is much larger than that today. The President sits atop this branch, but thousands of political and civil service government workers report directly or indirectly to the President.

The Cabinet

The President cannot be expected to make decisions based solely upon his or her own research or knowledge of an issue. The President's Cabinet serves as a board of senior advisors that meet frequently with the President to provide guidance on the issues of the day. At the outset of the republic, only three executive departments existed: the Department of Foreign Affairs (renamed the "Department of State"); the Department of War (renamed the "Department of Defense"); and the Department of Treasury. Today, the Cabinet consists of 15 executive departments, each led by a **Secretary** appointed by the President. These include, in order of succession to the President:[3]

- Vice President of the United States
- Department of State (1789)
- Department of the Treasury (1789)

> **Secretary**—the designated representative of the President leading a cabinet-level department.

- Department of Defense (1947)
- Department of Justice (1870)
- Department of the Interior (1849)
- Department of Agriculture (1889)
- Department of Commerce (1903)
- Department of Labor (1913)
- Department of Health and Human Services (1953)
- Department of Housing and Urban Development (1965)
- Department of Transportation (1966)
- Department of Energy (1977)
- Department of Education (1979)
- Department of Veteran's Affairs (1989)
- Department of Homeland Security (2002)

In addition to these Cabinet Secretaries, other Cabinet-rank advisors include:

- White House Chief of Staff
- Environmental Protection Agency Administrator
- Office of Management and Budget Director
- U.S. Trade Representative
- U.S. Ambassador to the United Nations
- Chairman of the Council of Economic Advisors
- Administrator of the Small Business Administration

Executive Agencies

Each Cabinet-level department operates under close political direction from the President. The President has the authority to not only appoint but also to remove any political appointee to these departments for any reason, including political affiliation or loyalty. As such, the appointees must be careful to balance their own aspirations in leading a department with the desires of the President.

As of fiscal year 2016, more than 1.8 million people are employed by the executive branch, led by the Departments of Defense, Veterans Affairs, and Homeland Security. This means that approximately 5.7% of the U.S. population is employed by the federal government.

Independent Agencies and Commissions

In addition to the 15 Cabinet-level agencies that advise the President, Congress has also created a number of independent agencies and commissions that are not part of any department. These executive agencies were created in most cases to address very narrow issues that require substantial depth and expertise and that would not benefit from the oversight (or politics) of a department. The authority and scope of each of these agencies is established in the **enabling acts** that Congress uses to create them.

No clear definition exists for an independent agency, but it is important to distinguish between two types. Independent agencies that are led by a single presidential appointee, usually termed the Director or Administrator, are under more direct presidential control. Thus, while termed "independent" due to their position outside of established departments, these agencies may be subjected to increased presidential influence. On the contrary, independent agencies are led by a board or commission

> Enabling act—legislation that creates an executive agency or commission.

and are deemed to be much more independent and able to operate in a less-politicized environment. The President appoints board members or commissioners, but their terms are staggered four-year terms, usually with requirements for bipartisan representation. Nevertheless, their budgets are approved by the Office of Management and Budget (part of the Executive Office of the President), and their chairperson is selected by the President, so they are not entirely independent either.

An important distinction between independent agencies and executive agencies is in the President's power to remove appointees. Appointees to executive agencies may be removed at any time and for any reason by the President. Appointees to independent agencies may only be removed for cause, such as neglect, malfeasance, or incapacity. A board member or commissioner may not be removed simply due to political party affiliation, for example.

According to www.USA.gov, there are (as of 2018) 67 independent executive agencies, which are more appropriately known as commissions.[4] These include bodies such as the Peace Corps, U.S. Postal Service, National Endowment for the Arts, National Science Foundation, Federal Trade Commission, and the Securities and Exchange Commission. Some of these, such as the Environmental Protection Agency, have a single administrator, whereas others, such as the Federal Reserve Board, are led by a commission. An example of each of these entities is provided in the following sections.

The Consumer Financial Protection Bureau

This independent regulatory agency was established in 2010 as part of the Dodd-Frank Act to regulate the banking industry. It is led by a single Director, appointed by the President and confirmed by the Senate. The enabling act establishing this agency is as follows:

> Title X, known as the Consumer Financial Protection Act of 2010, establishes the Consumer Financial Protection Bureau (CFPB or Bureau) as an independent agency within the Board of Governors of the Federal Reserve System (Federal Reserve). The CFPB regulates the offering and provision of consumer financial products and services under federal consumer financial laws. The organizing statute for the CFPB is below.
>
> **Purpose**
>
> CFPB ensures that the federal consumer financial laws are enforced consistently so that consumers may access markets for financial products, and so that these markets are fair, transparent, and competitive. July 21, 2011 was the official date on which the function and authority was transferred from other federal regulatory agencies to the CFPB.
>
> **Provisions**
>
> **Organization of Bureau**
>
> The Bureau is to be headed by a Director appointed by the President and confirmed by the Senate, and is to serve a five-year term. The Director is required to establish three

specific functional units within the Bureau focusing on research, community affairs, and collecting and tracking complaints. Additionally, the Director is required to establish the following four offices: (1) the Office of Fair Lending and Equal Opportunity, charged with oversight and enforcement of federal laws intended to ensure access to credit; (2) the Office of Financial Education, charged with educating consumers on financial decisions; (3) the Office of Service Member Affairs, charged with developing and implementing initiatives for military service members and their families; and (4) the Office of Financial Protection for Older Americans, charged with facilitating the financial literacy of individuals older than 62 years of age. Finally, the Director is required to establish a Consumer Advisory Board to advise and consult with the Bureau in the exercise of its functions.

Bureau Powers & Authority

The Bureau has the authority to administer, enforce, and otherwise implement federal consumer financial laws, which includes the power to make rules, issue orders, and issue guidance. The Financial Stability Oversight Council (FSOC) has the power to set aside any of the Bureau's regulations if the FSOC decides that the regulation would put the safety and soundness of the banking system, or the stability of the financial system of the United States, at risk.

The Bureau is authorized to engage in investigations and request information from covered persons, issue subpoenas or civil investigative demands, conduct hearings and adjudication proceedings, and commence civil actions in federal court seeking any appropriate or equitable relief against any person that violates a federal consumer financial law. The CFPB has exclusive authority to enforce federal consumer laws against nondepository covered persons., the Bureau has exclusive federal consumer law supervisory authority and primary enforcement authority over insured depository institutions or insured thrifts with assets totaling over $10 billion. The Bureau's authority over banks, thrifts, and credit unions with assets of $10 billion or less is more limited.

Preservation of State Law

Title X also deals with the role of state law and state intervention in the operation of federally-chartered depository institutions. The statute is not meant to preempt state consumer financial protection laws, as long as the state laws do not conflict with federal laws or regulations. State consumer protection laws that offer greater protection than federal law are not considered to be conflicting with federal laws. Further, state Attorney Generals and state regulators can bring civil actions to enforce provisions of Title X.

State consumer financial laws are preempted for national banks, federal thrifts, and their subsidiaries only if: (1) the application of the state law would have a discriminatory effect on the national bank or thrift; (2) the state law prevents or significantly interferes with the exercise of the national bank's or thrift's powers (codifying the Supreme Court's decision in *Barnett Bank v. Nelson*, 517 U.S. 25 (1996)); or (3) the state consumer law is preempted by another federal law other than this title. In accordance with the Supreme Court decision in *Cuomo v. Clearing House Assn., LLC*, 129 S. Ct. 2710 (2009), the Office of the Comptroller of the Currency's visitorial authority over national banks and federal thrifts is not to limit or restrict the authority of any state from bringing an enforcement action against a national bank or federal thrift. Finally, Title X does not preempt the applicability of state law to any subsidiary, affiliate, or agent of a national bank.

Transfer of Functions

The consumer financial protection functions of the Federal Reserve, Office of the Comptroller of the Currency, Office of Thrift Supervision, Federal Deposit Insurance Corporation, and National Credit Union Administration are transferred to the Bureau. The consumer financial protection functions of the Department of Housing and Urban Development that arise under the Real Estate Settlement Procedures Act, Secure and Fair Enforcement for Mortgage Licensing Act of 2008, and the Interstate Land Sales Full Disclosure Act are also transferred to the Bureau. The Federal Trade Commission retains its jurisdiction in implementing the Federal Trade Commission Act.

The Federal Communications Commission

This commission was established in 1934 to regulate interstate and foreign communications. It is an independent regulatory agency run by a group of seven commissioners. Notice how the statute creating the commission relies upon the Commerce Clause to assert federal authority over the regulation of communications. Relevant sections of the enabling act is below.

Title I—General Provisions

Purposes of the Act;

Creation of Federal Communications Commission

SEC. 1. For the purpose of regulating interstate and foreign commerce in communication by wire and radio so as to make available, so far as possible, to all the people of the United States a rapid, efficient, Nation-wide, and world-wide wire and radio communication service with adequate facilities at reasonable charges, for the purpose of the national defense, and for the purpose of securing a more effective execution of this policy by centralizing authority heretofore granted by law to several agencies and by granting additional authority with respect to interstate and foreign commerce in wire and radio communication, there is hereby created a commission to be known as the "Federal Communications Commission", which shall be constituted as hereinafter provided, and which shall execute and enforce the provisions of this Act.

Application of Act

SEC. 2. (a) The provisions of this Act shall apply to all interstate and foreign communication by wire or radio and all interstate and foreign transmission of energy by radio, which originates and/or is received within the United States, and to all persons engaged within the United States in such communication or such transmission of energy by radio, and to the licensing and regulating of all radio stations as hereinafter provided; but it shall not apply to persons engaged in wire or radio communication or transmission in the Philippine Islands or the Canal Zone, or to wire or radio communication or transmission wholly within the Philippine Islands or the Canal Zone.

(b) Subject to the provisions of section 301, nothing in this Act shall be construed to apply or to give the Commission jurisdiction with respect to (1) charges, classifications, practices, services, facilities, or regulations for or in connection with intrastate communication service of any carrier, or (2) any carrier engaged in interstate or foreign communication solely through physical connection with the facilities of another carrier not directly or indirectly controlling or controlled by, or under direct or indirect common control with, such carrier; except that sections 201 to 205 of this Act, both inclusive, shall, except as otherwise provided therein, apply to carriers described in clause (2).

***

Provisions Relating to the Commission

SEC. 4. (a) The Federal Communications Commission (in this Act referred to as the "Commission") shall be composed of seven commissioners appointed by the President, by and with the advice and consent of the Senate, one of whom the President shall designate as chairman.

(b) Each member of the Commission shall be a citizen of the United States. No member of the Commission or person in its employ shall be financially interested in the manufacture or sale of radio apparatus or of apparatus for wire or radio communication; in communication by wire or radio or in radio transmission of energy; in any company furnishing services or such apparatus to any company engaged in communication by wire or radio or to any company manufacturing or selling apparatus used for communication by wire or radio; or in any company owning stocks, bonds, or other securities of any such company; nor be in the employ of or hold any official relation to any person subject to any of the provisions of this Act, nor own stocks, bonds, or other securities of any corporation subject to any of the provisions of this Act. Such commissioners shall not engage in any other business, vocation, or employment. Not more than four commissioners shall be members of the same political party.

(c) The commissioners first appointed under this Act shall continue in office for the terms of one, two, three, four, five, six, and seven years, respectively, from the date of the taking effect of this Act, the term of each to be designated by the President, but their successors shall be appointed for terms of seven years; except that any person chosen to fill a vacancy shall be appointed only for the unexpired term of the commissioner whom he succeeds. No vacancy in the Commission shall impair the right of the remaining commissioners to exercise all the powers of the Commission.

(d) Each commissioner shall receive an annual salary of $10,000, payable in monthly installments.
(e) The principal office of the Commission shall be in the District of Columbia, where its general sessions shall be held; but whenever the convenience of the public or of the parties may be promoted or delay or expense prevented thereby, the Commission may hold special sessions in any part of the United States.
(f) Without regard to the civil-service laws or the Classification Act of 1923, as amended, (1) the Commission may appoint and prescribe the duties and fix the salaries of a secretary, a director for each division, a chief engineer and not more than three assistants, a general counsel and not more than three assistants, and temporary counsel designated by the Commission for the performance of special services, and (2) each commissioner may appoint and prescribe the duties of a secretary at an annual salary not to exceed $4,000. The general counsel and the chief engineer shall each receive an annual salary of not to exceed $9,000; the secretary shall receive an annual salary of not to exceed $7,500; the director of each division shall receive an annual salary of not to exceed $7,500; and no assistant shall receive an annual salary in excess of $7,500. The Commission shall have authority, subject to the provisions of the civil-service laws and the Classification Act of 1923, as amended, to appoint such other officers, engineers, inspectors, attorneys, examiners, and other employees as are necessary in the execution of its functions.
(g) The Commission may make such expenditures (including expenditures for rent and personal services at the seat of government and elsewhere, for office supplies, law books, periodicals, and books of reference, and for printing and binding) as may be necessary for the execution of the functions vested in the Commission and as from time to time may be appropriated for by Congress. All expenditures of the Commission, including all necessary expenses for transportation incurred by the commissioners or by their employees, under their orders, in making any investigation or upon any official business in any other place than in the city of Washington, shall be allowed and paid on the presentation of itemized vouchers therefor approved by the chairman of the Commission or by such other member or officer thereof as may be designated by the Commission for that purpose.
(h) Four members of the Commission shall constitute a quorum thereof. The Commission shall have an official seal which shall be judicially noticed.
(i) The Commission may perform any and all acts, make such rules and regulations, and issue such orders, not inconsistent with this Act, as may be necessary in the execution of its functions.
(j) The Commission may conduct its proceedings in such manner as will best conduce to the proper dispatch of business and to the ends of justice. No commissioner shall participate in any hearing or proceeding in which he has a pecuniary interest. Any party may appear before the Commission and be heard in person or by attorney. Every vote and official act of the Commission shall be entered of record, and its proceedings shall be public upon the request of any party interested. The Commission is authorized to withhold publication of records or proceedings containing secret information affecting the national defense.

(k) The Commission shall make an annual report to Congress, copies of which shall be distributed as are other reports transmitted to Congress. Such report shall contain such information and data collected by the Commission as may be considered of value in the determination of questions connected with the regulation of interstate and foreign wire and radio communication and radio transmission of energy, together with such recommendations as to additional legislation relating thereto as the Commission may deem necessary: Provided, That the Commission shall make a special report not later than February 1, 1935, recommending such amendments to this Act as it deems desirable in the public interest.

(l) All reports of investigations made by the Commission shall be entered of record, and a copy thereof shall be furnished to the party who may have complained, and to any common carrier or licensee that may have been complained of.

(m) The Commission shall provide for the publication of its reports and decisions in such form and manner as may be best adapted for public information and use, and such authorized publications shall be competent evidence of the reports and decisions of the Commission therein contained in all courts of the United States and of the several States without any further proof or authentication thereof.

(n) Rates of compensation of persons appointed under this section shall be subject to the reduction applicable to officers and employees of the Federal Government generally.

***

General Powers of Commission

SEC. 303. Except as otherwise provided in this Act, the Commission from time to time, as public convenience, interest, or necessity requires, shall-

(a) Classify radio stations;

(b) Prescribe the nature of the service to be rendered by each class of license stations and each station within any class;

(c) Assign bands of frequencies to the various classes of stations, and assign frequencies for each individual station and determine the power which each station shall use and the time during which it may operate;

(d) Determine the location of classes of stations or individual stations;

(e) Regulate the kind of apparatus to be used with respect to its external effects and the purity and sharpness of the emissions from each station and from the apparatus therein;

(f) Make such regulations not inconsistent with law as it may deem necessary to prevent interference between stations and to carry out the provisions of this Act: Provided, however, That changes in the frequencies, authorized power, or in the times of operation of any station, shall not be made without the consent of the station licensee unless, after a public hearing, the Commission shall determine that such changes will promote public convenience or interest or will serve public necessity, or the provisions of this Act will be more fully complied with;

(g) Study new uses for radio, provide for experimental uses of frequencies, and generally encourage the larger and more effective use of radio in the public interest;

(h) Have authority to establish areas or zones to be served by any station;

(i) Have authority to make special regulations applicable to radio stations engaged in chain broadcasting;

(j) Have authority to make general rules and regulations requiring stations to keep such records of programs, transmissions of energy, communications, or signals as it may deem desirable;

(k) Have authority to exclude form the requirements of any regulations in whole or in part any radio station upon railroad rolling stock, or to modify such regulations in its discretion;

(l) Have authority to prescribe the qualifications of station operator, to classify them according to the duties to be performed, to fix the forms of such licenses, and to issue them to such citizens of the United States as the Commission finds qualified;

(m) Have authority to suspend the license of any operator for a period not exceeding two years upon proof sufficient to satisfy the Commission that the licensee (1) has violated any provision of any Act or treaty binding on the United States which the Commission is authorized by this Act to administer or any regulation made by the Commission under any such Act or treaty; or (2) has failed to carry out the lawful orders of the master of the vessel on which he is employed; or (3) has willfully damaged or permitted radio apparatus to be damaged; (4) has transmitted superfluous radio communications or signals or radio communications containing profane or obscene words or language; or (5) has willfully maliciously interfered with any other radio communications or signals;

(n) Have authority to inspect all transmitting apparatus to ascertain whether in construction and operation it conforms to the requirements of this Act, the rules and regulations of the Commission, and the license under which it is constructed or operated;

(o) Have authority to designate call letters of all stations;

(p) Have authority to cause to be published such call letters and such other announcements and data as in the judgment of the Commission may be required for the efficient operation of radio stations subject to the jurisdiction of the United States and for the proper enforcement of this Act;

(q) Have authority to require the painting and/or illumination of radio towers if and when in its judgment such towers constitute, or there is a reasonable possibility that they may constitute, a menace to air navigation.

***

Because executive agencies are often given rulemaking or enforcement powers, they serve as the executioners of their enabling act powers. In a sense, this turns executive agencies into lawmaking bodies within the confines of their established authority. The President's influence over these agencies has a direct effect on the rules that they create, permitting the intermingling of presidential policy with legislative force. Accordingly, the appointment process to lead these agencies is of great importance to both the executive and legislative branches and often ends up as a partisan political process.

Senior posts within both departments and independent agencies are nominated by the President and confirmed by the Senate. Once they go through the **vetting process**, the nominees are examined by the Senate and, if they approve, the Senate gives their consent to appoint the nominees. A simple majority (51) of the Senate is required for confirmation. This process is explained in the Appointments Clause:

> Vetting process—the process of reviewing the credentials and interviewing a candidate for public office.

[The President] . . . shall nominate, and by and with the Advice and Consent of the Senate, shall appoint Ambassadors, other public Ministers and Consuls, Judges of the supreme Court, and all other Officers of the United States, whose Appointments are not herein otherwise provided for, and which shall be established by Law: but the Congress may by Law vest the Appointment of such inferior Officers as they think proper, in the President alone, in the Courts of Law, or in the Heads of Departments.

The President shall have Power to fill up all Vacancies that may happen during the Recess of the Senate, by granting Commissions which shall expire at the End of their next Session.

—U.S. Constitution, Art. II, Section 2

While heads of executive departments, federal judges, and other positions of substantial influence and power must proceed through the consent process, inferior officers may be appointed directly by the President or by the department itself. This refers to officers without significant authority who generally report to an appointee that was confirmed through the appointments process.[5]

Keep in mind that the vast majority of the government workforce is made up of the civil service—the core of non-political appointees that manage the operations of government agencies. The U.S. Office of Personnel Management estimates that there are approximately 4,000 political appointments to be made by each administration. This includes over 1,200 that require Senate confirmation, out of nearly 3 million civil service employees.

The President's Powers

To be elected President of the United States, a candidate must be a natural-born U.S. citizen of at least 35 years of age who has lived in the United States for at least 14 years. Unlike all other elected offices, the office of the President does not permit naturalized citizens to qualify. Once elected, the President serves for four years and may be re-elected once (due to the 22nd Amendment, which created term presidential limits).

The direct powers of the President are far more limited than many people realize; however, nor is the President a mere figurehead. Instead, the President serves as the country's policy guide, shepherding significant ideas through the legislative or regulatory process in order to more closely align domestic legislation with the President's vision for the country. The President is also the country's enforcer-in-chief of the laws, and the commander-in-chief of the military, giving that person vast power to carry out the laws laid down by the legislature. Article II provides the President with the powers to do this.

Enacting and Enforcing Laws

As discussed previously, before any bill can become a law, it must be presented by the Congress to the President for signature (or veto). This gives the President the power to enact or block enactment of legislation, within the constraints of the veto override. In addition, as the enforcer-in-chief of those laws, it is up to the President to see to it that those laws are implemented. This obligation is known as the **take care clause**.

> Take care clause—a clause of the U.S. Constitution requiring the executive to enforce the laws enacted by the legislature.

Appointment Power

The President also has the power to appoint the heads of executive agencies and commissions, federal judges including Justices to the U.S. Supreme Court, and ambassadors to foreign nations.

Treaty Power

The President is empowered to negotiate treaties with foreign nations. These treaties may include any issue, from environmental protection to trade. If the treaty will have any impact on U.S. law, the treaty requires the consent of the Senate before it can be ratified. Certain agreements between heads of state, known as executive agreements, may be concluded through diplomacy without the consent of the Senate.

Pardon Power

The President has the power to pardon anyone who has been convicted of federal crimes, with the notable exception of impeachment (i.e., the President cannot pardon himself).

Commander-in-Chief Power

The President serves as the commander of the army, navy, and militia of the United States.

Though not found in Article II of the Constitution, it is important to point out that the President also has the power to issue **Executive Orders**. These are orders directed at executive agencies or officers implementing specific policies. To be valid, the order must derive from an Article II power or from a delegated power by Congress. Executive Orders have been issued since President George Washington and have been used to free slaves (Emancipation Proclamation), declare bank holidays, seize control of steel mills, and create a bank (the Export/Import Bank), among other things. They are often controversial and frequently result in litigation. We will close out this section with a brief look at one of those cases.

> Executive Order—an order issued by the President under the authority of Article II of the U.S. Constitution.

President Trump issued Executive Order 13769 on January 27, 2017. That Order suspended immigrant and non-immigrant entry into the United States from several countries for 90 days and suspended the U.S. refugee program for 120 days. The Order was immediately challenged by a number of states, individuals, and civil rights groups, who argued that the ban was discriminatory and outside the scope of the President's powers.

In one of those cases (*State of Washington and State of Minnesota v. Trump*), two states argued that the ban on entry from certain Muslim-majority countries violated the Fifth Amendment Equal Protection clause by discriminating against citizens of those states on the basis of their national origin, race, and religion. They also argued that the ban violated the First Amendment Establishment clause by favoring Christianity over Islam. The District Court judge agreed and enjoined (blocked) the executive from enforcing the Executive Order. On appeal, the Ninth Circuit Court of Appeals upheld the injunction.

Subsequently, the government abandoned their appeal and instead crafted a new Executive Order that they hoped would not run afoul of the Constitution. A District Court judge in Hawaii entertained a challenge to the new Executive Order (No. 13780) and enjoined the administration from enforcing it. However, the U.S. Supreme Court reviewed the Order and found much of it to be constitutional, allowing it to go into effect in June 2016. This sequence of events reflects not only the important role that Executive Orders play in allowing the President to enforce his policy decisions, but also the key role played by the courts in keeping that power in check and avoiding constitutional overreach. We examine the courts next.

The Judiciary

The judicial Power of the United States, shall be vested in one supreme Court, and in such inferior Courts as the Congress may from time to time ordain and establish.
—U.S. Constitution, Art. III

It may not seem this way today, but the creation of a judiciary appears to have been an afterthought by the founding fathers. A court system was not seen as an essential apparatus of governance, but rather a means for resolving disputes. The precursor to the U.S. Constitution—the Articles of Confederation—made no mention of a judiciary. And the Constitution itself does not bestow any vast powers on the one court that it established in Article III—the U.S. Supreme Court. All of that changed very early on in the court's existence.

Article III of the U.S. Constitution established the U.S. Supreme Court as the locus of whatever judicial power there would be in the United States. It also established that the justices and judges of the federal courts would be appointed for life, helping to curb the possibility of political influence or loyalty to special interests by freeing the judges from the election and re-appointment process. The jurisdiction of the Court was laid out in Section 2 of that article, which vests the Supreme Court and inferior federal courts with the power to hear cases:

- arising under the Constitution
- arising under the laws of the United States and treaties (i.e., federal laws)
- affecting Ambassadors or other public officials
- involving admiralty and maritime law
- including the United States as a party
- affecting two or more states
- affecting citizens of different states or foreign countries

However, no specificity was provided about the scope of that judicial power. Did the Court have to defer to congressional or executive interpretations of law? Could the Court challenge the validity of a law or regulation? Could the Court overturn the decision of a state court? None of this was mentioned in the Constitution, leaving it up to the Congress and the Court itself to decide the scope of its jurisdiction.

Congress sought to resolve these concerns through enactment of the Judiciary Act of 1789. That Act established a Supreme Court bench consisting of one Chief Justice and five Associate Justices. It also established the federal court system that we know today, which includes federal district courts in each state as well as federal circuit courts to receive appeals from those district courts. Yet even with this Act, little actual authority was given to the Court, leaving it to the first justices to decide for themselves the scope of the Court's power. That is precisely what they did in *Marbury v. Madison*.

Marbury v. Madison, 5 U.S. (1 Cranch) 137 (1803)

The clerks of the Department of State of the United States may be called upon to give evidence of transactions in the Department which are not of a confidential character.

The Secretary of State cannot be called upon as a witness to state transactions of a confidential nature which may have occurred in his Department. But he may be called upon to give testimony of circumstances which were not of that character.

Clerks in the Department of State were directed to be sworn, subject to objections to questions upon confidential matters.

Some point of time must be taken when the power of the Executive over an officer, not removable at his will, must cease. That point of time must be when the constitutional power of appointment has been exercised. And the power has been exercised when the last act required from the person possessing the power has been performed. This last act is the signature of the commission.

If the act of livery be necessary to give validity to the commission of an officer, it has been delivered when executed, and given to the Secretary of State for the purpose of being sealed, recorded, and transmitted to the party.

In cases of commissions to public officers, the law orders the Secretary of State to record them. When, therefore, they are signed and sealed, the order for their being recorded is given, and, whether inserted inserted into the book or not, they are recorded.

When the heads of the departments of the Government are the political or confidential officers of the Executive, merely to execute the will of the President, or rather to act in cases in which the Executive possesses a constitutional or legal discretion, nothing can be more perfectly clear than that their acts are only politically examinable. But where a specific duty is assigned by law, and individual rights depend upon the performance of that duty, it seems equally clear that the individual who considers himself injured has a right to resort to the laws of his country for a remedy.

The President of the United States, by signing the commission, appointed Mr. Marbury a justice of the peace for the County of Washington, in the District of Columbia, and the seal of the United States, affixed thereto by the Secretary of State, is conclusive testimony of the verity of the signature, and of the completion of the appointment; and the appointment conferred on him a legal right to the office for the space of five years. Having this legal right to the office, he has a consequent right to the commission, a refusal to deliver which is a plain violation of that right for which the laws of the country afford him a remedy.

> To render a mandamus a proper remedy, the officer to whom it is directed must be one to whom, on legal principles, such writ must be directed, and the person applying for it must be without any other specific remedy.
>
> Where a commission to a public officer has been made out, signed, and sealed, and is withheld from the person entitled to it, an action of detinue for the commission against the Secretary of State who refuses to deliver it is not the proper remedy, as the judgment in detinue is for the thing itself, or its value. The value of a public office, not to be sold, is incapable of being ascertained. It is a plain case for a mandamus, either to deliver the commission or a copy of it from the record.
>
> To enable the Court to issue a mandamus to compel the delivery of the commission of a public office by the Secretary of State, it must be shown that it is an exercise of appellate jurisdiction, or that it be necessary to enable them to exercise appellate jurisdiction.
>
> It is the essential criterion of appellate jurisdiction that it revises and corrects the proceedings in a cause already instituted, and does not create the cause.
>
> The authority given to the Supreme Court by the act establishing the judicial system of the United States to issue writs of mandamus to public officers appears not to be warranted by the Constitution.
>
> It is emphatically the duty of the Judicial Department to say what the law is. Those who apply the rule to particular cases must, of necessity, expound and interpret the rule. If two laws conflict with each other, the Court must decide on the operation of each.
>
> If courts are to regard the Constitution, and the Constitution is superior to any ordinary act of the legislature, the Constitution, and not such ordinary act, must govern the case to which they both apply.

Chief Justice John Marshall, who had only been on the bench since 1801, used the *Marbury* case as an opportunity to clarify the role of the judiciary within the broader governing apparatus. The case established the principle of **judicial review**, which authorized the Court to determine the constitutionality of laws and other pronouncements by the legislative and executive branches of government. The reaction by some to this seemingly unauthorized usurpation of power to protect the Constitution was swift:

> Judicial review—the power of the courts to review the constitutionality of a statute or executive regulation.

> The question whether the judges are invested with exclusive authority to decide on the constitutionality of a law has been heretofore a subject of consideration with me in the exercise of official duties. Certainly there is not a word in the Constitution which has given that power to them more than to the Executive or Legislative branches.
> —Thomas Jefferson to W. H. Torrance, 1815. ME 14:303

The *Marbury* case was a major step toward the establishment of the judiciary as an equal branch with the legislature and executive. However, the decision itself did nothing more than clarify what the Court believed its authority to be—namely, to say what the law is. It was only a few years later when the Court applied this power in earnest by striking down a state statute that violated the *ex post facto* (after the fact) clause of the Constitution that we saw this power in action.

In the case of *Fletcher v. Peck*, 10 U.S. 87 (1810), the plaintiff brought a claim for contract breach against the defendant, Mr. Peck. The rather complicated fact scenario can be summarized as follows: The Georgia state legislature enacted a land grant in 1795 that awarded a large tract of land (54,000 square miles) to four development companies. Mr. Peck acquired title to part of that land while the Act was still in force. It was later discovered that the legislators who passed the land grant had received bribes to do so. Those legislators were voted out of office, and the new legislators immediately repealed the land grant and declared the previous grants void. After that repeal, Peck sold Fletcher his tract of land. Fletcher sued Peck for breach of contract, arguing that Peck did not have clean title to the land due to the rescission of the original land grant by the state legislature. In other words, Peck had nothing to sell but pretended to sell something anyway.

The question in the case for the parties was of course whether Peck had breached his contract. But the larger legal question here was whether the state legislature acted lawfully in rescinding the land grant and, if they did not, whether the Supreme Court had the authority to strike down the state law. The Court unanimously held that the Georgia legislature did not have the constitutional authority to invalidate a contract that had already been concluded. This was prohibited by the *ex post facto* clause of the U.S. Constitution. The Court used its power of judicial review to strike down the Georgia state law, thereby validating the contract between Mr. Peck and Mr. Fletcher.

The establishment of the judicial review power and its subsequent application in cases such as *Fletcher* helped to solidify the power of the judicial branch. Today, there is no doubt that the Court stands in final judgment of acts of Congress and of the executive branch and that its power to interpret and uphold the Constitution is broad. This allows the judiciary to serve as an additional check on the power of the other two branches. And while the Court's role is to uphold the Constitution, Congress retains the power to amend that document, allowing it to potentially undermine the judiciary, though this rarely happens.

Structure of the Judicial Branch

Though the Constitution created only one court, the Judiciary Act of 1789 established the more complete judiciary that we operate in today. As shown in Figure 3.1, the U.S. Supreme Court sits atop the federal court system, providing a court of final resort for any party seeking relief. Below the Supreme Court are 13 regional courts known as federal courts of appeal, or circuit courts. Those courts hear appeal from

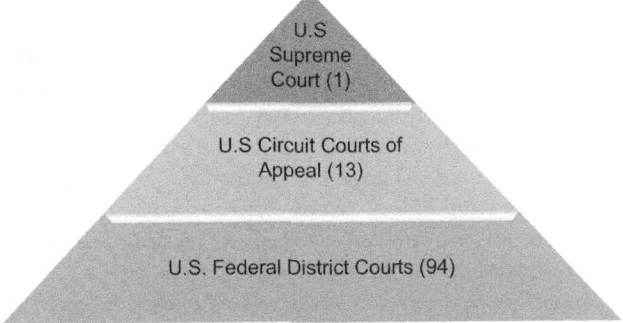

Figure 3.1 Federal Court Hierarchy.

the 94 federal district courts below them and situated across the country. Every state has at least one district court (and as many as four), usually located in a major city.

Not all cases qualify to be heard in federal court. As mentioned earlier, only cases that meet the subject-matter jurisdiction requirements of Article III can be heard by a federal court—other cases would have to be heard by a state court. In either case, however, the U.S. Supreme Court maintains **appellate jurisdiction** over the lower court's decision, even if the case did not qualify for federal jurisdiction.

While most cases can be heard by state courts, certain cases must generally go to federal court. These are called **federal question** cases, and they involve issues of exclusively federal law. These matters include the following:

- Suits between states
- Cases involving ambassadors and other high-ranking public officials
- Federal crimes (e.g., treason, piracy)
- Bankruptcy
- Patent, copyright, and trademark
- Admiralty and maritime law
- Antitrust
- Securities and banking regulation
- Other subjects assigned by statute (e.g., civil rights cases)

There are instances in which the federal and state court will have **concurrent jurisdiction**. If a federal statute or treaty has a direct bearing on a state matter or state law, a state court or a federal court may hear such a case. However, if a state court were to hear that matter, it would be subject to review by the U.S. Supreme Court.

Finally, there are certain cases in which the U.S. Supreme Court has **original jurisdiction**. This means that the Court can sit as a court of first instance to hear the matter. The Constitution identified two instances in which original jurisdiction can be applied—disputes between states and disputes involving ambassadors and other public ministers and consuls. Historically, the Court has principally applied this jurisdiction only over disputes between states and, more recently, between the United States and a particular state.

Rulings from a federal district court have limited applicability. While they may influence other jurisdictions, they are only binding on parties within their limited jurisdiction. As parties move up the ladder to higher-level courts, the scope of impact for the court's decision increases. A circuit court encompasses multiple states, and the U.S. Supreme Court encompasses the entire country. Thus, when seeking to effectuate broad public policy changes through litigation, it is important to bear in mind the jurisdictional limitations of the different court levels.

Bringing a case all the way to the U.S. Supreme Court is often a dream of activists seeking broad public policy change, but the road is long and treacherous. Unless the dispute is between states or public officials, a party generally must start their case at the trial court level in state or federal court. Following that process, they would next appeal to the state or federal appellate court. Finally, to bring a case to the U.S. Supreme Court, a party would file a **writ of certiorari** with the Court. If the Supreme Court grants the writ, it is granting a review of the record of the lower court. If they deny the writ, the decision of the previous court stands.

The U.S. Supreme Court today is made up of nine justices, each appointed by the President and confirmed by the Senate. This number was established by the Judiciary Act of 1869 and has remained consistent ever since. There is one Chief Justice, who

---

Appellate jurisdiction—the authority of a court to hear a certain type of case only when has been appealed from a lower court.

Federal question—a legal issue that involves a matter of federal law and can thus be heard by a federal court.

Concurrent jurisdiction—situation in which two or more courts with different jurisdictional requirements share jurisdiction over a particular matter.

Original jurisdiction—the authority of a court to hear a case without it going through the appellate process.

Writ of certiorari—a request for review (appeal) presented to the U.S. Supreme Court.

is nominated by the President and confirmed by the Senate and serves as the head of the Judicial Conference of the United States as well as the judge in a Senate trial in a case of impeachment of the President. The Chief Justice also decides who will write a court opinion, so long as he or she is in the majority for that decision.

All federal court judges are appointed for life and may only be removed through impeachment. Accordingly, a President may only fill slots that are opened due to retirement, death, elevation to other courts, or successful impeachment proceedings. There are approximately 677 federal district court judges, 179 courts of appeal judges, and nine Supreme Court justices. Since appointees sit for life, a President can have a lasting impact through the appointment of federal judges. The highest number of appointees in recent history was by President Ronald Reagan (402 appointments), followed closely by President Bill Clinton (387 appointments). The lowest number of appointees was by President Gerald Ford (63), followed by President John F. Kennedy (125). Because the appointment process takes time and can be politically contentious, some vacancies go unfilled.

The independence of the judiciary is crucial in ensuring effective governance. The fact that federal judges serve life terms is meant to insulate them from political pressure and from the election process. Appointed judges certainly bring their own political persuasions to bear on the court, but this independent structure ensures that they rule based upon their own experience and wisdom rather than that from donors, lobbyists, or others who might attempt to sway their views. This includes insulation from the very President that nominates them, leaving them free to adjust their public policy views once confirmed to the court.

The Power of Judicial Review

As the guardian of the Constitution, the U.S. Supreme Court has a critical role to play in governance. Their interpretation of the text of the Constitution and how it applies to a given case, statute, or rule reshapes the law itself, making the judicial branch, in effect, another lawmaking branch of government. Some have criticized the Court for being too *activist* and inserting its own interpretation over that of state and federal legislatures. Others have turned to the Court to rescue them from the decisions of the legislative and executive branches. And because justices serve for life and are not subject to the electoral process, the Court is both independent and insulated from public opinion.

The key mechanism that the public has to influence the Supreme Court is through their election of the President. While it is never a certainty, every President since Roosevelt, other than President Jimmy Carter, has been able to appoint at least one new justice to the Court. The changing makeup of the bench leads to compromise and conflict, but also leads to a Court that is loosely aligned with public opinion since the public elected the President that appointed the new justices.

Justices on the Court are often labeled *liberal* or *conservative* based upon their rulings. However, those designations are overly simplistic and miss the broader role of these individuals. The nature of the common law system in which we live requires a judge to follow past precedent (court decisions). Even the Supreme Court must adhere to their past rulings unless there is a good legal justification to differ. This means that even if a judge or justice differs politically from a particular conclusion, they are beholden to follow established precedent and rule on the basis of law, not on politics. That type of system ensures consistency and predictability in judicial proceedings and leads to very well-reasoned opinions based upon the foundations established by prior precedent. However, this system does not account for the power of interpretation.

The Constitution is not a detailed document. Unlike in a civil law system, where the constitution and related federal statutes are extensive and detailed, our founders designed a system that leaves a great deal of room for interpretation. We saw this earlier when reviewing the *Gibbons v. Ogden* case, or the *Marbury v. Madison* decision, in which the Court took extensive liberties in its assessment of certain constitutional provisions. We will examine this power of interpretation next.

Interpreting the Constitution

The explosive combination of judicial review power and a simple Constitution gives Supreme Court Justices an opportunity to rewrite history through judicial interpretations. This possibility has led commentators to place the justices in one of two camps: originalists and non-originalists.

Originalism is a school of thought that subscribes to the belief in maintaining the original meaning of the Constitution. A judge that subscribes to this theory would interpret the Constitution by strictly adhering to the words of that document and applying the meaning they would have had in the late 1780s. This approach limits opportunities for judges to insert their subjective interpretations into cases and forces the legislature to change the Constitution if it believes a new meaning is needed. Recent originalists on the Court include the late Antonin Scalia, Clarence Thomas, and Neil Gorsuch.

Non-originalists are said to follow the *living document* philosophy, which says that the founding fathers did not want to inject their own interpretations into the Constitution but rather desired to leave it to future policymakers to interpret the law as it would apply at the time of interpretation. Non-originalists are justices who use judicial *gap-filling* techniques to address modern issues with updated interpretations of the law, seeing the Constitution as a living document meant to grow and adapt to new circumstances. Federal judge Richard Posner has often been associated with a non-originalist ideology.

The debate over originalism and non-originalism can be clearly seen in cases during the mid-20th century addressing substantive due process rights. Also known as *fundamental rights*, this set of protections is meant to limit government interference with private affairs. The Fifth and 14th Amendments identify these rights as "life, liberty, or property," but they don't go any further than that in explaining what those rights are and what those words mean. Hence, it is up to the courts to make that determination.

In the early 20th century, the Court read into these rights the freedom of contract, meaning that the government would not interfere with someone's right to enter into any valid contract they wished, even if it ultimately harmed the other party. The Court made that interpretation in the case of *Lochner v. New York* (discussed at length in Chapter 5 on Economic Policy). Later, seeing that their opinion was largely being abused in commercial and labor contracts, the Court reinterpreted that clause to say that the freedom of contract is not an unlimited freedom and that government may be able to lay some restrictions on what can and cannot be accomplished through a contract. That interpretation opened the door to government regulation of commercial transactions.

The 1960s witnessed a significant rise in social movements favoring gender equality and women's rights. Among these was the right to use contraception and to seek an abortion. In 1965, the Supreme Court again interpreted the substantive due process clause, this time to include an implicit right to privacy. The Court used the term "penumbras" to define the shadowy edges of certain amendments, a term which would become synonymous with non-originalism. These penumbras were the logical outgrowths of the plain text found in the Constitution. In the *Griswold v. Connecticut* case, the Court found a right to privacy in the use of contraception in the penumbras of the 14th Amendment.

Even more recently, the Court struck down a federal statute that defined marriage as limited to opposite-sex couples, finding that distinguishing between different couples inherently violates the Equal Protection clause of the Fifth Amendment and is thus unconstitutional (*United States v. Windsor*). Later, the Court decided that states, like the federal government, could not prevent same-sex couples from marrying because it would violate the fundamental liberties guaranteed by the 14th Amendment. Through its interpretation, the Court effectively created a right to same-sex marriage that had been prevented by state and federal statutes before.

All of these decisions are controversial and usually result in a very close vote by the justices of the Court. And all of them are subject to further review in future challenges that raise novel arguments or that are presented to a Court with new justices or to override by congressional action. We can conclude from this discussion that the Court has a transformative impact on society and on public policy, and that the makeup of the Court, as determined by the President, can easily alter the outcome of public policy and law for decades.

Deference to Executive Agencies

Before we leave the topic of judicial review, it is imperative that we add one last point of analysis: deference. As we discussed earlier, executive power is largely carried out through either Executive Orders or through executive agencies (and those orders are usually directed at executive agencies). In the previous section we focused on the Supreme Court's ability to review legislation and to assess the constitutionality of state and federal laws, but what about the decisions made by executive agencies? We will spend a few moments looking at that issue now.

Recall that executive agencies are led by political appointees who serve at the pleasure of the President, and that independent commissions and boards are also led by political appointees and operate under slightly less presidential influence. But the agencies are also driven by a cadre of civil servants with the experience and expertise to carry out the long-term goals of the agency and to maintain a responsive approach to the public they serve.

Regulatory agencies, such as U.S. Customs and Border Protection or the Environmental Protection Agency, issue rules that interpret their authority to act in a given context. These rules may be simple and narrow, such as changing a digital interface to allow traders to make import duty payments online, or broad and extensive, such as guaranteeing equal access to information across the internet through net neutrality. In either case, they follow a rigid rulemaking process that involves public comment and often an economic impact assessment. Once the rule has been issued, it has the force of law behind it since it is an interpretation of a statute.

The agency's authority to interpret a statute might be seen as a narrow form of judicial review. They are exercising their discretion to find practical meaning within the language put together by legislators who often lack expertise in agency operations. How much, if any, discretion should regulatory agencies have to apply their own interpretation of the law in crafting their rules? Their interpretation may be practical and helpful, lending clarity to an ambiguous law, or it may be harmful or discriminatory, circumventing the intent of the law.

Agencies must interpret statutes in a way that meets their budgetary and other resource requirements. This may require them to prioritize certain efforts over others, or to enact rules that limit the scope of certain statutory pronouncements. Generally, the more specific and clear a statute is, the less room the agency will have to interpret it to their own policy positions. Some statutes, such as the Clean Water Act, specifically deny the agency any authority to interpret the statute differently from what is written.

When an agency interprets a statute to suit its needs and issues a regulation in accordance with that interpretation, it often faces legal challenge. The courts have traditionally viewed agencies as more expert than judges in developing a practical application of a statute and thus have generally deferred to their interpretation. The Supreme Court helped to give structure to this deferential approach by establishing a two-step test that balances the interests of legislators in having their statutes applied as written and the interests of agencies in clarifying the practical intent behind the law. The test is laid out in a case addressing the Environmental Protection Agency's interpretation of the Clean Air Act.

Chevron U.S.A. Inc. v. Natural Resources Defense Council, Inc., 467 U.S. 837 (1984)

In the Clean Air Act Amendments of 1977, Pub.L. 95–95, 91 Stat. 685, Congress enacted certain requirements applicable to States that had not achieved the national air quality standards established by the Environmental Protection Agency (EPA) pursuant to earlier legislation. The amended Clean Air Act required these "nonattainment" States to establish a permit program regulating "new or modified major stationary sources" of air pollution. Generally, a permit may not be issued for a new or modified major stationary source unless several stringent conditions are met. The EPA regulation promulgated to implement this permit requirement allows a State to adopt a plantwide definition of the term "stationary source." Under this definition, an existing plant that contains several pollution-emitting devices may install or modify one piece of equipment without meeting the permit conditions if the alteration will not increase the total emissions from the plant. The question presented by these cases is whether EPA's decision to allow States to treat all of the pollution-emitting devices within the same industrial grouping as though they were encased within a single "bubble" is based on a reasonable construction of the statutory term "stationary source."

The EPA regulations containing the plantwide definition of the term stationary source were promulgated on October 14, 1981. 46 Fed.Reg. 50766. Respondents filed a timely petition for review in the United States Court of Appeals for the District of Columbia Circuit pursuant to 42 U.S.C. § 7607(b)(1). The Court of Appeals set aside the regulations.

The court observed that the relevant part of the amended Clean Air Act "does not explicitly define what Congress envisioned as a stationary source, to which the permit program ... should apply," and further stated that the precise issue was not "squarely addressed in the legislative history." In light of its conclusion that the legislative history bearing on the question was "at best contradictory," it reasoned that "the purposes of the nonattainment program should guide our decision here." Based on two of its precedents concerning the applicability of the bubble concept to certain Clean Air Act programs, [Footnote 6] the court stated that the bubble concept was "mandatory" in programs designed merely to maintain existing air quality, but held that it was "inappropriate" in programs enacted to improve air quality. Since the purpose of the permit program its "raison d'etre," in the court's view—was to improve air quality, the court held that the bubble concept was inapplicable in these cases under its prior precedents. Ibid. It therefore set aside the regulations embodying the bubble concept as contrary to law. We granted certiorari to review that judgment, and we now reverse.

The basic legal error of the Court of Appeals was to adopt a static judicial definition of the term "stationary source" when it had decided that Congress itself had not commanded that definition. Respondents do not defend the legal reasoning of the Court of Appeals. Nevertheless, since this Court reviews judgments, not opinions, we must determine whether the Court of Appeals' legal error resulted in an erroneous judgment on the validity of the regulations.

When a court reviews an agency's construction of the statute which it administers, it is confronted with two questions. First, always, is the question whether Congress has directly spoken to the precise question at issue. If the intent of Congress is clear, that is the end of the matter; for the court, as well as the agency, must give effect to the unambiguously expressed intent of Congress. If, however, the court determines Congress has not directly addressed the precise question at issue, the court does not simply impose its own construction on the statute, as would be necessary in the absence of an administrative interpretation. Rather, if the statute is silent or ambiguous with respect to the specific issue, the question for the court is whether the agency's answer is based on a permissible construction of the statute.

> The power of an administrative agency to administer a congressionally created ... program necessarily requires the formulation of policy and the making of rules to fill any gap left, implicitly or explicitly, by Congress.

Morton v. Ruiz, 415 U. S. 199, 415 U. S. 231 (1974). If Congress has explicitly left a gap for the agency to fill, there is an express delegation of authority to the agency to elucidate a specific provision of the statute by regulation. Such legislative regulations are given controlling weight unless they are arbitrary, capricious, or manifestly contrary to the statute. Sometimes the legislative delegation to an agency on a particular question is implicit, rather than explicit. In such a case, a court may not substitute its own construction of a statutory provision for a reasonable interpretation made by the administrator of an agency.

We have long recognized that considerable weight should be accorded to an executive department's construction of a statutory scheme it is entrusted to administer, and the principle of deference to administrative interpretations

> has been consistently followed by this Court whenever decision as to the meaning or reach of a statute has involved reconciling conflicting policies, and a full

understanding of the force of the statutory policy in the given situation has depended upon more than ordinary knowledge respecting the matters subjected to agency regulations.

If this choice represents a reasonable accommodation of conflicting policies that were committed to the agency's care by the statute, we should not disturb it unless it appears from the statute or its legislative history that the accommodation is not one that Congress would have sanctioned.

In light of these well-settled principles, it is clear that the Court of Appeals misconceived the nature of its role in reviewing the regulations at issue. Once it determined, after its own examination of the legislation, that Congress did not actually have an intent regarding the applicability of the bubble concept to the permit program, the question before it was not whether, in its view, the concept is "inappropriate" in the general context of a program designed to improve air quality, but whether the Administrator's view that it is appropriate in the context of this particular program is a reasonable one. Based on the examination of the legislation and its history which follows, we agree with the Court of Appeals that Congress did not have a specific intention on the applicability of the bubble concept in these cases, and conclude that the EPA's use of that concept here is a reasonable policy choice for the agency to make.

***

When a challenge to an agency construction of a statutory provision, fairly conceptualized, really centers on the wisdom of the agency's policy, rather than whether it is a reasonable choice within a gap left open by Congress, the challenge must fail. In such a case, federal judges—who have no constituency—have a duty to respect legitimate policy choices made by those who do. The responsibilities for assessing the wisdom of such policy choices and resolving the struggle between competing views of the public interest are not judicial ones: "Our Constitution vests such responsibilities in the political branches." *TVA v. Hill*, 437 U. S. 153, 437 U. S. 195 (1978).

We hold that the EPA's definition of the term "source" is a permissible construction of the statute which seeks to accommodate progress in reducing air pollution with economic growth.

In what has become known as *Chevron Deference*, a court that is reviewing an agency's interpretation of a statute will ask the following two questions:

1. Is the language of the statute clear?
    a. If it is, that is the end of the matter and the agency must apply the statute as written.
2. If it is unclear or ambiguous, is the agency's interpretation reasonable?
    a. If it is, the court will defer to the agency's interpretation.

This keeps in place the careful balance between legislation that is meant to clearly guide agency actions in the achievement of a specific policy goal and legislation that is meant to provide an agency with the tools to carry out a broader policy goal.

Conclusion: Rule of Law and Effective Governance

The effectiveness of governing institutions is central to the functioning of any state. A weak or ineffective government that lacks the respect of the people can create instability and inconsistent market outcomes. While a government can take many forms, from parliamentary to presidential to party control, the key to successful governance may be rooted in strong **rule of law**.

Rule of law has no single definition but might be best characterized as the supremacy of law over the sovereign and respect for the institutions that implement the law.[6] This means that the law, created by the people, will always serve as a check on the government and that no official is above the law. Strong rule of law means not only that a government holds its own officials accountable, but also that the people perceive the government as obeying the law. This builds trust and facilitates a more effective environment for business development, risk-taking, and peaceful resolution of disputes.

> Rule of law—the subjugation of a government to the laws enacted by the citizens through their representatives.

Much has been written about the value of the rule of law for effective governance and economic growth. An annual index of factors that contribute to strong rule of law, including government transparency in decision-making, enforcement of private contracts by courts, and corruption, is published by the World Justice Project. Countries that score poorly on this index tend to have less stable economic and political environments. The United States tends to score highly on their rule of law index.

The institutions that wield political power in any democratic country are mechanisms by which the people can express their needs and wants and to shape the environment in which they want to live. These institutions operate at the local, state, and federal levels as well as cross-regionally to balance the interests of their constituents. The more legitimacy these institutions have, the more effective they can be in carrying out their duties; likewise, the more power they have, the more risk of corruption and abuse of power they face. A delicate balance must be maintained between empowering our institutions to serve our needs and over-empowering them to serve their own needs. The first step in achieving this balance is understanding the nature of those institutions and the limits that we place on them, which we have begun to do in this chapter.

Notes

1. John Phillip Reid, *Constitutional History of the American Revolution: The Authority of Law* 13 (2003).
2. Benjamin Franklin's Final Speech in the Constitutional Convention from the Notes of James Madison, 1789, www.pbs.org/benfranklin/pop_finalspeech.html
3. Note that between the Vice President and the Secretary of State, the Speaker of the House followed by the President pro tempore of the Senate would succeed the President. They are excluded here because they are not Cabinet members.
4. USA.gov Independent Agencies, www.usa.gov/independent-agencies
5. For more information on this process, see the cases of *Buckley v. Valeo* (1976), *Edmond v. United States* (1997), and *Morrison v. Olson* (1988).
6. Brian Z. Tamanaha, *On the Rule of Law: History, Politics, Theory* 30 (2004).

Additional Learning Resources

Annotated Case Bibliography

There are far too many important Supreme Court cases that address significant law and policy matters to list here, and many key cases will be identified and discussed throughout this text. Nevertheless, the following list is meant to be a foundational list of cases that address the power of the Supreme Court to effectuate public policy:

Dred Scott v. Sandford, 60 U.S. 393 (1857), Addressing the issue of slavery and the citizenship of slaves in the United States.

Plessy v. Fergusson, 163 U.S. 537 (1896), Addressing the equality of black and white citizens on public transport.

Brown v. Board of Education, 347 U.S. 483 (1954), Addressing the equality of black and white citizens in public schools.

Roe v. Wade, 410 U.S. 113 (1973), Addressing the fundamental right to have an abortion.

Citizens United v. Federal Election Commission, 558 U.S. 310 (2010), Addressing the First Amendment right of a corporation to influence elections.

Medellin v. Texas, 552 U.S. 491 (2008), Addressing state and federal power regarding decisions of an international tribunal.

INS v. Chadha, 462 U.S. 919 (1983), Addressing the power of Congress to veto the actions of the Executive branch.

United States v. Belmont, 301 U.S. 324 (1937), Addressing the Executive's power to enter agreements with foreign entities absent congressional approval.

New York Times v. United States, 403 U.S. 713 (1971), Addressing the power of the President to restrict the publication of documents ("The Pentagon Papers") from being printed.

Additional Readings

Politics, Institutions, and Rule of Law

John J. Langbein, *History of the Common Law: The Development of Anglo-American Legal Institutions* (2009).

Brian Tamanaha, *On the Rule of Law: History, Politics, Theory* 30 (2004).

James Q. Wilson & John J. Dilulio, *American Government: Institutions and Policies* (2017).

The U.S. Supreme Court

Stephen Breyer, *The Court and the World: American Law and the New Global Realities* (2016).

Peter Irons, *A People's History of the Supreme Court* (2006).

Jeffrey Toobin, *The Nine: Inside the Secret World of the Supreme Court* (2008).

4 Separating Facts and Fiction—How to Become a More Effective Researcher and a More Critical Reader

Science is built up of facts, as a house is built of stones; but an accumulation of facts is no more a science than a heap of stones is a house.
—Henri Poincarè

Introduction

In today's politically charged environment both within the United States and in many other parts of the world, information is the key to winning an election, making a wise business decision, or enacting smart public policies. And while facts change over time and no one has the foresight to predict every possible consequence of their actions, the more accurate information that we have access to, the better our decisions will be.

Information has never been easier to access than it is today. From traditional newspapers and radio and television broadcasts to more modern social media sources, we have no shortage of access to different viewpoints and analysis. However, with more access comes more risk that the information we are relying upon is in fact as accurate as it should be. The information that is presented to us may be misleading and, in some cases, may be intentionally false.

Misleading and false information may be harmless if we read it with a critical eye and understand the errors in the message. But the flood of information fed to us today in shallow bites and the blurring line between fact and opinion often leave us with little time to analyze and make judgments as to the veracity (truthfulness) of the material. Add to that the ease with which we can resend news stories and reports that may be false or misleading multiplies the impact of that material, lending the credibility of our name on "retweets" and "shares" that we may not have had an opportunity to fully assess. We are quickly building an information environment that makes no distinction between verified facts and conjecture, making the truth even harder to find.

If it were possible to contain false and misleading stories to within social media sites and treat them as entertainment rather than news, we may not need to address this issue in a book about law and public policy. Yet as the opening case highlights, some individuals take false information and act upon it as if it were true without taking the time to critically assess the origin and intent behind the story. Additionally, and perhaps even more concerning, the fact that public officials both participate in social media and act upon stories on social platforms raises significantly the level of importance of understanding how to evaluate and judge the truthfulness of political statements and commentary wherever they are found.

To combat the risk of confusing opinion for fact and of making conclusions on the basis of limited or biased information, we will take some time in this chapter to understand the critical analysis and reasoning process. Before delving into discussions of economic, environmental, and foreign policy issues, among others, it is of great importance that we strengthen our ability to break down arguments in order to assess their value, learn how to find and select reliable sources, and sharpen our ability to both create and respond to questionable claims. That will be our goal in the pages ahead.

Opening Case

In October 2016, a story about a hacked Twitter account of a white supremacist and the hacked email account of a Democratic campaign manager led to the beginning of unfounded allegations about a child sex trafficking ring supported by Democratic operatives. The news of a sex scandal was posted on a variety of mostly conservative websites and spread quickly across a number of platforms thanks to blog posts, retweets, and online promoters. Words in the leaked emails and messages such as "cheese pizza" were interpreted as code words for "child pornography," given the shared initial letters in the words. Soon, a location for the sex ring was identified as Comet Pizza in Washington, D.C.

The owner of Comet Pizza, a local family-oriented pizzeria, was targeted by followers of the rapidly spreading conspiracy theory. Photos from his Instagram account displaying customers as well as fake photos asserted as his own were shown as evidence that the sex ring was located in his restaurant. On December 4, 2016, Edgar Welch, a 28-year-old man from rural North Carolina, went to Comet Pizza with an AR-15 rifle to investigate the sex ring. He fired three shots inside as part of his investigation but found no evidence that the restaurant was harboring any child sex slaves. He told police that he went because of the news he had read online about the sex ring.

Welch pleaded guilty and was sentenced to four years in prison. Days after his arrest, Yusif Lee Jones from Louisiana made threatening calls to a nearby pizzeria, Besta Pizza, in an effort to finish what Welch could not. Jones faces up to five years in prison. Neither of the individuals has disavowed the conspiracy theory, and an active community online continues to propagate its tenets.

Major news sources, both liberal and conservative, have discredited the story. Yet the effects of the story were felt far and wide, leading to negative opinions of Democrats and Hillary Clinton, which were used by some mainstream politicians to generate public support of their campaigns.

Fundamentals of Critical Thinking

Critical thinking is a skill in high demand and short supply. Nearly every profession today requires it, yet only a handful of people possess it. Academic programs for some professions, such as law or economics, embed critical analysis into their curriculum. But in other areas, such as business, sociology, and even public policy, these skills are often seen as outside of the core curriculum. Without these skills, an education is simply incomplete.

At the outset, it is important to define critical thinking. Rather than a discipline in itself, critical thinking is a cross-disciplinary "soft" skill that enables you to organize ideas and form logical conclusions on the basis of a set of facts. Rather than teaching you how to find facts, critical thinking helps you to determine which facts are relevant and in what way in order to reach a given conclusion. Simply put, critical thinking is an effective mechanism to organize and evaluate ideas.

But critical thinking is more than that. It is also the ability to rationalize the logic behind an argument. A successful argument follows a logical pattern that a critical thinker can identify and evaluate. Similarly, an unsuccessful argument may be built upon logical fallacies or false statements, which an effective critical thinker can identify and disentangle to show its weaknesses. This skill is often understated but essential in analyzing everything from a legal argument to a business strategy to a proposed piece of legislation.

What Is Critical Analysis?

Historically, students at all levels of education would receive information from their teachers and the books and articles they were asked to read for class. They would digest and often discuss this information in the classroom, and possibly use it to prepare assignments or presentations. In some cases, they were asked to value this information and to determine its validity and strength as argument. It is in that valuation process that we begin to develop critical thinking skills.

Today, learning is far different from how it was in the past. Students are exposed to immense amounts of information, from their teachers and assigned readings, as well as from access to the Internet and exposure to social media, all of which provide analyses of every conceivable topic. Finding multiple opinions on a given topic is exceedingly easy today; however, determining the value of the sources for those opinions is exceedingly difficult. With increased access to information comes an increased risk that false or unsubstantiated information will infiltrate our research. This is why critical thinking and analysis is more important today than ever before.

The best way to start the critical thinking and analysis process is to *question everything*. This does not mean that you should set aside your manners and challenge every statement made to you. Rather, it means that you must always be on your guard for weak arguments, bias, and other logical problems that allow statements of opinion to appear as statements of fact. Consider the following statement from a recent news story:

> Some industry lobbyists have pointed out that rules ushered in after the financial crisis have in some ways been beneficial for the big banks, acting as a barrier to entry for any bank without the resources to handle the additional compliance costs.[1]

There is nothing obviously wrong with this statement, which forms part of a larger article about banking deregulation, but a critical eye will see a few reasons for concern. First, the statement asserts strong support by mentioning "several industry lobbyists," using that broad but undefined group to assuage any doubt about the words that follow. Then, "rules" are referenced in such a general tone that it is unclear exactly what rules this undefined group of lobbyists would be alluding to. Those rules have "in some ways been beneficial," though we don't know which rules and how they were beneficial to the "big banks" mentioned next. And finally, the author suggests that these rules may have prevented entry for "any bank without the resources to handle the additional compliance costs." Again, we don't know which banks this statement refers to, which resources would be short, and which additional compliance costs would prevent their entry. Of course, we are taking this single sentence out of context from the broader article, which does a nice job providing information about the topic. But what we can deduce is that statements like this are made to be swallowed without digesting, inserting the argument into your mind without valuation or analysis. Trusting without processing.

Critical thinking is a skill that slows down our ingestion of statements made in books, articles, news reports, social media, and by our learned professors, and gives our minds a moment to process and understand the logic behind those statements. The breadth of information access today is equivalent to drinking from a fire hose, meaning that we don't seem to have the time to understand what we are consuming. The downside of our increased access to information is the inability to understand it. Our goal must be to slow down the flow of data and enhance our critical eye on everything that we see. This doesn't mean turning off the flow of information, but rather focusing it on reliable sources.

The late-19th-century education reformer John Dewey is often seen as the father of critical thinking (though we could easily go back to Plato and others who applied similar skills). In his seminal work, *How We Think*, Dewey said that "[a]ctive, persistent and careful consideration of any belief or supposed form of knowledge in light of the grounds that support it, and the further conclusions to which it tends, constitutes reflective thought." His term for critical thinking was "reflection."

For him, our goal as critical thinkers must be to slow down our inquiries and understand the foundation of the argument:

> The essence of critical thinking is suspended judgment; and the essence of this suspense is inquiry to determine the nature of the problem before proceeding to attempts at its solution. This, more than any other thing, transforms mere inference into tested inference, suggested conclusions into proof.[2]

I wonder what Dewey would have said about 140-character political statements.

To be more precise, critical thinking is a technical process by which we can better understand how an argument is built. If each fact in an argument were a brick, critical analysis would help us to see what holds the bricks together and what structure they form when put together. As the opening quote alludes to, critical analysis helps us to distinguish between a house and a pile of bricks:

> Critical thinking is the intellectually disciplined process of actively and skillfully conceptualizing, applying, analyzing, synthesizing, and/or evaluating information gathered from, or generated by, observation, experience, reflection, reasoning, or communication, as a guide to belief and action. In its exemplary form, it is based on universal intellectual values that transcend subject matter divisions: clarity, accuracy, precision, consistency, relevance, sound evidence, good reasons, depth, breadth, and fairness. It entails the examination of those structures or elements of thought implicit in all reasoning: purpose, problem, or question-at-issue, assumptions, concepts, empirical grounding; reasoning leading to conclusions, implications and consequences, objections from alternative viewpoints, and frame of reference.[3]

Critical thinking involves asking questions, defining a problem, examining evidence, analyzing assumptions and biases, avoiding emotional reasoning, avoiding oversimplification, considering other interpretations, and tolerating ambiguity. In other words, critical thinking requires us to sharpen our analysis when reading and researching, looking not only at the substance of what we are reviewing but also the author of the work to understand any implicit bias or opinion, the sources of the work to understand the balance between conjecture and research, and the tone of the writing to understand if it is meant to move us through emotion or through fact.

So what does it mean to be an effective critical thinker? Based upon concepts outlined in a book on critical thinking by Beyer, we can define an effective critical thinker as someone who is:[4]

- skeptical;
- open-minded;
- respectful of evidence and reasoning;
- respectful of clarity and precision;
- able to look at different points of view and change positions when reason leads them to do so.

To become an effective critical thinker, it is important to develop a mechanism to evaluate the work of others. This requires the establishment of a set of criteria by which arguments can be assessed. A good starting point is to establish conditions that the argument must meet in order to be believable. These should include:

- Arguments must be based upon relevant, accurate facts;
- Arguments should be underpinned by credible, reliable sources;
- Arguments should be precise and avoid broad generalizations;
- Arguments should be free of bias and opinion; and,
- Arguments should be logically consistent.

You can apply these skills right away when you read a newspaper article, Facebook post, or anything else. You may find that nothing really meets all of these factors 100% of the time—and that is fine. Your goal is to weigh the argument's strength against its weaknesses so that you can decide how to use it. An argument that presents significant gaps in these conditions may be discarded or challenged rather easily, but an argument that meets most of these conditions may be suitable as a source for your own assertions and arguments.

Routinely applying these conditions in our reading can help us to avoid the traps of false statements asserted as true. Differentiating between opinion and fact is one thing, but how do we determine whether we can trust an assertion of fact that appears to be true? We will approach this issue in the following section on fake news.

Fake News and the Importance of Critical Analysis

Imagine that you open your daily newspaper (online or print version) and you see the following headline: "Great Astronomical Discoveries Made by NASA." The story references the *National Journal of Science* as its source of information and discusses the discovery of life on the moon. The author of the article is listed as Dr. Andrew Grant, who traveled with the NASA scientists to the moon during the great discovery. What would you do with this story—read it carefully with a critical eye? Share it on your social network? Or discard it as fake news?

This is a slightly modified version of a story printed in the *New York Sun* in 1835 discussing the discovery of life on the moon, including unicorns and flying bat-like creatures. Considering the time period, it was hard to disprove the story, but the facts certainly seem incredulous. But how would you go about researching whether there is any truth to the story?

Critical analysis is more important today than in the past largely because of the proliferation of fake and misleading stories delivered via a wide array of mediums, such as social media, news aggregators, and television. A fake or misleading story disseminated by a source that we trust alongside a seemingly real news story can add credibility and believability, despite any dubious claims in the story. As these stories gain traction, they spread like wildfire throughout a variety of news sources, building up their credibility until they are questioned by someone with the skills necessary to see the fallacies of the story.

One easy mechanism to assess the validity of sources comes from Sarah Blakeslee, a professor at California State University Chico, called the CRAAP test. She suggests asking the following about each source that you review:[5]

- Currency (When was it published? Has it been updated?)
- Relevance (Does it relate to your needs? Who is the audience?)
- Authority (Who are the author and publisher? What are their credentials?)
- Accuracy (Is it reliable and truthful? Is it supported by evidence?)
- Purpose (Why does this information exist? Is there a bias?)

A few other tips for online media analysis come from Melissa Zimdars at Merrimack College. She suggests the following to avoid the traps of fake news:

- Avoid websites with names ending in "lo" such as "Newslo" as these sites often blend real facts and false statements together.
- Ask whether mainstream media is also talking about the story.
- Look for author attribution to confirm the source of the article.
- Review the "About Us" page on the website to assess its legitimacy.
- Avoid articles that tend to use ALL CAPS in headlines or in the body of the article.

Fake news stories may begin as attempts at humor, such as posting a serious photo with a funny headline. Or those fake news stories may be meant to be taken seriously, either to influence opinions in a given way or to sow confusion and mistrust in news sources among readers. The spread of fake news stories perpetuates a sense of uncertainty about what to believe and what to discard. And this, in turn, leads many people to cocoon themselves within sources that they relate to without venturing out into any serious comparative research. In the next section, we will discuss how to distinguish facts from fiction and how to find sources of information to trust.

Social Media as a Source of News

More than one-third of Americans today get their news on social media sites, including Facebook, Twitter, SnapChat, and YouTube, among others (see Figure 4.1a). This means that, while some of the news stories we see online allow us to read the complete story, we are often viewing news on our smartphones and tablets without the benefit of time or readability to fully grasp a story and critically assess its validity. As I have repeated throughout this chapter, the increased access to news is potentially an excellent development; however, our limited ability to understand and assess that news may have the unintended effect of generating a population that relies on misinformation rather than no information to determine their actions and statements.

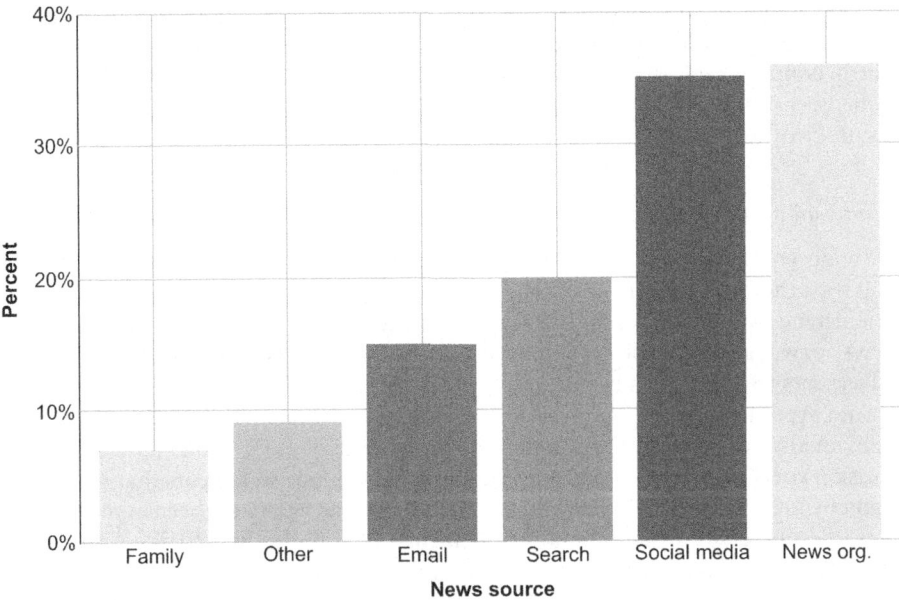

Figure 4.1a Sources of News for Americans.
Source: Pew Research Center Survey (Feb. 9, 2017).

An additional problem presented by accessing news on social media sites is the purpose of the site itself. Social media sites, by their nature, were created to facilitate social interactions—such as sharing family photos—and to ultimately show you advertisements that you may like that, if you click on them, will generate revenue for the social media site. Companies have invested heavily into developing analytics that ensure the personalization of each user experience, targeting ads for you based upon your past purchases, searches, and even comments that you make online.

In the 2011 book, *The Filter Bubble,* Eli Parsier discusses an experiment using Google to search for news. He asked friends across the political spectrum to search for the term "Egypt" in Google. Each of them, based on Google's algorithm, received different results, some focused on protests in Tahir Square, others about revolutionary turmoil, and still others about vacation spots in Egypt. Google gave the users what it thought they wanted to see. When it comes to advertising and social posts, this may be perfectly acceptable and even desirable. But what happens when these advanced algorithms are used to feed you news?

Searching for news on Google, or any of the popular social media platforms, is far different from reading news on traditional media. While you can certainly customize your *New York Times* or NPR preferences to certain categories, social media has mastered the ability to filter out stories that would not only fall outside your categorical preferences, but even those that fall outside your political preferences. By *liking* or *sharing* or even discussing a political topic, you are giving valuable information to the social media platform that it can use to cocoon you in a bubble of news stories that match your political preferences.

Ultimately, it is up to consumers to self-regulate their news feeds. This requires a conscious effort on the part of every user of social media to understand why certain news stories that interest them continue to dominate their feeds, how to access opposing views that will expand our understanding of key issues, and how to assess the validity of the stories that we read. The tips in this chapter provide a starting place, but it is up to each of us to be smart consumers of news from any source. And remember, unlike traditional media sources, social media does not depend on the accuracy of its reporting for its business to survive.

Who Can You Trust?

How do you know who to trust as a source of information (see Figure 4.1b)? Can you trust the *New York Times* or the *Wall Street Journal*, publications that have been in existence since 1851 and 1889, respectively? How about CNN, the first cable news network? Or National Public Radio, which relies on donations rather than advertisers to support its broadcasts?

And even if we can trust any of these sources in a general sense, can we trust the individuals reporting for those sources? For instance, in 2015, Fox News aired a terrorism expert from the CIA, Wayne Simmons, who made statements that were relied upon by many viewers. We later learned that Simmons had never been in the CIA and was later indicted for making false statements. And during the 2016 election cycle, the "20 largest fake stories generated 8.7 million shares, reactions, and comments, compared to 7.4 million generated by the top 20 stories from 19 major news sites."[6] The most popular story involved Pope Francis endorsing Donald Trump.

Once a news story is out, even if the information was incorrect and later retracted by the source, as was the case with Fox News, the damage is done. Some viewers will never learn of the retraction and will go on assuming the information was accurate. Others will see the retraction and begin to distrust other information given by that

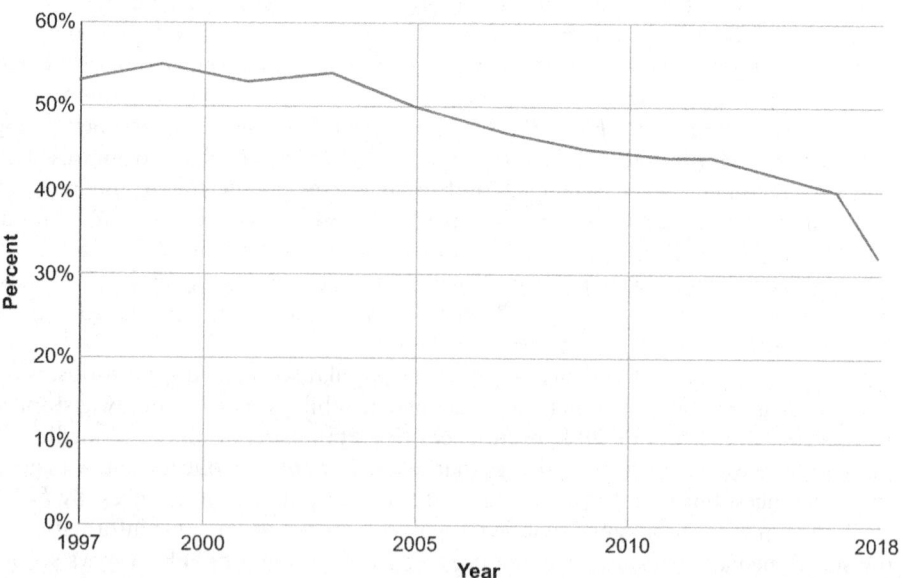

Figure 4.1b Americans' Trust in Traditional News Media (1997–2016).
Source: Gallup Poll (Sept. 14, 2016).

source. And still others will generalize that all mainstream media is unreliable due to these mistakes.

Our goal must be to become active participants in the media process, selecting our sources and stories carefully and reading with a critical eye. However, we should not discard sources on the basis of retracted stories; in fact, the act of retracting a story itself reflects the efforts of the source to give as accurate information as possible. Fake news is a significant and growing problem that we as consumers must address swiftly and directly through support for investigative journalism that provides solid research and analysis before reporting news, expanding critical thinking and analysis skills to be our own gatekeepers of what is real and what is not, and by not spreading unverified stories no matter how tempting it may be to do so.

News and Marketing: Which Is Which?

Though it may be difficult for some younger children to distinguish between substantive content and marketing on television—especially as marketers become better at making commercials appear to be shows in themselves—the transition between content and advertising is relatively easy to see by older children and adults. Online media today is in a different league altogether, often blending content with advertising in an effort to drive revenue to a website or to lead users to click on links that appear to be stories but in fact are part of marketing campaigns.

Online media sources today often survive on the basis of revenue earned through advertising. Consider the social media platform *Facebook*, which earns 98% of its revenue (2017) from advertising. Facebook executives may enjoy videos of your felines doing tricks, but their business model depends on their ability to convince viewers to click on ads as often as they click on cats. These sites have little obligation to evaluate the validity or accuracy of advertisements on their sites, though some have recently begun efforts to filter out potentially racist or other hateful speech with limited success.

Social media and other online sources generally have three types of materials on their sites: substantive content (e.g., news stories and editorial pieces), advertisements (e.g., clearly identified links to other sites or flyers), and **native advertising** (e.g., sponsored advertising content presented as substantive content). Native advertising is often the most difficult for viewers to distinguish because it uses design techniques and wording that make the advertisement appear very similar to a news story, and it is strategically placed alongside actual news stories. This is done to drive more viewers to click on the sponsored content and to thus drive revenue to the media site.

> Native advertising— paid advertising that mirrors the style or user experience of substantive material next to it.

Consider the two graphics in Figure 4.2 and Figure 4.3, one from the *New York Times* and another from the *Wall Street Journal*. Both of them include actual content alongside sponsored content, though distinctions between the two types of material are minimal. How easy is it for you to separate the real content from the sponsored content?

Perhaps even more difficult than distinguishing substantive content from native advertising is evaluating tweets. Twitter, especially in the United States, has become a widespread and effective tool for spreading information quickly from a number of other platforms, such as news and social media sites. Twitter has been used by politicians in the past, but the Trump Administration is the first to utilize the Twitter platform to express official political statements and opinions with constituents. This approach has given the platform more legitimacy as a means of sharing important information.

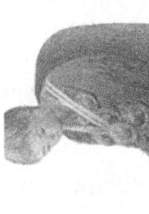  

J.M. Coetzee's Boyhood, in Black and White

Newly discovered photographs by the Nobel-winning novelist reveal a South African adolescence shaped by art and apartheid.

It's Time to Build a Less Addictive iPhone

Apple gave us the modern smartphone. Now, it can create a new take on the device by encouraging us to use it a lot less, our tech columnist writes.

Review: Gifted and Talented and Complicated

In "Off the Charts," Ann Hulbert examines the lives of child prodigies, who often fail to sustain their accomplishments, our reviewer writes.

FROM OUR ADVERTISERS

HPE
Computing's Next Big Thing?
It's happening at the edge, not in the cloud: Here's why.

AETNA
'A Holistic Approach'
Dr. Hal Paz on health care's move from the exam table to the kitchen table.

DESTINATION CANADA
Experience Unique Dining
See why Ontario is the place to please your palette.

WAZE
How Driving Changed in 2017
It's not just about getting from Point A to Point B anymore.

STANFORD CHILDREN'S HEALTH
High-Tech Children's Hospital
This hospital uses pioneering technology to treat kids.

Figure 4.2 Online Screenshot of the *New York Times* (Jan. 17, 2018).

Markets

GLOBAL MARKETS

U.S. Stocks Poised for Fresh Records as Bank Results Roll In

U.S. stocks were poised for fresh records as the earnings season continued, although markets in Europe and Asia mostly stalled after Wall Street's setback in the previous session.

PAID PROGRAM

How Cities Are Getting Smarter for Less

Advanced technologies are key to providing vital services as municipal budgets shrink.

ORACLE

Fed's Kapl Year, but S

Dallas Fed Pr Kaplan said h U.S. central b to raise inter times this yea even more to overheating.

U.S. Bank

U.S. Bancorp, regional bank country, said that the new boost its four earnings.

Figure 4.3 Online Screenshot of the *Wall Street Journal* (January 17, 2018).

Tweets are limited (as of 2018) to 240 characters. This leaves very little room for identifying sources and providing full details about assertions, leaving it up to the viewer to conduct their own research into the validity of assertions made in a tweet. However, with the ease of "retweeting" stories that we find interesting, and the limitless feed of customized tweets for our review, there is no shortage of opportunity for misleading or false stories to find their way into our Twitter feeds.

The further afield we move from clear delineations between facts and falsehoods, the closer we come to a world in which facts don't matter. Conclusions can be drawn from incorrect inferences, and decisions can be made on the basis of unsupported assertions. "Fake News" has become such a mainstream concept that the American Dialect Society named it the 2017 Word of the Year.[7] More disheartening, however, is that the proliferation of multiple news platforms with different degrees of journalistic ethics has led to the allegation of fake news against stories that are accurate but that we disagree with. Consider the following tweet from President Trump referring to a story aired on CNN:

> Jake Tapper of Fake News CNN just got destroyed in his interview with Stephen Miller of the Trump Administration. Watch the hatred and unfairness of this CNN flunky!
>
> —@realDonaldTrump, Jan. 7, 2018

Further damaging the trust in mainstream media, the Team GOP political action group lauded President Trump's "Fake News Awards" in January 2018 on their web siteand in numerous tweets, pointing out mistakes made by mainstream media as evidence that those sources propagate false information.

Major news media sites, such as CNN, the *New York Times*, National Public Radio, and the *Wall Street Journal*, have a reputation to protect in their publications.

Fake and misleading news stories on these platforms can quickly undermine trust in their reporting and dilute their brand, costing them subscribers. Non-mainstream media, such as bloggers, independent journalists, and politically motivated pundits, may build their brand off of advertising revenue, which can be driven by the number of likes and retweets that their stories receive, rather than the quality of the reporting. Some of their reporting may be highly regarded and well-researched; however, trust in journalism requires a reputation for accuracy and ethical reporting, which takes time to build.

The Society of Professional Journalists, a membership organization promoting journalistic integrity since 1909, identifies four precepts for ethical journalism:

- Seek Truth and Report It (i.e., take responsibility for work; don't sacrifice accuracy for speed; clearly identify sources);
- Minimize Harm (i.e., balance the public's need for information against potential harm; show compassion in reporting);
- Act Independently (i.e., avoid conflicts of interest; distinguish news from advertising); and,
- Be Accountable and Transparent (i.e., acknowledge mistakes and correct them).

The *New York Sun* article that we opened this section with was discredited shortly after being printed. There was no Dr. Grant, and no discoveries of life on the moon were made. However, the effects of the story continued to live on as readers persisted in the belief that the story, or at least parts of it, may have been true. Imagine the same scenario today. With the ease of retweeting, sharing, and simply skipping the hard task of critical analysis, we can serve as conduits for the perpetuation of fake news, further eliminating the line between facts and falsehoods.

Finally, if you are simply not sure about the accuracy of a story, try using a fact checker. These websites are dedicated to uncovering inaccuracies in reporting and they provide well-sourced documentation supporting their findings:

- Media Bias/Fact Check: https://mediabiasfactcheck.com
- FactCheck.org: www.factcheck.org
- Politifact: www.politifact.com
- Snopes.com: www.snopes.com
- Washington Post Fact Checker: www.washingtonpost.com/news/fact-checker/
- Hoaxy: http://hoaxy.iuni.iu.edu

Evaluating Sources

In an ideal world, every researcher would rely upon reputable, accurate research published in **peer-reviewed** scholarly journals and would use multiple sources to support each assertion of fact. However, we have to be realistic and understand the constraints upon us as researchers and work within a fast-moving information environment to capture the best possible information under the circumstances. This means that we need to become not only critical analysts but critical researchers as well.

> Peer-reviewed—evaluation by scholars of written submissions to assess the quality of the claims made in those submissions.

The gold standard in any research project is a peer-reviewed journal. These are publications that have built a reputation on accurate and well-sourced articles published by knowledgeable authors whose work has undergone double-blind review by experts in the field. Simply speaking, this means that the publication has been carefully checked to ensure that its assertions are well-supported, arguments are sound and logical, and that the conclusion follows from the asserted premises. This review is performed without any knowledge of the author or his or her affiliation, making it as unbiased as possible. The ultimate publication of a piece in a peer-reviewed journal does not speak to the importance of the claims or their relevance to current events—only to the soundness and structure of the article.

Peer-reviewed articles can be found online and in libraries. Online, they are accessible using a number of research databases, such as Lexis, ProQuest, and JSTOR. Many academic institutions provide access to these databases to their students. The database chosen usually depends on the field of study (e.g., Lexis for legal research). Articles are usually available directly from the journal website as well. Abstracts can usually be viewed free of charge, but downloading an article is often associated with a fee.

Determining whether an article is published in a peer-reviewed journal can be tricky. Just as a plethora of online media sources have appeared in recent years, online journals have also littered the research landscape. Here are a few things to look for when evaluating whether a journal is peer-reviewed and, even if it is, whether it is a wise choice for your research:

- On the journal's home page (or inside the cover of the print journal), look for language that identifies the journal as "peer-reviewed," "double-blind peer-reviewed," or "refereed."
- On the journal's submission page for authors, look for fees or credential requirements. Paying to download an article is reasonable, but some journals include a submission fee for authors—this is often a sign of less-reputable journals.
- Journals and magazines are often confused. Advertisements and non-research materials can be a sign that you are looking at a magazine rather than a journal.

It is important to note that some scholarly materials are not "peer-reviewed" by definition, but are equally valuable as research sources. These include law journals and law reviews, which are scholarly publications that utilize an editorial board to screen and evaluate the sources for submitted articles; many government documents, including legislation, regulations, and reports by government agencies; and reports by independent think tanks, which apply rigorous standards to their research and analysis, though they often write from one point of view and thus should be evaluated for bias. These are trustworthy research sources alongside your peer-reviewed journal articles.

Access to quality research is much easier today than in the past. Libraries used to be the principal place to conduct research, but today researchers can work from the comfort of their home to find everything a library might contain and more. But the researcher runs the high risk of finding and relying upon inaccurate or misleading research sources. The following tips may help to keep researchers focused on finding the most accurate materials for their research:

- Rather than *Googling* a research question, use an academically focused research database, such as *Google Scholar* (scholar.google.com);
- Apply the CRAAP method (discussed earlier) for evaluating the validity of any source that you intend to utilize;

118   *Separating Facts and Fiction*

- Never rely on a single source to support a significant assertion;
- News articles, blogs, and non-mainstream media sources can be used to inspire your research, but must always be supported by scholarly sources, such as journal articles and government reports; and,
- Try to have at least one scholarly source linked to each assertion of fact in your document.

The final step in the process of becoming an effective researcher is learning how to approach the research task. That is, how do you get started once you decide that you want to prepare a research analysis? We will approach this in the next section.

Developing a Research Plan

Thus far, we have discussed the importance of critical analysis in your research and review of daily news, social media, and scholarly works. We have also discussed how to separate fact from fiction when reviewing content. And lastly, we discussed the selection of sources to effectively provide structure to your own arguments and analysis. We conclude this chapter with a practical approach to developing the strongest and most effective arguments in your research papers, editorials, business reports, and every other analytical document that you create.

1. *Check your bias at the door.* No matter the issue, unless we have never been exposed to it before, we will have an underlying bias tilting us in one way or another toward a given outcome. Allowing this bias to creep into our analysis will lead us to favor certain sources over others, diminish the value of counterarguments, and interpret data more favorably when it supports our own beliefs. At the outset of your research, take a moment to write down how you personally feel about this topic. Be expressive and as opinionated as you want. Review what you've written and think about how your opinion might sway you toward a certain outcome in your research. Hold on to that document and refer to it regularly to remind you that bias ruins good research. Your search should ensure that you find sources that reflect arguments contrary to your own opinions, even if you disagree with them.
2. *Learn the language.* Today, many of us believe that we are experts in most things that we speak about, especially on social media. But to truly become an expert, a researcher has to first understand the language surrounding the research topic. Knowing the correct terminology is another way to avoid bias in our research. For instance, if we were researching immigration and we used search terms such as "illegal immigrant," we would be directed to more conservative media outlets. If we used the term "dreamer," we would be directed to more liberal media outlets. Our goal is to understand the neutral language that is used by researchers in order to find sources that let facts, rather than opinions, make their case. To do this, look for scholarly publications by using very bland search terms in your searches, such as "immigration" or "alien," and skim the text of those sources in search of terminology that will help you formulate your own focused search later. Become an expert by learning the language early on in your research process.
3. *Cast a wide net to start.* One of the problems with powerful databases is that they can bring us to key articles too quickly. That's right—*too* quickly. An

effective researcher does a good job in crafting narrow search terms that a good database will use to spit out one or two perfect articles to use as sources. The issue here is that the researcher likely left behind many equally important research articles that were missed by being too narrow in their search. My search for "protection of deferred action recipients" will lead me straight to the regulations affecting this class of immigrants, but it will also miss the many key issues related to this topic, such as executive power, alien work authorization, and legal status. A broader-based search at the outset allows you to use general search terms (from step 2) to begin identifying the range of possible sub-issues you will want to address. Skim the abstracts from the results of your broad searches and set aside those articles or links that you will want to revisit later. Anticipate about five sources per page of writing (e.g., a 20-page research paper assignment should yield about 100 articles to skim).

4. *Develop a focused search*. Now that you have a broad perspective on the topic, you need to begin narrowing down your sources to include only those that are most applicable and relevant to your research topic. The purpose of this narrowing process is to avoid taking the reader of your argument off on too many tangents. Your review of the abstracts from the sources that you already found should have given you a better sense of not only the language used around your topic area but also the key sub-issues. For instance, in my immigration research, I may have found discussions about the scope of executive power over immigration as well as the power of Congress to delegate certain constitutional powers to the executive historically. With these sub-issues in mind, use more complex searches to identify a more limited pool of results that match your criteria. I might search for the following: "executive power over immigration," for instance. And rather than using a broad search engine like Google Scholar, try to use a narrow search engine like Lexis or ProQuest to ensure that you only receive scholarly articles in the output. You should find about two articles for every page of text here.

5. *Keep track of your sources*. As you may have noticed, your research plan is intended to introduce you to many sources to support your analysis. It is easy to mix up sources and misplace ones that you reviewed. There are many ways to avoid the problem of knowing that you read it *somewhere* but not remembering where. For short research papers, I suggest printing out the first page and abstract of each source that you may use. Keep these in a research folder for the project that you are working on and add hand-written notes on those printouts to remind you of the context of the source. For longer pieces, develop an annotated bibliography. This is where you create an electronic document in which you list the citation for the source (or a weblink) and a sentence or two describing the content of that source. This is good for mid-sized research papers. Finally, for lengthier publications, theses, and dissertations, consider using software such as Zoltero or EndNote, both of which integrate nicely into word processing software to allow you to call upon the same source many times in the same document without having to dig through your files to find it.

6. *Check for balanced sources*. By this point, you likely have most of your research complete. Now is a good time to go back and ensure that you have all sides of the issue included. Picture yourself in a dressing room trying on a new outfit in front of three mirrors. Each mirror gives you a different

perspective and a potentially new piece of information to discuss. All of those perspectives are important in a complete analysis, and taking contrary positions into account will show that you have approached your research with a critical eye and a fair and balanced focus. Revisit your opinions from step 1 and ensure that you have included sources that contradict your line of thinking. Don't discount research that is disagreeable to you. So long as the source is reputable, that very research will give your article balance and completeness, reducing the chance that readers of your research will see only a one-sided analysis.

Closing Case: The Allegory of the Cave

> Imagine this: People live under the earth in a cavelike dwelling. Stretching a long way up toward the daylight is its entrance, toward which the entire cave is gathered. The people have been in this dwelling since childhood, shackled by the legs and neck. Thus they stay in the same place so that there is only one thing for them to look that: whatever they encounter in front of their faces. But because they are shackled, they are unable to turn their heads around.
>
> Some light, of course, is allowed them, namely from a fire that casts its glow toward them from behind them, being above and at some distance. Between the fire and those who are shackled [i.e., behind their backs] there runs a walkway at a certain height. Imagine that a low wall has been built the length of the walkway, like the low curtain that puppeteers put up, over which they show their puppets.
>
> So now imagine that all along this low wall people are carrying all sorts of things that reach up higher than the wall: statues and other carvings made of stone or wood and many other artifacts that people have made. As you would expect, some are talking to each other [as they walk along] and some are silent.
>
> . . . From the beginning people like this have never managed, whether on their own or with the help by others, to see anything besides the shadows that are [continually] projected on the wall opposite them by the glow of the fire.[8]

Sometimes it is difficult to see beyond what is right in front of us. Social media feeds us what it wants us to see; cable news broadcasts air what they believe will be most watched; and even conversations become talking points rather than critical analyses. Plato wrote about this problem 2,500 years ago by using an analogy—people raised to believe that what was right in front of them was reality without considering the possibility that there was more to the story than that.

Plato's story continued beyond the excerpt to discuss what would happen if these prisoners were freed and shown the daylight outside the cave. He describes how painful it would be to see the light and to discover the reality beyond the shadows. He considers this to be analogous to the attainment of true knowledge—facts. And he closes the story by asking what would happen if an informed person who broke free from the cave returned to tell the others that their reality is actually false: "And if they can get hold of this person who takes it in hand to free them from their chains and to lead them up, and if they could kill him, will they not actually kill him?"[9] As we have seen so often in modern times, even if we are aware of facts, convincing others of those facts may not only be difficult; it may result in such fierce rejection that a dispute could arise. Living with the shadows we know is often easier than trying to learn the truth of the matter.

Conclusion

Explain this to me like I'm a six-year old.
—- Attorney Joe Miller (played by Denzel Washington) in *Philadelphia* (1993)

If there is one thing that you take away from this chapter, it should be that critical thinking requires you to break down an argument into its simplest form so that you can see it for what it really is. Take away the rhetoric, the flowery language, the charts and graphs, and look at what is left. Take what remains and poke it and prod it until you understand not just what is being said, but why it is being said. Become a critical analyst in everything you write and in everything you read.

Critical Thinking and Analysis Exercises

Exercise 1: Evaluating the Validity of a Tweet

Review the tweet in Figure 4.4 from MoveOn.org. The tweet appears intended to persuade viewers about the accuracy of the assertion. If you were quickly reviewing your newsfeed and you agreed with this tweet, would you share it with others (i.e., retweet)? Now, take the time to evaluate the assertion. What elements of the tweet would you use to help you assess its validity and reliability?

Figure 4.4 Tweet from MoveOn.org, Nov. 17, 2015.

122 *Separating Facts and Fiction*

Exercise 2: Evaluating the Accuracy of an Article Found in a Database

Using one of the research databases discussed earlier (e.g., Google Scholar, JSTOR), search for the following scholarly article. Apply the techniques developed in this chapter to assess the validity of the claims made by the article as well as the reliability of the publication. Skim the article and explain how you might use this source in your own research (i.e., what assertions would you make on the basis of this source?).

Jennifer Hunt, *The Impact of Immigration on the Educational Attainment of Natives*, 52 Journal of Human Resources 1060 (2017).

Exercise 3: Evaluate a Claim

How concerned are you about the presence of high-fructose corn syrup in your food and beverages? Many states and cities have attempted to limit the use of this sugar alternative due to claims that it is higher in calories than natural sugar and that it can lead to obesity, increasing the costs of healthcare on communities. Do you believe those claims? Review the following article and then conduct research using at least two scholarly sources to evaluate the claim.

Dr. Mark Hyman, *Why You Should Never Eat High Fructose Corn Syrup*, Huffington Post, Nov. 12, 2013, www.huffingtonpost.com/dr-mark-hyman/high-fructose-corn-syrup_b_4256220.html

Exercise 4: Evaluate an Online News Story

Examine the story headline and graphic in Figure 4.5, which was initially published online using the imgur.com platform and subsequently published in the

Figure 4.5 UK Mirror, July 23, 2015.

British periodical, the *Mirror*, among other sites. Without conducting any additional research, what do you conclude from this news headline? Access the article using the following link and evaluate the claims made in that article. Without doing additional research, what do you conclude about the author's assertions? Finally, using Google Scholar or a similar search engine, investigate the claims made in the article. What did you discover, and does this change your opinion about the original article?

Link to Article: www.mirror.co.uk/news/world-news/fukushima-disaster-mutant-flowers-found-6123991

Notes

1. Alan Rappeport, *Democrats Add Momentum to G.O.P. Push to Loosen Banking Rules*, N.Y. Times, Jan. 15, 2018.
2. John Dewey, *How We Think* (1909).
3. Statement by Michael Scriven and Richard Paul, Presented at the 8th Annual International Conference on Critical Thinking and Education Reform, Summer 1987.
4. Barry Beyer, *Critical Thinking* (1995).
5. Sarah Blakeslee, *The CRAAP Test*, 31 LOEX Quarterly 6 (2004).
6. Darrell M. West, *How to Combat Fake News and Disinformation*, Brookings Institute (Dec. 18, 2017), www.brookings.edu/research/how-to-combat-fake-news-and-disinformation/
7. American Dialect Society, *'Fake News' Is 2017 American Dialect Society Word of the Year*, Jan. 5, 2018, www.americandialect.org/fake-news-is-2017-american-dialect-society-word-of-the-year
8. Plato, The Allegory of the Cave, *Republic*, VII (trans. Thomas Sheehan).
9. Id.

Additional Learning Resources

Additional Readings

Judith Binder, *Primary Research Tips and Techniques: Going beyond Online Searching*, 41.1 Online Searcher 10 (2017).

Stephan D. Brookfield, *Teaching for Critical Thinking: Tools and Techniques to Help Students Question Their Assumptions* (2012).

Natasha Holmes, et al., *Teaching Critical Thinking*, 112 Proceedings of the Nat'l Acad. of Sci. 11199 (2015).

David Hunter, *A Practical Guide to Critical Thinking: Deciding What to Do and Believe* (2014).

[Video] Katrina Sifferd, *Introduction to Philosophy: Critical Thinking and Logical Reasoning* (Discovery Education Film, 2012), www.films.com/ecTitleDetail.aspx?TitleID=119161

5 Economic Law and Policy

Introductory Case

"The only thing certain in life is death and taxes." But perhaps taxes are less certain than we thought. Prior to the 16th Amendment to the U.S. Constitution, which authorized Congress to tax individual income tax in order to fund government programs, the government was largely funded by tariffs on imported goods. When foreign manufacturers wanted to get their goods onto the U.S. market, they would be forced to pay significant taxes upon arrival, which in turn resulted in higher prices for their goods. Revenue from these import taxes increased following the second industrial revolution at the end of the 19th century, and tax rates came down, allowing U.S. consumers to more affordably purchase imported products. By the turn of the 20th century, however, it became clear that lower taxes on imported goods not only meant more access to those goods by U.S. consumers, but it also meant reciprocation by which our trading partners would lower their taxes on our exported goods. It was a win-win for businesses and consumers; however, it was a major loss of revenue to the U.S. government.

In 1913, the 16th Amendment passed, which allowed Congress to collect income taxes from individuals, an act that had previously been forbidden by law. This Amendment reflected a growing realization that import taxes caused more harm than good and restricted access to foreign goods and foreign markets, while also recognizing that an alternative mechanism was necessary to fund the federal government. Hence, the income tax was created, which today serves as the primary mechanism for keeping the government operating and funding the many programs that it took on since its inception.

Since passage of the 16th Amendment, debate has grown over tax policy, from conservative opinions pushing to reduce or eliminate income taxes as unlawful takings, to liberals arguing for broader or at least more egalitarian taxation that enables the funding of more social programs. These debates tend to center around a basic public policy question—what should the role of a central government be and how expansive should it be in individual affairs? While some see the federal government as the go-to solution for everything that ails the nation from poverty to health to infrastructure, others see it as an unnecessary obstruction to the progress of the free market and an unnecessary bureaucracy that is holding back economic growth.

Most economists support the idea of some taxation in order to provide essential programs for the country, such as national security, foreign policy, infrastructure, and in many cases, poverty alleviation. And the vast majority of economists agree that income taxes are preferred over import taxes. However, a small contingent of economists believe that income taxes (and import taxes) are not required to fund a central government. One of these proponents is Arthur Laffer.

Laffer popularized an idea from the 14th century that suggests that cutting income taxes will increase government revenue by unleashing the power of business growth and collecting a more substantial amount of tax from those businesses (though at a lower rate of taxation). Laffer argued that the higher the tax rate, the less incentive there is to operate or expand business operations. Thus, as a central government lowers their income tax rate, they are encouraging businesses to earn more revenue, which in turn will generate more taxes for the government. Like many economic concepts that we will discuss in this chapter, this theory is based on a number of likely unrealistic assumptions, such as a single marginal tax rate, a business environment capable of expansion, and potential revenue gains equal to or exceeding the losses realized with the lower tax rate. Yet putting those aside for now, we can examine a real-world application of this theory in the form of public policy.

Governor Sam Brownback of Kansas, a conservative, believed that the Laffer theory may be just the policy to jumpstart the stagnant Kansas state economy. Brownback sought the advice of Laffer on helping his economy to recover, and Laffer encouraged him to pursue supply-side economics, the policy by which growth comes from market freedom rather than taxation.[1] Laffer told Governor Brownback that states with no income tax (there are seven)[2] fare better economically *because* they have no income tax. Most economists disagree with this position and attribute their success to alternative revenue sources, such as oil or tourism.[3] Laffer, who was already influential within conservative circles and who served as an economic advisor to Ronald Reagan and an influencer to most Republicans after that, including Donald Trump, advised Brownback to slash income taxes in order to generate growth. Brownback did just that in what became known as the "Kansas Experiment."[4]

The Speaker of the House in Kansas, upon passage of the tax cut law, said:

> By reforming income taxes in Kansas, our state will start building a solid tax foundation that will create a strong economy for the years to come. We must continue down a path that brings prosperity to the residents of Kansas and HB 2117 will move our state toward a healthy and vibrant economy.

Specifically, HB 2117 (2012) collapsed the three-tier tax system taxes (rates of 3.5%, 6.25%, and 6.45%) into a two-tier system (rates of 3.0% and 4.9%). Some non-wage business income earned by small businesses was eliminated from the tax system, such as income earned by limited liability companies. And the law increased the standard tax deduction from $4,500 to $9,000 (single head of household) and $6,000 to $9,000 (married filing jointly). Estimates at the time on the high end projected growth through the creation of 22,000 jobs and more than $2 billion in additional individual income. However, skeptics predicted a budget shortfall within two years with a $2.5 billion deficit by 2018. Governor Brownback signed the bill into law in May 2012.

The real-world policy experiment of implementing supply-side, also known as trickle-down economics, in Kansas turned out to be a failure. The economic ramifications were quickly felt, though the political fallout took years to emerge. By 2014, Kansas was already running a deficit of roughly $600 million. Despite this shortfall and the below-average job growth in Kansas since the experiment began, Brownback won reelection in this largely conservative state. Immediately after being reelected in 2014, Governor Brownback, who had not significantly cut spending on government programs to account for the deficit, had to find other sources of revenue. He cut funding for education and ultimately proposed an increase in sales taxes and sin taxes (e.g., taxes on cigarettes).[5]

The deficit worsened and the economic experiment appeared to be failing as a public policy. When asked at the time why the experiment was not working, Laffer emphasized that analysts need to play the long game and view the data over at least ten years. Unfortunately, politicians rarely have that long to show that a policy can work. In February 2017, the Kansas Republican-led legislature passed a $1 billion tax increase to close the budget gap, but Brownback vetoed the increase. In March 2017, the Kansas Supreme Court ruled that the government was unconstitutionally underfunding public schools, causing disproportionately negative effects for black and Latino students.[6] And finally, in June 2017, Kansas legislators voted again to raise taxes by $1.2 billion, and they secured enough votes to override Governor Brownback's veto.[7]

The experiment was over.

Overview/Background

This chapter begins our exploration of topical issues. In each of these topics, we will begin with a look at historical elements that inform our current state of affairs. For instance, this chapter will explain competing economic theories in the early 20th century that led to a battle over liberal and conservative economic philosophies, which resonate more than ever in present-day policymaking. Following that brief history, we will use issue statements about key areas, such as trade policy, tax policy, or minimum wage policy, to develop a targeted policy analysis of key areas. Each area will include cases, statutes, and regulations, where appropriate, bridging the policy (idea) and law (application) divide.

Discussion Questions

What circumstances gave rise to the first period of economic regulation in the United States, and what impact did those regulations have on the economy?

Discuss the similarities and differences between economic policies in capitalist, socialist, and communist countries.

Which case would you say had the most substantial impact on the regulatory environment and why?

Economic Law and Policy

> Economics—the study of the production, consumption and transfer of wealth.

Economics refers to the study of the production, consumption, and transfer of wealth. In other words, the elements that make an economy function. As a concept, economics has been studied for centuries. But as a science, economics is a relatively young field, with research into the effects of different approaches to economic policy only beginning in the late 18th century. In this chapter, we will examine the history of economic policy by examining economic models prior to the establishment of "modern economics." We will then delve into economic policy—a dry-sounding concept but one of the most important areas of study in our policy environment. And finally, we will tackle one of the most perplexing problems of modern-day economics—inequality: why do some have more than others, and how does economic policy explain this?

Economic History: The Mercantilist Period

The same year that the United States proclaimed its independence from England, Adam Smith published his first text on economics, known as the *Wealth and Poverty of Nations*. This is arguably the first book examining economics through a scientific lens rather than a political one. And although the idea of rational economic policies had already been catching on in some economies, his work symbolized the beginning of a new era of economic progress based upon rational insights.

But Smith's text was not the beginning of our economic history. It is important that we go back just a bit before Smith to understand why we needed this scientific approach to markets and how that transformed what we had done for many years prior.

We begin with the theory of **mercantilism**, which guided many governments from the 16th through the 18th centuries, approximately. At its core, the theory of mercantilism positions the state at the center of the market, making it the driver of production, consumption, and wealth within its borders. The central government, often a monarch, set policies in accordance with its relationships with its neighbors rather than based upon market conditions. Access to foreign goods and services, then, depended upon royal relations.

Nationalism and **protectionism** were critical in the mercantilist model. Since economic growth and market expansion were not going to be driven by trade, it became important to protect domestic production from competition by foreign entities. This meant closing off access to domestic markets and blocking imports through taxes and heavy regulation. The policy goal was to increase reserves of precious metals (principally gold), which could be used to fund conquests and invest in the domestic economy.

Mercantilism is often discussed alongside **bullionism**, or the economic policy of pursuing precious metals. However, it should be clarified that mercantilism as an economic theory centered on wealth accumulation not simply to fill its vaults with gold bars, but rather to invest in the domestic market and facilitate growth in the absence of open trade.

The two principal ways for a government to increase its gold reserves are conquest and exports. The colonial period, during which mercantilism was particularly popular, enabled some European countries to leverage their military might toward this end by laying claim to foreign lands in Africa, Asia, and the Americas. Some of these colonizations were brutal; others less so. But all had the goal of extracting wealth from those colonies in order to enrich the mother country. An example of this pursuit of trade with colonies is the British East India Company (see Box 5.1).

> Mercantilism—an economic theory that defines wealth by the quantity of financial reserves.

> Nationalism—an emphasis on domestic pride and superiority over other countries.
>
> Protectionism—shielding domestic industry from competition through tariffs or other barriers.
>
> Bullionism—an economic theory that measures wealth by the quantity of precious metals owned.

Box 5.1: East India Company

British merchants came to control much of the trade between England and Southeast Asia following the 1588 defeat of the Spanish Armada. One group of merchants wisely sought a monopoly charter from Queen Elizabeth I of England to control merchant trade along these sea routes. The charter, granted in 1600, gave them exclusive control over trade with Southeast Asia and, principally, China. The British East India Company, as it was known, came to control 50% of world trade. They ventured into politics in the mid-18th century when they took control over the Bengal province of India. This grew into control over most of India and the beginnings of British rule over the country, which officially began in 1858. The Company charter was dissolved in 1874 due to financial problems.

The second way for a government to increase its gold reserves is to export more than it imports. Selling more of what a country produces to foreign buyers than that country buys from foreign sellers will result in a trade surplus—more gold will flow to the home country, thereby expanding its gold reserves. This can happen naturally when a country produces high-value goods that are in high demand by foreign buyers, but it is more likely to happen with government intervention. In this case, intervention meant regulations and trade barriers.

One of the earliest trade regulations that facilitated the mercantilist ideals of the time was the **British Navigation Acts**. These Acts, issued originally in 1651 and revised in subsequent years, were an effort by England to secure trade routes between England and its colonies. At the time, the Dutch posed a significant threat to the growing British Empire, a threat that was exacerbated by successful Dutch trade policies.

> British Navigation Acts—British legislation designed to strengthen control over trade between Britain and its colonies.

The first application of these Acts to block Dutch traders led to the Anglo-Dutch war in 1652, which was England's attempt to enforce the Navigation Acts and prevent Dutch merchant ships from trading with English colonies in the Americas. That war, fought entirely at sea, led the English navy to capture as many as 100 Dutch merchant ships and to further strengthen English trade routes.

The Navigation Acts, revised following the Anglo-Dutch war and the return to an English monarchy, enhanced English wealth by imposing taxes on all goods exported to or from British colonies. Any ship carrying commodities such as tobacco or sugar—principal exports from the colonies in the Americas—would have to pass through an English port first, even if their destination was Europe or elsewhere in the world, and pay a tax, which was collected by the crown. In addition, all ships trading with the British colonies had to be staffed with 75% Englishmen. These two restrictions aggravated merchants in the British colonies, as well as Dutch and other European merchants. However, it helped to secure England's position as an economic empire.

Mercantilism's fatal flaw was likely that it focused on enriching the state through a large empire, large military, and wealthy monarch rather than through the creation of wealth-building opportunities for a broader segment of the population. Some businessmen, through their political connections, could enrich themselves by becoming monopolists authorized to control certain sectors of the economy by the state, further disenfranchising the broader population. This approach led to a clear division between those who worked in order to support the crown and those who ruled the economic environment.

By the late 1700s, frustration with taxation and regulation reached a fever pitch, and many of the crown's subjects, particularly in the colonies, rebelled. In part, their rebellion against economic repression stemmed from the ideas circulating around a new economic model—**laissez-faire economics**. Roughly translated as "allow to do," *laissez faire* as an economic theory meant minimal government intervention in the marketplace—allowing free enterprise to grow without the constraints of extensive government regulation or oversight.

> Laissez-faire economics—an economic theory emphasizing free market policies and minimal government intervention in the economy.

It is important to note that these ideas, codified in the seminal work of Adam Smith, were not a call to throw off government completely. Rather, they reflected a reaction to overregulation of the markets and unfair practices with respect to trade. Smith himself supported the Navigation Acts, for instance, finding them to be an effective means of funding the government. But he also despised the monopolists, who were also preventing free and fair competition in the marketplace. Some economists have likened Smith's ideas to the Keynesian theory of the 20th century (discussed later). We will examine his ideas in more detail in the following section.

Capitalism and Free Markets

Adam Smith, often called the "Father of Economics," developed a theory of the market that emphasized trade as the driver of economic growth, rather than wealth accumulation. He developed the idea that through trade—with colonies and neighboring countries—an economy would be able to efficiently capitalize on its resources and create sustainable, long-term growth. Precious metals are an exhaustible resource, and they do not lead to economic development—only economic enrichment, and only for a short time.

To achieve sustainable economic growth, Smith focused on the theory of **absolute advantage**, which broke down the global marketplace into assets—land, labor, and capital. Each country has its own mix of those assets, and each mix results in certain production advantages. A country with large amounts of labor, for instance, might be able to produce labor-intensive goods, such as agriculture, more efficiently than countries with lower levels of labor. In such a country, Smith recommends devoting resources to the production of those advantageous goods in order to become even more efficient at doing so in order to trade with the world. That country would then export its agriculture and import most other things, produced by its more efficient trading partners, thereby maximizing the resource advantages of the world.

> Absolute advantage—an economic theory suggesting that a country should devote resources to the production of goods it can produce more efficiently than its trade partners.

According to this theory, if every country focuses on producing what it can produce best and trading that product with the rest of the world, then global markets will operate at their most efficient level. It does not necessarily mean that every country will grow equally wealthy or benefit from producing what they are best at producing. Rather, it will result in efficient world markets in the aggregate, yielding the best possible system of economic growth.

An important caveat to Smith's theory is that it depends on government non-intervention. This is where the concept of **free market capitalism** emerges from. Government regulations interfere with the *invisible hand* of the free market, which, according to Smith, guides the economy toward its natural equilibrium. The natural equilibrium is a state of affairs in which the market is operating efficiently and allocating resources appropriately. Since markets are neither moral nor self-serving, Smith believed that the incentives and disincentives to consume and produce in the marketplace would naturally drive stable and sustainable economic growth, and that government intervention, which creates artificial barriers to supply and demand, would interfere with that natural balance.

> Free market capitalism—an economic system in which the government plays a minimal.

Smith's absolute advantage theory has been modified over the years, including by David Ricardo, who posited that countries should look for **comparative advantages** relative to their trading partners rather than absolute global advantages in trade, and Robert Solow who added technology to the list of **factors of production**. But in essence, this economic theory has guided the laws and policies of capitalist countries from the 19th century through today.

> Comparative advantage—an economic theory suggesting that a country should devote resources to the production of goods it can produce at a lower opportunity cost than its trade partners.

Economics and the Regulatory State

Although Smith did not envision a non-existent government, he did long for a government that had limited involvement in the marketplace, allowing market forces to drive growth in the direction that markets see fit. That vision was not realized in any particular country to the degree promoted by Smith. Governments around the world adopted free market economics to some extent, but continued to play an important role in driving the direction of their markets by imposing regulations and taxes on certain industries and activities.

> Factors of production—traditionally, this refers to land, labor and capital. Today, it also includes entrepreneurship.

The United States had the advantage of being a young country that was born after many of the precepts of mercantilism were being abandoned in favor of free market economics. The founding fathers were keen on ensuring that the central government allowed entrepreneurs to take risks without the worries of an intrusive government. One of the clearest indications that the early U.S. government would follow the free market approach to governance is the U.S. Constitution itself.

One example of the protection that the new central government would provide to business came in a famous case dealing with navigation licenses—monopoly rights to exclusive trade along a river, in this case, the Hudson River. The case is well known because it reflected the desire at the time to prevent states from discriminating against out-of-state businesses by consolidating much of the power over trade within the federal government.

Gibbons v. Ogden

In 1808, New York granted a monopoly license to Robert Livingston and Robert Fulton to control navigation of the waters within the jurisdiction of New York. They requested similar licenses from other states but were unsuccessful in most cases. To undercut competition, Livingston and Fulton bought the boats of competitors and licensed franchisees who could operate by contract under their monopoly. Aaron Ogden purchased one of those licenses in 1815 and partnered with Thomas Gibbons to run a business along a water route in New York. The partnership failed but Gibbons maintained his right to operate his boats in New York, claiming that he had authorization under a 1793 federal boating law. Ogden sued Gibbons.

As preliminary to the very able discussions of the Constitution which we have heard from the bar, and as having some influence on its construction, reference has been made to the political situation of these States anterior to its formation. It has been said that they were sovereign, were completely independent, and were connected with each other only by a league. This is true. But, when these allied sovereigns converted their league into a government, when they converted their Congress of Ambassadors, deputed to deliberate on their common concerns and to recommend measures of general utility, into a Legislature, empowered to enact laws on the most interesting subjects, the whole character in which the States appear underwent a change, the extent of which must be determined by a fair consideration of the instrument by which that change was effected.

This instrument [the Constitution] contains an enumeration of powers expressly granted by the people to their government. It has been said that these powers ought to be construed strictly. But why ought they to be so construed? Is there one sentence in the Constitution which gives countenance to this rule? In the last of the enumerated powers, that which grants expressly the means for carrying all others into execution, Congress is authorized "to make all laws which shall be necessary and proper" for the purpose. But this limitation on the means which may be used is not extended to the powers which are conferred, nor is there one sentence in the Constitution which has been pointed out by the gentlemen of the bar or which we have been able to discern that prescribes this rule. We do not, therefore, think ourselves justified in adopting it. What do gentlemen mean by a "strict construction?" If they contend only against that enlarged construction, which would extend words beyond their natural and obvious import, we might question the application of the term, but should not controvert the principle. If they contend for that narrow construction which, in support or some theory not to be found in the Constitution, would deny to the government those powers which the words of the grant, as usually understood, import, and which are consistent with the general views and objects of the instrument; for that narrow construction which would cripple the government and render it unequal to the object for which it is declared to be instituted, and to which the powers given, as fairly understood, render it competent; then we cannot perceive the propriety of this strict construction, nor adopt it as the rule by which the Constitution is to be expounded. As men whose intentions require no concealment generally employ the words which most directly and aptly express the ideas they intend to convey, the enlightened patriots who framed our Constitution, and the people who adopted it, must be understood to have employed words in their natural sense, and to have intended what they have said. If, from the imperfection of human language, there should be serious doubts respecting the extent of any given power, it is a well settled rule that the objects for which it was given, especially when those objects are expressed in the instrument itself, should have great influence in the construction. We know of no reason for excluding this rule from the present case. The grant does not convey power which might be beneficial to the grantor if retained by himself, or which can enure solely to the benefit of the grantee, but is an investment of power for the general advantage, in the hands of agents selected for that purpose, which power can never be exercised by the people themselves, but must be placed in the hands of agents or lie dormant. We know of no rule for construing the extent of such powers other than is given by the language of the instrument which confers them, taken in connexion with the purposes for which they were conferred.

The words are, "Congress shall have power to regulate commerce with foreign nations, and among the several States, and with the Indian tribes."

The subject to be regulated is commerce, and our Constitution being, as was aptly said at the bar, one of enumeration, and not of definition, to ascertain the extent of the power, it becomes necessary to settle the meaning of the word. The counsel for the appellee would limit it to traffic, to buying and selling, or the interchange of commodities, and do not admit that it comprehends navigation. This would restrict a general term, applicable to many objects, to one of its significations. Commerce, undoubtedly, is traffic, but it is something more: it is intercourse. It describes the commercial intercourse between nations, and parts of nations, in all its branches, and is regulated by prescribing rules for carrying on that intercourse. The mind can scarcely conceive a system for regulating commerce between nations which shall exclude all laws concerning navigation, which shall be silent on the admission of the vessels of the one nation into the ports of the other, and be confined to prescribing rules for the conduct of individuals in the actual employment of buying and selling or of barter.

If commerce does not include navigation, the government of the Union has no direct power over that subject, and can make no law prescribing what shall constitute American vessels or requiring that they shall be navigated by American seamen. Yet this power has been exercised from the commencement of the government, has been exercised with the consent of all, and has been understood by all to be a commercial regulation. All America understands, and has uniformly understood, the word "commerce" to comprehend navigation. It was so understood, and must have been so understood, when the Constitution was framed. The power over commerce, including navigation, was one of the primary objects for which the people of America adopted their government, and must have been contemplated in forming it. The convention must have used the word in that sense, because all have understood it in that sense, and the attempt to restrict it comes too late.

If the opinion that "commerce," as the word is used in the Constitution, comprehends navigation also, requires any additional confirmation, that additional confirmation is, we think, furnished by the words of the instrument itself.

***

The word used in the Constitution, then, comprehends, and has been always understood to comprehend, navigation within its meaning, and a power to regulate navigation is as expressly granted as if that term had been added to the word "commerce."

To what commerce does this power extend? The Constitution informs us, to commerce "with foreign nations, and among the several States, and with the Indian tribes."

It has, we believe, been universally admitted that these words comprehend every species of commercial intercourse between the United States and foreign nations. No sort of trade can be carried on between this country and any other to which this power does not extend. It has been truly said that "commerce," as the word is used in the Constitution, is a unit every part of which is indicated by the term.

If this be the admitted meaning of the word in its application to foreign nations, it must carry the same meaning throughout the sentence, and remain a unit, unless there be some plain intelligible cause which alters it.

The subject to which the power is next applied is to commerce "among the several States." The word "among" means intermingled with. A thing which is among others is intermingled with them. Commerce among the States cannot stop at the external boundary line of each State, but may be introduced into the interior.

It is not intended to say that these words comprehend that commerce which is completely internal, which is carried on between man and man in a State, or between different parts of the same State, and which does not extend to or affect other States. Such a power would be inconvenient, and is certainly unnecessary.

Comprehensive as the word "among" is, it may very properly be restricted to that commerce which concerns more States than one. The phrase is not one which would probably have been selected to indicate the completely interior traffic of a State, because it is not an apt phrase for that purpose, and the enumeration of the particular classes of commerce to which the power was to be extended would not have been made had the intention been to extend the power to every description. The enumeration presupposes something not enumerated, and that something, if we regard the language or the subject of the sentence, must be the exclusively internal commerce of a State. The genius and character of the whole government seem to be that its action is to be applied to all the external concerns of the nation, and to those internal concerns which affect the States generally, but not to those which are completely within a particular State, which do not affect other States, and with which it is not necessary to interfere for the purpose of executing some of the general powers of the government. The completely internal commerce of a State, then, may be considered as reserved for the State itself.

But, in regulating commerce with foreign nations, the power of Congress does not stop at the jurisdictional lines of the several States. It would be a very useless power if it could not pass those lines. The commerce of the United States with foreign nations is that of the whole United States.

Every district has a right to participate in it. The deep streams which penetrate our country in every direction pass through the interior of almost every State in the Union, and furnish the means of exercising this right. If Congress has the power to regulate it, that power must be exercised whenever the subject exists. If it exists within the States, if a foreign voyage may commence or terminate at a port within a State, then the power of Congress may be exercised within a State.

This principle is, if possible, still more clear, when applied to commerce "among the several States." They either join each other, in which case they are separated by a mathematical line, or they are remote from each other, in which case other States lie between them. What is commerce "among" them, and how is it to be conducted? Can a trading expedition between two adjoining States, commence and terminate outside of each? And if the trading intercourse be between two States remote from each other, must it not commence in one, terminate in the other, and probably pass through a third? Commerce among the States must, of necessity, be commerce with the States. In the regulation of trade with the Indian tribes, the action of the law, especially when the Constitution was made, was chiefly within a State. The power of Congress, then, whatever it may be, must be exercised within the territorial jurisdiction of the several States. The sense of the nation on this subject is unequivocally manifested by the provisions made in the laws for transporting goods by land between Baltimore and Providence, between New York and Philadelphia, and between Philadelphia and Baltimore.

We Are Now Arrived at the Inquiry—What Is This Power?

It is the power to regulate, that is, to prescribe the rule by which commerce is to be governed. This power, like all others vested in Congress, is complete in itself, may be exercised to its utmost extent, and acknowledges no limitations other than are prescribed in the Constitution. These are expressed in plain terms, and do not affect the questions which arise in this case, or which have been discussed at the bar. If, as has always been understood, the sovereignty of Congress, though limited to specified objects, is plenary as to those objects, the power over commerce with foreign nations, and among the several States, is vested in Congress as absolutely as it would be in a single government, having in its Constitution the same restrictions on the exercise of the power as are found in the Constitution of the United States. The wisdom and the discretion of Congress, their identity with the people, and the influence which their constituents possess at elections are, in this, as in many other instances, as that, for example, of declaring war, the sole restraints on which they have relied, to secure them from its abuse. They are the restraints on which the people must often rely solely, in all representative governments.

The power of Congress, then, comprehends navigation, within the limits of every State in the Union, so far as that navigation may be in any manner connected with "commerce with foreign nations, or among the several States, or with the Indian tribes." It may, of consequence, pass the jurisdictional line of New York and act upon the very waters to which the prohibition now under consideration applies.

But it has been urged with great earnestness that, although the power of Congress to regulate commerce with foreign nations and among the several States be coextensive with the subject itself, and have no other limits than are prescribed in the Constitution, yet the States may severally exercise the same power, within their respective jurisdictions. In support of this argument, it is said that they possessed it as an inseparable attribute of sovereignty, before the formation of the Constitution, and still retain it except so far as they have surrendered it by that instrument; that this principle results from the nature of the government, and is secured by the tenth amendment; that an affirmative grant of power is not exclusive unless in its own nature it be such that the continued exercise of it by the former possessor is inconsistent with the grant, and that this is not of that description.

***

The grant of the power to lay and collect taxes is, like the power to regulate commerce, made in general terms, and has never been understood to interfere with the exercise of the same power by the State, and hence has been drawn an argument which has been applied to the question under consideration. But the two grants are not, it is conceived, similar in their terms or their nature. Although many of the powers formerly exercised by the States are transferred to the government of the Union, yet the State governments remain, and constitute a most important part of our system. The power of taxation is indispensable to their existence, and is a power which, in its own nature, is capable of residing in, and being exercised by, different authorities at the same time. We are accustomed to see it placed, for different purposes, in different hands. Taxation is the simple operation of taking small portions from a perpetually accumulating mass, susceptible of almost infinite division, and a power in one to take what is necessary for certain purposes is not, in its nature, incompatible with a power in another to take what is necessary for other purposes. Congress is authorized to lay and collect taxes, & to pay the debts and provide for the common defence and general welfare of the United States. This does not interfere with the power of the States to tax for the support of their own governments, nor is the exercise of that power by the States an exercise of any portion of the power that is granted to the United States. In imposing taxes for State purposes, they are not doing what Congress is empowered to do. Congress is not empowered to tax for those purposes which are within the exclusive province of the States. When, then, each government exercises the power of taxation, neither is exercising the power of the other. But, when a State proceeds to regulate commerce with foreign nations, or among the several States, it is exercising the very power that is granted to Congress, and is doing the very thing which Congress is authorized to do. There is no analogy, then, between the power of taxation and the power of regulating commerce.

***

But all inquiry into this subject seems to the Court to be put completely at rest by the act already mentioned, entitled, "An act for the enrolling and licensing of steamboats."

This act authorizes a steamboat employed, or intended to be employed, only in a river or bay of the United States, owned wholly or in part by an alien, resident within the United States, to be enrolled and licensed as if the same belonged to a citizen of the United States.

This act demonstrates the opinion of Congress that steamboats may be enrolled and licensed, in common with vessels using sails. They are, of course, entitled to the same privileges, and can no more be restrained from navigating waters and entering ports which are free to such vessels than if they were wafted on their voyage by the winds, instead of being propelled by the agency of fire. The one element may be as legitimately used as the other for every commercial purpose authorized by the laws of the Union, and the act of a State inhibiting the use of either to any vessel having a license under the act of Congress comes, we think, in direct collision with that act.

> As this decides the cause, it is unnecessary to enter in an examination of that part of the Constitution which empowers Congress to promote the progress of science and the useful arts.
>
> The Court is aware that, in stating the train of reasoning by which we have been conducted to this result, much time has been consumed in the attempt to demonstrate propositions which may have been thought axioms. It is felt that the tediousness inseparable from the endeavour to prove that which is already clear is imputable to a considerable part of this opinion. But it was unavoidable. The conclusion to which we have come depends on a chain of principles which it was necessary to preserve unbroken, and although some of them were thought nearly self-evident, the magnitude of the question, the weight of character belonging to those from whose judgment we dissent, and the argument at the bar demanded that we should assume nothing.
>
> Powerful and ingenious minds, taking as postulates that the powers expressly granted to the government of the Union are to be contracted by construction into the narrowest possible compass and that the original powers of the States are retained if any possible construction will retain them may, by a course of well digested but refined and metaphysical reasoning founded on these premises, explain away the Constitution of our country and leave it a magnificent structure indeed to look at, but totally unfit for use. They may so entangle and perplex the understanding as to obscure principles which were before thought quite plain, and induce doubts where, if the mind were to pursue its own course, none would be perceived. In such a case, it is peculiarly necessary to recur to safe and fundamental principles to sustain those principles, and when sustained, to make them the tests of the arguments to be examined.

The *Gibbons* case came at a time when the United States was largely an agrarian society, living off of the land and only minimally engaged in interstate commerce. In 1840, more than two-thirds of Americans were employed in agriculture. Yet, by the end of the 19th century, this number had dropped below half, with significant increases in industry and services (see Table 5.1).

Some historians argue that the railroad and its rapid expansion created most major industries in the United States.[8] Between 1850 and 1890, government and private sector funding led to a rapid expansion of railroad lines in the United States,

Table 5.1 Shift from Farming to Industry

	Employment %			Output % (1860 prices)			Services
Year	Agriculture	Industry	Services	Agriculture	Industry		
1840	68	12	20	47	21		31
1850	60	17	23	42	29		29
1860	56	19	25	38	28		34
1870	53	22	25	35	31		34
1880	52	23	25	31	32		38
1890	43	26	31	22	41		37
1900	40	26	33	20	40		39

Source: Joel Mokyr, Economics 323–2: *Economic History of the United States Since 1865* http://faculty.wcas.northwestern.edu/~jmokyr/Graphs-and-Tables.PDF.

Table 5.2 Ten Leading U.S. Industries by Value Added (millions of 1914 dollars)

1860		1880		1900		1920	
Industry	Value added	Industry	Value added	Industry	Value added	Industry	Value added
Cotton goods	59	Machinery	111	Machinery	432	Machinery	576
Lumber	54	Iron and steel	105	Iron and steel	339	Iron and steel	493
Boots and shoes	53	Cotton goods	97	Printing and publishing	313	Lumber	393
Flour and meal	43	Lumber	87	Lumber	300	Cotton goods	364
Men's clothing	39	Boots and shoes	82	Clothing	262	Shipbuilding	349
Machinery	31	Men's clothing	78	Liquor	224	Automotive	347
Woolen goods	27	Flour and meal	64	Cotton goods	196	General shop construction	328
Leather goods	24	Woolen goods	60	Masonry and brick	140	Printing and publishing	268
Cast iron	23	Printing	58	General shop construction	131	Electrical machinery	246
Printing	20	Liquor	44	Meatpacking	124	Clothing	239

Source: Joel Mokyr, Economics 323–2: Economic History of the United States Since 1865 http://faculty.wcas.northwestern.edu/~jmokyr/Graphs-and-Tables.PDF

dramatically reducing the cost of transport and opening opportunities for interstate commerce. Railroads were also the first major corporation in the United States, setting a model for business organizations in subsequent decades. Yet as the economy improved and business opportunities grew, the ill effects of business likewise grew, leading some states to consider intervention.

Agriculture was the principal business of the United States in the first part of 1800s. Cotton was the top export. In 1860, only 16% of Americans lived in cities, mostly in the Northeast.[9] However, this was beginning to change. The United States overtook Britain as the number-one economic power in the world in the late 1800s through its use of railroads and manufacturing.

Prior to the 1850s, fuel for energy was largely wood or coal-based. Oil was first refined and utilized as a fuel source in the 1850s, with an exploration boom following shortly thereafter. By 1870, John D. Rockefeller had formed his infamous oil corporation, Standard Oil, which monopolized the vast majority of oil wells in the United States and, by 1879, was responsible for 90% of oil production. The company was broken up in 1911 via the Supreme Court case, *Standard Oil Co. of New Jersey v. United States*.

The Slaughterhouse Cases (1873)

The Slaughterhouse Cases involve six consolidated appeals by an association of butchers in Louisiana in 1873.[10] At the time of this case, New Orleans residents got their drinking water from the Mississippi River. Just north of the city, hundreds of butchers prepared meats along the banks of the river, depositing blood and offal from the meats into the river. The toxins from these deposits polluted the drinking water of New Orleans residents and are blamed for a cholera outbreak in the city. As a result, the city took steps to relocate the butchers into a single slaughterhouse in the south of New Orleans, where space would be rented out to individual butchers. The city appealed to the state of Louisiana to assist. The state established the Crescent City Livestock Landing and Slaughter-House Company, a corporation that would coordinate the space for the butchers to use. The butcher's union sued the state, asserting a violation of the 14th Amendment due process clause, among other provisions.

These cases are brought here by writs of error to the Supreme Court of the State of Louisiana. They arise out of the efforts of the butchers of New Orleans to resist the Crescent City Livestock Landing and Slaughter-House Company in the exercise of certain powers conferred by the charter which created it, and which was granted by the legislature of that State.

The Slaughterhouse Cases (The Butchers' Benevolent Association of New Orleans v. The Crescent City Live-stock Landing and Slaughter-house Company, 83 U.S. 36 (1872).

***

The records show that the plaintiffs in error relied upon, and asserted throughout the entire course of the litigation in the State courts, that the grant of privileges in the charter of defendant, which they were contesting, was a violation of the most important provisions of the thirteenth and fourteenth articles of amendment of the Constitution of the United States. The jurisdiction and the duty of this court to review the judgment of the State court on those questions is clear, and is imperative.

***

[The Act] declares that the company, after it shall have prepared all the necessary buildings, yards, and other conveniences for that purpose, shall have the sole and exclusive privilege of conducting and carrying on the livestock landing and slaughterhouse business within the limits and privilege granted by the act, and that all such animals shall be landed at the stock landings and slaughtered at the slaughterhouses of the company, and nowhere else. Penalties are enacted for infractions of this provision, and prices fixed for the maximum charges of the company for each steamboat and for each animal landed.

***

It is not, and cannot be successfully controverted that it is both the right and the duty of the legislative body—the supreme power of the State or municipality—to prescribe and determine the localities where the business of slaughtering for a great city may be conducted. To do this effectively, it is indispensable that all persons who slaughter animals for food shall do it in those places and nowhere else.

The statute under consideration defines these localities and forbids slaughtering in any other. It does not, as has been asserted, prevent the butcher from doing his own slaughtering. On the contrary, the Slaughter-House Company is required, under a heavy penalty, to permit any person who wishes to do so to slaughter in their houses, and they are bound to make ample provision for the convenience of all the slaughtering for the entire city. The butcher then is still permitted to slaughter, to prepare, and to sell his own meats; but he is required to slaughter at a specified place, and to pay a reasonable compensation for the use of the accommodations furnished him at that place.

The wisdom of the monopoly granted by the legislature may be open to question, but it is difficult to see a justification for the assertion that the butchers are deprived of the right to labor in their occupation, or the people of their daily service in preparing food, or how this statute, with the duties and guards imposed upon the company, can be said to destroy the business of the butcher, or seriously interfere with its pursuit.

The power here exercised by the legislature of Louisiana is, in its essential nature, one which has been, up to the present period in the constitutional history of this country, always conceded to belong to the States, however it may now be questioned in some of its details.

***

The regulation of the place and manner of conducting the slaughtering of animals, and the business of butchering within a city, and the inspection of the animals to be killed for meat, and of the meat afterwards, are among the most necessary and frequent exercises of this power. It is not, therefore, needed that we should seek for a comprehensive definition, but rather look for the proper source of its exercise.

In Gibbons v. Ogden, [Footnote 5] Chief Justice Marshall, speaking of inspection laws passed by the States, says:

> They form a portion of that immense mass of legislation which controls everything within the territory of a State not surrendered to the General Government—all which can be most advantageously administered by the States themselves. Inspection laws, quarantine laws, health laws of every description, as well as laws for regulating the internal commerce of a State, and those which respect turnpike roads, ferries, &c., are component parts. No direct general power over these objects is granted to Congress, and consequently they remain subject to State legislation.

***

It can readily be seen that the interested vigilance of the corporation created by the Louisiana legislature will be more efficient in enforcing the limitation prescribed for the stock landing and slaughtering business for the good of the city than the ordinary efforts of the officers of the law.

Unless, therefore, it can be maintained that the exclusive privilege granted by this charter to the corporation is beyond the power of the legislature of Louisiana, there can be no just exception to the validity of the statute. And, in this respect, we are not able to see that these privileges are especially odious or objectionable. The duty imposed as a consideration for the privilege is well defined, and its enforcement well guarded. The prices or charges to be made by the company are limited by the statute, and we are not advised that they are, on the whole, exorbitant or unjust.

The proposition is therefore reduced to these terms: can any exclusive privileges be granted to any of its citizens, or to a corporation, by the legislature of a State?

***

To remove this difficulty primarily, and to establish clear and comprehensive definition of citizenship which should declare what should constitute citizenship of the United States and also citizenship of a State, the first clause of the first section was framed.

> All persons born or naturalized in the United States, and subject to the jurisdiction thereof, are citizens of the United States and of the State wherein they reside.

The first observation we have to make on this clause is that it puts at rest both the questions which we stated to have been the subject of differences of opinion. It declares that persons may be citizens of the United States without regard to their citizenship of a particular State, and it overturns the Dred Scott decision by making all persons born within the United States and subject to its jurisdiction citizens of the United States. That its main purpose was to establish the citizenship of the negro can admit of no doubt. The phrase, "subject to its jurisdiction" was intended to exclude from its operation children of ministers, consuls, and citizens or subjects of foreign States born within the United States.

The next observation is more important in view of the arguments of counsel in the present case. It is that the distinction between citizenship of the United States and citizenship of a State is clearly recognized and established.

Not only may a man be a citizen of the United States without being a citizen of a State, but an important element is necessary to convert the former into the latter. He must reside within the State to make him a citizen of it, but it is only necessary that he should be born or naturalized in the United States to be a citizen of the Union.

It is quite clear, then, that there is a citizenship of the United States, and a citizenship of a State, which are distinct from each other, and which depend upon different characteristics or circumstances in the individual.

We think this distinction and its explicit recognition in this amendment of great weight in this argument, because the next paragraph of this same section, which is the one mainly relied on by the plaintiffs in error, speaks only of privileges and immunities of citizens of the United States, and does not speak of those of citizens of the several States. The argument, however, in favor of the plaintiffs rests wholly on the assumption that the citizenship is the same, and the privileges and immunities guaranteed by the clause are the same.

The language is, "No State shall make or enforce any law which shall abridge the privileges or immunities of citizens of the United States." It is a little remarkable, if this clause was intended as a protection to the citizen of a State against the legislative power of his own State, that the word citizen of the State should be left out when it is so carefully used, and used in contradistinction to citizens of the United States in the very sentence which precedes it. It is too clear for argument that the change in phraseology was adopted understandingly and, with a purpose.

Of the privileges and immunities of the citizen of the United States, and of the privileges and immunities of the citizen of the State, and what they respectively are, we will presently consider; but we wish to state here that it is only the former which are placed by this clause under the protection of the Federal Constitution, and that the latter, whatever they may be, are not intended to have any additional protection by this paragraph of the amendment. If, then,

> there is a difference between the privileges and immunities belonging to a citizen of the United States as such and those belonging to the citizen of the State as such, the latter must rest for their security and protection where they have heretofore rested, for they are not embraced by this paragraph of the amendment.
>
> ***
>
> The adoption of the first eleven amendments to the Constitution so soon after the original instrument was accepted shows a prevailing sense of danger at that time from the Federal power. And it cannot be denied that such a jealousy continued to exist with many patriotic men until the breaking out of the late civil war. It was then discovered that the true danger to the perpetuity of the Union was in the capacity of the State organizations to combine and concentrate all the powers of the State, and of contiguous States, for a determined resistance to the General Government.
>
> Unquestionably this has given great force to the argument, and added largely to the number of those who believe in the necessity of a strong National government.
>
> But, however pervading this sentiment, and however it may have contributed to the adoption of the amendments we have been considering, we do not see in those amendments any purpose to destroy the main features of the general system. Under the pressure of all the excited feeling growing out of the war, our statesmen have still believed that the existence of the State with powers for domestic and local government, including the regulation of civil rights the rights of person and of property was essential to the perfect working of our complex form of government, though they have thought proper to impose additional limitations on the States, and to confer additional power on that of the Nation.
>
> But whatever fluctuations may be seen in the history of public opinion on this subject during the period of our national existence, we think it will be found that this court, so far as its functions required, has always held with a steady and an even hand the balance between State and Federal power, and we trust that such may continue to be the history of its relation to that subject so long as it shall have duties to perform which demand of it a construction of the Constitution or of any of its parts.
>
> The judgments of the Supreme Court of Louisiana in these cases are AFFIRMED.

The Contract Clause is found in Article I, Section 10 of the U.S. Constitution, and it prohibits states from interfering with private contracts. That clause was enacted in order to prevent state legislatures from giving special privileges, such as waivers from debts owed under private contracts, to their friends and supporters. This clause was interpreted most clearly in the 1810 case, *Fletcher v. Peck*.[11]

In *Fletcher v. Peck*, the state of Georgia granted territory to four companies. The following year, they rescinded that land grant. Several years later, Peck, who acquired land from the original land grant, sold his land to Fletcher. Fletcher discovered the Georgia legislation rescinding the original land grant and claimed that Peck breached the contract since he had no land to sell. The U.S. Supreme Court unanimously sided with Peck, concluding that Article 1, Section 10 of the U.S. Constitution prohibited states from passing retroactive legislation that would interfere with private contracts.

Fletcher established the precedent that legislatures cannot retroactively annul previous grants or contracts. The free market—a new concept at the time—should be left to operate absent government interference, in most cases. But this case dealt with a contract between private citizens. Would the result be different for corporations?

Early corporations were regulated and in many cases influenced by the state; however, it is important to understand how different early corporations were from modern corporations. In the late 18th and early 19th centuries, a group of investors that wanted to form a corporation had to request a charter from the state legislature, which required a bill to be passed through the legislature and signed into law by the state governor. The charter would specify the limited duration of the corporation, the rights of shareholders, and any restrictions that legislature thought appropriate. In return, the incorporators usually received benefits not available to private parties, such as grants of a monopoly or access to public land. Accordingly, early corporations were frequently created for the establishment of schools, roads, bridges, and other public projects where the state needed private investors to achieve a certain goal for the community at large.

Once a corporate charter has been granted, states were historically prohibited from interfering with the rights created in that charter. In the following case, the *Fletcher* precedent was extended to corporations, beginning a new era of corporate law.

Trustees of Dartmouth College v. Woodward involved a corporate charter that had been granted by King George III in 1769 to form Dartmouth College.[12] The charter set out the purpose of the school and granted it land on which to operate. Following the American Revolution, the state of New Hampshire, where Dartmouth is located, attempted to take over control of the college, arguing that the corporate charter was no longer valid since the United States had declared independence from Great Britain.

In a 6–1 decision written by Justice John Marshall, the Supreme Court found that a corporate charter, regardless of the fact that it is issued by a King or a state, is a private contract, and private contracts are sacrosanct. "An act of the State Legislature of New Hampshire altering the charter without the consent of the corporation in a material respect, is an act impairing the obligation of the charter, and is unconstitutional and void."[13] This decision was significant because it established precedent that the state had little control over contracts entered into by a corporation that was legitimately established.

Following this decision, many states passed incorporation laws meant to check corporate power and ensure that the state could amend a corporate charter if necessary. These restrictions, along with the difficult process of acquiring a corporate charter, led many businesses to utilize other legal forms to operate, such as limited partnerships and trusts. This began to change after the Civil War and passage of the 14th Amendment to the U.S. Constitution.

The 14th Amendment to the U.S. Constitution extended equal protection of the law to all U.S. citizens. The goal of that Amendment was largely to prohibit discrimination against African Americans, but corporations also saw this as an opportunity to acquire more rights as legal entities than their historic charters had afforded them. That is precisely what happened in 1886.

Three consolidated cases dealing with the taxation of railroads in California resulted in a Supreme Court opinion about whether private corporations, such as railroads, were entitled to the equal protection of the laws alongside natural citizens in accordance with the 14th Amendment.[14] The case, which was otherwise unremarkable, included a headnote written by the court reporter, who happened to be a former railroad president, that read as follows:

> Before argument, Mr. Chief Justice Waite said: "The Court does not wish to hear argument on the question whether the provision in the Fourteenth Amendment to the Constitution which forbids a state to deny to any person within its jurisdiction the equal protection of the laws applies to these corporations. We are all of opinion that it does."[15]

That reporter's note appeared in the final publication of the case and has since been used to guide future decisions about the rights of corporations. That case, which dealt with a state's efforts to tax improvements on land owned by a railroad company, became famous because it implied (though did not directly state) that corporations are owed the same equal protection rights under the 14th Amendment as individuals are. Thus began an era of seeing the corporation as an individual in the eyes of the law.

Early Business Regulation

By the turn of the 20th century, the population of the United States had increased, the land mass had expanded, and efficiency in agriculture had improved dramatically, lowering the cost of food. But several recessions, including the Long Depression between 1873 and 1876, which led hundreds of railroads to collapse and unemployment to exceed 14%, constrained economic growth. This began to change as electrification became widespread in homes and factories, allowing machines to produce goods more efficiently and workers to work after dark.[16] Improvements in the management of manufacturing facilitated mass production by using concepts such as specialization and the assembly line.[17]

The success of the economy also led to abuses of power, including the monopolization of oil production by Standard Oil, abuse of immigrant laborers in meatpacking plants, and the sale of falsely marketed and at times dangerous drugs and foods to unsuspecting consumers. The federal government made several attempts to fight back against this abuse of power, starting in earnest with the Interstate Commerce Act of 1887.

Throughout the 1800s, railroads had grown in power and began taking advantage of that power by soliciting political benefits in exchange for special treatment (e.g., free rides), and colluding within the railroad industry to fix rates against the interests of consumers. Upon objections, many from farmers who were hurt by the price discrimination,[18] states attempted to enact legislation preventing unfair practices by railroads. However, the U.S. Supreme Court, in *Wabash, St. Louis & Pacific Railway Company v. Illinois*,[19] ruled that such efforts violated the Interstate Commerce Clause, which made interstate trade regulation the business of the federal and not the state government.

In response to that decision, Congress enacted the Interstate Commerce Act. The Act established the first independent regulatory agency in U.S. history—the Interstate Commerce Commission (ICC). The ICC enacted rules that required railroads to offer reasonable and just rates for transport and also to publicize the rates they charge in order to deter price discrimination. The ICC was later (1935) empowered to regulate the bus and trucking industries. The agency was ultimately dissolved in 1995 following the deregulation of trains, busses, and other common carriers. However, the ICC represents the federal government's first significant foray into the regulation of business.

Further government involvement in business came about in the late 19th century as concerns over corporate malfeasance increased. The concerns were not new—Adam Smith had expressed them in 1776 when he suggested that corporate directors manage other people's money, making them more likely to engage in risky transactions that may hurt shareholders.[20] A pressing issue at the time was free competition and whether corporations were getting too large to allow small firms to get a foothold.

The Sherman Antitrust Act passed Congress in 1890 and was meant to prevent corporations from placing unreasonable restraints on trade through the use of monopolies or other barriers to interstate trade. That Act, still in effect today, was used to break up American Tobacco and Standard Oil in 1911, AT&T in 1982, and to facilitate several other pro-competition actions. Similarly, the Clayton Act of 1914 added price discrimination and exclusive dealing arrangements to the list of violations that can lead to criminal penalties.

In the early 20th century, other legislation considered **progressive** was being enacted to appease small businesses, workers, and consumers that were growing concerned about the direction of growth of the American economy. This included the Pure Food and Drug Act of 1906, the precursor to the Food and Drug Administration, the Immigration Act of 1924, which limited immigrant entry into the United States, and the creation of an income tax through passage of the 16th Amendment in 1913. Leaders of the progressive movement included Presidents Theodore Roosevelt, Woodrow Wilson, and Franklin Delano Roosevelt.

> Progressive—advocacy of improvements to society through political and economic reform.

The industrial revolution that generated tremendous economic growth in the United States and elsewhere also turned a largely equal agrarian society into an increasingly unequal industrialized society.[21] Income inequality began to increase in the early part of the 19th century as wages for unskilled laborers rose more slowly than wages for skilled laborers, such as clerks.[22] This differential of wages continued

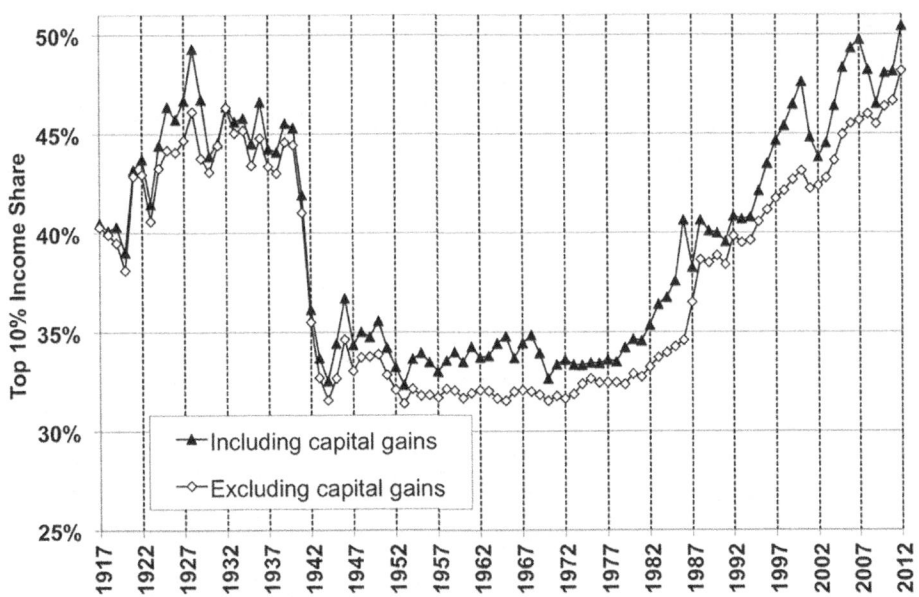

Figure 5.1 Percentage of Income Earned by Top 10% of U.S. Earners.
Source: Emmanuel Saez, University of California at Berkeley (2013).

to persist through the early 20th century and only subsided during World War II, when the National War Labor Board controlled wages.[23]

The famous economist Simon Kuznets, known for the Kuznets Curve, suggested the countries tend to go through a period of inequality as they develop economically and that they emerge from that process more equal. However, the little data that we have on U.S. income inequality in the 18th and 19th centuries suggests that, aside from the brief period during World War II, income inequality has been consistently rising in the United States.[24]

Whither Capitalism?

The history of all [previous] societies [has been] the history of class struggles.
—Karl Marx

Since the advent of the nation-state, there has been a debate over the best way for a central government to manage its economy. Earlier in this chapter, we discussed the idea of mercantilism, which was replaced by more market-oriented models. But even with a market-oriented model, there is a role to play for the central government, and the long-debated question has been about how much control that government should have over the market.

> Capitalism—an economic and political theory that emphasizes private ownership of capital.

Capitalism came into existence in roughly the 16th century as the medieval feudal system began to break down and large landowners hired laborers to work the land in exchange for money. European merchants led the way in expanding capitalism as they traded with distant buyers and sellers, leading to companies such as the British and Dutch East India companies (described earlier). The ideas of Adam Smith at the end of the 18th century helped to lead a push toward reduced government interference in trade. And the industrial revolution led to a new industrial capitalist that earned money not from labor, but rather from capital investments in land, factories, and other means of production.

As an economic theory, capitalism refers to private ownership of the means of production and the use of those means for private profit. Modern usage of the term refers to industrial capitalism, whereby individuals (and today corporations) use their capital to generate more capital through ownership of the means of production. The accumulation and investment of capital was encouraged through free market policies, which led to investments in productivity and technology that likely advanced industrialization, but also increased inequality by concentrating wealth in the hands of industrialists.

As industrial capitalism spread, some critics of rising inequality and concentration of wealth objected to free market government policies. Led by Count Henri de Saint-Simon, a new economic theory emerged that focused on organizing the chaotic "free for all" of capitalism by adding governmental controls to the free market. This approach, known as **socialism**, emerged in the mid-19th century as a way to leverage technology and administrative efficiency during the industrialization process by concentrating economic controls among **technocrats** in the central government.

> Socialism—an economic and political theory that emphasizes communitarian ownership of capital.
>
> Technocrat—in politics, a representative of an elite group of skilled decision makers.

The economic idea of socialism began to take hold toward the end of the 19th century, following a congress held in Geneva in 1866. Largely aligning with workers and trade unions, socialist (often termed "labor") parties began forming around the world, with the first official socialist party elected in Australia in 1904. Following that victory, labor parties in Britain and across Europe, as well as within the United States, began to gain influence in politics. The Russian Revolution of 1917, led by workers and peasants who had been living under the Romanov dictatorship, brought Vladimir Lenin to power and formed the first Socialist Republic. Lenin withdrew Russia from World War I and transferred land owned by the royal family to workers in Russia in an effort to facilitate wealth redistribution.

According to Karl Marx, who is most often associated with modern socialism and **communism**, all societies develop politically and economically with the ultimate goal of an equal, classless society. Marx predicted that societies would advance to become capitalist first, which would help them to develop the knowledge and resources needed to create a sustainable society; they would then advance to socialism, which would integrate central planning into the functioning economy by redistributing wealth and creating more equality; and then they would advance to communism, which would give power to the people and ultimately dissolve the state apparatus completely.[25]

> Communism—an economic and political theory that emphasizes communitarian ownership of all capital and property.

No country in the world has exhibited pure capitalism, which would involve complete market discretion and no government intervention or control; nor has any country exhibited pure communism, which would involve no state at all.[26] Each country mixes some elements of market control with some elements of state control. In the United States, state control has ebbed and flowed but has grown tremendously since the start of the industrial revolution (see following section). In Europe, state control has advanced steadily since democracy took hold following World War II, tilting most European countries closer to socialism than the United States is. And in China, the socialist economic model was the starting place for the post–Mao Zedong phase of Chinese development, yet elements of a capitalist free market have steadily grown since then.

The debate over which economic model—central planning or market driven—would be appropriate for the United States was highlighted by two key economists in the early 20th century: Friedrich Hayek and John Maynard Keynes. Hayek, an Austrian economist, followed a school of thought known as **libertarianism**, which argued that minimal government involvement in the economy is the best way to facilitate economic growth. Hayek believed that governments are not equipped to set prices—this task should be left to markets. Keynes, an English economist, disagreed. He argued that the government should use **fiscal policy** to stimulate economic growth and that, especially when the economy is in a slump, should run deficits in order to reenergize a slow-moving economy.

> Libertarianism—an extreme form of laissez-faire capitalism emphasizing minimal government intervention in the lives of citizens.
>
> Fiscal policy—government use of taxing and spending to influence the economy.

The stock market crash of 1929 and the ensuing economic depression that followed led many Americans to question the viability of a market-driven economy. Businesses took risks at the expense of workers and the broader economy; employers took advantage of laborers with low wages and poor working conditions; and industrialists continued to enrich themselves with little oversight. President Franklin Delano Roosevelt (FDR) tapped into the resentment of the American people toward the free market by enacting some of the most broad-sweeping regulations in history.

A Brief Political-Economic History of the United States

Coming to power in 1933, FDR applied Keynesian philosophy to attempt a reset of the sputtering American economy. With the help of a supportive Congress, FDR signed into law the Glass-Steagall Act, which separated investment and commercial banking; the Tennessee Valley Authority, which allowed dams to be built along the Tennessee River to generate low-cost power; and the Agricultural Adjustment Act, which paid farmers to withhold production of certain crops in order to allow the price for those crops to increase. The Glass-Steagall Act was repealed by Congress in 1999, and the Agricultural Adjustment Act was declared unconstitutional by the U.S. Supreme Court in 1936,[27] though Congress passed a modified version of the act in 1938, which is still valid today.[28]

Keynes's ideas aligned with the progressive political movement of the time and provided economic foundations to the New Deal policies of FDR. Roosevelt used government investment in order to stimulate the stagnant economy following the Great Depression, including investments in public works projects like the Works Progress Administration, created by Executive Order in 1933, which put about 3 million people to work restoring buildings, building highways and airports, and developing creative projects.

Among his other major economic achievements, FDR secured passage of the Social Security Act of 1935, which was the first American flirtation with socialist policies. In signing the Act, Roosevelt noted:

> We can never insure one hundred percent of the population against one hundred percent of the hazards and vicissitudes of life, but we have tried to frame a law which will give some measure of protection to the average citizen and to his family against the loss of a job and against poverty-ridden old age.[29]

The Act remains in effect today and helps millions of older and sick Americans.

While campaigning for his second term in office in 1936, FDR said,

> I should like to have it said of my first Administration that in it the forces of selfishness and of lust for power met their match, [and] I should like to have it said of my second Administration that in it these forces have met their master.

During his time in office, however, FDR faced stiff resistance from a conservative U.S. Supreme Court that believed he was extending the power of the federal government over the economy too far. In response, FDR threatened to "pack the court" with liberal Justices who would be sympathetic to his progressive agenda.

FDR's progressive agenda, while validated by the U.S. Supreme Court, lost steam when the economy failed to fully recover, and perceptions of FDR following his threats to pack the Supreme Court cost him political capital. All of this changed on December 7, 1941, when Japanese war planes bombed Pearl Harbor, Hawaii, sinking 20 American naval vessels and killing 2,000 American soldiers. FDR asked Congress to declare war on Japan, and subsequently on Japanese allies Germany and Italy, which Congress did nearly unanimously. Wartime production rejuvenated the American economy and effectively ended the Great Depression.

Boom (economic)—a period of sustained economic growth.

Following the war, the United States entered a **boom** period marked by significant economic growth, wage growth, and population growth. Figures 5.2 and 5.3 reflect the nature of that growth. Economic growth was strong for a few reasons. First, the wartime economy led to significant manufacturing growth and investments in technology. Second, the government continued to invest in public works projects, such as roads and bridges, allowing not only employment but also expansion to other parts of the country. Third, women joined the labor force in droves while men fought during World War II, and many remained in the workforce after the war ended in 1945.

The American middle class expanded in the 1950s as well, shrinking inequality. This is the result of steady employment and rising wages, but also of investments in education made because of the Servicemen's Readjustment Act of 1944, commonly known as the G.I. Bill. That law, signed by FDR, provided significant economic

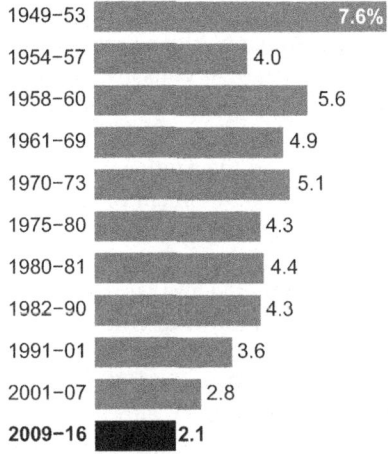

Figure 5.2 Periods of U.S. Economic Growth.
Source: *Wall Street Journal*, U.S. Commerce Department (2016).

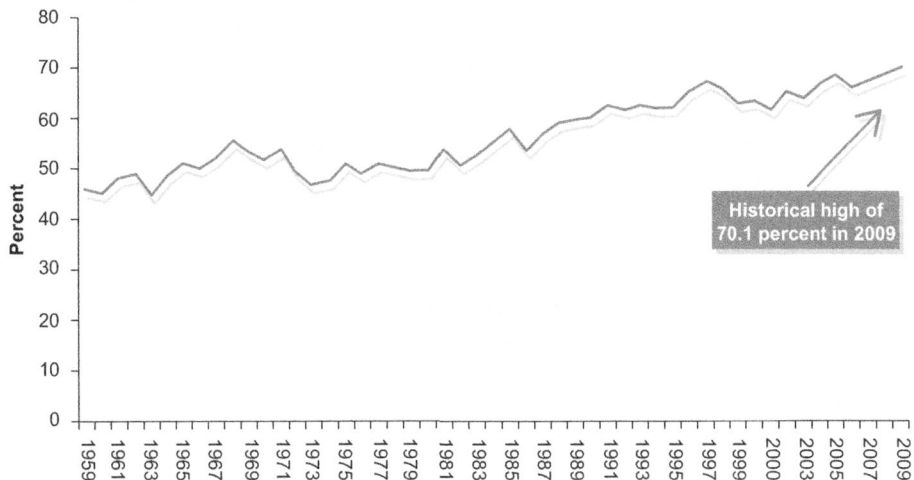

Figure 5.3 Enrollment in U.S. Colleges and Universities (1959–2009).
Source: *New York Times*, U.S. Bureau of Labor Statistics (2009).

benefits to returning veterans in the form of education payments for high school, college, or vocational training; low-interest mortgages to buy homes; and low-interest loans to start a business, among other things.

During World War II, the United States and the Union of Soviet Socialist Republics (USSR) were allies in the fight against Germany and Japan. The Red Army of the Soviets effectively fought off both the Nazi and Japanese attempts to expand their territory, all the while securing more territory for the USSR by expanding into Eastern Europe.

Following the war, the USSR, along with the United States, the United Kingdom, and China, served as the four world policemen. They were four of the five permanent members of the newly created United Nations Security Council (along with France), which allowed them to veto any global consensus they disagreed with. Relations between the United States and the Soviet Union began to deteriorate in the late 1950s as the Soviets effectively integrated the Eastern European countries that they occupied into the USSR and sought to expand their influence in the world.

Public policy shifted toward the containment of the expanding USSR. Policy arguments focused on the fundamental differences between democracy and communism, using the **Red Scare** to generate American support for anti-communist policies both within and outside of the United States. This threat justified heavy government investment in a large peacetime military industrial complex, leading the United States to make the largest investment in a military in the world.

> Red Scare—promotion of a broad fear of the potential rise of leftist, anarchist or communist policies.

The American economy in the 1960s shifted significantly away from the agrarian market that existed just a few decades earlier. Farm work declined as agricultural productivity increased, leading workers to relocate to cities or newly established suburbs (see Figure 5.4). Corporations consolidated their economic power by diversifying into different industries. And advances in understanding of fiscal policy led to better management of economic cycles, preventing the booms and busts of prior decades. American investors also began to engage in international trade, increasing foreign investment by 1000% in the 15 years following World War II.[30]

The 1960s period of strong economic growth and low inflation was also a period of increased government regulation. Concerns over increased pollution, inspired in part by the publication of Rachel Carson's famous book, *Silent Spring*, led to passage of the 1967 Clean Air Act. Concerns over safety in the workplace led to passage of the 1970 Occupational Safety and Health Act.

In 1962, author Michael Harrington published the famous book, *The Other America*, which was a detailed examination of both wealth and poverty in America

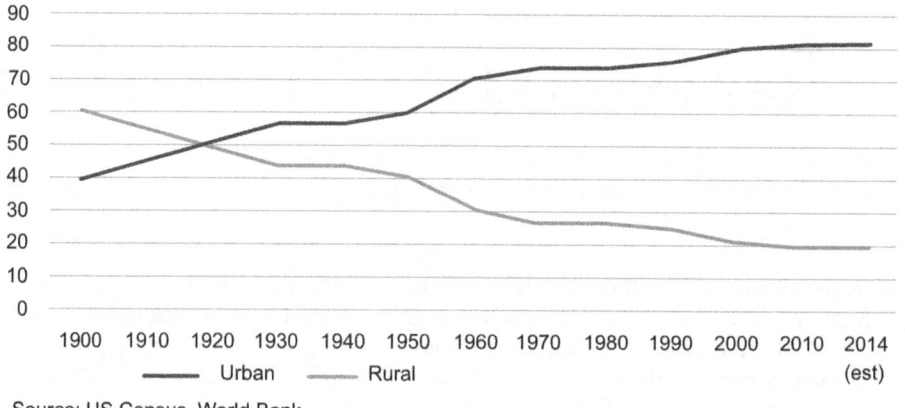

Figure 5.4 U.S. Urban and Rural Population (1900–2014).
Source: Urban Land Institute from U.S. Census and World Bank data.

and an examination of the then-increasing level of inequality. FDR had attempted to address the threat of poverty and inequality in his later package of economic and social reforms in the 1930s, but he was unable to secure congressional support. However, President Lyndon Johnson took up the issue with renewed vigor in 1964 with his War on Poverty, which was part of his Great Society program.

President John F. Kennedy faced a slowing economy in the early 1960s as the golden years of the 1950s began to wind down. He was advised to follow the Keynesian approach by investing federal reserves into public works projects to stimulate growth. Instead, Kennedy preferred using **supply-side economics** (see opening case to this chapter) to stimulate the economy through tax cuts. He was unable to implement them by the time of his 1963 assassination, leaving it to President Lyndon Johnson to do so. Johnson implemented the Kennedy tax cuts, which lowered tax rates significantly, dropping the highest individual rate from 91% to 70% and the corporate rate from 52% to 48%. Johnson also increased spending to fund his Great Society initiative, including the establishment of the Medicare and Medicaid national health insurance program passed in 1965.

> Supply-side economics—an economic theory suggesting that economic growth can be achieved by lowering taxes and reducing government regulation.

The U.S. economy enjoyed low unemployment and an array of new social programs by the end of the 1960s. Medicaid and investments in other anti-poverty programs dramatically reduced poverty in the United States, and Medicare greatly improved public health. But the costs for these programs, combined with increased costs for participation in the ongoing war in Vietnam, rose quickly. And since President Johnson had vowed not to raise taxes, Congress had to fund these programs through other means, such as **deficit spending**. This contributed to a rise in inflation, which made goods and services more expensive and reduced the value of the dollar.

> Deficit spending—government spending by borrowing rather than by taxing.

The economy of the 1970s was far less golden than that of the 1950s. President Nixon faced the highest level of inflation since 1951, which pushed the country into a recession. In 1973, in response to the Yom Kippur war among Egypt, Syria, and Israel, Arab oil-producing countries placed an embargo on oil exports to countries that supported Israel, including the United States. That embargo tripled the price of oil, leading to the first global oil crisis and worsening the U.S. economy. A negotiated settlement terminated the embargo in 1974, but a second embargo was levied in 1979 following the Iranian Revolution. Since then, largely because of oil exploration outside of the Middle East, oil prices have largely declined.

The end of the 1970s and the first two years of the 1980s were one of the worst economic periods in the United States since the Great Depression. Stagnating wage and income growth along with increasing inflation led to what was termed **stagflation**. Presidents Nixon, Ford, and Carter attempted to pull the country out of recession with price controls, regulations, and investment, but to no avail. When President Reagan took office in 1981, he focused on reducing inflation by reducing the money supply, which ultimately worked. However, not until 1983 did the economy begin sputtering forward once again.

> Stagflation—persistent high levels of inflation and unemployment.

The period of economic growth that began in 1982 was driven in large part by a **bull market** on Wall Street. Investors reaped tremendous returns during this period, leading to an eight-fold increase in the number of millionaires in five years.[31] Upper middle-class and wealthy investors did well during this period, but working-class Americans saw little improvement. Wages failed to rise and industrial jobs continued to disappear throughout the 1980s. Levels of inequality in the 1980s mirrored those of the 1920s (see Figure 5.5).

> Bull market—a market in which prices are rising, which encourages buying.

Unlike past administrations since Roosevelt, the Reagan Administration changed the fundamental economic policy approach of the United States in a significant way.

Figure 5.5 Income Inequality in the United States (1910–2010).
Source: Chart was made using data initially published as Thomas Piketty and Emmanuel Saez (2003), *Quarterly Journal of Economics*, 118(1), 2003, 1–39. Data (and updates) shown at http://inequality.org/income-inequality

Reagan was not a follower of Keynesian economics; rather, he believed that government intervention in and regulation of the economy was harmful rather than helpful or necessary. He argued that the free market does better when it is left alone, just as Adam Smith argued 200 years earlier and Hayek made the case for earlier in the 20th century. Reagan followed what was known as the **Chicago School of Economics**, a school of thought represented by the works of Milton Friedman and others who favored libertarian principles over liberal ones.

Reagan was the first U.S. president to associate democracy with capitalism. He convinced many people that political freedoms and economic freedoms are codependent and that a free market is essential for a functioning democracy. His ideas gained traction as the economy continued to expand throughout the 1980s and 1990s. Significantly, Reagan led the first major tax overhaul since the creation of the income tax in 1914. Among other things, he reduced the top tax rate from 70% to 50% in 1982 and then to 28% in 1988 (see Figure 5.6).

However, his **trickle-down economics** approach, which focused on income tax cuts for the wealthy and reduced regulation to stimulate investment that would ultimately trickle down to the working class, failed to produce even economic growth. Reagan believed firmly in the theory of Arthur Laffer (see the opening case to this chapter) that tax cuts would generate investment. After four years of tax cuts and no noticeable increase in investment, Reagan abandoned the theory and began raising taxes.

The Reagan Administration's approach to regulation was also a significant shift from prior administrations. His policy belief that government impeded economic growth meant that government regulations should be reduced or eliminated in order to pave the way to economic growth. Some **deregulation** had already started under the previous administration, but Reagan pushed for a broad array of legislative changes to allow businesses more freedom to operate.

One of the sectors that was deregulated was the financial sector—specifically, savings and loan banks. These banks received deposits from individuals and then

Chicago School of Economics—a school of economic thought associated with Milton Friedman and others at the University of Chicago emphasizing neoclassical economics.

Trickle-down economics—an economic theory emphasizing reduced taxes on business and the wealthy, which could encourage short-term investment.

Deregulation—the process of limiting or eliminating government regulation of the economy.

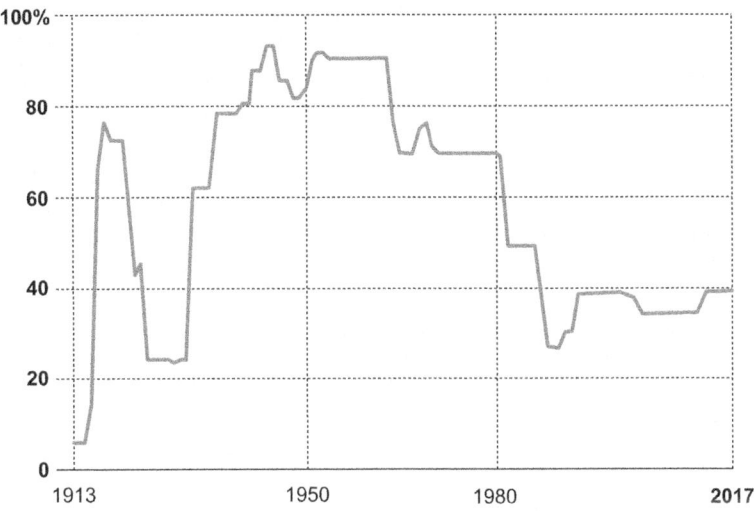

Figure 5.6 Highest Marginal U.S. Income Tax Rate (1913–2017).

Source: *Washington Post*; Tax Policy Center, www.taxpolicycenter.org/statistics/historical-highest-marginal-income-tax-rates

lent those monies out in the form of consumer loans for autos, mortgages, and similar items. These institutions had been regulated prior to the 1980s but were given more flexibility in how they invest their deposits under the Reagan Administration. When the Federal Reserve Bank raised the discount rate in 1989, many of these banks were unable to generate enough revenue from their investments to cover the interest owed to their clients, making them insolvent. Leveraging the weaker regulatory environment of the late 1980s, some of these banks ventured into high-risk investments in an effort to cover their losses. Most of those banks ultimately failed, causing the 1989 savings and loan crisis, which required substantial government bailouts that left the departing Reagan Administration with a serious deficit.

The one-term presidency of George H.W. Bush from 1988–1992 did little to boost economic growth. The savings and loan crisis, along with the 1990 Persian Gulf War, resulted in weak job growth, high interest rates, and unemployment above 6% by 1991. Voters soured on the economic policies of Reagan and Bush and looked to Bill Clinton to reinvigorate economic growth through new investments. Tax hikes, the Internet boom, and rapidly expanding globalization turned the economy around by 1994. By the end of his second term, President Clinton had converted a $290 billion budget deficit into a $236 billion budget surplus. The 1990s became known as the decade of the economic boom in the United States.

This boom began to fade in late 2000 as concerns over a technology bubble led the Federal Reserve to raise interest rates, and economic growth began to slow. By the start of George W. Bush's term in 2001, the United States was in a recession. The terrorist attack on the United States later that same year further worsened the economic recession. But the deregulatory approach started by President Reagan and continued, to a lesser extent, by President Clinton may also have paved the way to circumstances that led the 2000s to become known as the Lost Decade.

A housing boom that saw a dramatic increase in the number of homeowners in the United States by 2006 led to a spectacular crash in 2007. This sub-prime mortgage crisis resulted in part from risky investments made by under-regulated banks. Following the crash, U.S. GDP dropped precipitously, unemployment quickly rose, and many people lost their homes. At the time, economist Paul Krugman wrote:

> The prosperity of a few years ago, such as it was—profits were terrific, wages not so much—depended on a huge bubble in housing, which replaced an earlier huge bubble in stocks. And since the housing bubble isn't coming back, the spending that sustained the economy in the pre-crisis years isn't coming back either.[32]

No stranger to Keynesian economics, President Obama took office in 2009 with a plan to recover from the economic recession that began in 2007 through government investment in the economy. This started with an $800 billion government stimulus package that included tax cuts and spending on infrastructure, building upgrades, and similar investments. By 2011, the economy was growing again and the unemployment rate was decreasing. At that time, the Obama administration also sought to address the rising costs of healthcare with passage of the Patient Protection and Affordable Care Act, nicknamed *Obamacare* in 2010. And to address the 2007 housing crisis that caused much of the economic recession at that time, Obama also secured passage of the Dodd-Frank Wall Street Reform and Consumer Protection Act of 2010, which added new regulatory oversight of the banking sector.

The Obama Administration had several positive effects on the economy. According to the non-partisan Congressional Budget Office, the administration's increased taxes on wealthy earners reduced inequality significantly, unemployment dropped below 5% by the end of his second term, and average income rose by nearly 10%. However, these investments came at a cost. The trade deficit nearly doubled to $20 trillion, much of that due to the extension of the Bush-era tax cuts, and increasingly tense partisan politics made any progress on immigration, healthcare, or economic reform largely impossible.

Unlike President Obama's platform of *hope*, Donald Trump came into office in 2017 on a platform of *change*. The Trump Administration made the case that the economy was worsening for workers, whose jobs were being sent overseas due to outsourcing or being replaced by technology, and high taxes on the wealthy were holding back capitalist investment, slowing down potential economic growth. The first major legislative success of the Trump Administration was a significant $1 trillion tax cut enacted at the end of 2017, reducing the corporate tax rate from 35% to 21% and revising the tax code. As of the time of this publication, it is unclear what effect this tax cut will have on the overall economy.

Global Context

We have focused our attention in this chapter on economic policy in the United States. However, many of the economic theories that were discussed in this chapter have a global context as well. The United States is a relatively young nation, and it has not had any significant changes in governance that many other countries have endured. This final section will add a small window into the vast global economic policy landscape.

It is first and foremost essential to mention a recent analysis of the global economy that has garnered significant attention. French economist Thomas Piketty released his tome on global inequality in 2013.[33] His book, a historical analysis of global economic growth and inequality accompanied by dire predictions of future economic policy, gives us additional perspective on the global economy.

Piketty's thesis is quite simple—wealth (i.e., concentration of capital in the hands of one person or family) grows faster than economic output (i.e., the rate at which income from labor increases). In a nutshell, this means that the rich get rich faster than the working class, relatively speaking. And while that may not seem problematic *per se*, imagine that this has been the case since at least the 19th century and how the differing rates of increasing wealth have fed into massive inequality around the globe.

> When the rate of return on capital exceeds the rate of growth of output and income, as it did in the nineteenth century and seems quite likely to do again in the twenty-first, capitalism automatically generates arbitrary and unsustainable inequalities that radically undermine the meritocratic values on which democratic societies are based.[34]

This concentration of wealth in the hands of the rich, according to Piketty, created massive inequality in the 19th century that led to political upheaval. Inequality worsened prior to World Wars I and II, when significant wealth was lost, and in the era of high taxation following the war, which redistributed much of the accumulated capital more equally among the masses. However, Piketty contends that the accumulation of wealth is again on the rise, alongside levels of inequality, as tax rates have come down and growth has slowed.

> the decrease in the top marginal income tax rate led to an explosion of very high incomes, which then increased the political influence of the beneficiaries of the change in the tax laws, who had an interest in keeping top tax rates low or even decreasing them further and who could use their windfall to finance political parties, pressure groups, and think tanks.[35]

Piketty's lengthy book (696 pages) is filled with robust data and analysis and a few important recommendations. One is an answer to the long-held belief that, absent government intervention, inequality can be reduced through stronger economic growth. In his estimation, wealth accumulation will outpace economic growth in most scenarios. Another recommendation is that the best mechanism to attack inequality is with a wealth tax that transfers wealth from individuals to a state that can put it to broader use. And one final point that Piketty makes, which is very relevant to our discussion here, is that economics must be understood in the context of the policy environment in which it operates. Economics is more than mathematics and models—it is a theory for understanding and shaping the policies that we live by.

Conclusion

Economic policy has evolved significantly since the founding fathers drafted the U.S. Constitution. The largely agrarian, minimally populated United States of the 18th century radically transformed during the industrial revolution of the 19th century, leading to the creation of new industries and the expanded use of the corporation as a means of conducting business. These changes fueled population growth, geographic expansion, and immigration, but they also fueled externalities, such as pollution, unfair competition, questionable labor practices, and other possibly unethical behaviors.

Aside from the conduct of wars and diplomacy, and the prevention of interstate discrimination, the federal government had little role to play in the early United States. This role grew dramatically alongside the growth of the economy as the need for regulation became apparent. Yet disagreement quickly emerged over the shape of that government regulation. Would it be aggressive and centralized, as socialist economies preferred, or would it balance the needs of business with citizens and states, as free market economies preferred. This debate continued throughout much of the 20th century and has yet to be clearly resolved, as our policies ebb and flow from administration to administration.

The courts, and especially the U.S. Supreme Court, have been relied upon to interpret the legal rights and responsibilities of the government to manage the U.S. economy. This began as a non-interventionist approach most clearly evidenced during the *Lochner* era of the early 20th century. It was followed by a progressive approach to interpreting government involvement in the economy during the mid-20th century. And it is today a mix of both of those things, supporting limited government intervention in the economy but preventing a broader incursion into the marketplace that might stifle growth. What is critical for us to understand, however, is that the Court is an active participant in guiding the economic policy of the United States, with reverberations around the globe.

Additional Key Cases to Review

Lochner v. New York, 198 U.S. 45 (1905), *Lochner challenged a New York state law that set limits on labor practices for bakery employees. The Supreme Court struck down the law under the Due Process clause of the 14th Amendment.*

Wickard v. Filburn, 317 U.S. 111 (1942), *Filburn challenged the federal government's attempt to fine him for violating the Agricultural Adjustment Act, which regulated the growth of commodities during World War II. The Court found that Congress had power under the Commerce Clause to regulate even non-commercial production since it affected overall prices.*

Kelo v. City of New London, 545 U.S. 429 (2005), *Kelo sued the City of New London to challenge the government's use of Eminent Domain to transfer land from one private owner to another in the interest of economic development. The Supreme Court upheld this transfer as a public use within the meaning of the Takings Clause of the Constitution.*

Exercise and Discussion Questions

Exercise

Consider the following scenario and then answer the questions that follow:

> Assume that the current U.S. legislature has adopted a policy similar to the Laffer economic policy discussed in our opening case, which means that they are pursuing tax reductions with the expectation that such reductions will promote economic growth. That legislature enacts a series of reforms to the tax code that reduce the top tax bracket to 20% and that eliminates deductions that are largely favorable to the working class, such as child tax credits, student loan interest deductions, and mortgage deductions. The corporate tax rate is reduced to 15%. They believe that the lower tax rates for those who would invest in

the economy—namely, the wealthy—will encourage new investments and create jobs.

1. If you were a legislator who did not support this approach, what would be your central argument against the tax reform?
2. If you were a legislator who voted in favor of this reform, what argument would you make to your constituents to justify the increased taxes for the working class?
3. If you were asked at a global economic forum how this approach would make your country more competitive in world markets, what argument would you make to convince world leaders of the wisdom of this approach?

Additional Discussion Questions

1. What policies explain the judiciary's hesitation to allow government regulation during the late 19th and early 20th centuries?
2. Tax policy in the early 20th century dramatically differed from policies starting in the 1980s. This is often attributed to a shift from demand-side to supply-side economics. What does that mean and how does that explain the rationale for this shift in policy?
3. The *Gibbons v. Ogden* decision is often viewed as the seed for the growing federal government and its expanded role in the regulation of the marketplace. Some have argued that the Court read too broadly into the Commerce Clause in that decision. What is your opinion about the impact of that decision on the growth of the federal government and its authority to regulate the economy?
4. Thomas Piketty predicts that the global economy today is beginning to resemble the global economy leading up to the two world wars. Do you agree with his assessment and, if so, what do you see as the principal driver of this state of affairs?

Notes

1. Jim Tankersley, *Arthur Laffer Has a Never-Ending Supply of Supply-Side Plans for GOP*, Washington Post, Apr. 9, 2015.
2. Maurie Backman, *Here Are the U.S. States with No Income Tax*, Fox Business News, Nov. 23, 2016.
3. Steve Rose, *Arthur Laffer's View on the Kansas Economy: Prosperity Awaits Patient Tax Cutters*, Kansas City Star, Jan. 15, 2015.
4. Emily Behlmann, *Kansas Tax Cuts Signed into Law*, Wichita Business Journal (May 22, 2012).
5. Chris Sullentrop, *The Kansas Experiment*, N.Y. Times Magazine, Aug. 5, 2015.
6. Mitch Smith & Julie Bosman, *Kansas Supreme Court Says State Education Spending Is Too Low*, N.Y. Times, Mar. 2, 2017.
7. Celia Llopis-Jepsen, *Kansas Tax Cut Experiment Comes to an End as Lawmakers Vote to Raise Taxes*, Nat'l Pub. Rad., June 7, 2017.
8. Larry Haeg, *Harriman vs. Hill: Wall Street's Great Railroad War* (2013).
9. Walter Licht, *Industrializing America: The Nineteenth Century* (1995).
10. 83 U.S. 36 (1873).
11. *Fletcher v. Peck*, 10 U.S. 87 (1810).
12. 17 U.S. 518 (1819).
13. *Id.*
14. *Santa Clara County v. Southern Pacific Railroad*, 118 U.S. 394 (1886).

15. Ciara Torres-Spelliscy, *The History of Corporate Personhood*, Brennan Center for Justice, www.brennancenter.org/blog/hobby-lobby-argument
16. Harry Jerome, *Mechanization in Industry*, National Bureau of Economic Research 158 (1934).
17. David A. Hounshell, *From the American System to Mass Production, 1800–1932: The Development of Manufacturing Technology in the United States* (1984).
18. See, e.g., William D. Barnes, *Oliver Hudson Kelley and the Genesis of the Grange: A Reappraisal*, 41 Agricultural Hist. 229 (1967).
19. 118 U.S. 557 (1886).
20. Adam Smith, *An Inquiry into the Nature and Causes of the Wealth of Nations* (1776).
21. See, e.g., Kevin A. Bryan & Leonardo Martinez, *On the Evolution of Income Inequality in the United States*, 94 Econ. Quart. 97 (2008).
22. Robert A. Margo, *Wages and Labor Markets in the United States: 1820–1860* (2000).
23. Claudia Goldin & Robert Margo, *The Great Compression: The Wage Structure of the United States at Mid-Century*, 107 Quart. J. of Econ. 1 (1992) (describing the period that came to be known as the "Great Compression.").
24. See, e.g., Peter H. Lindert, *When Did Inequality Rise in Britain and America?*, 9 J. of Income Dist. 11 (2000).
25. See, e.g., Taner Cam & Mustafa Kayaoglu, *Marx's Distinction between Socialism and Communism*, 12 Int'l J. of Human Sci. 385 (2015).
26. See, e.g., Louis Fischer, *Has the United States Overextended It's Commitments to Resist Communism?*, 342 Annals of the Am. Acad. of Pol. and Social Sci. 59 (1962) (arguing that the Soviet Union should not consider itself communist because it operates more as an imperial capitalist state).
27. *U.S. v. Butler*, 297 U.S. 1 (1936).
28. Pub. L. No. 75-430, 52 Stat. 31 (1938).
29. Franklin Roosevelt's Statement on Signing the Social Security Act, Aug. 14, 1935, http://docs.fdrlibrary.marist.edu/odssast.html
30. Bernard Bailyn, et al., *The Great Republic: A History of the American People* 792–794 (1985).
31. Michael Schaller, *Reckoning with Reagan: America and Its President in the 1980s* 72 (1992).
32. Paul Krugman, *Life without Bubbles*, N.Y. Times, Dec. 22, 2008.
33. Thomas Piketty, *Capital in the Twenty-First Century* (2013).
34. Thomas Piketty, *Capital in the Twenty-first Century* 1 (2013).
35. Thomas Piketty, *Capital in the Twenty-First Century* 335 (2013).

Additional Learning Resources

Additional Readings

C.W., *What Was Mercantilism?*, The Economist, Aug. 23, 2013, www.economist.com/blogs/freeexchange/2013/08/economic-history

M. Foucault, *Security, Territory, Population: Lectures at the College de France 1977–1978* (2009).

John M. Keynes, *The General Theory of Employment, Interest and Money* (1935).

Lars Magnusson, *Mercantilism: The Shaping of an Economic Language* (2002).

Curtis P. Nettels, *British Mercantilism and the Economic Development of the Thirteen Colonies*, 12 J. of Econ. Hist. 105 (Spring 1952).

Thomas Piketty, *Capital in the Twenty-First Century* (2013).

Robert J. Samuelson, *The End of Free Trade*, Wash. Post, Dec. 26, 2007.

Adam Smith, *An Inquiry into the Nature and Causes of the Wealth of Nations* (1776).

6   Foreign Law and Policy

Astrid Schmidt-King

Introductory Case: Foreign Policy in Action

On January 27, 2017, after one week in office, President Donald Trump issued Executive Order 13769, "Protecting the Nation from Foreign Terrorist Entry Into the United States." The order read in part:

> The visa-issuance process lays a crucial role in detecting individuals with terrorist ties and stopping them from entering the United States. Perhaps in no instance was that more apparent than the terrorist attacks of September 11, 2001, when State Department policy prevented consular officers from properly scrutinizing the visa applications of several of the 19 foreign nationals who went on to murder nearly 3,000 Americans. . . . Deteriorating conditions in certain countries due to war, strife, disaster, and civil unrest increase the likelihood that terrorist will use any means possible to enter the United States. The United States must be vigilant during the visa-issuance process to ensure that those approved for admission do not intend to harm Americans and that they have no ties to terrorism. . . . The United States cannot, and should not, admit those who do not support the Constitution, or those who would place violent ideologies over American law.

The order also outlined the suspension of the issuance of visas and other immigrant benefits to nationals of countries of particular concern, calls for heightened screening standards for individuals seeking entry, and suspends the U.S. Refugee Admissions Program for 120 days.

The Federation for American Immigration Reform (FAIR) issued a press release in support of the Executive Order, noting:

> In taking these steps he [the President] is acting within his authority to protect the security and interests of the nation and the American people. A temporary time-out in refugee admissions will allow time for the new administration's intelligence leaders to review and enhance vetting procedures. Doing so will save American lives. ISIS has made it crystal clear that it intends to use the refugee flow to infiltrate the West, including the U.S., and these actions will hopefully stymie those plans and protect Americans from future attacks. By suspending the issuance of visas and other immigration benefits to nationals of countries that are hotbeds of terrorism, the administration is reducing the overall risk profile of the refugee program, and demonstrating its strong commitment to placing the interests and safety of Americans first.

Two days later, on January 29, 2017, Senators John McCain (R-AZ) and Lindsey Graham (R-SC) issued a statement in response to the President's Executive Order:

> It is clear from the confusion at our airports across the nation that President Trump's executive order was not properly vetted. We are particularly concerned by reports that this order went into effect with little to no consultation with the Departments of State, Defense, Justice, and Homeland Security. Such a hasty process risks harmful results. We should not stop green-card holders from returning to the country they call home. We should not stop those who have served as interpreters for our military and diplomats from seeking refuge in the country they risked their lives to help. And we should not turn our backs on those refugees who have been shown through extensive vetting to pose no demonstrable threat to our nation, and who have suffered unspeakable horrors, most of them women and children.
>
> Ultimately, we fear this executive order will become a self-inflicted wound in the fight against terrorism. At this very moment, American troops are fighting side-by-side with our Iraqi partners to defeat ISIL. But this executive order bans Iraqi pilots from coming to military bases in Arizona to fight our common enemies. Our most important allies in the fight against ISIL are the vast majority of Muslims who reject its apocalyptic ideology of hatred. This executive order sends a signal, intended or not, that America does not want Muslims coming into our country. That is why we fear this executive order may do more to help terrorist recruitment than improve our security.

> Executive Orders—directives issued by the President that can carry the force of federal law.

What Is an Executive Order?

Executive orders are directives issued by the President that can carry the force of federal law. While such presidential discretionary powers are implicitly authorized in accordance with Article II of the Constitution, they are not explicit.

Executive orders, presidential memoranda, and proclamations are used extensively by Presidents to achieve policy goals, set uniform standards for managing the executive branch, or outline a policy view intended to influence the behavior of private citizens. The U.S. Constitution does not define these presidential instruments and does not explicitly vest the President with the authority to issue them. Nonetheless, such orders are accepted as an inherent aspect of presidential power. Moreover, if they are based on appropriate authority, they have the force and effect of law.[1]

In response to an executive order, Congress does have the authority to pass a law that counters or overrides the order, however such Congressional acts are subject to presidential veto.

The business community, in support of immigration as a source of workforce, innovation, and entrepreneurship, responded to the executive order—which banned entry of citizens of seven Muslim-majority "countries of concern"—Iraq, Syria, Iran, Libya, Somalia, Sudan and Yemen—for 90 days.

> Tim Cook, Apple CEO: "Apple would not exist without immigration, let alone thrive and innovate the way we do."

Reed Hastings, Netflix CEO: "Trump's actions are hurting Netflix explores around the world, and are so un-American it pains us all. Worse these actions will make America less safe (though hatred and loss of allies) rather than more safe."

Howard Schultz, Starbucks CEO: Pledged to hire 10,000 refugees over 5 years from 75 countries where Starbucks does business as a testament to his opposition to the executive order and to "reinforce our belief in our partners around the world."

This sudden nature of the initial executive order was met with widespread confusion regarding its enforcement and questions regarding its constitutionality. The legal challenges focus on laws protecting immigrants from discrimination on the basis of their national origin, as noted in the Immigration and Nationality Act (INA) of 1965. While President Trump contends that as Executive-in-Chief and in accordance with 8 U.S. Code 1182 "Inadmissible aliens" (1952) he is able to "suspend the entry" of immigrants that he deems a threat to the nation, various judges, most notably a federal appeals court three-judge panel (9th Circuit Court of Appeals), struck down this argument, finding the executive order illegal pursuant to the INA (1965), which prohibits discrimination in the issuance of an immigrant visa on the basis of a "person's race, sex, nationality, place of birth or place of residence." The court ruling granted a temporary restraining order blocking the travel ban from taking effect. Though the White House argued that the executive order calls for the suspension of entry and the 1965 law focuses on the issuance of visas, those opposed to the order note that a visa is a prerequisite for entry, and therefore the 1952 law needs to be read in light of the 1965 law.

Instead of appealing the decision of the 9th Circuit U.S. Court of Appeals, the Department of Justice (DOJ), the federal executive department tasked with enforcing the law, defending U.S. interests, and ensuring public safety against domestic and foreign threats, issued an amended Executive Order 13780 on March 6, 2017. While the new order continued the 90-day travel ban, it removed Iraq from the original list of seven countries, clarified an exemption for permanent residents (U.S. green card holders), and limited the refugee ban from Syria to a 120-day freeze. Still, many people perceived the revised executive order as a "Muslim ban," and on March 15, 2017, Judge Derrick Watson of the U.S. District Court for the District of Hawaii issued a temporary restraining order on the basis that parts of the executive order were motivated by anti-Muslim bias and therefore violated the Establishment Clause of the First Amendment, which states that "Congress shall make no law respecting an establishment of religion, or prohibiting the free exercise thereof." The Lawyers' Committee for Civil Rights Under the Law stated, "The new executive order does not cure the discriminatory and unconstitutional effect of the travel ban. The order invites illegal profiling of minority and religious communities on the basis of race, national origin and religion" and violates the First and Fifth Amendments.

The White House appealed Judge Watson's ruling, which converted the temporary restraining order to an indefinite preliminary injunction to the U.S. Supreme Court. A legal showdown and procedural maze ensued, and a third executive order was issued modifying the list of countries banned—while Sudan was no longer subject to the ban, Chad, North Korea, and Venezuela were added to the list. President Trump's third attempt to ban travel from several predominantly Muslim nations met the same fate as the first two: It was blocked nationwide by a federal judge in Hawaii. The ban, "suffers from precisely the same maladies as its predecessor," Judge Derrick

Watson wrote. "It lacks sufficient findings that the entry of more than 150 million nationals from six specified countries would be 'detrimental to the interests of the United States,'" and it "plainly discriminates based on nationality." The White House explained that this travel ban was crafted in coordination with the departments of Homeland Security, State, Defense, and Justice and called Judge Watson's ruling "dangerously flawed" and a threat to national security.

Discussion Questions

What do you think? Is the travel ban legal? Should it be implemented in the name of national security? Or is its discriminatory impact too broad and therefore unconstitutional?

Immigration and Impact of Foreign Policy—in the Words of a Practitioner

Laura Reiff of Greenberg Traurig LLP co-chairs the Business Immigration & Compliance Practice and is the co-managing shareholder of the Northern Virginia office. She also co-chairs the firm's Labor & Employment Practice's International Employment, Immigration & Workforce Strategies group. Laura focuses her practice on business immigration laws and regulations affecting U.S. and foreign companies, as well as related employment compliance and legislative issues. Laura advises corporations on a variety of compliance-related issues and has been involved in audits and internal investigations and has successfully minimized monetary exposure as well as civil and criminal liabilities on behalf of her clients. She develops immigration compliance strategies and programs for both small and large companies. Laura's practice also consists of managing business immigration matters and providing immigration counsel to address the visa and work authorization needs of U.S. and global personnel, including professionals, managers and executives, treaty investors/ traders, essential workers, persons of extraordinary ability, corporate trainees, and students. She is an immigration policy advocacy expert and works on immigration reform policies.

> *As a business immigration attorney and policy advocate, my job is to help facilitate the movement of people into the U.S. for business purposes and to help any client deliver top notch services and to continue to expand both domestically and globally.*
>
> *Businesses need workers across the skill spectrum for innovation and production. In order to grow, businesses need access to talent and workers from outside the U.S. The current Administration's policies do not recognize immigration as the catalyst for growth that it is. Bad actors should be enforced against, but businesses should be permitted to utilize foreign born skilled workers, professionals and students to meet business needs. At full employment the U.S. should not stifle business immigration—to do so hampers goals of growth. This also includes respecting and expanding treaties and bilateral investment agreements which also support immigrant investors and professionals.*

Overview/Background

This chapter is structured so that the reader first is introduced to the foundations and key concepts related to foreign policy. With this foundation, the chapter examines significant events of the 19th and 20th centuries that shaped foreign policy, with a significant focus on the Cold War, *détente*, and the post–Cold War era. Understanding this background and historical context of foreign policy and international affairs is critical to appreciating the complexity of contemporary relationships and issues. The chapter then discusses how foreign policy is crafted, and it examines the role, powers, tools, and limitations of each branch of government—executive, legislative, and judicial—and it reviews the procedural policymaking process. In exploring the role of increased globalization, the chapter discusses the role of global governance and theories of international relations. In applying all of this to foreign policy in the 21st century, the chapter applies and links key concepts and examines contemporary issues. The chapter ends with concluding points, discussion questions, an exercise, and a list of recommended readings, including online resources. The chapter incorporates testaments from presidents and leading figures, vignettes from practitioners, charts and statistics, and discussion questions.

What Is Foreign Policy?

> *Foreign policy, unlike baseball, has no world championship; there are no permanent victories. In our era, moreover, neither the adversaries, nor the rules, nor even the location of the playing field are fully fixed. . . . The ultimate test of our foreign policy is how well our actions measure up to our ideals.*[2]
> —Madeleine K. Albright, first woman to serve as Secretary of State, 1997–2001

Whether marked by events such as World War II, the Cold War, and September 11th or defined by eras of intensified levels of globalization and technological advancement, foreign policy is critical to national **sovereignty** and international order. The term **foreign policy** refers to a state's reaction to and interaction with other states and non-state actors, such as terrorist groups. Foreign policy helps explain the behavior of a government, shapes national policies, and influences relations between **nation-states** (see Box 6.1).

Sovereignty—formally established by the Treaty of Westphalia in 1648, it is the fundamental principle that states have the right to operate as autonomous actors in the international political system.

Foreign policy—refers to a state's reaction to and interaction with other states and non-state actors, such as terrorist groups. Foreign policy helps explain the behavior of a government, shapes national policies, and influences relations among nation-states.

Nation-state—a sovereign state defined by borders, governed by an administration, and comprising people who share a national identity.

Box 6.1 Becoming a Nation-State System

Though critical political actors on the international stage, the idea of the sovereign nation-state is modern concept. As defined by Anthony D. Smith in Nationalism, *a nation is "a named human community residing in a perceived homeland, and having common myths and a shared history, a distinct public culture, and common laws and customs for all members." While "a nation is not a state" and it need be affiliated with a state* per se, *it often does seek recognition, nationhood, sovereignty, and territory (e.g., the Kurds and the Palestinians). States are governing bodies, defined by a sovereign territory,*

> borders, and a populace. As an institution, a state has the authority to promulgate laws, regulate policy, collect taxes, and maintain a military and police force; states impact the political, economic, and social well-being of its inhabitants and land. The relationship between a nation and a state is an important, complementary one; communities that constitute a nation are politically integrated into the organization of the state.
>
> The development of the nation-state system began primarily in Western Europe as resistance to feudalism increased and the influence of feudal lords diminished. As the medieval hierarchical model of government and political organization, feudalism centered on land ownership, whereby the feudal lord would provide land to a man in exchange for his labor and/or military service. At the same time, the Renaissance and the Reformation challenged long-standing senses of identity based on religion and compromised the political clout of the Catholic church. Sensing these shifting tides and a rising middle class, kings and queens sought to consolidate territories, demark new borders, and create new nations. As these consolidated centers became hubs of commerce and trade, there was a growing desire for independence from provincial feudal lords and a greater attraction to a monarchy system. A national monarch provided a more cosmopolitan political structure that facilitated the movement of people and goods. Inhabitants began to feel a sense of loyalty to the cities and towns, and beginning notions of nationalism emerged. Monarchs laid the foundation for the contemporary nation-state system, and the Treaty of Westphalia (1648) marked the modern system of international relations with sovereign states at the key political actors. The Westphalia system promoted the idea of peaceful co-existence between sovereign states (Westphalian sovereignty) and the balance of power as a critical components of foreign policy.

What Are the Goals of Foreign Policy?

The goal of foreign policy is captured in the mission of the U.S. Department of State: "to shape and sustain a peaceful, prosperous, just, and democratic world and foster conditions for stability and progress for the benefit of the American people and people everywhere." With 195 sovereign countries in the world as of 2017—each with their own national interests, concerns, and priorities—a state's foreign policy directly relates to its diplomatic, political, economic, social, military, security, and humanitarian interests. Therefore, foreign policy is fluid and dynamic; it adjusts based on changes that take place on the domestic, regional, or global level.

As a bridge between the state's domestic environment and the global environment, foreign policy is internally crafted and externally applied. The backdrop for creating foreign policy, a state's national interests can be shaped and influenced by many factors, including geography, regional interests and concerns, demographics, economic standing and level of development, political structure, social ideology, and history. Therefore, domestic concerns and national politics are directly related to a state's crafting of its foreign policy. "[T]oday's crucial foreign policy challenges arise less from problems between countries than from domestic politics within them."³ And as noted by President Bill Clinton (1993–2001),

> The more time I spend on foreign policy . . . the more I become convinced that there is no longer a clear distinction between what is foreign and domestic. . . . The longer I stay here, the more convinced I become that all my successors in the 21st Century will have to find different words for domestic and foreign. They'll probably talk about security and economic policy. And 10 years from now, the patterns of speech will be entirely different. People will be discussing things that happened within our borders and beyond our borders in general categories, rather than foreign and domestic, because they are tending to flow together in the global economy.

The Historical Context and Foundations of Foreign Policy

The 19th Century

With the Revolutionary War ending in 1783, the focus of the United States in the 19th century was on national independence from the more dominant European countries across the Atlantic Ocean and national expansion and development. As stated in his 1796 farewell address, George Washington observed that "Our detached and distant situation invites and enables us to pursue a different course." The 1800s were largely a time of **isolationism**, where the United States was less involved internationally and pursued a policy of non-interventionism. By focusing on nation-building, national interests, and the economic development and prosperity of the country, the United States did not seek "entangling alliances" or engage in global conflicts. In this spirit, President James Monroe (1817–1825) delivered his seventh annual speech to the U.S. Congress in 1823 where he warned against European interference in the affairs of the U.S. and the greater Western Hemisphere. This speech outlined what is referred to as the **Monroe Doctrine**, a critical element of U.S. foreign policy that warned European states (the Old World) against future colonization and interference in the New World while also reaffirming the U.S. policy of non-interventionism toward European countries. Though not viewed as a guiding principle at the time, the Monroe Doctrine came to be viewed as integral foreign policy and was invoked on several occasions.

> Isolationist—when a leader retreats from an active role in world affairs and international politics and is more focused on national and domestic concerns, including nation-building, national interests, and the economic development and prosperity.
>
> Monroe Doctrine—a critical element of U.S. foreign policy that warned European states (the Old World) against future colonization and interference in the New World while also reaffirming the U.S. policy of non-interventionism toward European countries.

As Noted by President Monroe in His Speech on December 2, 1823

The citizens of the United States cherish sentiments the most friendly in favor of the liberty and happiness of their fellow-men on that side of the Atlantic. In the wars of the European powers in matters relating to themselves we have never taken any part, nor does it comport with our policy to do so. It is only when our rights are invaded or seriously menaced that we resent injuries or make preparation for our defense. With the movements in this hemisphere we are of necessity more immediately connected, and by causes which must be obvious to all enlightened and impartial observers. The political system of the allied powers is essentially

> *different in this respect from that of America. This difference proceeds from that which exists in their respective Governments; and to the defense of our own, which has been achieved by the loss of so much blood and treasure, and matured by the wisdom of their most enlightened citizens, and under which we have enjoyed unexampled felicity, this whole nation is devoted. We owe it, therefore, to candor and to the amicable relations existing between the United States and those powers to declare that we should consider any attempt on their part to extend their system to any portion of this hemisphere as dangerous to our peace and safety. With the existing colonies or dependencies of any European power we have not interfered and shall not interfere. But with the Governments who have declared their independence and maintain it, and whose independence we have, on great consideration and on just principles, acknowledged, we could not view any interposition for the purpose of oppressing them, or controlling in any other manner their destiny, by any European power in any other light than as the manifestation of an unfriendly disposition toward the United States.*

While the policy of non-interventionism largely defined much of the 19th century, so did the United States' desire to expand geographically. To that end, the United States engaged in an armed conflict with Mexico from 1846–1848. The Mexican-American War (1846–1848), referred to by those in Mexico as the American Intervention in Mexico or the *Guerra de Estados Unidos a Mexico* ("War of the United States Against Mexico"), was a response to the U.S. annexation of Texas in 1845. The war officially ended with the signing of the Treaty of Guadalupe Hidalgo on February 2, 1848, whereby the United States acquired New Mexico and California—this purchased acquisition of 500,000 square miles expanded the U.S. border and positioned it as an emerging global leader.

Fifty years later in 1898, triggered by the inexplicable and mystifying sinking of the Battleship Maine in Havana (Cuba) harbor, the United States declared war on Spain. This marked the beginning of the Spanish-American War.[4] With a long-standing interest in Cuba, in part due to its sugar cane production, and with its continued interest in expansion, the United States intervened in the Cuban War of Independence and the Philippine Revolution, both lands that were still possessed by Spain; Spain also possessed Puerto Rico and Guam. The United States and signed a peace treaty in 1898 ending the war, establishing an independent Cuba, ceding Puerto Rico and Guam to the U.S., and allowing for the U.S. purchase of the Philippines from Spain. The once Spanish empire no longer existed.

The turn of the century—between the 19th and 20th—marked the beginning of the United States' **Open Door Policy**. As a superpower with increasing land, population, and influence, the United States was in a position to wield its political, economic, social, and military power in support of its 20th-century national interests. With populations concentrated in urban areas, the economic development and output of the United States increased with industrial production complementing, but outpacing, agricultural production. With an increase in manufacturing and industrial might came a heightened national and domestic interest in global marketplaces and trading partners. While often referred to as a doctrine encouraging free trade and international commerce, the Open Door Policy was specifically crafted in recognition

---

Open Door Policy—crafted in recognition of the various, potentially competing, spheres of influence in China. In a series of notes issued in 1899, U.S. Secretary of State John Hay called for the adherence to the principle of equal access and economic opportunity in China. Aimed at ensuring and protecting U.S. access into the China market against existing European trading partners, the Open Door Policy guided the U.S. policy toward the China market entering the 20th century.

of the various, potentially competing, spheres of influence in China. In a series of notes issued in 1899, U.S. Secretary of State John Hay called for the adherence to the principle of equal access and economic opportunity in China. Aimed at ensuring and protecting U.S. access into the China market against existing European trading partners, the Open Door Policy guided the U.S. policy toward the China market entering the 20th century.

The 20th Century

Key Events and Moments That Influenced 20th-Century Foreign Policy

- *The Great War—World War I (1914–1918)*
- *Fourteen Points (1918)*
- *Treaty of Versailles and League of Nations (1919)*
- *World War II (1939–1945)*
- *Bretton Woods System (1944)*
- *Establishment of the United Nations (1945)*
- *Marshall Plan and Truman Doctrine (1947–1948)*
- *Creation and U.S. recognition of Israel (1948)*
- *Formation of NATO (1949)*
- *Korean War (1950–1953)*
- *Cuban Revolution and creation of communist state (1959)*
- *Cuban Missile Crisis (1962)*
- *Vietnam War (1955–1975)*
- *U.S. détente policy efforts with Russia and China (1972)*
- *U.S. Embassy in Tehran seized by Iranian militants (1979)*
- *The Iran Contra Affair (1985–1987)*
- *Fall of the Berlin Wall (1989)*
- *End of the Cold War and dissolution of the Soviet Union (1991)*
- *Persian Gulf War (1990–1991)*
- *North American Free Trade Agreement (NAFTA) Treaty ratified by Congress (1993)*
- *World Trade Organization (WTO) established (1995)*
- *Conflict in the Former Yugoslavia and the Dayton Accords (1995)*

World War II

Following the roaring 1920s—a time of economic prosperity—was the Great Depression—a decade of economic depression lasting from 1929 to 1939. The end of the Depression marked the beginning of World War II. The Second World War was a global war involving various countries on different continents. With the end of the war in 1945 came a new international order and structure. To manage this new reality, the United States lead the creation of the **United Nations** (UN), an intergovernmental organization initially comprising 51 member states[5] and now consisting of 193 member states. Signed on June 26, 1945, the UN was established with the mission to facilitate international cooperation and prevent future conflict.

Article 1 - Purposes of the United Nations Are

1. To maintain international peace and security, and to that end: to take effective collective measures for the prevention and removal of threats to the peace, and for the suppression of acts of aggression or other breaches of the peace, and to bring about by peaceful means, and in conformity with the principles of justice and international law, adjustment or settlement of international disputes or situations which might lead to a breach of the peace;
2. To develop friendly relations among nations based on respect for the principle of equal rights and self-determination of peoples, and to take other appropriate measures to strengthen universal peace;
3. To achieve international co-operation in solving international problems of an economic, social, cultural, or humanitarian character, and in promoting and encouraging respect for human rights and for fundamental freedoms for all without distinction as to race, sex, language, or religion; and
4. To be a centre for harmonizing the actions of nations in the attainment of these common ends.[6]

The great powers emerging from the war—the United States, the Soviet Union, China, France, and the UK—were named permanent members of the **United Nations Security Council (UNSC)**.

Article 23 - Composition[7]

1. The Security Council shall consist of fifteen Members of the United Nations. The Republic of China, France, the Union of Soviet Socialist Republics, the United Kingdom of Great Britain and Northern Ireland, and the United States of America shall be permanent members of the Security Council. The General Assembly shall elect ten other Members of the United Nations to be non-permanent members of the Security Council, due regard being specially paid, in the first instance to the contribution of Members of the United Nations to the maintenance of international peace and security and to the other purposes of the Organization, and also to equitable geographical distribution.
2. The non-permanent members of the Security Council shall be elected for a term of two years. In the first election of the non-permanent members after the increase of the membership of the Security Council from eleven to fifteen, two of the four additional members shall be chosen for a term of one year. A retiring member shall not be eligible for immediate re-election.
3. Each member of the Security Council shall have one representative.

Article 24 - Functions and Powers[8]

1. In order to ensure prompt and effective action by the United Nations, its Members confer on the Security Council primary responsibility for the maintenance of international peace and security, and agree that in carrying out its duties under this responsibility the Security Council acts on their behalf.
2. In discharging these duties the Security Council shall act in accordance with the Purposes and Principles of the United Nations. The specific powers

---

United Nations (UN) and UN Security Council (UNSC)—an intergovernmental organization initially comprised of 51 member states now consists of 193 member states. Signed on June 26, 1945, the UN was established with the mission to facilitate international cooperation and prevent future conflict. The great powers emerging from the war—the United States, the Soviet Union, China, France, and the UK—were named permanent members of the United Nations Security Council (UNSC).

granted to the Security Council for the discharge of these duties are laid down in Chapters VI, VII, VIII, and XII.
3. The Security Council shall submit annual and, when necessary, special reports to the General Assembly for its consideration.

Post–World War II

The United States emerged from World War II as a powerful, strong economic state with increased global authority, which influenced U.S. foreign policy. The leader in establishing the UN, the United States also was responsible for the **Marshall Plan** in 1947. In the wake of the deadliest of wars, the Marshall Plan was created in response to the massive destruction on the European continent with the intention to economically assist, stabilize, and rebuild war-torn Europe.

> Marshall Plan—created in 1947 in the wake of World War II, the plan responded to the massive destruction on the European continent with the intention to economically assist, stabilize, and rebuild war-torn Europe.

Europe was devastated by years of conflict during World War II. Millions of people had been killed or wounded. Industrial and residential centers in England, France, Germany, Italy, Poland, Belgium and elsewhere lay in ruins. Much of Europe was on the brink of famine as agricultural production had been disrupted by war. Transportation infrastructure was in shambles. The only major power in the world that was not significantly damaged was the United States.

From 1945 through 1947, the United States was already assisting European economic recovery with direct financial aid. Military assistance to Greece and Turkey was being given. The newly formed United Nations was providing humanitarian assistance. In January 1947, U. S. President Harry Truman appointed George Marshall, the architect of victory during WWII, to be Secretary of State. In just a few months the State Department, under his leadership, with expertise provided by George Kennan, William Clayton and others crafted the Marshall Plan concept, which George Marshall shared with the world in a speech on June 5, 1947, at Harvard University.[9]

As noted in Marshall's speech,

Aside from the demoralizing effect on the world at large and the possibilities of disturbances arising as a result of the desperation of the people concerned, the consequences to the economy of the United States should be apparent to all. It is logical that the United States should do whatever it is able to do to assist in the return of normal economic health in the world, without which there can be no political stability and no assured peace. Our policy is directed not against any country or doctrine but against hunger, poverty, desperation and chaos. Its purpose should be the revival of a working economy in the world so as to permit the emergence of political and social conditions in which free institutions can exist. Such assistance, I am convinced, must not be on a piece-meal basis as various crises develop. Any assistance that this Government may render in the future should provide a cure rather than a mere palliative. Any government that is willing to assist in the task of recovery will find full cooperation, I am sure, on the part of the United States Government. Any government which maneuvers to block the recovery of other countries cannot expect help from us. Furthermore,

168 Foreign Law and Policy

> governments, political parties or groups which seek to perpetuate human misery in order to profit there from politically or otherwise will encounter the opposition of the United States.[10]

North Atlantic Treaty Organization (NATO)—created in 1949, the intergovernmental military alliance, the North Atlantic Treaty Organization (NATO), referred to in France as the Organisation du Traité de l'Atlantique Nord (OTAN), was created. An alliance of countries from North America and Europe, upon inception in 1949, NATO comprised 12 member states; today NATO has 29 member states. A collective approach to security and foreign policy, "NATO's purpose is to guarantee the freedom and security of its members through political and military means. NATO promotes democratic values and enables members to consult and cooperate on defence and security-related issues to solve problems, build trust and, in the long run, prevent conflict. NATO is committed to the peaceful resolution of disputes. If diplomatic efforts fail, it has the military power to undertake crisis-management operations. These are carried out under the collective defence clause of NATO's founding treaty - Article 5 of the Washington Treaty or under a United Nations mandate, alone or in cooperation with other countries and international organisations." Central to its mission is "the principle that an attack against one or several of its members is considered as an attack against all."

In 1949, nearly two years after the introduction of the Marshall Plan, the intergovernmental military alliance, the **North Atlantic Treaty Organization** (NATO), referred to in France as the Organisation du Traité de l'Atlantique Nord (OTAN), was created. An alliance of countries from North America and Europe, upon inception in 1949, NATO comprised 12 member states; today NATO has 29[11] member states. A collective approach to security and foreign policy,

NATO's purpose is to guarantee the freedom and security of its members through political and military means. NATO promotes democratic values and enables members to consult and cooperate on defence and security-related issues to solve problems, build trust and, in the long run, prevent conflict. NATO is committed to the peaceful resolution of disputes. If diplomatic efforts fail, it has the military power to undertake crisis-management operations. These are carried out under the collective defence clause of NATO's founding treaty - Article 5 of the Washington Treaty or under a United Nations mandate, alone or in cooperation with other countries and international organisations.

Central to its mission is "the principle that an attack against one or several of its members is considered as an attack against all." This principle, encapsulated in Article 5, has only been used one time in reaction to the terrorist attacks in the United States on 9/11.

> **Discussion Questions**
>
> What do you think? Is NATO a valuable alliance and foreign policy tool?

NATO has been a source of debate, especially as of late. When running for President, then candidate Donald J. Trump was dismissive of NATO and the role it plays in foreign policy. Calling it "obsolete" and an alliance based on old threats and not contemporary concerns, Trump was critical of the alliance and of the disproportionate financial burden placed on the United States. However, not long into his Presidency, Trump changed course, and while meeting with NATO's secretary general, he stated: "I said it was obsolete. . . . It's no longer obsolete." He now views NATO as a necessary tool for defending security and ensuring stability in the United States, Europe, and beyond. That said, at the NATO summit in May 2017, President Trump declined to directly affirm and support Article 5.

Trump Declines to Affirm NATO's Article 5: Speaking in front of the leaders of its member-nations, the president fails to make clear the United States still has the alliance's back. The Atlantic, May 25, 2017

BRUSSELS—President Trump did not explicitly endorse the mutual-aid clause of the North Atlantic Treaty at the NATO summit on Thursday *despite previous indications that he was planning to do so, keeping in place the cloud of ambiguity hanging over the relationship between the United States and the alliance. Speaking in front of a 9/11 and Article 5 Memorial at the new NATO headquarters, Trump praised NATO's response to the 9/11 attacks and spoke of "the commitments that bind us together as one." But he did not specifically commit to honor Article 5, which stipulates that other NATO allies must come to the aid of an ally under attack if it is invoked. The only time in history that Article 5 has been invoked was after the September 11 attacks, a fact that Trump mentioned. The memorial Trump was dedicating is a piece of steel from the North Tower that fell during the attacks.*

[. . .]

Trump has been a harsh critic of NATO overall, at one point calling it "obsolete." He has repeatedly criticized other allies for not paying their fair share of the defense burden of the alliance. He has pushed the alliance to do more to combat terrorism. At the NATO leaders summit, counter-terrorism and burden-sharing will dominate the agenda—not Russia. Trump did mention the Russian threat in his remarks on Thursday. "The NATO of the future must include a great focus on terrorism and immigration, as well as threats from Russia and on NATO's eastern and southern borders," he said. But he spent the bulk of the speech haranguing the other members of the alliance—standing only feet from him—for not meeting their spending obligations. "Twenty-three of the 28 member nations are still not paying what they should be paying and what they are supposed to be paying for their defense," Trump said. "We should recognize that with these chronic underpayments and growing threats, even two percent of GDP is insufficient to close the gaps in modernizing, readiness and the size of forces," he added. "Two percent is the bare minimum for confronting today's very real and very vicious threats."[12] *[see Figure 6.1]*

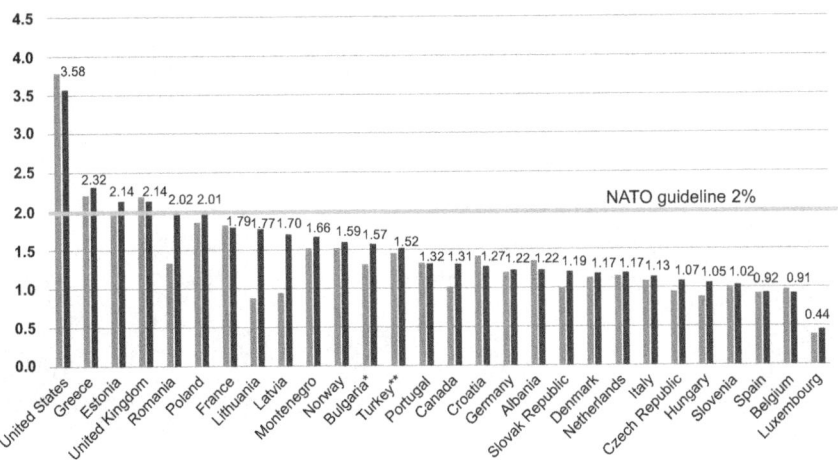

Figure 6.1 NATO Members' Military Expenditures (2014).
Source: NATO, Defence Expenditure of NATO Countries (2010–2017), June 29 2017.

The Cold War

> **Cold War (1947–1991)**—created a bipolar world order led by the then two superpowers, the United States and the U.S.S.R. Though actual war never materialized, the bipolar division following World War II created the Iron Curtain, closing off Eastern Europe from contact with the West. The end of the Cold War in 1991 marked the beginning of a new, more nuanced international order—one that was no longer primarily shaped by two countries practicing deterrence through military force and nuclear proliferation.
>
> **Containment**—a period following World War II that highlighted the ideological differences between capitalism and communism and the respective antipathy between the United States and the Soviet Union and the U.S. interest in containing the spread of communism and the Soviet Union.

The **Cold War** (1947–1991) created a bipolar world order led by the then two superpowers, the United States and the U.S.S.R. Though actual war never materialized, the bipolar division following World War II created the Iron Curtain, closing off Eastern Europe from contact with the West (see Figure 6.2). In a speech by Winston Churchill in 1946, he observed that "From Stettin in the Baltic to Trieste in the Adriatic, an iron curtain has descended across the Continent." Much of the foreign policy crafted at this time centered on this confrontational dynamic and alliances, coalitions, and policies were byproducts of this relationship built on rivalry. The United States was focused on containing the spread of communism and the Soviet Union. This period of **containment** following World War II highlighted the ideological differences between capitalism and communism and the respective antipathy between the United States and the Soviet Union. With tensions high

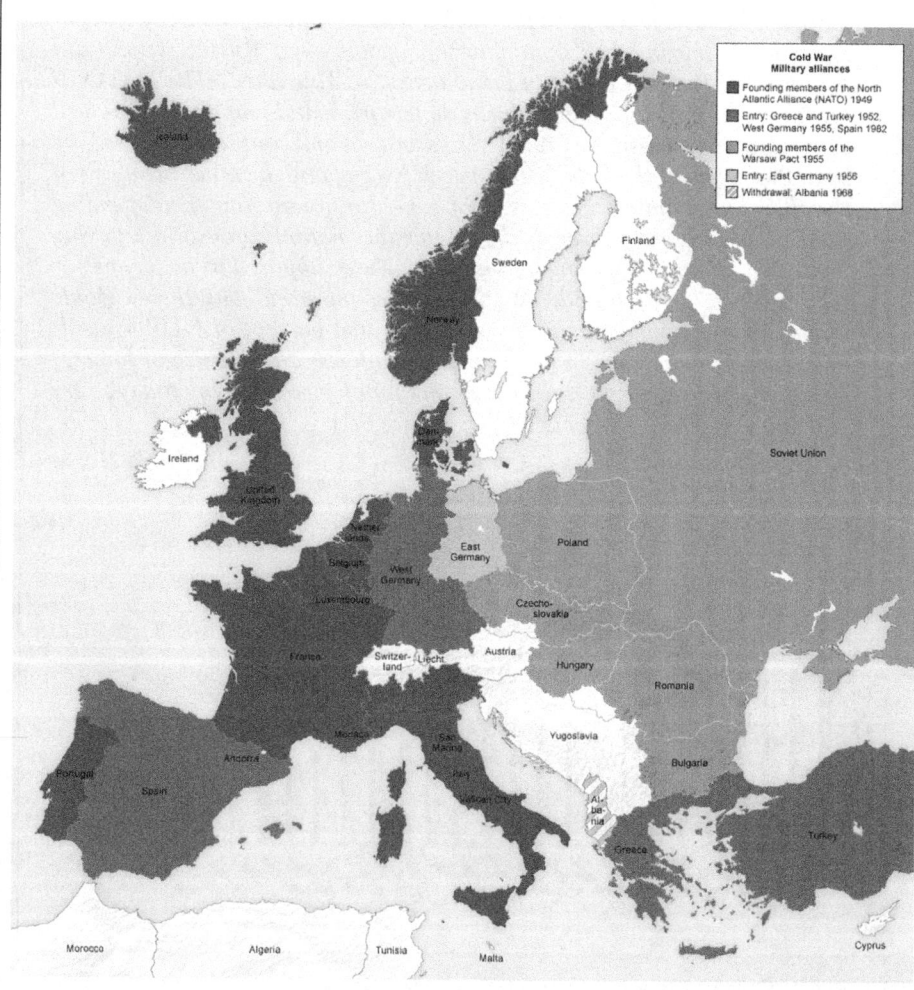

Figure 6.2 Europe during the Cold War.
Source: Wikimedia Commons

during the Cold War and with posturing against one another, the two countries disproportionately invested resources in their military power and prowess, including a nuclear arms and space race.

THE CUBAN MISSILE CRISIS

While the Cold War was defined by the ideological power struggle between the United States and the Soviet Union, Cuba posed the gravest foreign policy challenge to the United States. With just 106 miles between Key West, Florida and Havana, Cuba, this island came to represent a turning point in the Cold War. In 1959, the U.S.-backed leader of Cuba, Fulgencio Batista, was overthrown. The new leader, Fidel Castro, was a fierce Cuban nationalist who adopted a Marxist-Leninist political stance and ruled Cuba as a nationalized, communist, one-party state. Prime Minister from 1959 through 1976 and President from 1976 to 2008, Fidel Castro aligned with the Soviet Union and openly condemned the United States, declaring it an enemy of Cuba, its people, and its socialist ideology. In 1962, the United States discovered that medium- and intermediate-range missiles, which had the capability of carrying nuclear weapons, were being placed in Cuba at the urging of the Soviet Union. With Cuba's proximity to the United States, the missiles were intended to hit U.S. cities. This was a critical moment, and it is referred to as the Cuban Missile Crisis. In 1963, after intense weeks of governmental negotiations between the White House and the Kremlin, the missiles were removed from Cuba under the order of Nikita Khrushchev, the Secretary of the Communist Party of the Soviet Union from 1953 through 1964.

> The infamous "red telephone," also referred to as the "hotline," was established immediately following the Cuban Missile Crisis as a direct connection between the White House (U.S.) and the Kremlin (U.S.S.R.). The goal was to foster greater communication between the two superpowers.

The nuclear conflict between the two superpowers was averted, and, in the wake of the crisis, both the United States and the Soviet Union reconsidered the nuclear arms race that had come to define the Cold War. This begins the thawing of the Cold War.

EL BLOQUEO

A by-product of the Cold War era, *el bloqueo*, meaning "the blockade," refers to the embargo the United States placed against Cuba in the early 1960s. As noted on the State Department's website,

> The United States maintains a comprehensive economic embargo on the Republic of Cuba. In February 1962, President John F. Kennedy proclaimed an embargo on trade between the United States and Cuba, in response to certain actions taken by the Cuban Government, and directed the Departments of Commerce and the Treasury to implement the embargo, which remains in place today.[13]

In addition to trade, there are also travel restrictions placed on U.S. citizens and limitations on U.S. businesses seeking to do business in Cuba. Before leaving office, in

March 2016, President Barack Obama (2009–2017) announced that select embargo and travel restrictions against Cuba would be eased in an effort to strengthen relations between the countries. However, "[o]n June 16, 2017, President Trump issued a National Security Presidential Memorandum (NSPM) on Strengthening the Policy of the United States Toward Cuba."[14]

Many debate the value and purpose of the economic sanctions and travel restrictions. Proponents contend that if Cuba met the conditions outlined by the United States that focus on improving human rights and taking steps toward a democratic form of government, then the embargo would be lifted. Opponents argue that lifting the embargo would facilitate trade, business relations, and travel between the countries, which would induce democratic change in Cuba.

> **Discussion Question**
>
> Should the embargo remain in place?

> **On October 22, 1962, U.S. President John F. Kennedy Addressed the Nation and Cuba**[15]
>
> *This Government, as promised, has maintained the closest surveillance of the Soviet Military buildup on the island of Cuba. Within the past week, unmistakable evidence has established the fact that a series of offensive missile sites is now in preparation on that imprisoned island. The purpose of these bases can be none other than to provide a nuclear strike capability against the Western Hemisphere. . . . This urgent transformation of Cuba into an important strategic base—by the presence of these large, long range, and clearly offensive weapons of sudden mass destruction—constitutes an explicit threat to the peace and security of all the Americas, in flagrant and deliberate defiance of the Rio Pact of 1947, the traditions of this Nation and hemisphere, the joint resolution of the 87th Congress, the Charter of the United Nations, and my own public warnings to the Soviets on September 4 and 13. This action also contradicts the repeated assurances of Soviet spokesmen, both publicly and privately delivered, that the arms buildup in Cuba would retain its original defensive character, and that the Soviet Union had no need or desire to station strategic missiles on the territory of any other nation.*
>
> *Neither the United States of America nor the world community of nations can tolerate deliberate deception and offensive threats on the part of any nation, large or small. We no longer live in a world where only the actual firing of weapons represents a sufficient challenge to a nation's security to constitute maximum peril. Nuclear weapons are so destructive and ballistic missiles are so swift, that any substantially increased possibility of their use or any sudden change in their deployment may well be regarded as a definite threat to peace.*
>
> *For many years both the Soviet Union and the United States, recognizing this fact, have deployed strategic nuclear weapons with great care, never*

upsetting the precarious status quo which insured that these weapons would not be used in the absence of some vital challenge. Our own strategic missiles have never been transferred to the territory of any other nation under a cloak of secrecy and deception; and our history—unlike that of the Soviets since the end of World War II—demonstrates that we have no desire to dominate or conquer any other nation or impose our system upon its people. Nevertheless, American citizens have become adjusted to living daily on the Bull's-eye of Soviet missiles located inside the U.S.S.R. or in submarines.

But this secret, swift, and extraordinary buildup of Communist missiles—in an area well known to have a special and historical relationship to the United States and the nations of the Western Hemisphere, in violation of Soviet assurances, and in defiance of American and hemispheric policy—this sudden, clandestine decision to station strategic weapons for the first time outside of Soviet soil—is a deliberately provocative and unjustified change in the status quo which cannot be accepted by this country, if our courage and our commitments are ever to be trusted again by either friend or foe.

[...]

We will not prematurely or unnecessarily risk the costs of worldwide nuclear war in which even the fruits of victory would be ashes in our mouth—but neither will we shrink from that risk at any time it must be faced.

[...]

Many times in the past, the Cuban people have risen to throw out tyrants who destroyed their liberty. And I have no doubt that most Cubans today look forward to the time when they will be truly free—free from foreign domination, free to choose their own leaders, free to select their own system, free to own their own land, free to speak and write and worship without fear or degradation. And then shall Cuba be welcomed back to the society of free nations and to the associations of this hemisphere.

Fidel Castro in His Own Words

The duty of every revolutionary is to make the revolution. It is known that the revolution will triumph in America and throughout the world, but it is not for revolutionaries to sit in the doorways of their houses waiting for the corpse of imperialism to pass by. The role of Job doesn't suit a revolutionary. Each year that the liberation of America is speeded up will mean the lives of millions of children saved, millions of intelligences saved for culture, an infinite quantity of pain spared the people. Even if the Yankee imperialists prepare a bloody drama for America, they will not succeed in crushing the peoples' struggles, they will only arouse universal hatred against themselves. And such a drama will also mark the death of their greedy and carnivorous system. At [the] Punta del Este [inter-American conference in Uruguay in 1961] a great ideological battle unfolded between the Cuban Revolution and Yankee imperialism. Who did they represent there, for whom did each speak? Cuba represented the people; the United States represented the monopolies. Cuba spoke for America's exploited masses; the United States for the exploiting, oligarchical, and imperialist

Figure 6.3 Time Magazine Cover of Fidel Castro.
Source: http://content.time.com/time/covers/0,16641,19590126,00.html

interests; Cuba for sovereignty; the United States for intervention; Cuba for the nationalization of foreign enterprises; the United States for new investments of foreign capital. Cuba for culture; the United States for ignorance. Cuba for agrarian reform; the United States for great landed estates. Cuba for the industrialization of America; the United States for underdevelopment.... Cuba for peace among peoples; the United States for aggression and war. Cuba for socialism; the United States for capitalism.[16]

[The Soviet Union] could have installed a thousand [nuclear] missiles [in Cuba in 1962]! That's what I said to Biriouzov [the Soviet field marshal in charge of nuclear forces in Cuba]: a thousand missiles. I said to him: "Look, if it is in the interest and the defense of the entire socialist camp, we are prepared to install a thousand [nuclear] missiles here." Imagine my reaction when they told me that they would [only] install [40] missiles.... We defended these [nuclear] missiles with affection, with an incredible love. We were fighting for the first time almost on equal terms with an enemy [the United States] that had threatened and provoked us unceasingly. I wrote a letter [on October 26, 1962] to Khrushchev to give him courage. It was my opinion that, in case of an invasion, it was necessary to launch a massive and total nuclear strike [against the United States].... If they invade ... one should not waste time ... nor give the enemy the time to launch the first strike.[17]

THE WARMING OF THE COLD WAR

In the shadow of the Cuban Missile Crisis and with increased regional conflicts—the Korean War (1950–1953) and the Vietnam War (1955–1975)—and with U.S. domestic turmoil, there were new incentives to re-evaluate U.S. foreign policy and ease the Cold War geopolitical tensions between the United States and the Soviet Union. Upon becoming President, Richard Nixon (1969–1974) and the national Security Advisor, Henry Kissinger, pursued a new foreign policy of **détente**, which translated from French literally means "relaxation." This period of détente lasted beyond the Nixon Administration and was characterized by a closer working relationship between the United States and the Soviet Union, with increased communications, summits, arms control treaties (SALT I), regional cooperation and agreements (Helsinki Accords), and trade, namely exports from the United States to the Soviet Union.

The Soviet invasion of Afghanistan in 1979 (Soviet-Afghan War) marked the end of this period of détente, and Cold War tensions once again intensified. Often portrayed as a Cold War proxy war between the United States and the Soviet Union, the United States supported the *mujahideen* who fought against the communist party, who took power through a coup in 1978—People's Democratic Party of Afghanistan—and the Soviet Army who supported the communist government. The United States then boycotted the 1980 Olympics being hosted by Moscow as a demonstration of their disapproval of the Soviet Union's intervention into Afghanistan. U.S. President Ronald Reagan, an integral player in the Cold War, took office in 1981 and remained until 1989. Running as a presidential candidate on an anti-détente campaign, in one of his first press conferences, President Reagan stated that, "Détente's been a one-way street that the Soviet Union has used to pursue its aims." This shift in foreign policy and approach also served as the basis for President Reagan's famous speech made in 1987 in West Berlin, where he called on Mikhail Gorbachev, the General Secretary of the Communist Party of the Soviet Union, to "Tear down this wall!", which was constructed in 1961 to divide East and West Berlin and remained until 1989. The Berlin Wall (in German "Berliner Mauer" or simply, "Die Mauer" meaning "The Wall") physically represented the ideological divide between the communist Eastern German Democratic Republic run by the Soviet Union and the Western Federal Republic of Germany shared by the allied forces.

> Détente—translated from French literally means "relaxation." Often used in the context of the Cold War, the period of détente lasted beyond the Nixon Administration and was characterized by a closer working relationship between the United States and the Soviet Union with increased communications, summits, arms control treaties (SALT I), regional cooperation and agreements (Helsinki Accords), and trade, namely exports from the United States to the Soviet Union.

THE END OF THE COLD WAR

While it was believed that the end of the Cold War would result in a more peaceful, harmonious co-existence, arguably this was not the case. The end of the Cold War in 1991 marked the beginning of a new, more nuanced international order—one that was no longer primarily shaped by two countries practicing **deterrence** through military force and nuclear proliferation. The U.S./U.S.S.R.[18] détente—the easing of tensions between the two superpowers—ended the bipolar **balance of power** and geopolitical stability offered by **mutually assured destruction** (MAD), a doctrine that played an important role in the United States' defense and military policy against the U.S.S.R. MAD, formerly referred to as assured destruction (AD), is a term used with nuclear strategy, whereby states enter into a nuclear stand-off resulting in deterrence. This balance of power, also considered a balance of terror, acts as an incentive to exercise restraint given the massive risk and tragedy represented by nuclear war.

> Deterrence—a prevalent strategy during the Cold War whereby one actor uses the threat of force to convince an adverse actor to refrain from using force or prevent them from taking action.

> Balance of power—is a fundamental concept in international relations theory focused on the distribution of capabilities and resources resulting in a level of stability among nation-states and the maintenance of international order.

> **Mutually Assured Destruction (MAD)**—a doctrine that played an important role in the United States' defense and military policy against the U.S.S.R. MAD, formerly referred to as assured destruction (AD), is a term used with nuclear strategy whereby states enter into a nuclear stand-off resulting in deterrence. This balance of power, also considered a balance of terror, acts as an incentive to exercise restraint given the massive risk and tragedy represented by nuclear war.

Pursuant to the Treaty on the Non-Proliferation of Nuclear Weapons of 1970 (NPT), there are five Nuclear Weapon States (NWS): U.S., U.K., Russian Federation, China and France, all of which have a permanent seat on the United Nations Security Council (UNSC). In accordance with the UN Charter, the 15 members of the UNSC have primary responsibility for the maintenance of international peace and security. States who are not party to the NPT and possess nuclear weapons in violation of the treaty include: North Korea (who withdrew from the NPT in 2003), India, and Pakistan. It is surmised that Israel possesses nuclear weapons. NATO, also referred to as the Atlantic Alliance, allows for nuclear weapon sharing between member states. Under this policy, Belgium, Germany, Italy, the Netherlands and Turkey are hosting U.S. nuclear weapons. It is estimated that there are currently 150 nuclear weapons in Europe today, compared to 1971 when the number was 7,300.

No longer simply aligning on the side of the United States or the U.S.S.R., states began to re-examine and re-negotiate their relationships with one another, and they began to reconsider their relationships with international and regional organizations, interest groups, and the media. This not only influenced states' foreign policy, but it also impacted domestic politics, economics, and trade. This era of new post–Cold War national policies brought global issues and regional disputes to the vanguard.

In 2003, reflecting on the end of the Cold War, Robert McNamara, former U.S. Secretary of Defense (1961–1968), stated,

> I want to say, and this is very important: at the end we lucked out. It was luck that prevented nuclear war. We came that close to nuclear war at the end. Rational individuals: Kennedy was rational; Khrushchev was rational; Castro was rational. Rational individuals came that close to total destruction of their societies. And that danger exists today.

An article in *Foreign Policy* marking the 25th anniversary since the end of the Cold War notes:

> Twenty-five years ago, the Western conception of government—democracy, free markets, human rights—seemed to be proved to be the best, most stable, most moral way to govern. And it was decided that the Western way of government, 25 years ago, would govern the new Russia, too. As the USSR crumbled, many in the urban intelligentsia longed for a Westernization they believed would turn their country and their lives around. Just get rid of communism, they thought, and they'd start living like their American and European counterparts. And Westernization came. The first constitution written in Russia after the 1991 collapse of the USSR was drafted in the Western mold with the help of young Harvard University wonks. The era of Soviet one-party rule gave way to a raucous parliamentary system that, at one point, had more than 100 political parties, including one for beer lovers. There was suddenly a freewheeling and adversarial press in the Western mold. Those same Harvard wonks—young men like Jeffrey Sachs—helped push the painful transformation of the Soviet command economy into a market one. Western businessmen swarmed the country to make a killing but

also brought with them their new, seemingly superior ways of doing business: boards of directors, corporate governance, stocks and bonds. The dollar became the preferred, trusted currency. Western products flooded the Russian market: Coca Cola, Hollywood, cordless phones. At the same time, Russia quickly went from being a nuclear superpower to a backwater, culturally and geopolitically. Warsaw Pact countries and former Soviet republics lined up at NATO's door, and Russia came to be seen as the land of drunks and mail-order brides, a place to be mocked rather than feared.[19]

The Warsaw Pact was a collective defence treaty established by the Soviet Union and seven other Soviet satellite states in Central and Eastern Europe: Albania, Bulgaria, Czechoslovakia, East Germany, Hungary, Poland and Romania (Albania withdrew in 1968).[20]

Crafting U.S. Foreign Policy

All three branches of government, to varying degrees, play a role in crafting policies that shape the United States' relationship with other states and foreign entities.

The Role of the President

The executive branch of government has the greatest influence on foreign policy and international affairs and also has the greatest responsibility in carrying it out. Though the Commander-in-Chief of the U.S. Armed Forces, the President is also the Diplomat-in-Chief. The posture and position of the President influences the role the United States plays on the global stage. If, through the leadership of the President, the United States pursues policies that are outward looking and support the United States playing an active leadership role with regard to world affairs, then the President is viewed as an **internationalist**. If, however, the President retreats from an active role in world affairs and international politics and is more focused on national and domestic concerns, then the President is considered an **isolationist**. As discussed later in the chapter, during the Cold War the U.S. was largely focused on the external threat posed by the Soviet Union. Following the end of the Cold War, the United States turned its attention inward and focused on domestic concerns. This national focus shifted after 9/11. The terrorist attacks on U.S. soil highlighted the important relationship between national security and foreign policy, and the United States began to play an active role in world affairs, with an increased focus on terrorism.

> Internationalist—the pursuit of policies that are outward looking and support a country playing an active leadership role with regard to world affairs.

Essential Powers of the President Related to Foreign Policy

- Appoints the Secretary of State (head of the U.S. State Department)
- Negotiates and enters into international agreements and treaties
- Issues executive orders and executive agreements
- Hosts and attends summit meetings
- Appoints ambassadors of the U.S. Foreign Service

The case *U.S. v. Curtiss-Wright Export Corporation*, 299 U.S. 304 (1936), established the supremacy of the executive branch and the plenary power of the President with regard to foreign policy and affairs. The Supreme Court reversed the decision of the lower court, finding that absent explicit powers in the Constitution, the President nonetheless has implicit powers to conduct foreign affairs, greater than those of Congress and the Supreme Court. The proclamation that led to the Curtiss-Wright case is below:

> Now, therefore, I, Franklin D. Roosevelt, President of the United States of America, acting under and by virtue of the authority conferred in me by the said joint resolution of Congress, do hereby declare and proclaim that I have found that the prohibition of the sale of arms and munitions of war in the United States to those countries now engaged in armed conflict in the Chaco may contribute to the reestablishment of peace between those countries, and that I have consulted with the governments of other American Republics and have been assured of the cooperation of such governments as I have deemed necessary as contemplated by the said joint resolution, and I do hereby admonish all citizens of the United States and every person to abstain from every violation of the provisions of the joint resolution above set forth, hereby made applicable to Bolivia and Paraguay, and I do hereby warn them that all violations of such provisions will be rigorously prosecuted.
>
> And I do hereby enjoin upon all officers of the United States charged with the execution of the laws thereof the utmost diligence in preventing violations of the said joint resolution and this my proclamation issued there under, and in bringing to trial and punishment any offenders against the same.
>
> And I do hereby delegate to the Secretary of State the power of prescribing exceptions and limitations to the application of the said joint resolution of May 28, 1934, as made effective by this my proclamation issued there under.

On November 14, 1935, this proclamation was revoked (49 Stat. 3480), in the following terms:

> Now, therefore, I, Franklin D. Roosevelt, President of the United States of America, do hereby declare and proclaim that I have found that the prohibition of the sale of arms and munitions of war in the United States to Bolivia or Paraguay will no longer be necessary as a contribution to the reestablishment of peace between those countries, and the above-mentioned Proclamation of May 28, 1934, is hereby revoked as to the sale of arms and munitions of war to Bolivia or Paraguay from and after November 29, 1935, provided, however, that this action shall not have the effect of releasing or extinguishing any penalty, forfeiture or liability incurred under the aforesaid Proclamation of May 28, 1934, or the Joint Resolution of Congress approved by the President on the same date, and that the said Proclamation and Joint Resolution shall be treated as remaining in force for the purpose of sustaining any proper action or prosecution for the enforcement of such penalty, forfeiture or liability.[21]

United States v. Curtiss-Wright Export Corp., 299 U.S. 304 [1936]

The whole aim of the resolution is to affect a situation entirely external to the United States and falling within the category of foreign affairs. The determination which we are called to make, therefore, is whether the Joint Resolution, as applied to that situation, is vulnerable to attack under the rule that forbids a delegation of the lawmaking power. In other words, assuming (but not deciding) that the challenged delegation, if it were confined to internal affairs, would be invalid, may it nevertheless be sustained on the ground that its exclusive aim is to afford a remedy for a hurtful condition within foreign territory?

It will contribute to the elucidation of the question if we first consider the differences between the powers of the federal government in respect of foreign or external affairs and those in respect of domestic or internal affairs. That there are differences between them, and that these differences are fundamental, may not be doubted.

The two classes of powers are different both in respect of their origin and their nature. The broad statement that the federal government can exercise no powers except those specifically enumerated in the Constitution, and such implied powers as are necessary and proper to carry into effect the enumerated powers, is categorically true only in respect of our internal affairs. In that field, the primary purpose of the Constitution was to carve from the general mass of legislative powers then possessed by the states such portions as it was thought desirable to vest in the federal government, leaving those not included in the enumeration still in the states.

***

It results that the investment of the federal government with the powers of external sovereignty did not depend upon the affirmative grants of the Constitution. The powers to declare and wage war, to conclude peace, to make treaties, to maintain diplomatic relations with other sovereignties, if they had never been mentioned in the Constitution, would have vested in the federal government as necessary concomitants of nationality. Neither the Constitution nor the laws passed in pursuance of it have any force in foreign territory unless in respect of our own citizens (see *American Banana Co. v. United Fruit Co.*, 213 U. S. 347, 213 U. S. 356), and operations of the nation in such territory must be governed by treaties, international understandings and compacts, and the principles of international law. As a member of the family of nations, the right and power of the United States in that field are equal to the right and power of the other members of the international family. Otherwise, the United States is not completely sovereign. The power to acquire territory by discovery and occupation (*Jones v. United States*, 137 U. S. 202, 137 U. S. 212), the power to expel undesirable aliens (*Fong Yue Ting v. United States*, 149 U. S. 698, 149 U. S. 705 et seq.), the power to make such international agreements as do not constitute treaties in the constitutional sense, none of which is expressly affirmed by the Constitution, nevertheless exist as inherently inseparable from the conception of nationality. This the court recognized, and, in each of the cases cited, found the warrant for its conclusions not in the provisions of the Constitution, but in the law of nations.

In *Burnet v. Brooks*, 288 U. S. 378, 288 U. S. 396, we said, "As a nation with all the attributes of sovereignty, the United States is vested with all the powers of government necessary to maintain an effective control of international relations."

Not only, as we have shown, is the federal power over external affairs in origin and essential character different from that over internal affairs, but participation in the exercise of the power is significantly limited. In this vast external realm, with its important, complicated, delicate and manifold problems, the President alone has the power to speak or listen as a representative of the nation. He makes treaties with the advice and consent of the Senate; but he alone negotiates. Into the field of negotiation the Senate cannot intrude, and Congress itself is powerless to invade it. As Marshall said in his great argument of March 7, 1800, in the House of Representatives, "The President is the sole organ of the nation in its external relations, and its sole representative with foreign nations." The Senate Committee on Foreign Relations, at a very early day in our history (February 15, 1816), reported to the Senate, among other things, as follows:

The President is the constitutional representative of the United States with regard to foreign nations. He manages our concerns with foreign nations, and must necessarily be most competent to determine when, how, and upon what subjects negotiation may be urged with the greatest prospect of success. For his conduct, he is responsible to the Constitution. The committee consider this responsibility the surest pledge for the faithful discharge of his duty. They think the interference of the Senate in the direction of foreign negotiations calculated to diminish that responsibility, and thereby to impair the best security for the national safety. The nature of transactions with foreign nations, moreover, requires caution and unity of design, and their success frequently depends on secrecy and dispatch.

It is important to bear in mind that we are here dealing not alone with an authority vested in the President by an exertion of legislative power, but with such an authority plus the very delicate, plenary and exclusive power of the President as the sole organ of the federal government in the field of international relations—a power which does not require as a basis for its exercise an act of Congress but which, of course, like every other governmental power, must be exercised in subordination to the applicable provisions of the Constitution. It is quite apparent that if, in the maintenance of our international relations, embarrassment—perhaps serious embarrassment—is to be avoided and success for our aims achieved, congressional legislation which is to be made effective through negotiation and inquiry within the international field must often accord to the President a degree of discretion and freedom from statutory restriction which would not be admissible were domestic affairs alone involved. Moreover, he, not Congress, has the better opportunity of knowing the conditions which prevail in foreign countries, and especially is this true in time of war. He has his confidential sources of information. He has his agents in the form of diplomatic, consular and other officials. Secrecy in respect of information gathered by them may be highly necessary, and the premature disclosure of it productive of harmful results. Indeed, so clearly is this true that the first President refused to accede to a request to lay before the House of Representatives the instructions, correspondence and documents relating to the negotiation of the Jay Treaty—a refusal the wisdom of which was recognized by the House itself, and has never since been doubted. In his reply to the request, President Washington said:

The nature of foreign negotiations requires caution, and their success must often depend on secrecy, and even when brought to a conclusion, a full disclosure of all

> the measures, demands, or eventual concessions which may have been proposed or contemplated would be extremely impolitic, for this might have a pernicious influence on future negotiations or produce immediate inconveniences, perhaps danger and mischief, in relation to other powers. The necessity of such caution and secrecy was one cogent reason for vesting the power of making treaties in the President, with the advice and consent of the Senate, the principle on which that body was formed confining it to a small number of members. To admit, then, a right in the House of Representatives to demand and to have as a matter of course all the papers respecting a negotiation with a foreign power would be to establish a dangerous precedent.

Limits to Executive Power

The previous section highlights the broad and deep powers of the president, but Article II of the U.S. Constitution outlines the check and balances placed on the President by Congress.

Article II, Section 2

The President shall be commander in chief of the Army and Navy of the United States, and of the militia of the several states, when called into the actual service of the United States; he may require the opinion, in writing, of the principal officer in each of the executive departments, upon any subject relating to the duties of their respective offices, and he shall have power to grant reprieves and pardons for offenses against the United States, except in cases of impeachment.

He shall have power, by and with the advice and consent of the Senate, to make treaties, provided two thirds of the Senators present concur; and he shall nominate, and by and with the advice and consent of the Senate, shall appoint ambassadors, other public ministers and consuls, judges of the Supreme Court, and all other officers of the United States, whose appointments are not herein otherwise provided for, and which shall be established by law: but the Congress may by law vest the appointment of such inferior officers, as they think proper, in the President alone, in the courts of law, or in the heads of departments.

The President shall have power to fill up all vacancies that may happen during the recess of the Senate, by granting commissions which shall expire at the end of their next session.[22]

Treaties and Executive Agreements—Limitations and Legal Questions

In accordance with the Treaty Clause of the U.S. Constitution (Article II, Section 2), treaties are binding, formal written agreements entered into by the President with foreign nations, which require approval by the U.S. Senate by a two-thirds vote. While treaties are binding, there are limitations to their influence and enforcement. The decision in *Reid v. Covert*, 354 U.S. 1 (1957), highlighted some of these limitations including the following: "no agreement with a foreign nation can confer on Congress or any other branch of the Government power which is free from the restraints of the Constitution." Writing for the court, Justice Hugo Black noted that

> The United States is entirely a creature of the Constitution. Its power and authority have no other source. It can only act in accordance with all the limitations imposed by the Constitution. When the Government reaches out to punish a citizen who is abroad, the shield which the Bill of Rights and other parts of the Constitution provide to protect his life and liberty should not be stripped away just because he happens to be in another land.[23]

> Executive agreements—proffered by the President; they are not regulated by the U.S. Constitution and do not require a two-thirds approval by the U.S. Senate.

While **executive agreements** are proffered by the president, they are not regulated by the U.S. Constitution, nor do they require a two-thirds approval by the U.S. Senate:

> The power to enter into international agreements is a fundamentally important power of the American presidency. Historically, international agreements have played a prominent policy role—from the creation of important alliances and the ending of major wars to the emergence of critical international organizations and global trade structures.... [A] new policy innovation emerged during the twentieth century that enabled the president and Congress to effectively deal with the increased diplomatic demands of America's new leadership role: the executive agreement. Executive agreements do not require super-majority support in the Senate as do formal Article II treaties. Since the 1940s, the vast majority of international agreements have been completed by presidents as executive agreements rather than as treaties. This major policy evolution occurred without changes to the Constitution, though Supreme Court decisions and practice by the political branches have validated the change. This has led some scholars to conclude that the treaty power "has become effectively a Presidential monopoly.[24]

> This important innovation has created a conundrum for practitioners of foreign policy and students of separation of powers. Has the presidency usurped power and made unilateral what was intended by the framers to be shared? Are presidents routinely evading the Senate (and the Constitution's supermajority requirement for treaty consent) and completing consequential agreements as executive agreements rather than as treaties, while sending the less controversial agreements to the Senate as treaties? Or is the emergence of executive agreements a natural response to the complexities of the twentieth century by the American system of separate institutions sharing power, with the Congress complicit by allowing the evolution of the executive agreement as a policy tool?[25]

Discussion Questions

What do you think? Should executive agreements be subject to greater regulation? Should they be binding or subject to greater checks and balances? More broadly, what should the relationship between the executive and legislative branches be with regard to foreign policy?

Foreign Policy Advisors to the President

Established in Article II, Section 2 of the Constitution, the role of the President's Cabinet is to advise the President on any subject s/he may require relating to the duties of each member's respective office. The Cabinet generally consists of two dozen members, including the Vice President, Secretary of State, Secretary of the Treasury, Attorney General, Secretary of Commerce, Secretary of Labor, White House Chief of Staff, U.S. Trade Representative, and Representative of the United States to the United Nations.

Other key foreign policy advisors include:

- National Security Council (NSC) lead by the National Security Adviser
  - Established during President Harry Truman's Administration (1945–1953), the NSC is the primary forum that the President uses on issues related to security and foreign policy. The senior advisory group consist of the Vice President, Secretary of State, Secretary of Defense, leader of the Central Intelligence Agency, and chair of the Joint Chiefs of Staff.
- Joint Chiefs of Staff (Army, Marine Corp, Navy, Air Force): military policy experts
- Department of State: primary department responsible for state-to-state relations
- U.S. Foreign Service: U.S. Ambassadors
- Department of Defense: strategic coordination of military action
- Department of Treasury: enforces economic and trade sanctions
- Department of Homeland Security: secures the nation from threats including terrorism, cyber security, border security and natural disasters
- Intelligence Committee (Central Intelligence Agency, National Security Agency, Defense Intelligence Agency, Military Intelligence): monitor and provide national and global intelligence

---

The Unique Role of the U.S. Department of State (Also Referred to as the State Department)

> The Department's mission is to shape and sustain a peaceful, prosperous, just, and democratic world and foster conditions for stability and progress for the benefit of the American people and people everywhere. This mission is shared with the USAID, ensuring we have a common path forward in partnership as we invest in the shared security and prosperity that will ultimately better prepare us for the challenges of tomorrow.
>
> (Mission of the State Department)

The U.S. Secretary of State is the official position charged with diplomatic state relations. As a representative of the president, the Secretary of State leads the State Department, which is charged with developing foreign policy. The official diplomatic arm of the State Department, the U.S. Foreign Service consists of ambassadors, consuls, and foreign officers in

> support of the mission "to promote peace, support prosperity, and protect American citizens while advancing the interests of the U.S. Abroad." To access an organizational chart of the State Department, visit: www.state.gov/documents/organization/263637.pdf

Presidential Tools of Foreign Policy

The most influential branch with regard to foreign policy and affairs, the President utilizes various tools to conduct foreign policy including:

> **Diplomacy:** the art of dealing with and building relationships with leaders of other nations through meetings, discussions and negotiations. Diplomacy is the primary instrument of foreign policy and it is the first tool to be deployed. Often done behind the scenes, diplomatic relations also involve public messages, statements, press releases and invitations. Diplomacy can occur unilaterally (state acts alone), bilaterally (state works with another state) or multilaterally (state works with various other states)—how a state pursues diplomatic relations can impact levels of compromise, negotiation and positioning and influence.
>
> **Special Envoys:** As explained in *Foreign Affairs*,
>
> [a]mong all the instruments available to the President in his conduct of foreign relations, none is more flexible than the use of personal representatives. He is free to employ officials of the government or private citizens. He may give them such rank and title as seem appropriate to the tasks; these designations may be ambassador, commissioner, agent, delegate; or he may assign no title at all. He may send his agents to any place on earth that he thinks desirable and give them instructions either by word of mouth, or in writing, or through the Department of State, or in any other manner that seems to him fitted to the occasion. Some have been exceedingly formal; others completely informal. Many agents have borne commissions like those of Government officers, ensuring them diplomatic rights, dignities and immunities. Because of these circumstances many have mistakenly considered themselves officers. Others have had mere letters of introduction and have enjoyed no diplomatic privileges. Some have gone with no written credentials whatsoever, their errand described only verbally. Their functions have varied in importance from the trivial to the vital.[26]
>
> **Foreign aid:** Whether through economic aid, where states provide financial resources in the form of a loan, grant or donation or through military aid where states provide military resources including equipment, technology and know-how, the goal of foreign aid is to assist a state in furtherance of international relations and in support of foreign policy. Equally, if not more, influential is the role of economic sanctions and the threat and/or use of military force as a mechanism of foreign policy. As defined by the Council on Foreign Relations, "**economic sanctions** are defined as the withdrawal of customary trade and financial relations for foreign and security policy purposes."

Diplomacy—the primary instrument of foreign policy and the first tool to be deployed. Diplomacy, the art of dealing with and building relationships with leaders of other nations through meetings, discussions, and negotiations, can occur unilaterally (state acts alone), bilaterally (state works with another state), or multilaterally (state works with various other states)—how a state pursues diplomatic relations can impact levels of compromise, negotiation, and positioning and influence.

Foreign aid—often comes in the form of economic aid, where states provide financial resources in the form of a loan, grant, or donation or through military aid where states provide military resources including equipment, technology, and know-how, the goal of foreign aid is to assist a state in furtherance of international relations and in support of foreign policy.

Economic sanctions—the ceasing of customary trade, economic, and financial relations in support of foreign policy and/or in response to security concerns.

Diplomacy's Role in Foreign Policy—in the Words of a Former Diplomat

Ambassador Robert Finn is a Non-resident Fellow at the Liechtenstein Institute on Self-Determination and Lecturer in the Department of Near Eastern Studies at Princeton University. He served as the first U.S. Ambassador to Afghanistan in more than 20 years, from March 2002 until August 2003. He also served as U.S. Ambassador to Tajikistan from 1998–2001. He opened the U.S. Embassy in Azerbaijan in 1992.

Diplomacy is the essential tool of foreign policy. It is diplomats who prevent most wars from taking place, who negotiate the ends of wars, and who supervise the implementation of peace treaties. Teddy Roosevelt's adage "speak softly and carry a big stick" is as true today as it was a hundred years ago. To speak loudly and threaten without resolution or action is a recipe for failure. Many of the problems that still face us in Iraq stem from the mindset that ignored the importance of diplomacy and dismissed the role of the State Department. State Department representatives from the Bureau of Public Affairs numbered 16 in Iraq, whereas the military's public information sector numbered 200, including generals.

A successful integration of diplomacy and military presence can be the ticket for success. When the Serbian-held section of East Slavonia reintegrated with Croatia after long diplomatic talks twenty years ago, it was an international police force under the UN flag headed by an American general who managed the process, while NATO forces maintained peace in the larger area of the former Yugoslavia. The expertise and cultural knowledge of diplomats are the key tools for Washington to understand the world, just as the professional expertise and strategic abilities of the military make it possible to maintain global security.

The Turks have a saying: "All five fingers are not the same." When our government calls on all of its abilities, from the Department of Treasury to the Central Intelligence Agency, and National Security Agency to the National Institutes of Health and Citizenship and Immigration Services and conducts a conversation eliciting the merits of each, we arrive, certainly noisily, at the best consensus of "E pluribus unum." When we do not, we place our foreign and domestic policies at risk."

Powers of Congress

As mentioned in a previous chapter, the U.S. Congress, through the House of Representatives and, to an even greater degree, the U.S. Senate, provides checks and balances on executive power including the following:

- While the President appoints the Secretary of State and appoints ambassadors, they are all subject to the advice and consent of the Senate.
- While the President negotiates international treaties, treaties entered into by the President are subject to a two-thirds vote of the Senate.

- Congress has the power of the purse and the power to tax, and therefore it can limit or deny funding for proposed executive programs that relate to foreign policy, determine levels of foreign aid, and set the defense budget.
- Congress has the responsibility to create the civilian and military budget, which is directly related to foreign aid, military aid, and military action.
- Congress oversees international commerce with foreign nations and regulates tariffs on imports and exports.
- Congress creates policy that regulates federal immigration policy including quotas for immigration visas.
- Congress has the power to declare war. If the President decides to employ the military, the President often does so with the endorsement of Congress.

Article I, Section 8, Reads in Part[27]

- The Congress shall have power to lay and collect taxes, duties, imposts and excises, to pay the debts and provide for the common defense and general welfare of the United States; but all duties, imposts and excises shall be uniform throughout the United States;
- To declare war, grant letters of marque and reprisal, and make rules concerning captures on land and water;
- To raise and support armies, but no appropriation of money to that use shall be for a longer term than two years;
- To provide and maintain a navy;
- To make rules for the government and regulation of the land and naval forces;
- To provide for calling forth the militia to execute the laws of the union, suppress insurrections and repel invasions;
- To provide for organizing, arming, and disciplining, the militia, and for governing such part of them as may be employed in the service of the United States, reserving to the states respectively, the appointment of the officers, and the authority of training the militia according to the discipline prescribed by Congress;
- To make all laws which shall be necessary and proper for carrying into execution the foregoing powers, and all other powers vested by this Constitution in the government of the United States, or in any department or officer thereof.

Both the Senate and the House have standing committees specifically focused on foreign policy.

The U.S. Senate Committee on Foreign Affairs[28]

The Senate Foreign Relations Committee was established in 1816 as one of the original ten standing committees of the Senate. Throughout its history, the committee has been instrumental in developing and influencing United States foreign policy, at different times supporting and opposing the policies of presidents and secretaries of state. The committee has considered, debated, and reported important treaties and legislation, ranging from the purchase of Alaska in 1867 to the establishment of the United Nations in 1945. It also holds jurisdiction over all diplomatic nominations. Through these powers, the committee has helped shape foreign policy of broad significance, in matters of war and peace and international relations. Members of the committee have assisted in the negotiation of treaties, and at times have helped to defeat treaties they felt were not in the national interest.

The Foreign Relations Committee was instrumental in the rejection of the Treaty of Versailles in 1919 and 1920, and in the passage of the Truman Doctrine in 1947 and Marshall Plan in 1948. A bipartisan spirit prevailed as the committee confronted the perils of the Cold War. However, the state of almost constant crisis that the Cold War spawned eventually resulted in the vast expansion of presidential authority over foreign policy. Since the 1960s, the committee has sought to redress this imbalance of powers.

The U.S. House Committee on Foreign Affairs[29]

Jurisdiction. The Full Committee will be responsible for oversight and legislation relating to:

- *foreign assistance (including development assistance, Millennium Challenge Corporation, the Millennium Challenge Account, HIV/AIDS in foreign countries, security assistance, and Public Law 480 programs abroad);*
- *the Peace Corps;*
- *national security developments affecting foreign policy;*
- *strategic planning and agreements;*
- *war powers, treaties, executive agreements, and the deployment and use of United States Armed Forces;*
- *peacekeeping, peace enforcement, and enforcement of United Nations or other international sanctions;*
- *arms control and disarmament issues;*
- *the United States Agency for International Development;*
- *activities and policies of the State, Commerce and Defense Departments and other agencies related to the Arms Export Control Act, and the Foreign Assistance Act including export and licensing policy for munitions items and technology and dual-use equipment and technology;*
- *international law;*
- *promotion of democracy;*
- *international law enforcement issues, including narcotics control programs and activities;*
- *Broadcasting Board of Governors;*
- *embassy security;*
- *international broadcasting;*
- *public diplomacy, including international communication, information policy, international education, and cultural programs;*
- *and all other matters not specifically assigned to a subcommittee.*

The Committee will have jurisdiction over legislation with respect to the administration of the Export Administration Act, including the export and licensing of dual-use equipment and technology and other matters related

> to international economic policy and trade not otherwise assigned to a subcommittee and with respect to the United Nations, its affiliated agencies and other international organizations, including assessed and voluntary contributions to such organizations. The Committee may conduct oversight with respect to any matter within the jurisdiction of the Committee as defined in the Rules of the House of Representatives.

The Judicial Branch

Of all the branches of government, the courts play the most limited role with regard to creating foreign policy. When the courts do get involved it often concerns:

- Questions regarding the scope and limitations of presidential and congressional power
- International treaties
- Issues involving ambassadors and ministers
- Disputes between national and international states
- Issues related to admiralty law
- Issues related to maritime law

Discussion Question

Should the courts play a greater role in creating foreign policy?

> *In 2015, Richard Posner, a provocative and renowned jurist and trained economist who served as a judge in Chicago, Illinois on the U.S. Court of Appeals for the Seventh Circuit from 1981 through 2017, wrote an article, "The Law of the Land: How the Supreme Court Engages the World," in* Foreign Affairs *regarding the relationship between the Supreme Court and its justices and foreign affairs and policy.*[30] *The following quote is taken directly from the article:*
>
>> Justice Stephen Breyer of the U.S. Supreme Court has long been known as the most cosmopolitan justice—the justice most familiar with the laws of other nations and most concerned with how U.S. courts can cope with those laws when they impinge on American national interests or are invoked in U.S. courts. In his new book, The Court and the World, he sets forth his views on the interaction between the U.S. legal system and the legal systems of other countries. . . . The Court is an atypical judicial body in that it tends to decide relatively few cases in most of the areas of its jurisdiction, including the intersection between U.S. and foreign law. Those few cases tend to generate disagreement within the Court and uncertainty as to what exactly the law in a given area should be. It's difficult to get a coherent sense of a body of law from a handful of Supreme

Court cases; it might have been better to borrow material from summaries in treatises of the relevant legal doctrines and their applications. But Breyer's focus on the Supreme Court does cast light on what Supreme Court justices have learned and can learn from foreign legal practices and what foreign judges can learn in return. . . . In addition to comparing the Supreme Court's rules with the European approach of proportionality, Breyer catalogs differences between the U.S. legal system and the systems of foreign countries, such as India, Switzerland, and the United Kingdom. But he makes no attempt to arbitrate the differences among them. . . . In one section, for example, he discusses the application of American law to acts that occur in foreign countries. Suppose two foreign companies manufacture similar products, export them to the United States, and agree to sell them at the same price, thus eliminating competition between the two products, to the detriment of American consumers. They are deliberately injuring Americans, and such injurious conduct is usually deemed sufficient to trigger the applicability of U.S. antitrust law, even though enforcement may be difficult or even impossible (it may be impossible to obtain jurisdiction over the companies in an American court, for example). But to enforce U.S. antitrust law against such suppliers would, as Breyer emphasizes, violate "comity"—the respect that nations are expected to accord other nations in order to minimize international friction and conflict.

No formula has been devised to draw the line between permissible and impermissible extraterritorial applications of U.S. antitrust or other regulatory laws. The Supreme Court's approach, as described by Breyer, is distinctly ad hoc: it seeks harmony between overlapping U.S. and foreign laws, a goal that does not lend itself to the kind of formulaic approach that lawyers and judges prefer. . . . Breyer next focuses on the interpretation of treaties. He starts by stating that "interpreting treaties is usually a straightforward legal enterprise." The U.S. Supreme Court, he writes, "will normally proceed in much the same way as when it interprets any other legal text. It begins with the language, which it interprets in light of the treaty's context and purposes; it considers the treaty's drafting history; and it takes account of precedent." In fact, a dispute over a legal text—whether a statute, a regulation, a contract, a constitutional provision, or a treaty—rarely provokes serious litigation unless the dispute is over an issue that the drafters of the text did not foresee. And if they did not foresee it, then neither the language of the text nor its history will reveal how they wanted the issue resolved. In such cases, what is called "interpretation" is really completion—plugging a hole that the legislature left in the text—although judges rarely acknowledge this lest they come across as impolitic, belittling legislative foresight.

What Breyer rightly emphasizes is that the interpretation of a treaty, like its initial drafting, must take into account the views and interests of both (or all, if it is a multinational treaty) the nations that are parties to it. This makes it all the less likely that such litigation will be resolved by interpretation rather than through a compromise of the interests of the nations.

> **Discussion Question**
>
> *Disagreements between the Executive (president) and Legislative (Congress) branches of government arise regarding questions of jurisdiction, power, how foreign affairs are conducted, and how foreign policy is created. With the checks and balances discussed previously, what do you think the relationship between the executive, legislative, and judicial branches of government should be with regard to foreign policy?*

The Supreme Court's Role in a Globalized World

During the boom years of the 1990s, globalization emerged as the most significant development in our national life. With NAFTA and the Internet and big-box stores selling cheap goods from China, the line between national and international began to blur. In the seven years since 9/11, the question of how we relate to the world beyond our borders—and how we should—has become inescapable. The Supreme Court, as ever, is beginning to offer its own answers. As the United States tries to balance the benefits of multilateral alliances with the demands of unilateral self-protection, the court has started to address the legal counterparts of such existential matters. It is becoming increasingly clear that the defining constitutional problem for the present generation will be the nature of the relationship of the United States to what is somewhat optimistically called the international order.

This problem has many dimensions. It includes mundane practical questions, like what force the United States should give to the law of the sea. It includes more symbolic questions, like whether high-ranking American officials can be held accountable for crimes against international law. And it includes questions of momentous consequence, like whether international law should be treated as law in the United States; what rights, if any, noncitizens have to come before American courts or tribunals; whether the protections of the Geneva Conventions apply to people that the U.S. government accuses of being terrorists; and whether the U.S. Supreme Court should consider the decisions of foreign or international tribunals when it interprets the Constitution.

In recent years, two prominent schools of thought have emerged to answer these questions. One view, closely associated with the Bush administration, begins with the observation that law, in the age of modern liberal democracy, derives its legitimacy from being enacted by elected representatives of the people. From this standpoint, the Constitution is seen as facing inward, toward the Americans who made it, toward their rights and their security. For the most part, that is, the rights the Constitution provides are for citizens and provided only within the borders of the country. By these lights, any interpretation of the Constitution that restricts the nation's security or sovereignty—for example, by extending constitutional rights to noncitizens encountered on battlefields overseas—is misguided and even dangerous. In the words of the conservative legal scholars Eric Posner and Jack Goldsmith (who is himself a former member of the Bush administration), the Constitution "was designed to create a more perfect domestic order, and its foreign relations mechanisms were crafted to enhance U.S. welfare."

A competing view, championed mostly by liberals, defines the rule of law differently: law is conceived not as a quintessentially national phenomenon but rather as a global ideal. The liberal position readily concedes that the Constitution specifies the law for the United States but stresses that a fuller, more complete conception of law demands that American law be pictured alongside international law and other (legitimate) national constitutions. The U.S. Constitution, on this cosmopolitan view, faces outward. It is a paradigm of the rule of law: rights similar to those it confers on Americans should protect all people everywhere, so that no one falls outside the reach of some legitimate legal order. What is most important about our Constitution, liberals stress, is not that it provides rights for us but that its vision of freedom ought to apply universally.

[...]

International law, as even its staunchest defenders must acknowledge, often fails to accord with democratic principle. Such law is not passed by a democratically elected Congress and signed by a democratically elected president. It is true that the U.S. Constitution says that international treaties signed by the president and approved by the Senate shall be the supreme law of the land, thereby conferring some democratic legitimacy on treaties. But a great deal of international law derives not from treaties signed by consenting nations but rather from the vague category of international custom, which over time can harden into binding law. For hundreds of years, until more formal treaties were adopted, custom was the main way international law was created, giving rise to the laws of war, for instance, and condemning terrorism and torture. Even today, the existence of a treaty among only a select group of nations can be invoked in international forums as evidence of an established custom—and nonparticipating countries can come to be bound by treaties that they themselves never signed.

To conservatives, such international "law" is anathema. Even in cases in which explicit treaties among nations do exist, conservatives worry. Such treaties, after all, are increasingly interpreted by nondemocratic institutions like tribunals of the World Trade Organization or the United Nations' International Court of Justice. Two hundred years ago, treaties tended to be simple agreements between two parties, with each reserving the right to interpret (and, if necessary, enforce) the treaty's terms for itself. Today, though, many of the most important treaties—those governing trade, the environment and other crucial matters—involve a large number of nations that agree as a condition of the treaty to be bound by the decisions of an international body. To sign on to such a treaty, conservatives point out, confers future lawmaking authority on some unelected and thus undemocratic body.[31]

The Procedural Process of Creating Foreign Policy

While the role of the President and the executive branch of government was pronounced during the Cold War, the creation of foreign policy in the post–Cold War era is more balanced and seeks the input of various perspectives and stakeholders. While the actors and influencers may differ, the process by which policymakers craft foreign policy is similar to the public policy process (see Figure 6.4). As observed by James Scott in his book, *After the End*, "A changing agenda and increasing interdependence and transnational ties make foreign policy making more like domestic policy making: subject to conflict, bargaining, and persuasion among competing groups within and outside the government." As such, the creation of foreign policy has become more pluralistic in nature with state, governmental, and non-governmental actors and institutions playing a critical role and representing different perspectives and interests. While this is a positive development, it also increases the potential of divisive partisanship and political posturing.

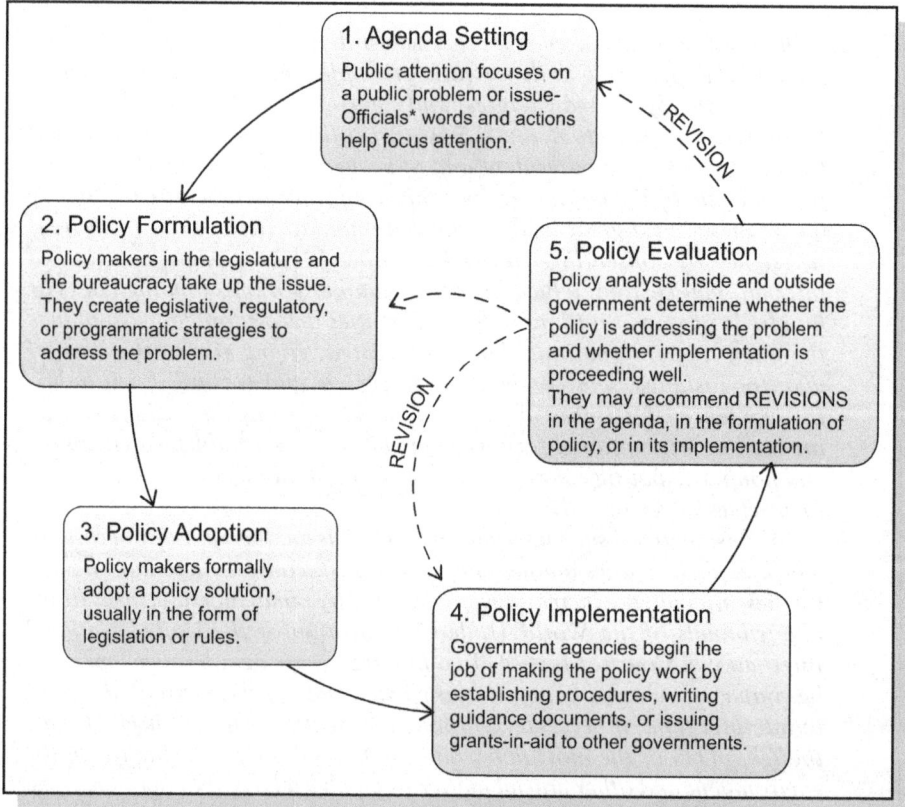

Figure 6.4 Policy Development Process.

Source: https://texaspolitics.utexas.edu/archive/html/bur/features/0303_01/policy.html

Increased Globalization and the Role of Global Governance

Another formidable influencer of foreign policy is the role of **globalization**. While the movement of people across borders is not a new phenomenon, the end of the Cold War bipolar world order and the fall of the Berlin Wall shaped a new global landscape and paved the way for greater interaction among states since global issues were no longer overshadowed by the preoccupation with the U.S.–Soviet Union superpower showdown. The increased global movement of people, technology, information, and goods, along with liberal policies supporting this greater economic and market integration and trade, is a testament to the power and influence of globalization—this interdependence presents new opportunities as well as new threats. This "intensification of worldwide social relations which link distant localities in such a way that local happenings are shaped by events occurring many miles away and vice versa" captures the importance of globalization in relation to U.S. foreign policy.[32] Globalization facilitates greater interconnectedness among states—politically, economically, and socially. The convergence of the end of the Cold War and an era of intensified globalization opened the field of foreign policy—the establishment of new international norms, the introduction of new actors, and the realization of a new global order resulted in a more open, but complex and political foreign policy process.

> Globalization—facilitates greater interconnectedness among states—politically, economically, and socially—and is marked by the increased global movement of people, technology, information, and goods, along with liberal policies supporting this greater economic and market integration and trade.

Globalization is closely related to technological and scientific advancements that influence foreign policy. As noted in a *Foreign Affairs* article, "Diplomacy for the 21st Century,"

> [s]cience and technology (S&T) play a critical role in a range of foreign policy issues, from driving economic development to responding to hostile governments and rogue organizations. Discoveries in nanotechnology, synthetic biology, and earth sciences offer new opportunities to improve human health, provide food and clean water, and issue warnings impending natural disasters. Advances in information and communications technologies are having remarkable impacts on every walk of life. International cooperation in science and technology is rapidly becoming an important element of foreign policies of nations throughout the world. The U.S. State Department is a critical focal pony for brining S&T to bear on an ever-growing array of challenges, from cyber crime to climate change.

Globalization has increased the interaction and interdependence among states economically, socially, and politically (see Figure 6.5). The changes brought about by globalization have also warranted a closer examination of the role and influence of **geopolitics** on globalization and global governance. **Global governance** seeks cooperation between states and transnational actors in support of responding to regional and global issues. Sovereign states have power over the multitude of non-state global governance actors and, in turn, these actors have influence over the political system. The power and authority of non-state actors is often determined by negotiations with the state. Global governance, the increased collaboration between state and non-state actors, can influence and establish new global norms, laws and rules that responds to world politics, globally and regionally.

> Geopolitics—examines the impact of geographic characteristics (e.g., location, demographics, resources, climate) on states' political power, foreign policy, and international relations.

> Global governance—also referred to as world governance, is a term used to denote a collaborative process among states, intergovernmental and regional organizations, transnational actors, and private groups to negotiate responses to global issues in support of greater global management.

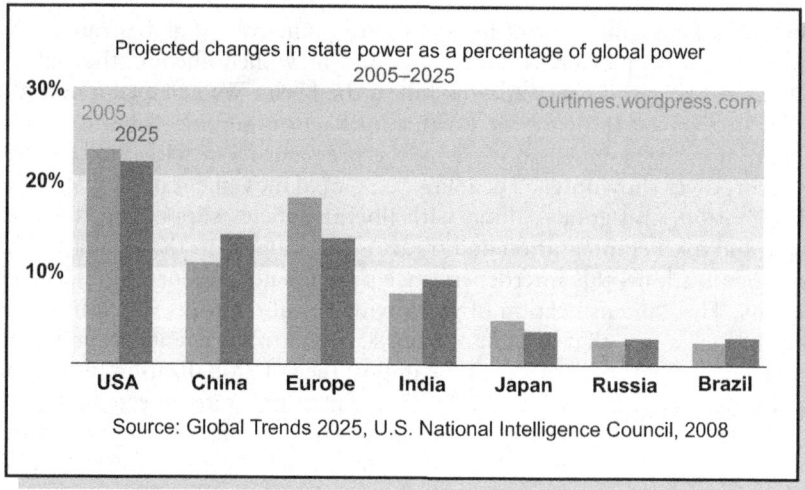

Figure 6.5 Projected Change in State/Global Power.
Source: U.S. Nat'l Intelligence Council (2008).

Theories of International Relations *influence the worldview of leaders, shape their perception of foreign affairs and impact the development of foreign policy. Motives, behaviors, actions and responses are interpreted and shaped by the theoretical lens by which it is viewed. The two leading theories connected with foreign policy are realism and liberalism—"[l]iberal and realist theories of international behavior present quite different vision of how states interact with one another."*[33]*In accordance with the realist school of thought the state is the primary actor and a state's foreign policy should be crafted and designed based on national interests, including security and economic.*

In 2008, the Governor of New Mexico and presidential candidate, Bill Richardson, wrote an article in Foreign Affairs *entitled "A New Realism: A Realistic and Principled Foreign Policy" where he promoted a new take on realism for foreign policy in the 21st century.* He said:

> To cope with this new world, we need a New Realism in our foreign policy—an ethical, principled realism that harbors no illusions about the importance of a strong military in a dangerous world but that also understands the importance of diplomacy and multilateral cooperation. We need a New Realism based on the understanding that what goes on inside of other countries profoundly impacts us—but that we can only influence, not control, what goes on inside of other countries. A New Realism for the twenty-first century must understand that to solve our own problems, we need to work with other governments that respect and trust us.

While liberal theory (sometimes referred to as pluralism or liberal institutionalism) views the state as important, it also believes that non-state actors play an integral role. Liberalism contends that formal and informal institutions, international organizations, and states can work together toward shared objectives and common goals. The liberal worldview holds that this level of cooperation is based on mutual benefit and reduces conflict and contributes to a more peaceful co-existence.

In 2009, Paul Wolfowitz wrote an article, "Think Again: Realism." In his article, Wolfowitz highlights the influence of international relations theories on presidents and their development of foreign policy. In discussing realism the doctrine, he notes,

> [i]n the words of one leading realist, the principal purpose of U.S. Foreign policy should be to manage "relations between states" rather than "alter the nature of states." . . . Critics of realism, like myself, do not think that the businesslike management of the "relations between states" should lead us to neglect issues regarding the "nature of states." In reality, the internal make-up of states has a huge effect on their external behavior—so it must be a significant consideration for U.S. foreign policy.

Foreign Policy in the 21st Century

The 21st century is significantly defined by September 11, 2001. The terrorist attacks on U.S. soil in New York (World Trade Center), Virginia (Pentagon), and in Pennsylvania fundamentally shaped U.S. foreign policy. In a *Brookings Report*, "September 11th and American Foreign Policy," written in November 2001, the author observed that,

> It is probably too soon to say for certain whether September 11 will prove to be such a "paradigm shift" along the lines of 1941 (when America abandoned isolationism), 1947 (when containment became the lens through which foreign policy was seen), or 1989 (when the "post-Cold War era" began). Much will depend on how the Administration responds, and whether it is able to maintain the level of focus and commitment on terrorism once the initial emotion and anger about the attack begins to subside. . . . The political and psychological impact of the September 11 attacks will have long term implications for the ways in which the United States engages in the world. Perhaps the most obvious affect on U.S. foreign policy will be through the new tradeoffs that a "war on terrorism" could require. If stopping terrorism really is now the country's top priority in the way that stopping Communism once was, competing priorities will inevitably be displaced. . . . The need for tradeoffs will also become clear when the economic and resources implications of the war on terrorism start to sink in. . . . Once the shock begins to wear off they are likely to realize just how consequential such a reordering of priorities will be, and their elected leaders—at present determined to preserve national unity—will have some hard decisions to make about allocating whatever resources are left.[34]

Key Events and Moments That Influenced 21st-Century Foreign Policy

- The terrorist attacks of 9/11 (2001)
- Operation Enduring Freedom (2001–2014)
- War in Afghanistan (2001–present)
- War against terrorism/War on Terror (2001–present)
- The Bush Doctrine (2002)
- Second Gulf War and weapons of mass destruction (WMD) (2003–2011)
- The Great Recession—Global Recession (2007–2009)
- Capture of Osama bin Laden (2011)
- "Arab Spring" (2011)
- Invasion of U.S. Consulate in Benghazi, Libya; the killing of Ambassador Christopher Stevens (2012)
- Boston Marathon bombing (2013)
- Seizing of the Crimean Peninsula by the Russian government (2014)
- Iran nuclear deal (2015)
- Paris Climate Accord (2015)
- China builds artificial islands in South China Sea (2015)
- Russia's intervention in Syria in support of Syrian President Bashar al-Assad (2015)
- European migrant/refugee crisis (2016)
- Brexit—Britain's vote to leave the European Union (EU) (2016)
- Election of U.S. President Donald J. Trump (2016)
- Attempted coup of President Recep Tayyip Erdogan in Turkey (2016)
- North Korea's testing and development of its missile and nuclear program (2016)
- Increase of right-wing populist movements on both sides of the Atlantic (2016–2017)
- Various terrorist acts by ISIS and lone wolf attacks (ongoing)

Contemporary Foreign Policy Issues

From concerns surrounding regions and states to topics including terrorism, national security, immigration, climate change, trade, nuclear **nonproliferation**, rogue regimes, regime change, technology, and the war on drugs, there are no shortage of foreign policy issues. Given the length of this chapter, it is not possible, nor responsible, to attempt to cover all of the pressing foreign policy concerns. Rather, Table 6.1 attempts to illustrate the complexity and multi-faceted nature of foreign affairs and policy.

Nonproliferation—methods and approaches aimed at preventing the acquisition, transfer, development, and spread of weapons of mass destruction and associated delivery systems.

Terrorism (War on Terror)

The turn of the 21st century is marked by September 11, 2001. 620 days into the 21st century, the United States was attacked on its homeland. With nearly 3,000 dead and 6,000 injured, the magnitude of the attack shifted Washington's focus to combating terrorism through domestic and foreign policy. While many believe that al Qaeda's

Table 6.1 Major Concerns by Region Show Divergences in Top Threat Assessment.
Regional medians saying _ is a major threat to our country

	Europe	Asia-Pacific	Middle East	Africa	Latin America
	%	%	%	%	%
ISIS	74	62	*	54	40
Global climate change	64	61	44	58	74
Cyberattacks from other countries	54	52	40	53	54
The condition of the global economy	37	46	59	51	61
A large number of refugees leaving countries such as Iraq and Syria	41	35	48	55	31
The United States' power and influence	31	35	50	37	47
Russia's power and influence	41	29	35	31	23
China's power and influence	30	47	20	32	25

Source: Spring 2017 Global Attitudes Survey. Q17a–h. Pew Research Center

Note: **Bolded** figures note the top concern in each region. Underlined figures note the second highest concern in each region.

* ISIS item only asked across four countries in the Middle East and North Africa. No median calculated. In these four countries, ISIS is the top threat.

coordinated attack under the leadership of the late Osama bin Laden was a response and reaction to U.S. foreign policy in the Middle East, others contend that it was an outright affront against American ideology and democratic values. In the aftermath of 9/11, the United States passed various laws designed to safeguard Americans and increase national security, and it took military action. On October 7, 2001, under the leadership of President George W. Bush (2001–2009), the United States and a coalition of forces—Operation Enduring Freedom (OEF)—began airstrikes on Afghanistan to combat al Qaeda and the Taliban, who was providing a safe haven and protection to the mastermind of the terrorist attacks, Osama bin Laden.

> **"After the Attacks: The Alliance; for the First Time, NATO Invokes Joint Defence Pact With U.S."**
> **(NY Times, September 13, 2001)**
>
> *NATO invoked a mutual defense clause in its founding treaty for the first time today, strongly suggesting that the United States would have the support of the allies if it takes military action against those responsible for attacks on the World Trade Center and the Pentagon. A NATO statement issued after a meeting of ambassadors to the 19-member alliance said, 'If it is determined that this attack was directed from abroad against the United States, it shall be regarded as an action covered by Article 5 of the Washington Treaty.' Article 5, the cornerstone of the alliance, says "an armed attack" against any of the allies in Europe or North America 'shall be considered an attack against them all.' It commits NATO members to take the necessary measures, including the*

> use of force, to restore security. The statement amounted to a powerful expression of European solidarity with the United States after a period in which trans-Atlantic relations have been strained by tensions over the Bush administration's policies in areas ranging from missile defense to the environment.[35]

The Bush Doctrine

In 2003, President George W. Bush (2001–2009) expanded the "war on terror" to Iraq. It was surmised that Saddam Hussein, Iraq's leader, possessed weapons of mass destruction (WMD) and that he was coordinating with al Qaeda. In October 2002, Congress pledged its support for the invasion of Iraq by a "coalition of the willing." Though Operation Iraqi Freedom did not receive much support from allies, nor approval of the UN Security Council, who did not believe Saddam Hussein possessed WMD, in March 2003 President Bush preemptively attacked Iraq, which later became known as the **Bush Doctrine**. With the objective to topple the regime, the preemptive strike was executed pursuant to the military doctrine, "shock and awe"—a rapid, intense bombing intended on destroying and disorienting the enemy. Though Saddam Hussein was ultimately captured in December 2003, U.S. and coalition forces were not viewed as liberators; rather, U.S. and coalition forces were attacked. In addition, an internal power struggle ensued between militias and insurgents trying to establish control amidst chaos.

Bush Doctrine—is a term used to denote President George W. Bush's preemptively attacked Iraq in March 2003, which was executed pursuant to the military doctrine, "shock and awe"—a rapid, intense bombing intended on destroying and disorienting the enemy.

PREEMPTIVE STRIKES—A TOOL OF PREVENTIVE WAR OR A PREMATURE WAR?

> We'll be deliberate, yet time is not on our side. I will not wait on events while dangers gather. I will not stand by as peril draws closer and closer. The United States of America will not permit the world's most dangerous regimes to threaten us with the world's most destructive weapons.
>
> —President George W. Bush

The War Powers Act

In seeking greater alignment between U.S. foreign policy and the nation's espoused democratic values, Congress passed the War Powers Act in 1973. As noted by the Library of Congress,

> The Constitution of the United States divides the war powers of the federal government between the Executive and Legislative branches: the President is the Commander in Chief of the armed forces (Article II, section 2), while Congress has the power to make declarations of war, and to raise and support the armed forces (Article I, section 8). Over time, questions arose as to the extent of the President's authority to deploy U.S. armed forces into hostile situations abroad without a declaration of war or some other form of Congressional approval. Congress passed the War Powers Resolution in the aftermath of the Vietnam War to address these concerns and provide a set of procedures for both the President and Congress to follow in situations where the introduction of U.S. forces abroad could lead to their involvement in armed conflict.

In a 2003 article entitled, "The Debate over War Powers,"[36] in the *Human Rights Magazine* of the American Bar Association, Mark R. Shulman and Lawrence J. Lee address questions regarding the constitutionality of the Bush Doctrine and they explore the tensions that exist:

> Constitutionally, the president has the unilateral authority to commit U.S. troops to Iraq or another rogue state under the newly promulgated preemption policy of the National Security Strategy only if he can show that such an action constitutes response to a sudden or imminent attack. The administration has provided no evidence that Iraq had invaded or intends to invade the United States (i.e., as a sponsor of September 11), let alone that it will do so imminently. Absent such evidence, congressional approval is needed. . . . The issues remain timely and relevant: must the president seek congressional authorization to order preemptive invasions of rogue states that may deliver weapons and aid to terrorists? What is the correct scope and allocation of war powers for preemptive invasions?

Discussion Questions

The legality of the Bush Doctrine is highly contested. Are preemptive strikes legal? Do they need to be authorized by Congress? What is the relationship between the War Powers Act and preemptive strikes authorized by the president?

BALANCING CIVIL LIBERTIES AND THE WAR ON TERROR: THE INTERSECTION OF THE SUPREME COURT AND EXECUTIVE POWER

Balancing civil liberties with national security is an issue that has been at the forefront since the terrorist attacks in 2001. In addressing this issue, the Supreme Court decision in *Hamdi v. Rumsfeld*, 524 U.S. 507 (2004) significantly influenced the development of foreign policy in the wake of the 9–11.

Argued in April 2004, *Hamdi v. Rumsfeld* (U.S. Secretary of Defense), 524 U.S. 507 (2004) addressed the delicate balance between national security and civil liberties. Delivered by Justice Sandra Day O'Connor, the opinion opens as follows:

> At this difficult time in our Nation's history, we are called upon to consider the legality of the Government's detention of a United States citizen on United States soil as an "enemy combatant" and to address the process that is constitutionally owed to one who seeks to challenge his classification as such. The United States Court of Appeals for the Fourth Circuit held that petitioner's detention was legally authorized and that he was entitled to no further opportunity to challenge his enemy-combatant label. We now vacate and remand. We hold that although Congress authorized the detention of combatants in the narrow circumstances alleged here, due process demands that a citizen held in the United States as an enemy combatant be given a meaningful opportunity to contest the factual basis for that detention before a neutral decision maker.

On September 11, 2001, the al Qaeda terrorist network used hijacked commercial airliners to attack prominent targets in the United States. Approximately 3,000 people were killed in those attacks. One week later, in response to these "acts of treacherous violence," Congress passed a resolution authorizing the President to "use all necessary and appropriate force against those nations, organizations, or persons he determines planned, authorized, committed, or aided the terrorist attacks" or "harbored such organizations or persons, in order to prevent any future acts of international terrorism against the United States by such nations, organizations or persons." Authorization for Use of Military Force ("the AUMF"), 115 Stat. 224. Soon thereafter, the President ordered United States Armed Forces to Afghanistan, with a mission to subdue al Qaeda and quell the Taliban regime that was known to support it.

This case arises out of the detention of a man whom the Government alleges took up arms with the Taliban during this conflict. His name is Yaser Esam Hamdi. Born an American citizen in Louisiana in 1980, Hamdi moved with his family to Saudi Arabia as a child. By 2001, the parties agree, he resided in Afghanistan. At some point that year, he was seized by members of the Northern Alliance, a coalition of military groups opposed to the Taliban government, and eventually was turned over to the United States military. The Government asserts that it initially detained and interrogated Hamdi in Afghanistan before transferring him to the United States Naval Base in Guantanamo Bay in January 2002. In April 2002, upon learning that Hamdi is an American citizen, authorities transferred him to a naval brig in Norfolk, Virginia, where he remained until a recent transfer to a brig in Charleston, South Carolina. The Government contends that Hamdi is an "enemy combatant," and that this status justifies holding him in the United States indefinitely—without formal charges or proceedings—unless and until it makes the determination that access to counsel or further process is warranted.

As noted in the syllabus, the official case summary:

Hamdi's father filed this habeas petition on his behalf under 28 U. S. C. §2241, alleging, among other things, that the Government holds his son in violation of the Fifth and Fourteenth Amendments. Although the petition did not elaborate on the factual circumstances of Hamdi's capture and detention, his father has asserted in other documents in the record that Hamdi went to Afghanistan to do "relief work" less than two months before September 11 and could not have received military training. The Government attached to its response to the petition a declaration from Michael Mobbs (Mobbs Declaration), a Defense Department official. The Mobbs Declaration alleges various details regarding Hamdi's trip to Afghanistan, his affiliation there with a Taliban unit during a time when the Taliban was battling U. S. allies, and his subsequent surrender of an assault rifle.

The District Court found that the Mobbs Declaration, standing alone, did not support Hamdi's detention and ordered the Government to turn over numerous materials for *in camera* review. The Fourth Circuit reversed, stressing that, because it was undisputed that Hamdi was captured in an active combat zone, no factual inquiry or evidentiary hearing allowing Hamdi to be heard or to rebut the Government's assertions was necessary or proper. Concluding that the factual averments in the Mobbs Declaration, if accurate, provided a sufficient basis upon which to conclude that the President had constitutionally detained Hamdi, the court ordered the habeas petition dismissed. The appeals court held that, assuming that express congressional authorization of the detention was required by 18 U.S.C. §4001(a)—which provides that "[n]o citizen shall be imprisoned or otherwise detained by the United States except pursuant to an Act of Congress"—the AUMF's "necessary and appropriate force" language provided the authorization for Hamdi's detention. It also concluded that Hamdi is entitled only to a limited judicial inquiry into his detention's legality under the war powers of the political branches, and not to a searching review of the factual determinations underlying his seizure.

Held: The judgment is vacated, and the case is remanded. Justice O'Connor, joined by The Chief Justice, Justice Kennedy, and Justice Breyer, concluded that although Congress authorized the detention of combatants in the narrow circumstances alleged in this case, due process demands that a citizen held in the United States as an enemy combatant be given a meaningful opportunity to contest the factual basis for that detention before a neutral decision maker. Justice Souter, joined by Justice Ginsburg, concluded that Hamdi's detention is unauthorized, but joined with the plurality to conclude that on remand Hamdi should have a meaningful opportunity to offer evidence that he is not an enemy combatant.

What Is a Habeas Corpus Petition?

Habeas corpus is Latin for "that you have the body." A writ of habeas corpus is invoked to determine the legality and validity of an individual's imprisonment or detention. A habeas petition is brought before a court against the state or federal government agent holding the individual in custody. The protections provided by habeas corpus are found in the U.S. Constitution, Article I, Section 9, Clause 2 which states: " The privilege of the writ of habeas corpus shall not be suspended, unless when in cases of rebellion or invasion the public safety may require it." While not explicitly stated in the Constitution, practitioners contend that "Since the Suspension Clause appears in Article I of the Constitution, which is predominately about the powers of Congress, there is a strong argument that only Congress can suspend the habeas writ."[37] Therefore, only Congress, through its own action or through its delegation to the Executive, has the authority to suspend a write; the Executive does not have this independent authority.

Fifth Amendment (Due Process)

"No person shall be held to answer for a capital, or otherwise infamous crime, unless on a presentment or indictment of a grand jury, except in cases arising

in the land or naval forces, or in the militia, when in actual service in time of war or public danger; nor shall any person be subject for the same offense to be twice put in jeopardy of life or limb; nor shall be compelled in any criminal case to be a witness against himself, nor be deprived of life, liberty, or property, without due process of law; nor shall private property be taken for public use, without just compensation."

Fourteenth Amendment (Equal Protection)

"All persons born or naturalized in the United States, and subject to the jurisdiction thereof, are citizens of the United States and of the state wherein they reside. No state shall make or enforce any law which shall abridge the privileges or immunities of citizens of the United States; nor shall any state deprive any person of life, liberty, or property, without due process of law; nor deny to any person within its jurisdiction the equal protection of the laws."

Discussion Questions

If you were a Supreme Court Justice, how would you have decided this case? How do you balance individual civil liberties with national security? What impact does the decision in this case have on foreign policy and international affairs?

The Intersection Between Privacy, National Security and Immigration—in the Words of a Practitioner

James Denvil is an attorney at Hogan Lovells, a multinational law firm with 45 offices and 2,800 attorneys across Africa, Asia, Europe, Latin America, the Middle East and the United States. The global legal practice helps corporations, financial institutions, and governments across the spectrum of their business and legal issues globally and locally. James helps companies navigate the complex challenges associated with deploying and managing today's information technologies and systems, develops policies and procedures, assists with responses to regulatory investigations and drafts advocacy materials and coordinates risk assessments. James' passion for privacy and security developed during his internship at the Department of Homeland Security's Privacy Office.

If you are an attorney who advises and counsels multi-national organizations, you have to be familiar with foreign policy. Foreign policy shapes the landscapes in which your clients operate, impacts your clients' business decisions, and affects the lives and perspectives of your client contacts. This was apparent at a privacy conference that I attended in early 2017.

One of the key issues to be discussed at the conference was whether European Union law would continue to support the transfer of personal information to the United States. There were concerns that some or all of the legal mechanisms supporting such transfers might be revoked due to concerns regarding U.S. national security access to the information. And less than a month before the conference took place, U.S. President Donald Trump signed an executive order that suspended the entry of Syrian refugees into the United States indefinitely and restricted entry for persons from Iran, Iraq, Libya, Somalia, Sudan, and Yemen. Now, this immigration policy might appear to be wholly unrelated to policy concerns about the free flow of information. But the immigration issues were a frequent topic of discussion at the conference.

U.S.-based organizations with European Union establishments worried that the European Union might express its dissatisfaction with U.S. immigration policy by making it harder for U.S. organizations to transfer personal information to their U.S. headquarters. Clients were considering whether it would be better to move data centers outside of the United States. And the immigration policy had a personal impact too. Conference participants were worried about co-workers who might be denied re-entry into the Unites States. And some non-U.S. participants considered whether they wished to or would be allowed to remain in the United States.

A privacy expert with no knowledge of foreign policy could have addressed many of the legal issues raised during the conference. But if you were not familiar with foreign policy, you could not appreciate the full context in which your clients and potential clients were viewing the issues.

Conclusion

While foreign policy is focused on a state's relation with other states, a state's foreign policy is very much shaped by internal domestic dynamics and political, economic, and social concerns—domestic and foreign affairs are intricately intertwined.

Globalization, including the greater role of technology, has changed the global landscape, challenges the traditional role of the nation-state, diminishes some of the limitations of territorial borders, expands access and communication between states, increases the role of state and non-state actors, intergovernmental organizations, non-governmental organizations and various other stakeholders, and highlights the potential role and importance of global governance.

A state's foreign policy is largely shaped by its executive leadership, which can determine whether a state is globally engaged or detached—whether a leader is an isolationist or internationalist is consequential for the state and can impact the international order and balance of power.

Discussion Questions

1. How has the role of the nation-state changed since the end of the Cold War?
2. What is the impact of globalization on 21st-century foreign policy?
3. How have the 9/11 terrorist acts influenced and shaped foreign policy?
4. What factors will shape future foreign policy? (e.g., technology, rising nationalism, etc.)

5. Regarding theories of international relations, which theory has been prevalent in the 19th century? 20th century? 21st century?
6. What role do domestic concerns and factors play in shaping foreign policy? Has the role increased or decreased in the 21st century?
7. Write a memo to the Secretary of State that frames and outlines what you perceive to be the most serious threat facing the United States. How does this significant threat influence and shape foreign policy? How does foreign policy influence the perception of the threat?

Exercise

Mutual Assured Destruction (MAD)

Earlier in the chapter, the nuclear doctrine of MAD was discussed in the context of the Cold War and the Soviet Union (see Figure 6.6, below). Now, in the 21st century, the discussion on MAD continues, as illustrated in the three excepts below.

MAD in the 21st Century, Mutually Assured Destruction May Have Been a Sensible Policy During the Cold War. It Isn't Now.
Clifford D. May, 2011, National Review

> "On Tuesday, June 28 [2011], outside the holy city of Qom, the rulers of the Islamic Republic of Iran test-fired 14 ballistic missiles, including long- and medium-range Shahab missiles and short-range Zelzal missiles. Also near Qom, new and improved centrifuges are turning out more enriched uranium for nuclear weapons.

Figure 6.6 U.S./Russia Nuclear Proliferation.
Source: Ploughshares Fund.

In addition, departing defense secretary Robert Gates noted last month that North Korea's nuclear weapons and missile development 'now constitute[] a direct threat to the United States. . . . They are developing a road-mobile [intercontinental ballistic missile]. . . . It's a huge problem.' For national-security experts, these developments raise a list of troubling questions. For the rest of us, they should raise just two: Do Iran and North Korea represent threats we should take seriously? The answer, clearly, is yes. Are we building the missile-defense system we need to protect America against these threats? The answer, just as clearly, is no. To understand how this situation has come about, recall a little history. During the Cold War, the United States adopted a strategic doctrine called MAD: Mutually Assured Destruction. The logic behind it was both perverse and compelling: So long as we were vulnerable to missile attack by the Soviets, and so long as the Soviets were vulnerable to missile attack by us, neither side would benefit by attacking first—on the contrary, a devastating retaliation would be assured. Assuming that both we and the Soviets were rational, the result would be a standoff, stability, and peaceful coexistence. Veterans of the Cold War, still influential in the foreign-policy establishment and the Obama administration, believe that if this kind of deterrence worked then, it can work now."

We Need Mutually Assured Destruction, But New Technologies May Make Mutually Assured Destruction Hard to Achieve, Alexander Velez-Green, 2017, National Review

"The cyber domain is being contested by militaries all over the world. This could pose a serious threat to the U.S. nuclear arsenal. U.S. officials fear that malicious code could delay the launch of U.S. nuclear missiles just long enough to allow a country like Russia—or maybe China in the future—to wipe them out. . . . But cyberspace is not the only place where MAD may be under threat. . . . Today, however, outer space is becoming a new battlefield. The United States especially relies on satellites to conduct military operations around the world. As a result, competitors are looking for ways to disable or destroy U.S. satellites in order to defeat the U.S. military asymmetrically."

"North Korea Sought Mutual Assured Destruction Relationship With U.S. in 2016" (Japan Times, *September 25, 2017*)

This article reported the following:[38]

"North Korea told the U.S. government it wanted to establish a mutual assured destruction relationship with Washington when the two countries held informal talks shortly after Pyongyang's nuclear test in January 2016, a former senior U.S. official said Sunday. During the informal talks in mid-January, the U.S. government replied to North Korean participants that it cannot accept such a deal, according to the official who declined to be named. . . . While expressing its intention to continue nuclear development, North Korea said in the meeting that Pyongyang and Washington could avoid a nuclear war by possessing nuclear weapons capable of retaliatory attacks, the official said. In response, the U.S. participants said the MAD strategy would not work like the relations between the United States and former Soviet Union during the Cold War, citing a gap in nuclear forces between the United States and North Korea. The U.S. participants also stressed it is necessary to denuclearize the Korean Peninsula for peace and stability in Asia, the official added."

Discussion/Debate Questions

Is MAD a doctrine that should be part of 21st-century foreign policy? Does it act as a deterrent to or a catalyst for war?

Notes

1. Vivian S. Chu & Todd Garvey, *Executive Orders: Issuance, Modification, and Revocation*, Congressional Research Service (2014).
2. Madeleine K. Albright, *The Testing of American Foreign Policy*, For. Aff. (Nov./Dec. 1998).
3. Jeff D. Colgan & Robert E. Keohane, *The Liberal Order Is Rigged*, For. Aff. (May/June 2017).
4. Following the U.S. declaration of war on Spain, in 1898 Senator Henry M. Teller of Colorado proposed what became known as the Teller Amendment. This amendment, which passed in April 1898, ensured that the U.S. would not establish permanent control of Cuba and stated that the U.S. "hereby disclaims any disposition of intention to exercise sovereignty, jurisdiction, or control over said island except for pacification thereof, and asserts its determination, when that is accomplished, to leave the government and control of the island to its people." In line with the amendment, the U.S. remained in Cuba for four years, leaving in 1902. In 1901, prior to leaving Cuba, Senator Orville Platt of Connecticut introduced the Platt Amendment, which secured the U.S. "the right to intervene for the preservation of Cuban independence, the maintenance of a government adequate for the protection of life, property, and individual liberty." The Platt Amendment, which superseded the Teller Amendment, remained in place until 1934.
5. Argentina, Australia, Belgium, Bolivia, Brazil, Byelorussian Soviet Socialist Republic, Canada, Chile, China, Colombia, Costa Rica, Cuba, Czechoslovakia, Denmark, Dominican Republic, Ecuador, Egypt, El Salvador, Ethiopia, France, Greece, Guatemala, Haiti, Honduras, India, Iran, Iraq, Lebanon, Liberia, Luxembourg, Mexico, Netherlands, New Zealand, Nicaragua, Norway, Panama, Paraguay, Peru, Philippine Republic, Poland, Saudi Arabia, Syria, Turkey, Ukrainian Soviet Socialist Republic, Union of South Africa, Union of Soviet Socialist Republics, United Kingdom, United States, Uruguay, Venezuela, Yugoslavia.
6. Charter of the United Nations, www.un.org/en/charter-united-nations/
7. United Nations Charter, Security Council Chapter, www.un.org/en/sections/un-charter/chapter-v/index.html
8. *Id.*
9. George C. Marshall Foundation, http://marshallfoundation.org/marshall/the-marshall-plan/
10. The Marshall Plan Speech, http://marshallfoundation.org/marshall/the-marshall-plan/marshall-plan-speech/
11. Albania, Belgium, Bulgaria, Canada, Croatia, Czech Republic, Denmark, Estonia, France, Germany, Greece, Hungary, Iceland, Italy, Latvia, Lithuania, Luxembourg, Montenegro, Netherland, Norway, Poland, Portugal, Romania, Slovakia, Slovenia, Spain, Turkey, United Kingdom and the United States. Russia, while once a member, is no longer a NATO member state. As noted by NATO,

    > For more than two decades, NATO has strived to build a partnership with Russia, developing dialogue and practical cooperation in areas of common interest. Cooperation has been suspended in response to Russia's military intervention in Ukraine, which the Allies condemn in the strongest terms. Political and military channels of communication remain open. NATO remains concerned by Russia's continued destabilising pattern of military activities and aggressive rhetoric, which goes well beyond Ukraine.
    >
    > www.nato.int/cps/en/natolive/topics_50090.htm

12. Rosie Gray, *Trump Declines to Affirm NATO's Article 5*, The Atlantic, May 25, 2017.

13. U.S. Dep't of State, Cuba Sanctions, www.state.gov/e/eb/tfs/spi/cuba/
14. *Id.*
15. Speech by President John F. Kennedy, Oct. 22, 1962, www.historyplace.com/speeches/jfk-cuban.htm
16. Fidel Castro, *The Duty of a Revolutionary Is to Make the Revolution: The Second Declaration of Havana*, speech delivered in Havana, Feb. 4, 1962, in Kenner and Petras, eds., Fidel Castro Speaks 104, 115 (1970).
17. Speech by Fidel Castro, *Report to the Central Committee of the Communist Party of Cuba*, Jan. 25–26, 1968.
18. The Union of Soviet Socialist Republics (U.S.S.R.), also referred to as the Soviet Union, existed from 1922 through 1991, at which point its successor state was renamed as the Russian Federation (Russia).
19. Julia Ioffe, *The End of the End of the Cold War*, For. Pol., Dec. 21, 2016.
20. North Atlantic Treaty Organization, *What Was the Warsaw Pact?*, www.nato.int/cps/en/natohq/declassified_138294.htm
21. *United States v. Curtiss-Wright Export Corp.*, 299 U.S. 304, 312–313 (1936).
22. U.S. Const., Art. II.
23. *Reid v. Covert*, 354 U.S. 1 (1957).
24. Thomas M. Franck & Edward Weisband, *Foreign Policy by Congress* 135 (1979).
25. Glen S. Krutz & Jeffrey S. Peake, *Treaty Politics and the Rise of Executive Agreements* (2009).
26. Henry F. Wriston, *The Special Envoy*, For. Aff. (Jan. 1960).
27. U.S. Const., Art I., Sec. 8.
28. U.S. Senate Committee on Foreign Relations, www.foreign.senate.gov
29. U.S. House of Representatives, Foreign Affairs Committee, https://foreignaffairs.house.gov
30. Richard A. Posner, *The Law of the Lands*, For. Aff. (Nov./Dec. 2015).
31. Noah Feldman, *When Judges Make Foreign Policy*, N.Y. Times Magazine, Sep. 25, 2008.
32. Anthony Giddens, The Consequences of Modernity 64 (1990).
33. Thomas S. Mowle, *Worldviews in Foreign Policy: Realism, Liberalism, and External Conflict* 24 Pol. Psych. 561 (2003).
34. Phillip H. Gordon, *September 11 and American Foreign Policy*, Brookings Institute (Nov. 1, 2001).
35. Suzanne Daley, *After the Attacks: The Alliance: For First Time, NATO Invokes Joint Defense Pact with U.S.*, N.Y. Times, Sep. 13, 2001.
36. Mark R. Shulman & Lawrence J. Lee, *The Debate over War Powers*, ABA J. of Hum. Rights (Winter 2003).
37. Nicholas Quinn Rosenkranz, *Obama Suspends the Law: What Would Lincoln Say?*, Wall St. J., Apr. 16, 2013.
38. The Japan Times, *North Korea Sought Mutual Assured Destruction Relationship with U.S. in 2016: U.S. Official*, Sep. 25, 2017.

Additional Learning Resources

Additional Readings

I. Bremmer, *Superpower: Three Choices for America's Role in the World* (New York: Penguin Publishing Group, 2015).

A renowned think tank, the **Brookings Institution** provides research and recommendations on a variety of policy areas, including foreign policy. www.brookings.edu

The **Center for Strategic and International Studies** is a bipartisan, nonprofit policy research organization providing strategic insights and policy solutions in support of global security and prosperity. www.csis.org

The **Council on Foreign Relations** is a think tank that serves as a key resource for U.S. foreign policy. www.cfr.org

The **Department of Defense** is a major player in the foreign policy process. www.defense.gov

The **Department of Homeland Security** is directly involved with foreign policy and focuses on "preventing terrorism and enhancing security; managing our borders; administering immigration laws; securing cyberspace; and ensuring disaster resilience." www.dhs.gov/about-dhs

Foreign Policy is a media organizations devoted to the coverage of global affairs. http://foreignpolicy.com/

The **Intelligence Community** is an umbrella website for 17 U.S. federal intelligence agencies. It focuses on issues including terrorism, technology, climate change, nuclear proliferation and more. www.intelligence.gov

G.F. Kennan, *After the Cold War*, New York Times, Feb. 5, 1989, www.nytimes.com/1989/02/05/magazine/after-the-cold-war.html

David Milne, *Worldmaking: The Art and Science of American Diplomacy* (New York: Farrar, Straus and Giroux, 2015).

Joseph S. Nye, Jr., *Presidential Leadership and the Creation of the American Era* (Princeton, NJ: Princeton University Press, 2013).

The **State Department** is the primary U.S. agency conducting foreign policy. www.state.gov

United States Institute of Peace is a nonpartisan organization promoting policies that encourage security and peace. www.usip.org

7 Security Law and Policy

Col. Michael W. Taylor

Introductory Case

On October 31, 2017, an immigrant from Uzbekistan, Sayfullo Saipov, drove a truck onto a crowded bicycle and pedestrian path in New York City, killing eight people and injuring a dozen more. Saipov got out of the truck shouting "Allahu Akbar," which is Arabic for "God is great." Saipov was seen carrying what appeared to be firearms, but which turned out to be a paintball gun and a pellet gun. Other items Saipov placed in the truck included several knives and a stun gun. Law enforcement officials shot Saipov and took him into custody.[1]

During questioning by law enforcement officers, Saipov said he was inspired to commit his crimes by watching videos produced by the Islamic State of Iraq and the Levant (commonly known as ISIL, or by its former acronym, ISIS). Saipov said he chose the date because he believed more people would be outdoors on Halloween and that would increase his chance of killing as many people as possible. Saipov said he was pleased with his actions and requested permission to display the ISIL flag in his hospital room. On November 1, 2017, the U.S. Attorney in the Southern District of New York charged Saipov with providing material support to a designated foreign terrorist organization and with killing people through use of a motor vehicle.[2]

President Donald Trump, a frequent user of the social media platform Twitter, commented about the case several times on Twitter. Shortly after the media began reporting on the attack, the President wrote "In NYC, looks like another attack by a very sick and deranged person. Law enforcement is following this closely. NOT IN THE U.S.A.!" and he followed that with "We must not allow ISIS to return, or enter, our country after defeating them in the Middle East and elsewhere. Enough!" In a comment the following day, the President wrote "NYC terrorist was happy as he asked to hang ISIS flag in his hospital room. He killed 8 people, badly injured 12. SHOULD GET DEATH PENALTY!" The President also wrote "Would love to send the NYC terrorist to Guantanamo but statistically that process takes much longer than going through the Federal system . . ."[3] Finally, President Trump used the case as an example of why he hoped to reform immigration laws.

Compare that attack with one that happened a few days later. On November 5, 2017, an American man by the name of Devin Kelley entered a church in Sutherland Springs, Texas during a Sunday worship service. Kelley used firearms to kill 26 people and injure 20 more. Kelley fled the church, and a local civilian shot and injured Kelley, who drove away in his car. The civilian followed Kelley, and after a high-speed chase Kelley's car crashed. Law enforcement officials arrived on the scene and found Kelley dead. Early media reports concerning Kelley noted that he may have had mental health problems and had been court-martialed and discharged from the U.S. Air Force.[4]

During a press conference shortly after the shooting, President Trump said, "I think that mental health is a problem here. Based on preliminary reports, this was a very deranged individual with a lot of problems over a very long period of time. We have a lot of mental health problems in our country, as do other countries, but this isn't a guns situation . . . we could go into it but it's a little bit soon to go into it. . . . This is a mental health problem at the highest level."[5]

Both tragic incidents share similarities. Individual men killed innocent bystanders. Law enforcement officials responded to investigate. The President quickly made public comments about the attacks. The motive for the attacks, however, is important and is the critical difference. While we may never know what motivated Kelley, Saipov proudly proclaimed the purpose of his attack was to support a terrorist organization.

Terrorist incidents like Saipov's have greatly influenced U.S. security policy over the past few decades. The U.S. concept of homeland security, profound changes in intelligence and surveillance laws and procedures, and the method of holding individuals accountable through the justice system have all changed, in part, due to terrorist attacks. Nevertheless, many questions remain. Should the motive for an attack make a difference in how U.S. officials respond to and ultimately prosecute the attacker? If the motive is unclear, should officials default to treating the case as one involving terrorism? Are U.S. law enforcement, intelligence, and court systems prepared for both types of situations? Are satisfactory law and policy in place? This chapter will explore these issues and help you form your own answers to these and other questions.

Overview/Background

Rulers throughout time have had a basic understanding of what we now call security policy, or else they probably were not rulers for long. For centuries before the rise of the nation-state, kings maintained armies and navies, established alliances, sent out spies, and had systems in place to protect themselves from being assassinated or overthrown. These topics still resonate today as the core of security policy.

The rise of democratic forms of government had little effect on the substantive aspect of security; the people still needed protection from enemies. What did change with security policy after the rise of democracies was similar to what changed for other types of policies: the impetus for making decisions shifted from a personal focus on what could keep the ruler in power to a focus on what was in the best interest of the nation as a whole, creation of more transparent processes, and accountability for actions through elections.

Within the United States, the people have always looked to the executive branch, and the President in particular, to set security policy for the country. Congress plays an important role in creating laws and through its function as a constitutional check on a powerful leader, but the President and his Cabinet determine the direction in which the nation will go. In the best-case scenario, the President will issue a clear statement on what his policy is. But more often than not, the **national security** policy is spread across many speeches, documents, orders, and occasionally laws. Not every President has made a lasting, significant contribution to the development of security policy. What follows is a brief synopsis of some of the Presidential policies that did.

President George Washington set a tone for the nation in his farewell address in September 1796. In his speech, he promoted national unity, warned of the dangers of

> National security—all threats to the United States, threats to the people, property, or interests of the United States, or actions taken to counter those threats.

geographical parties, and recommended international neutrality as keys to securing the fledgling nation. The next major policy came in December 1823, when President James Monroe gave a speech to Congress. During the speech, President Monroe famously set out important new elements of foreign policy and security policy in what would later be called the Monroe Doctrine. He said:

> We owe it, therefore, to candor and to the amicable relations existing between the United States and [European] powers to declare that we should consider any attempt on their part to extend their system to any portion of this hemisphere as dangerous to our peace and safety. With the existing colonies or dependencies of any European power we have not interfered and shall not interfere. But . . . we could not view any interposition for the purpose of oppressing [former colonies that have declared independence], or controlling in any other manner their destiny, by any European power in any other light than as the manifestation of an unfriendly disposition toward the United States.[6]

These few sentences set the tone for how the United States would relate to other nations for many decades. President James Polk, in his first address to Congress in 1845, continued the core elements of the Monroe Doctrine when he adopted what would eventually be called the Manifest Destiny doctrine. Polk called for an aggressive expansion of American territory in order to ensure peace for the nation from European powers and neighbors, such as Mexico. President Theodore Roosevelt reaffirmed the basic principles of the Monroe Doctrine in an address to Congress in December 1904.

In 1918, under President Woodrow Wilson, national security policy began to look beyond defense of the nation and beyond the Americas. While Wilson continued elements of Manifest Destiny in his policies, in his famous "Fourteen Points" speech to Congress in January 1918, he called for a diplomatic peace to end World War I, freedom of navigation of the sea, equal trade, resolution of colonial claims, and strengthening international law through the League of Nations.

President Harry Truman made substantial changes to the substance and processes involved in security policy. The important changes to the procedural elements are discussed later in the chapter. As for substance, the core elements of the Truman Doctrine were expressed in his speech to Congress in March 1947. Truman declared: "I believe that it must be the policy of the United States to support free peoples who are resisting attempted subjugation by armed minorities or by outside pressures . . . primarily through economic and financial aid."[7] President Dwight Eisenhower extended this policy by encouraging other countries to request economic or military aid in an address to Congress in January 1957.

The security policies of President Lyndon Johnson, expressed in May 1965, and President Ronald Reagan, as expressed in various speeches throughout the 1980s, were focused on containing and limiting Communist governments. President James Carter expressed in a State of the Union address in January 1980 that the United States would use military force to defend its interests in the Persian Gulf. By contrast, President Richard Nixon, in response to the ongoing Vietnam War, had expressed in a televised speech to the nation in November 1969 that the United States would keep treaty commitments and provide a shield if a nuclear power threatened a key ally. However, the United States would "look to the nation directly threatened to assume the primary responsibility of providing the manpower for its defense" when providing military and economic assistance when requested.[8]

From these examples we see that security policy is adaptable, changeable, and responds to current events around the globe. Later in the chapter, we will review the current U.S. security policies and compare them to their recent predecessors.

The complexity of the modern world, advances in technology, the rise of terrorism, and changes in communication have altered the way security policy is developed and expanded the area of focus beyond simply preservation of the United States and its sphere of influence. Today, security policy addresses numerous topics, including climate change, weapons of mass destruction, and cyberspace. Ultimately, security policy, as important as it is to the country's well-being, should not be viewed on its own; it is inextricably and overtly interwoven with the other policies discussed throughout this textbook.

> **Classified information**—"Information that has been determined pursuant to [Executive Order 13526] or any predecessor order to require protection against unauthorized disclosure and is marked to indicate its classified status when in documentary form."[9]
>
> **Security policy**—as used in this chapter, the term refers to policy matters involving both national security and homeland security.
>
> **National Security Council**—a council created by U.S. law to advise the President on matters concerning national security and whose membership includes the President, Vice President, and designated Cabinet officials.
>
> **Intelligence**—"The product resulting from the collection, processing, integration, evaluation, analysis, and interpretation of available information concerning foreign nations, hostile or potentially hostile forces or elements, or areas of actual or potential operations [or the] activities that result in the product."[10]

Discussion Questions

How do public statements from the President shape security policy, and is that the best mechanism for developing policy?

What constraints exist on the President's authority to implement security policy, and should there be more?

What is the relationship between security policy and other national policies, such as economic policy, foreign policy, and social policy?

Security Law and Policy

Before looking at the key substantive areas within national security policy, we first need to review two important procedural aspects: the structure of the organizations created to support the executive branch and the rules involving **classified information**.

The National Security Council and the Homeland Security Council

Ultimately, the President is responsible for the **security policy** of the country. Of course, this is too large a job for any one person, so within the executive branch there are organizations and processes to help the President execute that responsibility.

Soon after the end of World War II, President Truman wanted to substantially change the organization of the executive branch to enhance the security of the nation. Those efforts culminated in the National Security Act of 1947, which, among other changes, created the **National Security Council** (NSC). The statute has been amended several times, but the core function of the NSC has remained unchanged.

Title 50, United States Code, Section 3021 declares that the NSC shall "advise the President with respect to the integration of domestic, foreign, and military policies relating to the national security," with the goal of increasing cooperation among the agencies of the executive branch. The statute does not define what the term "national security" means, but we get some clues from the definition of the term "**intelligence** related to national security," which includes everything involving a threat to the

United States, its people, property, or interests, or anything else related to U.S. "national or **homeland security**."

The idea of homeland security as a concept separate from national security in the United States arose after the terrorist attacks of September 11, 2001. President Bush created the **Homeland Security Council** (HSC) as a distinct entity through an Executive Order on October 8, 2001. The following year, the Homeland Security Act of 2002 made the HSC permanent.

Title 6, United States Code, Section 492 states that the purpose of the HSC is to advise the President on homeland security matters. Again, there is no statutory definition of what the term "homeland security" means. The statutory purpose of the Department of Homeland Security (DHS), however, shows that the primary area of concern is preventing and responding to **terrorism** in the United States. DHS states that its missions are to prevent terrorism and enhance security, secure and manage the borders, enforce and administer immigration laws, safeguard and secure cyberspace, and strengthen national preparedness and resilience.

Significant overlap exists between national security and homeland security since they both deal with threats to the nation. Some people think of national security as the responsibility for activities occurring outside the United States and as homeland security for those within, but in reality, the dividing line is not so clearly defined. For example, consider the issue of ensuring the safety of passengers on commercial aircraft. While the Department of Transportation can establish requirements for passenger and baggage screening solely as a domestic aspect of homeland security, the threat often arises from flights originating in other countries. Working with the governments of those other countries to ensure proper screening implicates issues of national security, as the complex relationship with those governments has many layers beyond just transportation security.

Within the Executive Office of the President are numerous advisors in various areas who are not subject to confirmation by the Senate as cabinet officials are. Two positions related to the topic of security policy are the National Security Advisor, also known as the Assistant to the President for National Security Affairs, and the Homeland Security Advisor, also known as the Assistant to the President for Homeland Security and Counterterrorism.

The National Security Advisor takes the lead role in matters under the purview of the NSC and HSC. Under both President Barack Obama and President Donald Trump, the National Security Advisor has been responsible for setting the agenda and for other important tasks involved in directing both councils.[13] Furthermore, President Obama combined separate NSC and HSC staffs into a single NSC staff. While the councils remain distinct, as required by statute, the executive branch relies on extensive inter-agency cooperation on matters involving national and homeland security.

Both the NSC and HSC conduct their work primarily through committees. The **Principals Committee** (PC) is chaired by the National Security Advisor, rather than the President, as would be the case in a full NSC or HSC meeting. The PC meets as needed, but often a few times per month. Additionally, a **Deputies Committee** (DC), chaired by the Deputy National Security Advisor, is attended by the main deputy (for example, the Deputy Secretary of State) to the cabinet official. The role and meeting frequency of the DC varies with each President's administration, but the DC often does much of the work in shaping and developing the issues that need a decision from the PC or the full council.

Homeland security—efforts to prevent terrorist attacks, reduce vulnerability to terrorism, minimize damage from terrorist attacks, or recover from terrorist attack in the United States.[11]

Homeland Security Council—a council created by the United States to advise the President on matters concerning homeland security and whose membership includes the President, Vice President, and designated Cabinet officials.

Terrorism—"The unlawful use of force and violence against persons or property to intimidate or coerce a government, the civilian population, or any segment thereof, in furtherance of political or social objectives."[12]

Principals Committee—the senior Cabinet-level committee supporting the National Security Council and whose membership consists of Cabinet officials and senior White House advisors.

Deputies Committee—the senior sub-Cabinet interagency forum supporting the National Security Council.

Table 7.1 National and Homeland Security Council Membership (2017)

Position	NSC	HSC	PC
President	Statutory	Statutory	–
Vice President	Statutory	Statutory	–
Secretary of State	Statutory	Non-statutory	Non-statutory
Secretary of the Treasury	Statutory	Non-statutory	Non-statutory
Secretary of Defense	Statutory	Non-statutory	Non-statutory
Attorney General	Non-statutory	Statutory	Non-statutory
Secretary of Energy	Statutory	Non-statutory	Non-statutory
Secretary of Homeland Security	Non-statutory	Statutory	Non-statutory
United Nations Representative	Non-statutory	Statutory	Non-statutory
National Security Advisor	Non-statutory	Non-statutory	Non-statutory
Director of National Intelligence	Non-statutory	Non-statutory	Non-statutory
Homeland Security Advisor	Non-statutory	Non-statutory	Non-statutory
Director of Central Intelligence Agency	Non-statutory	Non-statutory	Non-statutory
Chairman of the Joint Chiefs of Staff	Non-statutory	Non-statutory	Non-statutory
Chief of Staff to the President	Invited	–	Non-statutory
Counsel to the President	Invited	–	Invited
Deputy Counsel for National Security	Invited	–	Invited
Director of Office of Management & Budget	Invited	–	Invited
Others as needed for specific issues*	Invited	Invited	Invited

Source: Compiled by author.

*Others specifically mentioned for consideration: Secretary of Commerce, U.S. Trade Representative, Assistant to the President for Economic Policy, Assistant to the President for Intragovernmental and Technology Initiatives, and Administrator of the U.S. Agency for International Development

> **Policy Coordination Committees**—various regional and issue-related committees that are the main day-to-day medium for coordinating security issues in support of the National Security Council.

In addition to the two main committees, several **Policy Coordination Committees** also support the NSC. These committees are issue based or regionally based and are typically chaired by members of the NSC staff. Attendance is at the Assistant Secretary level. Finally, the NSC staff, headed by an Executive Secretary and filled by individuals with extensive expertise in national security, works daily to ensure that the President and his administration are able to develop and implement security policy.

Table 7.1 shows which officials are required to attend council and PC meetings and whether membership is specified by statute or not, or whether the official is simply invited to attend. While the exact membership various from time-to-time due to changes implemented by the President, the table shows the membership as of President Trump's April 2017 memorandum.

Protecting Classified Information

One of the hallmarks of modern liberal democracies, such as the United States, is a strong preference for openness and transparency in government policies and operations. But even the most transparent governments have found that some information must be kept secret. After all, what good is a plan to keep the country safe if an adversary knows the details? Keeping the nation's sensitive information secret has long been a priority for policymakers and those responsible for implementing those policies. Militaries around the world have done this for centuries. For example, during World War II, the United States famously published posters using phrases such as "Loose Lips Sink Ships" to remind military service members and civilians to protect sensitive information.

For many years, the United States did not have a law protecting sensitive information. Congress eventually passed a Defense Secrets Act in 1911 and an Espionage Act in 1917, which provided limited statutory protection. Elements of those laws are still in place today as crimes in Title 18, United States Code, Chapter 37. However, the idea of systematically protecting information through government policy and regulation did not come about until 1951.

President Truman, through Executive Order 10290, created the first standardized system for classifying information. Prior to this order, the only sensitive information protected was related to the military. President Truman recognized that the concept of national security was broader than merely military activities and therefore extended the rules to all civilian agencies. The rules have been amended many times over the years, but the core idea of protecting a wide swath of sensitive information has remained. A month after issuing that order, President Truman signed into law the only statute making it a crime to misuse classified information, but that protection is limited to cryptographic technologies and communications intelligence.[14]

The current procedures for classifying, safeguarding, handling, and declassifying national security information are contained in Executive Order 13526 issued by President Obama in 2009. The order specifies which government officials have the authority to classify information, defines the levels of classification, the length of classification, and the circumstances under which information may be classified. In addition to the obvious traditional military categories, the order permits other categories of information to be classified, such as foreign relations activities of the United States and "scientific, technological, or economic matters relating to the national security."[15]

The Supreme Court has long recognized the importance of supporting executive branch decisions regarding classified information, even before the existence of a law or Executive Order. In 1875, the Supreme Court decided *Totten v. United States*. In *Totten*, the heirs of William Lloyd sued the United States for payment for services rendered under a contract. The contract was between Lloyd and President Abraham Lincoln during the Civil War and required Lloyd to travel to the southern states to gather and report military intelligence directly to the President. The existence of the contract itself and its terms, however, were a secret. The Court declared it had "no difficulty" in concluding that the President had the authority to enter into a secret contract and ruling against Lloyd's heirs. The Court reasoned if lawsuits for secret contracts could be brought in court, "the whole service . . . might be exposed, to the serious detriment of the public. A secret service, with liability to publicity in this way, would be impossible, and, such services are sometimes indispensable to the government."[16]

More recently, in *Department of the Navy v. Egan*,[17] the Court continued to give way to the executive branch on matters of national security. In this 1988 case, the Navy denied an employee a security clearance and subsequently removed him from his job due to the lack of the security clearance. The employee sued and the Court ruled for the United States. Recalling that the President is the Commander-in-Chief of the military, the Court noted his "authority to classify and control access to information bearing on national security . . . flows primarily from this constitutional investment of power in the President, and exists quite apart from any explicit congressional grant."[18] More significantly, the Court reaffirmed the precedent from several previous cases, holding that the judicial branch will traditionally defer to the executive branch and usually not intrude when the President is acting on matters involving the military and national security affairs.

The Supreme Court has, however, set some limits on respecting executive branch decisions concerning classified information. In 1971, two prominent newspapers published articles based on the "Pentagon Papers," which contained classified information about the Vietnam War. A Department of Defense employee leaked the documents to journalists, and the first article appeared in June 1971. The government brought suit two days later, seeking to enjoin the newspapers from further publication. Demonstrating the importance of the issue, the case was decided, appealed, and ultimately brought before the Supreme Court in a remarkable 11 days. In this case, *New York Times Co. v. U.S.*, the Court referenced cases pertaining to the First Amendment to conclude that the government would not get an injunction. The Court reasoned that the First Amendment imposes a heavy burden on the government to warrant an injunction, which would amount to "prior restraint" of the press and concluded the government failed to introduce evidence sufficient to meet that burden.[19]

The Justices sided six to three with the newspapers in that case, but the fractured nature of the opinions provided little practical guidance on how to resolve this issue in future cases. The law on this topic remains unsettled. Although many journalists believe it is unlikely they will be prosecuted for publishing classified information (as demonstrated by frequent publication of articles in recent years referring to classified government programs), a variety of existing criminal laws would allow for their prosecution. While journalists do not have a right to access classified information, once they obtain it, they have thus far been free to publish it without criminal consequences. The government's primary means of stopping leaks and deterring further unauthorized disclosures has been to discipline or prosecute the individuals who improperly released the classified data.

In the following sections, we will review official U.S. government policies on matters involving security. The source documents discussed are publicly available and are not classified. However, many of these documents are merely the releasable summaries of the full documents, which are classified. The classified versions are only available to those with the proper clearances and a need to know. Therefore, keep in mind that within the U.S. government, key officials are aware of security policy nuances that are not available to the general public.

National Security Strategy Report and Quadrennial Homeland Security Review

Now that we have explored how security policy is made and protected from disclosure, we can begin to examine the substance of the policy itself. Public opinion polls reveal that national security is a major factor in presidential elections. The U.S. electorate wants a President with a clear vision of how to protect them. During the campaign, the successful candidate will have made many statements and promises, some of which are relevant to security policy. However, that collection of comments is not the same as a complete strategy.

Since 1986, every new President has been required to submit a comprehensive report known as the **National Security Strategy Report** to Congress within 150 days of taking office and every year after that. The timeline and the annual requirement have not always been followed exactly. President William Clinton's administration submitted seven reports during his tenure, but President George H.W. Bush, President George W. Bush, and President Obama each submitted only two or three. President Trump's first report, in December 2017, was six months late, but that was earlier than the Clinton, Bush, or Obama Administrations published their first reports.

National Security Strategy Report—a report, due annually in accordance with U.S. law, from the President to Congress detailing the country's national security strategy.

Security Law and Policy 217

In accordance with the law, each report is supposed to set forth the national security strategy; detail goals and objectives related to national security; discuss foreign policy and defense capabilities; explain proposed uses of political, economic, military, and other elements of power; and evaluate the adequacy of the capabilities to carry out the strategy.[20] The reports do generally follow these requirements. The reports also broadly address several recurring themes: physical security, economic prosperity, spreading American values, and maintaining international order. Table 7.2 summarizes the key points under each of those themes using the last report prepared by each administration since 1993. While the details change depending on the historical context and the aspirations of the administration, the themes have remained remarkably constant.

Table 7.2 Comparison of National Security Strategies (1993–2017)

1993—G.H.W. Bush	2001—Clinton	2006—G.W. Bush	2015—Obama	2017—Trump
Security	*Security*	*Security*	*Security*	*Security*
• Strengthen national defense	• Shape international environment	• Prevent weapons of mass destruction	• Strengthen national defense	• Secure borders and territory
• Innovate defense industrial base	• Respond to threats and crises	• Transform security institutions	• Reinforce homeland security	• Pursue terrorist & transnational criminal organization threats to source
• Support non proliferation efforts	• Prepare for uncertain future	• Address globalization concerns	• Combat terrorism	• Keep U.S. safe in cyber era
• Develop ballistic missile defenses			• Build capacity to prevent conflict	• Promote resilience
• Improve intelligence capabilities			• Prevent weapons of mass destruction	• Renew security capabilities
• Stop terrorism			• Confront climate change	• Promote/protect national security innovation base
• Combat illegal drugs			• Assure access to shared spaces	
			• Increase global health security	
Prosperity	*Prosperity*	*Prosperity*	*Prosperity*	*Prosperity*
• Follow long-term growth strategy	• Strengthen financial coordination	• Ignite economic growth	• Put the economy to work	• Rejuvenate domestic economy
• Update economic policy	• Promote open trading system	• Expand development via democracy	• Advance energy security	• Promote free, fair, & reciprocal economic relationships
• Rebuild U.S. economic institutions	• Enhance U.S. competitiveness		• Lead in science & technology	• Lead in research, technology, invention, & innovation
• Focused foreign aid program	• Provide for energy security		• Shape global economic order	• Embrace energy dominance
• Protect the environment	• Promote sustainable development		• End extreme poverty	• Renew competitive advantages
• Use outer space effectively				

(*Continued*)

218 Security Law and Policy

Table 7.2 (Continued)

1993—G.H.W. Bush	2001—Clinton	2006—G.W. Bush	2015—Obama	2017—Trump
Values	*Values*	*Values*	*Values*	*Values*
• Enhance democracies world-wide • Create lasting global faith in U.S. • Champion fair immigration	• Strengthen emerging democracies • Adhere to human rights • Engage in humanitarian activities	• Champion human dignity	• Live U.S. values • Advance equality • Support emerging democracies • Empower civil society & leaders • Prevent mass atrocities	• Champion American values
International Order	*International Order*	*International Order*	*International Order*	*International Order*
• Exert influence at United Nations • Exert tailored regional influence	• Recognize regional differences	• Defeat terrorism via alliances • Defuse regional conflicts • Cooperate with global powers	• Advance rebalance to Asia/Pacific • Strengthen alliance with Europe • Seek peace/stability in Middle East • Invest in Africa's future • Deepen cooperation in the Americas	• Use effective diplomacy & statecraft • Encourage aspiring partners • Achieve better outcomes in multilateral forums • Implement policy in regional context

Source: Compiled by author.

The current U.S. security policy is detailed in President Trump's 2017 National Security Strategy Report, which was divided into four pillars: (1) protect the American people, the homeland, and the American way of life; (2) promote American prosperity; (3) preserve peace through strength; and (4) advance American influence. At the end, the report explained how the strategy would be contextually tailored based on six geographic regions around the world. In many ways, this was similar to President Obama's 2015 report, but Trump's policy emphasized security and economic prosperity more and in different ways. Trump's strategy also emphasizes competition with the rest of the world to a degree not seen in previous security strategies.

The reporting requirement for homeland security is different from that for national security. Even though the United States had no statutory requirement until 2009, President Bush published a National Strategy for Homeland Security in 2002. In 2009, Congress tasked the Secretary of the DHS to conduct reviews every four years and prepare reports. The DHS completed reports in 2010 and 2014, and another is due in 2018. The **Quadrennial Homeland Security Review** must include a complete examination of the homeland security strategy; provide recommendations for long-term strategy; recommend programs, assets, budget, policies, and authorities of

> Quadrennial Homeland Security Review—a report, due every four years in accordance with U.S. law, from the Secretary of Homeland Security to Congress detailing the country's homeland security strategy.

Table 7.3 Comparison of Homeland Security Missions (2002–2014)

2002	2010	2014
Domestic counterterrorism	Prevent terrorism & enhance security	Prevent terrorism & enhance security
Defend against terrorism		
Border & transportation security	Secure & manage borders	Secure & manage borders
Intelligence & warning	Enforce & administer immigration laws	Enforce & administer immigration laws
Protecting critical infrastructure	Safeguard & secure cyberspace	Safeguard & secure cyberspace
Emergency preparedness & response	Ensure resilience to disaster	Strengthen national preparedness & resilience

Source: Compiled by author.

DHS; and provide a prioritized list of missions, among many other requirements.[21] Table 7.3 summarizes the missions and focus areas detailed in each of the reports.

The 2002 strategy report explains the connection between national security and homeland security:

> The *National Security Strategy of the United States* aims to guarantee the sovereignty and independence of the United States, with our fundamental values and institutions intact. It provides a framework for creating and seizing opportunities that strengthen our security and prosperity. The *National Strategy for Homeland Security* complements the *National Security Strategy of the United States* by addressing a very specific and uniquely challenging threat—terrorism in the United States—and by providing a comprehensive framework for organizing the efforts of federal, state, local and private organizations whose primary functions are often unrelated to national security . . . Thus the *National Security Strategy of the United States* and *National Strategy for Homeland Security* work as mutually supporting documents, providing guidance to the executive branch departments and agencies.[22]

Homeland security is incorporated as a component of national security in the strategy report from President Obama in 2015. Although the concepts are separate but related, for the remainder of this chapter, we will not further distinguish between them and will simply use the term *security policy*. The following sections of the chapter are an overview of four key substantive aspects of security policy: **national defense**, homeland security, preventing terrorism, and **shared spaces**. As you consider these issues, remember that security policy covers a broad swath of topics, some of which are addressed in other chapters of this book. Therefore, this chapter only covers some of the topics under the "security" theme of the national security strategy.

National defense—"Programs for military and energy production or construction, military or critical infrastructure assistance to any foreign nation, homeland security, stockpiling, space, and any directly related activity [including] emergency preparedness activities . . . and critical infrastructure protection and restoration."[23]

Shared spaces—vital common areas consisting of the oceans, airspace, outer space, and cyberspace, that enable and support modern society and a global economy.

National Defense Policy and Law

Article II of the Constitution makes the President the Commander-in-Chief of the military. However, Article I gives Congress the power to declare war, something which it has done only a handful of times and never since World War II. Nevertheless, the Founding Fathers' carefully crafted system of checks and balances on this topic has, in practice, been lopsided in favor of the executive branch. Obviously, the United States has been in many armed conflicts since the 1940s. Those military actions are the result of presidents determining that use of military force was necessary to the country's security. Thus, each use of force is an example of security policy in action in the most direct, visible, and lethal way.

Since the close of the Cold War, many legal and policy limitations have arisen which are critical to planning and executing coalition military operations. These limitations exist as a result of different nations' views of international law, treaty obligations, and policies which become part of the rules of engagement. U.S. allies which joined in Afghanistan and Iraq agreed to an overall strategy, but almost immediately, difficulties arose in both campaigns, which the following examples illustrate.

The United States is not a signatory to the Ottawa Treaty outlawing the use of anti-personnel landmines, but close allies are. There were sound reasons for this treaty. Thousands of non-combatant civilians have been killed or maimed by these weapons, and landmines do not distinguish between combatants and non-combatants. On the other hand, there is an understandable reluctance to forswear the use of a weapon that can save the lives of one's own military forces. Close U.S. allies interpreted their agreement to the treaty as prohibiting even the transport of those weapons for U.S. forces. As a result, U.S. aircraft had to divert to other locations on short notice, and other military materiel was at risk of being supplied later than required. Another issue arose when a U.S. ally provided more fighter jets than pilots. The ally asked if U.S. pilots could fly the ally's aircraft, but only in accordance with the ally's more restrictive rules of engagement. Convincing the ally that the status of the pilot was paramount over the flag on the airplane took a bit of negotiating. I had a role in resolving both of these issues. I joined a small team which reviewed all of the allies' treaty and policy limitations—and there were quite a few—in order to assist U.S. military planners.

Other disagreements arose over the interrogation of captured belligerents as well as not assisting in psychological operations in Iraq. The Iraqi government at the time understood that sometimes in order to "ferret out" terrorist leaders while minimizing the risk to civilians, psychological operations—that is, employing sophisticated public and private influence media—was the best means possible. But, because the non-lethal use of this type of classified work may affect non-combatants, U.S. allies had a different view. Explaining the U.S. legal and policy basis for this type of operation was critical to removing allied opposition. It may be the case that U.S. allies did not approve of the methods, but they did understand U.S. determination to minimize the risk to civilians by not using gunfire or other weapons, but by using psychological campaigns to weaken the leadership of terrorist groups.

Joshua E. Kastenberg, J.D., LL.M.
Assistant Professor, University of New Mexico School of Law

Although the President as Commander-in-Chief has broad powers to use military forces, these powers are not unlimited. As a result of actions during the Vietnam War, Congress passed the War Powers Resolution over President Nixon's veto in 1973. The stated purpose of the statute is to limit the President's authority to use military force to situations when Congress has declared war, Congress has given statutory authorization, or the United States has been attacked. The law requires the President to submit a report to Congress within 48 hours of the use of military forces and provide updates at least every six months. Finally, the War Powers Resolution requires the President to terminate the use of armed forces within 60 days unless Congress approves of their continued use.[24]

The War Powers Resolution has resulted in an uneasy tension between the President and Congress. While all Presidents have consistently taken a position that the War Powers Resolution is unconstitutional, they have usually provided some reports to Congress and usually wait for Congressional authorization before large-scale uses of force. The most recent Congressional action in this area is known as the **Authorization for Use of Military Force** (AUMF). Passed in September 2001, the AUMF gives the President authority

> to use all necessary and appropriate force against those nations, organizations, or persons he determines planned, authorized, committed, or aided the terrorist attacks that occurred on September 11, 2001, or harbored such organizations or persons, in order to prevent any future acts of international terrorism.[25]

> **Authorization for Use of Military Force**—a statute passed after the terrorist attacks of September 11, 2001, giving the President the authority to use all necessary force in response to those attacks.

The AUMF is still in effect and has been cited as authority by Presidents Bush, Obama, and Trump to take offensive military action.

While Congress has considered the idea of repealing or updating the AUMF, the reality is that the Constitution and law impose few constraints on the ability of the President to implement security policy through the use of armed force. The 2000 case of *Campbell v. Clinton* illustrates this point.

Tom Campbell v. William Jefferson Clinton, 203 F.3d 19 (D.C. Cir. 2000)

On March 24, 1999, President Clinton announced the commencement of NATO air and cruise missile attacks on Yugoslav targets. Two days later, he submitted to Congress a report, "consistent with the War Powers Resolution," detailing the circumstances necessitating the use of armed forces, the deployments scope and expected duration, and asserting that he had "taken these actions pursuant to [his] authority ... as Commander in Chief and Chief Executive." On April 28, Congress voted on four resolutions related to the Yugoslav conflict: It voted down a declaration of war 427 to 2 and an "authorization" of the air strikes 213 to 213, but it also voted against requiring the President to immediately end U.S. participation in the NATO operation and voted to fund that involvement ...

Appellants, 31 congressmen opposed to U.S. involvement in the Kosovo intervention, filed suit prior to termination of that conflict seeking a declaratory judgment that the Presidents use of American forces against Yugoslavia was unlawful under both the War

Powers Clause of the Constitution and the War Powers Resolution ("the WPR") . . . The district court granted the Presidents motion to dismiss . . . and this appeal followed.

The government does not respond to appellants claim on the merits. Instead the government challenges the jurisdiction of the federal courts to adjudicate this claim on three separate grounds: the case is moot; appellants lack standing, as the district court concluded; and the case is nonjusticiable. Since we agree with the district court that the congressmen lack standing it is not necessary to decide whether there are other jurisdictional defects.

The question whether congressmen have standing in federal court to challenge the lawfulness of actions of the executive was answered, at least in large part, in the Supreme Court's recent decision in *Raines v. Byrd*, 521 U.S. 811, 117 S.Ct. 2312, 138 L.Ed.2d 849 (1997). *Raines* involved a constitutional challenge to the President's authority under the short-lived Line Item Veto Act. Individual congressmen claimed that under that Act a President could veto (unconstitutionally) only part of a law and thereby diminish the institutional power of Congress. Observing it had never held that congressmen have standing to assert an institutional injury as against the executive... the Court held that petitioners in the case lacked "legislative standing" to challenge the Act. The Court noted that petitioners already possessed an adequate political remedy, since they could vote to have the Line Item Veto Act repealed, or to provide individual spending bills with a statutory exemption.

Thereafter in *Chenoweth v. Clinton*, 181 F.3d 112, 115 (D.C.Cir. 1999), emphasizing the separation-of-powers problems inherent in legislative standing, we held that congressmen had no standing to challenge the Presidents introduction of a program through executive order rather than statute . . .

In this case, Congress certainly could have passed a law forbidding the use of U.S. forces in the Yugoslav campaign; indeed, there was a measure—albeit only a concurrent resolution—introduced to require the President to withdraw U.S. troops. Unfortunately, however, for those congressmen who, like appellants, desired an end to U.S. involvement in Yugoslavia, this measure was defeated by a 139 to 290 vote. Of course, Congress always retains appropriations authority and could have cut off funds for the American role in the conflict. Again there was an effort to do so but it failed; appropriations were authorized. And there always remains the possibility of impeachment should a President act in disregard of Congress authority on these matters.

Appellants constitutional claim stands on no firmer footing. Appellants argue that the War Powers Clause of the Constitution proscribes a President from using military force except as is necessary to repel a sudden attack. But they also argue that the WPR "implements" or channels congressional authority under the Constitution. It may well be then that since we have determined that appellants lack standing to enforce the WPR there is nothing left of their constitutional claim. Assuming, however, that appellants constitutional claim should be considered separately, the same logic dictates they do not have standing to bring such a challenge. That is to say Congress has a broad range of legislative authority it can use to stop a Presidents war making... and therefore under Raines congressmen may not challenge the Presidents war-making powers in federal court . . .

Accordingly, the district court is affirmed; appellants lack standing.

Although the *Campbell* case focuses on the War Powers Resolution, its implications are much more wide-ranging. Essentially, the Court of Appeals, relying on the Supreme Court case of *Raines v. Byrd*, ruled that policy disputes between the executive and legislative branches must be resolved between them; there can be no resort to the courts. If Congress disagrees with a President's policy, its options are to pass legislation, influence the policy through budgetary action, or possibly impeach the President if appropriate. This leaves a wide range of options open for a President in the area of national defense.

Homeland Security Policy and Law

For this section, we will examine one important concept that is not also covered by areas of national security policy or other chapters in this textbook: **critical infrastructure** protection. But first, we need to briefly review the organization tasked with that responsibility, the Department of Homeland Security.

Nine days after the September 11, 2001 terrorist attacks, President Bush addressed a joint session of Congress. During his speech, the President stated he had created a new Cabinet-level position, the Office of Homeland Security. The speech was followed a few weeks later with Executive Order 13228 that formalized the details. Finally, in November 2002, Congress passed the Homeland Security Act of 2002, which made the new organization, the Department of Homeland Security (DHS), permanent.[26] The Homeland Security Act established the missions of the DHS with a focus on preventing and responding to terrorism. The new organization was not created from scratch. Rather, the core of the department was formed from all or part of 22 different federal departments and agencies, each of which played a role in homeland security. One of the initial challenges for the DHS leadership was to integrate the disparate agencies into a more effective and unified organization in order to help the United States address the terrorist threat. One area of emphasis was on critical infrastructure.

> Critical infrastructure—"Systems and assets, whether physical or virtual, so vital to the United States that the incapacity or destruction of such systems and assets would have a debilitating impact on security, national economic security, national public health or safety, or any combination of those matters."[27]

Before September 11, 2001, little thought was given to systematically protecting vital parts of the American economy and way of life. Immediately afterward, that changed and Congress got involved. One of the most debated and far-reaching pieces of legislation in the aftermath of the attacks was the Uniting and Strengthening America by Providing Appropriate Tools Required to Intercept and Obstruct Terrorism Act (USA PATRIOT Act) of 2001.[28] The act is perhaps most well-known for its changes to surveillance procedures, which will be discussed later in this chapter. However, the act also contained a section on critical infrastructure protection.

Title 42, United States Code, Section 5195c declares it to be the policy of the United States that disruption of critical infrastructure be rare, short, localized, manageable, and minimally detrimental. Furthermore, the policy is to be carried out through cooperation with corporate and non-governmental organizations. Although there have been other policy implementation documents, most recently, this requirement was put into effect through a 2013 Presidential Policy Directive and refined in the same year in the National Infrastructure Protection Plan (NIPP 2013).[29]

NIPP 2013 delineates 16 critical infrastructure sectors: chemical, commercial facilities, communication, critical manufacturing, dams, defense industrial base, emergency services, energy, financial services, food and agriculture, government facilities, healthcare/public health, information technology, nuclear reactors/materials/waste, transportation systems, and water/wastewater systems. Each of these sectors has its own annexes supporting the national plan, but even these annexes lack detail. For example, clearly every nuclear reactor must be protected, but which farms and train stations are critical? In aggregate, they all are, but the country does not have sufficient resources to protect every element of every sector.

To help resolve this problem, the policy creates many formal and informal councils to help identify risks, plan for contingencies, and coordinate responses when necessary. These bodies include councils to coordinate in and across sectors as well as councils to coordinate between government agencies and commercial entities. Collectively, the councils are responsible for ensuring that limited resources are allocated in the best interests of the nation as a whole while recognizing that homeland security issues frequently transcend U.S. borders and will often require collaboration with non-U.S. entities.

The 2014 Quadrennial Homeland Security Review provides overall guidance on the risks that the council structure should be prepared to address. The review declares the following areas to be the focus in the near term: terrorism, cyber threats, biological hazards (such as disease and agricultural threats), transnational criminal organizations, and natural disasters.

Preventing Terrorism: Policy and Law

The topic of terrorism has featured prominently as a security issue for several decades, and especially since September 11, 2001. While the United States does not have a unified statutory definition of terrorism, the regulations governing the Federal Bureau of Investigation (FBI), referenced earlier in the definition, provide a useful starting point. By any meaning of the word, there have been thousands of terrorist acts in the world in the past few decades and many hundreds within the United States. The difference between an act of criminal violence and an act of terrorism usually boils down to the motive for the attack or the object of the attack, but the policy implications for acts of terror are vastly different from those for ordinary criminal activity.

In the 1993 National Security Strategy under President George H. W. Bush, terrorism warranted only two brief paragraphs that focused on return of hostages and a no-negotiation strategy for accomplishing that objective. By 2001 under President Clinton, the discussion on terrorism expanded to two pages with additional comments throughout the document. President Clinton noted that the United States would address terrorism, domestically and internationally, through preventative measures and by appropriate response when acts of terror occur. The prevention strategy called for a heavy emphasis on intelligence collection and enhancing the political will to prevent terrorism and security capabilities of other countries. The response strategy included bringing the perpetrators of terrorist acts to justice when possible, and, if law enforcement, diplomatic, and economic tools fail to work, using military force in other countries.

What changed in those few years? Fundamentally, the nature, quantity, and scope of the attacks. President Clinton's policy document identified several significant attacks, including the 1993 World Trade Center bombing, a 1993 shooting outside the Central Intelligence Agency headquarters, simultaneous bombings of two U.S. embassies in Africa in 1998, and the 2000 attack on the *USS Cole* while in a harbor in Yemen. The strategy document did not mention the bombing of the Murrah Federal Building in Oklahoma City in 1995, which the FBI calls the "worst act of homegrown terrorism" in U.S. history.[30] Two Americans upset with specific acts of their own government committed the Oklahoma City attack. Foreigners with ties to international terror groups carried out the other attacks. Preventing both types of attacks are important to national security and homeland security policy, but the national focus has primarily been on attacks with links to terror groups, especially after September 11, 2001.

By the time President George W. Bush submitted his second National Security Strategy in 2006, the United States had been fighting the War on Terror for five years. The document began "America is at war. This is a wartime national security strategy required by the grave challenge we face."[31] This strategy was full of references to terrorism, and the strategy to defeat terrorism received an entire chapter by becoming one of nine key points in the document. President Bush noted that the nature of the fight against terrorism had changed. He identified several successes in the fight, including international cooperation in law enforcement, intelligence, military, and diplomatic efforts. He declared that the long-term solution to the problem of terrorism was to spread democracy and thereby increase human freedom and dignity. Finally, he set the short-term policy objectives: prevent attacks by terrorist networks, deny weapons of mass destruction to rogue states and terrorists, and deny terror groups support and sanctuary or control of any nation, especially rogue states.

In President Obama's second National Security Strategy in 2015, he noted the terrorism threat had decreased but was not eliminated. Spending two pages on what is a sub-heading for his overall security strategy, he noted that the approach had shifted from large ground wars to targeted counterterrorism operations with partners. Obama focused largely on two main terror groups, al-Qa'ida and ISIL. Among other things necessary to enhancing national defense, he called for growing intelligence, surveillance, and reconnaissance capabilities. Finally, he commented that the goal is to "detain, interrogate, and prosecute terrorists through law enforcement" when outside of areas of active hostilities.[32]

In President Trump's first National Security Strategy in 2017, he commented repeatedly about the terrorist threat in general, and the jihadist terror threat in particular throughout the document. Trump noted success against some terrorist organizations, especially ISIL. However, he remained concerned about multiple threats. Trump called for improvements to the **intelligence community**, seeking improved understanding and the ability to harness and merge all information available. Trump's strategy did not address the prosecution of suspected terrorists.

Two important themes emerge from these documents. First, intelligence collection is paramount to ending terrorism. Second, the U.S. policy has generally been to hold terrorists accountable through the criminal justice process when possible rather than treating them as enemy combatants. Both themes are examined in the following sections.

> Intelligence community—those offices and organizations that conduct intelligence activities, including the Central Intelligence Agency, the National Security Agency, the Defense Intelligence Agency, the National Reconnaissance Office, and more than a dozen other organizations through the U.S. government.

Preventing Terrorism: Intelligence

Gathering accurate and timely information about an enemy has been a foundation to successful strategies for centuries. Sun-Tzu, a famous fifth-century BC military strategist from China, said:

> By perceiving the enemy and perceiving ourselves, there will be no unforeseen risk in any battle. By not perceiving the enemy yet perceiving ourselves, there will be partial victory and partial loss. By not perceiving the enemy and not perceiving ourselves, every battle will be an unforeseen risk.[33]

In modern terms, the information about and the analysis of the enemy is called intelligence.

Collecting information about both internal and external threats has gone by many names: espionage, spying, reconnaissance, surveillance, and others. Traditionally, human agents gathered the information directly by interacting with other people or clandestinely stealing or reviewing documents or other items. Two changes from this historical norm have made the process of intelligence gathering in the United States more complicated: democratic freedoms enshrined in the Constitution and advances in communications technology.

The Fourth Amendment to the Constitution creates a "right of the people to be secure in their persons, houses, papers, and effects, against unreasonable searches and seizures . . . and no Warrants shall issue, but upon probable cause . . . particularly describing the place to be searched, and the persons or things to be seized."[34] Each word in this amendment has been litigated many times over in criminal cases. The basic principle that we can draw from this vast body of case law is that intelligence collection within the United States or involving **U.S. persons** is restricted by the Fourth Amendment, as the Supreme Court recognized in the 1967 case *Katz v. U.S.*[35] Conversely, intelligence collection everywhere else and against all other individuals or entities is subject only to law or policy. The laws and policy concerning collection against non-U.S. persons are generally very permissive.

> **U.S. person**—"A United States citizen, an alien known by the intelligence element concerned to be a permanent resident alien, an unincorporated association substantially composed of United States citizens or permanent resident aliens, or a corporation incorporated in the United States, except for a corporation directed and controlled by a foreign government or governments."[36]

The other factor, communications technology, is linked to the first. A large majority of important intelligence data is electronic. The data is stored on computers or phones and transferred through wired or wireless means. Intelligence agencies have the technical capability to intercept and review much of this stored and transmitted data, which has greatly expanded the reach and influence of those agencies. While discrimination between U.S. persons and non-U.S. persons is relatively easy to do in human-to-human interactions, it is enormously complex, if not impossible, in machine-to-machine processes. Thus, one main dilemma for the United States has been how to limit the collection of information involving U.S. persons to avoid violation of the Fourth Amendment, and how to handle information about U.S. persons that is collected.

Turning to the law and policy regulating intelligence, the first major statute enacted was the National Security Act of 1947. The law created the Central Intelligence Agency (CIA) and instituted an absolute prohibition on the CIA exerting any law enforcement or security functions inside the United States. Under the law, the FBI would remain the primary agency for domestic investigations.

Following some controversial activities and organizational disputes, President Gerald Ford issued the first Executive Order regarding intelligence matters in 1976, and in 1978 Congress passed the Foreign Intelligence Surveillance Act (FISA). Through FISA, Congress sought to balance privacy interests and foreign intelligence collection using electronic surveillance and physical searches. The law also created two special courts—the **U.S. Foreign Intelligence Surveillance Court** (FISC) and the U.S. Foreign Intelligence Surveillance Court of Review. The purpose of the new courts was to provide a special forum for federal judges to review and, if appropriate, authorize surveillance and searches in accordance with FISA and the Constitution. Proceedings before the FISC are not open to the public and usually involve classified information. Generally, all intelligence collection under FISA must be approved in advance by the FISC unless the collection is targeted against foreign governments or entities controlled by foreign governments.[37]

> **U.S. Foreign Intelligence Surveillance Court**—a special court created by the Foreign Intelligence Surveillance Act to review government requests to collect intelligence.

In 1981, President Ronald Reagan issued Executive Order 12333, which, as amended several times, is still the main policy document regulating intelligence collection and the organization of the intelligence community. The order establishes the goals of the intelligence program: (1) to obtain information for the President, NSC, and HSC in order to develop and implement foreign, defense, and economic policies; and (2) to protect the United States from foreign security threats. The collection emphasis is to be directed towards espionage against the United States, terrorist threats to the United States, and threats concerning weapons of mass destruction.[38]

The Executive Order reaffirms that in implementing the intelligence program, the government must protect the rights of U.S. persons, including civil liberties and privacy rights. The order also requires each element of the intelligence community to develop procedures concerning the collection, retention, and dissemination of information concerning U.S. persons and obtain Attorney General approval of the procedures. Collection involving U.S. persons or taking place within the United States must use the least intrusive techniques feasible. Finally, the order severely limits the use of physical surveillance and physical searches in the United States or of U.S. persons except when conducted by the FBI. The FBI has bifurcated procedures concerning domestic investigation of terrorist activity and for international terrorist acts.

Unsurprisingly, the September 11, 2001 terrorist attacks resulted in changes to intelligence law and policy. The main changes came through the USA PATRIOT Act of 2001, mentioned previously. A primary goal of the act was to authorize enhanced investigative tools to prevent future terrorist attacks. Accordingly, the USA PATRIOT Act made it easier to obtain FISC approval to gather intelligence. Another law, the Intelligence Reform and Terrorism Prevention Act of 2004, also lessened restrictions within FISA.[39] Congress, recognizing that changing FISA could tip the balance between national security and democratic freedoms too far, inserted sunset provisions into some parts of the two laws. Originally, the modified provisions were set to expire in 2005, but that date has been extended multiple times. Currently, those provisions are set to expire on December 15, 2019.

Of the modifications with sunset provisions, the most controversial and well publicized is Section 215 of the USA PATRIOT Act. Prior to the change in 2001, FISA authorized collection of records from only four types of businesses: common carriers, public accommodation facilities, storage facilities, and vehicle rental facilities. Section 215 extended that authority to "any tangible things," although there are additional requirements for library, firearms sales, tax, education, or medical records.[40] Section 215 also substantially lowered the evidentiary standard, making it easier for the government to obtain approval from the FISC.

Acting under the relaxed standards in the USA PATRIOT Act, the government began collecting enormous quantities of telephone data to help identify individuals affiliated with terrorist groups. This activity became public knowledge following the leaks in 2013 by Edward Snowden, a former contractor supporting the U.S. intelligence community. The leaks led to a number of lawsuits and to one more change to FISA. In 2015, Congress enacted the Uniting and Strengthening America by Fulfilling Rights and Ensuring Effective Discipline Over Monitoring Act (USA FREEDOM Act). This Act restricted the government's ability to obtain bulk telephone data by requiring that government requests to the FISC be substantially more specific than was previously required.

While the general policy in Executive Order 12333 has changed little, this area of the law remains fluid, with Congress constantly expanding, limiting, and fine-tuning the limits of executive branch authority. Media reporting on intelligence community activities has increased, and further scrutiny from Congress may be forthcoming. Absent additional Congressional involvement, all the provisions of FISA will return to their pre-2001 more restrictive state in 2019. Generally, the administrations of Presidents Bush and Obama maximized their use of the expanded surveillance authorities in order to prevent terrorism. How President Trump's administration will influence or respond to changes in surveillance law remains to be seen.

Preventing Terrorism: Justice

In December 2001, a British passenger on a flight from Paris to Miami attempted to blow up the plane using explosives hidden in his shoes. The man, Richard Reid, declared himself to be part of al-Qa'ida. Reid's attempt was unsuccessful, as the crew and passengers subdued him. The flight landed in Boston, where authorities took Reid into custody. He later pled guilty and was sentenced to life in prison.

Reid's crime was processed through the federal criminal justice system: investigated by the FBI, prosecuted by the Department of Justice, and tried in United States District Court. Hundreds of terrorists have been tried and convicted in this same manner; some are infamous, but most go unnoticed by the public. This standard process is what President Obama meant when he said that the goal is to use law enforcement methods to prosecute acts of terror to increase national security. The United States has at its disposal other methods for responding when terrorism suspects are located abroad and not readily subject to arrest by U.S. law enforcement. One alternative is the use of military force. This can take the form of targeted killings, such as through raids or drone strikes. For example, in May 2011, U.S. special forces military personnel raided the home of Osama bin Laden in Pakistan and killed him. Military action also might be designed to capture and detain suspected terrorists. The treatment of captured terrorism suspects as "enemy combatants" and the use of indefinite detention and **military commissions**, rather than civilian criminal trials, have proven to be especially controversial features of the U.S. approach to terrorism since September 11, 2001.

> Military commission—a military tribunal created in order to try civilians for misconduct through a process other than court-martial or by a regularly constituted civilian criminal court.

Recall the 2001 Authorization for Use of Military Force discussed previously. As a result of that Congressional mandate, President Bush authorized the detention and trial of international terrorists later that year. In turn, that order led to the decision to move captured terrorists out of the battlefield in Afghanistan and onto the U.S. Navy facility in Guantanamo Bay, Cuba. President Bush's administration intentionally chose a location outside of the United States because of the Supreme Court decision in *Johnson v. Eisentrager*,[41] which held that U.S. courts did not have jurisdiction over non-citizens detained outside the United States. Litigation contesting the detainee's confinement began within a month of the first detainees arriving at the Guantanamo Bay facility in January 2002. The litigation began a long series of legislative, judicial, and executive actions and reactions that is still ongoing as the three branches of government attempt to refine and strike the appropriate balance and separation of powers in the areas of security and counter-terrorism.

In 2004, the Supreme Court decided in the case of *Rasul v. Bush*[42] that the detainees could use the existing federal habeas corpus statute to challenge their detention. President Bush and Congress modified that statute in 2005 in an effort to stop detainee litigation. In 2006, the Supreme Court decided in *Hamdan v. Rumsfeld*[43] that the new law did not apply to the many cases already in progress. That case also struck down President Bush's initial attempt to establish military tribunals to try enemy combatants. Therefore, later in 2006, Congress passed another law denying detainees the right to habeas corpus in any existing or future case. This is the background for the following Supreme Court case, *Boumediene v. Bush*, which looked beyond statutory habeas corpus to the constitutional right of habeas corpus.

Lakhdar Boumediene v. George W. Bush, 533 U.S. 723 (2008)

Petitioners present a question not resolved by our earlier cases relating to the detention of aliens at Guantanamo: whether they have the constitutional privilege of habeas corpus, a privilege not to be withdrawn except in conformance with the Suspension Clause, Art. I, §9, cl. 2. We hold these petitioners do have the habeas corpus privilege. Congress has enacted a statute, the Detainee Treatment Act of 2005 (DTA), 119 Stat. 2739, that provides certain procedures for review of the detainees' status. We hold that those procedures are not an adequate and effective substitute for habeas corpus. Therefore §7 of the Military Commissions Act of 2006 (MCA), 28 U. S. C. A. §2241(e) (Supp. 2007), operates as an unconstitutional suspension of the writ. We do not address whether the President has authority to detain these petitioners nor do we hold that the writ must issue. These and other questions regarding the legality of the detention are to be resolved in the first instance by the District Court.

[...]

In deciding the constitutional questions now presented we must determine whether petitioners are barred from seeking the writ or invoking the protections of the Suspension Clause either because of their status, i.e., petitioners' designation by the Executive Branch as enemy combatants, or their physical location, i.e., their presence at Guantanamo Bay. The Government contends that noncitizens designated as enemy combatants and detained in territory located outside our Nation's borders have no constitutional rights and no privilege of habeas corpus. Petitioners contend they do have cognizable constitutional rights and that Congress, in seeking to eliminate recourse to habeas corpus as a means to assert those rights, acted in violation of the Suspension Clause.

[...]

[W]e conclude that at least three factors are relevant in determining the reach of the Suspension Clause: (1) the citizenship and status of the detainee and the adequacy of the process through which that status determination was made; (2) the nature of the sites where apprehension and then detention took place; and (3) the practical obstacles inherent in resolving the prisoner's entitlement to the writ.

[...]

We hold that Art. I, §9, cl. 2, of the Constitution has full effect at Guantanamo Bay. If the privilege of habeas corpus is to be denied to the detainees now before us, Congress must act in accordance with the requirements of the Suspension Clause. Cf. *Hamdi*, 542 U. S., at 564 (Scalia, J., dissenting) ("[I]ndefinite imprisonment on reasonable suspicion is not an available option of treatment for those accused of aiding the enemy, absent a suspension of the writ"). This Court may not impose a de facto suspension by abstaining from these controversies. See *Hamdan*, 548 U. S., at 585, n. 16 ("[A]bstention is not appropriate in cases ... in which the legal challenge 'turn[s] on the status of the persons as to whom the military asserted its power' " (quoting *Schlesinger v. Councilman*, 420 U. S. 738, 759 (1975))). The MCA does not purport to be a formal suspension of the writ; and the Government, in its submissions to us, has not argued that it is. Petitioners, therefore, are entitled to the privilege of habeas corpus to challenge the legality of their detention.

[...]

Our holding with regard to exhaustion should not be read to imply that a habeas court should intervene the moment an enemy combatant steps foot in a territory where the writ runs. The Executive is entitled to a reasonable period of time to determine a detainee's status before a court entertains that detainee's habeas corpus petition. The [Combatant Status Review Tribunal (CSRT)] process is the mechanism Congress and the President set up to deal with these issues. Except in cases of undue delay, federal courts should refrain from entertaining an enemy combatant's habeas corpus petition at least until after the Department, acting via the CSRT, has had a chance to review his status.

[...]

In considering both the procedural and substantive standards used to impose detention to prevent acts of terrorism, proper deference must be accorded to the political branches. See *United States v. Curtiss-Wright Export Corp*. Unlike the President and some designated Members of Congress, neither the Members of this Court nor most federal judges begin the day with briefings that may describe new and serious threats to our Nation and its people. The law must accord the Executive substantial authority to apprehend and detain those who pose a real danger to our security.

Officials charged with daily operational responsibility for our security may consider a judicial discourse on the history of the Habeas Corpus Act of 1679 and like matters to be far removed from the Nation's present, urgent concerns. Established legal doctrine, however, must be consulted for its teaching. Remote in time it may be; irrelevant to the present it is not. Security depends upon a sophisticated intelligence apparatus and the ability of our Armed Forces to act and to interdict. There are further considerations, however. Security subsists, too, in fidelity to freedom's first principles. Chief among these are freedom from arbitrary and unlawful restraint and the personal liberty that is secured by adherence to the separation of powers. It is from these principles that the judicial authority to consider petitions for habeas corpus relief derives.

Our opinion does not undermine the Executive's powers as Commander in Chief. On the contrary, the exercise of those powers is vindicated, not eroded, when confirmed by the Judicial Branch. Within the Constitution's separation-of-powers structure, few exercises of judicial power are as legitimate or as necessary as the responsibility to hear challenges to the authority of the Executive to imprison a person. Some of these petitioners have been in custody for six years with no definitive judicial determination as to the legality of their detention. Their access to the writ is a necessity to determine the lawfulness of their status, even if, in the end, they do not obtain the relief they seek.

Because our Nation's past military conflicts have been of limited duration, it has been possible to leave the outer boundaries of war powers undefined. If, as some fear, terrorism continues to pose dangerous threats to us for years to come, the Court might not have this luxury. This result is not inevitable, however. The political branches, consistent with their independent obligations to interpret and uphold the Constitution, can engage in a genuine debate about how best to preserve constitutional values while protecting the Nation from terrorism. Cf. *Hamdan*, 548 U. S., at 636 (Breyer, J., concurring) ("[J]udicial insistence upon that consultation does not weaken our Nation's ability to deal with danger. To the contrary, that insistence strengthens the Nation's ability to determine—through democratic means—how best to do so").

> It bears repeating that our opinion does not address the content of the law that governs petitioners' detention. That is a matter yet to be determined. We hold that petitioners may invoke the fundamental procedural protections of habeas corpus. The laws and Constitution are designed to survive, and remain in force, in extraordinary times. Liberty and security can be reconciled; and in our system they are reconciled within the framework of the law. The Framers decided that habeas corpus, a right of first importance, must be a part of that framework, a part of that law.
>
> The determination by the Court of Appeals that the Suspension Clause and its protections are inapplicable to petitioners was in error. The judgment of the Court of Appeals is reversed. The cases are remanded to the Court of Appeals with instructions that it remand the cases to the District Court for proceedings consistent with this opinion.

Despite the language in *Boumediene* that the President's power was vindicated, in reality an important part of the nation's security policy—indefinite detention without trial—was now subject to challenge in the court system on a case-by-case basis. Eventually, litigation, political pressure, and more complete evaluations of the facts concerning each individual detainee would result in the transfer or release of most of the detainees at Guantanamo Bay. While the United States attempted a handful of detainee prosecutions through military commissions, those cases would not go as well as President Bush hoped.

> *The attempt to try terrorism suspects in military commissions failed for several reasons. One reason is that the Military Commissions Act conflated two distinct concepts: the concept of terrorism and the concept of war crimes. Military commissions are appropriate forums in which to try captured combatants for violations of the law of war, but terrorism, and material support for terrorism, the primary offenses that Guantanamo detainees were accused of committing, are not recognized war crimes. Rather these crimes have traditionally been charged under federal criminal law. Although a few detainees were convicted or pled guilty to these crimes, these convictions were later overturned by the federal courts on appeal.*
>
> *Another reason for the failure of the military commissions is that the rules and regulations which govern them were hastily put together and poorly thought out. As a legal system created wholly from scratch, many issues that have arisen were not anticipated and are not covered in the authorizing legislation or the implementing regulations. Since there are no prior precedents to guide the lawyers and judges who are participating in the process, every single issue that arises must be decided anew, which has caused endless delays in getting cases to trial.*
>
> *But the overriding reason for the failure of the military commissions is torture. The abuse of detainees, particularly the so-called "high value detainees" who were held in secret CIA-run "black" sites and brutally mistreated before eventually being brought to Guantanamo to face trial, has greatly complicated efforts to prosecute them, as much of the evidence that the government hopes to introduce against them was acquired through coercive methods. The torture of some detainees has so badly affected the mental state of some that they could not be put on trial. In other cases, the interrogation methods used against the detainees, and much of the evidence the government seeks to use*

> against them, is highly classified and cannot be presented in open court. This leaves the commissions open to criticism for lack of transparency, and making it appear that the U.S. is simply hiding embarrassing information.
>
> David J. R. Frakt, J.D.
> Former Military Commissions Defense Counsel

The current military commissions process began in 2001 with a system that barely provided rights to the detainees. Through court challenges and Congressional intervention, that system has been modified several times until it mostly resembles the American criminal justice system, with a few notable and significant differences that are still being litigated. One of the key problems with the early system involved the extent to which statements derived from torture could be used against the detainee.

Many credible reports documented abuses of detainees while in U.S. custody at locations such as Abu Ghraib in Iraq, Bagram in Afghanistan, and at Guantanamo Bay in Cuba. These abuses led to massive public outcry, image problems for the United States, and eventually to changes in law and policy. It takes little imagination to see how detaining individuals indefinitely, without a process for which they could petition for release, and while at risk for torture, created the need for legislative and policy fixes. Meanwhile, justice for the victims of those accused of perpetrating the attacks of September 11, 2001, against the *USS Cole*, and other major terrorist attacks has been delayed because of U.S. policy decisions. The military commission trials have been slow, repeatedly delayed, and largely ineffective; indeed, most of the few successful prosecutions have been overturned on appeal.

The debate over whether to use the standard criminal justice system or military detention and military commissions for suspected terrorists is ongoing. For example, in 2011, the United States captured Ahmed Warsame, who was affiliated with a Somali terrorist group. The Navy held him aboard a ship for two months, where he was interrogated by federal law enforcement and intelligence agents, before transferring him to the Department of Justice, where he ultimately plead guilty in federal court. While he was in the custody of military personnel, however, many people demanded that he be taken to Guantanamo Bay, Cuba instead. Warsame is not the only recent alleged terrorist to have been detained and interrogated abroad. In October 2017, the United States detained an unnamed individual ISIL fighter in Iraq. For months, the government fought releasing his name and challenged the right of advocacy groups to petition for habeas corpus on the individual's behalf.[44]

Whether future individuals captured in similar circumstances will be handled in the same manner remains to be seen. The policy decisions are still in flux as President Trump has repeatedly called for more alleged terrorists to be sent to Guantanamo Bay, as the introductory case to this chapter demonstrated.

Shared Spaces: Policy and Law

President Obama's 2015 National Security Strategy was the first national strategy to link the concepts of ocean, air, outer space, and cyberspace into a combined category he called shared spaces. President Obama's previous national security strategy from 2010 addressed cyberspace, but the shift to cover all four mediums was a significant expansion. Several previous publications at lower governmental levels or by independent scholars had recognized the similarities and interconnected nature of the mediums, which are sometimes also referred to as the "global commons."

These shared spaces are vitally important to U.S. security policy because they, as described in the 2015 National Security Strategy, "enable the free flow of people, goods, services, and ideas. They are the arteries of the global economy and civil society, and access is at risk due to increased competition and provocative behaviors."[45] President Trump's 2017 policy also addressed the importance of each of the shared spaces individually, with a particular focus on space and cyber, but his strategy did not combine them together as a group.

These shared spaces generally differ from the security policy areas discussed previously because the link between law and policy is different in the international context. In a domestic matter such as the rules concerning intelligence collection, the three branches of government often engage in a back-and-forth dialogue to create, shape, and revise both the law and the policy. When the underlying rules are written collectively by the international community, however, U.S. security policy is more constrained, with little expectation that the executive branch can modify the foundational set of rules. As you will see, the U.S. security policy in each of these areas is often little more than a statement that the United States wants all nations to follow the rules so the shared spaces remain safe and free to use. Despite the unimaginative policy, each of the following areas is profoundly important to U.S. security.

Shared Spaces: Oceans

Commerce, transportation, piracy, and war have been commonplace on the oceans for millennia. Each of these pose considerable risk or reward for the parties involved. The U.S. interests in the oceans are substantially the same as every other country's interests—maintain the freedom of navigation and the sustainability of the environment. Over centuries of practice, the law of the sea has developed to do just that. Ultimately, much of that customary international law has been reflected in a treaty, the United Nations Convention on the Law of the Sea (UNCLOS), which took effect in 1994. UNCLOS replaced several other treaties that had been in force since the early 1960s. Virtually every country is a party to the treaty. The notable exception is the United States, which has not ratified the treaty, but by policy has declared it recognizes that the treaty reflects international law and will comply with its provisions.

The basics of the law of the sea are fairly straightforward and both guide and limit U.S. policy involving the oceans. Each country with a coast has a territorial sea extending out 12 nautical miles, a contiguous zone out to 24 nautical miles, and an exclusive economic zone extending out 200 nautical miles. Everything outside the territorial sea boundary is known as international waters, and everything outside the exclusive economic zone is called the high seas. The territorial sea is part of each country's **sovereign** area subject to its law and regulations, except that any ship may pass through another country's territorial waters, without seeking permission, on its way to somewhere else. This right is referred to as innocent passage. Within the contiguous zone, countries have the right to enforce only customs, tax, immigration, and pollution laws. Within the exclusive economic zone, a country has the sole right to exploit natural resources, including fishing and oil and natural gas. On the high seas, no country may generally assert any rights other than the right to defend its vessels. UNCLOS also has general provisions for protecting the marine environment from both pollution and from over-fishing. Finally, the treaty reaffirms that piracy is illegal.

Despite near-universal agreement on these basic principles, much conflict remains over the details and the implementation. For example, the exact boundaries for the different categories of ocean areas are in dispute in many regions of the world. Of particular importance to the United States currently is the area around the Arctic. As the sea ice in the Arctic has been receding in the past decades, the six countries

> Sovereign—an independent entity vested with absolute political authority over itself and subordinate to no other.

that border the Arctic Ocean are attempting to maximize their areas of influence and resource production. President Trump's 2017 policy barely mentions maritime issues. However, President Obama had set out the following basic objectives:

- Maintain the capability to ensure the free flow of commerce and deter aggressors
- Demand safe and responsible behaviors
- Reject illegal and aggressive claims to territory
- Condemn deliberate attacks on commercial traffic
- Denounce coercion and assertive behaviors on territorial disputes
- Build international cooperation in the Arctic and to combat piracy and drugs
- Obtain Senate advice and consent in order to become a party to UNCLOS

Shared Spaces: Air

Air travel, while only about 100 years old, has rapidly developed its own set of rules, which are embodied in the Convention on International Civil Aviation, also known as the Chicago Convention, which went into effect in 1947. Virtually all countries are party to the treaty. The Chicago Convention replaced a treaty from 1922. The driving need for rules shortly after World War I arose because of the revolution in military technology that aircraft brought to the fight. The ability to fly over territory was such a drastic change that the international community created a treaty to address the security concern. The first article of the 1922 treaty recognized that all countries, not just the parties to the treaty, maintained absolute sovereignty over the air space above their territory.

Generally, the current legal regime concerning aircraft is much simpler and less contested than the rules governing the oceans. From a security policy standpoint, only a few of the rules are relevant. The Chicago Convention maintains the most important element as its first article—every country has sovereignty over the airspace above its territory, including the territorial sea out to 12 nautical miles. Unlike with the law of the sea, there is no automatic authority to fly over another country's territory. The treaty prohibits the use of weapons against civil (non-military) aircraft while flying. Finally, the treaty states that each country generally has the right to regulate the aircraft flying over its territory. Several other treaties address matters of aviation safety and security, but the Chicago Convention contains the basic principles. The Chicago Convention has proven to be remarkably adaptable and flexible. Numerous annexes and amendments have changed it from time to time to keep up with advances in technology.

Military forces have, despite the treaty, on a few occasions shot down commercial aircraft. For example, in 1983, a Soviet fighter shot down Korean Air Lines Flight 007, which had strayed into Soviet airspace. Also, in 1988, a U.S. Navy ship shot down Iran Air Flight 655 when Navy personnel mistook the civilian aircraft for an Iranian war plane. Other than a handful of these type of incidents, instances of hijacking or bombing, and drug smuggling, there are no current important security issues related to aviation. In fact, the 2015 National Security Strategy discussed air and maritime security in the same section, and the 2017 strategy barely mentioned them at all.

Shared Spaces: Outer Space

Space travel, an even more recent development, began about 60 years ago. Like the other physical environments (air and ocean) previously discussed, the international community saw the need for specialized agreements to address issues related to outer space. Thus, several treaties address the rights and duties of spacefaring countries. The Treaty on Principles Governing the Activities of States in the Exploration and Use of Outer Space, Including the Moon and Other Celestial Bodies (commonly known as the Outer Space Treaty) entered into force in 1967. A slight majority of the countries in the world have joined the Outer Space Treaty. The international community created three other widely accepted treaties during the 1960s and 1970s, but those are not relevant to security matters.

The basic concept of the Outer Space Treaty is that national sovereignty does not exist in space, unlike on land, air, and sea. The exploration and use of outer space is to be done for the benefit and interests of all countries. The moon and other celestial bodies are to be used exclusively for peaceful purposes. Note, however, that the text intentionally did not say that space itself was only for peaceful purposes. Through this artful language, the lead drafters of the agreement—the United States and the former Soviet Union—ensured the possibility of future military use of empty space. Nevertheless, the treaty forbids nuclear weapons from being placed in orbit. Finally, the treaty requires each country to be responsible for and supervise its own (governmental or commercial) activities in space and establishes rules for liability for accidents.

> *Services provided by space-based systems have become an integral part of modern society. From financial transactions, to navigation, to communications, to precision farming, to weather forecasting and disaster relief, most of us do not realize such services as we know them today would be impossible without space. We do not think about space when we make a withdrawal at an ATM; watch a televised sporting event taking place live on the other side of the globe; or follow our automobile's navigation system to a previously unknown location. We just expect the services to be there when we need them.*
>
> *Modern society is completely dependent on space. So too is national security. Modern militaries of the world rely on space-based capabilities and the services they provide to conduct modern-day military operations. No military is more dependent on space than that of the United States. The soldiers, sailors, airmen and Marines of the U.S. military all rely on space for intelligence, surveillance, and reconnaissance; missile warning and defense; precision navigation; precision targeting; command and control; communications; weather; and more.*
>
> *It is an unfortunate reality that wherever humans have wandered, war has followed. Threats to space systems are real and increasing and with them the possibility that armed conflict might one day extend to outer space. From a legal perspective, space really is not all that special when it comes to armed conflict. The international legal regime governing activities in outer space specifically provides that activities in the exploration and use of outer space shall be carried on in accordance with international law, including the Charter of the United Nations. Hence, well-established legal rules on the use of force and the law of armed conflict apply in outer space. The challenge of armed conflict in outer space from a legal perspective is applying those well-established legal rules in an environment vastly different from the air, land, and maritime domains. This is an environment where operational norms are yet to be established, situational awareness may be lacking, and indications, warnings, and intentions unclear. As the prospect for armed conflict in space increases, it is incumbent on the national security legal community to be prepared to address the difficulty in applying well-established legal principles to armed conflict in the final frontier.*
>
> Michael R. Hoversten, J.D., LL.M.
> Chief, Space, Cyber, International and Operations Law
> Headquarters, Air Force Space Command

Unlike in air law, the legal regime in space has not been updated or revised despite the advances in technology and the shift in the use of space from governmental entities to commercial ones. Since the Outer Space Treaty was written, the way countries access and use space has changed significantly. From a security policy perspective, the most important change is the view that space is increasingly seen as a future military battlefield with potentially devastating and worldwide consequences. In the past 20 years, several countries have demonstrated the capability to physically destroy satellites, interrupt telecommunications transmitted through satellites, and jam Global Positioning System navigation signals. These capabilities have the potential to disrupt the modern way of life and make large regions of space unusable for hundreds or thousands of years.

Addressing these concerns, the 2015 National Security Strategy predictably reiterated themes from the Outer Space Treaty and was consistent with the concepts concerning the other shared spaces. The security strategy called for international cooperation to manage threats, develop a code of conduct on outer space activities, and expand partnerships with the private sector. The policy also called for additional development of capabilities to identify and attribute attacks on space systems, deter and defeat efforts to attack space systems, and increase resiliency of U.S. space capabilities.

President Trump's 2017 policy called on the United States to maintain leadership in and freedom of action in space. It also clearly stated that the United States would respond to harmful interference with space architecture directly affecting vital U.S. interests. President Trump sought to advance space as a priority domain, promote space commerce, and maintain the U.S. lead in exploration. Because of its special nature, however, the topic of outer space has an additional, stand-alone national policy document.

In 2010, President Obama issued the latest national space policy. It updated guidance from 1996 and 2006. The space policy reaffirmed basic principles in the Outer Space Treaty and set goals, which were largely adopted in the 2015 National Security Strategy. Obama's space policy established broad guidelines for each of the three space sectors (commercial, civil, and national security) and for areas where the sectors overlap: increasing international cooperation, preserving the space environment, improving export policies for space-related items, developing space nuclear power, protecting the radiofrequency spectrum, and assuring resilience of mission-essential functions. In December 2017, President Trump changed one paragraph of Obama's 2010 policy to make human exploration of the moon and Mars a priority.

Shared Spaces: Cyberspace

Cyberspace is, of course, the newest development in the concept of shared spaces. Cyberspace only bears a passing resemblance to the other three mediums as it is not physical in the same sense that the others are. While physical wires and the electromagnetic spectrum are the realm of cyberspace, they only serve to transmit information and only through areas of physical space. Cyberspace technology also changes much more rapidly than the technology used in the other shared spaces. Furthermore, the rules governing cyberspace are primarily domestic, national law.

The international community has not developed an overarching set of principles or rules that apply to activities or information in cyberspace, although Russia and others have suggested negotiating an agreement that would essentially disarm cyberspace. One scholarly publication, the 2017 Tallinn Manual 2.0 on the International Law Applicable to Cyber Operations, purports to describe emerging international law on governmental use of cyberspace for national security purposes, but the international community has not developed consensus on what cyberspace law actually entails.

Within the United States, the law governing cyberspace is an eclectic, ad hoc collection still currently in development. The United States has few rules governing content due to the First Amendment, but it has some limitations on criminal behavior. A large body of criminal law, including a treaty on cybercrime, applies in cyberspace and makes certain activities illegal. The case law concerning cyberspace, which is still in development, focuses mainly on search and seizure issues and is therefore linked to the surveillance issues discussed previously.

> *It was clear from the late 1990s that cyber security threats would eventually become among the most serious to U.S. national security, and that time has arrived. Unfortunately, despite its seemingly insurmountable advantage in cyberspace capabilities from the advent of the internet in the late 1960s, U.S. dominance has begun to fade, leaving it vulnerable to aggressive actions by other States. One of the major reasons for the closing gap between the United States and its international competitors is that U.S. national security leaders have been unable to agree on how best to combine the various aspects of cyber power—intelligence gathering, enhancing military capabilities, and leveraging the distribution of information—to advance U.S. national security interests.*
>
> *The founding of U.S. Cyber Command in 2010 did little to advance military cyber capabilities, and the U.S. Intelligence Community suffered a series of devastating leaks of information, including specific techniques, that seriously eroded its technical lead in cyber spying. In the meantime, China, Russia, Israel, and, to a lesser extent, Iran and North Korea all found ways to cut the U.S. lead in specific areas, including corporate espionage, network exploitation, and manipulating the flow of information.*
>
> *The United States is somewhat hamstrung in its attempts to compete in some of the most promising cyber areas because of constitutional and legal mandates in the national security framework. Strategies to advance national security in cyberspace can appear to run counter to constitutionally protected aspects of personal information, often rendering proposed operations in the informational and private economic spheres out of bounds. The fate of U.S. cyber national security going forward depends on how well it can navigate the competing interests of privacy, free speech, and national security.*
>
> *Unless another technology such as genetically engineered bioweapons, quantum computing, or nanotechnology develops to change the mix, four areas will determine whether the United States is able to maintain its dominant position in international affairs: a high-performance economy, an effective nuclear deterrent, continuing innovation, and strong cybersecurity. Although all are under threat, cyberspace provides the quickest path for adversaries to undermine the United States. Preventing that from happening must be a U.S. priority.*
>
> Gary D. Brown, J.D., LL.M.
> First Senior Legal Counsel to U.S. Cyber Command

Despite the lack of substantive law, the United States does not lack cyber policy. The number of policy documents is orders of magnitudes higher than what is available for the other shared spaces, although not all of them relate directly to security policy. The earliest presidential-level policy can be traced back to 1995, when cyberspace appeared

238 *Security Law and Policy*

as an aspect of critical infrastructure protection in a memorandum about terrorism. References to cyber first appear in the National Security Strategy in 1999, and the first stand-alone policy document was in 2000. Since then, the policies have changed and adapted with internet technology, but usually lag behind technological developments.

In the 2015 National Security Strategy, President Obama declared the United States would take several cyber-related actions to ensure security, including: securing federal networks, working with Congress to pursue legislation, defending against cyber attacks, prosecuting illegal cyber acts, and developing norms of international behavior. In the 2017 National Security Strategy, President Trump established the following priorities:

- Countering cyber criminals
- Identifying and prioritizing risk
- Deterring and disrupting malicious cyber actors
- Improving information sharing and sensing
- Deploying layered defenses
- Improving attribution, accountability, and response
- Enhancing cyber tools and expertise
- Improving integration and agility

Global Context

While we have focused on U.S. security policy and processes in this chapter, it should come as no surprise that most nations have a security policy in some form. As mentioned at the beginning of the chapter, the idea of preserving and protecting a nation is at least as old as the idea of government itself. Not all the themes or ideas are universal, but a few examples from around the globe demonstrate that most major world powers recognize the need to systematically develop a security policy.

One outlier in this regard is the Republic of India, which has never written a national security strategy document. In the 1990s, India's Defence Secretary commented that all the elements of the doctrine are well known throughout the government, and there is no confusion or lack of clarity despite the lack of a written document.[46] This situation has not changed, and the world has little insight into India's policy. As you read through each of the varied examples that follow, which have been made public, note the similarities and differences with U.S. security policy.

The first policy for comparison comes from the Russian Federation. It published its most recent national security strategy in 2015, which established the following as its long-term national interests:[47]

- Strengthening national defense
- Strengthening political and social stability, including developing democratic institutions
- Increasing the standard of living, including medical care
- Maintaining traditional Russian values
- Improving the economy
- Enhancing standing as a world power

The second policy for comparison comes from the People's Republic of China. China is substantially less transparent than the United States or Russia concerning its overall national security strategy. In January 2015, according to a report by the official news agency of the Chinese government, the ruling party adopted the outline of a national security strategy. The available summary, which is much shorter than the written policies of other nations, did not provide specific details but did list some areas of concern and general goals:[48]

- Responding to profound changes in the international economic and societal situation
- Safeguarding China's core and vital interests and protecting its citizens
- Enhancing state security while simultaneously preserving the rule of law
- Promoting the common prosperity of all nations
- Increasing national security education and developing national security professionals
- Building a prosperous society
- Reinforcing the prominence of the Politburo of the Communist Party of China

As a third example, the United Kingdom prepared a National Security Strategy and Strategic Defence and Security Review in 2015. The UK's review identified several challenges driving security priorities, including terrorism, the impact of technology, and the erosion of rules-based international order. The UK established three national security priorities: protecting its people, protecting its global influence, and promoting its prosperity. Under each of these priorities are a number of sub-objectives. which are very similar to those in U.S. policies. For example, under the protecting people priority, the UK identifies the need to enhance the armed forces, maintain a nuclear deterrent, combat terrorism, and respond to cyberspace threats, among other issues.

Conclusion

From ancient times, to the early days of the United States, and continuing through the present, security policy has played an important role in every nation's growth. As we have seen, many of the key themes in security policy throughout history and across the world are similar. One element that has changed is the development of a formalized process for preparing, reviewing, approving, and publishing security policy. The United States created such a requirement in 1986 for national security and in 2009 for homeland security. Putting the process into U.S. law ensured that security policy would be regularly updated, knowledgeable participants would be involved, and transparency would increase. Security policy will continue to evolve in response to world changes, but maintaining a robust process for developing and publicizing that policy is important to a democratic nation.

Two developments in the past few decades have been the primary shapers of U.S. security policy: terrorism and technology. Throughout much of U.S. history, the primary focus of security policy was national defense; the threat posed by peer nation-states was the biggest risk. The rise of terrorist attacks around the world, and especially within U.S. borders, caused the United States to reconsider security policy and stress areas that were previously ignored or under-emphasized. Terrorists have been aided by the rapid advancement of inexpensive technology, transportation, and methods of communication. Those same developments, however, increase the risks presented by nation-states as well. Furthermore, technology, especially in the area of cyberspace, advances so rapidly that U.S. security policy struggles to keep pace.

In the area of security policy, the U.S. Constitution's system of checks and balances is perhaps at its most unbalanced point, tipping in favor of the executive branch. Undoubtedly, a fundamental role for the President is to ensure the safety and security of the country. Neither Congress nor the courts desire to decrease U.S. security by taking ill-advised or uninformed actions. Congress certainly can set certain boundaries in the area of national security, as it did with the National Security Act of 1947, the War Powers Resolution, and many other instances. Or Congress can expand executive branch power, as it did in several key laws after September 11, 2001. Only the executive branch, however, is able to directly and rapidly respond to security threats; Congress must allow the executive branch the freedom to do so. Similarly, the courts are at their most deferential to the executive branch in matters of security and foreign policy. The U.S. court system has decided few cases directly involving matters of security policy. In the few cases that do exist, the courts usually acknowledge they are not equipped to second-guess the executive branch on matters involving the nation's security.

Exercise/Discussion Questions

Exercise

Consider the following scenario and then answer the questions that follow:

Assume there is a well-known terrorist group with strong ties to a government that is not friendly to the United States. The terrorist group has agents within the United States. The intelligence community is monitoring the activities and communications of those agents. U.S. government officials learn that the group is planning to use large quantities of small, autonomous drone aircraft in a swarming attack to try and damage a nuclear power plant near the U.S.–Canada border.

1. Is this a matter of national security, homeland security, or both? Does it matter what label this situation is given?
2. Is U.S. security policy sufficiently well-developed in order to allow government agencies to respond to the threat? In what ways could the policy be improved?
3. What are the main constitutional and legal principles governing how U.S. government agencies can react in this situation?
4. How would the U.S. response options change if a well-meaning whistleblower leaked information about the situation to the press because he/she felt the government's response was inadequate and slow?
5. Other than security policy, what other national policies are implicated by this situation and how?

Additional Discussion Questions

1. What are the advantages of not publicly disclosing a security strategy (for example, India) or of withholding portions of a strategy due to the classified nature of the information (for example, the U.S.)? What are the disadvantages?
2. What are the ramifications to U.S. security policy if a President makes statements and takes actions inconsistent with the published National Security Strategy Report?
3. In the area of intelligence collection, has Congress appropriately balanced the need to protect civil liberties with the need to prevent terrorist attacks?
4. Should enemy combatants be tried through military commissions or the federal criminal system and why?
5. Which of the shared spaces poses the most risk to the future security of the U.S. and why?

Notes

1. *Complaint against Suspect in Manhattan Terror Attack*, N.Y. Times, Nov. 1, 2017, www.nytimes.com/interactive/2017/11/01/us/document-U-S-v-Sayfullo-Saipov-Complaint.html?_r=0
2. *Id.*
3. Donald Trump Twitter Account, https://twitter.com/realDonaldTrump
4. David Montgomery, et al., *Gunman Kills at Least 26 in Attack on Rural Texas Church*, N.Y. Times, Nov. 5, 2017.
5. Justin McCurry, et al., *'This Isn't a Guns Situation', Says Trump after Texas Church Shooting*, The Guardian, Nov. 6, 2017.
6. The Monroe Doctrine (1823), www.ourdocuments.gov/doc.php?flash=false&doc=23
7. Harry S. Truman, *Address of the President to Congress, Recommending Assistance to Greece and Turkey*, Mar. 12, 1947, www.trumanlibrary.org/whistlestop/study_collections/doctrine/large/documents/index.php?documentid=5-9&pagenumber=4
8. Richard Nixon, *Address to the Nation on the War in Vietnam*, Nov. 3, 1969, www.presidency.ucsb.edu/ws/?pid=2303
9. E.O. No. 13526, *Classified National Security Information*, Dec. 29, 2009.
10. Joint Publication 1–02, DOD Dictionary of Military and Associated Terms (Aug. 2017).
11. 50 U.S.C. § 4552(11).
12. 28 C.F.R. § 0.85(l).
13. The White House, *National Security Presidential Memorandum 4, Organization of the National Security Council, the Homeland Security Council, and Subcommittees*, April 4, 2017.
14. 18 U.S.C. § 798.
15. E.O. No. 13526, *Classified National Security Information*, Dec. 29, 2009.
16. 92 U.S. 105 (1875).
17. 484 U.S. 518 (1988).
18. *Id.*
19. 403 U.S. 713 (1971).
20. 50 U.S.C. § 3043.
21. 6 U.S.C. § 347.
22. Department of Homeland Security, *National Security Strategy for Homeland Security*, July 16, 2002.
23. 50 U.S.C. § 4552(14).
24. 50 U.S.C. §§ 1541–1544.
25. P.L. No. 107–140 (2001).
26. P.L. No. 107–296 (2002).
27. 42 U.S.C. § 5195c(e).
28. P.L. No. 107–156 (2001).
29. Department of Homeland Security, *NIPP 2013: Partnering for Critical Infrastructure Security and Resilience* (2013).
30. Oklahoma City Bombing, *FBI History, Famous Cases & Criminals*, www.fbi.gov/history/famous-cases/oklahoma-city-bombing
31. The White House, *National Security Strategy* (2006).
32. The White House, *National Security Strategy* (2015).
33. J.H. Huang, *Sun-Tzu: The New Translation* (1993).
34. U.S. Const. amend. IV.
35. 389 U.S. 347 (1967).
36. E.O. No. 12333, *United States Intelligence Activities*, Dec. 4, 1981 as amended in 2003, 2004, and 2008.
37. 50 U.S.C. §§ 1801–1805.
38. E.O. No. 12333, *United States Intelligence Activities*, Dec. 4, 1981 as amended in 2003, 2004, and 2008.
39. P.L. No. 108–458 (2004).
40. 50 U.S.C. § 1861(a).
41. 339 U.S. 763 (1950).
42. 542 U.S. 466 (2004).
43. 548 U.S. 557 (2006).
44. Benjamin Wittes, *The Taste of Crow: Okay, I'm Alarmed Now*, LawFare Blog (Dec. 12, 2017), www.lawfareblog.com/taste-crow-okay-im-alarmed-now

242   Security Law and Policy

45. The White House, *National Security Strategy* (2015).
46. Brig Deepak Sinha, *Divergent Paths: India's National Security Strategy & Military Doctrine*, 30.1 Indian Defence Rev. (Jan.–March 2015), www.indiandefencereview.com/news/divergent-paths-indias-national-security-strategy-military-doctrine/0/
47. Olga Oliker, *Unpacking Russia's New National Security Strategy*, Center for Strategic and Int. Stud. (Jan. 7, 2016), www.csis.org/analysis/unpacking-russias-new-national-security-strategy. An unofficial English translation is available at www.ieee.es/Galerias/fichero/OtrasPublicaciones/Internacional/2016/Russian-National-Security-Strategy-31Dec2015.pdf
48. The Politburo examined and adopted the Outline of the National Security Strategy, Xinhua News Agency (Jan. 23, 2015), http://news.sina.com.cn/c/2015-01-23/180531437149.shtml (unofficial translation provided by Google).

Additional Learning Resources

Additional Readings

Lamont Colucci, *The National Security Doctrines of the American Presidency: How They Shape Our Present and Future*. 2 Volumes (Praeger, 2012). *A review of U.S. national security policies from Presidents Washington to Obama.*

Andrew M. Dorman & Joyce P. Kaufman, Eds., *Providing for National Security: A Comparative Analysis* (Stanford University Press, 2014). *An overview of the national security priorities for several key countries around the world.*

Susan N. Herman, *Taking Liberties: The War on Terror and the Erosion of American Democracy* (Oxford University Press, 2011). *A review of government intrusions into and limitations of democracy after September 11, 2001.*

Arthur S. Hulnick, *Keeping Us Safe: Secret Intelligence and Homeland Security* (Praeger, 2004). *An argument to revamp intelligence and homeland security to a more flexible system in the post–September 11, 2001 world.*

Karl F. Inderfurth & Loch K. Johnson, Eds., *Fateful Decisions: Inside the National Security Council* (Oxford University Press, 2004). *A selection of articles, essays, and documents providing insight on the National Security Council from 1947 to 2003.*

Scott Jasper, Ed., *Securing Freedom in the Global Commons* (Stanford University Press, 2010). *A discussion of how outer space, the oceans, airspace, and cyberspace impact national security.*

Franklin D. Kramer, et al., Eds., *Cyberpower and National Security* (National Defense University Press, 2009). *A collection of articles and essays exploring cyber policy, infrastructure, security, military, and criminal activities.*

Keith Gregory Logan, Ed., *Homeland Security and Intelligence* (Praeger Security International, 2010). *A collection of expert articles on homeland security and the intelligence community.*

Sam C. Sarkesian, et al., *U.S. National Security: Policymakers, Processes & Politics* (5th ed., Lynne Rienner Publishers, 2007). *An overview of the participants and processes involved in U.S. national security.*

Glenn Sulmasy, *The National Security Court System: A Natural Evolution of Justice in an Age of Terror* (Oxford University Press, 2009). *A history of non-traditional U.S. courts, with a focus on the system in place at Guantanamo Bay, Cuba.*

Cynthia A. Watson, *U.S. National Security: A Reference Handbook* (2nd ed., ABC-Clio, 2008). *An assessment of security challenges facing the* United States.

8 Food and Agriculture Law and Policy

Ann C. Bliss and Autumn T. Johnson

Hors d'oeuvres: Vertical Integrity

On Making Chicken

"Broilers" is the standard industry term used for chickens raised to be eaten as meat. The business model that changes broilers into meals or menu items that feature chicken is known as "vertical integration." High-volume, low-cost production of poultry meat for consumption by humans and pets is accomplished through concentrated feeding, slaughter, and production operations.

Centralization and specialization are the key components of vertical integration. Policy decisions and cost controls reside with the "Integrator." As owners of the flock, the Integrator determines feed formulary, pharmaceutical and chemical applications (such as antibiotic and supplemental nutrients), as well as veterinary care and maintenance. To the extent that the meat product is branded as part of a marketing program, the Integrator would be the name most consumers recognize: Tyson and Perdue being the most familiar.

"Growers" (also known as "Operators") own the land and "grow-out houses" in which the flock is confined. Their role is that of caretaker for the growth of sufficient broiler-weight to meet their contract obligations to the Integrator, who guarantees them payment according to the weight gained from hatchling to carcass.

On the way from being broilers to becoming chicken, an animal must be killed, cleaned, and cut. These activities take place at "Processing Plants," and are performed by a combination of machine and human labor. One such processing plant is owned and operated by Simmons Foods, Inc. Workers at the Simmons plant slaughter and process broilers into pet food. Chicken sold by Walmart, KFC, and other national brand retailers and restaurant chains is also made by the workers at Simmons.

On Learning to Work

The local Simmons Processing Plant had a problem. Hours needed on the killing, cleaning, and production lines could not be filled adequately to keep up with delivery of ready broilers—at least at a cost of labor that would maintain profitability. Smooth and efficient as the Vertical Integration model had proven itself to be, it would be the victim of its own success unless a continuing labor force could be identified and guaranteed. And so it was.

Facing sentencing in a Marshall County, Oklahoma courtroom, 23-year-old Brad McGahey was about to become a member of that workforce, integrated into a vertical production sequence as smoothly and efficiently as one of its broilers. "You need to learn a work ethic," the judge told him on a wintry day in early 2010. "I'm sending you to CAAIR." CAAIR stands for Christian Alcoholics and Addicts in Recovery, a tax-exempt charitable organization founded in 2007.

According to Amy Julia Harris and Shoshanna Walter of the Center for Investigatory Reporting, approximately 200 men lived in dormitory-style housing on the CAAIR campus when Brad was "diverted" there, rather than sent to jail. Most worked at the nearby Simmons plant. The discounted hourly wage Simmons paid went directly to CAAIR. Instead of a paycheck, the men got bunkbeds, meals, and access to Alcoholics and Narcotics Anonymous meetings or other counseling classes if there was time between shifts. Church attendance was mandatory during the first four weeks of residency, but after that only weekly Bible group was required. The men were not allowed cell phones or money.[1]

Because they had to sign a Disclaimer of Employment that labeled them as "clients" of CAAIR, the men also didn't receive basic coverage for on-the-job injuries through Worker's Compensation or accrue Unemployment Benefits. As it turns out, Brad's need for "rehabilitation" was non-existent when the criminal justice system sent him to CAAIR. His pre-sentencing report made clear that he had no prior convictions for—and no significant use of—alcohol or other addictive substances. The charges that brought him before the judge that day were for property-based offenses. But if he left the program, as he did when his hand was accidentally crushed in a processing machine, he would be sent to prison. And he was.

On Building Community

Simmons Foods ranked first place among the largest privately held companies in the listing published by the *Northeast Arkansas Business Journal* in 2017. The Journal reports that Simmons had 5,800 employees, down from 6,085 in 2011. According to CAAIR's 2013 IRS filings, it received $150,000 from Simmons Foods that year, earmarked for construction of additional dormitory space. "It's about building relationships with our community and supporting the opportunity to help people become productive citizens," said a spokesperson for Simmons Foods. After being released from prison, Brad McGahey was eventually able to obtain surgery for his injured hand. More than three years had passed since the injury occurred that day he tried to assist another Simmons worker whose glove had gotten caught in the processing lines, and the operation was less than fully successful. At the time of his interview with the Center for Investigative Reporting, he admitted to being dependent on the hydrocodone pills his doctors prescribed for pain. "I can't live without them," he said.[2]

On Asking

When ordering chicken with your salad or on your bun, ask yourself: when, in the process of making chicken out of broilers, did we stop asking what happens?

On Answers

If a valid answer includes accountability, then law and the legal system are only the lowest levels of a "vertically integrated" analysis. At the apex, we answer ourselves only by asking again and again: Do the products I'm offered feed me with calories at the cost of my conscience? Does the cost of the food I buy equal the real cost of what I consume?

Soup or Salad? An Overview

"De Gustibus non est disputandum"—This Latin maxim that dates back to early Roman times tells us "There is no arguing about taste." And yet: What people eat, what they should (or shouldn't) eat, how food should (or shouldn't) be produced and distributed, and how it is provided drives debate at all levels and of policy and across multiple administrative agencies. Not unlike other contemporary issues in America, the debate reveals substantial divides.

There are two divergent trends in the American food system: "(1) consumer demand for 'real' food that is sustainably produced and (2) the economic and political forces that continue to encourage consolidation and industrialization in agricultural production."[3] There are four related goals of the food movement.

First, the movement seeks "good food," which is defined by a variety of related characteristics, including healthy, natural, and wholesome—often prioritizing quality over cost savings. Second, it calls for more information about how food is produced and greater transparency regarding production and processing, and it ultimately rejects practices that are found to be inappropriate. Third, it reflects concern for sustainability and the environmental effect of food production and food waste. And fourth, it seeks a return to more local and regional sourcing of food. Defined as such, the food movement combines the goals of public health advocates, environmentalists, social justice advocates, and those concerned with farm animal welfare.

While consumer-interest trends move markedly toward good food, social justice in food production practices, sustainability, and an emphasis on local sourcing, mainstream agricultural production has continued its march toward concentration, industrialization of production practices, and production of food products associated with unhealthy eating patterns.[4]

The key focus of American agriculture is efficiency. More production is better, which leads to dependency on chemical and pharmaceutical products, genetic engineering, confinement of animals, and striving for those new and highly marketable products that are edible "food like substances."[5]

When positions are founded on a bedrock of layered legislative benefit, bolstered against change by entrenched belief, and powered by special interests, is there hope for meaningful insight and responsive reform? We are consumers in a market economy, and we have made that power known in furtherance of greater purposes than filling our own plates. We are citizens graced with constitutional protections for free expression, living in a society ensured against aggregation of governing power in one branch by separation into three. Our voices register in legislative chambers, agency hearing rooms, and polling places. We can speak to truths beyond our next drive-thru. And we have.

This chapter explores the legal and policy issues surrounding both food and agriculture. It is by no means comprehensive and should be read as a survey of some of the major issues of the day. Juxtaposing the "food movement" (i.e. what people want in their food) and the prevalent industry practices provides for a window into many of the present conflicts. The authors of this chapter believe that conscientious and honest exploration of past policy has only begun, and already produced significant moral outcomes. More are yet to come.

The Entrée: Food Law and Policy

Introduction and Background

> **Electronic Benefits Transfer (EBT)**—the method by which SNAP benefits are provided to beneficiaries, in the form of a pre-loaded debit card that can be presented for payment at a licensed retail food outlet. This acronym is commonly used by recipients and retailers in lieu of the term Food Stamps.
>
> **Supplemental Nutrition Assistance Program (SNAP)**—the federal food assistance program originally known as Food Stamps.

When you see gas stations and convenience stores advertising **EBT**, you are seeing the largest and most important public assistance program this country provides for its citizens. Although the letters EBT actually stand for Electronic Benefits Transfer, this is the acronym by which millions of Americans refer to the benefits they receive from **SNAP**, the USDA's Supplemental Nutrition Assistance Program. Originally created as the Food Stamp Program, its history begins during the years of the Great Depression. The following sections examine the development of America's nutrition assistance policies by examining the major themes of access, eligibility, benefit levels, and administration over the program's history.

The first Food Stamp Program was initiated in 1939. Designed as a commodities distribution program, government purchases of excess harvest through its non-profit Food Surplus Commodities Corporation helped shore up market prices for growers. Making that food available to those in need provided a source of relief for the unemployed. The Secretary of Agriculture's 1939 annual report included the following description of the FSCC's mission:

> In times of great agricultural surpluses, which usually are accompanied by great unemployment, it will be there to do a minimum job in terms of minimum diets below which the public health would be endangered. The broader market it made possible for farmers in times of stress will help to stabilize our whole economy.[6]

Bringing Food Home—Access

Over the course of nearly four years, the first Food Stamp Program reached approximately 20 million people in nearly half of the counties in the United States.[7] To get your food, you applied for and were given two kinds of stamps: orange stamps and blue stamps. You paid for orange stamps out of your own pocket. These stamps had a dollar-for-dollar face value. For every dollar you paid, you received that value in orange stamps with a face value of $1 each. Orange stamps could be used for any kind of food you wanted to buy. For every $1 worth of orange stamps you paid for, you also received 50 cents worth of blue stamps for free, but blue stamps could only be used as payment for food determined by the USDA to be surplus.

The "bonus value" you received in blue stamps was therefore a function of the number of orange stamps you bought. You couldn't get blue stamps without buying orange stamps, and you were required to buy orange stamps in an amount equal to what was considered a normal proportion of your income on food. This became known as the "purchase requirement," because you had to turn a determined number of your dollars (that you may or may not have actually spent on food) into orange stamps—stamps that could only buy food from grocers who were authorized retailers under the Food Stamp Program (see Figure 8.1).

Your local county relief office made the determination about whether you were eligible for the program at all and what your monthly food budget was expected to be. It didn't matter if you were growing or raising your own food and using dollars for other household expenses. Getting those blue stamps "cost" you dollars out of pocket for the purchase of orange stamps in the amount required by your county.

It's important to note that at inception, the Food Stamp Program did not include federal regulatory provisions that determined either eligibility or benefits as uniform

Food and Agriculture Law and Policy 247

Figure 8.1 Grocery Store Poster Provided to Retailers by the USDA as Part of the Original Food Stamp Program.

standards. These were determined by county. Mabel McFiggin, an unemployed factory worker living in Rochester, New York, was the first recipient of Food Stamps through the USDA. On May 16, 1939, she bought butter, eggs, flour, and prunes. The first retailer caught violating the program was Nick Salzano, in October 1939. The program came to an end in 1943. By that time, food surpluses faded due to the war effort, and unemployment had declined.[8]

Filling Promises—Access for All

Despite its limitations, the success of the first Food Stamp program remained in the family memories of those it helped long after it officially ended. Interest continued and emerged again as a national issue during John F. Kennedy's presidential campaign in West Virginia. Having promised to start a Food Stamp Program if elected, his first Executive Order on January 21, 1961 expanded food distribution programs. The success of several pilot programs initiated by the USDA pursuant to that order led to President Johnson's request that a permanent program be enacted as part of his War on Poverty. The Food Stamp Act of 1964 was signed into law with the stated purpose of strengthening the agricultural economy and providing improved levels of nutrition for low-income families.

> **Looking Past Your Plate [Discussion Question]**
>
> 1. *Many people would be surprised to know that SNAP benefit funding is brought before Congress as part of the Farm Bill. Historically, the USDA has been charged with serving the food and agriculture industries by "fostering new or expanded markets" and finding ways to move "larger quantities of agricultural products through the private marketing system to consumers," and the stated design goals of the original Food Stamp Program reiterate that mission. Are these organizational mandates compatible with USDA's administration of a public health program such as food assistance?*

Key provisions of the 1964 Food Stamp Act were as follows:

- Except for alcoholic beverages and imported foods, all food items were eligible for purchase with food stamps.
- Although the "purchase requirement" was continued, the program was based on a "coupon" or single-stamp system: Color-coded value and product qualifications were eliminated. Recipients still paid to purchase their food stamps with dollars, but they bought the stamps at a fraction of their face value, up to a maximum total. Therefore, the "bonus value" (previously stored on blue stamps as a fixed amount) could be increased or reduced, depending on the price paid for the stamps. As household income rose, so did the price of the stamps—effectively providing more bonus value dollars to those with greater need, who could buy the stamps at a lower price.
- Each state was required to develop eligibility standards that would apply to all its residents, and a plan of operation that would ensure implementation, including issuance to all qualified beneficiaries. The Act included specific language prohibiting discrimination based on race, religious creed, national origin, or political belief.
- The federal government took sole responsibility for funding benefits and retained power to authorize retailers using standardized licensing requirements. The state's cost to administer the program was to be offset, in part, with federal contributions.

> **Looking Past Your Plate [Discussion Question]**
>
> 1. *Compare the 1964 Food Stamp Act's requirements for state-wide eligibility standards and prohibition against discrimination with the way applicants*

> obtained food assistance in the previous program. What problems or practices were the new requirements intended to prevent? If you were an African American family in need when this Act became law, would it have changed your willingness to apply for Food Stamp benefits? Would it have had on impact on the likelihood you could get them?

Filling Plates—Eligibility and Benefit Levels, Shared Funding

The early 1970s were a period of growth in food stamp participation, due in part to increased geographic availability. However, concerns emerged about the cost of providing food stamp benefits, with attendant questions about administration. Delays and barriers that prevented timely certification and receipt of benefits were also identified. It was during this time that the issue dominating food stamp legislation ever after was framed: How to balance program access with program efficiency and accountability? Three major pieces of legislation shaped this period:

- P.L. 91–671 (Jan. 11, 1971) established uniform national standards of eligibility and work requirements. It also required that allotments be equivalent to the cost of a nutritionally adequate diet. Participants' purchase requirements were limited to 30% of their income, and Congress authorized the USDA to pay 62.5% of specific administrative costs incurred by states.[9]
- The Agriculture and Consumer Protection Act of 1973 (P.L. 93–86, Aug. 10, 1973) required States to expand the program to every political jurisdiction before July 1, 1974, and expanded the program to drug addicts and alcoholics in treatment and rehabilitation centers. It also established semi-annual allotment adjustments, SSI cash-out, and bi-monthly issuance; introduced statutory complexity into the definition of "income" for purposes of computing the price participants paid for stamps. This legislation also added a new category of eligible purchases with SNAP benefits—seeds and plants which produce food for human consumption.
- P.L. 93–347 (July 12, 1974) authorized the Department to pay 50% of all States' costs for administering the program (as opposed to offsetting specified costs, as provided for in the 1971 amendments.) This law also established the requirement for efficient and effective administration by the States.

In accordance with P.L. 93–86 (August 10, 1973), the Food Stamp Program began operating nationwide on July 1, 1974. Participation for July 1974 was almost 14 million.

How Much Is Enough?

As a result of the 1971 amendments, the USDA created Food Plans that represent a nutritious diet at four different cost levels. The most basic plan at the lowest cost level was the Economy Plan, now known as the **Thrifty Food Plan**. By creating a "market basket" of the food items needed to fill each dietary plan, the retail cost to purchase those items is determined and used to establish the maximum benefit available for food stamp participants. In addition to cost, differences among plans are in specific foods and quantities of foods. Another basis of the Food Plan cost computation is the

> **Thrifty Food Plan (TFP)**—the food plan used to determine maximum SNAP benefits for qualified recipients. It is based on USDA determinations of the food items necessary to provide an adequate level of nutrition at minimum cost.

assumption that all meals and snacks are prepared at home. Each month, the USDA posts the current monthly cost of the Thrifty Food Plan on its website. The decision in *Rodway v. USDA* reveals a major policy change in food assistance. The decision is excerpted as follows.

Rodway et al. v. United States Department of Agriculture, 514 F2d 809 (D. C. Cir) (1975)

Plaintiffs-appellants began this litigation in December 1971. The individual appellants are members of nine low-income households, all of which receive food stamps. In District Court appellants charged the Secretary was violating the [Food Stamp] Act in two ways: (1) the Secretary's Economy Food Plan allegedly did not provide a nutritionally adequate diet and so its use violated the Act; and (2) the allotment system, because it was based on an average family and on average food prices and preferences, and because it did not continually reflect the current cost of food, did not provide all food stamp recipients with the opportunity to purchase even the Economy Food Plan.

The Food Stamp Act (the Act) was first passed in 1964. Its purposes were to distribute the agriculture surplus of this nation in a beneficial manner, to safeguard the health and well-being of our citizens, and to raise the level of nutrition among low-income households. The Act allows eligible recipients to purchase food stamps (coupons) at prices significantly below their face value. The stamps, in turn, may be used at face value to purchase food at certain retail stores. The cost of the coupons for each household is variable; the Act directs that it "shall represent a reasonable investment on the part of the household, but in no event more than 30 per centum of the household's income...." The original Act directed the Secretary of Agriculture (the Secretary) to administer the program so that "eligible households ... shall be provided with an opportunity *more nearly* to obtain a nutritionally adequate diet through the issuance to them of a coupon allotment..." In 1971, however, the Act was amended and this language was significantly altered. The italicized words "more nearly" were deleted from the Act, so that the Secretary's duty became to provide food stamp recipients "with an opportunity to obtain a nutritionally adequate diet...." Essentially, it is the effect of this change that is here at issue.

At oral argument USDA conceded that the present system results in the individual appellants receiving substantially less than that necessary for them to purchase even the Economy Food Plan. In part this is so because, by USDA's own figures, the cost (and composition) of a nutritionally adequate diet varies according to an individual's age and sex. The allotment regulations, however, do not consider age and sex at all. Rather they calculate the cost of the Plan for a family composed of two adults, ages 20–35, one child, age 6–9, and one boy, age 9–12. Thereafter, this cost is adjusted only for the number of persons in each eligible household, without regard to its individual composition. Thus every four-person household receiving food stamps receives the same amount each month that necessary to feed the hypothetical family of four although some households need substantially more than the hypothetical family of four and some need substantially less.

USDA's failure to account for the composition of each recipient household by age and sex is not the only reason why appellants receive less than they need to purchase a nutritionally adequate diet. The recipient's health and the amount of his daily physical activity also influence the cost to him of a nutritionally adequate diet. The fact that, in accordance with the Act, 7 U.S.C. § 2016(a), the Secretary adjusts the allotment figures for inflation only twice a year, and in so doing uses cost of food data current six months prior to the effective date of the new allotment schedules, means that the actual cost of the Economy Food Plan is frequently higher than the allotment even for the hypothetical family of four. Moreover, appellants are all from Northeastern states where the cost of food is higher than the national average, which the Secretary uses in pricing the Economy Food Plan.

All this the Secretary concedes. He defends the allotment system not on its accuracy but on the ground of administrative necessity. He further suggests, that appellants' allotments fall short because they are members of "unusual families." We agree that there is room for administrative convenience and necessity in the administration of the food stamp program. The number of variables affecting the needs of individual recipients is, ultimately, infinite, and we certainly do not expect the Secretary to embark upon extensive metabolic examinations of each food stamp recipient to determine individual need. But we do not think that justifies automatically ignoring generalized, easily quantified, and easily verified differences among recipients under the rubric of administrative necessity.

This conclusion is bolstered by reference to the legislative history. Most significant is the change, mentioned earlier, from the promise of the 1964 Act, "an opportunity more nearly to obtain a nutritionally adequate diet" to that of the 1971 amendments, "an opportunity to obtain a nutritionally adequate diet." At the same time, the purpose of the Act was changed from "raising levels of nutrition" to enabling eligible households "to purchase a nutritionally adequate diet."

We are thus convinced by the language of the statute and by the legislative history that the 1971 amendments marked a major shift in the policy of the Food Stamp Act, a shift from supplementing the diets of low-income households to guaranteeing those households the opportunity for an adequate diet. Congress plainly intended the 1971 amendments to assure that no eligible family need go malnourished; the Government would provide all the opportunity to be healthfully fed. Manifestly, that congressional intent is frustrated if the food stamp program is administered in such a way that a substantial number of eligible households do not receive sufficient coupons to purchase what the Secretary determines to be a nutritionally adequate diet. For a family that needs a loaf of bread, the offer of a slice is poor comfort. We think such an administrative system would violate the Act.

The purposes of the Food Stamp Act and the health and well-being of our populace are too important, and the legislative intent that those purposes be achieved for substantially all recipients too clear, for us to allow their administrative evisceration. We think that an averaging system such as that now used can be sustained only if the Secretary can show that such a system will deliver coupons to substantially all recipients sufficient to allow them to purchase a nutritionally adequate diet. If such an "efficient" system does not meet this test, which we think is congressionally mandated, then the Secretary must individualize his computations to the extent necessary to achieve this result, or increase the amount of the "average" allotment so that virtually all recipients are swept within it. And, needless to say, whatever approach is utilized must be supported by the administrative record developed on remand.

Looking Past Your Plate [Discussion Questions]

1. *How did the Rodway court address the conflict between administrative efficiency and congressional intent? Visit the USDA website to find the current month's Thrifty Food Plan. Do you see evidence of the Rodway decision's impact in the way the USDA compiles and displays this information?*
2. *Why does the USDA produce the Low Cost, Moderate Cost, and Liberal Food Plans in addition to the Thrifty Food Plan? Use the USDA Center for Nutrition Policy and Promotion website (www.cnpp.usda.gov) to find the current month's "USDA Food Plans: Cost of Food Report."*
3. *Compare the market baskets of food items that are the basis for those plans and their cost. Consider your own food choices and budget. Which food plan would your eating habits most nearly match?*

More Platters, Less Paperwork—Access and the Food Stamp Act of 1977

In 1977, both the outgoing Republican Administration and the new Democratic Administration led by President Jimmy Carter offered Congress proposed legislation to reform the Food Stamp Program. The Republican bill stressed targeting benefits to the neediest, simplifying administration, and tightening controls on the program; the Democratic bill focused on increasing access to those most in need and simplifying and streamlining a complicated and cumbersome process that delayed benefit delivery, as well as reducing errors and curbing abuse. Amidst all the themes, the Purchase Requirement was recognized as the single most significant barrier to participation. The rallying cry for reform was **EPR**—Eliminate the Purchase Requirement. The bill that became the law did exactly that. It also:

- established statutory income eligibility guidelines based on the poverty line and created 10 categories of excluded income as well as other income adjustments for determining participant eligibility;
- raised the general resource limit to $1,750 and established a fair market value test for evaluating vehicles as resources;
- penalized households whose heads voluntarily quit jobs;
- restricted eligibility for students and aliens;
- eliminated the requirement that households must have cooking facilities;
- allowed stores to give Food Stamp users cash change up to 99 cents;
- established the principle that stores must sell a substantial amount of staple foods to be authorized retailers;
- created a 30-day processing standard and the concept of expedited service; and
- provided joint processing for **SSI** applications and coordination with **AFDC** (Aid for Families with Dependent Children, aka "Welfare").

EPR was implemented on January 1, 1979. Participation that month increased 1.5 million over the preceding month.

Eliminate the Purchase Requirement (EPR)—early versions of the food assistance program required beneficiaries to buy stamps using their own dollars. Recognized as an obstacle to participation, calls to revise the program included the urge to eliminate this purchase requirement.

Supplemental Security Income (SSI)—a form of cash assistance to disabled individuals who qualified by virtue of their poverty. Provided by the federal government and administered by the Social Security Administration.

Aid for Families with Dependent Children (AFDC)—a form of cash assistance for low-income households who qualified by virtue of their poverty. Funded in part by federal subsidies and administered by state and county government. Replaced by PRWORA in 1996.

Looking Past Your Plate [Discussion Question]

1. *On April 30, 1975, Frances J. Woods of Fort Worth, Texas filed U.S. Patent application #573–036 for a Container for Microwave Heating of Frozen*

> Sandwiches. Use the web to research the history of microwave ovens and the development of prepared, packaged foods for heating in a microwave oven. Can you place those developments in time with provisions of this Act?
> 2. As a general rule, SNAP benefits may not be used for buying hot foods or for food items to be consumed on-site. Can you identify any policy reasons behind these prohibitions? How does this rule restrict nutrition options for the homeless? Given increased availability of microwave-ready meals and reliance on these prepared foods, would you change the policy?

Who's at the Table?—Eligibility, Expectation, and Culture

By December 1979, participation surpassed 20 million. In the early 1980s, the size and expense of the Food Stamp Program came under close scrutiny. Major legislation in 1981 and 1982 prohibited using federal funds for outreach. In addition, significant attention was given to the definition of "household." In 1981 the Senate noted that small households of one, two, or three persons received more food stamps per person than did larger households, based on economies of scale. For example, $70 in stamps for a household of one, $128 for two, $183 for three. In a household of four, the total benefit of $233 works out to $58.25 per person—$11.75 less than each individual would receive if living separately. By 1982, this gave rise to concern that larger households could fragment into separate, smaller households by purchasing and preparing food separately—or claim to do so—allowing those individuals to obtain benefits they would not otherwise be entitled to.

Thus, amendments to the Food Stamp Act made in 1981 and 1982 re-defined a "household" as:

1. an individual who lives alone or who, while living with others, customarily purchases foods and prepares meals for home consumption separate and apart from the others, or
2. a group of individuals who live together and customarily purchase food and prepare meals together for home consumption; *except that parents and children*, or siblings, *who live together shall be treated as a group of individuals who customarily purchase and prepare meals together for home consumption even if they do not do so, unless one of the parents, or siblings*, is an elderly or disabled member." (emphasis added). (Section 3(i) of the Food Stamp Act of 1964, 78 Stat. 703, as re-designated and amended, 7 U. S. C. § 2012(i). Omnibus Budget Reconciliation Act of 1981, Pub. L. 97–35, 95 Stat. 358. The clause extending the proviso to siblings, was added by the Omnibus Budget Reconciliation Act of 1982, Pub. L. 97–253, 96 Stat. 772.)

The constitutionality of the new definitional tests was challenged on equal protection grounds by several beneficiary families who sought to be treated as separate households but did not qualify under this language. Deciding that the statutory definition had a rational basis, the District Court upheld the new definitions. It found that the amendments made it more difficult for individuals who lived together to manipulate the rules so as to obtain separate household status and receive greater benefits. The District Court concluded that attempting to make individual case determinations as to household status would be so time consuming as to create an excessive administrative burden and that unrelated persons who live together for reasons of economy or health are more likely to actually be separate households than related families who live together. However, the U.S. Supreme Court reversed, determining that the District Court erred by treating parents, children, and siblings (the disadvantaged class created by the amendments) as "suspect" or "quasi-suspect" for purposes of equal protection analysis.[10]

Today, the detailed federal regulations that define households for purposes of SNAP benefits require several pages of print. As the litigation history shows, two basic sources of complexity compete and contribute to the problem of deciding exactly who is at the table and who counts: Difficulties in applying the basic definition to the broad range of possible living situations that exists in the United States, and programmatic concern with excluding persons or households not targeted for benefits within the intent of the law.[11]

Still Hungry: Eligibility, Enforcement, and Expectations

Recognition of the severe domestic hunger problem in the latter half of the 1980s led to incremental improvements in the Food Stamp Program in 1985 and 1987, such as elimination of sales tax on food stamp purchases, eligibility for the homeless, and expanded nutrition education. The Hunger Prevention Act of 1988 and the Mickey Leland Memorial Domestic Hunger Relief Act in 1990 foretold the improvements that would be coming. The 1988 and 1990 legislation increased benefits by applying a multiplication factor to Thrifty Food Plan costs, authorized nutrition education grants, and increased the severity of penalties for individuals or firms who violated program rules. And EBT was established as the preferred means of benefit issuance.

No Second Helpings, Welfare Reform: The Personal Responsibility and Work Opportunity Act of 1996

The mid-1990s was a period of welfare reform. Many states were given waivers of the rules for the cash welfare program, Aid to Families with Dependent Children (**AFDC**) well before major welfare reform legislation was enacted in 1996. The Personal Responsibility and Work Opportunities Reconciliation Act of 1996 (**PRWORA**) removed the entitlements to AFDC and replaced that with a new block grant to states called Temporary Assistance to Needy Families (**TANF**). Major changes to the Food Stamp Program were enacted under PRWORA, even as the program itself was reauthorized in the 1996 Farm Bill. Among them were the following:

> Personal Responsibility and Work Opportunities Reconciliation Act of 1996 (PRWORA)—this federal legislation removed the entitlements to AFDC and replaced the program with block grants to states called Temporary Assistance to Needy Families (TANF).

- Receipt of food stamp benefits was limited to three out of 36 months for able-bodied adults without dependents (ABAWDs) who were not working at least 20 hours a week or participating in a work program;
- Maximum allotments were reduced by setting them at 100% of the change in the Thrifty Food Plan (down from 103% of the change in the TFP);
- Eliminating eligibility for most legal immigrants.

Then There Was More: The Early 2000s and the Farm Bill of 2002

Participation declined throughout the late 1990s, even more so than expected based on the changes in PRWORA and falling unemployment. Program access and simplification of program rules were a major focus of proposed legislation and of major regulations promulgated by the Department. In May 2002, the Food Security and

Rural Investment Act of 2002 was enacted, including reauthorization of the Food Stamp Program. Major changes included the following:

- Restoration of eligibility for food stamps to qualified aliens who had been in the United States at least five years. Eligibility was provided for immigrants who received certain disability payments and for their children, regardless of how long they have been in the country.
- The income adjustments used to qualify applicants for program participation were indexed each year for inflation and were tied to family size.
- The quality control system by which state administration was monitored was reformed. Financial sanctions were based on consecutive years of high error rates. States with low error rates received a performance bonus, rather than enhanced funding. Other changes were made to simplify the program and align its requirements with TANF.

Word Salad

We need to eat. The daily task of getting enough to eat, and what it's like when you don't, is the stuff of stories. Hunger is a character in the stories we tell each other. The word is one we recognize at least from personal sensation and at worst as ongoing experience. For a nation, the story is different. It can only be told accurately and meaningfully with data: discrete units of information drawn from each individual story and gathered to tell the tale of whether our collective, national response has made a difference (see Figure 8.2).

As part of its mission, the USDA gathers data. Food assistance (including SNAP, related forms of nutrition assistance for women and infants, and for seniors and the institutionalized), school lunch, and other feeding programs cost money to fund and to administer. Evaluating benefit usage and the success of program design are fair questions for the money spent, and the USDA provides answers in a variety of forms.

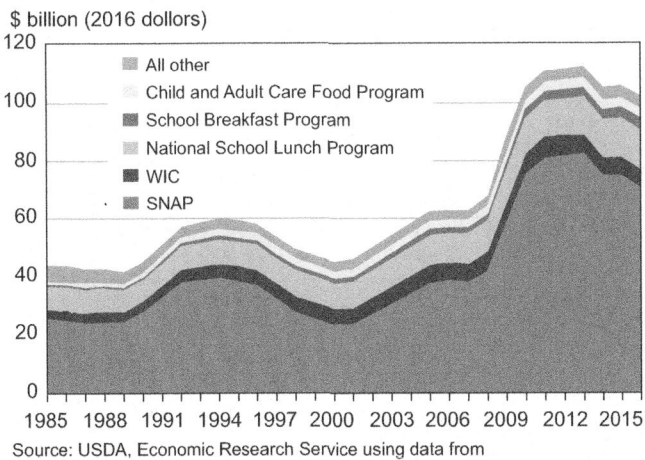

Figure 8.2 USDA—ERS, Administrative Publication 078, & Charting the Essentials, 2017.

Table 8.1 Food Insecure

The Old Words Were:	The New Words Are:	They Mean:
Food insecurity without hunger	Low food security	Reports of reduced quality, variety, or desirability of diet. Little or no indication of reduced food intake.
Food insecurity with hunger	Very low food security	Reports of multiple indications of disrupted eating patterns and reduced food intake.

Table 8.2 Food Secure

The Old Words Were:	The New Words Are:	They Mean:
Food Security	High food security	No reported indications of food-access problems or limitations.
Food Security	Marginal food security	One or two reported indications, typically of anxiety over food sufficiency or shortage of food in the house. Little or no indication of changes in diets or food intake.

> Food insecurity/security—the basic terms from which all USDA data regarding food assistance programming is derived; used for collecting, compiling, and analyzing data for purposes of policy development and program implementation.

How does the USDA gather data that will tell us the national story about hunger? Besides program usage and design, how do we determine national need? A vocabulary that will capture more than personal experience is essential. "**Food insecurity**" is the term that serves as a basis for that vocabulary.

In 2006, the USDA introduced new language to describe ranges of severity of food insecurity. The USDA made these changes in response to recommendations by an expert panel convened at the USDA's request by the Committee on National Statistics (CNSTAT) of the National Academies. Even though new labels were introduced, the methods used to assess households' food security remained unchanged, so statistics for 2005 and later years are directly comparable with those for earlier years for the corresponding categories. These are the labels the USDA uses to collect data for and about the food assistance programs it administers (see Tables 8.1 and 8.2).

> Looking Past Your Plate [Discussion Question]
> 1. Do you find the USDA vocabulary compelling?
> 2. What words or issues are important in public debate about food policy?
> 3. What words or evidence are meaningful in public debate about food policy?
> 4. Does compassion look different at the level of individual action than it does at the level of national policy?

Re-Branding: The Food, Conservation and Energy Act of 2008

The Food Stamp Program was officially renamed as the Supplemental Nutrition Assistance Program. This legislation also renamed the Food Stamp Act of 1977 the Food and Nutrition Act of 2008 and became effective in October of 2008.

Digging In: An Exercise

1. *Refer to Tables 8.1 and 8.2 comparing "old" and "new" terminology used by the USDA in fulfilling its congressional mandate under the laws that provide food assistance.*
2. *Notice that the old lexicon provided three terms, but now there are four.*
3. *Notice that the old lexicon included the word "hunger." Neither the new words nor their definitions include that term.*
4. *What purpose does the new vocabulary serve in developing survey questions? Is data more reliable if it is gathered from subjective reports of physical sensation, or from objective counts of behavioral change?*
5. *What purpose does the new vocabulary serve in conveying information to citizens and their congressional representatives?*
6. *Using Figure 8.3, would you be able to talk to another person about the policy and funding issues underlying food assistance programs in the United States? What words would you use (or not) to tell the story the numbers in this figure show?*

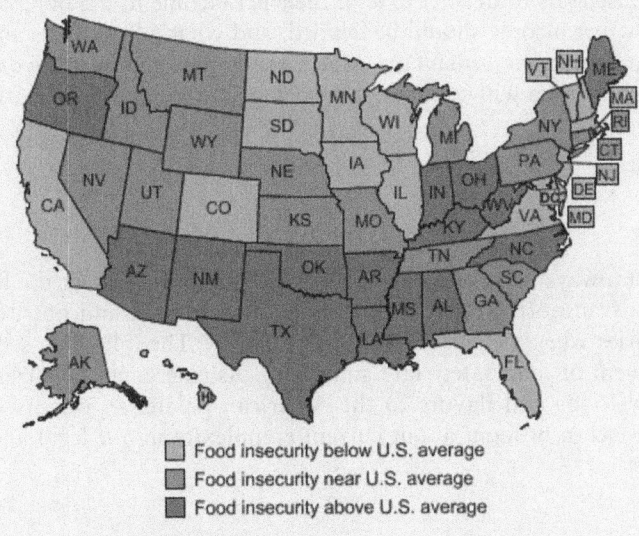

Source: USDA, Economic Research Service, using data from the December 2014, 2015, and 2016 Current Population Survey Food Security Supplements.

Figure 8.3 Prevalence of Food Insecurity (2016).
Source: USDA, Economic Research Service.

In a Wrap: Conclusions

Although the basic design of SNAP (with the exception of national eligibility standards and elimination of the purchase requirement) has remained unchanged since the 1964 law was enacted, the program has undergone many substantial changes that have resulted in its expansion and retraction over the years. These changes have often brought new complexities to program administrators and applicants. The legislation governing today's program has specific eligibility requirements and administrative procedures that make SNAP more complex than other social programs. Even as many features of the program limit its ability to be responsive to an individual household's needs, many other features, such as income deductions, are designed to make it more responsive. Striking a balance between a more targeted and a more accessible benefit has been an ongoing tension in the program. The size and cost of the program make it a political target for budget cuts, and even relatively small adjustments have the potential to impact a significant number of Americans.[12]

Over the years, debates have continued. Should the program be more of a nutrition program or serve as an income-maintenance benefit, including whether an in-kind benefit (such as the early form of commodity distribution) should be replaced by a cash allotment? Should the program limit food choices, and if so to what extent? What responsibilities should participants be expected to meet (e.g., be required to seek employment if able-bodied, or participate in job training)? Should geographic distinctions be applied in determining need and/or benefit levels? To what extent does the program's role include providing nutrition education? To what extent should program funding include the costs of outreach to eligible non-participants?[13]

Other debates have centered on the adequacy of the Thrifty Food Plan and whether expecting households to devote 30% of their net income to the purchase of food is realistic. How net income should be defined, and what adjustments and exclusions for income qualifications, remain the subject of complex administrative examination. These and other issues will continue to be debated as long as people are hungry.[14]

Food Safety

Introduction

Food has not always been safe. Our everyday assumptions about the foods we eat, their origins, transport, production, storage, distribution, and nutritive value are relative luxuries when viewed in the light of history. The following sections review the development of food safety law and policy. As emerging globalization of trade brought new foods and flavors to the American palate, so increased awareness and public concern brought about current complexity in our legal and regulatory environment.

Beginnings

Early conditions in the U.S. food and drug industries can hardly be imagined today. Use of chemical preservatives and toxic colors was virtually uncontrolled. Changes from an agricultural to an industrial economy had made it necessary to provide the rapidly increasing city population with food from distant areas, but sanitation was primitive in the light of modern standards. Ice was still the principal means of refrigeration. Milk was still unpasteurized. Cows were not tested for tuberculosis. The great pioneers of bacteriology were just starting their string of victories over infectious diseases: In 1883, Robert Koch discovered the cholera bacteria and established that the disease was transmitted by contaminated water and food.[15]

Not until interstate commerce began its great expansion after the Civil War did the need for federal rulemaking become widely realized. The Pure Food Movement—a grass-roots phenomenon that germinated in the 1870s—was the original and principal source of political support for the Food and Drugs Act of 1906.

The United States had been slow to recognize the need for a national food and drug law. Frederick Accum's "Treatise on Adulterations of Food and Methods of Detecting Them" had been published in London in 1820, and Great Britain's first national food law was passed in 1860. However, such food laws as existed in the United States focused on standardizing weights and measures. Inspection and quality standards were limited to only a few commodity products and were essentially intended to promote foreign sales by protecting brand. As such, they were unique to each state and often dated back to colonial times.[16]

In 1902, a group of young men known as the "Poison Squad" captivated the country's attention. As part of an experiment under the supervision of the "Bureau of Chemistry" headed by Harvey W. Wiley, these volunteers agreed to eat only foods treated with measured amounts of chemical preservatives. The object was to demonstrate whether these substances were injurious to health. Ingredients on the menu included borax; salicylic, sulphurous, and benzoic acids; and formaldehyde. Wiley (as well as other food scientists) concluded that chemical preservatives should be used in food only when necessary, that the burden of proving safety should fall squarely on the producer, and that none should be used without informing the consumer on the product label.

These key concepts remain basic principles in food policy and law today, the result of those first five years of continuing and controlled research. William H. Carter, an African American, played a significant role in establishing the credibility of Wiley's research. First hired as a cook for the Squad in 1902, he completed a degree in pharmaceutical chemistry and served in the FDA laboratories for 43 years.

Wiley took his findings to the public, becoming a popular speaker at women's clubs, civic and business organizations. National magazines, such as *Colliers Weekly*, the *Ladies Home Journal*, and *Good Housekeeping* contributed to an energized public opinion with cartoons, articles, and editorials. Historians and Dr. Wiley himself credited club women and the Pure Food Movement for turning the tide, but final action by Congress is often credited to the single chapter in Upton Sinclair's novel *The Jungle* that portrayed conditions in the Chicago meat-packing industry. Two bills became law on June 30, 1908: The Wiley Act and the Food and Drug Act of 1906.

Administration of the new laws was assigned to the Bureau of Chemistry. Scientific methods of analysis as well as inspection techniques and administrative enforcement actions, including legal procedures for seizing violative products that are still in use today, were developed in those early years. The Bureau continued its enforcement role until 1927. At that time, law enforcement functions were separated from agricultural research. This was the genesis of the Food, Drug and Insecticide Administration, renamed the Food and Drug Administration (FDA) in 1931. In 1940, to prevent recurring conflicts between producer interests and consumer interests, the FDA was transferred from the U.S. Department of Agriculture to the Federal Security Agency, which became the Department of Health, Education and Welfare in 1953. Today, we know this important federal agency as the Department of Health and Human Services.

The original Food and Drugs Act passed by Congress and signed by President Theodore Roosevelt addressed food safety as a national concern by crafting its prohibitions in terms of interstate commerce, consistent with congressional authority as expressed in constitutional terms. It prohibited interstate commerce in misbranded and adulterated foods, drink, and drugs. Early federal law identified and defined two legal terms that remain foundational in U.S. law: "adulterated" and "misbranded" foods: The first Certified Color Regulations, issued in 1907 at the request of manufacturers and users, listed seven colors found suitable for use in foods. (An example of the "adulteration" issue in food law.) The Gould Amendment (passed in 1913) required that food package contents be "plainly and conspicuously marked on the outside of the package in terms of weight, measure, or numerical count." (An example of the "misbranding" issue in food law.)[17]

In 1914 the Supreme Court issued its first ruling interpreting the language of the Food and Drugs Act. The decision in *U.S. v. Lexington Mills and Elevator Company* (232 U.S. 399, 1914) held that the burden of proof to establish that a food was unsafe was on the government.

> **Looking Past Your Plate [Discussion Questions]**
>
> 1. *The original Act had no requirements for pre-market safety testing of treated foods. How did this affect the Court's decision in the Lexington Mills case? How does the current legislative and regulatory emphasis on the prevention of foodborne illness change the consequences for food businesses whose products cause harm?*

Changes

In 1933 the FDA recommended a complete revision of the original 1906 Act. A five-year battle for legislative reform ensued. Two tragedies fueled the public demand for legislative reform: Sales of "Elixir of Sulfanilamide," a raspberry-flavored antibiotic syrup that contained a poisonous solvent, killed 107 persons, many of whom were children. "Jamaica Ginger" was a stimulant drink that became popular during the Prohibition years. "Jake Walk"—a distinctive pattern of toe-to-heel gait—was found to be the result of neuromotor impairment due to organophosphate poisoning in production of the drink.

On June 25, 1938, President Franklin D. Roosevelt signed the Federal Food, Drug, and Cosmetic Act. Many of the new law's provisions focused on medical, pharmaceutical, and cosmetic products. Some of the substantive changes which applied to food were as follows:

- Known poisons were prohibited as additions to foods except where unavoidable or required in production. Safe tolerances for residues (e.g., for pesticides) were authorized, as determined by industry and the USDA. Factory inspections were specifically authorized.
- Food standards were required to be set up when needed "to promote honesty and fair dealing in the interest of consumers."
- Injunctions issued by the Federal court against violators was added to the list of legal remedies, which previously included product seizures and criminal prosecutions.
- The definition of "adulteration" was broadened—and the burden of proof to establish the safety of a given additive was placed on the industry. Compare this to the conclusion of the *Lexington Mills* case.

> **Looking Past Your Plate [Discussion Questions]**
>
> 1. *Food safety legislation often appears to follow public tragedy, but are such events the sole cause of these regulatory initiatives? What is the role of industry, trade and retail groups, consumers, and other government agencies in laying the groundwork for congressional action?*

In addition, several specific provisions of the new Act targeted marketing and packaging practices, especially in regard to new foods that were promoted as improved substitutes. The 1938 law:

- Prohibited false statements about the food item.
- Addressed labeling of imitation foods, such as margarines that were meant as substitutes for butter. If a product imitated another food, the label had to clearly state that fact.
- Required food labels to affirmatively provide the name, quantity, contents, and manufacturer.
- Required special labeling information for dietary foods.
- Prohibited misleading containers.

The Wheeler-Lea Act, also passed in 1938, expanded regulatory reach over "food safety" concerns by charging the Federal Trade Commission with oversight of advertising products otherwise regulated by the FDA, with the exception of prescription drugs. The "misbranding" prohibitions, rooted in the original 1906 Act, now encompass food advertising as a matter understood to impact the safety and health of consumers.[18]

> **Vitamin Donuts**
>
> *Around 1940, the results of two small studies set off a panic. A handful of subjects deprived of Vitamin B1 (thiamine) became sluggish and apathetic. One researcher concluded that thiamine deficiency was causing Americans to lack energy and motivation—conditions a country mobilizing for war could not afford. Consequently, the Government endorsed products enriched with thiamine. After many letters, the Nutrition Division allowed the Doughnut Corporation to call their product "enriched flour donuts" but not "enriched donuts" or their original choice, "vitamin donuts."*[19]

In 1949, the FDA used its delegated authority to publish industry guidance for the first time. The Procedures for the Appraisal of the Toxicity of Chemicals in Food came to be known as the Black Book. Its successor, the Red Book (officially known as Toxicological Principles for the Safety Assessment of Direct Food Additives and Color Additives Used in Food) was published by the FDA in 1982.

Looking Past Your Plate [Discussion Questions]

Besides rulemaking authority, federal agencies have the power to issue guidelines that supplement regulations by providing the agency's interpretation of the laws it enforces. Guidelines do not have the same force of law as rules.

1. As food technologies and consumer trends evolve at an ever-increasing pace, should the FDA rely on issuing guidelines to update or modify existing standards without having to mandate specific standards? Why or why not?
2. What incentives would a manufacturer, distributor, or retailer have to comply with non-mandatory guidelines?

In 1949, Congress began a series of investigative hearings to investigate the presence of chemicals in food and, later, cosmetics. The hearings, chaired by Rep. James T. Delaney of New York, went on for two years. From the committee's work came three amendments that fundamentally changed the character of the U.S. food and drug law: the Pesticide Amendment (1954), the Food Additives Amendment (1958), and the Color Additive Amendments (1960). Very significant was a proviso in the food and color additive laws that no additive could be deemed safe (or given FDA approval) if it was found to cause cancer in humans or experimental animals. Known as the Delaney Clause, the section was initially opposed by the FDA and by scientists who agreed that an additive used at very low levels need not necessarily be banned because it may cause cancer at high levels. Proponents justified the clause on the basis that cancer experts had not been able to determine a safe level for any carcinogen. This was the underlying basis in 1959 for a nationwide FDA recall of cranberries contaminated by the weed killer aminotriazole.

With these laws on the books, it could be said for the first time that no substance can legally be introduced into the U.S. food supply unless there has been a prior determination that it is safe. By shifting the burden onto manufacturers to do the research, costs of administration and agency oversight were significantly reduced. Preventing violations through clearance before marketing gave consumers immeasurably better protection than merely prosecuting the few violations that could be proved after injuries were reported and investigated. Notwithstanding publicity critical of the FDA, the fact of congressional attention and action has arguably had beneficial results, particularly in convincing growers that pesticides must be used with care and raising public awareness.[20]

The year 1962 ushered in a broadened perspective on the issue of food safety: informed choice. President John F. Kennedy proclaimed The Consumer Bill of Rights in his message to Congress, including articulated rights to safety, to be informed, to choose, and to be heard. In subsequent years, this focus expanded to include consumer education, the better to prepare consumers for making the health and nutrition choices that information offers.

> **Looking Past Your Plate [Discussion Questions]**
> 1. *As applied to food and diet, how do the rights identified by President Kennedy relate to the two foundational concepts of food law identified earlier: Misbranding and Adulteration?*
> 2. *Can you discern the presence of these consumer rights in current issues regarding GMO and Country of Origin labeling?*

After many years of intervening initiative, often targeted to specific industries or trades, Congress passed the Nutrition Labeling and Education Act in 1990. It required all packaged foods to bear nutrition labeling and all health claims for foods to be consistent with terms defined by the Secretary of Health and Human Services. The law preempted state requirements about food standards, nutrition labeling, and health claims. Terms such as "low fat" and "light" were standardized for use on the food ingredient panel, and the panel itself was formatted in a standard display. For the first time, some health claims for foods were permitted. The Act also:

- Mandated nutrition labeling of food products (previously voluntary).
- Applied nutrition labeling requirements to imported food products as well as domestic products.
- Required that nutrition information on labels had to be based on serving size, rather than package size.
- Replaced extensive state food laws in some jurisdictions that address food misbranding. The effect was to accommodate compliance for interstate companies by creating one uniform standard set by the FDA.
- Mandated more detailed declaration of ingredients on package label to include color, peanut, and juice content.
- Defined the difference between butter, margarine, and spread and between fruit drink and fruit juice.
- Allowed combinations of food ingredients that may have been prohibited by some state laws, but the ingredients must be accurately labeled (e.g., canola oil added to butter).

The year 1990 also saw Congress pass the Organic Foods Production Act, requiring the USDA to develop national standards for organically produced agricultural products to assure consumers that agricultural products marketed as organic meet consistent, uniform standards. For perspective, consider the history of the 1870s Pure Food Movement.

The FDA Food Safety Modernization Act (FSMA) has been described as the single most sweeping legislative reform of the food system since the original 1906 Food and Drug Act. It was signed into law by President Obama on January 4, 2011. The legislation focused on using the power of regulatory authority in the FDA to shift from responding to food contamination to preventing it. Its official title is "To Amend the Federal Food, Drug, and Cosmetic Act with respect to the Safety of the Food Supply."

Food for Thought . . . Food Safety [Vignette]

In the spring of 2007, I was asked to testify before the U.S. House of Representative's Energy and Commerce Committee, which was the committee tasked with modernizing our food safety system. From those hearings, which stretched from 2007 to 2009, came the Food Safety Modernization Act (FSMA).

My testimony, which only lasted for about 15 minutes with questions, was part of a hearing entitled, "A Diminished Capacity: Can the FDA Assure the Safety and Security of the Nation's Food Supply?" My pitch was pretty straightforward—modernize our food safety system and deny me the opportunity to sue food companies on behalf of my clients.

After me came a table full of CEOs whose companies had caused some of the larger foodborne illness outbreaks in the preceding years. Producers of lettuce, pot pies, beans, and chili sauce were forced to stand and swear under oath to tell the truth. Their army of lawyers was right behind them.

It was clear that all of them wished they were anywhere in the world other than where they were now sitting. Just months before, all spinach grown in the U.S. was recalled after 205 people were sickened and five died from spinach that came from one California farm. Spinach sales tanked. Then there was the peanut recall, prompted by more than 700 illnesses and nine deaths. That one ended up causing more than 4,000 products to be recalled and peanut sales to plummet, at an estimated cost of nearly $500 million.

It was amazing to see CEOs, who may have previously thought that "government was the problem," admit that it was past time to enact comprehensive food safety legislation to allow for thoughtful hazard analysis of the food supply. Being hauled in front of a congressional committee, realizing the burden on the consumers, or feeling the hit to their company's bottom line may have awakened them to a newfound desire for a partnership between business, government, and consumers.

With this partnership—especially between some consumer groups and the food industry—the outlines of FSMA began to emerge. The FDA was tasked with creating new regulations in consultation with both industry and consumers. The FDA also was given—although not necessarily wanted—mandatory recall authority. Although still not frequently used, it is an "arrow in the quiver," along with mandatory registration, mandatory reporting, and increased product testing, all of which adds a bit of muscle to an agency without the necessary resources for enough inspections.

In my view, a CEO and board embracing FSMA makes sense. Playing by the rules and not poisoning customers is good for business. I would be remiss if I didn't mention one final reason why the CEO and board need to pay attention to FSMA. That would be these two words: "criminal sanctions." There have been more criminal prosecutions in the past five years of food company managers than in the prior two decades combined. Hefty fines and jail time do have a way of focusing one's attention.[21]

Bill Marler, Attorney[22]
Marler Clark

The FDA Food Safety Modernization Act (FSMA) is global in its approach to assuring the safety and security of the food supply. It can be described as a world in itself, as it addresses world production, marketing, transportation, and distribution of food.

Overview of the Food Safety Modernization Act[23]

With planetary intention, how does the FSMA impact the "local food" movement, and those whose production, marketing, transportation, and distribution models may be as close at hand as your local farmer's market?

Food for Thought . . . Local Food [Vignette]

Food safety issues that led to Congressional and Administration interest in a new produce food safety law (FSMA) were few and far between considering that Americans eat 1 billion meals a day. The single major event that created the final push involved an *E. coli* contamination in spinach that was not easy to understand or explain. Rather than this event prompting research activity, the response was legislation and regulation. The law, designed to reduce food safety risk to the public, has created a hysteria within the FDA that works to decrease the number of smaller growers in favor of larger operations that can afford new and stringent standards. Although there are certain exemptions built within the law, buyers are becoming increasingly convinced that everyone should comply.

While it can be argued that there is a risk in any size operation, the intent was to reduce risk to the food supply. One way to do that is to encourage a greater diversity in operations so that a problem within any one operation does not significantly impact the larger population. The need for additional research on how food can become contaminated in growing, harvesting, and packing operations, combined with education on the basic food safety practices throughout the farming community, would have been a better approach.

One part of the supply chain issue involved food that is at least partially processed after it is harvested. These items often are comingled in packing houses, end up in bags (e.g., salad mixes), and may be more likely to bring harm to the food supply than items that are not comingled and processed. To reflect this issue, exemptions for smaller growers on the growing, harvesting, and packing side may disappear when a product is processed, even fresh processed. This puts greater financial and regulatory pressure on those smaller growers. Usually, comingling does not happen on smaller operations and, perhaps, comingling should have been a trigger for compliance.

The result of much of this can be explained as hourglass economics. Very small growers are either exempted or can operate below the radar screen while large growers, by virtue of their size, can afford to hire individuals to help them comply with the regulations. There is not much space left in the middle for smaller and medium-sized family farms to operate, and I fear this will get worse.

A. Richard Bonanno, Associate Dean[24]
NC State University

> **Agency Roles Today**
>
> The USDA is responsible for regulating meat and poultry, egg products, and catfish, whereas the U.S. Food and Drug Administration (FDA) oversees food safety for almost all other foods. The FDA conducts periodic inspections of food businesses. The USDA is required to conduct continuous inspection at meat processing plants.

The Entrée: Agriculture Law and Policy

Historical Background

> **Homestead Act**—federal law that accelerated the settlement of the western territory by granting adult heads of families 160 acres of surveyed public land for a minimal filing fee and five years of continuous residence on that land.

> **U.S. Department of Agriculture (USDA)**—agency responsible for federal regulations regarding agriculture, farming, forestry, and food.

While it has been stated that agriculture, including the domestication of animals, had its origins in the Ice Age, more than 10,000 years ago, within the United States we will start our conversation with the **Homestead Act** of 1862. This Act encouraged settlement in the western United States by providing 160 acres of land to settlers in exchange for a filing fee and five years of residence on the land.[25] Indeed, Thomas Jefferson was a champion of the concept of democratic agrarianism, the notion that our nation needed an agrarian foundation, which encouraged independence and self-reliance.[26] According to the **USDA**, agriculture policy can be categorized into four periods.

In the first period, roughly 1785–1890, the focus of "farm" policy was land distribution and expansion of settlement through numerous private farm operations. The second period, from about 1830 to 1914, focused on improving the productivity of farm operations, through support of research and education. The third period, approximately 1870–1933, ushered in limited regulation of markets, infrastructure improvements, and provision of economic information to help farmers compete. The fourth period, since 1924, focused on direct government intervention to provide farm income support. Whether we are currently in a time of transition toward a new type of policy remains to be seen, but over the last 15 years or so, debate about farm income support policies has accelerated. Movements toward more open global trade, an increasing emphasis on market-driven production decisions, and attention to environmental costs of agricultural production have all influenced current policy discussions.[27]

> **Agricultural exceptionalism**—agriculture is not subject to the same regulations are other industries.

The idea that farms and farmers are central to democracy and thus America, led to policies that reiterated the belief in **agricultural exceptionalism**. For example, agriculture is exempted or given special treatment in the realms of labor law, bankruptcy, anti-trust regulation, and environmental law. Numerous institutions exist solely to promote and serve the interests of the industry, such as the Department of Agriculture, land grant colleges, the Bureau of Reclamation, the Rural Electrification Administration, and the Agricultural Extension Service, amongst others. Furthermore, federal farm programs exist to provide benefits that are unique to agriculture, such as farm insurance, the subsidization of specific crops, farm loan programs, etc. Aside from the historical and often romanticized view of farms, several factors distinguish agriculture from other industries. First, food is a necessity essential for survival. Second, agriculture produces living things, which adds an ecological and ethical component not present in industries that produce inanimate objects. Third, agriculture is dependent on the natural world.[28]

Food for Thought... Agricultural Exceptions to Environmental Laws [Vignette]

Over the last several decades, researchers have documented that factory farms—industrial-style animal agricultural operations—generate and discharge into groundwater, streams, rivers, and the ocean. Likewise, air pollution from factory farms contributes to unhealthy air quality and oppressive, harmful nuisance conditions for nearby residents. As our climate change awareness expands, we also understand the significant greenhouse gases emitted by on-field agriculture (nitrous oxide) and factory farms (methane), with the latter consuming vast amounts of feed produced by the former and simultaneously comprising the leading source of methane emissions in states like California.

The problem is not that agriculture enjoys a *de jure* exemption from Congress, but rather the environmental cops on the beat actually choose non-enforcement. The Clean Air Act, which became law in 1970, has never exempted agricultural sources. After factory farms were held accountable by citizens in the late 1990s and early 2000s, the U.S. EPA under George W. Bush granted 14,000 factory farms a far-ranging amnesty deal in 2005. The EPA was supposed to research and determine whether such sources emitted enough pollution to trigger controls, but the agency failed to follow through and carry out its responsibilities as determined by its own inspector general in 2017. The Clean Water Act passed in 1972 with provisions explicitly subjecting factory farms—termed **Concentrated Animal Feeding Operations**—to industrial source pollution controls. Again, factory farms found an accommodating EPA, which changed its regulations to make permitting and pollution controls effectively nonexistent.

Non-enforcement is bipartisan when it comes to agriculture. President Obama's EPA turned a blind eye to agricultural pollution under the watch of Lisa Jackson and Gina McCarthy. While the EPA embarked on a series of major climate change regulations using its newly found Clean Air Act authority, targeting the power sector, cars and trucks, and new oil and gas wells, the EPA declined to regulate factory farms. As Supreme Court Justice William Brennan famously wrote, "enforcement of the law is what really counts."

Brent Newell, Legal Director
Center on Race, Poverty & the Environment

> Concentrated Animal Feeding Operation (CAFO)—a specific type of large-scale industrial agricultural facility that raises animals, usually at high density, for the consumption of meat, eggs, or milk. To be considered a CAFO, a farm must first be categorized as an animal feeding operation (AFO). An AFO is a lot or facility where animals are kept confined and fed or maintained for 45 or more days per year, and crops, vegetation, or forage growth are not sustained over a normal growing period.

Today, the number of farms and the people employed in the agricultural sector has decreased dramatically.[29] In 1935, farms peaked at 6.8 million. According to the USDA, that number has dropped to around 2 million.[30] According to the Bureau of Labor Statistics, in 2016, agriculture, forestry, huntingm and fishing provided 1.5% of the jobs in the United States (see Figure 8.4)[31] The USDA states that farms contribute about 1% of the U.S. GDP.[32] In 2016, the median pay of agricultural workers, those actually working in the fields or tending to livestock, was $22,540 annually.[33] The overwhelming goal of U.S. agricultural policy has been efficiency, to produce the most food for the least amount of money.

As a result, while the largest number of farms are small family farms, they account for only 24.2% of production.[34] The primary components that have contributed to

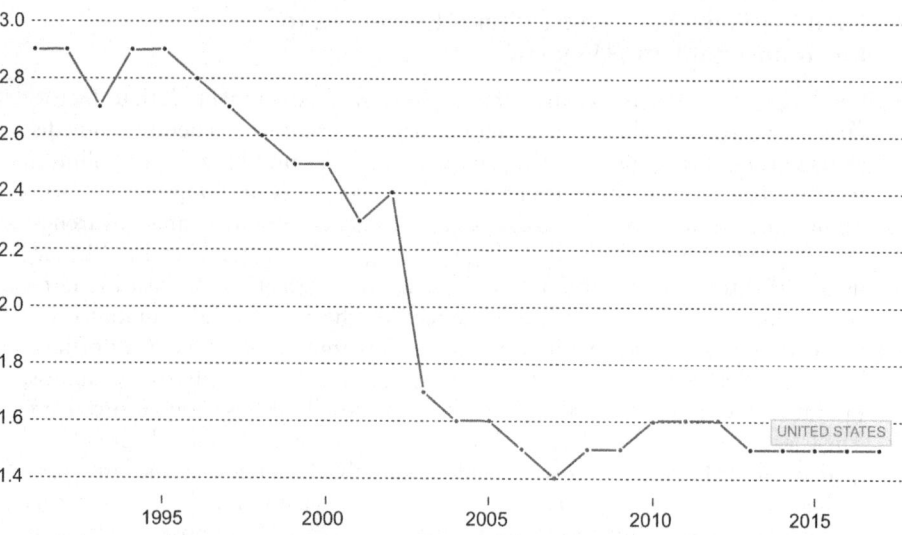

Figure 8.4 Employment in the U.S. Agriculture Sector (1991–2015).
Source: World Bank, International Labor Organization.

the industrialization of agriculture are large-scale production of specialized products (i.e., monoculture); technology (i.e., pesticides, fertilizers, antibiotic use in animals, GMOs, and automation); vertical integration in which various stages of production are controlled by one company (i.e., marketing and production contracts in which the farmer does not own the product); and factory farming (i.e., concentrated animal feeding operations).[35] These themes will be explored throughout this chapter.

Food for Thought . . . Agriculture Policy Overview [Vignette]

Agriculture is a tremendously complex policy area. It affects how we feed our children, what we do to protect the environment, and even the ways we preserve the security of our nation. Before contemplating agriculture's macro effects, though, one must remember a more fundamental principle: Agriculture is not just a business; it is a way of life. A farm is often more a part of a farmer's identity than it is a place on a map. Policymakers must understand the deeply personal nature of farming and ranching before attempting to craft policy.

Anyone wanting a true understanding of agriculture must also eschew preconceived ideas. Farmers aren't relics of the past. They constantly are incorporating the latest technology to better adapt to changing markets, volatile weather, and shrinking revenue margins. As importantly, early technology adoption has afforded farmers to be even better stewards of land and resources.

Effective policy must also account for the unique aspects of agriculture such as region and production sector. In the arid West, our concerns often revolve around water and the vast swaths of our states that are publicly owned, but the top-tier issues for Southern agriculture will be different. Likewise, a production sector's concerns vary. Ethanol incentives may be popular in states with robust corn production, but they could be less well-received by states with wide-scale livestock production, which is dependent on feed prices.

Lastly, agriculture is in a period of change. Never before has the United States produced more food and never before have there been so few people—less than 2% of the population—involved in the process. Americans care passionately about their food, but they may not have the practical context of what it takes to produce it. That creates a vacuum where distrust and half-truths can take root. The nuances of agriculture can't be explained in a soundbite, but misinformation can be. This is agriculture's great challenge, and the stakes are high.

Celia Gould, Director
Idaho State Department of Agriculture

Looking Past Your Plate [Discussion Questions]

1. What are the reasons for and against treating agriculture differently from a legal and policy standpoint? Do you agree that agriculture should be exempted from environmental, labor, and antitrust laws?
2. When you think of a farm, what comes to mind? Do you equate farming with small family farms or industrial-size farms? Why? Which is producing your food?
3. Do you have any experience on a farm or working in agriculture? Do you know anyone else who does?

Major Themes

Regulation and Oversight

There are three primary agencies tasked with regulating food and agriculture:

The **Food and Drug Administration** (FDA) has direct regulatory authority over most of our food system, yet the **Environmental Protection Agency** (EPA) regulates the appropriate use of pesticides, including those applied to food crops. The Department of Agriculture (USDA) has jurisdiction over most meat products, yet the FDA approves and regulates the drugs that can be administered to livestock.[36]

The safety and quality of the U.S. food supply is governed by a highly complex system stemming from at least 30 laws related to food safety that are collectively administered by 15 agencies. The two primary food safety agencies are USDA and FDA. USDA is responsible for the safety of meat, poultry, processed egg products, and, as soon as recently proposed regulations are finalized, catfish. FDA is responsible for virtually all other food, including seafood.[37]

> U.S. Food and Drug Administration (FDA)—agency under the Department of Health and Human Services responsible for federal regulations regarding human and veterinary drugs, vaccines, medical devices, cosmetics, supplements, tobacco, and food (except meat and eggs regulated by the USDA).
>
> Environmental Protection Agency (EPA)—federal agency created to protect human health and the environment, by writing and enforcing regulations.

> **Farm Bill**—an omnibus, multi-year law (renewed every five years) that governs an array of agricultural and food programs. Titles in the most recent farm bill encompassed farm commodity price and income supports, agricultural conservation, farm credit, trade, research, rural development, bioenergy, foreign food aid, and domestic nutrition assistance.

Food for Thought . . . The Farm Bill [Vignette]

If you look at how law affects you on a regular basis in your daily life, the **Farm Bill** is more important than the Constitution. The "Farm Bill" is actually a collection of laws that govern an array of agricultural and food programs. It is re-negotiated in its entirety every five years. The US Department of Agriculture implements the Farm Bill and therefore it is a government agency that wields a lot of power.

The Farm Bill's core programs financially support farms through a "social safety net." This includes programs that ensure that farmers of some crops (such as wheat, corn, soybeans, peanuts, and rice) receive price support against low market prices that would otherwise put farmers out of business. Other programs provide farmers with subsidized insurance. But the Farm Bill's scope is extensive since it also covers things like environmental policy, food stamps, school lunches, foreign aid, international trade, rural economic development and infrastructure, and energy. More recently, the Farm Bill has included provisions to support new farmers, socially disadvantaged farmers, and organic farming.

Because it is regularly renegotiated and covers such a wide scope of issues, the Farm Bill forces different groups to form coalitions that belie regular partisan divisions in U.S. politics. Only recently, however, have a large number of people engaged with the law and politics of the Farm Bill. As a result, there are a host of new ideas. Since the 1970s, the Farm Bill has primarily ensured that agriculture is an industry geared towards producing as much product as possible. Recently, however, different social movements and community groups have come together to push for a different kind of Farm Bill that is instead driven by a national policy focused on providing everyone in the United States with healthy and delicious food.

Michael Fakhri, Associate Professor
University of Oregon School of Law

Looking Past Your Plate [Discussion Questions]

1. *Does it help or hurt food safety to have numerous different government agencies involved in regulating our food system? Why?*
2. *Summarize the Farm Bill in your own words. What programs are included?*

Livestock Production and Slaughter

Year-round mass production of meat in the late 19th century led slaughterhouses to an assembly-line process staffed by unskilled workers, some of whom were children. The four largest meatpackers ("the big four") drew the ire of butchers and ranchers and were accused of being a "beef trust," which essentially controlled the industry as an "unjust monopoly." In the 1880s, Congress began investigating the "beef trust," as well as other anticompetitive practices in sugar, whiskey, and cotton. The Sherman Antitrust Act was passed in 1890. The Justice Department began investigating the meatpacking companies under the Sherman Act in 1902.

In 1906, Upton Sinclair published his book, *The Jungle*. It was inspired by a labor strike between the Amalgamated Meat Cutters and the Butcher Workmen of North

America in 1903. The book relays egregious working conditions within slaughterhouses and is based on Sinclair's own undercover work and interviews with workers. Sinclair had intended to highlight the treatment of the working class and reveal abuses by large businesses; however, instead readers became concerned with slaughterhouses and meat production and consumption specifically. It is estimated that 1 million people read *The Jungle* in its first year of publication. Other nations actually banned the importation of American meat. "Despite Sinclair's focus on the plight of industrial workers and his relative disinterest in the issue of food safety, *The Jungle* would ultimately play a prominent role in the development of American meat regulation."[38]

After *The Jungle*'s release, President Roosevelt initiated investigations of meatpacking plants. Upon findings by the Labor Commissioner consistent with the recitation of circumstances in the novel, Roosevelt called for new legislation. In 1906, the **Meat Inspection Act** and the **Pure Food and Drug Act** were passed, the latter of which led to the creation of the Food and Drug Administration (FDA). In 1921, the **Packers and Stockyards Act** was passed, which goes beyond the Sherman Antitrust Act in "broadly prohibiting monopolistic, unfair, deceptive, and unjustly discriminatory practices" specifically with the marketing of livestock, meat, and poultry.[39] Other relevant statutes related to food safety and inspection include the **Poultry Products Inspection Act** of 1957, which requires mandatory inspection of domesticated birds intended for human consumption; the **Agricultural Marketing Act** of 1946, which provides for voluntary inspection of animals (mostly non-domesticated) by the USDA, even though they are under the purview of the FDA; and the **Egg Products Inspection Act**, passed in 1970.[40]

Humane Treatment of Farm Animals

The USDA's Animal and Plant Health Inspection Service (APHIS) is responsible for enforcing the Animal Welfare Act (AWA; 7 U.S.C. 2131 et seq.), which requires minimum standards of care for certain warm-blooded animals bred for commercial sale, used in research, transported commercially, or exhibited to the public. However, the act excludes farm animals raised for food and fiber from coverage.

The **Humane Methods of Slaughter Act** (7 U.S.C. 1901 et seq.), enforced by the USDA's Food Safety and Inspection Service (FSIS), governs the slaughter and handling of livestock (but not poultry) at packing plants. Also, under the so-called Twenty-Eight Hour Law (49 U.S.C. 80502, last amended in 1994), many types of farm animal carriers "may not confine animals in a vehicle or vessel for more than 28 consecutive hours without unloading the animals for feeding, water, and rest."[41]

According to the Government Accountability Office (GAO), more than 150 million animals are slaughtered annually in the United States as food for human consumption at 800 slaughterhouses. If the animals travel across state borders (i.e., are involved in interstate commerce), the slaughterhouse must have FSIS inspectors on site. These inspectors are supposed to ensure that the animals are humanely treated while in the plant, in accordance with the Humane Methods of Slaughter Act. Once the animals arrive on site, they are to be stunned, so as not to be conscious during slaughter. After they are stunned, they are shackled and hoisted onto the processing line and then bled, before further processing commences. The FSIS has issued guidance as to what treatment is egregious under the Act, which includes skinning or dismembering live animals, beating animals, repeated stunning, dragging conscious animals, running animals over with equipment, etc.

If an inspector determines an egregious act has occurred, they can take a variety of actions, including shutting down the plant. However, a study conducted by the GAO revealed inconsistent enforcement by FSIS inspectors. Individual inspectors have discretion in deciding how to address violations of the Act. The pie chart,

---

Meat Inspection Act—federal law that makes it illegal to adulterate or misbrand meat and meat products sold as food, also ensures sanitary slaughter conditions.

Pure Food and Drug Act—federal law intended to remove harmful and misrepresented foods and drugs from the market, as well as regulate the sale and manufacture of food and drugs sold in interstate commerce.

Packers and Stockyards Act—federal law intended to ensure competition in the livestock, meat, and poultry markets.

Poultry Products Inspection Act—federal law requiring USDA to inspect all domesticated birds intended for human consumption during slaughter.

Agricultural Marketing Act—federal law that established the Federal Farm Bureau. It aims to promote agricultural cooperatives that could stabilize farm prices.

Egg Products Inspection Act—federal law that requires inspection of plants that break, dry, and process shell eggs into liquid, frozen, or dry eff products.

Humane Methods of Slaughter Act—federal law that requires the proper treatment and humane handling of all food animals slaughtered in USDA-inspected slaughter plants. It does not apply to chickens or other birds.

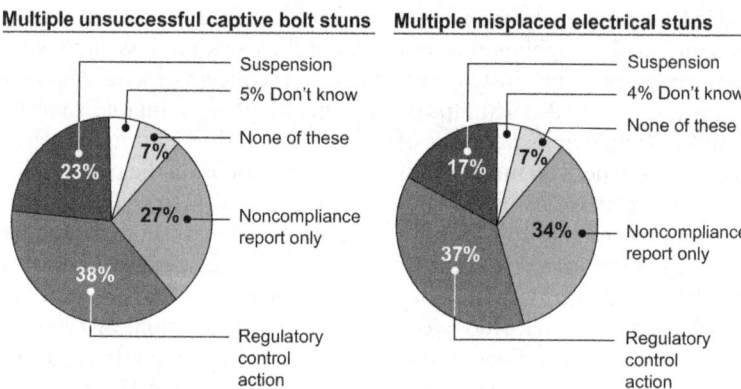

Figure 8.5 Food Safety Inspector Enforcement Actions.
Source: Government Accountability Office.

Figure 8.5, displays the enforcement actions available to an inspector and the significant inconsistency in an inspector's choice of enforcement actions. The GAO study revealed that the inspectors themselves want more guidance and training on appropriate enforcement actions. The GAO concluded:

> It is difficult to know whether the reported incidents of egregious animal handling at the slaughter plants in California and Vermont are isolated cases or indicative of a more widespread problem. Either way, it is evident from our survey results and our analysis of HMSA enforcement data that inspectors did not consistently identify and take enforcement action for humane handling violations for the period we reviewed.[42]

Concentrated Animal Feed Operations (Factory Farms)

As has been referenced throughout this chapter, the longstanding policy in U.S. agriculture has been efficiency, to make more with less. One result of this is the industrialization of farming. Farms are bigger, have less diversity in crops, and utilize techniques commonly associated with factory farming. A concentrated animal feeding operation (CAFO) has a lot of animals in a small area, such as 1,000 cows or 10,000 chickens. You have likely seen a CAFO if you've spent time in California's Central Valley, along Idaho's I-84 highway, or in much of the Midwest. "Large numbers of swine CAFOs are now located in Iowa and North Carolina, dairy CAFOs in California, and broiler chicken CAFOs in Arkansas and Georgia."[43]

Poultry are often kept in long, windowless barns, and the cows are crowded together in dirt lots, feeding through a metal railing. Because there are so many animals in such a close area, numerous environmental issues result, largely from waste, as well as disease among the animals. More than 50% of our meat comes from CAFOs. There are nearly 10,000 CAFOs in the United States. CAFOs produce two times more waste than the entire U.S. human population in one year. CAFOs also do not produce crops. **Environmental justice** issues have also been raised as the people living within the sight and smell of these operations are often poor.

CAFOs produce water and air pollution that harms fisheries and forests, drinking water, and recreational facilities. Other externalities include health problems caused

> **Environmental justice**—the fair treatment and meaningful involvement of all people regardless of race, color, national origin, or income, with respect to the development, implementation, and enforcement of environmental laws, regulations, and policies.

by fine particles that lodge in the lungs, foul odors, and antibiotic-resistant pathogens. All of these problems are caused largely by the excessive numbers and crowding of animals in CAFOs, which result in too much manure in too small an area and the overuse of antibiotics to compensate for the stressful and unsanitary conditions.[44]

Pharmaceuticals in Livestock Production

Livestock production in the United States routinely utilizes antimicrobials, hormones, and beta-agonists. All antibiotics are antimicrobials, which are used to prevent the growth of microorganisms, such as bacteria and viruses. Antimicrobials can be used for medical treatment, but they are often used to increase efficiency (i.e., bigger animals faster) and as a disease preventative. Approximately 60–80% of livestock receive antimicrobials. Roughly half of these compounds are also used to treat disease in humans. Steroidal hormones are also given to livestock to increase their rate of growth, such as estrogen, progesterone, and testosterone. "Dairy cows may receive the genetically engineered hormone, recombinant bovine somatotropin (rBST), often referred to as recombinant bovine growth hormone (rBGH), to increase milk production."[45] Even in 1999, it was reported that 39% of beef weighing below 700 pounds and 82% weighing more than 700 pounds received hormones. Beta-agonists manipulate the metabolism of livestock to increase muscle growth. Approximately, 60–80% of pork and 70% of beef in the United States receive a beta-agonist. It is also used in turkey. "The **Food, Drug, and Cosmetic Act** (FDCA) governs the approval of animal drugs and gives regulatory authority to the Secretary of the Department of Health and Human Services (HHS)."[46]

> Food, Drug and Cosmetic Act—a set of federal laws giving authority to the FDA to oversee the safety of food, drugs, and cosmetics.

Antibiotics are essential to treat infections caused by bacteria, and the rise of antibiotic resistance is one of the biggest threats to global health, according to the World Health Organization (WHO). In 2013, the U.S. Department of Health and Human Services' (HHS) Centers for Disease Control and Prevention (CDC) estimated that antibiotic-resistant bacteria cause at least 2 million illnesses and 23,000 deaths in humans each year in the United States alone. WHO has stated that the emergence and spread of antibiotic-resistant bacteria have been linked to the overuse and misuse of antibiotics in veterinary and human medicine. According to the CDC's website, there is strong evidence that some antibiotic resistance in bacteria is caused by antibiotic use in food animals—dairy and beef cattle, poultry (chicken and turkey), and swine raised for human consumption. Antibiotics are used in food animals to prevent, control, and treat disease as well as to promote efficient growth. Although any use of antibiotics can lead to resistance, certain uses in food animals expose bacteria to low doses of these drugs over a long period. This long-term, low-level exposure to antibiotics may lead to the survival and growth of resistant bacteria, according to the CDC. Also, once the resistant bacteria grow in food animals, they may pass to humans through the consumption or handling of meat, poultry, or other food animal products; contact with animals by farm workers or food processors; or runoff of animal waste into water or soil used for growing food crops. This can lead to foodborne illness, including outbreaks from resistant bacteria in animal products.

Two federal departments are primarily responsible for ensuring the safety of the food supply, including the safe use of antibiotics in food animals—HHS and the U.S. Department of Agriculture (USDA). Within HHS, the Food and Drug Administration (FDA) approves for sale, and regulates the manufacture and distribution of, antibiotics used in animals. Agencies within the USDA, including the Food Safety and Inspection Service (FSIS) and the Animal and Plant Health Inspection Service (APHIS), collect information about antibiotic use and resistance in food animals and educates producers and other users about appropriate antibiotic use, respectively, among other things.[47]

Table 8.3 Agency Efforts Regarding Antibiotic Resistance

Agency	Type of activity	Agency efforts
U.S. Department of Health and Human Services		
Centers for Disease Control and Prevenuon	Data collection, education	Conduct surveillance of antibiotic resistance in foodbome bacteria in ill humans.
		Promote appropriate use of antibiotics in food animals though educational activities.
Food and Drug Administration	oversight, data collection, education	Approve for sale and regulate the manufacture and distribution of antibiotics for food animals.
		Collect and report annual veterinary antibiotic sales data by drug class—a drug may be classified by the chemical type of the active ingredient or by the way it is used to treat a particular condition.
		Conduct surveillance of antibiotic resistance in isolates—a bacterial strain that has been isolated—of foodbome bacteria from retail meat and poultry.
		Promote appropriate use of antibiotics in food animals though educational activities.
U.S. Department of Agriculture (USDA)		
Animal and Plant Health Inspection Service	Data collection. education	Manage periodic, national surveys of producers that focus on animal health, welfare, and production.
		Manage the program that certifies private veterinarians to carry out certain federal animal health programs.
		Promote appropriate use of antibiotics in food animals though educational activities.
Agricultural Research Service	Data collection	Conducted surveillance of antibiotic resistance in food animal isolates of foodbome bacteria (ended by 2013).
		Conduct research on antibiotic resistance, which may include data collection.
Economic Research Service	Data collection	Manage and conduct producer surveys; principally focused on farm finances and also used to track and analyze practices, including antibiotic use.
Food Safety and Inspection Service	Data collection	Conduct inspections at slaughler plants in the United States.
		Conduct surveillance of antibiotic resistance in food animal isolates of foodbome bacteria (started in 2013).
National Agricultural Statistics Service	Data collection	With USDA's Economic Research Service, manage and conduct producer surveys principally focused on farm finances and also used to track and analyze practices. including antibiotic use.

Source: Centers for Disease Control and Prevention.

National Meat Association v. Harris, 132 S.Ct. 965 (2012)

The Federal Meat Inspection Act (FMIA) regulates the inspection, handling, and slaughter of livestock for human consumption. We consider here whether the FMIA expressly preempts a California law dictating what slaughterhouses must do with pigs that cannot walk, known in the trade as nonambulatory pigs.

In 2008, the Humane Society of the United States released an undercover video showing workers at a slaughterhouse in California dragging, kicking, and electro-shocking sick and disabled cows in an effort to move them. The video led the federal government to institute the largest beef recall in U.S. history in order to prevent consumption of meat from diseased animals. Of greater relevance here, the video also prompted the California legislature to strengthen a pre-existing statute (599f) governing the treatment of nonambulatory animals and to apply that statute to slaughterhouses regulated under the FMIA.

Petitioner National Meat Association (NMA) is a trade association representing meat-packers and processors, including operators of swine slaughterhouses. It sued to enjoin enforcement against those slaughterhouses, principally on the ground that the FMIA preempts application of the state law. The District Court granted the NMA's motion for a preliminary injunction, reasoning that 599f is expressly preempted because it requires swine "to be handled in a manner other than that prescribed by the FMIA" and its regulations. But the United States Court of Appeals for the Ninth Circuit vacated the injunction. According to that court, the FMIA does not expressly preempt 599f because the state law regulates only "the kind of animal that may be slaughtered," and not the inspection or slaughtering process itself.

The FMIA's preemption clause sweeps widely—and in so doing, blocks the applications of 599f challenged here. The clause prevents a State from imposing any additional or different—even if non-conflicting—requirements that fall within the scope of the Act and concern a slaughterhouse's facilities or operations. And at every turn 599f imposes additional or different requirements on swine slaughterhouses: It compels them to deal with nonambulatory pigs on their premises in ways that the federal Act and regulations do not. In essence, California's statute substitutes a new regulatory scheme for the one the FSIS uses. Where under federal law a slaughterhouse may take one course of action in handling a nonambulatory pig, under state law the slaughterhouse must take another.

The FMIA's scope includes not only "animals that are going to be turned into meat," but animals on a slaughterhouse's premises that will never suffer that fate. The Act's implementing regulations themselves exclude many classes of animals from the slaughtering process. Swine with hog cholera, for example, are disqualified; so too are swine and other livestock "affected with anthrax." Indeed, the federal regulations prohibit the slaughter of any nonambulatory cattle for human consumption. As these examples demonstrate, one vital function of the Act and its regulations is to ensure that some kinds of livestock delivered to a slaughterhouse's gates will not be turned into meat. Under federal law, nonambulatory pigs are not among those excluded animals. But that is to say only that 599f's requirements differ from those of the FMIA—not that 599f's requirements fall outside the FMIA's scope.

The FMIA regulates slaughterhouses' handling and treatment of nonambulatory pigs from the moment of their delivery through the end of the meat production process. California's 599f endeavors to regulate the same thing, at the same time, in the same place—except by imposing different requirements. The FMIA expressly preempts such a state law. Accordingly, we reverse the judgment of the Ninth Circuit, and remand this case.

For Further Reading: US v. Stevens, 559 U.S. 460 (2010).

Food for Thought . . . Ag-Gag Laws [Vignette][48]

The animal agriculture industry has advocated for the passage of "ag-gag" laws in over half of U.S. states over the past decade. These laws effectively "gag" whistleblowers from disclosing abuses on factory farms by criminalizing undercover investigations of operations and banning recording or distribution of photos, video, or audio (see Figure 8.6).

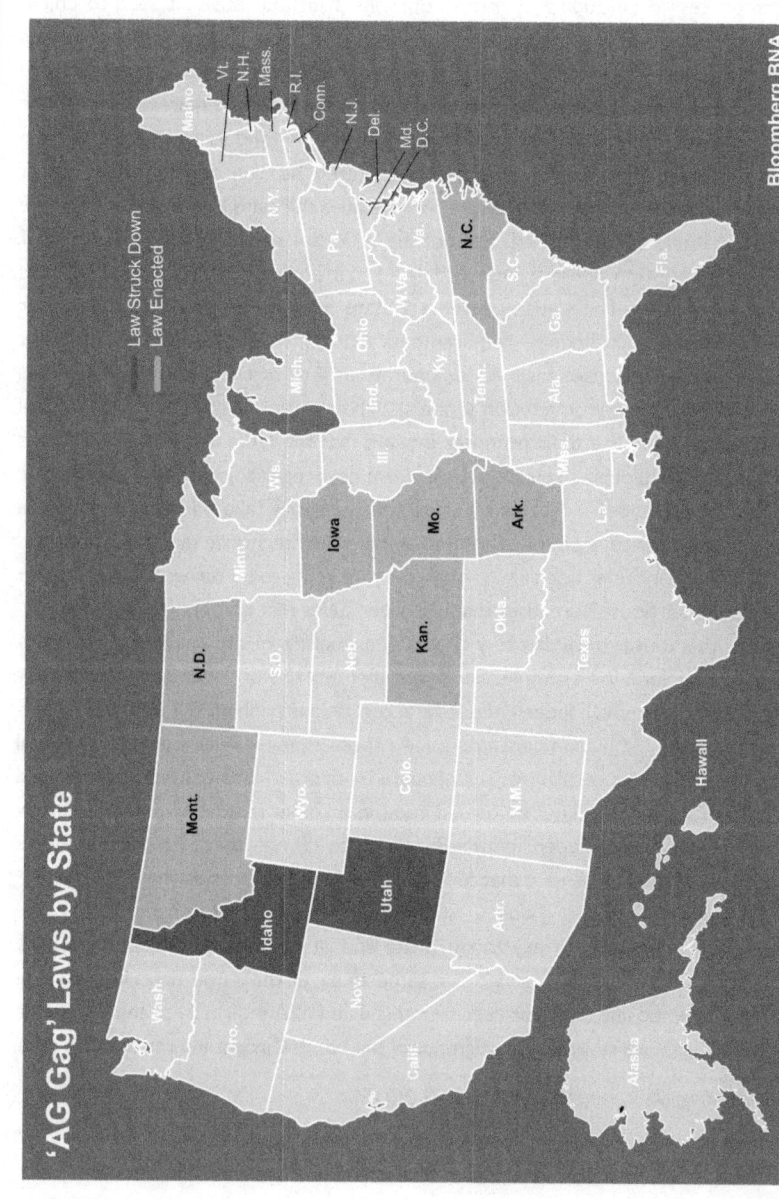

Figure 8.6 Whistleblower Gag Laws.
Source: Bloomberg.

Factory farms, referred to in regulatory terms as "concentrated animal feeding operations" (CAFOs), are industrial facilities in which thousands or even millions of food animals are raised in confinement. Passage of ag-gag laws is a tactic used by the industry to combat investigations that often reveal violations of environmental, food safety, or workplace safety standards—along with severe animal abuse—in factory farms or other industrial agricultural facilities.

In polls, Americans consistently indicate support for humane treatment of food animals, and public outrage over abuses is well justified. The 1906 publication of Upton Sinclair's *The Jungle* has given way to more recent investigations documenting downed cows, dead and rotting hens alongside those laying for human consumption, and the exploitation of poorly trained migrant dairy workers. The ability of citizens to document these abuses increases transparency and compliance to ensure the safety of our food supply and the welfare of food animals.

As of October 2017, ag-gag laws were in effect in seven states but have been ruled unconstitutional under the First Amendment in Idaho, Wyoming, and Utah. Iowa and North Carolina's ag-gag laws are currently under challenge.

Wenonah Hauter, Executive Director
Food & Water Watch

Looking Past Your Plate [Discussion Questions]

1. Are you concerned about the use of antibiotics in your food? Why?
2. What are the reasons for and against laws that preclude videoing or photographing inside of an agriculture facility? Do you agree with these laws? Why?
3. What kinds of regulations do you think are appropriate regarding the treatment and slaughter of livestock?

Genetically Modified Organisms and Pesticides

The Environmental Protection Agency (EPA) is responsible for implementing federal pesticide policies under two statutes: the Federal Insecticide, Fungicide, and Rodenticide Act (FIFRA), governing the sale and use of pesticide products within the United States, and the Federal Food, Drug, and Cosmetic Act (FFDCA), which limits pesticide residues on food in interstate commerce (including imports).

There are an estimated 18,000 pesticide products currently in use. These generally are regulated under FIFRA, but approximately 5,800 pesticide products used in food production also are regulated under the FFDCA, as discussed later. FIFRA requires the EPA to regulate the sale and use of pesticides in the United States through registration and labeling. Pesticides are broadly defined in FIFRA Section 2(u) as chemicals and other products used to kill, repel, or control pests. Familiar examples include pesticides used to kill insects and weeds that can reduce the yield, and sometimes harm the quality, of agricultural crops, ornamental plants, forests, wooden structures (e.g., through termite damage), and pastures.[49]

Numerous policy issues stem from the use of pesticides in agriculture. For example, the use of glyphosate (also known as Roundup), which is a commonly used herbicide on crops. Its widespread use has led to the development of genetically modified crops so that the herbicide can be sprayed directly onto the crops and kill everything but them. Of course, as discussed, this results in issues with cross-contamination due to cross-pollination and then patent issues. Approximately 93% of U.S. soybean crops and 85% of U.S. corn crops are genetically modified. Much like with the overuse of antibiotics, resulting in antibiotic-resistant super bugs, the widespread use of glyphosate has led to "super weeds." As of 2014, 14 such super weed species had been identified, which result in crop loss. The WHO has categorized glyphosate as "probably carcinogenic to humans."[50]

Another major policy issue stemming from the widespread use of pesticides in agriculture is the impact on bee health:

> Reports worldwide indicate that populations of managed honey bees, wild bees, and native bees have been declining, with colony losses in some cases described as severe or unusual. Other reports indicate that many insect pollinator species may be becoming rarer, which some say may be a sign of an overall global biodiversity decline.
>
> Since 2006, USDA estimates that bee colony losses have averaged nearly 30% annually. . . . Reasons cited for bee population declines include a wide range of possible factors. Potential identified causes include bee pests and diseases, diet and nutrition, genetics, habitat loss and other environmental stressors, agricultural pesticides, and beekeeping management issues.
>
> Studies have shown that bees are exposed to pesticides in many ways throughout the foraging period: from planter exhaust material produced during the planting of treated seed; from the soil of both planted and unplanted fields; in flowers growing near these fields; as well as applications in or near bee hives. Pesticides are reported to have adverse local impacts on honey bees and some native bees. Widespread use of herbicides reduces habitat available to bees; many pesticides are known to be lethal to bees, given sufficient levels of exposure; and some reports of local bee kill incidents have been well documented.[51]

In addition to these policy issues, pesticides also create long-term negative health effects for farmworkers. Worker Protection Standards (WPS)

> limit the application of pesticides when workers are present in the fields, provides time requirements for re-entry into a treated area, requires protective equipment in certain circumstances, mandates signage for treated areas, and requires training for workers who may be exposed to pesticides and who apply pesticides, and mandates access to decontamination resources.[52]
>
> EPA has reported that of the 1.2 billion pounds of pesticides used in the United States annually, 76 percent, or about 950 million pounds, is used in the agriculture industry. According to EPA, farmworkers are among the primary populations exposed to these pesticides. . . . The Department of Labor estimates that there are about 2.5 million hired farmworkers and that about 1.8 million of them work on crops. . . . [R]esearchers at the National Cancer Institute have reported that farmworkers and their children are frequently exposed to potentially carcinogenic pesticides. . . . Some studies have reported associations between pesticide exposure

and a range of chronic effects on humans, including fetal deaths and deformities, cancers, and neurological and developmental effects.[53]

Food for Thought... Crop Cross-Contamination [Vignette]

Although U.S. federal agencies approve **genetically engineered** (GE) crops for cultivation and human consumption, there are gaps in the legal framework for dealing with other risks from GE crops. Due to the licensing agreements required by GE patent holders, farmers bear much of the legal risk when GE crops cross-pollinate compatible non-GE crops.

Patent infringement liability is one legal risk for farmers who find GE material on their land due to cross-contamination. After *OSGTA v. Monsanto* (2013), Monsanto was ordered to not sue farmers whose fields had less than 1% patented material; however, higher levels of contamination are likely and can give rise to a lawsuit. In *Bowman v. Monsanto* (2013), the U.S. Supreme Court found that a farmer who knowingly planted GE seeds was liable for patent infringement, but noted that the law may view innocent cross-contamination differently in a future case. At this time the uncertainty in future enforcement results in non-GE farmers bearing the risk of cross-contamination.

Non-GE farmers whose crops are contaminated may also lose organic certification or access to export markets. They may turn to state common law of torts (negligence, trespass, nuisance) to sue their GE crop-producing neighbors as the source of contamination. Because GE license agreements shift all risks of use to the GE farmer, they bear the risk of legal liability, costs of litigation, and strife between neighbors.

Current contract, patent, and tort law allocates risks arising from GE cross-contamination, but there is still considerable uncertainty in how future lawsuits will be resolved. State or federal policy could be designed to equitably allocate the risk between GE creators, GE growers, and non-GE growers such that all growers are free to choose their production practices and markets without uncertainty about legal liability.

Christy Anderson Brekken, Instructor
Oregon State University

> **Genetically Modified Organism (GMO) or Genetically Engineered (GE)**—a GMO is an organism whose genome has been altered by the techniques of genetic engineering so that its DNA contains one or more genes not normally found there. Note: A high percentage of food crops, such as corn and soybeans, are genetically modified.

Vernon Bowman v. Monsanto Company, 133 S.Ct. 1761 (2013)

Vernon Bowman is a farmer in Indiana. He purchased Roundup Ready each year, from a company affiliated with Monsanto, for his first crop of the season. Bowman, however, devised a less orthodox approach for his second crop of each season. Because he thought such late-season planting "risky," he did not want to pay the premium price that Monsanto charges for Roundup Ready seed. He therefore went to a grain elevator; purchased "commodity soybeans" intended for human or animal consumption; and planted them in his fields. And because most of those farmers also used Roundup Ready seed, Bowman could anticipate that many of the purchased soybeans would contain Monsanto's patented technology. When he applied a glyphosate-based herbicide to his fields, he confirmed that this was so; a significant proportion of the new plants survived the treatment, and produced in their turn a new crop of soybeans with the Roundup Ready trait. Bowman saved seed from that crop to use in his late-season planting the next year—and then the next, and the next, until he had harvested eight crops in that way.

After discovering this practice, Monsanto sued Bowman for infringing its patents on Roundup Ready seed. Bowman raised patent exhaustion as a defense, arguing that Monsanto could not control his use of the soybeans because they were the subject of a prior authorized sale (from local farmers to the grain elevator). The District Court rejected that argument, and awarded damages to Monsanto of $84,456. The Federal Circuit affirmed.

The doctrine of patent exhaustion limits a patentee's right to control what others can do with an article embodying or containing an invention. Under the doctrine, "the initial authorized sale of a patented item terminates all patent rights to that item." And by "exhaust[ing] the [patentee's] monopoly" in that item, the sale confers on the purchaser, or any subsequent owner, "the right to use [or] sell" the thing as he sees fit. Consistent with that rationale, the doctrine restricts a patentee's rights only as to the "particular article" sold; it leaves untouched the patentee's ability to prevent a buyer from making new copies of the patented item. Bowman himself disputes none of this analysis as a general matter: He forthrightly acknowledges the "well settled" principle "that the exhaustion doctrine does not extend to the right to 'make' a new product."

Unfortunately for Bowman, that principle decides this case against him. Under the patent exhaustion doctrine, Bowman could resell the patented soybeans he purchased from the grain elevator; so too he could consume the beans himself or feed them to his animals. Monsanto, although the patent holder, would have no business interfering in those uses of Roundup Ready beans. But the exhaustion doctrine does not enable Bowman to make additional patented soybeans without Monsanto's permission. And that is precisely what Bowman did. He took the soybeans he purchased home; planted them in his fields at the time he thought best; applied glyphosate to kill weeds; and finally harvested more beans than he started with. Because Bowman thus reproduced Monsanto's patented invention, the exhaustion doctrine does not protect him.

Our holding today is limited. In another case, the article's self-replication might occur outside the purchaser's control. Or it might be a necessary but incidental step in using the item for another purpose. In the case at hand, Bowman planted Monsanto's patented soybeans solely to make and market replicas of them, thus depriving the company of the reward patent law provides for the sale of each article. Patent exhaustion provides no haven for that conduct. We accordingly affirm.

For Further Reading: Monsanto v. Geertson Seed Farms, 561 U.S. 139 (2010); *Bates v. Dow Agrosciences*, 544 U.S. 431 (2005).

Organic Standards

Organic labeling is regulated by the USDA's Agriculture Marketing Service (AMS). Organic farming did not really take off until the late 1980s, because prior to that the system that existed supported conventional agriculture. At the outset, because of a lack of action at the federal level, organic farming had success at the state level (see Figure 8.7). New York, California, Maine, and Connecticut were leaders in organic legislation. By 1990, 26 states had acted regarding organic legislation. This number

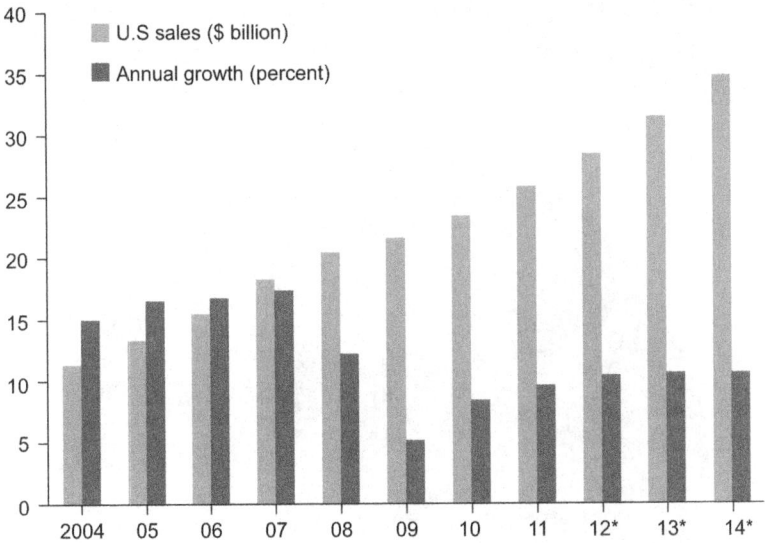

Figure 8.7 U.S. Organic Food Sales (2005–2014).
Source: U.S. Department of Agriculture.

grew to 38 by 2010. Additionally, there was a push for self-regulation amongst some farming organizations.

The U.S. Congress acted in 1990 with the **Organic Foods Production Act** (OFPA) as part of the Farm Bill. The OFPA did not preclude state efforts, but instead required accreditation via third-party certifications. The USDA proposed rules in 1997. The National Organic Program (NOP) was officially implemented in 2002. There are numerous roles for the states to play in organic certification. First, states can apply to operate their own organic program, which would allow states to have more stringent standards. Second, states can become certifying agents; as of 2013, 16 states were accredited certifying agents. Third, states can participate in cost-sharing programs.

"Organically produced food cannot be produced using the products of genetic engineering, sewage sludge, or ionizing radiation. Most synthetic chemicals, including fertilizers are prohibited."[54] When transitioning to organic farming, the land cannot be treated with pesticides, herbicides, or synthetic fertilizers for three years. Livestock cannot be treated with hormones or antibiotics, and medical treatment can only be utilized in the event of illness. The feed must also be organic.[55]

> Organic Foods Production Act— federal law that authorizes the National Organic Program (NOP) to be administered by the USDA. NOP is the regulatory framework governing organic food.

Looking Past Your Plate [Discussion Questions]

1. *Had you heard of GMOs before? Do you have any concerns about eating genetically modified food? Why?*
2. *Do you agree that the government should issue patents on living organisms? Why?*
3. *Do you agree that the living conditions of organic animals should be different than those of conventional or non-organic animals for human consumption? Why?*

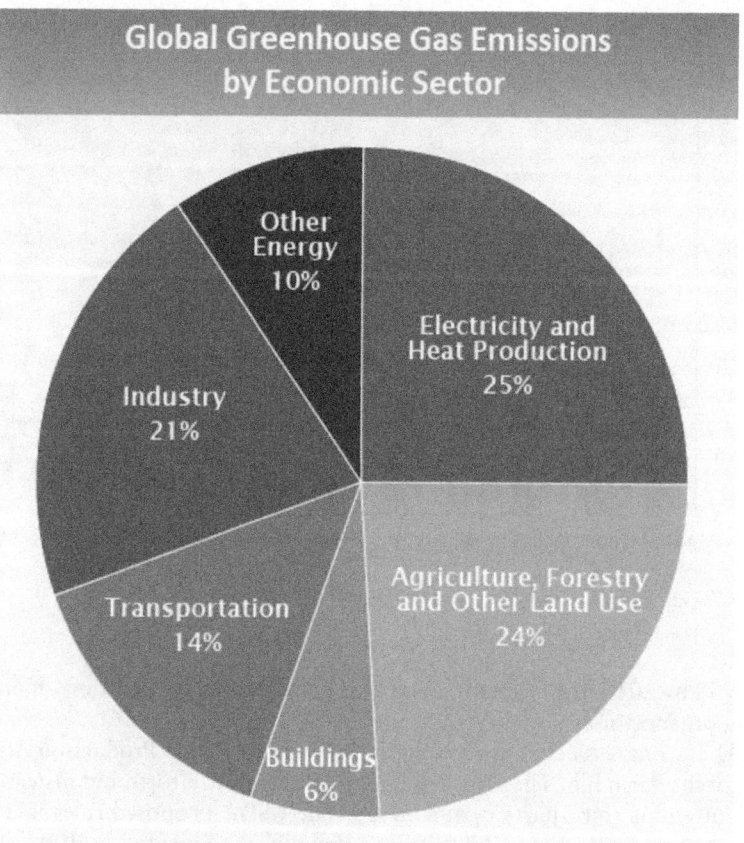

Figure 8.8 Greenhouse Gas Emissions by Economic Sector.
Source: IPCC (2014).

Other Significant Issues

Ag and Climate Change

The overwhelming consensus in the scientific community is that the climate is warming and that human activities are the cause, due to greenhouse gas emissions (GHGs) (see Figures 8.8 and 8.9). Agriculture plays both a cause and effect role in climate change. First, agriculture is a source of GHGs. Emissions from agriculture are estimated to range from 51%[56] of worldwide GHG emissions to 18%, which is greater than the transportation sector.[57]

> The two key types of GHG emissions associated with agricultural activities are methane (CH_4) and nitrous oxide (N_2O). Agricultural sources of CH_4 emissions mostly occur as part of the natural digestive process of animals and manure management at livestock operations; sources of N_2O emissions are associated with soil management and fertilizer use on croplands. . . . Emissions from agricultural activities account for 6%-8% of all GHG emissions in the United States.[58]

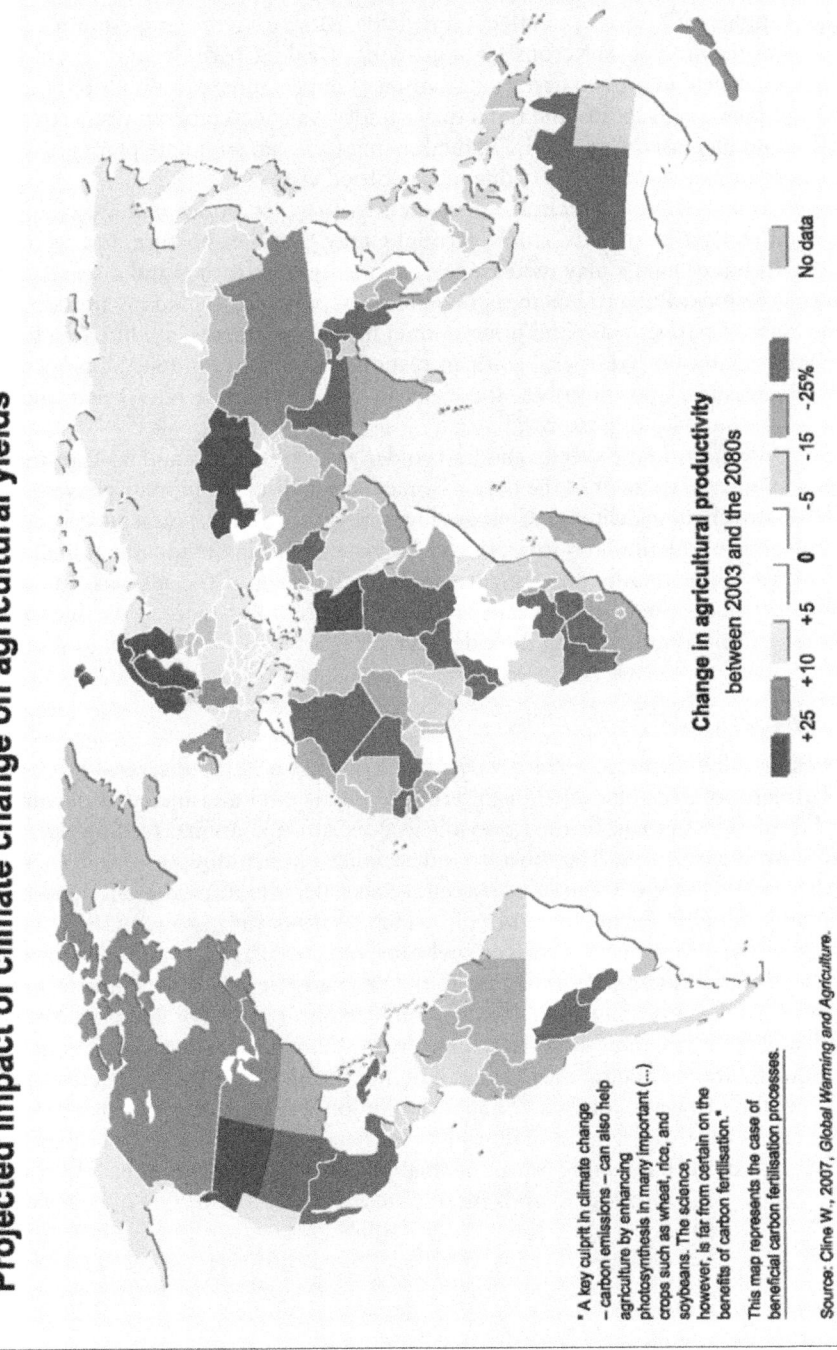

Figure 8.9 Greenhouse Gas Emissions by Source.
Source: IPCC (2006).

Secondly, the agricultural sector is impacted by climate change. From drought, to floods, to other natural disasters, agriculture is very susceptible to the impacts of climate change. Changes are expected to crops, livestock, and fisheries. According to the EPA,

> Higher CO_2 levels can affect crop yields. More extreme temperature and precipitation can prevent crops from growing. Dealing with drought could become a challenge in areas where rising summer temperatures cause soils to become drier. Many weeds, pests, and fungi thrive under warmer temperatures, wetter climates, and increased CO_2 levels. Though rising CO_2 can stimulate plant growth, it also reduces the nutritional value of most food crops.
>
> Heat waves, which are projected to increase under climate change, could directly threaten livestock. Drought may threaten pasture and feed supplies. Climate change may increase the prevalence of parasites and diseases that affect livestock. Potential changes in veterinary practices, including an increase in the use of parasiticides and other animal health treatments, are likely to be adopted to maintain livestock health in response to climate-induced changes in pests, parasites, and microbes. Increases in carbon dioxide (CO_2) may increase the productivity of pastures, but may also decrease their quality.
>
> Many aquatic species can find colder areas of streams and lakes or move north along the coast or in the ocean. Some marine disease outbreaks have been linked with changing climate. Changes in temperature and seasons can affect the timing of reproduction and migration. Many steps within an aquatic animal's lifecycle are controlled by temperature and the changing of the seasons. In addition to warming, the world's oceans are gradually becoming more acidic due to increases in atmospheric carbon dioxide (CO_2).[59]

Biodiversity and Monoculture

Historically, farmers raised a variety of livestock and grew several types of crops. Farmers rotated the crops on different tracts of land and included pasture land in the rotation. As you learned previously, concentrated animal feeding operations do not grow any crops. The move to industrialized agriculture has resulted in a system that, while more efficient, also encourages a reduction in biodiversity and the rise of mono-cropping (or **monoculture**), in which a farmer only grows massive amounts of one or two crops, such as corn or soybeans, often that are genetically engineered to be resistant to pesticides. With regard to the raising of livestock, often the farm will only raise one species of animal in massive, confined operations. The animals do not graze at all and sometimes may not ever go outside. In addition to concerns over animal welfare, industrialized agriculture also raises a number of environmental concerns, such as the generation of waste and water and air pollution. Furthermore, this change in farming practices has had a significant impact on farmers. As agribusiness has become vertically integrated, the bargaining power of small or independent farmers has decreased.[60]

Monoculture—the cultivation of a single crop in a given area.

For Further Reading: *Corporate Agriculture: JEM AG Supply v. Pioneer Hi-Bred*, 534 U.S. 124 (2001).

Labor and Immigration

Immigration and labor issues are particularly relevant to agriculture. Many of the people who work in the fields, slaughterhouses, and livestock operations are immigrants. The Fair Labor Standards Act did not protect farmworkers until 1966. The Migrant and Seasonal Agricultural Worker Protection Act was passed in 1983.

However, concerns over immigration and labor policies regarding farmworkers remain present. Concerns within the industry over the deportation of workers remain in the news and garnered much national attention after the 2016 presidential election. Though this chapter cannot adequately discuss both of these issues, consider the extent to which you rely on farms for your food and who the workers are that make sure your food reaches your plate.

Food for Thought . . . Gender, Labor, and Food Systems [Vignette]

Gender is an analytical tool that is often left out of agricultural and food (agrifood) scholarship and policy. However, women are actively engaged in the agrifood system, including as laborers, and experiences within the agrifood system can be highly gendered. For instance, research has demonstrated that women still remain predominantly responsible for the labor of food provisioning in the United States, as well as globally. Food provisioning refers to the work of providing food for families, and includes planning meals, acquiring food, preparing meals, and cleaning up after meals. In addition to this work within the household, women are also often actively engaged in labor in the agrifood system outside of the home. For instance, women are increasingly acting as farm operators, particularly on small-scale farms. Farmwork is becoming increasingly feminized, as women make up a greater share of those who labor in agricultural fields in the United States and beyond. And women labor in restaurants, grocery stores, and food processing facilities. In each of these types of agrifood labor there are potential benefits, including economic benefits, but also challenges. These challenges include lower well-being associated with being responsible for work in both the public and private spheres (e.g., working a second shift), often working in unsafe conditions, and more broadly dealing with gender inequality in the workplace.

Although women play such an important role as laborers in the agrifood system, and face potentially unique (or gendered) challenges, most agrifood policies are written from a gender-neutral standpoint. While the subjects of policy are often referred to in gender-neutral terms, like workers, individual, or family, the implications of policy are far from gender neutral. Looking forward we need to pay greater attention to the ways in which experiences within the agrifood system are gendered, and the role that public policy and law can play in shaping the lives of individuals and communities in the United States and beyond.

Rebecca L. Som Castellano, Assistant Professor
Boise State University

Looking Past Your Plate [Discussion Questions]

1. *Do you think there are categories of workers that should not be protected by labor laws? Why?*
2. *How much of your food plays a role in climate change? Do different kinds of food (like meat versus vegetables) have a different impact on the environment? Why?*

286 Food and Agriculture Law and Policy

Global Context

Food and agricultural policy are not solely of national concern. Due to trade, the policies of the United States and other trading partners have global impact. From labeling to the use of GMOs and antibiotics and hormones, there are many issues contested on a global scale. While this chapter has primarily looked at law and policy impacts domestically, this section offers a snippet into their implications worldwide, including on trade via trade agreements and in disputes at the World Trade Organization (WTO).

Food for Thought . . . Agriculture and Trade [Vignette]

The importance of trade to American agriculture is hard to overstate. At the national level, more than a quarter of ag production is exported, which contributes to a significant agricultural trade surplus (see Figure 8.10). Trade is perhaps disproportionately important for very rural states like Montana, where much more food is produced than can be consumed. When 95% of potential buyers are outside of the U.S. borders, access to foreign markets is essential for the success of an industry that is the backbone of rural America.

A trade agreement is the primary mechanism for opening up foreign markets. The goal of a trade agreement is to reduce or eliminate tariff and non-tariff barriers to trade, thereby making exports between those countries more competitive as compared to domestic production or other foreign imports. Each country sets tariffs for all imports, including agricultural imports. With

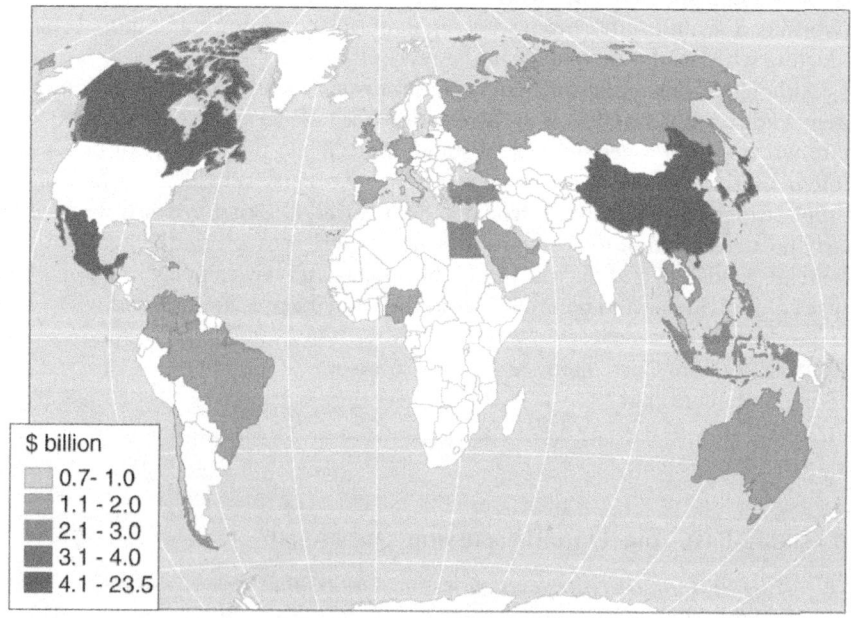

Figure 8.10 Top U.S. Agricultural Export Destinations.
Source: U.S. Department of Agriculture, Economic Research Service.

the goal of either raising revenues or protecting their domestic production, tariffs, especially if they are inappropriately high, reduce demand for foreign products by making them more expensive than goods produced domestically.

Aside from tariffs, every country sets up import restrictions that are intended to protect health and the environment. For example, consumers expect that imported food is produced with the same food safety standards that are applied to domestic food. Similarly, restrictions are put in place to protect against unwanted pests or disease that may have an impact on the environment or on human or animal health. While these sanitary and phytosanitary (SPS) measures are necessary to protect health or the environment, they may also be used to restrict imports, even in the absence of tariffs. For this reason, trade agreements set up requirements around the implementation of SPS measures to ensure that they are not simply barriers to trade disguised as safety measures.

Trade agreements are ultimately political agreements in that they are created through often years of negotiations by the executive branch, and must then be ratified by the legislature in order to come into effect. Once an agreement is in place, enforcement and compliance of that agreement is a matter of law. Lawyers working for the government, private industry, and special interest groups engage in either courts of law, arbitration, or trade tribunals to ensure all signatories to the agreement comply with the terms. Without meaningful enforcement and compliance efforts, any trade agreement will fail to fully advance trade.

Benjamin Thomas, Director
Montana Department of Agriculture

The United States and the European Union (EU) have disputed the EU's ban on beef from cows treated with hormones since the 1980s. This dispute has resulted in numerous appearances before the WTO. While the EU continues to ban the hormone-treated beef, the United States has been permitted to retaliate against the EU by imposing various tariffs on products imported from the EU. The Congressional Research Service (CRS) provides a comprehensive chronology of this dispute starting in 1981 and concluding in 2013.[61] A summary of the dispute is provided as follows:

> Starting in 1981, the EU adopted restrictions on livestock production limiting the use of natural hormones to therapeutic purposes, banning the use of synthetic hormones, and prohibiting imports of animals and meat from animals that have been administered the hormones. In 1989, the EU fully implemented its ban on imports of meat and meat products from animals treated with growth promotants. Initially the ban covered six growth promotants that are approved for use and administered in the United States. The EU amended its ban in 2003, permanently banning one hormone—estradiol-17β—while provisionally banning the use of the five other hormones.
>
> The United States has suspended trade concessions with the European Union by imposing higher import tariffs on EU products. The first U.S. action in 1989 imposed retaliatory tariffs of 100% ad valorem duty on selected food products, and remained in effect until 1996. The second U.S. action in 1999 again imposed a 100% ad valorem duty on selected foods from EU countries.

Over the years, the United States and the EU have attempted to resolve this dispute through a series of WTO dispute consultations, settlement panels, arbitration proceedings, and formal appeals. One of the earlier WTO panel decisions in 1997 ruled against the EU on the grounds that the ban is inconsistent with the EU's WTO obligations under the Sanitary and Phytosanitary (SPS) Agreement because the EU had not conducted a risk assessment. In response, the EU commissioned studies and reviews to address the scientific basis of its ban on hormone-treated meat. Following each of these reviews, the EU reaffirmed its position that there are possible risks to human health associated with hormone-treated meat, given the available scientific data. The EU claims it has complied with its WTO obligations and has challenged the United States for maintaining its prohibitive import tariffs on EU products. The United States disputes whether the EU has conducted an adequate risk assessment to support its position and maintains there is a clear worldwide scientific consensus supporting the safety to consumers of eating hormone treated meat. In October 2008, the WTO issued a mixed ruling allowing the United States to continue its trade sanctions, but allowing the EU to maintain its ban.[62]

For Further Reading: International Food Security Indicators, www.ers.usda.gov/topics/international-markets-trade/global-food-security/interactive-chart-international-food-security-indicators/

Conclusion

Food and agriculture law and policy are large, complex areas that cannot be adequately explained in depth in one textbook chapter. We hope this chapter has opened your eyes to the numerous legal and policy issues of the day. If this subject has been of interest to you, we invite you to review the Additional Learning Resources. Food is so important to our lives that we actually organize our day around eating. It is the focal point of most of our holidays and special events. We invite you to consider the ethical choices you make every time you sit down for a meal.

In America, September is Hunger Action Month. October is National Farm to School Month. In 1937, we began celebrating National Milk Month every June, now known as National Dairy Month. Food is always on our calendar—and on our national agenda. At best, this chapter offers you a menu of policy debates and issues, literally from farm to fork. Where *our* food comes from, where *your* food comes from; how *we* eat, how *you* eat, and how others are fed—may this survey serve a feast for further thought. Bon Appétit.

Dessert: Digging In—Exercises

1. You want to open a small corner grocery in an underserved area in your community. Use the USDA website "Retailers Information" pages (www.fns.usda.gov/snap/retail-store-eligibility-usda-supplemental-nutrition-assistance-program) to determine what requirements your store must meet to be able to sell to shoppers using SNAP benefits for their purchases.

    - Discuss these requirements in terms of food and nutrition assistance policies.
    - Discuss these requirements in terms of their impact on your business.

2. You are part of a product design team that is charged with developing a new energy drink. The product must qualify for purchase with SNAP benefits, but

must also meet consumer demand for foods that are healthy, convenient, and natural. Use the USDA website for "Eligible Foods" (www.fns.usda.gov/snap/eligible-food-items) to research both content and packaging requirements for your product.

- Discuss these requirements in terms of food and nutrition assistance policies.
- Discuss these requirements in terms of food choices and current consumer trends.

3. Open your preferred social media site. Review photos and posts from the previous two months. Count the number of entries that involve food. How many of those entries:

   - Involve preparing or eating something that was home-cooked?
   - Involve eating out at a restaurant or in another group environment (like a cafeteria)?
   - Involve or include a nationally branded food item, product, or provider?

   Discuss how your own eating habits and choices are impacted by food policy "from farm to fork." Identify one area or theme from this chapter that might change the way you eat, and why.

4. Do you have a favorite family recipe or dish that dates back generations? Research the origins of the dish, including the person or persons who that dish is associated with and when they lived. Ingredient by ingredient, which items do you think might have been obtained with "Blue" Food stamps during the Depression Era? Which with "Orange" stamps? *(Alternative version: Instructor finds several vintage recipes online and distributes them to students.)*

5. How close is your nearest CAFO? Starting with that map, use state, county, or local government agency resources to find a CAFO in your area. As you research, make note of each obstacle or challenge you faced in finding the facility. Was it easy to identify? Should it be? Should these facilities be indicated by highway or other road signage, the way historical and recreational sites are posted? Imagine such a sign or posting that would provide public information about these food sources. What should it include?

6. Research media coverage regarding immigration and customs enforcement (ICE) enforcement actions at food production or farm facilities. Analyze the impact of those actions on the business owner, the industry, and the community.

7. Research media coverage of labor conditions at food production or factory-farm facilities. Do you think there are categories of workers that should not be protected by labor laws? Why or why not?

8. Research the history of various food movements in the United States since the end of the Civil War. Can you recognize any of your own beliefs about food in the precepts of a prior movement or activist? How do your beliefs align with (or differ from) current food policy in the United States?

Notes

1. Ana Julia Harris & Shoshana Walter, *They Thought They Were Going to Rehab: They Ended Up in Chicken Plants*, Reveal from the Center for Investigative Reporting, www.revealnews.org/article/they-thought-they-were-going-to-rehab-they-ended-up-in-chicken-plants/
2. Jeff Della Rosa, *Poultry Producer Simmons Tops Private Companies List in Northwest Arkansas, for Smith Areas*, Northwest Arkansas Business Journal (2017), https://talkbusiness.net/2017/07/poultry-producer-simmons-tops-private-companies-list-in-northwest-arkansas-fort-smith-areas/

3. S. Schneider, *Moving in Opposite Directions? Exploring Trends in Consumer Demand and Agricultural Production*, 43 Mitchell Hamline L. Rev. 400 (2017).
4. *Id.*
5. Michael Pollan, *In Defense of Food* (2008).
6. Julie Caswell & Ann Yaktine, *Supplemental Nutrition Assistance Program: Examining the Evidence to Define Benefit Adequacy* (2013).
7. U.S. Department of Agriculture, *Supplemental Nutrition Assistance Program (SNAP)* (Washington, DC: U.S., 2017), www.fns.usda.gov/snap/short-history-snap
8. Julie Caswell & Ann Yaktine, *Supplemental Nutrition Assistance Program: Examining the Evidence to Define Benefit Adequacy* (2013), https://doi.org/10.17226/13485
9. J.C. Ohls & H. Beebout, *The Food Stamp Program: Design Tradeoffs, Policy, and Impacts: A Mathematica Policy Research Study* (1993).
10. *Lyng v. Castillo*, 477 U.S. 635 (1986).
11. J.C. Ohls & H. Beebout, *The Food Stamp Program: Design Tradeoffs, Policy, and Impacts: A Mathematica Policy Research Study* (1993).
12. *Id.*
13. *Id.*
14. *Id.*
15. North Dakota State University, *Milestones in U.S. Food Law*, 2017, www.ag.ndsu.edu/foodlaw/overview/history/milestones
16. W. Janssen, *The Story of the Laws Behind the Labels* (1981).
17. *Id.*
18. *Id.*
19. A. Kamps & A. Perez, *What's Cooking, Uncle Sam? The Government's Effect on the American Diet*, 2014, www.archives.gov/publications/ebooks/whats-cooking.html
20. North Dakota State University, *Milestones in U.S. Food Law*, 2017, www.ag.ndsu.edu/foodlaw/overview/history/milestones
21. B. Marler, *MarlerBlog*, 2015, www.marlerblog.com/2015/09/page/3/
22. Attorney Bill Marler is a personal injury and products liability attorney. He began litigating foodborne illness cases in 1993, when he represented Brianne Kiner, the most seriously injured survivor of the Jack in the Box *E.coli* bacterial outbreak. Under the auspices of the non-profit Outbreak, Inc., Bill spends much of his time traveling to address food industry groups, fair associations, and public health groups about foodborne illness litigation and issues surrounding it. He is a frequent writer on topics related to foodborne illness.
23. Lloyds Register Quality Assurance, www.lrqausa.com/Certification/FDA-Food-Safety-Modernization-Act-FSMA/
24. Richard Bonanno has served as President of the Massachusetts Farm Bureau, as a member of the American Farm Bureau Board, as Chair of Science Policy for the regional and national weed science societies, and served on the Scientific Advisory Board for the Massachusetts Secretary of Environmental Affairs. Rich Bonanno also owns and, for 27 years, operated his family's vegetable and bedding plant farm north of Boston. During those same years, he was an Educator for UMass Extension specializing in both weed management and on-farm food safety practices.
25. Library of Congress, Primary Documents in American History: Homestead Act, www.loc.gov/rr/program/bib/ourdocs/Homestead.html
26. R. Kirkendall, *Up to Now: A History of American Agriculture from Jefferson to the Revolution to Crisis*, in S. Schneider (Ed.), *Food, Farming, and Sustainability: Readings in Agricultural Law* 3–4 (1987).
27. A. Effland, *U.S. Farm Policy: The First 200 Years*, 2000, www.farmlandinfo.org/sites/default/files/US_Farm_Policy_March_2000_1.pdf
28. Susan Schneider, *A Reconsideration of Agricultural Law: A Call for the Law of Food, Farming, and Sustainability*, 34 William and Mary Environmental Law & Policy Review 935–963 (2010).
29. Food and Water Watch, *Factory Farm Nation 2015 Edition*, www.foodandwaterwatch.org/sites/default/files/factory-farm-nation-report-may-2015.pdf
30. USDA, Census of Agriculture, www.agcensus.usda.gov/Publications/2012/Online_Resources/Highlights/Farm_Demographics/
31. Bureau of Labor Statistics, *Employment by Major Industry Sector*, www.bls.gov/emp/ep_table_201.htm

32. USDA, Economic Research Service, *Ag and Food Sectors and the Economy*, www.ers.usda.gov/data-products/ag-and-food-statistics-charting-the-essentials/ag-and-food-sectors-and-the-economy/
33. Bureau of Labor Statistics, *Occupational Outlook Handbook*, www.bls.gov/ooh/farming-fishing-and-forestry/agricultural-workers.htm
34. USDA, *Farming and Farm Income*, www.ers.usda.gov/data-products/ag-and-food-statistics-charting-the-essentials/farming-and-farm-income/
35. Susan Schneider, *Food, Farming, and Sustainability: Readings in Agricultural Law* (2016).
36. Susan Schneider, *Examining Food Safety from a Food Systems Perspective: The Need for a Holistic Approach*, 2014 Wisconsin Law Review 397, 397–419 (2014).
37. Government Accountability Office, *Federal Food Safety Oversight* (2011).
38. D. Moss & M. Campasano, *The Jungle and the Debate over Federal Meat Inspection in 1906*, Harvard Business Review, N9–716–045 (2016).
39. C. Kelley, *Introduction to the Packers and Stockyards Act*, in Susan Schneider, *Food, Farming, and Sustainability: Readings in Agricultural Law* 442–464 (2003).
40. G. Becker, *Meat and Poultry Inspection: Background and Selected Issues* (2010).
41. T. Cowan, *Humane Treatment of Farm Animals: Overview and Issues* (2011).
42. Government Accountability Office, *Humane Methods of Slaughter Act* (2010).
43. Union of Concerned Scientists, *CAFOs Uncovered: The Untold Costs of Confined Animal Feeding Operations* (2008).
44. Id.
45. Susan Schneider, *Beyond the Food We Eat: Animal Drugs in Livestock Production*, 25 Duke Environmental Law & Policy Forum, 227, 227–280 (2015).
46. Id.
47. Government Accountability Office, *Antibiotic Resistance* (2017).
48. P. Hayes, *Fate of 'Ag Gag' Laws May Ride on Utah, Idaho Cases*, Bloomberg BNA (2017), www.bna.com/fate-ag-gag-n73014463296/
49. L. Schierow & R. Esworthy, *Pesticide Law: A Summary of the Statutes* (2012).
50. Susan Schneider, *Food, Farming and Sustainability: Readings in Agricultural Law* (2016).
51. R. Johnson, *Bee Health: The Role of Pesticides* (2015).
52. Id.
53. Government Accountability Office, *Pesticides* (2000).
54. Susan Schneider, *Food, Farming and Sustainability: Readings in Agricultural Law* (2016).
55. H. Pitman, *A Legal Guide to the National Organic Program*, The National Agricultural Law Center (2011), http://nationalaglawcenter.org/wp-content/uploads/assets/articles/pittman_organicprogram.pdf
56. World Watch, *Livestock and Climate Change*, 2009, www.worldwatch.org/files/pdf/Livestock%20and%20Climate%20Change.pdf
57. Food and Agriculture Organization, *Livestock's Long Shadow*, United Nations (2006). Also see, www.fao.org/climatechange/41521-0373071b6020a176718f15891d3387559.pdf
58. R. Johnson, *Climate Change: The Role of the U.S. Agriculture Sector* (2009).
59. EPA, *Climate Impacts on Agriculture and Food Supply* (2017).
60. Susan Schneider, *Food, Farming and Sustainability: Readings in Agricultural Law* (2016).
61. R. Johnson, *The U.S.-EU Beef Hormone Dispute* (2015).
62. Id.

Additional Learning Resources

Additional Readings

1. National Food and Agriculture Law Center, http://nationalaglawcenter.org/research-by-topic/
2. Susan Schneider, *Food, Farming and Sustainability: Readings in Agricultural Law* (North Carolina: Carolina Academic Press, 2016). Also see, www.foodfarmingsustainability.com/
3. Food Politics by Marion Nestle, www.foodpolitics.com/
4. Animal Legal Defense Fund, *Taking Ag-Gag to Court*, http://aldf.org/cases-campaigns/features/taking-ag-gag-to-court/

5. Food and Water Watch, *Factory Farm Map*, http://factoryfarmmap.org/
6. Last Week Tonight with John Oliver, *Chickens*, https://youtu.be/X9wHzt6gBgI
7. Neal Fortin, *Food Regulation: Law, Science, Policy, and Practice* (NJ: Wiley, 2009).
8. Theodore Feitshans, *Agricultural and Agribusiness Law: An Introduction for Non-Lawyers* (New York: Routledge, 2016).
9. Vandana Shiva, *Seed Sovereignty, Food Security* (CA: North Atlantic Books, 2016).
10. Maryn McKenna, *Big Chicken: The Incredible Story of How Antibiotics Created Modern Agriculture and Changed the Way the World Eats* (Washington, DC: National Geographic Partners, 2017).
11. Mette Vaarst, et al., *Animal Health and Welfare in Organic Agriculture* (MA: CABI, 2004).
12. Matthew Garcia, *From the Jaws of Victory: The Triumph and Tragedy of Cesar Chavez and the Farm Worker Movement* (Berkeley, CA: University of California Press, 2012).
13. Tim Josling, et al., *Food Regulation and Trade: Toward a Safe and Open Global System* (Washington, DC: Institute for International Economics, 2004).
14. Temple Grandin, *Improving Animal Welfare 2nd Edition: A Practical Approach* (MA: CABI, 2015).
15. Frontline, *The Trouble with Chicken*, www.pbs.org/wgbh/frontline/film/trouble-with-chicken/
16. Frontline, *Rape in the Fields*, www.pbs.org/wgbh/frontline/film/rape-in-the-fields/
17. PBS, *Dirty Birds: A Story of Chickens in America*, www.pbs.org/video/original-fare-dirty-birds-story-chickens-america/
18. Kathryn Peters, *Keeping Bees in the City? Disappearing Bees and the Explosion of Urban Agriculture Inspire Urbanites to Keep Honeybees: Why City Leaders Should Care and What They Should Do about It*, 17.3 Drake Journal of Agricultural Law 597–644 (2013).
19. Jeffrey M. Berry, *Feeding Hungry People: Rulemaking in the Food Stamp Program* (Rutgers University Press, 1984).
20. Ali Berlow, *The Mobile Poultry Slaughterhouse: Building a Humane Chicken-Processing Unit to Strengthen Your Local Food System* (North Adams, MA: Storey Publications, 2013).
21. Recommended documentaries:

    a. Food Inc., www.takepart.com/foodinc/index.html
    b. King Corn, www.kingcorn.net/
    c. Forks Over Knives, www.forksoverknives.com/
    d. Cowspiracy, www.cowspiracy.com/
    e. Food Chains, www.foodchainsfilm.com/
    f. Fed Up, http://fedupmovie.com/#/page/home

9 Environmental Law and Policy

Inara Scott

Opening Case: Children Sue to Stop Climate Change

In 2015, an unusual group of plaintiffs, with ages ranging from eight to nineteen,[1] filed a bombshell case. In their complaint, they alleged that the federal government was taking actions that were contributing to a variety of negative health impacts, including increases in allergies, asthma, cancer, cardiovascular disease, stroke, heat-related deaths, foodborne diseases, injuries, and toxic exposures.[2] Furthermore, they claimed, the federal government's actions were threatening basic requirements for human health—things like "clean air, pure water, sufficient food, and adequate shelter"[3]—as well as jeopardizing the United States' national security.[4] If action was not taken to change current policies, their complaint alleged, the very survival of the plaintiffs and future generation was threatened.[5]

The basis of the complaint, of course, was climate change. The actions complained about were the federal government's support of the fossil fuel industry and failure to implement policies to restrict carbon dioxide and greenhouse gas emissions. By failing to address climate change—and even exacerbating it through policies that provided subsidies for the fossil fuel industry—the plaintiffs claimed that the government was infringing on their fundamental rights to life, liberty, and property.

While the impacts of climate change the plaintiffs pointed to may sound dire, they were by no means exaggerated. In the Fourth National Climate Assessment, released in November 2017, the U.S. Global Change Research Program (USGCRP) concluded that global average temperatures increased 1.8°F from 1901–2016, and are projected to increase up to 11.9°F by 2100. The cause of this warming was an increase in greenhouse gas emissions, which accumulate in the atmosphere and act as a sort of heat-trapping blanket around the earth. As the USGRCP concludes, "For the warming over the last century, there is no convincing alternative explanation" for changes to the climate other than human activity.[6] Most alarmingly, the report emphasizes that "unanticipated and difficult or impossible-to-manage" changes are increasingly likely as climate events multiply and key thresholds are crossed.[7]

Global climate change, already occurring, will bring significant impacts to U.S. and global communities. Global average sea levels are expected to increase between 1–4 feet by 2100, and a rise of 8 feet *cannot be ruled out*,[8] putting megacities such as Shanghai, Bangkok, Miami, and Tokyo at risk and potentially displacing millions. The changing climate will cause increases in extreme weather events, flooding, forest fires, and drought. The negative impact of climate change on a variety of health conditions has been well documented and includes an increase in heat-related deaths, increased risks for cardiovascular and respiratory illnesses, and increases in illness such as Lyme disease and water-related infections.[9]

With this sobering backdrop, the lawsuit raises questions that go to the very heart of the relationship between the government, individual citizens, and the environment. Does the U.S. government owe citizens a duty to maintain a "stable climate system capable of sustaining human life"? Does the Due Process Clause of the U.S. Constitution and the fundamental right to liberty prohibit the federal government from taking actions that threaten the long-term sustainability of the planetary system? Even if the answers to these questions is yes, is a court of law the right place to compel the government to act, or must citizens wait and rely on legislatures to act on their behalf?

Beyond these big-picture questions, the lawsuit raises other, more specific questions that run through much of the study of environmental law. If someone pollutes the air that I breathe, or cuts down trees in a forest where I occasionally hike, do I have a right to sue? What if I cannot show that I have been physically injured, or that my property has been damaged? How can laws and courts account for damages that may occur generations in the future? Should laws protect species, landscapes, or ecosystems based purely on their value to people, or do they have some inherent worth the law should recognize? How can we place an economic value on a beautiful view? How should scientific studies, including those lacking absolute certainty, be incorporated into legal proceedings?

History of Environmental Law

The study of environmental law and policy encompasses all of these questions and many more. But what exactly is **environmental law**? What does it include and how has it evolved?

Environmental law—a broad area of law that governs the interactions between human beings and their environment, including the regulation of pollution, natural resources, chemical use and disposal, and the clean-up of hazardous waste. Environmental law includes international treaties, and federal, state, and local laws and regulations.

Most people, when asked to describe environmental law, would probably point to laws like the Endangered Species Act, which seeks to protect threatened and endangered species and their habitat, or the Clean Water Act, which limits the dumping of pollutants into public waterways. Indeed, while there is no single definition of environmental law, at a minimum, studies of environmental law generally include those laws and policies addressing the use and preservation of the natural environment and the plants and animals that inhabit it. The focus of many environmental statutes is limiting pollution, whether that is pollution to air, land, or water. Environmental statutes today regulate the use and disposal of toxic and hazardous substances; the use of public lands, coastal areas, and natural resources like fisheries; and the development of urban open spaces, parks, and recreation.

The scope of environmental laws continues to grow over time. More recently, the regulation of the energy industry, including the extraction of fossil fuels and generation of electricity, which was once considered a separate field, has been included in the larger discussion of environmental law and policy. Many consider laws related to animal welfare and the regulation of property development—for example, zoning laws—to be environmental law as well.

The growth in the scope and nature of what we might call environmental law reflects the history of the field. For much of the early history of the United States, Americans looked upon the wilderness as something to be conquered. As Aldo Leopold said in 1918, "a stump was our symbol of progress." The government's role with regard to the environment was to hand out land—including that taken by force, fraud, or coercion from native peoples[10]—and encourage development.

Yet by the same token, many recognized that the identity of the United States was bound up in its wilderness. Popular American icons, including John Muir, Henry David Thoreau, and George Perkins Marsh, brought national attention to the impact of humans on their environment, and argued for the preservation of wilderness as a part of the essential character of America. As John Muir argued in an 1897 article advocating for the passage of federal statutes to protect U.S. forests,

> The forests of America, however slighted by man, must have been a great delight to God; for they were the best he ever planted. The whole continent was a garden, and from the beginning it seemed to be favored above all the other wild parks and gardens of the globe.[11]

A desire to protect iconic U.S. lands did result in what has been called America's "best idea"[12]—the preservation of large tracts of land purely for scenic enjoyment. In 1864, in the midst of the Civil War, President Lincoln signed a bill to protect the Yosemite Valley and Mariposa Grove of Giant Sequoias from development. The first official national park, however, was created in 1872, when President Ulysses S. Grant signed legislation to set aside the land that would become Yellowstone. In 1906, with the strong support of President Theodore Roosevelt, the passage of the Antiquities Act created protection for archeological sites on public lands. Roosevelt, a dedicated outdoorsman, hunter, and conservationist, went on to extend the reach and authority of the Antiquities Act to create the first "national monument" in 1907—the Grand Canyon.

While these early days did establish a framework for the preservation of wilderness areas, the environmental law movement as it is currently known can most closely be linked to the work of a woman writing about the impact of commonly used chemicals on songbirds, insects, and human health. In 1962, Rachel Caron's book *Silent Spring* shook many people in America as it exposed the danger of exposure to DDT, a powerful pesticide that had been widely applied for many years for insect control. Carson's research showed that the indiscriminate use of DDT had significant impacts on wildlife, particularly birds, and also on human health. Carson died of breast cancer in 1964. *Silent Spring* is widely credited with drawing national attention to concerns about the use of pesticides, as well as sparking a national conversation about the limitations and dangers of relying on chemicals to reshape the natural world and ensure human "progress."

The publication of *Silent Spring* came in the midst of a post–World War II era that saw massive expansion of industries creating a variety of pollutants, including toxic and hazardous wastes. Though industrialization brought improvements to the standard of living for many Americans, the negative health effects of industrialization became impossible to avoid. In 1948, a weather inversion trapped a cloud of smog over Donora, Pennsylvania, resulting in a toxic soup of pollution so thick that visibility in the town was reduced to zero. The Donora Death Fog, as it was later named, killed 20 people and sickened over 7,000. In 1952, a similar fog killed thousands in London—up to 12,000, according to a recent study.[13] Hundreds more died in New York City in 1966.

The waters of the United States were similarly, visibly, polluted. Waste, including raw sewage and industrial pollutants, was commonly disposed directly into waterways. The Cuyahoga River was so heavily polluted that it caught fire a number of times, most notoriously in 1969, becoming a symbol of environmental degradation. Other rivers were similarly contaminated. In 1970, the Department of Health, Education, and Welfare found that 30% of drinking water samples contained unsafe levels of chemicals. In the Hudson River, bacteria levels were reported at 170 times the safe limit.[14] In 1969, an enormous oil spill—at the time, the largest in U.S. history—near the city of Santa Barbara, in Southern California, coated miles of coastline, killed thousands of birds and marine mammals, including dolphins, seals, and sea lions, and sparked a debate over the future of offshore oil drilling along the California coast.

As concern about the effects of pollution grew, environmental organizers worked to bring national attention to the problem. On April 22, 1970, the first Earth Day, inspired in part by the Santa Barbara oil spill, surprised everyone with a turnout of over 20 million throughout the country. Recognizing environmental protection as an increasingly popular issue among Americans, President Nixon came to champion environmental protection. In July 1970, he proposed the establishment of a single federal agency to oversee the creation and administration of environmental law and regulation, and to strengthen fragmented environmental enforcement within the federal government.[15] Congress approved the agency and the appointment of its first administrator, William D. Ruckelshaus, in late 1970. Ruckelshaus, who served twice as the head of the Environmental Protection Agency (once under Nixon and again under President Ronald Regan) was sworn in on December 4, 1970, and a new era of environmental regulation was begun.

In quick succession, a number of environmental statutes were passed, including the Clean Air Act (CAA, 1970), the Clean Water Act (CWA, 1972) and the Endangered Species Act (ESA, 1973). Support for environmental regulation was strikingly bipartisan, as Democrats and Republicans alike embraced the need to address the unmistakable environmental crises. The Clean Air Act passed in the Senate on a vote of 73–0. An only slightly more moderate version of the bill passed the House on a vote of 374–1.[16]

The flurry of statutes passed in the 1970s continued at a blistering pace, with an emphasis on the management and conservation of species and land for future generations. Congress passed laws to protect marine mammals (Marine Mammal Protection Act, 1972); encourage the development of coastal management plans (Coastal Zone Management Act, 1972); require plans for the management of national forests (National Forest Management Act, 1976); protect the health of the public by regulating the production, use, importation, and disposal of chemicals (Toxic Substances Control Act, 1976); and regulate, on a "cradle-to-grave" basis, the generation, production, and disposal of hazardous wastes (Resource Conservation and Recovery Act, 1976).

Most of these statutes, which today form the backbone of environmental law, operate on a *proactive* basis, using regulatory controls, planning, and management to limit pollutants and ensure resources will be preserved into the future. However, a crisis that erupted in the late 1970s required a different sort of response. In the neighborhood of Love Canal, in the city of Niagara Falls, residents discovered that their homes and children's schools had been built upon the site of a former chemical waste dumpsite—and that toxic wastes had been leaching for years into their homes, playgrounds, and backyards. Studies found high levels of cancer-causing chemical in the air, water, and soil. Residents experienced liver and kidney damage and high rates of birth defects and miscarriages. Chromosome damage was found in more than one-third of residents.

It took determined activism by journalists and a local resident, Lois Gibbs, to uncover the extent of the problem and to shame public officials into taking action to address it. Eventually over 700 families had to be relocated. In 1978, President Carter was forced to declare Love Canal a federal health emergency and direct the first-ever use of federal funds to assist in an emergency other than a natural disaster. Clean-up of the site was extensive, costing hundreds of millions of dollars.

In this case, a proactive approach to eliminate *future* disasters wasn't enough. Instead, Congress drew up a law called the Comprehensive Environmental Response, Compensation, and Liability Act (CERCLA), also known as the Superfund Act. CERCLA created a *retroactive* liability scheme that imposed strict liability (liability without fault or negligence) for the clean-up of sites contaminated with hazardous wastes on a wide group of potentially responsible parties, including owners, former owners, and people who arranged for the disposal of hazardous wastes.

A unique feature of almost all of these environmental statutes was the inclusion of citizen suit provisions. A citizen suit provision allows individual citizens or citizen groups to sue either a private individual or the government for violating environmental laws, or for failing to carry out a duty prescribed by a law. In some cases, the person bringing the suit can even recover their attorney fees or other costs of enforcement. Thus, under the Clean Air Act, a private citizen can sue an individual or business she believes is violating limits on emissions of toxic substances. She can also sue the EPA for failing to make or enforce rules as the statute requires. Citizen suits are often facilitated by mandatory reporting requirements. Under laws such as the Clean Water Act, those who dump pollutants into waterways are required to keep and post records of their dumping; this information may be useful to activists if permits are violated, chemicals are found in places where they are not allowed, or the amount of pollutants exceeds the regulated limits.

* * *

> Quite often, we think of relationships between environmental regulators and businesses as adversarial, and sometimes that traditional view is accurate. But business-regulator relationships are also often collaborative, and those collaborative relationships have played a huge part in improving our environmental quality in many ways at the same time our economy has grown.[17]
> —Dave Owen, University of California Hastings School of Law

* * *

Even as the environmental law movement took off in the 1970s, however, there were cracks in the façade. Some who supported the new environmental legislation weren't fully prepared for its impacts, and litigation began to test the boundaries of the new laws. In 1978, the Supreme Court decided *Tennessee Valley Authority v. Hill*,[18] a case that pitted a tiny endangered fish, the snail darter, against the Tellico Dam, a project on which over $100 million had already been spent and was nearing completion.

Evidence suggested that completion of the dam would wipe out the last remaining habitat for the snail darter, causing it to go extinct. Supporters of the dam felt that the project should be completed anyway, based on the money that had already been spent and the potential benefit of the dam in producing electricity. The Supreme Court found that the Endangered Species Act contemplated precisely this type of conflict between human development and species preservation, and that it was intended to make species preservation the ultimate priority. It found no room in the statute for exceptions, including those based on economics or cost-benefit analyses:

> It may seem curious to some that the survival of a relatively small number of three-inch fish among all the countless millions of species extant would require the permanent halting of a virtually completed dam for which Congress has expended more than $100 million.... We conclude, however, that the explicit provisions of the Endangered Species Act require precisely that result.... Concededly, this view of the Act will produce results requiring the sacrifice of the anticipated benefits of the project and of many millions of dollars in public funds. But examination of the language, history, and structure of the legislation under review here indicates beyond doubt that Congress intended endangered species to be afforded the highest of priorities.[19]

Ultimately, Congress passed an exception to the law for the Tellico Dam project and the dam was completed, but the Endangered Species Act became a symbol of the conflict between human development and the preservation of non-human species. Many would say it symbolized the *overreach* of environmental laws, in putting the needs of animals and plants above those of landowners and communities.

Other fights would follow, gradually reversing the bipartisan agreement over the need for increased environmental protection and the benefit of government regulation. In particular, President Ronald Reagan's Administration was openly hostile to

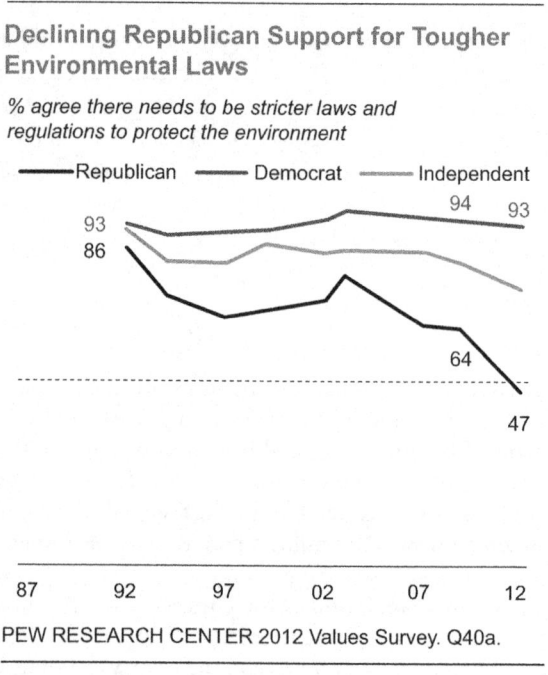

Figure 9.1 Partisan Polarization Surges in Bush, Obama Years.

Source: Pew Research Center (Jun. 4, 2012), www.people-press.org/2012/06/04/partisan-polarization-surges-in-bush-obama-years/

environmental regulation and began seeking ways to push back against environmental policies they saw as limiting business and economic growth.

One issue in particular became a focal point and lightning rod for the dispute between the parties: climate change. Though scientists began to link increased levels of carbon dioxide (CO_2) to the warming of the earth in the 1800s, national and international attention became focused on the issues in the 1980s. In 1983, the U.S. National Academy of Sciences and the EPA both issued reports warning of potentially dangerous consequences from global warming. Meanwhile, the 1992 United Nations Framework Convention on Climate Change (UNFCCC) was the first major international treaty to address climate change. The UNFCCC set into motion subsequent international climate change agreements, including the 1997 Kyoto Protocol and Paris Agreement of 2015.

***

My generation—the millennials—watched while we passed legislation to address acid rain, and signed global agreements to fix the ozone hole. We thought that surely we'd be able to fix climate change, especially since we knew we were the cause. Three decades later, sadly, we haven't been able to do that. We don't need any more reports or assessments detailing the problem despite massive disinformation campaigns meant to undermine scientific credibility. We need to talk solutions. We know it's real. We know it's us. I still have hope.
—Kathie Dello, Associate Director of Oregon Climate Change Research Institute

***

In less than three decades, fueled by arguments over regulation and climate change, a small gap between Republicans and Democrats turned into a chasm. In 1987, 61% of Republicans and 50% of Democrats agreed that government regulation of business usually does more harm than good; in 2012, that nine-point gap had turned into a 35-point gap. In 2016, 58% of Republicans said stricter environmental laws hurt the economy and cost too many jobs, while only 17% of Democrats agreed (from 39% (R) and 29% (D) in 1994).[20]

From 1992 to 2012, support for greater regulation to protect the environment dropped 41 percentage points among Republicans.[21] By 2017, environmental protection—and climate change in particular—had become one of the most divisive public policy issues in the United States. Perhaps as a result, CERCLA remains the last major piece of environmental legislation passed by the U.S. Congress. Since its passage in 1980, the only major changes that have occurred in the field have been made through regulation and litigation.

In summary, this short history of environmental law emphasizes the following points:

1. Environmental law is wide-ranging and covers a variety of areas, but deals primarily with the control of pollution and the management of natural resources.
2. Environmental law is overwhelmingly statutory and regulatory. While the second decade of the 2000s brought a resurgence of interest in older, **common law**

> Common law—law that derives primarily from precedent developed from previous judicial decisions.

doctrines to fight climate change, such as the public trust doctrine, control of pollution and the management of natural resources still take place primarily through laws and complex regulations.
3. Lawsuits and litigation are central to environmental enforcement, with a high level of participation by private individuals and activist groups.
4. Environmental protection and climate change are areas of significant political dispute.
5. Environmental law is both national and international in scope. National divides over environmental policy, and the impacts of U.S. environmental actions on international parties, make environmental regulation particularly challenging.

Environmental law is a broad and complex field. Instead of trying to introduce or describe all of the major environmental laws, this chapter focuses on major themes and policy conflicts. By presenting a small number of key court cases and a brief description of two of the most important environmental laws, this chapter seeks to describe how the field of environmental law is organized and the way it operates.

Discussion Questions

As you read the rest of this chapter, consider the following questions:

1. *Silent Spring* (1962) was published during a period of enormous economic growth—sometimes called the Golden Age of Capitalism—that began following the end of World War II in 1945 and ended with a recession in the United States that began in 1973. Why do you think significant economic growth might be accompanied by increasing environmental regulations?
2. *Compare and contrast:* China and India have seen significant economic growth and rising per capita incomes in the past two decades, while major cities in these countries are often choked by crippling pollution and smog. Have these countries seen a similar wave of environmental regulation as was seen in the United States? Research the history of environmental regulation in these countries. Find a copy of the Chinese documentary film *Under the Dome* by Chai Jing,[22] which was widely compared to *Silent Spring*, and learn a little about the history and impact of the film. What happened after the film was released? What impact has it had on Chinese environmental law and regulation?
3. A major challenge of environmental law is illustrated by the snail darter case, which pitted a tiny fish against a massive dam. Environmental regulators must frequently decide how to balance the growth and profits of an industry against individual health and the development of public lands. A 2013 study concluded that air pollution leads to 200,000 early deaths each year in the United States.[23] A 2015 study found that air pollution was the leading contributor to early death worldwide. Does this mean we need stricter environmental laws? How do we decide when environmental regulation is enough? How "clean" do you think the environment should be? How "safe" is safe enough?
4. Climate change is increasingly seen as a political, not simply a scientific, debate. Similarly, debates over environmental regulations increasingly break on political lines. As the results of pollution and climate change can be catastrophic for people both within and outside the United States, what strategies do you think could help bridge the partisan gap over environmental policies?

5. The plaintiffs described in the introductory case study were neither the first nor the last group of children to challenge government inaction over climate change. Research some of these cases and find out how the children have fared. What does their success—or lack thereof—tell you about how effective current laws are as a tool for preventing future environmental damage?

Keep in mind that this case only addresses the direct impacts of climate change on these particular plaintiffs. Climate change also has a number of indirect impacts. Increased drought, loss of arable lands, extreme weather events, and impaired access to food and fresh water can lead to increased migration and an escalation of national and international conflicts. For this reason, the U.S. Department of Defense has labeled climate change a "threat multiplier" that can "enable terrorist activity and other forms of violence."[24]

Major Themes in Environmental Law and Policy

Overview

Human societies are utterly dependent on the natural environment. From the food they grow to the water they drink to the air they breathe, without a healthy environment, human societies cannot function. If the essence of effective public policy is the manner in which a government chooses to act (or not act) to ensure the health and welfare of its citizens, then public policy cannot be separated from environmental policy. When natural resources are clean and abundant, the need for government intervention is small; as resources become threatened or constrained, the need for intervention increases.

A government's ability to ensure economic growth and prosperity is a fundamental aspect of effective public policy. **Natural capital**—including air, water, soil, and all manner of natural resources—is essential to economic growth. If we think of the economy as being dependent on the society in which it functions, we can also think

> Natural capital—value provided from natural resources, including clean air, water, soil, plants, and living organisms.

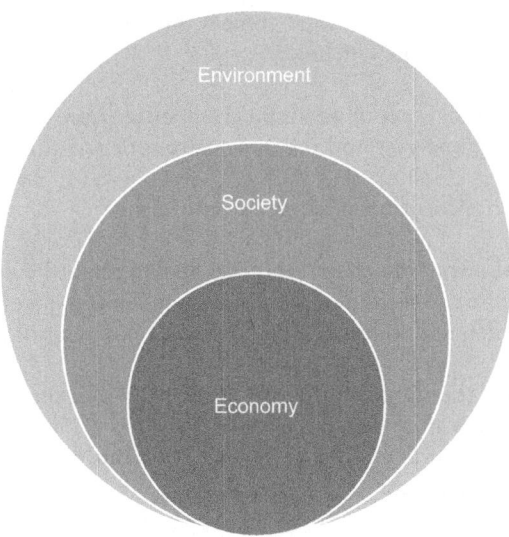

Figure 9.2 Highlighting the centrality of environmental policy in public policy.

about society as being dependent on the environment. Thus while many position the environment as one aspect of public policy, and economics as a separate aspect of public policy, it may be more helpful to think of public policy—and economics in particular—as being nested within environmental policies.

It should come as no surprise that as the population of the earth has increased and access to natural resources had become constrained, environmental policy has become an area of increasing interest and controversy. This is true on a national and international level. Many of the earth's resources are shared; if one nation pollutes the ocean or depletes a fish population, other nations are also impacted. The centrality of environmental policy to all public policy, at both a national and international level, is becoming clear in the early 21st century. This is particularly true as the specter of climate change and its related challenges—water shortages, loss of arable land to drought and changing weather patterns, sea level rise—threatens nations on an existential level.

Faced with both the undeniable challenge and need to determine effective environmental policy, it can be helpful to break down the study of environmental policy into three "buckets" of issues. We might call the first bucket the foundational of environmental policy. The questions we wrestle with here include:

- What steps should the government take to regulate the use of shared public resources?
- How should a society balance protection of human and non-human interests?
- What actions should a government take today to preserve the availability of resources for future generations?
- How should society balance individual property rights with impacts on non-property owners?

Based on the answer to these foundational questions, regulators must then determine what specific strategies will be adopted to implement fundamental policy choices. We might lump these strategic choices into a second bucket. Key strategic choices in environmental policy include:

- use of market-based vs. command-and-control measures;
- use of cost-benefit analyses and the integration of economic and non-economic data; and
- use of science to inform or guide decision-making.

As environmental laws take shape, the last bucket might be said to include the administrative details of adopting, implementing, and enforcing environmental policies. These issue, which are no less central to the development of policy, include:

- Who should have the right to bring a lawsuit related to the use or development of natural resources they do not own?
- What role should courts play in reviewing decisions by agencies like the EPA or the U.S. Forest Service?

Rather than thinking of these three types of issues as a linear, or even circular, process, it is important to note that environmental policy is continually being reconsidered and reshaped as elements within one bucket shift or change. For example, in

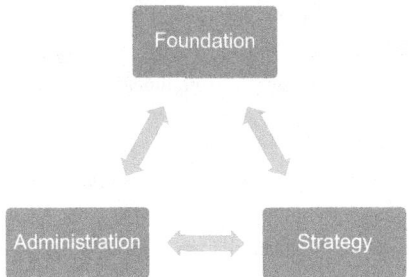

Figure 9.3 The interrelated linkages in environmental strategy and policymaking.

a time of unconstrained resources, public policy choices may weigh heavily in favor of private landowner rights. But in a time of constrained or polluted natural resources, private landowner rights may be curtailed for the good of the whole. Higher levels of government intervention may drive different strategic or administrative choices, even as strategic policies drive questions around administrative or foundational choices. For example, if we decide to employ a cost-benefit analysis (strategic), what kind of data should be considered (administrative), and how should laws address non-economic values (foundation)?

The next sections illustrate policy issues that have been raised and addressed in U.S. environmental law in each of these three categories, and discuss how they are likely to continue to evolve and remain relevant in years to come.

Foundation

Garrett Hardin's *Tragedy of the Commons* is one of the best-known illustrations of the central challenge at the heart of environmental law and policy: how do we protect shared resources such as air, water, and soil from overuse and degradation? As you read the following excerpt, think about how the air and water represent commons, and how those commons were used before environmental laws such as the Clean Air Act and Clean Water Act.

Tragedy of the Commons

Garrett Hardin

....The tragedy of the commons develops in this way. Picture a pasture open to all. It is to be expected that each herdsman will try to keep as many cattle as possible on the commons. Such an arrangement may work reasonably satisfactorily for centuries because tribal wars, poaching, and disease keep the numbers of both man and beast well below the carrying capacity of the land. Finally, however, comes the day of reckoning, that is, the day when the long-desired goal of social stability becomes a reality. At this point, the inherent logic of the commons remorselessly generates tragedy.

As a rational being, each herdsman seeks to maximize his gain. Explicitly or implicitly, more or less consciously, he asks, "What is the utility to me of adding one more animal to my herd?" This utility has one negative and one positive component.

1. The positive component is a function of the increment of one animal. Since the herdsman receives all the proceeds from the sale of the additional animal, the positive utility is nearly +1.
2. The negative component is a function of the additional overgrazing created by one more animal. Since, however, the effects of overgrazing are shared by all the herdsmen, the negative utility for any particular decision-making herdsman is only a fraction of -1.

Adding together the component partial utilities, the rational herdsman concludes that the only sensible course for him to pursue is to add another animal to his herd. And another; and another.... But this is the conclusion reached by each and every rational herdsman sharing a commons. Therein is the tragedy. Each man is locked into a system that compels him to increase his herd without limit-in a world that is limited. Ruin is the destination toward which all men rush, each pursuing his own best interest in a society that believes in the freedom of the commons. Freedom in a commons brings ruin to all.

Some would say that this is a platitude. Would that it were! In a sense, it was learned thousands of years ago, but natural selection favors the forces of psychological denial (8). The individual benefits as an individual from his ability to deny the truth even though society as a whole, of which he is a part, suffers.

Education can counteract the natural tendency to do the wrong thing, but the inexorable succession of generations requires that the basis for this knowledge be constantly refreshed.

***

In an approximate way, the logic of commons has been understood for a long time, perhaps since the discovery of agriculture or the invention of private property in real estate. But it is understood mostly only in special cases which are not sufficiently generalized. Even at this late date, cattlemen leasing national land on the western ranges demonstrate no more than an ambivalent understanding, in constantly pressuring federal authorities to increase the head count to the point where overgrazing produces erosion and weed-dominance. Likewise, the oceans of the world continue to suffer from the survival of the philosophy of the commons. Maritime nations still respond automatically to the shibboleth of the "freedom of the seas." Professing to believe in "the inexhaustible resources of the oceans," they bring species after species of fish and whales closer to extinction.

The National Parks present another instance of the working out of the tragedy of the commons. At present, they are open to all, without limit. The parks themselves are limited in extent— there is only one Yosemite Valley—whereas population seems to grow without limit. The values that visitors seek the parks are steadily eroded. Plainly, we must soon cease to treat the parks as commons or they will be of no value anyone.

What shall we do? We have several options. We might sell them off as private property. We might keep them as public property, but allocate the right enter them. The allocation might be on *the basis of wealth, by the use of an auction system. It might be on the basis merit, as defined by some agreed-upon standards. It might be by lottery. Or it might be on a first-come, first-served basis, administered to long queues. These, I think, are all the reasonable possibilities. They are all objectionable. But we must choose-or acquiesce in the destruction of the commons that we call our National Parks.*

Pollution

In a reverse way, the tragedy of the commons reappears in problems of pollution. Here it is not a question of taking something out of the commons, but of putting something in—sewage, or chemical, radioactive, and heat wastes into water; noxious and dangerous fumes into the air, and distracting and unpleasant advertising signs into the line of sight. The calculations of utility are much the same as before. The rational man finds that his share of the cost of the wastes he discharges into the commons is less than the cost of purifying his wastes before releasing them. Since this is true for everyone, we are locked into a system of "fouling our own nest," so long as we behave only as independent, rational, free-enterprises.

The tragedy of the commons as a food basket is averted by private property, or something formally like it. But the air and waters surrounding us cannot readily be fenced, and so the tragedy of the commons as a cesspool must be prevented by different means, by coercive laws or taxing devices that make it cheaper for the polluter to treat his pollutants than to discharge them untreated. We have not progressed as far with the solution of this problem as we have with the first. Indeed, our particular concept of private property, which deters us from exhausting the positive resources of the earth, favors pollution. The owner of a factory on the bank of a stream—whose property extends to the middle of the stream, often has difficulty seeing why it is not his natural right to muddy the waters flowing past his door. The law, always behind the times, requires elaborate stitching and fitting to adapt it to this newly perceived aspect of the commons.

Discussion

The tragedy of the commons tells us that when resources are shared, there must be some legal/regulatory structure to ensure that they are not overused. This principle might be said to lie at the heart of environmental law. Few would argue that there should be *no* limitations on the chemicals that can be dumped into shared waterways, or the pollutants that can be emitted into the air we all breathe. The question is one of *degree* (how much should we limit? how much should we allow?) and *cost* (who should bear the cost of the limitations?).

The issue of cost can be understood using the economic principle of **externalities**. Externalities are the side effects of private actions, typically commercial, that are borne by third parties rather than their creator. The classic example in the environmental context is the waste generated by a factory that is dumped in the river, or the pollution that the factory emits that is dispersed into the air. The factory owners create the waste, but they do not pay for it. Individuals also create externalities—everyone who drives a car or heats their home with fossil fuels generates greenhouse gases. When externalities provide a benefit, society is generally willing to take advantage of that benefit. But when the externality creates harm, who pays for the harm, and how should it be rectified?

> Externalities—the side effects of private actions, typically commercial, that are borne by third parties rather than their creator.

> **Polluter pays principle**—the principle that the entities that create pollution should be the ones to bear the costs of managing it.

The **polluter pays principle** requires the generator of the externality to pay for its effects. This principle can be seen in many of the major environmental statutes, including the Clean Air Act and Clean Water Act. But even when a polluter pays strategy is adopted, significant questions remain at both the fundamental policy and strategic level, including: what form should the payment take? Should society adopt a *preemptive* strategy and make the factory pay to implement devices to prevent pollution, or should it take a *retroactive* approach and make the factory pay to clean up the air after it is polluted? What if the impacts of the externalities aren't known for years, or even decades? Even if the polluter pays, how much should it pay? Is there some amount of emissions for which they get a free pass? In the commercial context, what responsibility should the end user/consumer have for externalities associated with their purchases?

***

> [O]ne of economics' fundamental principles [is] that negative externalities create social welfare losses.... We can argue over the amount of benefit and make cases against regulations that cannot survive a rigorous cost-benefit analysis. We can argue that even regulations whose benefits exceed their costs should also be subject to cost-effectiveness analysis. But let's not pretend that externalities don't exist.[25]
>
> —Seth Jaffe, Environmental Practice Group Coordinator, Foley Hoag LLP

***

One assumption of the tragedy of the commons is that all of the residents of the commons share equally in the negative effects of its degradation. But what if some individuals can ensure their externalities are disposed of in one commons, while they live in another? Consider communities that are directly adjacent to factories or power plants that emit toxic chemicals. These communities bear a disproportionate share of the negative impacts of the externalities associated with production of commercial or industrial goods. The goal of achieving "fair treatment and meaningful involvement of all people regardless of race, color, national origin, and socioeconomic status, with regard to the creation and implementation of environmental laws, regulations, and policies,"[26] is known as **environmental justice**.

> **Environmental justice**—the goal of achieving fair treatment and meaningful involvement of people regardless of race, color, national origin, and socioeconomic status, with regard to the creation and implementation of environmental laws, regulations, and policies.

The beginning of the environmental justice movement coincided with the civil rights movement, as African Americans began to protest the repeated siting of hazardous and chemical waste sites in African American communities. In 1987 a highly regarded, first-of-its-kind study by the United Church of Christ (UCC) found persistent and substantial disparities between communities of color and white communities when it came to the disposal of toxic wastes.[27] A follow-up study 20 years later reached a similar conclusion:

> Host neighborhoods of commercial hazardous waste facilities are 56% people of color whereas nonhost areas are 30% people of color. Percentages of African Americans, Hispanics/Latinos and Asians/Pacific Islanders in host neighborhoods are 1.7, 2.3 and 1.8 times greater (20% vs. 12%, 27% vs. 12%, and 6.7% vs. 3.6%), respectively.[28]

Since the first UCC study in 1987, new studies have repeatedly found significant disparities in the exposure of communities of color, including racial and ethnic minorities, to toxic environmental hazards, including hazardous waste sites, vehicle and diesel traffic, and outdoor and industrial pollution. Most recently, a 2017 study by the National Association for the Advancement of Colored People (NAACP) and the Clean Air Task Force (CATF) noted that:

> African Americans are exposed to 38 percent more polluted air than Caucasian Americans, and they are 75 percent more likely to live in fence-line communities than the average American. Fence-line communities are communities next to a company, industrial, or service facility and are directly affected in some way by the facility's operation (e.g., noise, odor, traffic, and chemical emissions). Most fence-line communities in the United States are low-income individuals and communities of color.[29]

Enforcement of existing environmental laws has also been found to disproportionately favor whites. A study published in the *National Law Journal* in 1992 found significant delays in placing hazardous waste sites in minority communities on a national priority list for clean-up as compared to white communities. The same study found that penalties for violations of environmental laws were 46% higher in white communities than in minority communities, and that the EPA was significantly more likely to "cap" and leave hazardous wastes in place in minority communities, as opposed to permanent treatment and elimination of the waste, which occurred more frequently in white communities.[30]

***

In my work in finance and energy, I realized that there are laws today that create structural inequality, but law can also be used to create sustainable outcomes for the planet and for people. When we look at new legal structures we must ask, what is lost, and what remains, if the status quo ante persists? What might a new system, incorporating principles of economic fairness, energy democracy, and climate and environmental justice, look like?

—Shalanda Baker, Northeastern University Professor of Law, Public Policy and Urban Affairs, Global Resilience Institute, founding director of the Energy Justice Program

***

In 1994, President Clinton issued Executive Order 12898, which directed federal agencies to "make achieving environmental justice part of its mission by identifying and addressing, as appropriate, disproportionately high and adverse human health or environmental effects of its programs, policies, and activities on minority populations and low-income populations."[31] However, the subjective nature of the order left environmental justice to an essentially discretionary process. Although President Obama made environmental justice a priority for his administration, including the development of an EPA action plan to advance environmental justice from 2016–2020 (EJ

2020 Action Agenda[32]), early actions by the Trump Administration to roll back environmental regulations, limit the collection and release of environmental data, and reduce funding to programs to clean up communities of color appear to be limiting the environmental justice movement's progress.[33]

1. A challenging extension of the polluter pays principle can be seen in international negotiations over greenhouse gas emissions and climate change mitigation. Even if there is no debate over the science of climate change, there remains much debate over how to allocate and share the responsibility for addressing the problem. If the international community wants to limit future emissions, how should those limits be calculated? How should we account for the fact that the United States has historically contributed the largest individual country percentage share of cumulative world emissions? How do we account for emissions going forward? For an enlightening look at different ways of capturing and accounting for global emissions, visit https://wri.org/blog/2014/11/6-graphs-explain-world%E2%80%99s-top-10-emitters.
2. If you were to design a global mechanism to limit future increases in global warming, what basis would you use to limit emissions? per capita? country by country? emissions intensity? historic contributions? Research the principle of *"common but differentiated responsibilities"* and the way this principle has been adopted in global climate change treaties.

Fundamental Right to a Healthy Environment?

The opening case study presented a snapshot of the children's lawsuit against the United States' government for their contribution to climate change and failure to address the potential for future harm caused by the emission of greenhouse gasses. The following is an excerpt from an order in that case, in which the judge considers whether the climate change plaintiffs can move forward with their claim that the government has violated a fundamental right by failing to preserve the environment for future generations.

This is no small question for a judge to decide. Like the question of abortion or same-sex marriage, the plaintiffs are asking the court to decide if individual U.S. citizens have a legal right that is not written down in a statute and does not expressly appear in the Constitution. In effect, the plaintiffs are arguing that the right to life, liberty, and property includes the right to a healthy environment. They also argue that this right preexisted the Constitution, and is something that the U.S. government cannot bargain away or delegate to someone else.

How would it change our environmental laws if people had a fundamental right to a healthy environment?

Juliana v. United States, 217 F. Supp. 3d 1224 (D. Or., 2016)

Plaintiffs in this civil rights action are a group of young people between the ages of eight and nineteen ("youth plaintiffs"); Earth Guardians, an association of young environmental activists; and Dr. James Hansen, acting as guardian for future generations.[2] Plaintiffs filed this action against defendants the United States, President Barack Obama, and numerous executive agencies. Plaintiffs allege defendants have known for more than fifty years that the carbon dioxide

("CO_2") produced by burning fossil fuels was destabilizing the climate system in a way that would "significantly endanger plaintiffs, with the damage persisting for millennia," ... Plaintiffs argue defendants' actions violate their substantive due process rights to life, liberty, and property, and that defendants have violated their obligation to hold certain natural resources in trust for the people and for future generations.

***

Background

This is no ordinary lawsuit. Plaintiffs challenge the policies, acts, and omissions of the President of the United States, the Council on Environmental Quality, the Office of Management and Budget, the Office of Science and Technology Policy, the Department of Energy, the Department of the Interior, the Department of Transportation ("DOT"), the Department of Agriculture, the Department of Commerce, the Department of Defense, the Department of State, and the Environmental Protection Agency ("EPA"). This lawsuit challenges decisions defendants have made across a vast set of topics—decisions like whether and to what extent to regulate CO_2 emissions from power plants and vehicles, whether to permit fossil fuel extraction and development to take place on federal lands, how much to charge for use of those lands, whether to give tax breaks to the fossil fuel industry, whether to subsidize or directly fund that industry, whether to fund the construction of fossil fuel infrastructure such as natural gas pipelines at home and abroad, whether to permit the export and import of fossil fuels from and to the United States, and whether to authorize new marine coal terminal projects. Plaintiffs assert defendants' decisions on these topics have substantially caused the planet to warm and the oceans to rise. They draw a direct causal line between defendants' policy choices and floods, food shortages, destruction of property, species extinction, and a host of other harms.

***

Discussion

***

The Due Process Clause of the Fifth Amendment to the United States Constitution bars the federal government from depriving a person of "life, liberty, or property" without "due process of law." U.S. Const. amend. V. ... When the government infringes a "fundamental right," ... a reviewing court applies strict scrutiny. Substantive due process "forbids the government to infringe certain 'fundamental' liberty interests at all, no matter what process is provided, unless the infringement is narrowly tailored to serve a compelling state interest." ... Resolution of this part of the motions to dismiss therefore hinges on whether plaintiffs have alleged infringement of a fundamental right.

Fundamental liberty rights include both rights enumerated elsewhere in the Constitution and rights and liberties which are either (1) "deeply rooted in this Nation's history and tradition" or (2) "fundamental to our scheme of ordered liberty[.]" ...

I have no doubt that the right to a climate system capable of sustaining human life is fundamental to a free and ordered society. Just as marriage is the "foundation of the family," a stable climate system is quite literally the foundation "of society, without which there would be neither civilization nor progress." ... Plaintiffs do not object to the government's role in producing any pollution or in causing any climate change; rather, they assert the government has caused pollution and climate change on a catastrophic level, and that if the government's actions continue unchecked, they will permanently and irreversibly damage plaintiffs' property, their economic livelihood, their recreational opportunities, their health, and ultimately their (and their children's) ability to live long, healthy lives.... [P]laintiffs allege a stable climate system is a necessary condition to exercising other rights to life, liberty, and property.

In framing the fundamental right at issue as the right to a climate system capable of sustaining human life, I intend to strike a balance and to provide some protection against the constitutionalization of all environmental claims. On the one hand, the phrase "capable of sustaining human life" should not be read to require a plaintiff to allege that governmental action will result in the extinction of humans as a species. On the other hand, acknowledgment of this fundamental right does not transform any minor or even moderate act that contributes to the warming of the planet into a constitutional violation. In this opinion, this Court simply holds that where a complaint alleges governmental action is affirmatively and substantially damaging the climate system in a way that will cause human deaths, shorten human lifespans, result in widespread damage to property, threaten human food sources, and dramatically alter the planet's ecosystem, it states a claim for a due process violation. To hold otherwise would be to say that the Constitution affords no protection against a government's knowing decision to poison the air its citizens breathe or the water its citizens drink. Plaintiffs have adequately alleged infringement of a fundamental right.

***

Public Trust Claims

In its broadest sense, the term "public trust" refers to the fundamental understanding that no government can legitimately abdicate its core sovereign powers.... Plaintiffs' public trust claims arise from the particular application of the public trust doctrine to essential natural resources. With respect to these core resources, the sovereign's public trust obligations prevent it from "depriving a future legislature of the natural resources necessary to provide for the well-being and survival of its citizens."

***

The public trust doctrine defines inherent aspects of sovereignty. The Social Contract theory, which heavily influenced Thomas Jefferson and other Founding Fathers, provides that people possess certain inalienable rights and that governments were established by consent of the governed for the purpose of securing those rights.[13] Accordingly, the Declaration of Independence and the Constitution did not create the rights to life, liberty, or the pursuit of happiness—the documents are, instead, vehicles for protecting and promoting those already-existing rights. Governments, in turn, possess certain powers that permit them to safeguard the rights of the people; these powers are inherent in the authority to govern and cannot be sold or bargained away.[13]

> The Founding Fathers were also influenced by intergenerational considerations. They believed the inalienable rights to life, liberty, and property were rooted in a philosophy of intergenerational equity. Thomas Jefferson, for example, thought that each generation had the obligation to pass the natural estate undiminished to future generations....

Although the public trust predates the Constitution, plaintiffs' right of action to enforce the government's obligations as trustee arises from the Constitution. I agree ... that plaintiffs' public trust claims are properly categorized as substantive due process claims. As explained, the Due Process Clause's substantive component safeguards fundamental rights that are "implicit in the concept of ordered liberty" or "deeply rooted in this Nation's history and tradition." Plaintiffs' public trust rights ... satisfy both tests.

***

Conclusion

Throughout their objections, defendants and intervenors attempt to subject a lawsuit alleging constitutional injuries to case law governing statutory and common-law environmental claims. They are correct that plaintiffs likely could not obtain the relief they seek through citizen suits brought under the Clean Air Act, the Clean Water Act, or other environmental laws. But that argument misses the point. This action is of a different order than the typical environmental case. It alleges that defendants' actions and inactions—whether or not they violate any specific statutory duty—have so profoundly damaged our home planet that they threaten plaintiffs' fundamental constitutional rights to life and liberty.

A deep resistance to change runs through defendants' and intervenors' arguments for dismissal: they contend a decision recognizing plaintiffs' standing to sue, deeming the controversy justiciable, and recognizing a federal public trust and a fundamental right to climate system capable of sustaining human life would be unprecedented, as though that alone requires its dismissal. This lawsuit may be groundbreaking, but that fact does not alter the legal standards governing the motions to dismiss. Indeed, the seriousness of plaintiffs' allegations underscores how vitally important it is for this Court to apply those standards carefully and correctly.

***

DISCUSSION

The journey of the plaintiffs in the case of *Juliana v. United States* is in early stages, but it represents a growing interest in redefining environmental law and policy around a fundamental, constitutional right to a healthy environment. Of course, this issue has sparked enormous controversy. In particular, many ask if a fundamental right to a healthy environment exists, how far does that right go, and how would a court determine what was "healthy" enough?

In this case, the judge contends that she intends to "strike a balance" by defining the right as one to "*a climate system capable of sustaining human life.*" This way, she says, only the most extreme cases could be addressed by this standard. Although this may sound like an uncomfortably vague standard for a court to apply, many constitutional rights sit on a continuum that is similarly undefined. For example, the Fourth Amendment guarantees that people will be free from "unreasonable searches and seizures," despite the fact that it is enormously difficult for a court to define what is "reasonable" and interpret how that definition might change over time.

The Supreme Court has recognized that the definition of "fundamental rights" can evolve and new rights can be created. In *Obergefell v. Hodges*,[34] which recognized a constitutional right to same-sex marriage, Justice Kennedy wrote:

> The generations that wrote and ratified the Bill of Rights . . . did not presume to know the extent of freedom in all its dimensions, and so they entrusted to future generations a charter protecting the right of all persons to enjoy liberty as we learn its meaning. When new insight reveals discord between the Constitution's central protections and a received legal stricture, a claim to liberty must be addressed.[35]

On the other hand, if a right to a healthy environment—in whatever form—does exist, it will almost certainly create unprecedented upheaval in the administration of environmental policy. Faced with such a right, the U.S. government might be required to overturn years of settled law regarding the regulation and oversight of fossil fuel development, water use, and agriculture. Regulation of transportation and energy, two of the greatest contributors to climate change, could come under more stringent federal government oversight. The fuel sources used for electricity generation, which are generally regulated at the state level, could also become a matter of federal oversight.

However this case is ultimately decided, there is little doubt the obligation of the U.S. government with regard to maintaining certain minimum standards for environmental health and safety will continue to be the subject of controversy for years to come.

Personal Property Rights

A fundamental aspect of the U.S. legal system is the recognition of private property and the rights that go along with property ownership. The Fifth Amendment of the U.S. Constitution protects individuals from being "deprived of life, liberty, or property, without due process of law." It also ensures that private property cannot be taken for public use "without just compensation." The ability of the government to regulate what an individual landowner can or cannot do with his or her private property is certainly a key issue in environmental law and policy. However, a separate issue relates to the interactions *between* private property owners, and the effects of private actions on shared environmental resources and private property alike.

The next case addresses such a conflict. On one side of the case stood a group of small farmers and individual landowners. On the other stood the owner of a large cement factory. The conduct at issue was, quite simply, the operation of the plant. It was not illegal and took place within the private property of the cement plant owner. Yet the pollution, dirt, smoke, and vibrations (akin to mini-earthquakes that could shake items from bookcases and cause cracks in walls) caused by the plant's operation directly impacted surrounding landowners and community members. It impacted their private property and also impacted their health.

Because this case predated the major environmental laws, the only avenue available to the plaintiffs was to sue under a common law claim of nuisance. A *nuisance* is generally defined as an unreasonable and substantial interference with an individual's use and enjoyment of their land. The concept of nuisance has existed for centuries, dating back to 12th-century England. With a long history of judicial decisions defining and describing a nuisance, the court in *Boomer* had no trouble concluding a nuisance existed. The question was, what to do about it? How should the court address private conduct that creates public environmental harms?

Boomer v. Atlantic Cement Co., 26 NY2d 219 (Ct. App. NY, 1970)

Defendant operates a large cement plant near Albany. These are actions for injunction and damages by neighboring land owners alleging injury to property from dirt, smoke and vibration emanating from the plant. A nuisance has been found after trial, temporary damages have been allowed; but an injunction has been denied.

The public concern with air pollution arising from many sources in industry and in transportation is currently accorded ever wider recognition accompanied by a growing sense of responsibility in State and Federal Governments to control it. Cement plants are obvious sources of air pollution in the neighborhoods where they operate.

But there is now before the court private litigation in which individual property owners have sought specific relief from a single plant operation. The threshold question raised by . . . . this appeal is whether the court should resolve the litigation between the parties now before it as equitably as seems possible; or whether, seeking promotion of the general public welfare, it should channel private litigation into broad public objectives.

A court performs its essential function when it decides the rights of parties before it. Its decision of private controversies may sometimes greatly affect public issues. Large questions of law are often resolved by the manner in which private litigation is decided. But this is normally an incident to the court's main function to settle controversy. . . .

Effective control of air pollution is a problem presently far from solution even with the full public and financial powers of government. In large measure adequate technical procedures are yet to be developed and some that appear possible may be economically impracticable. It seems apparent that the amelioration of air pollution will depend on technical research in great depth; on a carefully balanced consideration of the economic impact of close regulation; and of the actual effect on public health. It is likely to require massive public expenditure and to demand more than any local community can accomplish and to depend on regional and interstate controls.

A court should not try to do this on its own. . . .

The cement making operations of defendant have been found [to be a nuisance.] . . . The total damage to plaintiffs' properties is, however, relatively small in comparison with the value of defendant's operation and with the consequences of the injunction which plaintiffs seek. . . .

The rule in New York has been that such a nuisance will be enjoined although marked disparity be shown in economic consequence between the effect of the injunction and the effect of the nuisance. . . . To follow the rule literally in these cases would be to close down the plant at once. This court is fully agreed to avoid that immediately drastic remedy; the difference in view is how best to avoid it.

One alternative is to grant the injunction but postpone its effect to a specified future date to give opportunity for technical advances to permit defendant to eliminate the nuisance; another is to grant the injunction conditioned on the payment of permanent damages to plaintiffs which would compensate them for the total economic loss to their property present and future caused by defendant's operations. For reasons which will be developed the court chooses the latter alternative.

> ... [T]echniques to eliminate dust and other annoying by-products of cement making are unlikely to be developed by any research the defendant can undertake within any short period, but will depend on the total resources of the cement industry Nationwide and throughout the world. The problem is universal wherever cement is made.
>
> For obvious reasons the rate of the research is beyond control of defendant. If at the end of [an injunction] the whole industry has not found a technical solution a court would be hard put to close down this one cement plant if due regard be given to equitable principles.
>
> On the other hand, to grant the injunction unless defendant pays plaintiffs such permanent damages as may be fixed by the court seems to do justice between the contending parties. All of the attributions of economic loss to the properties on which plaintiffs' complaints are based will have been redressed....
>
> Jason, J. (Dissenting).
>
> ***
>
> This type of pollution, wherein very small particles escape and stay in the atmosphere, has been denominated as the type of air pollution which produces the greatest hazard to human health. We have thus a nuisance which not only is damaging to the plaintiffs, but also is decidedly harmful to the general public.... In permitting the injunction to become inoperative upon the payment of permanent damages, the majority is, in effect, licensing a continuing wrong. It is the same as saying to the cement company, you may continue to do harm to your neighbors so long as you pay a fee for it. Furthermore, once such permanent damages are assessed and paid, the incentive to alleviate the wrong would be eliminated, thereby continuing air pollution of an area without abatement....
>
> [In addition,] the promotion of the interests of the polluting cement company has, in my opinion, no public use or benefit.
>
> ... I would enjoin the defendant cement company from continuing the discharge of dust particles upon its neighbors' properties unless, within 18 months, the cement company abated this nuisance.... I am aware that the trial court found that the most modern dust control devices available have been installed in defendant's plant, but, I submit, this does not mean that better and more effective dust control devices could not be developed within the time allowed to abate the pollution.
>
> Moreover, I believe it is incumbent upon the defendant to develop such devices, since the cement company, at the time the plant commenced production (1962), was well aware of the plaintiffs' presence in the area, as well as the probable consequences of its contemplated operation. Yet, it still chose to build and operate the plant at this site.
>
> In a day when there is a growing concern for clean air, highly developed industry should not expect acquiescence by the courts, but should, instead, plan its operations to eliminate contamination of our air and damage to its neighbors.

Discussion

1. This case illustrates a number of key environmental policy issues. The first issue the court had to decide was whether it should limit its opinion to simply deciding the dispute between the parties, or if it should use its opinion to try to address broader policy objectives. How did it decide this question? What

should the role of courts be in deciding private disputes that have significant public consequences? How do you think the court in *Juliana v. United States* should apply this principle?

2. A second key environmental policy issue has to do with the balance of rights between property owners. When conduct by one property owner causes damage to another property owner, whose rights are more important? How should a court decide what kind of conduct is "unreasonable"? Many courts use a rule that finds conduct is unreasonable if "the gravity of the harm outweighs the utility" of the conduct. But harm to whom? Should the court consider harm to the surrounding community, or just harm to the individual plaintiff? Do you think, based on this test, that the court reached the right outcome? How does the scope of this balancing test relate to the principle discussed in #2?

3. A third key policy challenge raised by this case is how policymakers and the courts should weigh non-economic environmental attributes. If the court is to award "permanent damages" for harm to the plaintiff's land, should it look simply at the reduction in the fair market value of the land? What other types of factors should the court consider? A common mechanism used in environmental regulation is a cost-benefit analysis. But how can a cost-benefit analysis take into account non-economic costs and benefits?

4. The rule in New York had previously been that a private nuisance causing substantial ongoing harm would generally be enjoined—that is, the defendant would have to stop whatever conduct was causing the nuisance. Here, that conduct was the operation of the cement plant, but the court concludes it will not take that step. What was the basis for the court's decision? The majority opinion points to two alternatives to the old rule. What were the alternatives and which did it choose? How would the dissent have decided this case differently?

Strategy

In this section, we look at how several major environmental laws illustrate strategic choices in creating environmental law and policy.

First, we consider how the Clean Air Act splits authority for environmental protection between the federal and state governments. This system is known as **cooperative federalism**, and it is a key principle in many environmental statutes. We will also consider how the CAA does, and does not, consider cost-benefit analyses when setting limits for emissions of air pollutants. Next, we look at the Clean Water Act, and how it uses a **command-and-control** mechanism to improve water quality. Finally, we will consider a **market-based** approach to environmental regulation: the cap-and-trade system used in California to address greenhouse gas emissions.

> Cooperative federalism—a system in which federal, state, and local governments share legislative and regulatory authority. In environmental law, a cooperative federalism approach recognizes the historic interest of states in regulating their own natural resources.
>
> Market-based regulation—in environmental law, market-based regulation uses economic signals, such as price or profits, to incentivize desired behavior and limit undesirable behavior.

Clean Air Act

The CAA is one of the United States' most important environmental statutes, and it promises to continue to play an important role in the future of environmental law. It is also enormously complex, with a variety of provisions. We will only consider a few of those provisions here.

By 1970, the potentially deadly health impacts of poor air quality and hazardous air pollutants were well known. The tough policy question was how to set limits for emissions of common pollutants. Previous efforts at regulating air quality had left much of the work of determining the appropriate standards to states. This system was ultimately ineffective, in part because states lacked the resources to determine the health effects of major pollutants and determine safe levels for their emissions. However, there was a strong desire to limit the federal government's role in setting environmental policies for states. In some states, pollution came from heavy industry; in others, it came from transportation. How could policymakers create a one-size-fits-all approach to pollution control?

The CAA solved this problem with cooperative federalism. In this system, the EPA determined limits for the amount of certain major pollutants that could be in the **ambient air**. These major pollutants, known as **criteria pollutants**, were ones that were both known to be unsafe and were present all over the country. After setting limits for the amount of each of the criteria pollutants that could be present in the air (the National Ambient Air Quality Standards, or NAAQS), the federal government then left it to the states to determine how to achieve these limits. States were required under the CAA to create state plans to ensure they would meet the NAAQS; the EPA reviewed and oversaw those plans to ensure they achieved the standards.

When setting the NAAQS, policymakers could have gone two different routes. One route would be to set standards based on health; that is, researchers could figure out what was "healthy air" and then set limits based on that, regardless of how expensive or difficult they would be. This is a *health-based standard*. Another route would be similar to the one chosen in the Boomer case. Policymakers could ask, "What technology exists today, and how clean can we get the air based on the existing technology?" This is a *technology-based standard*.

As you read the following case, consider whether the CAA uses health-based or technology-based standards when setting the NAAQS.

> Ambient air—atmospheric air in its natural state; generally understood as the air we breathe.
>
> Criteria pollutants—under the Clean Air Act, the EPA must list air pollutants present in the ambient air due to numerous or diverse mobile or stationary sources that "reasonably may be anticipated to endanger public health or welfare" and develop air quality criteria for these pollutants. 42 U.S.C. § 7408 (2016). As of 2017, there are seven of these "criteria pollutants": carbon monoxide, lead, ground-level ozone, particulate matter, nitrogen dioxide, and sulfur dioxide.

Whitman v. American Trucking Associations, 531 U.S. 457 (2001)

[The Clean Air Act (CAA) requires the EPA to promulgate NAAQS for each of the criteria pollutants. Once the NAAQS have been set, the EPA must review them every five years. This case arose when the EPA revised the NAAQS for particulate matter and ozone and made them much more stringent. The American Trucking Association argued that the EPA should have set the NAAQS based on a cost-benefit analysis. They also argued that the language of the statute was so vague it was unconstitutional, because it essentially allowed the EPA to create its own laws.] . . .

[The CAA] instructs the EPA to set primary ambient air quality standards "the attainment and maintenance of which . . . are requisite to protect the public health" with "an adequate margin of safety." Were it not for the hundreds of pages of briefing respondents have submitted on the issue, one would have thought it fairly clear that this text does not permit the EPA to consider costs in setting the standards. . . .

[T]o prevail in their present challenge, respondents must show a textual commitment of authority to the EPA to consider costs in setting NAAQS [and] that textual commitment must be a clear one. Congress, we have held, does not alter the fundamental details of a regulatory scheme in vague terms or ancillary provisions—it does not, one might say, hide elephants in mouseholes. . . . [We do not find such clear language here.]

> *[With regard to the argument that the statute is too vague] ... [w]e agree with the Solicitor General that the ... CAA at a minimum requires that "for a discrete set of pollutants and based on published air quality criteria that reflect the latest scientific knowledge, [the] EPA must establish uniform national standards at a level that is requisite to protect public health from the adverse effects of the pollutant in the ambient air." [This charge to the EPA is not impermissibly vague.]*
>
> *... [A] certain degree of discretion, and thus of lawmaking, inheres in most executive or judicial action. [T]he CAA, which to repeat we interpret as requiring the EPA to set air quality standards at the level that is "requisite"—that is, not lower or higher than is necessary—to protect the public health with an adequate margin of safety, fits comfortably within the scope of discretion permitted by our precedent.*

Discussion

The Whitman case settled a question that had been plaguing the implementation of the CAA: how should cost-benefit analyses be factored into limits on air pollutants? In short, although industry thought it would be better to consider how expensive it would be to achieve certain standards, the Supreme Court found that statute required the EPA to ignore cost-benefit data and focus instead on what was necessary to preserve human health.

The case also made it clear that the CAA both allowed and required the EPA to consider "the latest scientific knowledge" when determining how to protect Americans from the adverse health effects of pollutants. Although this may sound like a straightforward principle, it ties environmental policy much more closely to scientific data and research than many other policy areas. It also limits the ability of the EPA to be guided solely by powerful lobby groups or industry. Although it may choose positions advocated by those groups, in doing so it opens itself to challenge in court.

The final point illustrated by this case is the enormous amount of discretion the EPA has to set standards under the CAA. Although the Court ultimately held that the statute was not too vague to survive a constitutional challenge, there can be little doubt that the EPA holds a great deal of power to set policy. Some would argue that an unelected administrative agency should not have such authority. Consider what the EPA can do: by changing the NAAQS, it can determine the profitability of entire industries (such as the trucking industry) and also influence the health outcomes for millions of Americans. Whether this structure is appropriate from a policy perspective remains a continuing area of controversy.

Clean Water Act

After the Clean Air Act, probably the best-known environmental statute is the Clean Water Act (CWA). Like the CAA, this statute also uses a command-and-control mechanism and a system of cooperative federalism to clean up heavily polluted waterways. **Command and control** refers to a regulatory system in which the government sets a limit (command) and then has enforcement power if the regulated entity doesn't meet that standard (control). The cooperative federalism in the CWA, like the CAA, relies on the federal government to set national standards and the states to determine how best to implement those standards.

The heart of the CWA is quite simple: it makes it unlawful for any person to discharge a pollutant into a waterway without having a permit. Permits are issued

> **Command and control**—in environmental law, command-and-control regulations set specific limits and standards for behavior, commonly in emissions of pollutants, and employ enforcement mechanisms to ensure standards are met.

under the National Pollutant Discharge Elimination System (NPDES). Permits may be issued by federal agencies or by states, if they request the authority to issue permits. Enforcement generally takes place at the state level.

Unlike the NAAQS, which are entirely health-based, the limits for permits under the NPDES are set in a number of ways. Some are technology-based, whereas others are based on the water-quality standard intended for a particular waterway. For example, the rules for permits may be different in a body of water that serves as a source of drinking water than in a river that is used for barging cargo. Some highly toxic pollutants also have special standards.

Most of the controversy under the CWA has centered around the definitions given to key terms in the statute. For example, what kind of waterways are subject to limitations? What about a wetland that is dry part of the year but filled with water for part of the year? What about a small pond that is not connected to any other waterway? What is a pollutant? Can sand be a pollutant? What about heat? All of these questions have been, and continue to be, the subject of lawsuits and rulemaking processes by the EPA.

Market Mechanisms

In the late 1980s, an environmental issue of significant concern was the emissions of sulfur and nitrogen oxides into the air in the United States that were contributing directly to acid rain in Canada and the Northeastern United States. Acid rain, primarily created by emissions from coal-fired power plants, severely damaged Canadian and U.S. waterways and forests. The question was how to limit it.

In this case, rather than using another command-and-control mechanism, policymakers developed a market-based emissions trading program. Under the terms of the program, an aggressive cap was placed on the amount of emissions from the most-polluting coal-fired power plants, which required a significant reduction in the amount of total emissions from those plants. Then, a certain number of allowances for emissions were distributed to covered plants. Plants could continue to emit pollutants, but only if they had an allowance. Plants that reduced their emissions below the limit could trade (sell) their extra allowances to other plants, thus creating a market for these allowances.

This type of system, known as a "cap and trade" system, was remarkably successful. Emissions were reduced and forest ecosystems that had been damaged by acid rain began to recover. Perhaps most notably, the reduction in emissions also had a health benefit for people living in communities affected by the power plants. Estimates suggest that $50 billion in health benefits were achieved for $0.5 billion in program costs.[36]

Market-based mechanisms are particularly popular among people who believe command-and-control mechanisms can limit economic growth. Others believe a market-based system creates incentives to develop new technology to address environmental challenges. California has implemented a cap and trade system to reduce greenhouse gas emissions. The goal of California's program is to achieve an 80% reduction from 1990 levels of greenhouse gas emissions by 2050. The California program uses a cap on emissions that declines each year, along with a market mechanism to trade emission allowances.[37]

Market-based mechanisms have also been proposed at the federal level to address climate change. In 2009, a bill known as the Waxman-Markey Bill passed the House of Representatives, though it ultimately failed to move forward in the Senate. In Spring 2017, a bipartisan group calling itself the Climate Leadership Council proposed a system that included a carbon tax and carbon dividends to be distributed to all Americans as an alternative market-based mechanism for addressing climate change.[38]

Administration

The last bucket of issues concerns the administrative details of environmental law. Though they are no less important, these questions may draw less attention outside of legal circles because they deal with the way laws are structured and implemented. One issue in particular, however, is crucial to understanding how environmental law and policy is pursued. This is the notion of **standing**.

Standing is a constitutional requirement that limits the kind of cases that federal courts can decide. Under this rule, the case or "controversy" to be decided must be a live, actual dispute, and the party bringing the case must be the injured party. The stakes here are very high: if a party bringing a case does not have standing, then their case will be dismissed and their arguments on the merits of a case will never be heard.

In cases involving the environment, the standing requirement can get tricky. Who is the injured party when the damage being complained about is harm to a forest, or the ambient air, or an entire ecosystem? In the next case, the Supreme Court sets forth standards that still guide courts today.

> **Standing**—the legal right to bring a lawsuit in a court of law.

Lujan v. Defenders of Wildlife, et al., 504 U.S. 555 (1992)

[In this case, the Secretary of the Interior interpreted the Endangered Species Act in a way that it only applied to actions within the United States or on the high seas, and created a rule to that effect. The issue the court addressed was whether the plaintiffs had standing to seek judicial review of the rule.]

... Over the years, our cases have established that the irreducible constitutional minimum of standing contains three elements. First, the plaintiff must have suffered an "injury in fact"—an invasion of a legally protected interest which is (a) concrete and particularized, and (b) "actual or imminent, not 'conjectural' or 'hypothetical.'" Second, there must be a causal connection between the injury and the conduct complained. ... Third, it must be "likely," as opposed to merely "speculative," that the injury will be "redressed by a favorable decision."

... Respondents' claim to injury is that the lack of consultation with respect to certain funded activities abroad "increas[es] the rate of extinction of endangered and threatened species." ... [But it is not enough to show that the animals would be injured by the action. Respondents had to show that they would be directly affected and harmed.]

... [To establish this injury, one of the plaintiffs claimed that she traveled to Egypt in 1986 and observed an endangered crocodile species that was threatened by development in Egypt. Another plaintiff claimed that she traveled to Sri Lanka in 1981] and "observed the habitat" of "endangered species such as the Asian elephant and the leopard"... although she "was unable to see any of the endangered species".... [She further claimed that development threatening these species] harmed her because she "intend[s] to return to Sri Lanka in the future and hope[s] to be more fortunate in spotting at least the endangered elephant and leopard."...

[The plaintiffs' have produced] ... no facts, however, showing how damage to the species will produce "imminent" injury. ... That the women "had visited" the areas of the projects before the projects commenced proves nothing. ... [T]he affiants' profession of an "intent" to return to the places they had visited before—where they will presumably, this time, not be deprived of the opportunity to observe animals of the endangered species—is simply not

> enough. Such "some day" intentions—without any description of concrete plans, or indeed even any specification of when the some day will be—do not support a finding of the "actual or imminent" injury that our cases require.
>
> ***
>
> We hold that respondents lack standing to bring this action . . .

Discussion

The issue of standing continues to be a concern for environmental plaintiffs today. For example, the plaintiffs in *Juliana v. United States* had to show their concrete, particularized injury caused by climate change. One of the plaintiffs did so by showing that record-setting temperatures harmed his family's hazelnut orchard; another showed that hot, dry conditions and pollutants from forest fires exacerbated her asthma. Environmental plaintiffs seeking to protect distant or remote land or animals with which they do not have direct contact, on the other hand, may be unable to proceed.

Synthesis

As you review this chapter, consider the following questions to synthesize your learning:

1. How is the study of environmental law like other areas of law and policy you have studied? How is it different?
2. If you could wipe the slate clean and start developing a brand-new policy for dealing with pollution of air and water, what kind of policy would you develop? Consider the following elements:
    a. How much control should the government have over a private citizen's use of their own land?
    b. Who should pay for externalities?
    c. Should your new law be proactive or retroactive?
    d. Will you use a market-based or command-and-control mechanism?
    e. Will you include health-based or technology-based targets?
    f. Who will have the ability to enforce your statute? Will citizens be involved?
3. How should the government address the problem of climate change? How is this problem categorically different from other environmental challenges addressed by the Clean Air Act or the Clean Water Act? How is it similar?

Conclusion

The study of environmental law and policy raises more questions than it answers. These questions go to the heart of our understanding of the role of the government in everything from the way we regulate shared resources to the way disputes over actions on private property will be handled by courts. As competition for shared resources increases and threats to public health from climate change, pollution, and overuse compound, the pressure on the legal system and policymakers to develop new, dynamic, and responsive policies will increase. How these policies will be developed remains to be seen.

Notes

1. The child plaintiffs were also joined by the organization Earth Guardians and Dr. James Hasen.
2. First Amended Complaint for Declaratory and Injunctive Relief at ¶ 237, Juliana v. United States, No. 6:15-cv.01517-TC (D. Or. Sept. 10, 2015), https://static1.squarespace.com/static/571d109b04426270152febe0/t/57a35ac5ebbd1ac03847eece/1470323398409/YouthAmendedComplaintAgainstUS.pdf
3. *Id.*
4. *Id.* at ¶ 239.
5. *Id.* at ¶ 241.
6. USGCRP, *Climate Science Special Report: Fourth National Climate Assessment* 1 (Wuebbles, D.J., et al., Eds., 2017), https://science2017.globalchange.gov/
7. *Id.* at ES-33.
8. *Id.* at ES-10.
9. USGCRP, *The Impacts of Climate Change on Human Health in the United States: A Scientific Assessment* (Crimmins, A., et al., Eds., 2016), https://health2016.globalchange.gov/
10. For an overview of the history of American Indian law, see William Canby, Jr., *American Indian Law in a Nutshell* (2014). Though it is not directly a part of environmental law, laws relating to the treatment of Native Americans are closely linked to environmental law, as the lives of the native people were closely bound to the land they inhabited.
11. John Muir, *The American Forests*, The Atlantic, Aug. 1897, www.theatlantic.com/magazine/archive/1897/08/the-american-forests/305017/
12. This quote is attributed to Wallace Stegner, who wrote that national parks were "the best idea we ever had. Absolutely American, absolutely democratic, they reflect us at our best rather than our worst." www.nps.gov/americasbestidea/.
13. Michelle L. Bell, et al., *A Retrospective Assessment of Mortality from the London Smog Episode of 1952: The Role of Influenza and Pollution*, 112 Environmental Health Perspectives 6 (2004), www.ncbi.nlm.nih.gov/pmc/articles/PMC1241789/pdf/ehp0112-000006.pdf
14. *A Brief History of the Clean Water Act*, Oregon Public Broadcasting, www.pbs.org/now/science/cleanwater.html (last visited Nov. 29, 2017).
15. Pres. Richard Nixon, *Reorganization Plan No. 3 of 1970*, July 9, 1970, https://archive.epa.gov/epa/aboutepa/reorganization-plan-no-3-1970.html
16. E.W. Kenworthy, *Tough New Clean-Air Bill Passed by Senate, 73 to 0*, NY Times, Sep. 23, 1970, http://query.nytimes.com/mem/archive/pdf?res=9802E0D71038EE34BC4B51DFBF66838B669EDE
17. Dave Owen, *Seven Reasons Why Gutting EPA Is Bad for Business*, Environmental Law Prof Blog (Apr. 12, 2017), http://lawprofessors.typepad.com/environmental_law/2017/04/seven-reasons-why-gutting-epa-is-bad-for-business.html
18. 437 U.S. 153 (1978).
19. *Id.* at 172–174.
20. Monica Anderson, *For Earth Day, Here's How Americans View Environmental Issues*, Pew Research Center (Nov. 29, 2017), www.pewresearch.org/fact-tank/2017/04/20/for-earth-day-heres-how-americans-view-environmental-issues/
21. Dan Farber, *Environmental Values and Political Polarization*, LegalPlanet (Nov. 6, 2012), http://legal-planet.org/2012/11/06/environmental-values-and-political-polarization/
22. Chai Jing, Under the Dome: Investigating China's Smog (Full Translation), Mar. 1, 2015, www.youtube.com/watch?v=T6X2uwlQGQM
23. Jennifer Chu, *Study: Air Pollution Causes 200,000 Early Deaths Each Year in the U.S.*, MIT News, Aug. 29, 2013, http://news.mit.edu/2013/study-air-pollution-causes-200000-early-deaths-each-year-in-the-us-0829
24. U.S. Department of Defense, Quadrennial Defense Review 2014 at 8 (2014), www.defense.gov/pubs/2014_Quadrennial_Defense_Review.pdf
25. Seth Jaffe, *It's the Externalities*, Stupid, Law & the Environment (Oct. 24, 2017), www.lawandenvironment.com/2017/10/24/its-the-externalities-stupid/
26. *Learn about Environmental Justice*, U.S. Envtl. Protection Agency, www.epa.gov/environmentaljustice/learn-about-environmental-justice (last visited Jan. 2, 2018).
27. *A Movement Is Born*, United Church of Christ (2017), www.ucc.org/a_movement_is_born_environmental_justice_and_the_ucc

28. Robert Bullard, et al., Toxic Wastes and Race at Twenty: 1987–2007 at x (2007), http://d3n8a8pro7vhmx.cloudfront.net/unitedchurchofchrist/legacy_url/13611/contents-and-executive-summary.pdf?1418440224
29. Lesley Fleischman & Marcus Franklin, Fumes across the Fence-Line: The Health Impacts of Air Pollution from Oil & Gas Facilities on African American Communities at 6 (Nov. 2017), www.naacp.org/wp-content/uploads/2017/11/Fumes-Across-the-Fence-Line_NAACP_CATF.pdf
30. Marianne Lavelle & Marcia Coyle, *Unequal Protection: The Racial Divide in Environmental Law*, Nat'l L. J. (Sep. 21, 1992).
31. Executive Order 12898, 59(32) Fed. Reg. (Feb. 16, 1994), www.archives.gov/files/federal-register/executive-orders/pdf/12898.pdf
32. *EJ 2020 Action Agenda: The U.S. EPA's Environmental Justice Strategic Plan for 2016–2020*, Env. Protection Agency (Oct. 2016), www.epa.gov/sites/production/files/2016-05/documents/052216_ej_2020_strategic_plan_final_0.pdf
33. Nadja Popovich & Livia Albeck-Ripka, *52 Environmental Rules on the Way Out Under Trump*, N.Y. Times, updated Oct. 6, 2017, www.nytimes.com/interactive/2017/10/05/climate/trump-environment-rules-reversed.html
34. 135 S. Ct. 2584 (2015).
35. *Id.* at 2598.
36. Gabriel Chan, et al., *The SO2 Allowance Trading System and the Clean Air Act Amendments of 1990: Reflections on Twenty Years of Policy Innovation* 5 (Jan. 2012), https://sites.hks.harvard.edu/m-rcbg/heep/papers/SO2-Brief_digital_final.pdf
37. *Cap-and-Trade Program*, California Air Resources Board (reviewed Nov. 21, 2017), www.arb.ca.gov/cc/capandtrade/capandtrade.htm
38. *Council Announces Its Founding Members*, Climate Leadership Council, www.clcouncil.org (last visited Nov. 29, 2017).

Additional Learning Resources

Additional Readings

Drawdown: The Most Comprehensive Plan Ever Proposed to Reverse Global Warming (Paul Hawken, Ed.) (Penguin Books, 2017). A thoroughly-researched compendium of positive actions that can be taken to reverse global warming and address carbon pollution.

Jonathan Harr, *A Civil Action* (Vintage, 2011). An engrossing movie describing an environmental "toxic tort" case involving a cluster of childhood leukemia cases in Woburn, Massachusetts. Illustrates the challenges of environmental litigation and a small law firm trying to stand up against a team of corporate lawyers.

Oliver A. Houck, *Taking Back Eden: Eight Environmental Law Cases That Changed the World* (Island Press, 2011). A set of eight illustrative case studies of environmental law cases brought in eight different countries.

Richard J. Lazarus, *The Making of Environmental Law* (University of Chicago Press, 2006). A history of environmental law told by one of the leading figures in the law.

Robert V. Percival, et al., *Environmental Regulation: Law, Science, and Policy* (Aspen, 2013). A comprehensive casebook including both legal and policy developments with an emphasis on real-world implications.

Zygmunt J. B. Plater, *The Snail Darter and the Dam* (Yale University Press, 2013). Tells the story behind one of the most important environmental law cases in U.S. history.

Walter A. Rosenbaum, *Environmental Politics and Policy* (Cq Press, 2016). Useful for students of political sciences, environmental studies, and policy that includes a historical narrative interwoven with current policy issues.

Norman J. Vig & Michael E. Kraft, *Environmental Policy: New Directions for the 21st Century* (CQ Press, 2015). An accessible history of environmental policy with attention to future implications.

10 Employment Law and Policy

Elizabeth Brown, Keith Diener, Lucien Dhooge, Leora Eisenstadt, and Natalie Pedersen

Overview/Background

Employment-at-Will

Employment law in the United States is a constant struggle between the employer's desire to retain as much freedom as possible in how to operate his or her business and the employees' rights to be protected in some way within the workplace. America is built on freedom of choice, and that freedom is certainly a founding principle of employment law. We seek to allow employers and employees as much choice in the employment relationship as possible. However, throughout time, the need for government and judicial intervention has become apparent. Such intervention often necessarily impedes employer freedom in order to expand employee rights. This chapter will focus on that tension and how the pull and push between employer freedom and employee rights has shaped the current legal framework in which employers operate.

Employment law in America generally operates under the presumption that employment for an unspecified or indefinite term is considered to be **employment-at-will**. This is the default rule in 49 out of the 50 states. Montana is the only exception. This means that in the vast majority of states, employment can be terminated at any time for any reason (excepting improper discriminatory reasons) or for no reason at all. Over the past three decades, the once almost-irrebuttable presumption that such employment is at-will has been increasingly weakened by courts. Through a combination of both tort and contract doctrine, courts have mitigated the sometimes harsh results of the rigid at-will presumption.

> Employment-at-will—an employment relationship in which the employee can be fired by the employer at any time for any reason (no just cause is required).

The American common law presumption that employment for an unspecified period of time is considered "at-will" can generally be traced to Horace Wood's 1877 *A Treatise of the Law of Master and Servant*. There Wood stated:

> With us the rule is inflexible, that a general or indefinite hiring is prima facie a hiring at will, and if the servant seeks to make it out a yearly hiring, the burden is upon him to establish it by proof.[1]

The employment-at-will rule quickly spread across America and, by 1895, had been adopted by many American courts, including the New York Court of Appeals, New York's highest court. In *Martin v. New York Life Ins. Co.*, the Court held that an indefinite hiring was presumed to be at-will and that a specific rate of payment per year did not negate the presumption of at-will employment.[2] This development was obviously quite advantageous, expanding employer freedom exponentially and minimizing the voice of the worker. Obviously, if a worker can be fired at any time and for any reason, the worker's voice in workplace conditions and treatment is all but muted.

Eventually, courts and legislatures began to chip away at the presumption of employment-at-will. This has happened in several ways. On the federal level, Congress passed anti-discrimination laws such as Title VII of the Civil Rights Act of 1964, the Age Discrimination in Employment Act, and the Americans with Disabilities Act. These laws have all limited employer freedom to make employment decisions based on characteristics unrelated to job performance (specifically race, sex, religion, national origin, color, age and disability). The expansion of employee rights to be treated equally at work necessarily led to a contraction of employer freedom to make hiring, promotion, demotion, pay, and termination decisions. For, if employers must hire without regard to these protected characteristics, they are necessarily being constrained in their decision-making to the extent that they may have a taste for discrimination or feel that their employees or clients may have such a taste. Obviously, it is socially desirable to have such regulations in the workplace, but they do, nonetheless, curtail employer freedom in favor of employee rights.

Courts have also been steadily eroding the irrefutable nature of the at-will presumption through recognition of common law exceptions to the presumption crafted in torts and contract. Here, we will discuss the most common exceptions.

Wrongful Discharge in Violation of Public Policy

The majority of states now recognize a cause of action for wrongful discharge in violation of public policy. Examples of discharges made in violation of public policy include those made in bad faith, those made because the employee refuses to participate in criminal activity, those made for exercising a statutory right, those made in retaliation for whistleblowing or invoking a public duty, and those made out of malice. Courts that have recognized such an exception do so on the understanding that employees may take certain actions that could be against the employer's interest but are for the good of society. For instance, participating in jury duty or testifying against an employer in court are both societally beneficial but costly to the employer. Courts have protected these activities at the expense of the employer—thus, once again limiting employer freedom to promote the public good.

Covenant of Good Faith and Fair Dealing

Some courts have recognized an implied duty of good faith and fair dealing within the employment relationship that requires the employer and employee not to do anything to impede the other from enjoying the benefits of that relationship. Thus, an employer who terminates an employee after a sale, but before the employee's commission comes due in order to prevent the collection of that commission, may violate the implied duty of good faith and fair dealing in those states that recognize it in the employment context.

Implied Contracts

In one of the most interesting developments in the latter part of the 20th century, some courts have interpreted employee handbooks to be contractually binding on employers, thus limiting the employer's ability to terminate an employee at-will. For instance, in *Woolley v. Hoffmann-LaRoche*,[3] the plaintiff was hired without a written employment contract, but received an employee handbook one month after being hired. He was later fired and sued his former employer, claiming the termination clauses of the personnel manual requiring certain procedures before termination were contractually enforceable. The New Jersey Supreme Court ultimately sided with the employee because the handbook set up the reasonable expectation in the employee that the procedures would be followed before termination and, thus, created an implied contract between employer and employee. Thus, employers need to be clear in their handbooks if they do not intend them to be contractually binding. The *Woolley* court and other courts have suggested the addition of prominent disclaimers to employee handbooks that inform employees that the handbook does not, in fact, create a contract and that the employee is still an at-will employee. Employee handbooks will be discussed in more detail later in this chapter.

Promissory Estoppel

Some courts have allowed employees to rely on the doctrine of **promissory estoppel** in order to sustain a cause of action for wrongful termination. The elements of promissory estoppel are as follows: (1) a promise, (2) the promisor's foreseeability of the promisee's reliance thereon, and (3) substantial reliance by the promisee to his detriment. Thus, in cases where an employer has offered an employee a job and the employee has quit his or her current job and moved cross-country to take the new job, some courts have held that under the theory of promissory estoppel, the employee could no longer be fired at-will because there is a quasi-contract requiring the employment.

> Promissory estoppel—a legal principle that allows enforcement of a promise even though there is no formal consideration, when the promisee foreseeably relies on the promise or her detriment.

Thus, it is becoming clear that the presumption of at-will employment, and the degree of employer freedom that accompanies it, are not nearly as strong as in past times. Both statutory and common law exceptions to the doctrine have been and continue to be carved in a way that favors employees while limiting the freedom of employers. Table 10.1 shows certain common law exceptions to employment-at-will that indicates the states in which those exceptions have been recognized. For the remainder of this chapter, we will discuss, in detail, certain areas where the struggle between employer freedom and employee rights has become particularly salient recently. We will first look at covenants not to compete and employee handbooks. We will then turn our attention to employee privacy rights. Finally, we will finish up looking at the policy effects of Title VII of the Civil Rights Act of 1964, specifically examining the areas of religious discrimination, pregnancy in the workplace, and sexual harassment.

Table 10.1 Common law exceptions to employment-at-will

State	Public Policy	Implied Contract	Covenant of Good Faith & Fair Dealing
Alabama	No	Yes	Yes
Alaska	Yes	Yes	Yes
Arizona	Yes	Yes	Yes
Arkansas	Yes	Yes	Yes
California	Yes	Yes	Yes
Colorado	Yes	Yes	No
Connecticut	Yes	Yes	Yes
Delaware	Yes	No	Yes
District of Columbia	Yes	Yes	No
Florida	No	No	No
Georgia	No	No	No
Hawaii	Yes	Yes	No
Idaho	Yes	Yes	Yes

(*Continued*)

Table 10.1 (Continued)

State	Public Policy	Implied Contract	Covenant of Good Faith & Fair Dealing
Illinois	Yes	Yes	Yes
Indiana	Yes	No	Yes
Iowa	Yes	Yes	No
Kansas	Yes	Yes	No
Kentucky	Yes	Yes	No
Louisiana	No	No	Yes
Maine	No	Yes	No
Maryland	No	Yes	No
Massachusetts	Yes	Yes	Yes
Michigan	Yes	Yes	No
Minnesota	Yes	Yes	No
Mississippi	Yes	Yes	No
Missouri	Yes	No	No
Montana	Yes	Yes	No
Nebraska	Yes	Yes	No
Nevada	Yes	Yes	Yes
New Hampshire	Yes	Yes	Yes
New Jersey	Yes	Yes	Yes
New Mexico	Yes	Yes	No
New York	No	Yes	No
North Carolina	Yes	No	No
North Dakota	Yes	Yes	No
Ohio	Yes	Yes	No
Oklahoma	Yes	Yes	Yes
Oregon	Yes	Yes	No
Pennsylvania	Yes	Yes	Yes
Rhode Island	No	No	No
South Carolina	Yes	Yes	Yes
South Dakota	Yes	Yes	No
Tennessee	Yes	No	No
Texas	Yes	Yes	No
Utah	Yes	Yes	No
Vermont	Yes	Yes	Yes
Virginia	Yes	Yes	No
Washington	Yes	Yes	No
West Virginia	Yes	Yes	No
Wisconsin	Yes	Yes	No
Wyoming	Yes	Yes	Yes

Policy Implications of Employer-Employee Contracts

Contracts are regularly utilized to govern employer-employee relationships. The United States promotes a broad public policy in favor of freedom of contract that permits contractual parties considerable discretion to formulate conscionable and legal contract provisions. This overarching public policy allows employers and employees to tailor contracts to meet the individual business needs of each relationship. Contracts may be categorized as *express* or *implied*. In an **express contract**, the parties, either orally or through writing, reach an explicit agreement. A written agreement

Express contract—a contract created either orally or through writing, wherein the parties reach an explicit agreement.

that offers an employee a definite term of employment, such as a one-year guaranteed term, is an express contract that may modify an otherwise at-will relationship. An **implied contract** is one that is implied by the conduct of the parties, that arises even without an express oral or written agreement. An implied contract may arise from promises made by an employer in employee handbooks, personnel policies, or through practices or assurances made by an employer to an employee. The freedom of contract, however, is not without limits, and certain contract provisions will be deemed unenforceable even if freely agreed between the parties.

> Implied contract—a contract that arises by the conduct of the parties, and is inferred by a court to exist. It may arise from promises made by an employer in employee handbooks, personnel policies, or through practices or assurances made by an employer to an employee.

Noncompete Agreements

Noncompete agreements, sometimes called "covenants not to compete" or "restrictive covenants," provide an employer with a means of protecting its legitimate interests from being infringed by an employee. Noncompete agreements are express contracts through which an employee agrees not to compete with his or her employer for a certain amount of time after the employment relationship ends. There is considerable variation across the states as to when a noncompete agreement will be enforced. Generally, if an employee signed a noncompete agreement through which she commits not to compete with her employer for a certain amount of time after the end of the employment relationship, then the agreement is enforceable so long as it supports legitimate interests, is reasonable, and has adequate consideration.[4]

> Noncompete agreement—express contracts through which an employee agrees not to compete with his or her employer for a certain amount of time after the employment relationship ends. They are sometimes also used for the sale of a business.

In deciphering the legitimacy of interests, courts typically balance the interests of the employer, the employee, and the public. Legitimate employer interests may include protecting proprietary or confidential business information, maintaining goodwill, maintaining customer relationships, and protecting trade secrets. Legitimate employee interests may include maintaining income to support oneself or one's family, promoting employee mobility, and ensuring marketability. Even if an employer has a legitimate interest, at times the public interest will outweigh that interest to render a noncompete agreement unenforceable. The public's interest may include the broad public policy that restraints on trade can harm the economy, particularly in specific fields, such as the practice of law or medicine, where the public is benefited by having doctors or attorneys in a community. Nevertheless, some states still permit noncompete agreements for doctors, but most states prohibit lawyers from being restricted by noncompete agreements pursuant to their rules of professional conduct (based on the policy rationale of ensuring the public's right to counsel of choice). The public's interest in a noncompete agreement that prohibits a doctor from working in a specific area may be impacted by how many doctors in the same specialty are available to serve the public in that area.[5]

Noncompete agreements must be reasonable as to time, location, and industry.[6] The scope of a noncompete agreement cannot be broader than reasonably necessary to ensure that the legitimate interests of the employer are preserved. The reasonableness of the agreement involves a case-specific inquiry into reasonableness that accounts for the employer, employee, and public interests involved. A restriction against competing in a larger region (e.g., the state of North Carolina) may be reasonable for large internet companies that distribute nationwide, but unreasonable for smaller, local companies. The industry must also be narrowly tailored to certain business activities. For example, a court refused to prohibit an oral surgeon from practicing in general dentistry when he worked only as an oral surgeon with his previous employer that did not practice general dentistry.[7] Similarly, a two-year restriction may be reasonable to protect a software company from misappropriation of its technology, but may be unreasonably long in other situations, such as in the Jimmy John's example described in Box 10.1.

> **Box 10.1: Jimmy John's Noncompete Controversy**
>
> *Jimmy John's sandwich shop came under scrutiny for including a very restrictive noncompete clause in the employment agreements of its sandwich makers. The clause read, in relevant part:*
>
>> *Employee covenants and agrees that, during his or her employment with the Employer and for a period of two (2) years after . . . he or she will not have any direct or indirect interest in or perform services for . . . any business which derives more than ten percent (10%) of its revenue from selling submarine, hero-type, deli-style, pita and/or wrapped or rolled sandwiches and which is located within three (3) miles of either [the Jimmy John's location in question] or any such other Jimmy John's Sandwich Shop.*[8]
>
> **Legal Reasoning Questions**
>
> 1. Can you identify the employer's legitimate interest? If so, what is it? If no, why not?
> 2. What is the public's interest in this agreement? Should the public interest supersede the employer's interest and this agreement be deemed unenforceable? Why or why not?
> 3. Does this noncompete agreement seem reasonable to you? Why or why not?

> Consideration—the value given in return for a promise or performance, such as money or services, that is exchanged between parties to form a contract.

Noncompete agreements must have adequate consideration. **Consideration** is the value given in return for a promise or performance, such as money or services, that is exchanged between parties to form a contract. In cases of signature of a noncompete at hire, the new employment is considered adequate consideration to support a contract. That is, in exchange for the job (and wages), the employee agrees to perform the work and not to compete with the employer for a certain amount of time after the employment relationship ends. While noncompete agreements signed upon hire have adequate consideration (i.e., the job and wages), if a current or ongoing employee is required to sign a noncompete agreement, states diverge as to whether the ongoing employment is sufficient consideration to support a valid contract.

In the case *of Poole v. Incentives Unlimited, Inc.*,[9] the Supreme Court of South Carolina had to decide whether continued at-will employment was sufficient consideration to support a noncompete agreement that was signed during an ongoing employment-at-will relationship. Poole began working for Incentives, a travel agency, in 1992 and, almost four years later, was asked by her employer to sign a noncompete agreement. She signed it. After Poole left Incentives to work for another travel agency, Incentives sought a temporary injunction to prevent Poole from competing and monetary damages for her breach of the noncompete agreement. The lower courts held that ongoing at-will employment was insufficient consideration to support a noncompete agreement, and that separate consideration is required, so the covenant was deemed not enforceable.

In affirming the lower court's decision, the Supreme Court of South Carolina agreed that separate consideration, and not merely ongoing employment, is needed for an enforceable noncompete agreement. It quoted its prior opinion that "A covenant not to compete is enforceable if it is not detrimental to the public interest, . . . is reasonably limited as to time and territory, and is supported by valuable consideration," and recalled that such covenants shall be "critically examined and construed against the employer."[10] In other situations of ongoing employment, such as if the covenant is made in exchange for a promotion, changes in pay, or changes in duty, then there may be separate consideration sufficient for an enforceable covenant. However, in Poole's case, the position, salary, and duties did not change, and there was no separate consideration, and so the covenant was deemed unenforceable.

Although the Supreme Court of South Carolina deemed ongoing at-will employment insufficient consideration to support a noncompete agreement, other states do not.[11] In most jurisdictions, for a noncompete agreement between an employer and employee to be enforceable, it must promote legitimate interests, be reasonable, and have adequate consideration. Yet, when noncompete agreements are utilized to protect a buyer's interest when purchasing an ongoing business, they are more likely enforceable. In these cases, the seller will agree in a contract not to start a competing business within a certain geographic region of the old business (which the seller is selling to the buyer). This covenant allows the buyer to purchase the ongoing business, along with its reputation and goodwill, without concern that the seller will open a new competing business in that region. If the restrictive covenant is reasonable and an ancillary part of the contract, it is generally enforceable.

Box 10.2: Practitioner Quote

The majority of non-competes that are presented to employees are legally unenforceable. . . . In New Jersey, courts are less motivated to enforce non-compete agreements incidental to one's employment than they are to enforce a non-compete agreement incidental to the sale of one's business.
—Michelle Douglass, Esq. *New Jersey Certified Civil Trial Attorney*

Under common law, if a noncompete agreement is deemed unenforceable, courts implement the **blue pencil doctrine** to strike out unenforceable clauses but leave the enforceable clauses in effect. The modern trend is that courts cannot just strike out clauses, but they can reform the noncompete to make the entire noncompete enforceable. While some states still adhere to the traditional blue pencil rules,[12] and some states void overly broad noncompete agreements entirely,[13] most today allow for the judicial reformation of noncompete agreements.[14] In other words, in most states judges have the power to modify an otherwise unenforceable noncompete to make it enforceable by, for example, limiting the time, location, or industry stated in the agreement.

> Blue pencil doctrine—a rule in common law that allows courts to strike out unenforceable clauses in noncompete agreements but leave the enforceable clauses in effect.

Employee Handbooks

Employee handbooks are often utilized to notify employees of personnel policies. Employee handbooks have both advantages and disadvantages. The advantages include that uniform policies aimed at treating all employees consistently and fairly may minimize the potential for discrimination against protected classes if such policies are consistently applied. Employee handbooks provide a clear and concise statement of company ideals and processes so to prevent miscommunications with employees. Written protocols relating to the terms and conditions of employment, hiring, and firing must be administered consistently to reduce the risk of lawsuits. The disadvantages of employee handbooks include the cost of implementation and regularly updating the handbooks, and that these handbooks do limit the discretion of the employer. Thus, while giving the employee some degree of predictability, employee handbooks simultaneously limit the flexibility that employers have to address unique circumstances of employment. Additionally, employee handbooks may provide a basis for lawsuits against employers, based on theories of implied contract.

In the case of *Dent v. Fruth*,[15] the Supreme Court of Appeals of West Virginia was tasked with deciding whether an implied contract was created through an employee handbook. Dent was terminated from her job and subsequently brought a lawsuit against Fruth, a pharmacy, for wrongful termination based on a violation of an implied contract created by the employee handbook. The court focused on the language of the handbook itself to decipher whether an implied contract was created, and concluded that the disclaimers were insufficient to bar an implied contract claim.

The employee handbook said that an employee may be terminated if that employee receives two written warnings in a 12-month period. Dent was terminated without receiving two written warnings, and so claimed that the employer breached its implied contract by terminating her. Fruth argued that its disclaimers shielded it from implied contract liability, and the lower courts agreed, granting summary judgment to Fruth.

The Supreme Court of Appeals of West Virginia reversed, holding that material issues of fact remained as to whether Fruth's disclaimers were sufficient. It reasoned that a clear and conspicuous disclaimer that clearly articulates at-will status (that an employee could be terminated at any time) and that the handbook is not a contract, could be sufficient to bar an implied contract claim. Yet, in Dent's case, the disclaimers did not state "explicitly that the employees in that case were employees at will and could be terminated at any time and without any prior notice."[16] Such an explicit disclaimer was not present in Dent's case, and so she was permitted to proceed on her implied contract claim and the case was remanded for trial.[17]

Contracts play an important role in defining the boundaries of employer-employee relationships, but public policy places limits upon what contracts, whether express or implied, courts will enforce. As the Supreme Court of the United States recognizes,

> freedom of contract is a qualified, and not an absolute, right. There is no absolute freedom to do as one wills or to contract as one chooses. The guaranty of liberty does not withdraw from legislative supervision that wide department of activity which consists of the making of contracts, or deny to government the power to provide restrictive safeguards. Liberty implies the absence of arbitrary restraint, not immunity from reasonable regulations and prohibitions imposed in the interests of the community.[18]

Courts may monitor and refuse to enforce employer-employee agreements when these agreements undermine legitimate public interests.

Privacy in Employment Law

It has never been easier or more important for employers to measure and monitor all aspects of their business, from productivity to communication to employee health and wellness. In certain matters, it is the employers' obligation to monitor what their employees do. For example, employers are bound by law to take steps to minimize the chances of sexual harassment in the workplace, which often involves a certain amount of training and supervision. At the same time, employers must understand that their interest in monitoring their workforce is limited by their workers' rights of privacy.

Employee privacy is a fast-moving area of law, both because the technology available to employers is changing rapidly and because employees' expectations of privacy, which are important in determining privacy violations, are shifting as well. Technological advances such as biometric measuring create new and arguably more intrusive ways for employers to monitor employees. Each such advance presents a challenge for employers, as courts may not determine whether certain technologically advanced practices violate employee privacy until those practices are widespread.

In general, employers may not engage in practices that violate an employee's **objective and subjective expectation of privacy.** There are various ways in which an employer can limit the objective expectation of privacy, such as alerting employees to the practices used to monitor their behavior or communication (for example, through a carefully crafted social media policy). Consistent enforcement of privacy policies may bolster an employer's ability to claim that its policies established a lower objective expectation of privacy, while inconsistent enforcement may have the opposite effect.

Whether an employer is public or private affects the level of privacy afforded to employees. Government employees have greater rights of privacy than do private employees because the Fourth Amendment's protections against unreasonable search and seizure limit what a government employer may do.

> **Objective expectation of privacy**—an objective, legitimate, reasonable expectation of privacy; correlating with the expectation of privacy generally recognized by society.
>
> **Subjective expectation of privacy**—a certain individual's opinion that a certain location or situation is private. This may vary from person to person.

Social Media Use

While many employers have policies regarding their employees' social media use, there are important checks on the extent to which employers can take action in response to such use. Courts have held that it is a violation of the National Labor Relations Act (NLRA) to prohibit employees from social media use that reflects poorly on their employer.

In the *National Captioning Institute* case,[19] for example, the National Labor Relations Board (NLRB) evaluated the National Captioning Institute's policy that told employees: "If you opt to post about your job on social media, it must be done responsibly." The policy went on to prohibit posts about NCI's software as well as personal commentary that "could reflect poorly upon NCI's professionalism or reputation." NCI also warned employees not to "use the NCI name on any posts that are Google-searchable." An NLRB judge found that these policies could be read to violate the workers' rights under the NLRA to collectively criticize their employer or workplace. The ban on using the company name on searchable posts was also held to violate the NLRA because it could be construed to stop employees from naming their employer in statutorily protected complaints about their terms of employment. The NLRB judge ordered NCI to remove its social media policy and inform its employees of the change. As a result, employers should be cautious about suggesting that they will monitor the social media use of their employees, and they should not dissuade employees from talking about the employer on social media to ensure that the employer does not violate the NLRA.

Internet and Phone Usage

Employees generally have reasonable expectations of privacy in their social media passwords, but they have less privacy in their email or social media communications, except for the rights provided under the NLRA and similar laws. Employers regularly monitor email usage, and emails are often used in trial to establish or limit an employer's liability. Employers also have the right to track websites that their employees visit and block certain sites and programs on employer networks and devices.

While employers can also monitor calls made to and from their offices, there are limitations on the extent to which they can listen to personal calls made at work. Under the Electronics Communications Privacy Act (ECPA), an employer may not monitor employees' personal phone calls unless the employee is aware of and consents to its monitoring. The ECPA also limits the extent to which they review, delete, or block access to their employees' voicemail messages.

Drug and Alcohol Testing

Whether an employer may subject its employees to drug and alcohol screening tests depends on where the employer is located, what the employees do, and the rationale for the testing. Many states have laws limiting the extent to which employers can use screening tests and the kinds of tests they can use. In general, courts uphold employee drug and alcohol testing when the employee's performance can affect public health and safety. Employers are also generally able to test employees for drug and alcohol use when the particular employee has a recent history of such use or when the employer has an objectively reasonable basis to suspect that the employee is using illegal substances, such as observing certain changes in the employees' behavior.

Biometric Privacy

> **Biometric data**—data about humans that is used in biometric analysis and in identifying specific humans by their unique traits.
>
> **Personally identifiable information (PII)**—information that can be used on its own or with other information to identify, contact, or locate a single person, or to identify an individual in context.

Many employers use fingerprints, voice prints, facial recognition technology, and other **biometric data** to assess or monitor their employees. For example, some businesses use biometric time clocks that allow employees to clock in or out with a fingerprint or retina scan. Others use biometric screening in their health and wellness plans to assess health risks and target incentives for improving employee health, which often correlates with lower health insurance costs. These technologies can be useful in increasing security and convenience for the employer, but they also raise privacy and security concerns. Biometric data can comprise **personally identifiable information (PII)** that can be misused if not adequately protected.

Some states have laws limiting the extent to which employers can collect and use the biometric data or PII of their employees and establishing safeguard for such collection and use. Illinois's Biometric Information Privacy Act, for example, requires that employers get informed consent before collecting biometric data and mandates certain safeguards against unauthorized disclosure and misuse. Employers subject to this law have to protect and store biometric data with the same degree of care with which they protect other PII.

Salary History

Employees and putative employees are also entitled to privacy regarding their salary history in many states. In 2017, California became the fourth state to enact a law preventing an employer from asking any applicant about their salary history. New York City and other large cities have similar laws. Other states are considering similar legislation. These laws are designed to protect prior salary information and prevent employers from relying on an applicant's salary history in determining how much a new employee should be paid. In some cases, these laws are also intended to help minimize the gender wage gap. The New York City Council announced that one of its goals in passing its salary history inquiry ban was "reducing the likelihood that women will be prejudiced by prior salary levels."

Criminal Conviction History

Some states also ban the once-common practice of asking job applicants to state whether they have ever been convicted of a crime. These laws, popularly known as **ban the box laws** because of the checkboxes used to ask about criminal conviction history, are in effect in California, Massachusetts, and several other states. The rationale for these laws is that asking about an applicant's criminal history makes it harder for ex-offenders to find a job, which in turn makes it likelier that they will re-offend.

> Ban the box laws—state laws that forbid employers from asking job applicants whether they have ever been convicted of a crime.

Title VII and Religion

Title VII of the Civil Rights Act of 1964 prohibits employers from discriminating against employees on the basis of religion unless the employer is a religious organization.[20] The term "religion" has a very broad meaning. The term includes not only large organized religions such as those in the Judeo-Christian tradition or Islam but also includes religious beliefs that are not part of a formal faith or church, are held by a small group of people, or are based upon ethical and moral principles. It is irrelevant whether the individual is a new convert, consistently observes his or her faith, or engages in practices different from those commonly accepted in the religion. Rather, the most important factor is whether the individual's beliefs and associated practices are sincerely held. However, the Equal Employment Opportunity Commission (EEOC) has specifically noted that "[s]ocial, political, or economic philosophies, or personal preferences are not 'religious' beliefs under Title VII."[21]

Religious organizations are permitted to favor individuals of their particular religions in employment decisions. Religious organizations are defined as corporations, associations, educational institutions, or societies whose "purpose and character are primarily religious."[22] Significant factors in this determination include the purpose of the organization as stated in its organizational documents, the religious affiliation of those individuals and entities participating in its management and membership, the extent to which its operations are religious or involve religious practices, and whether it is a non-profit organization.

The EEOC defines religious discrimination as "treating a person (an applicant or employee) unfavorably because of his or her religious beliefs . . . [or] because that person is married to (or associated with) an individual of a particular religion."[23] Religious discrimination takes many different forms. Employers may not engage in **disparate treatment** based upon religious beliefs and practices. For example, an employer may not disqualify an individual from eligibility for a job based upon the religious preferences of the employer or its employees, clients, or customers. Another example of religious discrimination is harassment. Harassment of an individual on account of his or her religion is illegal when its frequency and severity create a hostile or offensive work environment or result in an adverse employment

> Disparate treatment—differing treatment of an employee from that accorded to similarly situated employees based upon protected status or membership in a protected class.

decision such as a demotion or termination. Potential harassers include supervisors, co-workers, clients, and customers. Employers are also prohibited from segregating employees based upon their religious beliefs and practices. An example in this regard is an employer who assigns a religious employee to a position involving minimal customer contact due to the employee's dress or grooming practices. Employers are also prohibited from retaliating against religious employees based upon their beliefs, practices, requests for workplace accommodations, or actions associated with a claim of religious discrimination. Finally, employers cannot mandate or prohibit employee participation in religious activities as a condition of future or continued employment.

Non-religious employers must reasonably accommodate their employee's beliefs unless to do so would result in undue hardship. Employers may be asked to accommodate a wide variety of religious beliefs and practices in the workplace. **Religious accommodations** include flexibility in scheduling, allowing voluntary shift trades, and modifications to employer rules and policies. For example, an employer should allow its employees time off from work for devotional activities such as a Roman Catholic requesting time away from work to receive the blessing of ashes on Ash Wednesday. Another example is a Jewish employee who requests time off to mark various holidays or to leave work early on the Sabbath in order to arrive at home before sundown. Employer-mandated grooming policies are fraught with potential conflicts with religious practices of affected employees. Examples in this regard include policies relating to hair length and the wearing of beards and religious clothing and jewelry.

> Religious accommodations—the requirement that an employer adjust its work environment to allow employees to practice their religions, such as scheduling, shift substitutions, reassignments, and modifications to workplace policies, procedures, and practices.

An example of grooming policies conflicting with religious expression rights may be found in *Equal Employment Opportunity Commission v. United Parcel Service*.[24] UPS prohibits male employees who are in contact with customers or in supervisory positions from wearing beards or growing their hair below collar length. UPS also refuses to hire, promote, or accommodate such individuals. These policies were challenged by two individuals who claimed that their grooming choices were mandated by their respective faiths. One individual, a practicing Muslim, was advised to shave his beard in order to be hired for a driver helper position despite his protestations that the wearing of a beard was part of his religious observance. Another individual employed as a part-time load supervisor was instructed to cut his hair despite the fact that it was part of his observance of his Rastafarian faith.

More problematic for employers are religious beliefs that have the possibility of interfering with the employee's performance of his or her job duties or causing conflict in the workplace. How should an employer proceed if an employee claims that job duties conflict with his or her religious beliefs? For example, how should a pharmacy proceed if one of its pharmacists refuses to fill prescriptions for contraceptives for unmarried women or those products which he or she believes to be abortifacients? What approach should an employer take with respect to an employee whose faith requires proselytization, including to fellow employees in the workplace?

> Undue hardship—an exception to the requirement of reasonable accommodation of an employee's religious beliefs based upon cost, decreases in workplace safety or efficiency, or infringements upon the rights of other employees including increases in their share of work.

In answering these questions, it is important to remember that an employee's free exercise rights are not absolute if they result in an **undue hardship** to the employer. There are numerous grounds upon which an employer's hardship in accommodating an employee's religious practices may be considered undue. Employers are under no obligation to accommodate religious practices that are unduly costly, compromise workplace safety or efficiency, violate an existing seniority system, or infringe upon the rights of other employees.

An example of undue hardship may be found in *Peterson v. Hewlett-Packard Company*.[25] The *Peterson* case involved HP's diversity program. Launched in 2000, the program included posters showing different employees with labels (including one individual labeled "gay") with the accompanying slogan "Diversity is our Strength." Richard Peterson, who worked in HP's Boise, Idaho office, responded to this campaign and the placement of a poster with the label "gay" by posting scriptural passages on homosexuality in public view outside his cubicle. Peterson stated that it was his religious duty "to expose evil when confronted with sin."[26] Among the scriptural passages Peterson posted was Leviticus 20:13, which states "[i]f a man also lie with mankind, as he leith with a woman, both of them have committed an abomination; they shall surely be put to death; their blood shall be put upon them."[27] Peterson admitted his postings were intended to be "hurtful so that people would repent (change their actions) and experience the joys of being saved."[28]

HP's managers met with Peterson and advised him that his messages violated a company policy barring comments or conduct relating to a person's race, gender, religion, disability, age, sexual orientation, or ethnic background as harmful to the dignity and feelings of individual employees. However, Peterson stated he would continue to post the scriptures on his cubicle until the poster was removed. Peterson was subsequently suspended with pay but re-posted the scriptural passages upon his return, at which time he was terminated. Peterson subsequently initiated litigation against HP, claiming that it had engaged in disparate treatment and failed to reasonably accommodate his religious beliefs.

In upholding his firing, the U.S. Court of Appeals for the Ninth Circuit held that HP had a right to enforce its policy if done so in an even-handed manner and even if certain messages were suppressed. HP's efforts to eradicate discrimination in the workplace, including discrimination against members of the LGBTQ+ community, were "entirely consistent with the goals and objectives of our civil rights statutes generally."[29] HP had accommodated Peterson's beliefs as expressed in other forums, including a letter to the *Idaho Statesman* newspaper, in which he called the diversity campaign a "platform to promote the homosexual agenda."[30] HP also did not prevent Peterson from parking his car, which bore a bumper sticker with the legend "Sodomy is Not a Family Value," in the company parking lot.

Peterson was not subject to treatment different from employees who placed the diversity posters in the HP workplace as these individuals "were simply communicating [HP's] views as they were directed to do by management whereas Peterson was expressing his own personal views which contradicted those of management."[31] Furthermore, HP's posters were intended to "promote tolerance of the diversity that exists within [HP's] workforce," whereas Peterson's postings were an attack on a group of employees based upon an individual characteristic.[32] HP's refusal to require removal of posters of all employees from the workplace was not evidence of disparate treatment as those posters were not "intended to be hurtful to, or critical of, any other employees" and were not in violation of the company's anti-harassment policy.[33] The court concluded Peterson was not discharged because of his religious beliefs but rather due to his violations of HP's anti-harassment policy and insubordination.

HP could not be required to make either of the accommodations Peterson indicated he would accept, specifically, permitting him to post his scriptural messages or eliminating references to homosexuality from the workplace diversity campaign. Peterson's first proposed accommodation would have required HP to "permit an employee to post messages intended to demean and harass his co-workers."[34] Peterson's second proposed accommodation "would have forced the company to exclude sexual orientation from its workplace diversity program."[35] Either choice would have created undue hardship for HP as "it would have inhibited its efforts to attract and retain a qualified, diverse workforce, which the company reasonably views as vital to its commercial success."[36]

A related question is whether affected individuals must request a religious accommodation from their employer in order to trigger the employer's obligation to provide accommodation. This question was answered in the negative by the U.S. Supreme Court in *Equal Employment Opportunity Commission v. Abercrombie & Fitch Stores, Inc.*[37] Seventeen-year-old Samantha Elauf applied for a job in a children's clothing store owned by Abercrombie & Fitch at the Woodland Hills Mall in Tulsa, Oklahoma in 2008. Elauf wore a head scarf to her interview but did not inform the employer of her reason for covering her head. Abercrombie & Fitch refused to hire Elauf because her head scarf clashed with its "Look Policy," which called for employees to dress in a "classic East Coast collegiate style."

Elauf filed a complaint with the EEOC, which agreed to file a lawsuit on her behalf. Elauf won a $20,000 jury verdict at trial, but the result was overturned on appeal by the U.S. Court of Appeals for the Tenth Circuit on the basis that Elauf never informed Abercrombie & Fitch that she wore a head scarf for religious reasons. The court held that "[j]ob applicants should not be allowed to remain silent and assume that the employer recognizes the religious motivations behind their fashion decisions."[38]

The U.S. Supreme Court reversed this result on appeal. Writing for the 8–1 majority, Associate Justice Antonin Scalia concluded that, contrary to Abercrombie & Fitch's assertion, the reason Elauf was not hired was in order for it to avoid accommodating her religious beliefs. Elauf was not required to make a specific request for a religious accommodation. Rather, the Court held that Title VII prohibits adverse employment decisions made with a forbidden motive, whether this motive derives from actual knowledge, a well-founded suspicion, or a hunch regarding the applicant's religious affiliation. Employers could not "make an applicant's religious practice, confirmed or otherwise, a factor in employment decisions."[39]

Sexual Harassment and Workplace Culture

In 2017, there was an eruption of public allegations of sexual harassment against major media figures, CEOs, Hollywood celebrities, and others that brought to light an issue with which companies have been grappling for several decades. In fact, for two years prior to this opening of the floodgates, tech companies like Uber and Google had faced public allegations of sexual harassment, often made by former employees who later took to Twitter, Facebook, or their own blogs to describe the harassment they had endured at the hands of supervisors and top executives. In nearly every case, the employees contended that when they complained to Human Resources, they received little response, that they faced retaliation for making complaints, or that they were too afraid to come forward.

Title VII of the Civil Rights Act of 1964 makes sexual harassment prohibited sex discrimination and recognizes the detrimental impact that harassment has on its victims and their ability to be effective workers. As a result, the law regulates behavior and comments in the workplace when they rise to the level of unlawful harassment. At the same time, companies have the freedom to create workplace cultures that meet their needs, that assist in recruiting new talent, and that create productive and innovative workers. The line between an employer's ability to control its culture and prohibited harassment is sometimes questionable, and courts must decide, on a case-by-case basis, whether the behaviors at issue constitute unlawful sexual harassment or were simply offensive to one particular employee.

Box 10.3: THINX, Taboo-Smashing, and Sexual Harassment

THINX, a company that produces "period-proof underwear," is also known for its taboo-smashing former CEO and an unusual workplace culture. Mika Agrawal, the former CEO, commented in a promotional video, "My favorite thing to talk about are the things you're not supposed to talk about."[40] *In addition to selling the period-proof underwear, the company sees as its mission the breaking down of taboos regarding women's bodies and menstruation.*[41] *But this approach offended at least one former employee. A sexual harassment complaint to the City of New York Commission on Human Rights by the former head of Public Relations for THINX alleged that Agrawal, among other things, openly talked about and touched her employees' breasts, discussed her own sexual exploits in detail, routinely changed clothes in front of employees, and conducted video-conference meetings nude and in bed or from the toilet. At the time, the company had no Human Resources managers, training, or policies. The complaint was ultimately dismissed after a confidential settlement. Nonetheless, the episode raises important questions about the line between a company's freedom to create a workplace culture that represents its brand and legal restrictions on permissible behavior and comments of a sexual nature.*

Where do you think that line should be drawn? Should employees of a company like THINX be viewed as forewarned that the company's mission of breaking taboos would bleed into its culture? Can a company require its employees to be comfortable with sexual discussions and bodily freedom, or should the law step in to protect employees in this scenario?

Sexual Harassment Law

Although Title VII was passed in 1964, the EEOC did not recognize sexual harassment as a form of sex discrimination until 1980. It was not until 1986 that the Supreme Court defined sexual harassment. In *Meritor Savings Bank v. Vinson*,[42] the plaintiff, a bank teller who ultimately became assistant branch manager, alleged that her supervisor suggested sexual relations and that, after first refusing, she later agreed out of fear of losing her job. The plaintiff claimed that her supervisor then made repeated demands upon her for sexual favors, that he fondled her in front of other employees, followed her into the women's restroom, exposed himself to her, and forcibly raped her on several occasions. The plaintiff contended that she never reported the harassment and never attempted to use the bank's complaint procedure because she was terrified of her supervisor. The Court concluded that "a plaintiff may establish a violation of Title VII by proving that discrimination based on sex has created a hostile or abusive work environment."[43] An analogy between sexual harassment and conduct outlawed as race discrimination provided the reasoning for the Court's conclusion:

> Sexual harassment which creates a hostile or offensive environment for members of one sex is every bit the arbitrary barrier to sexual equality at the workplace that racial harassment is to racial equality. Surely, a requirement that a man or woman run a gauntlet of sexual abuse in return for the privilege of being allowed

to work and make a living can be as demeaning and disconcerting as the harshest of racial epithets.

For its part, the EEOC has issued regulations defining sexual harassment as follows:

> Unwelcome sexual advances, requests for sexual favors, and other verbal or physical conduct of a sexual nature constitute sexual harassment when (1) submission to such conduct is made either explicitly or implicitly a term or condition of an individual's employment, (2) submission to or rejection of such conduct by an individual is used as the basis for employment decisions affecting such individual, or (3) such conduct has the purpose or effect of unreasonably interfering with an individual's work performance or creating an intimidating, hostile, or offensive working environment.[44]

Quid pro quo harassment—demands that make sexual conduct a condition of employment.

Hostile work environment harassment—language or conduct in the workplace that interferes with the employee's ability to work or creates an unbearable work environment.

Severe or pervasive harassment—a requirement for sexual harassment to be unlawful. These terms are interpreted by courts in the context of a case and may have different meanings to different judges.

Objectively and subjectively offensive conduct—a requirement for a court to find harassing behavior unlawful. It must be conduct that "a reasonable person would find hostile or abusive, and one that the victim in fact did perceive to be so."

Retaliation—behavior that punishes a victim of discrimination for reporting the unlawful conduct.

These guidelines dictate that there are two basic forms of prohibited sexual harassment: (1) quid pro quo harassment and (2) hostile work environment harassment. **Quid pro quo harassment** typically involves demands that make sexual conduct a condition of employment. In this form of harassment, there is an express or implied link between submission to sexually oriented behavior and a tangible job consequence. For example, an employee is terminated after refusing to date or have sex with her supervisor. In contrast, **hostile work environment harassment** involves language or conduct in the workplace that interferes with the employee's ability to work or creates an unbearable work environment. The Court in *Meritor Savings Bank* made clear that not all offensive conduct creates an unlawful hostile work environment and that "[f]or sexual harassment to be actionable, it must be sufficiently **severe or pervasive** to alter the conditions of [the victim's] employment and create an abusive working environment."[45] Constant sexual remarks, comments about an employee's body, or unwelcome physical touching may all give rise to a claim of hostile work environment harassment.

The Supreme Court has also clarified in subsequent cases that for harassing conduct to be actionable, it must be both **objectively and subjectively offensive conduct**. In other words, it must be conduct that "a reasonable person would find hostile or abusive, and one that the victim in fact did perceive to be so." The Court has regularly repeated its admonishment that "'simple teasing,' offhand comments, and isolated incidents (unless extremely serious) will not amount to discriminatory changes in the 'terms and conditions of employment.'"

In addition to prohibiting sexual harassment, Title VII also includes a prohibition against **retaliation** in order to protect employees who come forward and make complaints. This retaliation protection is not specific to sexual harassment and protects anyone who opposes a practice made unlawful under Title VII, whether it involves race, sex, religion, color, or national origin discrimination. Title VII provides:

> It shall be an unlawful employment practice for an employer to discriminate against any of his employees or applicants for employment . . . because he has opposed any practice made an unlawful employment practice by this subchapter, or because he has made a charge, testified, assisted, or participated in any manner in an investigation, proceeding, or hearing under this subchapter.[46]

The retaliation provisions of Title VII are often raised in sexual harassment suits because of the difficult nature of coming forward to complain about sexual harassment and because so many employees claim that they were fired, demoted, or otherwise punished for speaking up about this particular form of discrimination.

Company Practices and Policies on Harassment

A pair of cases at the Supreme Court in 1998 created inducements for employers to develop company policies on prohibited sexual harassment and reporting mechanisms that encourage employees to come forward. The cases, *Burlington Industries Inc. v. Ellerth*[47] and *Faragher v. City of Boca Raton*,[48] discussed the concept of **vicarious liability** for harassment—the notion that an employer could be liable for the conduct of its employees, both managers and underlings, in different circumstances. The Court held that, in general, employers are liable for an actionable hostile work environment created by a supervisor. However, when no **tangible employment action** is taken (i.e. termination, demotion, etc.), the employer can raise an **affirmative defense** to liability by demonstrating (1) that the employer "exercised reasonable care to prevent and correct promptly any sexually harassing behavior," and (2) that "the plaintiff employee unreasonably failed to take advantage of any preventive or corrective opportunities provided by the employer or to avoid harm otherwise." In essence, a company can avoid liability in a hostile work environment case if it can demonstrate both that it put in place policies prohibiting harassment and reasonable procedures for reporting complaints and that the plaintiff failed to make use of these procedures.

This pair of cases had major implications for the way that companies should and do educate and train their managers and their workforce in general. In practice, employers should have basic prevention and reporting systems in place both as a means of avoiding liability in sexual harassment suits and in an effort to create a healthy workplace in which employees are productive contributors. Companies should have good anti-harassment policies that are widely distributed and discussed. They should provide training to managers and lower-level employees about what the policies entail and behaviors that are prohibited under them. In addition, companies should put in place complaint procedures that allow for multiple routes for a complaint depending on who the alleged harasser is and his or her relationship to the complaining employee. Finally, when complaints are lodged, companies should take those complaints seriously, investigate allegations thoroughly, and take action to stop any unlawful behavior immediately.

> **Vicarious liability**—the notion that an employer could be liable for the conduct of its employees.
>
> **Tangible employment action**—a significant change in employment status, including hiring, firing, failing to promote, a significant change in benefits, etc.
>
> **Affirmative defense**—a defense in which the defendant introduces evidence, which, if found to be credible, will negate liability, even if it is proven that the defendant committed the alleged acts.

Oncale v. Sundowner Offshore Servs., 523 U.S. 75 (1998)

In late October 1991, Oncale was working for respondent Sundowner Offshore Services on a Chevron U.S.A., Inc., oil platform in the Gulf of Mexico. He was employed as a roustabout on an eight-man crew which included respondents John Lyons, Danny Pippen, and Brandon Johnson. Lyons ... and Pippen ... had supervisory authority. On several occasions, Oncale was forcibly subjected to sex-related, humiliating actions against him by Lyons, Pippen and Johnson in the presence of the rest of the crew. Pippen and Lyons also physically assaulted Oncale in a sexual manner, and Lyons threatened him with rape.

Oncale's complaints to supervisory personnel produced no remedial action; in fact, the company's Safety Compliance Clerk ... told Oncale that Lyons and Pippen "picked [on] him all the time too," and called him a name suggesting homosexuality. Oncale eventually quit—asking that his pink slip reflect that he "voluntarily left due to sexual harassment and verbal abuse." When asked at his deposition why he left Sundowner, Oncale stated "I felt that if I didn't leave my job, that I would be raped or forced to have sex."

Oncale filed a complaint against Sundowner in the United States District Court for the Eastern District of Louisiana, alleging that he was discriminated against in his employment because of his sex. Relying on the Fifth Circuit's decision in Garcia v. Elf Atochem North America, the district court held that "Mr. Oncale, a male, has no cause of action under Title VII for harassment by male co-workers." On appeal, a panel of the Fifth Circuit concluded that Garcia was binding Circuit precedent, and affirmed. We granted certiorari.

Title VII of the Civil Rights Act of 1964 provides, in relevant part, that "it shall be an unlawful employment practice for an employer ... to discriminate against any individual with respect to his compensation, terms, conditions, or privileges of employment, because of such individual's race, color, religion, sex, or national origin." We have held that this not only covers "terms" and "conditions" in the narrow contractual sense, but "evinces a congressional intent to strike at the entire spectrum of disparate treatment of men and women in employment." "When the workplace is permeated with discriminatory intimidation, ridicule, and insult that is sufficiently severe or pervasive to alter the conditions of the victim's employment and create an abusive working environment, Title VII is violated."

Title VII's prohibition of discrimination "because of ... sex" protects men as well as women, and in the related context of racial discrimination in the workplace we have rejected any conclusive presumption that an employer will not discriminate against members of his own race. "Because of the many facets of human motivation, it would be unwise to presume as a matter of law that human beings of one definable group will not discriminate against other members of that group." In Johnson v. Transportation Agency, Santa Clara Cty., a male employee claimed that his employer discriminated against him because of his sex when it preferred a female employee for promotion. Although we ultimately rejected the claim on other grounds, we did not consider it significant that the supervisor who made that decision was also a man. If our precedents leave any doubt on the question, we hold today that nothing in Title VII necessarily bars a claim of discrimination "because of ... sex" merely because the plaintiff and the defendant (or the person charged with acting on behalf of the defendant) are of the same sex.

[W]hen the issue arises in the context of a "hostile environment" sexual harassment claim, the state and federal courts have taken a bewildering variety of stances. Some, like the Fifth Circuit in this case, have held that same-sex sexual harassment claims are never cognizable under Title VII. Other decisions say that such claims are actionable only if the plaintiff can prove that the harasser is homosexual (and thus presumably motivated by sexual desire). Still others suggest that workplace harassment that is sexual in content is always actionable, regardless of the harasser's sex, sexual orientation, or motivations.

We see no justification in the statutory language or our precedents for a categorical rule excluding same-sex harassment claims from the coverage of Title VII. As some courts have observed, male-on-male sexual harassment in the workplace was assuredly not the principal evil Congress was concerned with when it enacted Title VII. But statutory prohibitions often go beyond the principal evil to cover reasonably comparable evils, and it is ultimately the provisions of our laws rather than the principal concerns of our legislators by which we are governed.

***

Respondents and their amici contend that recognizing liability for same-sex harassment will transform Title VII into a general civility code for the American workplace. But that risk is no greater for same-sex than for opposite-sex harassment, and is adequately met by careful attention to the requirements of the statute. Title VII does not prohibit all verbal or physical harassment in the workplace; it is directed only at "discrimination . . . because of . . . sex." We have never held that workplace harassment, even harassment between men and women, is automatically discrimination because of sex merely because the words used have sexual content or connotations. "The critical issue, Title VII's text indicates, is whether members of one sex are exposed to disadvantageous terms or conditions of employment to which members of the other sex are not exposed."

Courts and juries have found the inference of discrimination easy to draw in most male-female sexual harassment situations, because the challenged conduct typically involves explicit or implicit proposals of sexual activity; it is reasonable to assume those proposals would not have been made to someone of the same sex. The same chain of inference would be available to a plaintiff alleging same-sex harassment, if there were credible evidence that the harasser was homosexual. But harassing conduct need not be motivated by sexual desire to support an inference of discrimination on the basis of sex. A trier of fact might reasonably find such discrimination, for example, if a female victim is harassed in such sex-specific and derogatory terms by another woman as to make it clear that the harasser is motivated by general hostility to the presence of women in the workplace. A same-sex harassment plaintiff may also, of course, offer direct comparative evidence about how the alleged harasser treated members of both sexes in a mixed-sex workplace.

***

And there is another requirement that prevents Title VII from expanding into a general civility code: As we emphasized in Meritor and Harris, the statute does not reach genuine but innocuous differences in the ways men and women routinely interact with members of the same sex and of the opposite sex. The prohibition of harassment on the basis of sex requires neither asexuality nor androgyny in the workplace; it forbids only behavior so objectively offensive as to alter the "conditions" of the victim's employment.

***

We have emphasized, moreover, that the objective severity of harassment should be judged from the perspective of a reasonable person in the plaintiff's position, considering "all the circumstances." In same-sex (as in all) harassment cases, that inquiry requires careful consideration of the social context in which particular behavior occurs and is experienced by its target. A professional football player's working environment is not severely or pervasively abusive, for example, if the coach smacks him on the buttocks as he heads onto the field—even if the same behavior would reasonably be experienced as abusive by the coach's secretary (male or female) back at the office. The real social impact of workplace behavior often depends on a constellation of surrounding circumstances, expectations, and relationships which are not fully captured by a simple recitation of the words used or the physical acts performed.

***

Because we conclude that sex discrimination consisting of same-sex sexual harassment is actionable under Title VII, the judgment of the Court of Appeals for the Fifth Circuit is reversed, and the case is remanded for further proceedings consistent with this opinion.

It is so ordered.

Pregnancy in the Workplace

The issues associated with pregnancy in the workplace have been the cause of intense confusion, even for the most well-meaning employers. Because only women get pregnant, employers often find themselves in a situation where biological differences necessitate differences in treatment. However, as views on pregnancy and parenting have evolved, it is becoming more and more clear that new mothers and fathers need to be treated the same in many circumstances, while differing treatment will be allowed by courts in others. Even today, large companies such as Estée Lauder, UPS, and JP Morgan Chase are facing lawsuits stemming from issues surrounding pregnancy. Questions of how much leave should be given, to whom it should be given, what accommodations need to be made for pregnant workers on the job, and when an employee can refuse to hire a pregnant employee are all still sources of potential liability for employers.

As a society, we, of course, want to encourage and support reproduction in general. However, the question becomes how much responsibility we put on employers to support this societally desirable action. Employers want the freedom to determine how to respond to an employee's pregnancy in the way they see fit. For instance, some employers would like to be able to force pregnant employees to take on different and more lenient jobs while pregnant or even force employees to take unpaid leave before becoming pregnant. Employees, on the other hand, would like to be entitled to a different job during pregnancy, to the extent that they cannot perform the one they currently have. These issues of employer freedom versus employee rights in the pregnancy area have come front and center in recent years, as will be discussed in the following sections. Specifically, disputes involving job accommodations, pregnancy as a bona fide occupational qualification, and parental leave have found courts tackling issues at the core of what it means to treat employees equally.

Title VII of the Civil Rights Act of 1964 and the Pregnancy Discrimination Act of 1978

Title VII of the Civil Rights Act of 1964 prohibits employers from discriminating against their employees because of sex. In a series of early cases, the United States Supreme Court held that employee benefits programs that exclude pregnancy from coverage were not discriminatory under Title VII because such policies discriminated against pregnant versus non-pregnant women and not against women versus men.[49] In 1978, Congress repudiated these holdings with the passage of the Pregnancy Discrimination Act (PDA). The PDA amends Title VII to include discrimination because of pregnancy as discrimination because of sex. Specifically, the PDA provides that an employer may not discriminate against an employee on the basis of pregnancy, childbirth, or a related medical condition. Additionally, the PDA provides that women affected by pregnancy, childbirth, or a related medical condition must be treated the same as other non-pregnant employees who are similar in their ability or inability to work. We will take each of these provisions in turn.

Discrimination Based on Pregnancy, Childbirth, or Other Related Medical Conditions

Under Title VII, as amended by the PDA, an employer may not discriminate against an employee because of pregnancy, childbirth, or any related medical conditions.

Therefore, an employer cannot fire someone simply for becoming pregnant. In *Asmo v. Keane, Inc.*,[50] the court held that a two-month period between the time the employer became aware of the plaintiff's pregnancy and the time the employer fired the plaintiff showed a causal link between the pregnancy and the discharge. Additionally, courts have held that an employer is not allowed to discriminate against an employee because of the employee's intention to become pregnant. Thus, when hiring, employers should not ask women whether they intend to become pregnant. Furthermore, employers need to be mindful of how they treat mothers who return to work after childbirth. Specifically, adverse treatment of a lactating employee may raise an inference of discrimination under Title VII because lactation is a medical condition related to pregnancy and childbirth. In sum, employers need to be careful to not take any adverse employment actions simply because a woman is pregnant, intends to become pregnant, or has a medical issue related to pregnancy and childbirth.

Accommodation of Pregnancy in the Workplace

The second requirement of the PDA has been the subject of much confusion among courts trying to figure out what it means to treat similarly situated pregnant and non-pregnant employees equally. This confusion has been particularly obvious in the area of **job accommodation**. That is, to what extent does an employer have to place an employee in a different job while the employee is pregnant? Courts have held that the employer has a legal duty to reassign a pregnant woman if the employer has reassigned non-pregnant individuals who have work limitations similar to the pregnant employee. For instance, if an employer has reassigned all men with lifting limitations to light-duty work, then they would likely have to grant the same accommodation to pregnant women similarly limited in their ability to lift. For a greater discussion of this issue, see the *Young* case at the end of this section.

> Job accommodation—finding a position or job within an organization for an employee who is no longer able to complete the essential tasks of their job (can be due to pregnancy, religion, or disability).

Pregnancy as a Bona Fide Occupational Qualification

Title VII provides a very narrow affirmative defense for employers that allows hiring with regard to certain protected characteristics. Specifically, pursuant to Section 703(e) of Title VII,

> it shall not be an unlawful employment practice for an employer to hire and employ employees . . . on the basis of his religion, sex, or national origin in those certain instances where religion, sex, or national origin is a **bona fide occupational qualification (BFOQ)** reasonably necessary to the normal operation of that particular business or enterprise.

Since this provision of Title VII allows for discrimination in certain instances, courts have interpreted it extremely narrowly. When it comes to pregnancy, courts have held that concern for a pregnant mother or fetus is not enough to meet the standards for a BFOQ under Title VII. For instance, the Supreme Court rejected a battery manufacturing company's efforts to only employ women incapable of becoming pregnant in jobs in which employees could come into contact with high lead levels.[51] The Court reasoned that potential fertility had nothing to do with the actual qualifications to be able to make sound batteries and, therefore, was not a BFOQ. However, that does not mean pregnancy can never serve as a BFOQ. In *Levin v. Delta Air Lines, Inc.*,[52] the court held that not being pregnant was a BFOQ for flight attendants since pregnancy

> Bona fide occupational qualification (BFOQ)—employment qualities or attributes of a prospective or current employee that an employer is allowed to consider under law for the purpose of hiring or retention. The qualifications may include gender, age, and national origin, if those characteristics are considered essential to the job requirements.

could lead to unexpected complications mid-flight that could compromise a flight attendant's ability to keep passengers safe in an emergency. Notably, the BFOQ of non-pregnancy was not based on risk to the mother or fetus, but rather to third parties—here, the passengers. As noted previously, the BFOQ is a very narrow defense and rarely recognized as a reason for discriminating against pregnant employees.

Parental Leave

Under the Family and Medical Leave Act (FMLA), eligible employees are entitled to up to 12 weeks unpaid leave upon the birth or adoption of a child. In recent years, many companies have decided to voluntarily offer much more generous leave. For instance, in August 2015, Netflix introduced a parental leave policy that allowed

> unlimited leave policy for new moms and dads that allows them to take off as much time as they want during the first year after a child's birth or adoption. . . . Parents can return part-time, full-time, or return and then go back out as needed. We'll just keep paying them normally, eliminating the headache of switching to state or disability pay.[53]

Additionally, companies like Amazon, Google, and Bloomberg have offered generous paid leave policies to their employees after the birth of a child.

The benefits to paid parental leave are clear—when parents have more bonding time with their babies without the pressure of lost compensation, this results in everything from reduced instances of sickness for the baby to long-term higher IQ scores. Additionally, paid leave is beneficial for employers because it tends to increase employee commitment to the company once they return from leave, as well as increasing employee productivity since employees don't feel that they have to choose between work and family in the early stages of parenthood.

However, even well-meaning employers can sometimes get themselves into trouble. In 2013, Estée Lauder adopted a new parental leave policy that not only provided paid time off to new mothers to recover from childbirth, but also granted new mothers another six weeks of paid parental leave for child bonding. Under the new policy, the company offered new fathers two weeks of paid leave for such bonding. On August 30, 2017, the EEOC announced a class action lawsuit against Estée Lauder, claiming the company's parental leave policy violates Title VII of the Civil Rights Act of 1964 and the Equal Pay Act of 1963. Both laws prohibit discrimination based on sex in pay and benefits. The EEOC argued that in providing new mothers and fathers unequal amounts of time for bonding, the company violated the law. So what should a well-meaning employer who would like to offer paid leave to new parents do? The employer should continue to do so, while reevaluating its policies to be sure they stay within the confines of the law. Most importantly, employers need to be sure they are treating workers equally. This does not mean that they have to give equal periods of paid leave to birth mothers and fathers. The law actually does not require that. Because birth mothers are recovering from the medical consequences of pregnancy, employers are allowed, under the law, to offer birth mothers paid time off to recover from pregnancy without offering such similar time to fathers. According to EEOC Guidelines on Parental Leave, what employers cannot do is offer parental leave time not associated with medical recovery (say, for bonding with the child) on an unequal basis to mothers and fathers. Instead, any time given to women for bonding with their new babies must also be offered to men.

Young v. United Parcel Service, Inc. 575 U.S. ___ (2015)

Peggy Young worked as a part-time driver for the respondent, United Parcel Service (UPS). Her responsibilities included pickup and delivery of packages that had arrived by air carrier the previous night. In 2006, after suffering several miscarriages, she became pregnant. Her doctor told her that she should not lift more than 20 pounds during the first 20 weeks of her pregnancy or more than 10 pounds thereafter. UPS required drivers like Young to be able to lift parcels weighing up to 70 pounds (and up to 150 pounds with assistance). UPS told Young she could not work while under a lifting restriction. Young consequently stayed home without pay during most of the time she was pregnant and eventually lost her employee medical coverage. Young subsequently brought this federal lawsuit. We focus here on her claim that UPS acted unlawfully in refusing to accommodate her pregnancy-related lifting restriction. Young said that her co-workers were willing to help her with heavy packages. She also said that UPS accommodated other drivers who were "similar in their ... inability to work." She accordingly concluded that UPS must accommodate her as well.

UPS responded that the "other persons" whom it had accommodated were (1) drivers who had become disabled on the job, (2) those who had lost their Department of Transportation (DOT) certifications, and (3) those who suffered from a disability covered by the Americans with Disabilities Act of 1990 (ADA). UPS said that, since Young did not fall within any of those categories, it had not discriminated against Young on the basis of pregnancy but had treated her just as it treated all "other" relevant "persons."

Title VII of the Civil Rights Act of 1964 forbids a covered employer to "discriminate against any individual with respect to ... terms, conditions, or privileges of employment, because of such individual's ... sex." In 1978, Congress enacted the Pregnancy Discrimination Act, which added new language to Title VII's definitions subsection. The first clause of the 1978 Act specifies that Title VII's "ter[m] 'because of sex' ... include[s] ... because of or on the basis of pregnancy, childbirth, or related medical conditions." The second clause says that "women affected by pregnancy, childbirth, or related medical conditions shall be treated the same for all employment-related purposes ... as other persons not so affected but similar in their ability or inability to work...." This case requires us to consider the application of the second clause to a "disparate-treatment" claim—a claim that an employer intentionally treated a complainant less favorably than employees with the "complainant's qualifications" but outside the complainant's protected class.

***

The District Court granted UPS' motion for summary judgment. It concluded that ... those with whom Young compared herself—those falling within the on-the-job, DOT, or ADA categories—were too different to qualify as "similarly situated comparator[s]."

***

On appeal, the Fourth Circuit affirmed. It wrote that "UPS has crafted a pregnancy-blind policy" that is "at least facially a 'neutral and legitimate business practice,' and not evidence of UPS's discriminatory animus toward pregnant workers." It also agreed with the District Court that Young could not show that "similarly-situated employees outside the protected class received more favorable treatment than Young." Specifically, it believed that Young was different from those workers who were "disabled under the ADA" (which then protected only those with permanent disabilities) because Young was "not disabled"; her lifting limitation was only "temporary and not a significant restriction on her ability to perform major life activities." Young was also different from those workers who had lost their DOT certifications because "no legal obstacle stands between her and her work" and because many with lost DOT certifications retained physical (i.e., lifting) capacity that Young lacked. And Young was different from those "injured on the job because, quite simply, her inability to work [did] not arise from an on-the-job injury." Rather, Young more closely resembled "an employee who injured his back while picking up his infant child or ... an employee whose lifting limitation arose from her off-the-job work as a volunteer firefighter," neither of whom would have been eligible for accommodation under UPS' policies.

The parties disagree about the interpretation of the Pregnancy Discrimination Act's second clause. As we have said ... the Act's first clause specifies that discrimination "'because of sex'" includes discrimination "because of ... pregnancy." But the meaning of the second clause is less clear; it adds: "[W]omen affected by pregnancy, childbirth, or related medical conditions shall be treated the same for all employment-related purposes ... as other persons not so affected but similar in their ability or inability to work." Does this clause mean that courts must compare workers only in respect to the work limitations that they suffer? Does it mean that courts must ignore all other similarities or differences between pregnant and nonpregnant workers? Or does it mean that courts, when deciding who the relevant "other persons" are, may consider other similarities and differences as well? If so, which ones?

***

The parties propose very different answers to th[ese] question[s]. Young and the United States believe that the second clause of the Pregnancy Discrimination Act "requires an employer to provide the same accommodations to workplace disabilities caused by pregnancy that it provides to workplace disabilities that have other causes but have a similar effect on the ability to work." In other words, Young contends that the second clause means that whenever "an employer accommodates only a subset of workers with disabling conditions," a court should find a Title VII violation if "pregnant workers who are similar in the ability to work" do not "receive the same [accommodation] even if still other non-pregnant workers do not receive accommodations." UPS takes an almost polar opposite view. It contends that the second clause does no more than define sex discrimination to include pregnancy discrimination. Under this view, courts would compare the accommodations an employer provides to pregnant women with the accommodations it provides to others within a facially neutral category (such as those with off-the-job injuries) to determine whether the employer has violated Title VII.

***

We cannot accept either of these interpretations.... The problem with Young's approach is that it proves too much. It seems to say that the statute grants pregnant workers a "most-favored-nation" status. As long as an employer provides one or two workers with an accommodation—say, those with particularly hazardous jobs, or those whose workplace presence is particularly needed, or those who have worked at the company for many years, or those who are over the age of 55—then it must provide similar accommodations to all pregnant workers (with comparable physical limitations), irrespective of the nature of their jobs, the employer's need to keep them working, their ages, or any other criteria.

***

We find it similarly difficult to accept the opposite interpretation of the Act's second clause. UPS says that the second clause simply defines sex discrimination to include pregnancy discrimination. But that cannot be so. The first clause accomplishes that objective when it expressly amends Title VII's definitional provision to make clear that Title VII's words "because of sex" and "on the basis of sex" "include, but are not limited to, because of or on the basis of pregnancy, childbirth, or related medical conditions." We have long held that "'a statute ought, upon the whole, to be so construed that, if it can be prevented, no clause'" is rendered "'superfluous, void, or insignificant.'" But that is what UPS' interpretation of the second clause would do.

***

Thus, a plaintiff alleging that the denial of an accommodation constituted disparate treatment under the Pregnancy Discrimination Act's second clause may make out a prima facie case by showing, as in McDonnell Douglas, that she belongs to the protected class, that she sought accommodation, that the employer did not accommodate her, and that the employer did accommodate others "similar in their ability or inability to work." The employer may then seek to justify its refusal to accommodate the plaintiff by relying on "legitimate, nondiscriminatory" reasons for denying her accommodation. But, consistent with the Act's basic objective, that reason normally cannot consist simply of a claim that it is more expensive or less convenient to add pregnant women to the category of those ("similar in their ability or inability to work") whom the employer accommodates.... If the employer offers an apparently "legitimate, nondiscriminatory" reason for its actions, the plaintiff may in turn show that the employer's proffered reasons are in fact pretextual. We believe that the plaintiff may reach a jury on this issue by providing sufficient evidence that the employer's policies impose a significant burden on pregnant workers, and that the employer's "legitimate, nondiscriminatory" reasons are not sufficiently strong to justify the burden, but rather—when considered along with the burden imposed—give rise to an inference of intentional discrimination.

***

Under this interpretation of the Act, the judgment of the Fourth Circuit must be vacated. Viewing the record in the light most favorable to Young, there is a genuine dispute as to whether UPS provided more favorable treatment to at least some employees whose situation cannot reasonably be distinguished from Young's.... Young also introduced evidence that UPS had three separate accommodation policies (on-the-job, ADA, DOT). Taken together, Young argued, these policies significantly burdened pregnant women. (shop steward's testimony that "the only light duty requested [due to physical] restrictions that became an issue" at UPS "were with women who were pregnant"). The Fourth Circuit did not consider the combined effects of these policies, nor did it consider the strength of UPS' justifications for each when combined. That is, why, when the employer accommodated so many, could it not accommodate pregnant women as well? We do not determine whether Young created a genuine issue of material fact as to whether UPS' reasons for having treated Young less favorably than it treated these other nonpregnant employees were pretextual. We leave a final determination of that question for the Fourth Circuit to make on remand, in light of the interpretation of the Pregnancy Discrimination Act that we have set out above.

For the reasons above, we vacate the judgment of the Fourth Circuit and remand the case for further proceedings consistent with this opinion.

It is so ordered.

Conclusion

As you can see from the variety of topics discussed in this chapter, employment law in the United States requires a constant balancing between the employer's freedom to run his or her workplace as he or she sees fit and employees' rights within that workplace. From privacy rights, to rights to be free from discrimination and sexual harassment, to rights to work after leaving a particular employer, this area of law is replete with policy issues that force courts and legislatures to confront questions about what rights both employers and employees should enjoy every day. In the future, the tensions are likely to continue and will likely center on religious beliefs that come in conflict with one's ability to do a job, sexual harassment after the Me Too Movement, and privacy in a world of ever-changing technology. Although we cannot absolutely predict how these legal issues will unfold in the court or legislatures, one thing is certain—they will all require careful balancing of employee rights versus employer freedom.

Discussion Questions

1. In this chapter, you read about how noncompete agreements can be held unenforceable because they prevent the public from receiving medical or legal services. What other public policies do you think could outweigh an otherwise valid noncompete, so as to lead a court to hold a noncompete unenforceable because the public interest outweighs competing employer interests?
2. What are the advantages and disadvantages of employee handbooks? If you were starting your own business, would you utilize an employee handbook? Why or why not?
3. What are some industries that you think noncompete agreements should be used in? Why?
4. Employers are held responsible, in many ways, for the safety and well-being of their employees. To what extent does employee monitoring help employers carry out that responsibility? In what ways might monitoring undermine employee well-being?
5. Do you think current employment privacy laws give employees too little privacy or too much protection at the expense of legitimate employer concerns?
6. How do you think courts should go about determining what a "reasonable expectation of privacy" is, and why?
7. To what extent do you think an employer should have to accommodate an employee's desire to proselytize within the workplace? What are the consequences of such accommodation for the employer and other employees?
8. Do you think employers should have to accommodate an employee's religious beliefs that prevent the employee from actually performing some of his or her job duties (e.g., a county clerk who won't issue marriage licenses to same-sex couples)? Why or why not?
9. Justice Scalia notes in Oncale that "The real social impact of workplace behavior often depends on a constellation of surrounding circumstances, expectations, and relationships which are not fully captured by a simple recitation of the words used or the physical acts performed." What does this mean? What factors should courts consider when deciding if behavior rises to the level of unlawful harassment?

10. The Supreme Court has remarked that Title VII is not meant to be a "general civility code." What do you think this means? How can courts distinguish offensive conduct from unlawful conduct? Would your analysis be the same or different if the case involved racial harassment rather than sexual harassment?
11. In nearly all of the recent cases involving allegations of sexual harassment, the alleged perpetrators have been male and the alleged victims have been female. What characteristics of the modern workplace and of society generally have led to this dynamic?
12. In *Oncale*, Justice Scalia comments that "[S]tatutory prohibitions often go beyond the principal evil to cover reasonably comparable evils, and it is ultimately the provisions of our laws rather than the principal concerns of our legislators by which we are governed." Do you agree? Should the Court consider more than the intentions of the legislators when interpreting the scope of protection provided by a statute? Can you think of other areas of law where this comment might be applicable?
13. Do you think employers should ever be able to refuse to hire someone who is pregnant, even if they would make the same decision about another similarly situated non-pregnant individual? Why or why not?
14. Do you think pregnancy should ever be a bona fide occupational qualification that justifies wholesale exclusion of pregnant women from certain jobs? If so, when?

Notes

1. H.G. Wood, a Treatise of The Law of Master and Servant 272 (1877).
2. 42 N.E. 416, 417 (N.Y. 1895).
3. 491 A. 2d 1257 (N.J. 1985).
4. Some states, such as California, North Dakota, and Oklahoma, prohibit noncompete agreements in employment. See Cal. Business & Professions Code § 16600, N.D. Cent. Code § 9–08–06, and OK Stat. § 15–219A.
5. *The Community Hospital Group, Inc. v. More*, 183 N.J. 36, 49 (2005).
6. Michael J. Garrison & John T. Wendt, *The Evolving Law of Employee Noncompete Agreements: Recent Trends and an Alternative Policy Approach*, 45 Am. Bus. L. J. 107 (2008).
7. *Karpinski v. Ingrasci*, 268 N.E.2d 751, 755–756 (1971).
8. Dave Jamieson, *Jimmy John's Makes Low-Wage Workers Sign 'Oppressive' Noncompete Agreements*, HuffPost, Oct. 15, 2014, www.huffingtonpost.com/2014/10/13/jimmy-johns-non-compete_n_5978180.html
9. 345 S.C. 378 (2001).
10. *Id.* at 381.
11. *Compare to Systems Concepts, Inc. v. Dixon*, 669 P. 2d 421, 425–426 (Utah 1983).
12. *Beverage Systems of the Carolinas, LLC v. Associated Beverage Repair*, LLC 268 N.C. 693 (2016).
13. Wis. Stat. § 103.465 (2016).
14. Restatement (Second) of Contracts § 184 (1981).
15. 192 W. Va. 506 (1994).
16. *Id.* at 510.
17. *Compare to Woolley v. Hoffmann-La Roche, Inc.*, 491 A.2d 1257 (N.J. 1985).
18. *W. Coast Hotel Co. v. Parrish*, 300 U.S. 379, 392 (1937).
19. *Nat'l Captioning Inst. v. Nat'l Ass'n. of Broadcast Employees & Technicians Communication Workers of America, AFL—CIO*, ALJ Ruling JD-71-17 (Sep. 18, 2017).
20. 42 U.S.C. § 2000e-2(a)(1–2) (2018).

21. U.S. Equal Emp. Opportunity Comm'n, *What You Should Know about Workplace Religious Accommodation* 1.
22. 42 U.S.C. § 2000e-1(a) (2018).
23. U.S. Equal Emp. Opportunity Comm'n, *Religious Discrimination* 1 (2017).
24. Case No. 15–04141 (E.D.N.Y. July 15, 2015).
25. 358 F.3d 599 (9th Cir. 2004).
26. *Id.* at 601.
27. *Id.* at 601–602.
28. *Id.* at 602.
29. *Id.* at 603.
30. *Id.* at 604.
31. *Id.*
32. *Id.* at 605.
33. *Id.*
34. *Id.* at 607.
35. *Id.*
36. *Id.*
37. 135 S. Ct. 2028 (2015).
38. 731 F.3d 1106 (10th Cir. 2013).
39. *Abercrombie & Fitch Stores, Inc.*, 135 S. Ct. at 2033.
40. Noreen Malone, *Sexual-Harassment Claims against a 'She-E.O.' Thinx Boss Miki Agrawal Wanted to Break Taboos about the Female Body: According to Some Employees, She Went Too Far*, The Cut, Mar. 20, 2017, www.thecut.com/2017/03/thinx-employee-accuses-miki-agrawal-of-sexual-harassment.html
41. Thinx, www.shethinx.com (last visited Jan. 8, 2018) (asking customers to provide an email address to "get taboo-smashing updates, must-know period info, and answers to all your health Qs").
42. 477 U.S. 57 (1986).
43. 477 U.S. 57, 66 (1986).
44. 29 C.F.R. § 1604.11(a).
45. 477 U.S. 57, 67 (1986).
46. 42 U.S. Code § 2000e—3(a).
47. 524 U.S. 742 (1998).
48. 524 U.S. 775 (1998).
49. *See Gilbert v. General Electric*, 425 U.S. 989 (1976); *see also Nashville Gas Co. v. Satty*, 434 U.S. 136 (1977).
50. 471 F.3d 588 (6th Cir. 2006).
51. *Int'l Union v. Johnson Controls*, 499 U.S. 187 (1991).
52. 730 F.2d 994 (5th Cir. 1984).
53. Tawni Cranz, *Starting Now at Netflix: Unlimited Maternity and Paternity Leave*, Netflix US & Canada Blog (Aug. 4, 2015, 1:42 PM), http://blog.netflix.com/2015/08/starting-now-at-netflix-unlimited.html. Note that this policy only applies to certain employees. Employees involved in the DVD and call center aspects of the company (generally, the hourly employees) are subject to a different, less generous policy. *See* Shane Ferro, *Netflix Just Made Huge Strides on Parental Leave*, Huff Post, Dec. 9, 2015, www.huffingtonpost.com/entry/netflix-paid-parental-leave-hourly-workers_us_56685ae1e4b009377b233a79

Additional Learning Resources

Additional Readings

ANITA: *Speaking Truth to Power* (Samuel Goldwyn Films, 2014), a documentary about Anita Hill's testimony in October 1991 at the Senate Judiciary Committee in which she described sexual harassment by now US Supreme Court Justice Clarence Thomas.

Deborah L. Brake & Joanna Grossman, *Unprotected Sex: The Pregnancy Discrimination Act at 35*, 21 Duke J. Gender L. & Pol'y 67 (Fall 2013).

Jessica K. Fink, *In Defense of Snooping Employers*, 16 J. of Bus. L. 551 (2014).

Michael J. Garrison & John T. Wendt, *The Evolving Law of Employee Noncompete Agreements: Recent Trends and an Alternative Policy Approach*, 45 Am. Bus. L. J. 107 (2008).

Tristin K. Green, *Discrimination Laundering: The Rise of Organizational Innocence and the Crisis of Equal Opportunity Law* (2017), describes how employers' organizational and legal efforts to minimize discrimination often does the opposite and how and why judges are changing the law to protect them.

Kevin D. Horvitz, *An Unreasonable Ban on Reasonable Competition: The Legal Profession's Protectionist Stance against Noncompete Agreements Binding In-House Counsel*, 65 Duke L. J. 1007–1053 (2016).

Saru M. Matambanadzo, *Reconstructing Pregnancy*, 69 SMU L. Rev. 187 (Winter 2016), This article explores the definition of pregnancy under the Pregnancy Discrimination Act and arguing for a more comprehensive and culturally defined meaning.

Paula C. O'Callaghan & Jerome D. O'Callaghan, *Facebook's 'Like': The First Amendment and Free Speech in the Workplace*, 15 ALSB J. of Emp't and Labor L. Volume 26–44 (2014).

Griffin Toronjo Pivateau, *Putting the Blue Pencil Down: An Argument for Specificity in Noncompete Agreements*, 86 Neb. L. Rev. (2007).

Joseph A. Seiner, *The Supreme Court's New Workplace: Procedural Rulings and Substantive Worker Rights in the United States* (2017), describes how the US Supreme Court has eroded the rights of minority workers through subtle changes in procedural law.

11 Civil Rights Law and Policy

Ehsan Zaffar

Introduction

> **Civil rights**—rules and laws that protect various freedoms from infringement by the state to which citizens belong. Civil rights often allow for individuals to freely participate in and criticize the state.
>
> **Human rights**—norms and moral principles, sometimes expressed as laws, that describe and proscribe standards of human behavior. Human rights are inalienable (i.e., all humans have these rights merely because they are human). An example of a human right is "freedom from slavery."

Civil rights and, more broadly, **human rights** are sets of moral principles or norms that describe standards of human behavior. They are often practically expressed as laws and policies both obligatory on and protected by the government. Human rights are more appropriately understood as "inalienable" or fundamental rights that cannot be separated from the person. In other words, a person has the right to life, liberty, or safety merely because they are a human who exists. Thus, human rights apply to all humans irrespective of their nationality, language, religion, or ethnicity. On the other hand, civil rights are a more specific subset of human rights. They must take effect through the rule of law (i.e., in a statute or governing constitution). Thus, because the laws and people of each nation are different, civil rights protect a specific class or classes of people and differ from country to country. For instance, in the United States, the Second Amendment to the United States Constitution guarantees Americans the right to bear arms. This right to bear arms is unique to only a few other countries besides the United States.

Some examples of modern human rights would be the right to life, the right to free movement, and the right to safety and security. Examples of civil rights, for instance, those found in the United States, would be the freedom of expression and speech, the right to vote, and the freedom to petition the government for grievances.

Limitations

It is important to note that, in almost all cases, rights are not unlimited. Reasonable limitations are applied by law and policy to the expression of all human and civil rights. For instance, though Americans enjoy freedom from government interference in their speech, this right is not unlimited: all U.S. law students learn that they are not protected from yelling "fire" in a crowded theater lest their exclamation cause a stampede and trample other patrons. In the United States, as in many other countries, speech is not protected if it causes imminent harm to another person, especially if the harm intended by the speech was intentional. Later parts of this chapter will explore some other limitations on speech and protections granted to certain kinds of speech such as political speech.

Human rights as moral principles, and then later as codified rules and laws, have been around since the dawn of civilization. As the idea of nation-states has become refined, so too have the laws that govern them, including human rights laws. The efficacy of rights is often determined by the consistent application of the rule of law, and by extension the quality and character of the biases of legal and government institutions. Thus, the strength of human and civil rights laws is often mediated by institutional and structural discrimination, and furthered by racial equity and a recognition of identity-based privilege.

Rights Before the Republic

Ideas of liberty, freedom, and rights have existed throughout human history, but what we would today consider human rights did not come about until the 20th century. Nonetheless, societies around the world began conceptualizing ideas of human dignity, justice, and well-being from the earliest flourishing of civilization. These ideas, and the institutions that supported them, can be thought of as "proto-human rights," and they find their earliest expression in the Cyrus Cylinder, an ancient sixth-century BCE clay cylinder, upon which are written the rights and privileges to be assigned to the Jewish people by the ancient Persian king, Cyrus the Great. The Cyrus Cylinder is the first known example of a governing body affirmatively granting a people under its rule liberty and holding itself obligated to guarantee this liberty under penalty and punishment.[1]

Further advancements in proto-human rights occurred in ancient Athens with the development of the idea of "citizenship" (albeit citizenship was conferred only on certain males in Athenian society), where those with citizenship could vote and had the right to speak in the political assembly.[2]

In South Asia, the ancient inscriptions of stone pillars known as the Edicts of Ashoka, emphasized the importance of tolerance in public policy by the government, forbid the slaughter of prisoners of war, and according to some interpretations, outlawed slavery.

Throughout Chinese history, but perhaps most importantly during the rise of Confucianism in the sixth century BCE, the idea closest to human rights was that of *jen*: treating others as you would wish to be treated yourself. This idea of a morally superior, loving, and just ruler was studied by many in China. This humanistic approach to man, independent of rank and status, led to a formulation of human rights in the sense of a philosophical recognition of the worth of man and his potentiality.

Roman jurisprudence further strengthened the idea of the state's obligations to its people, especially citizens of the Roman empire. The idea of the Roman *jus*, or "right due to a Roman," was the precursor to the modern American right of petitioning the state for redress of grievances. Indeed, the word "justice" derives from *jus*.

The fall of Rome presaged a degradation of legal progress as many concepts of Athenian democracy and Roman citizenship were overtaken by patron-client relationships between feudal lords and peasant farmers. The Magna Carta, an English charter issued in 1215, was a rare exception in these dark times. Written due to a disagreement between King John, the Pope, and other landed English nobility, the Magna Carta required the King to renounce certain powers, respect certain legal procedures, and accept that his will could be bound by the law and not just divine mandate. These ideas eventually ended up transforming into modern American concepts of civil liberties, due process, and the rule of law, respectively.

As Rome fell and the Dark Ages swallowed much of continental Europe, the Early Islamic Caliphate introduced innovative social reforms in the Middle East, many of which were later adopted by Renaissance thinkers in Europe. These included the denunciation of aristocratic privilege, an expansion in the rights of women to own property and assert legal claims against men as well as represent themselves in divorce proceedings, an expansion of certain rights to ethnic minorities, and perhaps most remarkably, the enshrining of religious freedom in the Charter of Medina, a formal agreement between Muslims and those living under their rule from different faiths. These practices continued relatively unabated through to the end of the Ottoman Empire after World War I.[3]

The Renaissance, the Protestant Reformation, and the disappearance of feudal authoritarianism in Europe from the 1400s to 1600s led to transformation of "proto-human rights" into the modern conception of "rights" as a set of laws and precepts, independent of divine mandate, and similar to the way they are perceived today in the United States. Prior to this time, the Magna Carta, and other efforts in the Islamic world and antiquity, constituted a form of limited political and legal agreements to address specific rather than broad-ranging political circumstances.

The conquest of the Americas in the 15th and 16th centuries by Spain, during the Age of Discovery, resulted in vigorous debate about human rights in Colonial Spanish America. This led to the issuance of the Laws of Burgos by Ferdinand the Catholic on behalf of his daughter, Joanna of Castile. Among the provisions of the Laws of Burgos were novel ideas regarding child labor, women's rights, wages, suitable accommodations, and rest/vacation, among others.

Several 17th- and 18th-century European philosophers, most notably John Locke, developed the concept of natural rights, the notion that people are born free and equal irrespective of who they are. Though Locke believed natural rights were derived from divinity since humans were creations of God, his ideas were important in the development of the modern notion of rights. Locke's conception of rights is at the core of what Western democracies today view as human rights: natural rights that do not rely on citizenship nor any law of the state, nor are they necessarily limited to one particular ethnic, cultural, or religious group.

The U.S. Declaration of Independence essentially adopted Locke's ideas wholesale and, along with the French Declaration of the Rights of Man and Citizen, defined a set of individual and collective rights (e.g., "certain unalienable rights, that among these are life, liberty and the pursuit of happiness") that apply not only to French or American citizens, but to all men without exception (though "men" as defined in these documents excluded many males and all women).

A similar seminal document, the Virginia Declaration of Rights, also incorporated many of Locke's ideas regarding natural rights. The Virginia Declaration of Rights was one of the earliest documents to emphasize the protection of individual rights, rather than advocating for the protection of only members of Parliament or consisting of simple laws that can be changed as easily as passed. For instance, it was the first declaration of rights to call for a free press.[4] The Virginia Declaration went on to influence both the U.S. Declaration of Independence and the U.S. Constitution and, more importantly, the Bill of Rights—a set of amendments to the U.S. Constitution outlining specific rights to be given to all persons.

From the Revolution to World War II

I confess that there are several parts of this Constitution which I do not at present approve, but I am not sure I shall never approve them. For having lived long, I have experienced many instances of being obliged by better information, or fuller consideration, to change opinions even on important subjects, which I once thought right, but found to be otherwise.

—Benjamin Franklin

As originally ratified, the U.S. Constitution primarily addressed the structure of the government and provided for few individual liberties. Instead, these rights were set forth later in the Bill of Rights, comprised of the first ten amendments to the Constitution. A bill of rights was demanded by many states in return for ratification of the Constitution itself. Though the Constitution continues to undergo a process of formal amendment and interpretation by courts, the fundamental principles on which this country was founded remain at the core of this document more than 200 years later.

The Bill of Rights remained little more than an empty promise of individual freedom until 1803, when the U.S. Supreme Court held in *Marbury v. Madison* that the Supreme Court had the authority to strike down legislation it found unconstitutional. Even then, the Bill of Rights applied only to the federal government and failed to bind individual states until the late 1890s, when the **Incorporation Doctrine** began to take shape.

Through a series of decisions beginning in 1897, the Supreme Court held that the 14th Amendment ensured that portions of the Bill of Rights were enforceable against the states and not just the federal government. Since then, the rights enshrined in the Bill of Rights have been progressively enumerated by the Supreme Court as worthy of constitutional protection irrespective of whether government interference is the result of state or federal action. These rights are said to be "incorporated" against the states through the 14th Amendment.

A prominent and relatively recent example of this incorporation can be found in *Gideon v. Wainwright*, where the Supreme Court unanimously held that states were required under the Sixth Amendment to provide counsel in criminal cases to represent defendants who were unable to afford their own attorneys. 375 U.S. 335 at 372. The *Gideon* decision dramatically transformed the rights of indigent, low-income, and unsophisticated litigants throughout the country. The decision effectively created and then expanded the need for public defenders, which had previously been rare for non-federal cases. For example, immediately following the decision, the state of Florida required public defenders for all parties in need in each of the state's circuit courts.[5]

> Incorporation doctrine—a legal doctrine through which the first ten amendments to the U.S. Constitution (the Bill of Rights) are found to be applicable to all U.S. states through the Due Process clause of the 14th Amendment. Prior to the Incorporation Doctrine, the Bill of Rights applied only to the federal government.

Chief among the ten amendments is the first one. The First Amendment is primary for a reason: it bestows among the most comprehensive and expansive of rights upon the American polity. The First Amendment protects the free exercise of religion, the freedom of speech and the press, and the freedom to petition the government and assemble as a group to protest or express grievances. A discussion of the development of a few of the most important of these rights: the freedom of religion and the freedom of speech and the press is instructive because these rights are foundational to the American ethos, due mostly to the circumstances of religious and state-sponsored persecution that spurred the creation of the United States.

Freedom of Religion

> *Congress shall make no law respecting an establishment of religion, or prohibiting the free exercise thereof . . .*
> —First Amendment to the United States Constitution

The First Amendment protects religious freedom in two ways: It forbids Congress from establishing a national religion (Establishment Clause) and prohibits Congress from passing any law that impedes the freedom of Americans to practice their faith however they wish (Free Exercise Clause). In general, both clauses proscribe governmental involvement with and interference in religious matters.

The freedom to practice a faith, or no faith at all, arose from the historical sense of persecution many American colonists felt under British rule. Up until the late Renaissance, almost every nation in Western Europe had an established and official church.

Those Europeans who did not join the church were often denied rights, banished, jailed, tortured, or murdered. Some of these persecuted communities fled England and other nearby nations to become the first American colonists. During this time, wars driven by religious feuds were also common in mainland Europe. The Americas were seen as a refuge from these religious conflicts. It was natural then for many of the framers of the Constitution, such as Thomas Jefferson, to seek to wall off the excesses of a religious state by creating a "wall of separation between church and state."

Despite these noble intentions, in practice, religious freedom has not always been guaranteed in the United States. Throughout the 18th and 19th centuries, non-Protestants were often not seen as trustworthy leaders, and "religious tests" were common for those who wanted to hold public office. Though the Constitution banned such tests for federal office, states were slow to implement non-discriminatory provisions; it wasn't until 1961 that the Supreme Court found Maryland's religious test for public office unconstitutional.[6]

Like other civil rights, the Supreme Court has placed freedom of religion on a spectrum of rights, from most protected to least protected. Given the United States' history, the "freedom to believe or not believe" is given the highest judicial deference, meaning that the government cannot interfere with a person's right to practice their faith, except in cases where other fundamental rights, such as the right to life, may be at risk.

Despite these significant protections, the Supreme Court has drawn a distinction between religious belief and religious conduct. Unlike religious belief, religious conduct must occasionally yield to government interests. The Free Exercise Clause "embraces two concepts—freedom to believe and freedom to act. The first is absolute, but in the nature of things, the second cannot be."[7] In such instances, courts must consider both the government's interest in taking a particular action and the religious rights affected by that action. Only if the governmental interest in limiting conduct is "compelling" and if no alternative forms of regulation would serve that interest, can the individual asserting their rights be forced to yield.[8]

More recently, the Supreme Court has gone so far as to uphold government action that affects religious conduct so long as the resulting restriction is not the purpose of the action but merely incidental to it. For instance, Oregon passed a law prohibiting the possession of peyote, a powerful hallucinogenic traditionally used in Native American religious rituals. Although the new law infringed on the religious conduct of Native Americans, the Supreme Court upheld the constitutionality of the law because the primary purpose of the law was to protect people from a harmful drug, not to target Native American religion. A few years later, however, a different decision was reached in a case involving the Santeria religion, which practices animal sacrifice. That case stemmed from a city ordinance passed in Hialeah, Florida, after city leaders learned a Santeria church was about to be established within city limits. The ordinance prohibited the "unnecessary killing of an animal in a public or private ritual ceremony not for the primary purpose of food consumption." The Supreme Court found the ordinance unconstitutional because it targeted the Santeria religion without a compelling reason to do so.[9]

As is often the case, when conflicting court decisions are not resolved by the Supreme Court, Congress can and does step in. In light of these divergent decisions on religious conduct, Congress decided to take action to safeguard long-held religious protections. In 1993, Congress passed the Religious Freedom Restoration Act, which restored the requirement that the federal government have a "compelling interest" before intruding in religious practices. The Supreme Court subsequently held that the law did not apply to states. To overcome this judicial decision, Congress then passed the **Religious Land Use and Institutionalized Persons Act** of 2000 (RLUIPA), which protects religious institutions from burdensome zoning law restrictions and protects inmates' rights to exercise religious practices. RLUIPA has most frequently been used to prevent local states and municipalities from discriminating against minority religious congregations by using zoning regulations in a discriminatory manner, often without the need for a lawsuit.

> Religious Land Use and Institutionalized Persons Act—A U.S. federal law that prohibits burdens on the religious freedom of the incarcerated and affords religious institutions avenues for redress against discriminatory property laws.

For instance, in Berkeley, Illinois, a mosque had operated in a former school building on a 4.5-acre parcel for more than 20 years. The mosque sought to build a 13,000-square-foot addition to accommodate its congregation (which had grown to the point that worshipers spilled into the hallways during services) and to make exterior changes to give the building a more mosque-like appearance, including adding a minaret. The expansion project faced community opposition and repeated permit denials. The Civil Rights Division of the Department of Justice opened an investigation under RLUIPA in 2007, and in March 2008, the city agreed to allow the mosque project to move forward.

Most recently, the First Amendment's religious freedom guarantees have been implicated in the form of a challenge to President Trump's "travel ban," which barred non-citizens from mostly majority-Muslim countries entry into the United States. Challengers to the executive order asserted that the order "targeted Muslims for opprobrium, denigration, and discrimination based solely on their faith."[10,11]

Freedom of Speech and Press

The First Amendment protects individual expression by guaranteeing the freedom of speech. The Supreme Court has broadly interpreted "speech" to include Internet communication, art, music, clothing, and even **"symbolic speech,"** such as flag burning. Freedom of the press generally allows for newspapers, radio, television, and many online sources to publish articles and express opinions representing the public dialogue without interference or constraint by the government.

> Symbolic speech—legal term describing actions that convey a specific message to those viewing it

At the time it was written, the Constitution's First Amendment established one of the strongest standards for the guarantee of free speech worldwide. Although the First Amendment as stated is rather absolute in its protection of free speech, the Bill of Rights' protection required the promulgation of revised judicial standards over time. In the United States, these standards evolved through decisions of the Supreme Court to expand freedom and reduce restrictions on the media and other means of expression. For example, slander and national security were traditionally common justifications for restricting speech until recent times.

Likewise, the freedom of the press was written into the Constitution primarily to allow an appropriate outlet for free expression. Unlike other nations, the United States does not police its press but nonetheless expects them to be responsible and inform the public on current events and important issues so that citizens can make sound decisions, such as which electoral candidates and ballot measures to support. In many ways, the media also provide a check on the government by asking questions of public officials that citizens may not be able to ask.

The First Amendment's free speech and freedom of press guarantees are seen as the cornerstone of the Bill of Rights and are generally premised on three deeply held beliefs by the original drafters of the Constitution:

> First, the belief that the government "of the people by the people" cannot exist without unfettered debate and disagreement within a free and open space,

which allows citizens to engage in self-government by using reason and practical judgment. Thus, because people communicate on political matters so that they can intelligently participate in the democratic process, without free speech, self-government becomes impossible.[12]

Second, that the idea first articulated in Western thought by John Stuart Mill, and found later in the court's rationale in *Abrahms v. United States*, is that freedom of speech is important because, in a marketplace of ideas, the better ideas will eventually prevail through competition.[13] Under this framework, one form of speech isn't more valuable than any other form of speech; rather, the value of speech depends on its popularity.

Lastly, the idea that free speech promotes every individual's self-fulfillment and autonomy was an important one valued by the founding fathers. Under this rationale, non-political speech such as artistic expression is fully covered; as with the marketplace of ideas rationale, there is no hierarchy of speech. On the other hand, under this approach one wonders what is so special about freedom of speech inasmuch as other provisions of the Constitution (like substantive due process) similarly promote self-fulfillment and autonomy.

None of these rationales captures the complexity of free speech issues or the actual free speech jurisprudence of the Supreme Court and the policies and regulations that are informed by that set of laws. For example, the self-government rationale does not explain why artistic expression and scientific speech should be protected by the First Amendment. Similarly, the marketplace of ideas and self-fulfillment/individual autonomy rationales do not satisfactorily explain why obscene speech or child pornography is not protected by the First Amendment.

Like other rights guaranteed in the Constitution, freedom of speech has its limits. The Supreme Court has found that the First Amendment prohibits the state and federal government from restricting speech based on content or by imposing prior restraints on speech.

Limitations on Speech

Thus, most forms of speech are protected by the First Amendment, but there are exceptions for speech that does not add to public debate or may cause harm. Those exceptions include obscenity (though the laws in the United States regarding what is obscene are relatively progressive), defamation, incitement to violence, "fighting words," harassment, privileged communications (such as those between an attorney and her client), trade secrets, classified material (or other material critical for the national security of the nation), copyright, patents, military conduct, political speech, and some commercial speech (such as advertising). Moreover, speech that is part of an act the law traditionally considers criminal is not protected by the First Amendment. For example, publishers cannot distribute magazines containing child pornography since the manufacturing, distribution, and possession of child pornography is illegal. In instances like this, protecting children from exploitation is deemed to be more important than any message provided in the magazine.

Additional nuances exist that effectively act as limitations on speech. For instance, the First Amendment by its terms applies only to laws enacted by Congress and not to the actions of private persons. (Through interpretation of the 14th Amendment, the prohibition extends to the states as well.)[14] Therefore, social media companies such as Facebook or Twitter may freely limit the speech of their customers without legal consequence.

Another important limitation on speech is defamation, or speech that contains false or derogatory statements that injure a person's reputation. Defamation can occur though the spoken word (slander) or written communication (libel). Issues of defamation arise most frequently when public figures are involved.

The Supreme Court established the legal standard for libel, and by doing so, the limits of written speech, in the landmark case, *New York Times Co. v. Sullivan*. *New York Times* was not only a landmark freedom of speech case, but a case that further strengthened the freedom of the press in the United States. As you read *New York Times Co.* as follows, consider the various ways in which the justices balance freedom of speech with privacy and permissible speech with speech that may not be in the public interest.

New York Times Co. v. Sullivan, 376 U.S. 254 (1964)

We are required in this case to determine for the first time the extent to which the constitutional protections for speech and press limit a State's power to award damages in a libel action brought by a public official against critics of his official conduct....

L.B. Sullivan, a city commissioner in Montgomery, Alabama, sued the New York Times Company and four African-American clergymen for libel based on a full-page advertisement published in the New York Times in 1960. The ad asked readers to help fund the civil rights movement and decried an "unprecedented wave of terror" in the South. The ad listed the names of 64 persons, including the clergymen, who purportedly endorsed its content. Sullivan's libel claim focused on two of the ad's ten paragraphs:

> In Montgomery, Alabama, after students sang "My Country, 'Tis of Thee" on the State Capitol steps, their leaders were expelled from school, and truckloads of police armed with shotguns and tear-gas ringed the Alabama State College Campus. When the entire student body protested to state authorities by refusing to re-register, their dining hall was padlocked in an attempt to starve them into submission.
>
> Again and again the Southern violators have answered Dr. King's peaceful protests with intimidation and violence. They have bombed his home almost killing his wife and child. They have assaulted his person. They have arrested him seven times—for "speeding," "loitering" and similar "offenses." And now they have charged him with "perjury"—a felony under which they could imprison him for ten years.

Sullivan contended that the ad accused him of overseeing a campaign of violence in his capacity as supervisor of the police, and he brought witnesses who testified that they understood the ad to refer to him. He established that he had not participated in the events attributed to the police but brought no evidence of any pecuniary loss resulting from the libel. The Times conceded that the ad contained several minor inaccuracies: the students sang the National Anthem rather than "My Country, 'Tis of Thee"; nine students were expelled for demanding service at a lunch counter in the county courthouse, not for leading a demonstration; the police never literally "ringed" the campus; and Dr. King had been arrested four times, not seven. The trial judge instructed the jury that the statements in the ad were libelous per se and not privileged. He also instructed that the jury could impose liability if it found petitioners had published the statements "of and concerning" Sullivan. The judge also told jury members they could award presumed and punitive damages even if no actual damages were shown and punitive damages could be awarded if they found "evidence of actual malice or malice in fact." [The jury returned a verdict of $500,000, and the judge did not require the jury to designate which portion, if any, of the award constituted punitive damages. The Supreme Court of Alabama affirmed.]

I

We may dispose at the outset of two grounds asserted to insulate the judgment of the Alabama courts from constitutional scrutiny. The first is the proposition relied on by the State Supreme Court—that "The Fourteenth Amendment is directed against State action and not private action." That proposition has no application to this case. Although this is a civil lawsuit between private parties, the Alabama courts have applied a state rule of law which petitioners claim to impose invalid restrictions on their constitutional freedoms of speech and press.... The second contention is that the constitutional guarantees of freedom of speech and of the press are inapplicable here, at least so far as the Times is concerned, because the allegedly libelous statements were published as part of a paid, "commercial" advertisement.... The publication here was not a "commercial" advertisement.... it communicated information, expressed opinion, recited grievances, protested claimed abuses, and sought financial support on behalf of a movement whose existence and objectives are matters of the highest public interest and concern.... Any other conclusion would discourage newspapers from carrying "editorial advertisements" of this type, and so might shut off an important outlet for the promulgation of information and ideas by persons who do not themselves have access to publishing facilities—who wish to exercise their freedom of speech even though they are not members of the press....

II

The question before us is whether (Alabama libel law), as applied to an action brought by a public official against critics of his official conduct, abridges the freedom of speech and of the press that is guaranteed by the First and Fourteenth Amendments. Respondent relies heavily, as did the Alabama courts, on statements of this Court to the effect that the Constitution does not protect libelous publications. Those statements do not foreclose our inquiry here. None of the cases sustained the use of libel laws to impose sanctions upon expression critical of the official conduct of public officials.... Like insurrection, contempt, advocacy of unlawful acts, breach of the peace, obscenity, solicitation of legal business, and the various other formulae for the repression of expression that have been challenged in this Court, libel can claim no talismanic immunity from constitutional limitations. It must be measured by standards that satisfy the First Amendment.

***

(W)e consider this case against the background of a profound national commitment to the principle that debate on public issues should be uninhibited, robust, and wide-open, and that it may well include vehement, caustic, and sometimes unpleasantly sharp attacks on government and public officials... The present advertisement, as an expression of grievance and protest on one of the major public issues of our time, would seem clearly to qualify for the constitutional protection. The question is whether it forfeits that protection by the falsity of some of its factual statements and by its alleged defamation of respondent. Authoritative interpretations of the First Amendment guarantees have consistently refused to recognize an exception for any test of truth—whether administered by judges, juries, or administrative officials—and especially one that puts the burden of proving truth on the speaker. The constitutional protection does not turn upon "the truth, popularity, or social utility of the ideas and beliefs which are offered."

What a State may not constitutionally bring about by means of a criminal statute is likewise beyond the reach of its civil law of libel. The fear of damage awards under a rule such as that invoked by the Alabama courts here may be markedly more inhibiting than the fear Of prosecution under a criminal statute. Alabama, for example, has a criminal libel law which subjects to prosecution "any person who speaks, writes, or prints of and concerning another any accusation falsely and maliciously importing the commission by such person of a felony, or any other indictable offense involving moral turpitude," and which allows as punishment upon conviction a fine not exceeding $500 and a prison sentence of six months. Presumably a person charged with violation of this statute enjoys ordinary criminal-law safeguards such as the requirements of an indictment and of proof beyond a reasonable doubt. These safeguards are not available to the defendant in a civil action. The judgment awarded in this case—without the need for any proof of actual pecuniary loss—was one thousand times greater than the maximum fine provided by the Alabama criminal statute, and one hundred times greater than that provided by the Sedition Act. And since there is no double-jeopardy limitation applicable to civil lawsuits, this is not the only judgment that may be awarded against petitioners for the same publication.

Whether or not a newspaper can survive a succession of such judgments, the pall of fear and timidity imposed upon those who would give voice to public criticism is an atmosphere in which the First Amendment freedoms cannot survive.... The state rule of law is not saved by its allowance of the defense of truth.... Allowance of the defense of truth, with the burden of proving it on the defendant, does not mean that only false speech will be deterred. Even courts accepting this defense as an adequate safeguard have recognized the difficulties of adducing legal proofs that the alleged libel was true in all its factual particulars. Under such a rule, would-be critics of official conduct may be deterred from voicing their criticism, even though it is believed to be true and even though it is in fact true, because of doubt whether it can be proved in court or fear of the expense of having to do so. They tend to make only statements which "steer far wider of the unlawful zone." The rule thus dampens the vigor and limits the variety of public debate. It is inconsistent with the First and Fourteenth Amendments.

The constitutional guarantees require, we think, a federal rule that prohibits a public official from recovering damages for a defamatory falsehood relating to his official conduct unless he proves that the statement was made with "actual malice"—that is, with knowledge that it was false or with reckless disregard of whether it was false or not. An oft-cited statement of a like rule, which has been adopted by a number of state courts, is found in the Kansas case of *Coleman v. MacLennan*, 78 Kan. 711, 98 P. 281 (1908)....

Such a privilege for criticism of official conduct is appropriately analogous to the protection accorded a public official when he is sued for libel by a private citizen. In *Barr v. Matteo*, 360 U.S. 564, 575, this Court held the utterance of a federal official to be absolutely privileged if made "within the outer perimeter" of his duties. The States accord the same immunity to statements of their highest officers, although some differentiate their lesser officials and qualify the privilege they enjoy. But all hold that all officials are protected unless actual malice can be proved. The reason for the official privilege is said to be that the threat of damage suits would otherwise "inhibit the fearless, vigorous, and effective administration of policies of government" and "dampen the ardor of all but the most resolute, or the most irresponsible, in the unflinching discharge of their duties." Analogous considerations support the privilege for the citizen-critic of government. It is as much his duty to criticize as it is the official's duty to administer. As Madison said, "the censorial power is in the people over the Government, and not in the Government over the people." It would give public servants an unjustified preference over the public they serve, if critics of official conduct did not have a fair equivalent of the immunity granted to the officials themselves.

We conclude that such a privilege is required by the First and Fourteenth Amendments.

III

We hold today that the Constitution delimits a State's power to award damages for libel in actions brought by public officials against critics of their official conduct. Since this is such an action, the rule requiring proof of actual malice is applicable. While Alabama law apparently requires proof of actual malice for an award of punitive damages, where general damages are concerned malice is "presumed." Such a presumption is inconsistent with the federal rule.... Since the trial judge did not instruct the jury to differentiate between general and punitive damages, it may be that the verdict was wholly an award of one or the other. But it is impossible to know, in view of the general verdict returned.

Because of this uncertainty, the judgment must be reversed and the case remanded. Since respondent may seek a new trial, we deem that considerations of effective judicial administration require us to review the evidence in the present record to determine whether it could constitutionally support a judgment for respondent. This Court's duty is not limited to the elaboration of constitutional principles; we must also in proper cases review the evidence to make certain that those principles have been constitutionally applied. This is such a case, particularly since the question is one of alleged trespass across "the line between speech unconditionally guaranteed and speech which may legitimately be regulated."

In cases where that line must be drawn, the rule is that we 'examine for ourselves the statements in issue and the circumstances under which they were made to see ... whether they are of a character which the principles of the First Amendment, as adopted by the Due Process Clause of the Fourteenth Amendment, protect." We must "make an independent examination of the whole record," so as to assure ourselves that the judgment does not constitute a forbidden intrusion on the field of free expression. Applying these standards, we consider that the proof presented to show actual malice lacks the convincing clarity which the constitutional standard demands, and hence that it would not constitutionally sustain the judgment for respondent under the proper rule of law. The case of the individual petitioners requires little discussion. Even assuming that they could constitutionally be found to have authorized the use of their names on the advertisement, there was no evidence whatever that they were aware of any erroneous statements or were in any way reckless in that regard. The judgment against them is thus without constitutional support.

As to the Times, we similarly conclude that the facts do not support a finding of actual malice.... The Times' failure to retract upon respondent's demand, although it later retracted upon the demand of Governor Patterson, is ... not adequate evidence of malice for constitutional purposes. Whether or not a failure to retract may ever constitute such evidence, there are two reasons why it does not here. First, the letter written by the Times reflected a reasonable doubt on its part as to whether the advertisement could reasonably be taken to refer to respondent at all. Second, it was not a final refusal, since it asked for an explanation on this point—a request that respondent chose to ignore.... It may be doubted that a failure to retract which is not itself evidence of malice can retroactively become such by virtue of a retraction subsequently made to another party. But in any event that did not happen here, since the explanation given by the Times' Secretary for the distinction drawn between respondent and the Governor was a reasonable one, the good faith of which was not impeached.

Finally, there is evidence that the Times published the advertisement without checking its accuracy against the news stories in the Times' own files. The mere presence of the stories in the files does not, of course, establish that the Times "knew" the advertisement was false, since the state of mind required for actual malice would have to be brought home to the persons in the Times' organization having responsibility for the publication of the advertisement. With respect to the failure of those persons to make the check, the record shows that they relied upon their knowledge of the good reputation of many of those whose names were listed as sponsors of the advertisement, and upon the letter from A. Philip Randolph, known to them as a responsible individual, certifying that the use of the names was authorized....

We also think the evidence was constitutionally defective in another respect: it was incapable of supporting the jury's finding that the allegedly libelous statements were made "of and concerning" respondent. Respondent relies on the words of the advertisement and the testimony of six witnesses to establish a connection between it and himself.... There was no reference to respondent in the advertisement, either by name or official position.... Moreover, the statements about the police were false only in that the police had been "deployed near" the campus but had not actually "ringed" it and had not gone there in connection with the State Capitol demonstration, and in that Dr. King had been arrested only four times rather than seven. The ruling that these discrepancies between what was true and what was asserted were sufficient to injure respondent's reputation may itself raise constitutional problems, but we need not consider them here. Although the statements may be taken as referring to the police, they did not on their face make even an oblique reference to respondent as an individual. Support for the asserted reference must, therefore, be sought in the testimony of respondent's witnesses. But none of them suggested any basis for the belief that respondent himself was attacked in the advertisement beyond the bare fact that he was in overall charge of the Police Department and thus bore official responsibility for police conduct.... Thus, proof that the ad pertained to Sullivan relied "on the bare fact of respondent's official position."

This proposition has disquieting implications for criticism of governmental conduct. For good reason, "no court of last resort in this country has ever held, or even suggested, that prosecutions for libel on government have any place in the American system of jurisprudence.". . . The present proposition would sidestep this obstacle by transmuting criticism of government, however impersonal it may seem on its face, into personal criticism, and hence potential libel, of the officials of whom the government is composed. There is no legal alchemy by which a State may thus create the cause of action that would otherwise be denied for a publication which, as respondent himself said of the advertisement, reflects not only on me but on the other Commissioners and the community." Raising as it does the possibility that a good-faith critic of government will be penalized for his criticism, the proposition relied on by the Alabama courts strikes at the very center of the constitutionally protected area of free expression. We hold that such a proposition may not constitutionally be utilized to establish that an otherwise impersonal attack on governmental operations was a libel of an official responsible for those operations. Since it was relied on exclusively here, and there was no other evidence to connect the statements with respondent, the evidence was constitutionally insufficient to support a finding that the statements referred to respondent. The judgment of the Supreme Court of Alabama is reversed and the case is remanded to that court for further proceedings not inconsistent with this opinion.

Justice BLACK, with whom Justice DOUGLAS joins, concurring.

. . . I vote to reverse exclusively on the ground that the Times and the individual defendants had an absolute, unconditional constitutional right to publish in the Times advertisement their criticisms of the Montgomery agencies and officials. . . . The half-million-dollar verdict does give dramatic proof, however, that state libel laws threaten the very existence of an American press virile enough to publish unpopular views on public affairs and bold enough to criticize the conduct of public officials.

The factual background of this case emphasizes the imminence and enormity of that threat. . . . Briefs before us show that in Alabama there are now pending eleven libel suits by local and state officials against the Times seeking $5,600,000, and five such suits against the Columbia Broadcasting System seeking $1,700,000.

In my opinion the Federal Constitution has dealt with this deadly danger to the press in the only way possible without leaving the free press open to destruction—by granting the press an absolute immunity for criticism of the way public officials do their public duty. Stopgap measures like those the Court adopts are in my judgment not enough. . . .

Discussion

> **Actual malice**—a legal standard in libel law that requires public figures to prove that the actions of a publisher of allegedly libelous material be affirmatively malicious in their intent.

The *New York Times Co.* case established the **"actual malice"** standard, which to this day has to be met before public reports about individuals can be legally actionable. By setting a high standard, the Court helped secure the freedom of speech and freedom of press in the United States.

There is also a practical outcome of such a high judicial standard: because it is so difficult to prove a newspaper's knowledge and intentions, claims of libel made by public figure plaintiffs rarely succeed.

How do you think the *New York Times Co.* case is playing out in a modern political climate that often makes a target of the press and other news organizations?

Do you think the Supreme Court would have ruled differently if the case was being heard today and if the defendant was a scrappy blogger instead of an established newspaper? How does the identity of the party publishing the allegedly libelous information affect an understanding of their malicious intent?

> **Discussion Question**
>
> In his concurring opinion, Justice Hugo Black wrote, "I doubt that a country can live in freedom where its people can be made to suffer physically or financially for criticizing their government, its actions, or its officials.... An unconditional right to say what one pleases about public affairs is what I consider to be the minimum guarantee of the First Amendment." How did Justice Black come to the same conclusion as the majority, but for a different reason? With which opinion do you agree?

How and when the government limits speech is a continual question for the nation's courts. Courts prefer that the government limit speech on the basis of time, place, and manner of the speech rather than its content. Generally, the government may limit speech based on its content only when the government has a compelling interest in limiting speech, such as when the speech presents a clear danger to public safety. This is often a difficult standard for the government to meet. In *New York Times Co. v. United States* (1971), Daniel Ellsberg, a former national security employee, intended to interfere with the Vietnam War by releasing information that was critical of government policy to the *New York Times*. The Supreme Court held that the First Amendment protected the right of the *New York Times* to print the materials, irrespective of who leaked them and how they were leaked. The Court found that despite the sensitive nature of the documents, the government had not set forth compelling evidence of danger to the public if the materials were published. Notably, the court said that embarrassment of the government was not sufficient to restrict speech.

However, government regulations that limit the time, place, and manner of speech—but NOT the content—are generally permissible. Thus, a local police department may ask protestors to assemble at a park away from an elementary school to ensure the safety of young children. In *Frisby v. Schultz*, the town board passed an ordinance prohibiting any person from "picketing before or about the residence or dwelling of any individual" within the town limits. The Supreme Court upheld the ordinance, finding that protecting privacy in residential homes outweighed the rights of protestors to express grievances (or more specifically their desire to target a specific home with unwelcome speech).

You can see by now that three areas become important when thinking about speech: (1) the content of the speech, (2) the forum where the speech is expressed, and (3) the medium of dissemination. Courts and policymakers often ask questions about the content, medium, and forum when attempting to determine how and when speech should be regulated:

Content: "WHAT" is being said? Courts usually ask this question when seeking to categorize the type of speech, and thus the level of protection it is due. There are several tiers of protected speech, some which receive higher protection (i.e., less or no government interference) and some which receive lower protection (significant government interference). At the top of this hierarchy is political speech (such as campaign speeches) followed closely by artistic and scientific expression. At the bottom is speech that has no legal or policy-based protections: for example, fighting words, true threats of imminent violence, and obscenity (such as child pornography). Speech dealing with a commercial purpose is somewhere in the middle.

Medium: "HOW" is the speech being expressed? Speech in person (oral) and written speech have the highest protections. Electronic speech, such as radio broadcasts or television programs, are occasionally given lesser protection. This includes the Internet. Novel areas for consideration are whether computer code is speech and, if so, what kind of code constitutes speech. Consider also that different media have different physical characteristics that sometimes play a determinative role in First Amendment analysis. For example, a sound truck with blaring announcements that are difficult to ignore is quite different from a person handing out leaflets who can be ignored or otherwise avoided.

Forum: "WHERE" is the speech taking place? This is usually only a consideration regarding public property (since the government is the actor guaranteeing the right to free speech, not a private entity). Thus, different kinds of public property where individuals intend to communicate may have different levels of protection. First Amendment protection is highest in open public lands such as city parks, voluntary public forums created by the government, plazas and streets. At the other end is public property which has a purpose incompatible with (usually because of safety reasons) free speech access. Examples of these kinds of places include a secure government facility or a public library.

Other Important Amendments

The Third Amendment stems from the anger the colonists felt when the King of England forced them to house military troops, even in times of peace. Although not a problem in recent times, the Supreme Court has held that the Third Amendment's prohibition against the quartering of soldiers, "in any house in time of peace without the consent of the owner," is the foundation of the right to privacy. Thus, while the Constitution does not specifically provide for a right to privacy, the First, Third, Fourth, and Fifth Amendments create "zones of privacy" around a citizen's property and person.

The Seventh Amendment protects the right to a jury trial in most federal civil lawsuits. The right to a jury trial was especially important to the framers of the Constitution, who felt unfairly treated by the British government, which often forced colonists to be tried by a single military judge. Both the Ninth and Tenth Amendments explain that if certain rights are not explicitly set forth in the Bill of Rights, they are retained by the people. Finally, the Fifth Amendment also protects the property rights of citizens by limiting the government's power of eminent domain, which is the government's right to take property (usually land) for public use. For example, if the government proposes to build a new highway where a house now stands, the government may legally take the land, but it must pay the homeowner the fair market value for the property.

Despite these aforementioned rights, their application prior to modern times was laughably discriminatory. When the Declaration of Independence was signed in 1776, discriminatory treatment was rampant among different races, social classes, and genders. Since the founding of the United States, virtually every race and nationality has fallen victim to discriminatory treatment at one time or another. To understand the development of liberty protections, we focus the remainder of this chapter on understanding this gap between civil rights as they are enumerated in law versus how they are enforced in practice.

From the founding of the United States, reality did not reflect the rights guaranteed under the law. Despite "all men being equal," slavery was permissible in large parts of the United States. Moreover, the Constitution counted slaves as just three-fifths of a person. Slavery went on to plague political debate for decades, and by the 1850s slavery had been eradicated in the northern states and the Northwest Territory but still thrived in the South. In 1857, the *Dred Scott* decision intensified the division between the states and contributed to the start of the Civil War.[15]

The government's victory in the U.S. Civil War ensured the passage of the 13th Amendment. Far more than ensuring an end to slavery, it ensured that no people, regardless of race or other characteristic, may be forced into labor against their will. Because of the 13th Amendment's guarantee against forced labor, courts today generally refuse to require specific performance as a remedy for breach of a service contract. For example, if someone enters into a house-cleaning contract at a hotel but fails to follow through, the hotel may sue for breach of contract, but the court most likely will impose financial damages rather than order the individual to complete the house-cleaning tasks. Following the civil rights movement of the 1950s and 1960s, the Supreme Court validated Congress's power under the 13th Amendment to enact civil rights legislation that prohibited private racial discrimination. In *Jones v. Alfred H. Mayer Company* (1968), a real estate developer refused to sell housing or property to African Americans. An African American couple sued the developer under a federal law mandating that all U.S. citizens have the same property rights as white citizens. The Supreme Court upheld the law, ruling that Congress has the power to enact laws that directly affect the acts of individuals, thereby making the 13th Amendment the first and only constitutional provision applicable to private citizens as well as to the state and federal government.

The Modern Civil Rights Movement

Although amendments to the Constitution after the Civil War guaranteed equal rights to all Americans, many U.S. citizens—especially African Americans—still experienced discrimination and segregation on a wide scale. Southern states passed **"Jim Crow" laws**, which required African Americans and white people to be separated in most public places, such as schools or restaurants. African Americans had to ride in the back of buses and use separate public restrooms. In the North, African Americans could vote, and segregation was less noticeable, but prejudice still restricted opportunities for them. From an early time, many Americans objected to the unfair treatment of African Americans, and in 1909, a group of mostly African Americans founded the National Association for the Advancement of Colored People (NAACP). The NAACP worked through the courts to challenge laws and customs that denied African Americans their constitutional rights. In 1910, other concerned citizens formed the National Urban League to help African Americans find jobs and reach economic parity with other Americans. These and other groups built a civil rights movement supported by millions of people across the United States.

Jim Crow laws—state and local laws in the United States (but mostly in the South) that enforced racial segregation.

In 1948, President Harry Truman ordered an end to segregation in the nation's armed forces; and in 1954, the Supreme Court ruled in favor of NAACP lawyers in *Brown v. Board of Education*, deeming racial segregation in public schools unconstitutional under the 14th Amendment's equal protection principle. In the 1950s, Dr. Martin Luther King, Jr., a Baptist minister and a central leader in the civil rights movement, inspired others to join the movement through marches, boycotts, and demonstrations that expressed non-violent resistance to and peaceful protest of discriminatory laws and practices. Some African American students participated in "sit-ins" at lunch counters reserved for white people, while other African Americans, along with many white citizens, teamed up as "Freedom Riders" to ride buses together throughout the South to protest segregation. On August 23, 1963, more than 200,000 people marched in Washington, D.C. to demand equal rights regardless of skin color.

Finally, in 1964, Congress listened to the demands of the people and passed the Civil Rights Act, which prohibited discrimination in public facilities, employment, education, and voter registration based on race, color, gender, religion, and national origin. Then, in 1965, the Voting Rights Act was enacted, further ensuring that minorities gained equal access to the polls.

This broad period from the end of World War II until the late 1960s is often referred to as the "Second Reconstruction," a time when grassroots movements, coupled with gradual but progressive actions by elected leaders and the judiciary, granted all Americans full political rights (at least in name).

This "Second Reconstruction" and the civil rights movement that arose before, during, and after Dr. King's assassination encouraged the passage of statutes expanding the application of constitutional amendments in other, more modern, areas of public life. State and federal statutes passed throughout the 1950s and 1960s addressed civil rights in the context of education, employment, and housing. These statutes typically outline the scope of the penalties and remedies against interference with the right, and often create a government agency or office (such as the Equal Employment Opportunity Commission, EEOC) to enforce the right through investigation, penalties, and prosecution.[16]

Who Is Protected?

Civil rights legislation and policy promulgated since the civil rights movement is ordered around the idea of "protected classes" or characteristics. Protected characteristics include the aforementioned gender, age, or religion but can also include other categories such as pregnancy or sexual orientation. Some characteristics are only protected against discrimination at work or school or only in certain states, such as gender identity or criminal record.

Arguably the most influential civil rights law since the end of the civil war is the Civil Rights Act of 1964. This law prohibits discrimination on the basis of race, color, national origin, or religion in public establishments with connections to interstate commerce or those that the state supports with financial assistance. Certain parts of the Civil Rights Act prohibit specific areas of discrimination. For instance, Title VI prohibits discrimination in educational programs that receive federal financial assistance, and Title VII prohibits employment discrimination when an employer engages in interstate commerce.

Additional anti-discrimination statutes include the Voting Rights Act of 1965, the the Age Discrimination in Employment Act of 1967, Americans with Disabilities Act

(ADA) of 1990, and the Civil Rights Act of 1991. As seen previously, these statutes are codifications of situations Congress has thought deserve remedies, primarily because they occur often or are widespread. Despite these laws, the Supreme Court and other state and federal courts frequently interpret situations that are not covered by statute. For example, the Supreme Court's interpretation of Title IX of the Civil Rights Act of 1964 found that a victim of intentional sex discrimination has the private right to bring a civil action for damages against a recipient of federal financial assistance.[17] Federal courts were also crucial in mandating school desegregation.

In some cases, multiple civil rights statutes are implicated. For example, if a pregnant female applicant of Middle Eastern descent over the age of 40 does not get a job for which she is qualified in California, her civil rights under Title VII of the Civil Rights Act of 1964, the Pregnancy Discrimination Act that is part of Title VII, and California's Fair Employment and Housing Act may all be implicated. Similarly, a pregnant and disabled teenager who is banned from attending high school because of her pregnancy may have grounds to file suit or obtain other remedies under Title IX, the Americans with Disabilities Act (ADA), the Individuals with Disabilities Education Act (IDEA), and Section 504 of the Rehabilitation Act of 1973 (Section 504).

Often, retaliation related to the exercise of an individual's civil rights is also prohibited, both in law and policy. This means that an employer or academic institution cannot take an adverse action against someone merely because they seek to address a civil rights–related grievance. The Equal Employment Opportunity Commission's (EEOC) policy is illustrative:

> A manager may not fire, demote, harass or otherwise "retaliate" against an individual for filing a complaint of discrimination, participating in a discrimination proceeding, or otherwise opposing discrimination. The same laws that prohibit discrimination based on race, color, sex, religion, national origin, age, disability and genetic information also prohibit retaliation against individuals who oppose unlawful discrimination or participate in an employment discrimination proceeding.
>
> It is important to understand how retaliation manifests and to prevent it from occurring. If retaliation for such activities were permitted, it would have a chilling effect upon the willingness of individuals to speak out against employment discrimination or to participate in the EEOC's administrative process or other employment discrimination proceedings. Thus, EEO practitioners must work diligently with managers to ensure that retaliation is not permitted in the workplace.
>
> It is obvious that the cause and effect of interpersonal conflicts can potentially implicate a legal process. This is particularly apparent with retaliation law because the legal standard requires an examination of the behavior after the allegation. The standard for proving a retaliation claim requires showing that the manager's action might deter a reasonable person from opposing discrimination or participating in the EEOC complaint process.[18]

Beyond Civil Rights

Since the 1960s, *overt* discrimination, such as the segregation of public facilities on the basis of race, has diminished or vanished completely. Nonetheless, *circumstantial* discrimination remains a persistent problem. The ability to address much of this indirect discrimination lies beyond the confines of the law discussed thus far. Thus, a 150 years after the end of slavery, African American families remain on average 13 times poorer than their white counterparts. School segregation and housing discrimination have been illegal since the passage of the Housing Discrimination Act, yet African Americans live in poorer school districts and neighborhoods that remain informally segregated. The Civil Rights Act of 1964 addressed voting rights, and the Supreme Court's seminal *Brown v. Board of Education* decision did away with "separate but equal," but a law cannot change the underlying problems, such as poverty, that create the conditions in which inequality thrives.

Modern civil rights movements (often referred to as "social justice movements"), such as Black Lives Matter and the Occupy Wall Street movement, are consciously or subconsciously calling attention to a long-held legal and policy doctrine known as **disparate impact**. In the United States, disparate impact refers to practices in employment, housing, and other areas that adversely affect one group of people (usually referring to those with a protected characteristic) more than another, even though the rules applied by employers, teachers, the government, landlords, etc. are *prima facie* neutral (i.e., neutral on their face). In most cases, a civil rights violation can be shown if an official practice has a disproportionally adverse effect on members of the protected class as compared with non-members of the protected class. The impact of policies that disparately impact a group of people are often felt over time and indirectly. For instance, state-sponsored surveillance of a group of individuals with a specific last name isn't facially discriminatory against Orthodox Jews, but nonetheless if the last name is one commonly shared by many Orthodox Jews and is a name chosen due to their faith, they end up being discriminated against merely because of their religion.

> Disparate impact—refers to practices that adversely affect one group of people more than another, even though the rules and laws applied to all people are the same.

As communities attempt to come to term with these more nuanced civil rights issues, they often find that legal concepts and policies are inadequate to address multilayered and circumstantial discrimination. Thus, though adequate, legal concepts of disparate impact are nonetheless insufficient descriptors of the kinds of nuanced, hidden, and indirect discrimination that is part of American life today. To describe these problems more accurately, modern social justice movements rely on ideas of structural racism, institutional racism/sexism, privilege, and racial/gender equity. For example, even though the First Amendment guarantees freedom of speech, how powerful is that speech as an advocacy tool if you are an African American in jail, a woman working in a male-dominated profession, or an American Muslim in the armed forces? What barriers silence or chill your speech? What institutions and cultural values perpetuate a system whereby you self-censor your thoughts for fear of retaliation or discrimination?

Structural and Institutional Discrimination vs. Individual Discrimination

Structural discrimination is the first of the ideas that are helpful in understanding and answering these questions. Structural discrimination is a system in which public policies, institutional practices, cultural representations, and other norms work in various, often reinforcing ways to perpetuate racial group inequality. Ideas of structural discrimination identify dimensions of American history in particular that have allowed privileges associated with "whiteness" and disadvantages associated with "color" to endure, perhaps lessen, but nonetheless adapt over time.[19] Structural discrimination is often viewed as systemic: a feature of the social, economic, and political systems in which society exists.

> Structural discrimination—a system in which public policies, institutional practices, cultural representations, and other norms work in various, often reinforcing ways to perpetuate racial group inequality.

Closely related are ideas of **institutional discrimination**: policies and practices within and across institutions that, intentionally or not, produce outcomes that repeatedly favor a specific group or put another group at a disadvantage. Unlike individual discrimination, institutional discrimination is the aggregate behavior of social institutions themselves, the embedded culture of the institution itself. Institutional discrimination is most often found in larger institutions such as schools, and can be evidenced by the way many schools discipline students of color at much higher rates than their white counterparts, even when the extent of bad behavior is identical across race. Likewise, the American criminal justice system incarcerates a far higher percentage of people of color as a portion of the population. Closely related are ideas of institutional sexism or institutional gender bias. Institutional gender bias can contribute to disparities between women and men, often in complex ways. For example, a common bias is the leadership bias stereotype: this is where women face prejudice in the workplace because characteristics associated with leadership are viewed as incongruent with women's gender roles. For example, women who display assertiveness may be perceived as competent but unpleasant.[20]

> Institutional discrimination—policies and practices within and across institutions that, intentionally or not, produce outcomes that repeatedly favor a specific group or put another group at a disadvantage.

The term "institutional racism" found meaningful description in *Black Power: The Politics of Liberation* by Stokely Carmichael:

> When white terrorists bomb a black church and kill five black children, that is an act of individual racism, widely deplored by most segments of the society. But when in that same city—Birmingham, Alabama—five hundred black babies die each year because of the lack of power, food, shelter and medical facilities, and thousands more are destroyed and maimed physically, emotionally and intellectually because of conditions of poverty and discrimination in the black community, that is a function of institutional racism. When a black family moves into a home in a white neighborhood and is stoned, burned or routed out, they are victims of an overt act of individual racism which most people will condemn. But it is institutional racism that keeps black people locked in dilapidated slum tenements, subject to the daily prey of exploitative slumlords, merchants, loan sharks and discriminatory real estate agents. The society either pretends it does not know of this latter situation, or is in fact incapable of doing anything meaningful about it.
>
> p. 4, Nov. 1992

Institutional racism or discrimination should be contrasted with the individual discrimination we have been discussing primarily thus far. Individual discrimination refers to the behavior of individual members of one identity group that is intended to have a differential and/or harmful effect on the members of another identity group. In individual, institutional, and structural forms of discrimination, the term *dominant* refers to groups that have most of the power in society (e.g., are "privileged"). Concomitantly, the term *minority* refers to groups that lack power; it does not refer to groups that are small. In the United States, people of color and women are minority groups, as are certain non-Christian religious groups like Jews and Muslims. People of color also happen to be a numerical minority, but women are not.

Examples of individual discrimination include an employer who rejects all African American job applicants, a landlord who refuses to rent an apartment to a woman wearing a religious headdress, a group of high school students who paint derogatory comments about gay and lesbian classmates. All of these are examples of individuals acting against other individuals merely because of their identity and affiliation.

Contrast this with "acceptable" discrimination where penalties accrue against an individual not because of who they are, but because of what they have done. The latter bases consequences on behavior rather than identity. Insidious and indirect forms of discrimination such as structural and institutional discrimination often conflate the two judgments, placing punitive or bureaucratic burdens on a population because of its identity or a perceived correlation between identity and bad behavior.

Recent examples surrounding the deaths of unarmed African Americans by law enforcement officers provides a vehicle to discuss these issues. If a death is not justified and is an isolated incident, we would define it as individual discrimination. However, when these deaths become a pattern, such as the deaths of several African Americans from 2014 through 2017 in Ferguson, Missouri, Eric Garner in New York City, Tamir Rice in Cleveland, and Freddie Gray in Baltimore, then they can be seen as an example of institutional discrimination because the incidents involve the actions of an institution like a large police department. One can assess the nature of the discrimination by grassroots community responses to the results of discrimination. For instance, discrimination at the institutional level often gives rise to a set of new institutions to counter it. The rise of the Black Lives Matter movement in the aftermath of the Brown shooting in Ferguson is an example of this trend.[21]

The subsequent trials and frequent acquittals of the officers charged with the shootings mentioned earlier illustrates the structural discrimination present in the system. Remember that structural discrimination is often never *overt* discrimination. Thus, when the defense attorneys for the police department request a change of venue to a more conservative, predominantly white or racially homogenous community, this is not overtly discriminatory against African American jurors or victims, but nonetheless ends up having a disparate impact on those populations when the officers end up being acquitted by sympathetic jurors. This was the case with the 1992 trial and acquittal of the officers involved in the beating of Rodney King Jr. in Los Angeles. As the rise of social institutions happens to combat institutional discrimination, structural discrimination often encourages large-scale public responses. Sometimes, these responses can be violent and counterproductive in their own right, as was the case with the riots in Los Angeles, which occurred after the acquittal of the LAPD officers who beat Rodney King.[22]

Institutional discrimination does not just involve the public sector, however. Almost since its rebranding in 1992, the 100-year-old retailer Abercrombie & Fitch was the subject of lawsuits about its discriminatory hiring and employment practices. In all of its almost 1,000 storefronts, the company perpetuated an effective apartheid-like policy of hiring a certain kind of individual for the front of the store and a certain kind of individual for the back of the store. As CEO Mike Jeffries discussed candidly in an interview,

> In every school there are the cool and popular kids, and there are the not-so-cool kids. Candidly, we go after the cool kids. We go after the attractive, all-American kid with a great attitude and a lot of friends. A lot of people don't belong in our clothes and they can't belong. Are we exclusionary? Absolutely.[23]

In 2004, the company agreed to pay $50 million to several thousand employees in order to settle a class-action lawsuit charging that it discriminated against African Americans, Latinos, and Asian Americans in both its hiring practices and its advertising. Among other things, the suit alleged that non-whites were regularly shoehorned into back-of-the-store jobs where customers wouldn't see them as much. More recently in 2015, the Supreme Court sided with Samantha Elauf, an American Muslim woman who wore a headscarf and was denied employment because the way she looked violated Abercrombie's "look policy." The Court found that Abercrombie's policies violated the Civil Rights Act of 1964, effectively asserting that the retailer's blanket policy, which called for banning of minority or visibly religious employees from working on the store floor, was institutional discrimination.

Like institutional discrimination, structural discrimination can take place outside of large public institutions or the government. Consider the lending industry: Significant evidence indicates that people of color or those from minority religious communities are less likely than White Americans to get business loans or home mortgages—even when both applicants have identical credit ratings and financial profiles. In some cases, this is despite the greater growth and profitability of minority-owned firms in the United States. Structural discrimination on the basis of gender is also widespread. Studies have found that female-owned businesses in the same financial condition as male-owned businesses are 33% less likely to receive small-business funding.[24]

Who Can Discriminate?

It is important to note that individual discrimination is not limited to the majority racial or religious community. If a woman refuses to hire a man because of his gender, or a Hispanic man refuses to hire a white person because of his race, these are also examples of discrimination, irrespective of underlying privilege issues. The key issue is assessing the intent of the person taking the alleged action: was their intent to treat another unequally or to cause harm to the alleged victim due to their membership in a specific group?

Institutional discrimination, however, is usually carried out by the majority group (or a group dominant in some other way besides sheer numbers) against a minority group, because the dominant group controls the institutions and has incentive to continue creating policy that further upholds those institutions.

All forms of discrimination—from individual to structural—have significant impacts, even if an individual never experiences the discrimination. For instance, knowledge of pre-existing biases held by banks may discourage a minority business owner from obtaining lending to expand a pre-existing business or open a new one or discourage someone from applying to college because they feel that they may never get a student loan. Likewise, examples of retaliation against religious minorities, violent or otherwise, may discourage members of the religious group from speaking out or advocating for their community for fear of reprisal, thus interfering with their free speech rights. We call this inhibition or indirect discouragement of the legitimate exercise of someone's rights a "**chilling effect**" on a person's rights. In the legal context, a chilling effect can be a law or other official action that discourages the exercise of rights, and in the policy context this can manifest in the form of social or popular discouragement, anger, or threats.

> Chilling effect—a law or other official action that discourages the exercise of rights. In the policy context this can manifest in the form of social or popular discouragement, anger, or threats.

Privilege and Equity

Structural or institutional racism, sexism, and so forth is often perpetuated by privilege, which often refers to historical and contemporary advantages in access to quality of education, jobs, and livable wages, homeownership, retirement benefits, wealth, and the like., The following quotation from a publication by Peggy Macintosh can be helpful in understanding what is meant by white privilege, a specific form of racial privilege:

> As a white person I had been taught about racism that puts others at a disadvantage, but had been taught not to see one of its corollary aspects, white privilege, which puts me at an advantage. . . . White privilege is an invisible package of unearned assets which I can count on cashing in every day, but about which I was meant to remain oblivious.[25]

The average white household had nearly $800,000 in assets in 2011, compared with $154,000 for African Americans.[26]

Issues of structural or institutional racism perpetuated by privilege can be ameliorated by policies that favor **racial equity** (or gender parity, etc.). Racial equity refers to what a non-racist society would and should look like. In a racially equitable society, the distribution of society's benefits and burdens would not be skewed by race. Thus, a poor Hispanic neighborhood, a poor African American neighborhood, and a poor white neighborhood would have equal access to benefits and privileges. This is in contrast to the current state of affairs in which a person of color is more likely to live in poverty, be imprisoned, drop out of high school, be unemployed, and experience poor health outcomes like diabetes and other fatal diseases in comparison with other identity counterparts in a similar situation. Ideas of racial equity thus hold society to a higher standard and force individuals to consider not only individual-level discrimination protected by the Constitution but also overall social outcomes that lead to disparate impact discrimination and social injustice.

Thus, affirmative action policies, which provide some institutional benefits to a minority community that previously was discriminated against, are an example of a policy promoting racial equity through the recognition of privilege and that seeks to redress grievances arising from structural and/or institutional discrimination.

> Racial equity—Racial equity refers to what a non-racist society would and should look like. In a racially equitable society, the distribution of society's benefits and burdens would not be skewed by race.

Looking Ahead

> *What used to be racial segregation now mirrors itself in class segregation.*
> —Barack H. Obama

A growing movement for economic civil rights is now taking hold in the United States. One that acknowledges that racial and religious bigotry in the United States isn't over, but that there is a parallel set of worsening problems, chief among them a division of the populace by extremes of the economic classes. Even Dr. Martin Luther King, Jr. recognized this issue half a century earlier when he advocated for a "Poor People's Campaign" to supplement civil rights efforts for low-income African Americans. Since that time, as economic inequality in the United States has worsened, a movement to address class inequality has only grown.

Consider the issue of marriage across racial and class lines. Whereas interracial marriage was illegal in many states half a century ago, today it is common. By contrast, while marriage across class lines was increasingly accepted in the first half of the 20th century, that trend has reversed itself as educated people have become less likely than in the past to marry those with less education.

Discussion Questions

As you review this chapter, consider the historical context within which civil rights have evolved. When the United States was founded, the population of modern-day Houston was spread out among 13 states. Almost everyone lived on farms, not in cities. They lived with extended families and relied upon strong social networks for support. The Bill of Rights spoke to grievances not borne of income inequality but of the excesses of the state. Those grievances haven't gone away, but additional problems have arisen in the last 250 years that require solutions by a concerted movement of people and ideas—a movement that thinks critically about what a "right" is; a movement that tackles laws blocking the poor from better housing due to exclusionary zoning practices; a movement that integrates schools not only on the basis of color but also in terms of economic disparity; a movement that advocates for Election Day as a national holiday to make voting easier for everyone, not just low-income Americans; a movement that holds responsible those who prevent the formation of economic unions, even by well-off professionals, like lawyers and doctors; and a movement that asks why we protect the right to own a lethal weapon but not to obtain a square meal.

Indeed, Dr. Martin Luther King, Jr. himself closed a seminal speech on civil rights with a similar call to action:

> The contemporary tendency in our society is to base our distribution on scarcity, which has vanished, and to compress our abundance into the overfed mouths of the middle and upper classes until they gag with superfluity. If democracy is to have breadth of meaning, it is necessary to adjust this inequity. The curse of poverty has no justification in our age. It is socially as cruel and blind as the practice of cannibalism at the dawn of civilization, when men ate each other because they had not yet learned to take food from the soil or to consume the abundant animal life around them. The time has come for us to civilize ourselves by the total, direct and immediate abolition of poverty.

1. What would your movement look like? Would it focus on the civil rights issues of old, such as free speech and freedom of religion? Or would it seek to redefine issues of income inequality and pay equity as modern-day civil rights issues?
2. Think also about what the idea of a movement says about the area of civil rights law. Is the study of civil rights a unique area of the law? Or does it encompass all areas of law and policy and thus act more like threads that weave the law than a separate subject in and of itself?
3. This chapter has also exposed you to the balance of power between the people and their government. Does the government today possess too much power? Is the people's "voting power" enough to encourage change in government policy? What other checks or balances would you impose on the government if you believe it is too powerful? What unintended consequences can you see arising from these additional restrictions?

Notes

1. Antoine Simonin, The Cyrus Cylinder, *Ancient History Encyclopedia* (Jan. 18, 2012).
2. Dinah Shelton, *An Introduction to the History of International Human Rights Law*, 2007, https://scholarship.law.gwu.edu/cgi/viewcontent.cgi?referer=www.google.com/&httpsredir=1&article=2045&context=faculty_publications
3. Firestone (1999) p. 118; *Muhammad*, Encyclopedia of Islam Online. *See also*, Muhammad Watt & R.B. Serjeant, *The Constitution of Medina*, 8 Islamic Quarterly 4 (1964).
4. Craig R. Smith, *To Form a More Perfect Union*, Long Beach, CA: Center for First Amendment Studies 21 (1993).
5. *Gideon's Promise, Still Unkept*, N.Y. Times, Mar. 18, 1993. As funding for public defender programs has increased, novel ways of representing the poorest have emerged. For instance, in 2010, a public defender's office in the South Bronx called The Bronx Defenders created the Center for Holistic Defense, which has helped other public defender offices, from Montana to Massachusetts, develop a model of public defense called holistic defense or holistic advocacy. In it, criminal defense attorneys work on interdisciplinary teams, alongside civil attorneys, social workers, and legal advocates, to help clients with direct and collateral aspects of their criminal cases. *See* Daniel June, How Well are the Poor Publicly Defended?, May 7, 2013, jdjournal.com
6. *Torcaso v. Watkins*, 367 U.S. 488, 494 (1961).
7. *Cantwell v. Connecticut*, 310 U.S. 296, 304 (1940).
8. *Herbert v. Verner*, 374 U.S. 398, 403, 406–409 (1963).
9. *Adapted from Know Your Rights, a Guide to the United States Constitution*, U.S. Attorney's Office—District of Minnesota 3 (2011).
10. Americans United, *The Muslim Ban*, https://au.org/files/Muslim%20Ban%20Amicus%20Brief%20SCOTUS%209.18.170.pdf. *As of print, the case is still winding its way back and forth the federal circuits and the Supreme Court.*
11. Jan Herrick, *Supreme Court Brief: Muslim Ban Violates Religious Freedom*, People for the American Way Foundation (Sept. 22, 2017).
12. See, e.g., Ilya Shapiro, *The First Amendment's Protection of Political Speech Extends to Both Donations and Spending*, ScotusBlog (April 3, 2014).
13. This idea is articulated more fully by Justice Brandeis in *Whitney v. California*, a seminal free speech case. Incidentally, this foundational premise also gives rise to the uniquely American belief that even "hate speech," or offensive and abhorrent speech, is as protected as pleasant speech. Thus, in the United States, the best way to combat hate speech isn't to censor it, it is to respond with "good speech."
14. *See Bill of Rights: The Fourteenth Amendment and Incorporation, infra. Herbert v. Lando*, 441 U.S. 153, 168 n.16 (1979).
15. In *Dred Scott v. Sanford*, African Americans, whether enslaved or free, were not permitted to become U.S. citizens, and therefore were unable to enjoy the rights and protections afforded citizens. Furthermore, the Supreme Court found slaves to be a property interest that could not be taken away from the states by the federal government because of the Fifth Amendment's due process clause.
16. Though federal law pre-empts state and local laws, in many cases state and local laws can provide greater civil rights protections than can federal law. For instance, California's Unruh Civil Rights Act outlaws workplace discrimination based on not only the federal categories of sex, race, religion, age, and national origin, but it also extends these protections to discrimination on the basis of medical condition, genetic information, marital status, and sexual orientation.
17. *Barnes v. Gorman*, 536 U.S. 181, 185 (2002).
18. Equal Employment Opportunity Commission, *Retaliation Considerations*, www.eeoc.gov/laws/types/retaliation_considerations.cfm
19. We most often use **structural racism** as an example in this chapter, but these ideas apply just as readily to other forms of discrimination, including but not limited to structural sexism, structural ethnocentrism, etc.
20. Claartje Vinkenburg, et al., *An Exploration of Stereotypical Beliefs about Leadership Styles: Is Transformational Leadership a Route to Women's Promotion?*, 22.1 The Leadership Quarterly 10–21 (2011).
21. Vox.com, *U.S. Police Racism*, www.vox.com/cards/police-brutality-shootings-us/us-police-racism

22. *Rodney King Case and the Los Angeles Uprising*, UCLA Film & Television Archive, www.cinema.ucla.edu
23. Benoit Denizet-Lewis, *The Man behind Abercrombie & Fitch Salon*, 2011, www.salon.com/2006/01/24/jeffries/ (last visited Feb. 4, 2018).
24. Biz to Credit, *Women's Small Business Outlook Webinar*, www.biz2credit.com/appfiles/biz2credit/pdf/webinar/Womens-Small-Business-Outlook-2016.pdf
25. See: Peggy Macintosh, "Unpacking the Invisible Knapsack." excerpted from Working Paper #189 White Privilege and Male Privilege a Personal Account of Coming to See Correspondences through Work in Women's Studies. Wellesley, MA: Wellesley College Center for the Study of Women (1989). Adapted from The Aspen Institute's "Glossary for Understanding the Dismantling Structural Racism/Promoting Racial Equity Analysis." The average white household had nearly $800,000 in assets in 2011, compared with $154,000 for African Americans.
26. USA Today, *Equality Still Elusive 50 Years after Civil Rights Act*, www.usatoday.com/story/news/nation/2014/01/19/civil-rights-act-progress/4641967/ (Accessed Feb. 5, 2018).

Additional Learning Resources

Additional Readings

Taylor Branch, *Parting the Waters: America in the King Years 1954–63* (Simon and Schuster, 1989). The first book in a formidable three-volume social history.

The Civil Rights Resource Guide, Library of Congress, www.loc.gov/rr/program/bib/civil-rights/external.html

Geoffrey R. Stone, *The First Amendment* (Aspen Casebook Series, 2016). A seminal casebook on First Amendment jurisprudence written by some of the leading figures in the field.

Jeanne Theoharis, *A More Beautiful and Terrible History: The Uses and Misuses of Civil Rights History* (Beacon Press, 2018). "A bracing corrective to a national mythology" (*New York Times*) that has been created about the civil rights movement."

Index

16th Amendment, U.S. Constitution 1, 7, 124, 143
23rd Amendment, U.S. Constitution 39
1964 Food Stamp Act 248

able-bodied adults without dependents (ABAWD) 254
absolute advantage 129
actual malice 360–364
Adam Smith 127–129, 143–144, 150
administrative expansion 27
Administrative Procedure Act of 1946 (APA), the 23
Age Discrimination in Employment Act 324, 368
agencies: executive 24–26; independent 24–26; regulatory 24–26
Ag-Gag Laws 275–277
Agricultural Adjustment Act, the 16, 145–146, 154
agricultural exceptionalism 266
Agricultural Marketing Act, the 271
Agriculture and Consumer Protection Act of 1973, the 249
Agriculture Marketing Service (AMS) 280
Aid For Families with Dependent Children (AFDC) 252
Airline Deregulation Act 28
ambient air 316–317, 319
Amendment XII, U.S. Constitution 41–42
American Civil Liberties Union 50
Americans with Disabilities Act 324, 345, 368–369
Antiquities Act, the 295
appellate jurisdiction 94, 96
apportionment 42–45
Arizona State Legislature v. Arizona Independent Redistricting Commission (2015) 46
Arthur Laffer 28, 124, 150
Article II, Section 1, Clause 3, U.S. Constitution 40
Articles of Confederation, the 38, 63–64, 69
Authorization for Use of Military Force 200, 221, 228

Baker v. Carr 43
balance of power 162, 175–176, 187, 203
bank run 14
biodiversity 278, 284
biometric data 332
biometric privacy 332
Black Lives Matter Movement, the 370, 372
black market 7
Black Power: The Politics of Liberation 371
Black Thursday 14
blue pencil doctrine 329
Boomer v. Atlantic Cement Co., 26 NY2d 219 (Ct. App. NY, 1970) 313–314
boom period 146
Boston Tea Party 63
British Navigation Acts, the 62, 128
Brown v. Board of Education, 1954 368, 370
bullionism 127
bull market 149
Burlington Industries Inc. v. Ellerth 339
Bush Doctrine, the 30, 196, 198–199

Cabinet, the 81–89
capitalism 129, 144–145
caucus 53
Centers for Disease Control and Prevention (CDC) 273–274
Chevron Deference 102
Chevron U.S.A. Inc. v. Natural Resources Defense Council, Inc., 467 U.S. 837 (1984) 100
Chicago School of Economics, the 150
Christian Alcoholics and Addicts in Recovery (CAAIR) 244
Chy Lung v. Freeman, 92 U.S. 275 (1875) 71
citizen suit provisions 297
Civil Rights Act of 1964 26, 80, 324–325, 333, 336, 340, 342, 345
Civil Rights Act of 1991, the 369
Civil Service Act of 1883, the 2
classified information 212, 214–216
Clayton Act of 1914, the 143
Clayton Antitrust Act of 1914 7

Clean Air Act, the 315–317
Clean Water Act (CWA), the 317–320
closed primary 53
cloture 67
Coal Conservation Act, the 16
Cold War (1947–1991), the 28–29, 161, 165, 170–171, 175–177, 187, 192–193
command and control mechanism 315, 317–318, 320
commerce clause 16, 75–76, 80, 85, 142, 154–155
common law 23–24, 97, 161–162, 279, 299, 311, 323–325, 329
communism 22, 26–29, 145, 148, 170, 176, 195
comparative advantage(s) 129
Comprehensive Environmental Response, Compensation, and Liability Act (CERCLA), the 297
concentrated animal feeding operations 267–268, 277, 284
concurrent jurisdiction 96
congressional districts 42–47
Connecticut Compromise, the 38–39
consideration 94, 108, 130, 133, 325, 327–329
constituents 64–65
Constitutional Convention (1787) 37, 44, 64, 103
Consumer Financial Protection Act of 2010, the 83–85
Consumer Financial Protection Bureau 25, 83–85
Contract Clause, the, Article I, Section 10, U.S. Constitution 140
cooperative federalism 315–317
Copper v. Harris (2017) 47
Covenant of Good Faith and Fair Dealing 324
CRAAP Test 110
cracking 46
criteria pollutants 316–317
critical analysis 106–110, 116, 118
critical infrastructure 219, 223, 238
Cuban Missile Crisis, the 165, 171–175

Defense Secrets Act of 1911 215
deficit spending 149
Department of Health, Education, and Welfare, the 295
Department of the Navy v. Egan, 1988 215–216
Deputies Committee 213
deregulation 28–30, 150
deregulatory era 28–30
détente 161, 165, 175
deterrence 26, 170, 175–176, 205
diplomacy 184–185, 187, 190, 194
disenfranchisement 37, 51
disparate treatment 333, 335, 340, 345, 347
Dodd-Frank Act, the 83

early business regulation 142–144
East India Company, the 62, 127
economic history 127–128
economic sanctions 172, 184
Egg Products Inspection Act of 1970, the 271
el bloqueo 171–174
elector 38–39
Electoral College, the 38–40
Electronics Benefits Transfer (EBT) 246, 254
Eliminate the Purchase Requirement (EPR) 252
Eli Parsier 30, 111
employee handbooks 324–325, 327, 329–330
employment-at-will 323–325, 328
Enabling Acts 82
Endangered Species Act, the 294, 296–298
enumerated powers 67–68, 71, 130, 179
environmental justice 272, 306–308
Environmental Law 266–267, 272, 293–294, 298–300
Environmental Protection Agency (EPA), the 82–83, 99–100, 269, 277, 296
Equal Employment Opportunity Commission (EEOC), the 333–334, 336, 368–369
Equal Employment Opportunity Commission v. Abercrombie & Fitch Stores, Inc 336
Equal Employment Opportunity Commission v. United Parcel Service 334
Equal Protection Clause 44–45, 91, 99
Espionage Act of 1917 215
Evenwel v. Abbott (2016) 47
executive agencies 25, 308, 82–83, 89, 94
executive agreements 91, 177, 181–182, 187
executive orders 91–92, 158–159, 203
express contract 326–327
externalities 272, 305–306

factors of production 129
faithless electors 39
fake news 109–110, 113, 115, 116
Faragher v. City of Boca Raton 339
Farm Bill 270
Farm Bill of 2002, the 254–255
Federal Communications Commission, the 24–25, 85–86
federalism 53
federal question 96
Federation for American Immigration Reform (FAIR), the 157
Fidel Castro 171, 173–174
filibuster 67
Filter Bubble, the 111
First Continental Congress, the 63
fiscal policy 145, 148
Fletcher v. Peck, 10 U.S. 87 (1810) 95, 140
Food, Drug, and Cosmetic Act (FDCA), the 21, 260, 263, 270, 277

Food and Drug Administration (FDA), the 25, 143, 259, 269, 271, 273
food insecurity 256–257
food safety 271–274, 277, 287
Food Safety Modernization Act (FSMA), the 263–265
foreign aid 184, 186, 217, 270
Foreign Intelligence Surveillance Act (FISA) 226
Foreign Policy in the 21st Century 195–198
Frederick Taylor 8
freedom of religion 355–357
free market(s) 128–130, 144–145, 150, 154
free market capitalism 129

Garn-St. Germain Depository Institutions Act 29
general election 50, 53
Genetically Modified Organisms (GMOs) 277–279
geopolitics 193
gerrymandering 45–46, 52
Gibbons v. Ogden, 22 U.S. 1 (1824) 75–76, 98, 130–136
Gilded Age, the 1–3, 7, 14
Glass-Steagall Act 145–146
global governance 161, 193, 203
globalization 151, 161, 190, 193, 203
Government Accountability Office (GAO) 271–272
Greenhouse Gas Emissions (GHGs) 282, 293, 308, 315, 318
Gulf of Tonkin Resolution, the 27

Hamdi v. Rumsfield, 524 U.S. 507 (2004) 199–201, 229
Harris v. Arizona Independent Redistricting Commission (2016) 47
Heart of Atlanta Motel 77–79
homeland security 202, 210, 212–213, 215–219, 223–225, 239
Homeland Security Act of 2002 213
Homeland Security Council, the 213
Homestead Act of 1862, the 266
hostile work environment harassment 338
house of representatives 30, 38, 41, 44, 64–65, 180–181
How a Policy Becomes a Law 66
Humane Methods of Slaughter Act, the 271
human rights 352–354

immigration 284–285
Immigration Act of 1924, the 143
Immigration and Nationality Act of 1965 (INA) 27, 159
implied contracts 324–325
implied powers 68–69, 71, 179
Inadmissible alien(s) 159
incorporation doctrine 355

independent agencies and commissions 82–90
independent regulatory agency 83, 85, 142
individual discrimination 370–373
Individuals with Disabilities Education Act (IDEA), the 369
industrial capitalist 144
institutional discrimination 370–373
intelligence community 225–227, 237
internationalist 22, 26, 177
interpreting the constitution 98–99
Interstate Commerce Act of 1887, the 7, 23, 142
Interstate Commerce Commission 9, 25, 142
ISIS 196–197, 209
Islamic State of Iraq and the Levant (ISIL) 158, 209, 225, 232
isolationism 15, 163, 195
isolationist 163, 177

Jim Crow 367
John Dewey 108
Jones v. Alfred H. Mayer Company (1968) 367
judicial review 43, 94–95, 97–98, 319
judiciary, the 21, 31, 38, 67–68, 92–102, 368
Juliana v. United States, 217 F. Supp. 3d 1224 (D. Or., 2016) 308–311

Kansas Experiment 125
Katzenbach v. McClung, 379 U.S. 294 (1964) 76–80
Katz v. U.S., 1967 226
Keynesian 128, 145, 149–150, 152
Kuznets Curve 144
Kyoto Protocol 30, 299

laissez-faire 14–15, 16, 22, 32, 128, 145
Lakhdar Boumediene v. George W. Bush, 533 U.S. 723 (2008) 229–231
Lawmakers, the 64–67
Lawyers' Committee for Civil Rights Under the Law, the 159
Leonard White 8
libertarianism 145
limits to executive power 181–182
literacy tests 51–52
Livestock Production & Slaughter 270–271
Lochner Era 13, 21–22, 154
Lochner v. New York, 198 U.S. 45 (1905) 10–13
Lujan v. Defenders of Wildlife, et al. 504 U.S. 55 (1992) 319–320

Majority Leader 66
Manifest Destiny Doctrine, the 211
Marbury v. Madison, 5 U.S. (1 Cranch) 137 (1803) 93–94, 355
Marshall Plan 22, 165, 167–168, 187

Martin v. New York Life Ins. Co, 1895 323
Massengill and Elixir sulfanilamide 21–23
McCulloch v. Maryland, 17 U.S. (4 Wheat) 316 (1819) 69–71
Meat Inspection Act of 1906, the 271, 274
mercantilism 127–128, 130, 144
Meritor Savings Bank v. Vinson 337–338
Mexican-American War (1846–1848) 164
military commissions 228–232
Mobile v. Bolden (1980) 52
monoculture 268, 284
Monroe Doctrine 163, 211
Morehead v. New York ex rel. Tipaldo 16–17
muckraking 3
mutually assured destruction 175–176, 204–205

National Assessment of Educational Progress, the 35
National Association for the Advancement of Colored People (NAACP), the 307, 367–368
National Captioning Institute 331
national defense 217, 219, 223, 225, 238
National Industrial Recovery Act 16
National Infrastructure Protection Plan 223
nationalism 127, 161–162
National Labor Relations Act 23, 78–80, 331
National Meat Association v. Harris, 132 S.Ct. 965 (2012) 274–275
National Popular Vote Interstate Compact 40
national security 177, 183, 196–197, 199, 202–203, 212–239, 265, 357–358
National Security Act of 1947, the 212, 226
National Security Advisor 213–214
National Security Council, the 183, 212–214
National Security Strategy Report 216–219
National War Labor Board 144
nation-states 161, 175, 239, 352
native advertising 113
Nat'l Labor Relations Board v. Hearst, 322 U.S. 111 (1944) 23
natural capital 301
New Deal 15–21, 25–27
New Jersey Plan, the 38
New York Times Co. v. Sullivan. New York, 376 U.S. 254 (1964) 359–364
New York Times Co. v. United States (1971) 365
noncompete agreements 327–329
nonproliferation 196
North American Free Trade Agreement (NAFTA) 29–30, 165, 190
North American Treaty Alliance (NATO) 22
North Atlantic Treaty Organization (NATO) 168

Objective and Subjective Expectation of Privacy 331
Occupational Safety and Health Act of 1970, the 27, 148
Oncale v. Sundowner Offshore Servs., 523 U.S. 75 (1998) 339–341
Open Door Policy 164–165
open primary 53
Organic Foods Production Act of 1990 (OFPA) 263, 281
organic standards 280–281
original jurisdiction 96
Other America, the 148, 367

Packers and Stockyards Act of 1921, the 271
packing 46
Paris Agreement, 2015 299
Parrish v. West Coast Hotel, 300 U.S. 379 (1937) 16–21
Patient Protection and Affordable Care Act (ACA), the 31, 36, 152
peer-reviewed 116–117
Pendleton Act, the 2–3
Personally Identifiable Information (PII) 332
Personal Responsibility and Work Opportunity act of 1996 (PRWORA), the 252, 254
Peterson v. Hewlett-Packard Company, 2000 334
Pew Research Center 35–36
Policy Coordination Committees 214
political appointee 2
political boss 6
political machine(s) 3, 6
political parties 4, 37, 39, 47–53, 153, 168, 176
polluter pays principle 306–308
pollution 100–102, 148, 153, 233, 267, 272, 284, 294–296, 305–306, 312–316
Poor People's Campaign 374
Poultry Products Inspection Act of 1957, the 271
powers of congress 67–80
Pregnancy Discrimination Act of 1978, the 342, 345–347
presentment 67, 201
Presidential Tools of Foreign Policy 184–185
President's Powers, the 90–92
preventing terrorism 219, 224, 225–232
Preventing Terrorism Policy and Law 224–232
primary 39, 50, 53
Principals Committee, the 213
privilege and equity 373–375
Procedural Process of Creating Foreign Policy 192
progressive 143, 146
Progressive Era, the 3–8
promissory estoppel 325–326
protectionism 127

Index

Pure Food and Drug Act of 1906, the 6, 9, 143, 271

Quadrennial Homeland Security Review 216–219
quid pro quo harassment 338

racial equity 374
Reagan Administration 28, 149–151
redistricting 45–47, 55
Red Scare 148
Reid v. Covert, 354 U.S. 1 (1957) 181
Religious accommodations 334
Religious Land Use and Institutionalized Persons Act of 2000 (RLUIPA), the 357
Revolutionary War 63, 163
Reynolds v. Simms 44
riders 67
Rodway et al. v. United States Department of Agriculture, 514 F2d 809 (D.C.) (1975) 250–252
rulemaking 23, 89
rule of law 103

Schedule-C Appointee 2
Scientific Management Theory 8
security policy 212
Servicemen's Readjustment Act of 1944, the (G.I. Bill) 146
shared spaces 219
Shared Spaces Policy and Law 232–239
Shelby County v. Holder 53
Sherman Antitrust Act, the 7, 143, 270–271
Silent Spring 148, 295
Simon Kuznets 144
Slaughterhouse Cases, the (1873) 136–140
socialism 25, 144–145
social media 209, 289, 331–332, 358
Social Security Act of 1935 15, 146
Society of Professional Journalists, the 116
sovereignty 161
Soviet Union, the 22, 28–30, 148, 166, 170–175, 177, 193, 205, 235
Speaker of the House 65, 67
spoils system 2
stagflation 149
Standard Oil 136, 142–143
structural discrimination 353, 370–373
sub-prime mortgage crisis 152
Supplemental Nutrition Assistance Program (SNAP) 246, 256, 288
supply-side economics 152
supremacy clause 71

take care clause 91
Tea Act of 1773, the 62
technocrats 144
Temporary Assistance to Needy Families (TANF) 254–255

Tennessee Valley Authority, the 145
Tennessee Valley Authority v. Hill 297
terrorism 195–203, 210, 212–213, 218–219, 221, 223–232, 238–239
theories of international relations 194–195
Thrifty Food Plan, the 249–250, 252, 254, 258
Title VII of the Civil Rights Act of 1964, the 324–325, 335–347, 368–369
Title IX of the Civil Rights Act of 1964 369
Tom Campbell v. William Jefferson Clinton, 203 F. 3d 19 (D.C. Cir. 2000) 221–222
Totten v. United States, 1875 215
Townshend Acts of 1767, the 62
tragedy of the commons 303–305
travel ban 159–160, 357
Treaties And Executive Agreements 181–183
Treatise of the Law of Master and Servant, A 323
trickle-down economics 28, 150
Truman Doctrine, the 22, 165, 187, 211
Trustees of Darmouth College v. Woodward 141

undue hardship 334
Union of Soviet Socialist Republics (USSR), the 147, 166
United Nations 165–166
United Nations Framework Convention on Climate Change (UNFCCC), the 299
United Nations Security Council 148, 166, 176
Uniting and Strengthening America by Providing Appropriate Tools Required to Intercept and Obstruct Terrorism (USA Patriot Act) of 2001 30, 223, 227
U.S. Foreign Intelligence Surveillance Court (FISC) 226–227
U.S. Global Change Research Program (USGCRP), the 293
U.S. Senate 38, 65, 181, 186–188
U.S. v. Curtiss-Wright Export Corporation, 299 U.S. 304 (1936) 177–178

Vernon BOWMAN v. Monsanto Company, 133 S.Ct. 1761 (2013) 279–280
vertical integrity 243, 268
veto 67, 91, 222
vetting process 90
Virginia Plan, the 38
voter registration 50, 53, 368
voting 38, 48–49
Voting Rights Act of 1965 27, 51–52, 54

Wabash, St. Louis & Pacific Railway Company v. Illinois 142
War on Poverty 26
War Powers Act, the 198
Warsaw Pact, the 177

Watergate Scandal 27
welfare reform 254
Wesberry v. Sanders, 376 U.S. 1 (1964) 43–44
Wheeler-Lea Act of 1938, the 261
Whitman v. American Trucking Associations, 531 U.S. 457 (2001) 316–317
Wickard v. Filburn, 317 U.S. 111 (1942) 78
World Health Organization (WHO) 273
World War II 22, 144, 161, 165, 170, 172–173, 295, 354
writ of certiorari 96
writ of habeas corpus 72–74, 201
wrongful discharge in violation of public policy 324

Young v. United Parcel Service, Inc. (2015) 345

Made in the USA
Middletown, DE
16 January 2024

47989814R00223